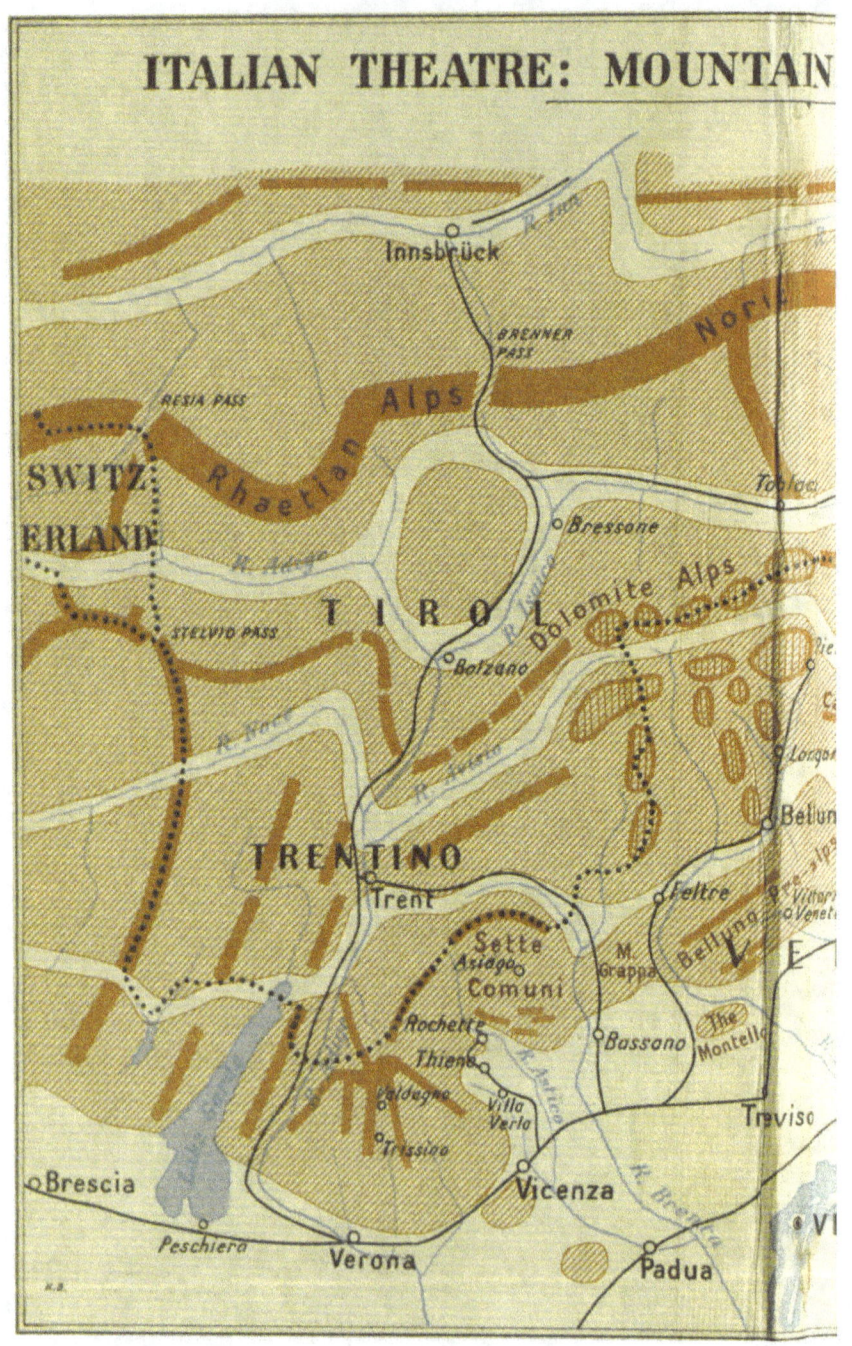

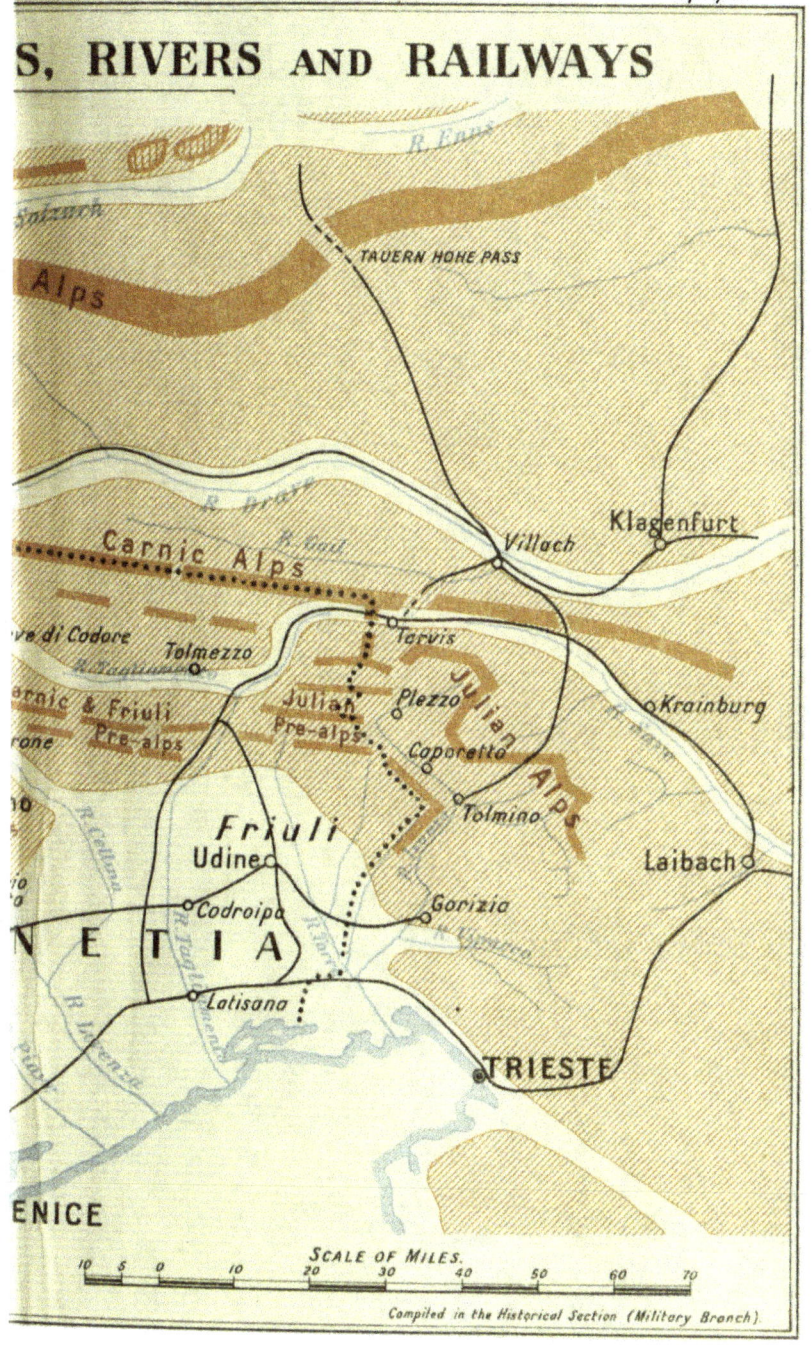

Frontispiece

The FLUCTUATIONS of the ITALIAN FRONT
23rd April 1915 to 26th November 1917

REFERENCE.
Frontier.
Italian Front on 23rd April 1915.
Austrian gains before 24th Oct. 1917
Loss in May–June 1916.
Limit of Austrian advance June 1916.
Italian front on 26th Nov. 1917
South Limit of mountain area

HISTORY OF THE GREAT WAR

BASED ON OFFICIAL DOCUMENTS
BY DIRECTION OF THE HISTORICAL SECTION OF THE
COMMITTEE OF IMPERIAL DEFENCE

MILITARY OPERATIONS ITALY
1915-1919

Compiled by
BRIGADIER-GENERAL SIR JAMES E. EDMONDS, C.B., C.M.G.,
D. LITT. (*Oxford*), R.E. (*Retired*), p.s.c.†,
and
MAJOR-GENERAL H. R. DAVIES, C. B.

The Naval & Military Press Ltd

Published by

The Naval & Military Press Ltd
Unit 5 Riverside, Brambleside
Bellbrook Industrial Estate
Uckfield, East Sussex
TN22 1QQ England

Tel: +44 (0)1825 749494

www.naval-military-press.com
www.nmarchive.com

In reprinting in facsimile from the original, any imperfections are inevitably reproduced and the quality may fall short of modern type and cartographic standards.

PREFACE

This volume contains an account of the war in Italy 1915–18 with special reference to the part played by the British force which was engaged in it. The first military aid given to the Italian Armies by the French and British took the form of a few heavy artillery batteries sent to them in April 1917. Provision of troops was discussed at the same time, and a special mission went to Italy to make all preliminary arrangements for the transport from France of a number of divisions. It was not until six months later, however, after the disaster of Caporetto, that a contingent of six French and four British divisions was detached to Italy, although " Passchendaele " was still in progress and " Cambrai 1917 " in immediate prospect.

Instead of beginning the story at the arrival of the British divisions in Italy, it was considered desirable to include as an introduction a sketch of the events which brought Italy into the war and of the operations which had already taken place, also to describe shortly the operations as a whole. This seemed the more necessary as there is no good account of the campaign in English. Two accounts, both written by Italians, were in existence ;[1] but both—as also do the Italian official battle-monographs—tend to glorify the part played by the Italian Armies and say very little about the decisive part played by the French and British divisions, a point referred to again in the " Reflections " at the end of Chapter XXIV.

The extraordinary feats of the British contingents in forcing a passage of the Piave in the final phase and in the pursuit of the Austrians in the mountains to Trent, are thus known to very few except those who took part, one of whom, an Italian Army commander, the Duke of Aosta, cousin of the King, said that without the presence of British troops and their commander " there would have been no Vittorio " Veneto ".

---

[1] See Tosti, Villari and Vittorio Veneto in Book List. The value of the official monographs may be judged by reference to p. 323, where an incident at Sacile is discussed.

PREFACE

Besides the British official records and Italian documents supplied to British G.H.Q. such as "Notizie Militari", there was plenty of material, as will be seen from the "List of Books". The Italian Official Account unfortunately had not in 1939 gone farther than May 1917, and no additional volumes have since come to hand; but the Austrian account had been completed and has been found to be a reliable guide, provided with excellent maps. The "Enciclopedia Italiana" contains a 115-page article on the war superbly illustrated. Further, the absence of an Italian official account of the final period is partly compensated for by the monographs on the later battles issued by the Italian General Staff, and by the number of books written by Italian and Austrian commanders. These enabled a narrative to be pieced together, but did not contain sufficient data for the compilation of detailed objective and situation maps. The maps indeed gave a good deal of trouble, as no two of the many available agreed—this was markedly the case with the course of the river Piave and the features of the country round Asiago.

"A Summary of the Campaign in Italy and an account of the Battle of Vittorio Veneto" in the "Army Quarterly" of October 1921 by Major-General the Hon. J. F. Gathorne-Hardy, Lord Cavan's Chief General Staff Officer, has proved a useful first guide to the study of the campaign.

Amongst the documents available were Field-Marshal Lord Cavan's private papers; the reports of Br.-General Sir Charles Delmé-Radcliffe, Chief of the British Mission at Italian Headquarters and formerly Military Attaché in Rome; and the reports of Colonel C. A. Lamb, attaché to the British Embassy in Rome, and of Br.-General J. H. V. Crowe, who was head of two special missions sent to Italy.

For the French operations the French Official Account, Tome VII. Second Volume was available. The German share in the war was recounted in an official monograph by the Bavarian General Krafft von Delmensingen, who was Chief of Staff of the German contingent in Italy.

Of English books there were histories of four of the five British divisions which were employed in Italy, that of the 23rd Division by Lieut.-Colonel H. R. Sandilands being particularly detailed in the Italian part; the 7th Division besides has a most vivid narrative of the last phase in

" The Defeat of Austria as seen by the 7th Division " by its senior chaplain the Rev. Canon E. C. Crosse ; and the 48th Division in " With the 48th Division in Italy ", by the late Lieut.-Colonel G. H. Barnett, its A.A. and Q.M.G. " With the British Guns in Italy ", by Lieut. Dalton (now the Right Hon. Hugh, Chancellor of the Exchequer 1945), and the "Diary of a Liaison Officer in Italy in 1918", by C. H. Goldsmid of the 9th Lancers, furnished excellent descriptions of what their authors had witnessed.

Much of the information about communications, supply and transport is taken from two lectures delivered by Colonel W. S. Swabey and printed in the "R.A.S.C. " Quarterly ", Vol. IX, pp. 207 and 477, and from an administrative report by Brigadier E. Felton Falkner, former A.A. and Q.M.G. of the 23rd Division. I have again had the benefit of the invaluable criticism of Mr. C. T. Atkinson M.A. (Oxon), Major-General Sir Henry Thuillier and Captain Wilfred Miles, and of the assistance throughout of Mr. A. W. Tarsey. The maps and sketches were fairdrawn for reproduction by Mr. H. Burge.

The draft chapters were sent for comment and criticism to all available officers who had been in Italy, and I have to thank in particular for assistance rendered in that way: Field-Marshal Lord Cavan, General Sir Alexander Wardrop, General Sir Richard Haking, Lieut.-General Sir Geoffrey Howard, Lieut.-General Sir Richard O'Connor, Major-General Sir Robert Fanshawe, Major-General Sir Henry Thuillier, Major-General Hon. Maurice Wingfield, Major-General C. R. Buckle, Br.-General J. H. V. Crowe, Brigadier H. R. Sandilands, Brigadier E. Felton Falkner, Brigadier H. S. G. Schomberg, Colonel G. Badham Thornhill, Colonel R. H. Beadon, Lieut.-Colonel C. N. Buzzard, Lieut.-Colonel W. M. Pryor, Lieut.-Colonel F. M. Tomkinson, Major Sir Owen Morshead, and Major P. E. Longmore.

All officers concerned may not, however, have seen the draft or the proof sheets, or may not agree with what has been printed, so I beg, as I have done in previous volumes, that corrections or additions, and any criticism thought necessary may be sent to the Historical Section, Cabinet Office, Great George Street, Westminster, S.W.1.

May 1948 J. E. E.

NOTES

The location of troops is written from right to left of the front of the Allied Forces, unless otherwise stated.

The distinguishing numbers of formations are written in words for Armies, in Roman figures for corps and in Arabic figures for divisions: thus First Army, I Corps, 1st Division. To save space and follow the custom observed as regards divisions, " Infantry Brigades " are invariably called " Brigades " only, as distinguished from " Cavalry Brigades " and " Artillery " Brigades ". The usual Army abbreviation of regimental titles are employed: thus " R. West Kent " for " The Queen's Own " Royal West Kent Regiment ", " K.O.Y.L.I." for the " King's " Own Yorkshire Light Infantry ".

First-line and Second-line Territorial Force units, if both existed, are distinguished by a figure before the number: thus 1/8th London, 2/8th London.

Austrian and German formations are printed in italics: thus *First Army, 125th Regiment.*

Austrian custom as regards the use of "von", which is followed, differed in 1914–18 from the German. Thus General Edler von Horsetzky may be mentioned as General Horsetzky; whereas in Germany he would be either Horsetzky or General von Horsetzky.

To save space " Austrian " is generally used instead of " Austro-Hungarian ". The divisions distinguished as *Honved* (literally " Home Guard ", usually translated as Militia) were Hungarian. The armed forces of the Dual Monarchy after the defeat by Prussia in 1866 formed three categories:

(1) The main army under the Common Ministry of War, recruited from both parts of the Empire;

(2) forces (*Landwehr*) administered by the Austrian Ministry of Defence;

(3) forces (*Honved*) administered by the Hungarian Ministry of Defence and recruited from Hungary alone;

Those under (2) and (3) consisted of first-line troops, reserves, *Ersatz* reserves and *Landsturm*. All three received the same training.

The established English form of Italian place names has been followed: thus Trent not Trento, Venice not Venezia; Mantua and Padua, not Mantova and Padova; and when places have both Italian and German or Slav names, the first have been adopted: thus Bolzano not Botzen, Fiume not Reka, Gorizia not

Görz ; where the spelling of the Italian form varies on different maps, as for instance Vazzolo (Vazzola), Tezze (Tezza), endeavour has been made to be consistent.

German-Austrian-Italian (Mid-European) time was one hour ahead of the Entente time. Both belligerents adopted Summer Time in 1916, the Allies on the night of the 9th/10th March and the Central Powers on the 14th/15th April ; it ended each year for both sides on the 30th September/1st October.

Owing to printing restrictions, map references instead of being in the margin, as in earlier volumes, are given in footnotes. To save the man-power involved by inserting the sketches and photographs in the text, they are bound together at the end of the volume.

CONTENTS

CHAPTER I

PAGE

PRELIMINARY 1
  The Triple Alliance and Italy's Neutrality : Plans for Italy's Military Aid to Germany against France : Italy's Plans against Austria-Hungary : The Outbreak of War The Pact of London.
  Note : Treaty of the Triple Alliance 1882 7

CHAPTER II

FROM THE OPENING OF HOSTILITIES UNTIL THE END OF 1916 9
  State of the Italian Army : The Theatre of War : The Opposing Austro-Hungarian Forces : The First Four Battles of the Isonzo : Allied Plans for 1916 and the Fifth Isonzo Battle : Italian Requests for Heavy Artillery : The Austrian Trentino Offensive : The Sixth Battle of the Isonzo (Battle of Gorizia), 6th–17th August 1916 : The Autumn Offensive, 14th September–4th November 1916 ; The Seventh, Eighth and Ninth Battles of the Isonzo.
  Note : Financial Loans to Italy 23

CHAPTER III

THE YEAR 1917 UNTIL THE EVE OF THE BATTLE OF CAPORETTO 24
  Plans for 1917 : Assistance to Italy Discussed : General Cadorna's Views and the Visits to him of Generals Nivelle and Robertson : Br.-General Crowe's Mission : Projects for Transport of Troops to Italy : Loan of Heavy Batteries to Italy : The Tenth Battle of the Isonzo (12th May–5th June) : The Battle of Ortigara (10th June) : The Eleventh Battle of the Isonzo (The Bainsizza, 17th August–12th September) : The Austrian Retreat : Results of the Eleventh Battle.
  Note : Austrian-German Consideration of a Campaign against Italy at the Beginning of 1917 ... 38

CONTENTS

Chapter IV

THE TWELFTH BATTLE OF THE ISONZO. THE BATTLE OF CAPORETTO 40

Cadorna abandons the Offensive : Information of Enemy's Offensive : The Italian Defence : Cadorna's Orders : The Austro-Hungarian Plan : The First Day of Battle (24th October) : The Second Day (25th October) : The Third Day (26th October).

Chapter V

AFTER CAPORETTO. THE RETREAT TO THE TAGLIAMENTO 58

Organization of British Assistance : Organization of French Assistance : Administrative and Transport Arrangements : The Italian Retreat : 27th October : 28th October : 29th October : 30th October ; Loss of Codroipo : 31st October ; The Italians on the Tagliamento : Arrival of Generals Foch and Robertson.

Chapter VI

THE RETREAT FROM THE TAGLIAMENTO TO THE PIAVE 1ST–10TH NOVEMBER 1917 74

The Halt on the Tagliamento : Visit of Generals Foch and Robertson : The Austrian-German Break into the Tagliamento Front : Cadorna Orders a Retreat to the Piave : The Rapallo Conference : Diaz Succeeds Cadorna : Foch and Wilson remain in Italy : The Retreat from the Tagliamento : The Italians on the Piave : The Asiago Plateau : The Monte Grappa Offensive (13th November).

Chapter VII

THE ARRIVAL OF THE BRITISH AND FRENCH DIVISIONS.. 88

The Move of the XIV Corps to Italy : Lord Cavan in Italy : Decision as to the Area of Concentration : Arrival of General Sir Herbert Plumer : General Plumer's First Report : Move of the XI Corps to Italy : Arrival of the French Contingent : Inter-Allied Consultations : Appointment of General Fayolle : Advance of the XIV Corps : Anglo-French Troops ordered into the Line : The End of the Caporetto Offensive.

CONTENTS

CHAPTER VIII

THE BRITISH ENTER THE LINE **104**

The Montello Position : The XIV Corps takes over the Montello Sector : Artillery of the XIV Corps : Air Support : The Group Plan of Defence : General Diaz's Indecision : Arrival of the XI Corps : General Plumer's Report of the 14th December 1917 : Instructions of the Supreme War Council : The Closing Days of 1917 : Italy's Shortage of Coal and Foodstuffs : Reports of the Military Representatives of the Supreme War Council.

CHAPTER IX

BEHIND THE FRONT. ADMINISTRATION, SCHOOLS, SIGNALS, INTELLIGENCE **122**

Reinforcements and Postings : Prisoners of War : Medical : Engineer Services : Ordnance : Ammunition : Supplies : Transportation : Remounts : Veterinary : Canteens : Lines of Communication and Base : Training and Schools of Instruction : Signals : Intelligence.

CHAPTER X

THE FIRST QUARTER OF 1918 UNTIL GENERAL SIR HERBERT PLUMER'S RECALL TO FRANCE **131**

General Situation and Air Activity : General Plumer's Report of 13th January 1918 : General Plumer's Report of 20th January 1918 : The Breaking Up of the Grouping for Defence : The XI Corps Takes Over the Arcade Sector on the Piave : Italian Winter Operations : Projected Operations by the 5th Division

Notes : I. Reorganization of the Austrian-German Forces in Italy **142**

II. The Reorganization of the Italian Army... **142**

III. Summary of a Report on the Situation of the Italian Army by General Fayolle, 26th December 1917 ... ... **143**

CONTENTS

Chapter XI

WITHDRAWAL OF PART OF THE BRITISH AND FRENCH TROOPS FROM ITALY 146

The Return of the British Troops from Italy envisaged : Discussions in the War Cabinet and the Decision to Recall Two Divisions : Protests by the Italian Government : Departure of the 41st Division and the XI Corps and Reorganization of the British Force in Italy ; Departure of General Plumer : Final Decision of the War Cabinet and the Reduction of the British Force : Reduction of the French Force.

Chapter XII

THE MOVE OF THE FRENCH AND BRITISH CONTINGENTS TO THE ASIAGO PLATEAU... 158

General Fayolle's Proposals for an Allied Offensive from the Asiago Plateau : The Italian Modifications of General Fayolle's Proposals and the Redistribution of the Italian Armies : The Plan of Operations : The French and British Troops Remaining in Italy : Relief of the British in the Montello Sector : The Occupation of the Asiago Position.

Chapter XIII

THE ASIAGO SECTOR : MARCH TO MID-JUNE 1918 ... 167

Description of the Asiago Sector and the British Position : Communications : Method of Supply : Housing, Canteens and Recreation : Schools of Instruction : Discussions on Policy : Offence or Defence : Decision to Launch an Offensive : British Ground and Air Activity in April and May : The Offensive Postponed : Italian Plans for Minor Offensives : Proposed Anglo-Italian Army.

Chapter XIV

THE AUSTRIAN PLANS FOR AN OFFENSIVE IN 1918 ... 187

First Proposals : The High Command's Plan : Discussions : Final Modifications.

Note : The Opposing Forces 193

CONTENTS

CHAPTER XV

THE BATTLE OF ASIAGO, 15TH–16TH JUNE 1918 ... **194**
  Situation on the morning of the 15th June : Influenza : The Opposing Forces : Warnings of an Enemy Offensive : The Enemy Bombardment : The Beginning of the Infantry Assault : The Assault on the 23rd Division ; It holds its ground : The Assault on the 48th Division ; a Pocket made in its Front : The Situation of the 48th Division about Midday : The Afternoon Counter-Attacks : The 4.30 a.m. Counter-Attack on the 16th : Action after the Battle : Reflections.
  Note : The Austrian Account of the Battle of Asiago   **219**

CHAPTER XVI

THE BATTLE OF THE PIAVE, 15TH–24TH JUNE 1918 ... **221**
  The Initial Situation : The Opening Phase on the 15th June : The Montello : The Opening Phase on the Lower Piave : Result of the First Day : 16th June ; a Wasted Day : 17th June ; the Austrians enlarge their Bridgeheads : 18th June ; Little Change in the Situation : Austrian Discussions on the Continuation of the Battle : The Italian Decision to take the Counter-Offensive : The Austrian Decision to Withdraw across the Piave : Casualties : Action on the Mountain Front : Italian Advance from the Sile (old Piave) to the Piave : Reflections on the Austrian Offensive.

CHAPTER XVII

PRELIMINARY DISCUSSIONS ON AN ITALIAN OFFENSIVE ... **242**
  Generals Foch and Diaz : Generals Lord Cavan and Diaz.
  Note : The Austrian Plans after the Battle of the Piave **249**

CHAPTER XVIII

THE FRONT DURING THE LONG PAUSE IN THE OPERATIONS 25TH JUNE—24TH OCTOBER **251**
  Trench Warfare on the Asiago Front : July : August ; a Multiple Raid : September ; Reduction and Partial Relief of the British Contingent : October.

CONTENTS xiii

Chapter XIX

PAGE

THE BATTLE OF VITTORIO VENETO, 24TH OCTOBER–4TH
  NOVEMBER 1918. THE CONQUEST OF PAPADOPOLI
  ISLAND, 23RD–24TH OCTOBER 264

The Opposing Forces : General Diaz's Plan : Concentration for Battle : The 7th Division takes over a Piave Front : Lord Cavan's Instructions to the Tenth Army : The Preparations to seize Papadopoli Island : Passage of the Piave by the 22nd Brigade : British portion of Papadopoli Island secured : The Main Attack is Postponed : The 22nd Brigade captures the rest of the Island : Construction of Pontoon Bridge : The Monte Grappa Fighting.

Chapter XX

THE BATTLE OF VITTORIO VENETO (*continued*). THE
  PASSAGE OF THE PIAVE, 27TH OCTOBER 1918 ... 284

The Twelfth and Eighth Armies : The Tenth Army ; Preparations for the Assault : Orders for the Attack : The Assault of the 7th and 23rd Divisions : Advance to the Second and Third Objectives : Completion of Bridging Operations : The Austrian Account.

Chapter XXI

THE BATTLE OF VITTORIO VENETO (*continued*). THE
  FORCING OF THE MONTICANO, 28TH–29TH OCTOBER
  1918 297

28th October : The Expansion of the Piave Bridgeheads : The Orders of the Tenth Army : Trouble at the Bridges : The Attack of the Italian XVIII Corps : Advance of the British XIV Corps : The Attack of the 23rd Division : The Attack of the 7th Division : The Attack of the Italian XI Corps : The Armies other than the Tenth Army.

29th October : The Forcing of the Monticano 304
The Orders of the Tenth Army : The Attack of the British XIV Corps : The Italian XI Corps : The Attack of the Italian XVIII Corps : The Italian Eighth Army : The Italian Twelfth Army : The Italian Fourth Army.

Note : The Austrians on the 28th and 29th October ... 314

CONTENTS

CHAPTER XXII

PAGE

THE BATTLE OF VITTORIO VENETO (*continued*). THE PURSUIT FROM THE MONTICANO TO THE LIVENZA, 30TH–31ST OCTOBER 1918 317

30th October : The XIV Corps in Pursuit : The Italian Armies 317
31st October : Halt on the Livenza 321
Note : The Austrians on the 30th and 31st October ... 325

CHAPTER XXIII

THE END OF THE WAR ON THE MOUNTAIN FRONT... ... 327

The Austrians abandon Asiago : The Attack on the Austrian *Winterstellung* : 1st November ; The Pursuit begins : 2nd November ; Entry into the Val d'Assa : The Austrian Frontier crossed : Difficulties of Supply : 3rd November : The Austrians prematurely announce an Armistice : Terms offered to the Austrians : Pursuit down into the Val Sugana ; disposal of prisoners : 4th November : The Armistice takes effect at 3 p.m.

Note : Lessons in Mountain Warfare. Report by Major-General Sir H. A. Walker, commanding the 48th Division 346

CHAPTER XXIV

THE BATTLE OF VITTORIO VENETO (*concluded*). THE END OF THE WAR ON THE VENETIAN FRONT. 1ST–4TH NOVEMBER 1918 : FROM THE LIVENZA TO THE TAGLIAMENTO 348

1st November ; Halt on the Livenza : 2nd November ; Crossing of the Livenza : 3rd November ; the Tagliamento reached : The Austrians assert Signature of Armistice : 4th November ; Passage of the Tagliamento. Captures and Casualties : Strength and Total Casualties : Reflections.

CONTENTS

Chapter XXV

How THE ARMISTICE CAME ABOUT... 359

Early Austrian Efforts to obtain Peace : The Emperor Karl Proclaims his Empire a Federal State : Disastrous Effects of the Emperor's Proclamation : The Emperor Karl Decides to ask for an Armistice : The Hungarian Government Decides to Lay Down Arms : Delay in the Reception of the Austrian Armistice Commission : The *Entente* Prepares Armistice Terms : The Austrian Armistice Commission is Received by the Italians : The Austrian Armistice Commission Refer the Terms to Vienna : Difficulties of Communication : Reception of the Terms by the Austrian High Command : The Armistice Terms Accepted : The Emperor Karl changes his mind and hands over Command of the Troops : The Signing of the Armistice at Villa Giusti.

Note : Economic Condition of Austria-Hungary in 1917–18 379

Chapter XXVI

THE END OF THE BRITISH FORCES IN ITALY 380

Plans to Invade Bavaria : Withdrawal of the XIV Corps to the Trissino Area : Withdrawal of the 48th Division : The Concentration of the British Force and Demobilization.

TABLE OF APPENDICES

No.		PAGE
I.	Order of Battle of the British Forces in Italy, November–December 1917	389
II.	Order of Battle of the British Forces in Italy, 15th June 1918	399
III.	Order of Battle of the French Forces in Italy, November 1917	404
IV.	Order of Battle of the Italian Armies, 24th October 1917	405
V.	Order of Battle of the Italian Armies (including French and British contingents), 15th June 1918	406
VI.	Order of Battle of the Austro-German Forces in the Italian theatre at the beginning of the Caporetto offensive : October 1917	407
VII.	Order of Battle of the Austro-Hungarian Forces, 15th June 1918	409
VIII.	The Secret Treaty with Italy (The Pact of London), 26th April 1915	411
IX.	Official Report of the Convention in the Event of Co-operation of British Troops in Italy, 7th May 1917	416
X.	Instructions by the Chief of the Imperial General Staff to General Sir Herbert Plumer when leaving for Italy, 9th November 1917	424
XI.	Protocol of the Conditions of Armistice between the Allied and Associated Powers and Austria-Hungary, Signed at Villa Giusti at 3 p.m. on 3rd November 1918	426

MAPS AND SKETCHES

PHOTOGRAPHS[1]

No.	Date	Title	
1.	30th October 1918	Pontoon Bridges over the Piave at Maserada...	*Between pages*
2.	2nd May 1918 ...	Entrance to Val d'Assa	*xxx & 1*

MAPS
(In Pocket)

1. The Asiago Battle-Ground.
2. The Battle of the Piave, 15th June–6th July 1918.
3. Vittorio Veneto. The Break-Through on the Piave, 27th–29th October 1918.
4. Final Advance from Asiago, 1st–4th November, 1918.
5. The Advance of the XIV Corps, 27th October–4th November 1918.

SKETCHES
(Bound in Volume)

	Italian Theatre : Mountains, Rivers and Railways ...	*End-paper*
	The Fluctuations of the Italian Front, 23rd April 1915 to 26th November 1917...	*Frontispiece*
1.	Ground Gained in the Eleven Battles of the Isonzo...	*At end*
2.	Routes from France into Italy	,,
3.	Eve of Caporetto. 23rd October 1917	,,
4.	The Italian Retreat to the Piave	,,
5.	The Front in Italy, 13th December 1917	,,
6.	Situation in Mid-November 1917	,,
7.	The Austrian Plan for the Offensive 1918	,,
8.	The Battle of Asiago, 15th–16th June 1918...	,,
9.	The British Multiple Raid of the 8th/9th August and the Austrian Retirement 17th/18th August 1918	,,
10.	Italian Plan and Situation on the 24th October 1918...	,,
11.	Capture of Papadopoli Island, 23rd–26th October 1918...	,,
12.	Campaign of Vittorio Veneto. Daily Advances	,,

---

[1] Kindly supplied by the Imperial War Museum.

LIST OF BOOKS

TO WHICH MOST FREQUENT REFERENCE IS MADE

ALBERTI : " Il Generale Falkenhayn. Le Relazione tra i Capi di S.M. della Triplici ". By General Adriano Alberti. (Rome : Liberia dello Stato.) •

As its title indicates, this book deals with two subjects : an appreciation of General Falkenhayn and an account of the relations between the Chiefs of the General Staff of the three Powers of the Triple Alliance. As it was issued (1924) by the State printing press and contains copies of important official documents (General Pollio's official report of the conference with the German and Austrian Chiefs of Staff 1913, and the report of the Italian military attaché of his interview with General Falkenhayn just before Italy's entry into the War), it may be assumed to be inspired.

ARZ : " Zur Geschichte des Grossen Krieges 1914–19 ". By General-Colonel Freiherr Arz von Straussenburg. (Vienna : Rikola Verlag.)

The war reminiscences of the Austrian general who, after commanding a division, a corps, and an Army in the earlier part of the War, in February 1917 succeeded Field-Marshal Conrad von Hötzendorf as Chief of the General Staff.

A.O.A. (Austrian Official Account) : " Oesterreich-Ungarns Letzter Krieg 1914–18 ". (Vienna : Verlag der Militärwissenschaftlichen Mitteilungen.)

The Austrian Official Account in seven volumes, with annexes and maps, compiled by the *Kriegsarchiv*. The final volume was published in 1939. As it takes up the information elicited by the Italian Commission of Enquiry into the defeat at Caporetto, not available in England, Volume VI is particularly valuable for that period.

BALDINI : " Diaz ". By General Alberto Baldini. (Florence : G. Barbèra.)

A military account of the actions and policy of General Diaz from the time he became Chief of the General Staff.

BERNDT : " Letzter Kampf und Ende der 29 Division ". By General Berndt. (Reichenberg : Verlag der Heimatsöhne im Weltkrieg.)

Deals with the last fight and collapse of the German-Bohemian 29th Division in October 1918 and is written by the Austrian General who commanded it. Its opponents were British troops, and the account relates the operations from the other side of the hill described in " The Defeat of Austria As Seen by the 7th Division ".

LIST OF BOOKS

CADORNA : " La Guerra alla Fronte Italiana ". Two volumes. By Generale Luigi Cadorna. (Milan : Fratelli Treves.)

This book, by the Italian Chief of the General Staff, covers the whole period of his command (24th May 1915–9th November 1917), that is until the Italian army, after its retreat from Caporetto, was established on the Piave. It is a commentary and apologia rather than a history.

CADORNA II : " Altre Pagine sulla Grande Guerra ". By Generale Luigi Cadorna. (Milan : Mondadori.)

This gives the plans drawn up by the Italian General Staff, previous to the author succeeding General Pollio as Chief of the General Staff, for despatching troops by railway to the Rhine front to assist Germany.

CAPELLO I : " Note di Guerra ". By General Luigi Capello. (Milan : Fratelli Treves.)

General Capello (born in 1859), who was in Libya as an infantry brigadier, in 1915, commanded the 25th Division, then the VI and other corps, the Gorizia Zone and the Second Army. His book describes in detail, with good maps, the successes of the Italian army in 1917, Caporetto, the retreat, and the final victory, in which he took part as a corps commander.

CAPELLO II : " Per la Verita ". By General Luigi Capello. (Milan : Fratelli Treves.)

In this the commander of the Italian Second Army defends himself against the remarks made about him by a Parliamentary Commission of Enquiry.

CAVIGLIA : " La Dodicesima Battaglia (Caporetto) ". By Marshal Enrico Caviglia. (Milan : Mondadori.)

The author (born in 1862) at the beginning of the war commanded an infantry brigade. By July 1917 he was in command of the XXIV Corps, which played an important part in the battle of the Bainsizza in August, and held its ground for some time in the Caporetto battle. In June 1918 he was appointed to command the Eighth Army. His book, published in 1933, deals authoritatively with Caporetto and with the retreat to the Piave. It contains some very useful sketch maps.

CAVIGLIA'S PIAVE : " Le Tre Battaglie del Piave ". By Marshal Enrico Caviglia. A French translation has been published by the Bibliothèque, Paris.

A military account of the three battles of the Piave.

CRAMON : " Unser Österreich-Ungarischer Bundesgenosse im Weltkrieg ". By General von Cramon. (Berlin : Mittler.)

The author was for four years, from January 1915, German Military plenipotentiary at Austro-Hungarian Supreme

Command Headquarters. His book gives a good account of the relations of the two Headquarters as regards plans and mutual assistance.

48TH DIVISION : " With the 48th Division in Italy ". By Lieut.-Colonel G. H. Barnett, C.M.G., D.S.O. (Blackwood.)

The author was A.A. & Q.M.G. of the division in 1917–18, and provides a narrative compiled from his own diary and personal notes.

F.O.A. (French Official Account) : " Les Armées française dans la Grande Guerre ". Ministère de la Guerre. Etat-Major de l'Armée. Service Historique. (Paris : Imprimerie Nationale.)

Tome VI. Volumes I and II cover the period dealt with in this volume and have chapters devoted to the Italian theatre.

GERMAN MONOGRAPH : " Der Durchbruch am Isonzo ". By General Krafft von Dellmensingen. (Oldenburg : Stalling.)

The compiler of this official monograph on the battle of Caporetto and the subsequent pursuit, was Chief of the Staff to General Otto von Below, commander of the German Fourteenth Army, which played the principal part. It is a most valuable record, as it is seldom that the staff officer in charge of a great operation writes an account of it.

GIARDINO : " Rievocasioni e Riflessione di Guerra ". By General (later Marshal) Gaetano Giardino (Milan : Mondadori.)

Two volumes by the commander of the Italian Fourth Army from April 1918. He had previously been commander of the 48th Division and XXV Corps, and Sub-Chief of the General Staff under General Diaz.

GOOCH : " Studies in Diplomacy and Statecraft ". By G. P. Gooch. (Longmans.)

The author was, among other things, joint-editor, with the late Mr. Temperley, of the Foreign Office publication, " British Documents on the Origin of the War, 1898–1914 ", and thereby had access to Foreign Office records. The book contains a series of studies, made either for lectures or magazine articles.

I.O.A. (Italian Official Account) : " L'esercito Italiano nella Grande Guerra (1915–18) ". (Rome : Istituto Poligrafico dello Stato.)

The Italian official account compiled by the General Staff. The last volume received, the fourth, takes the story of the operations to May 1917.

KRAUSS : " Das Wunder von Karfreit ". By General Alfred Krauss. (Munich : Lehmann.)

LIST OF BOOKS

This Austrian General (born in 1862) commanded the group of four divisions on the right of the Austrian-German forces at Caporetto. His book deals in detail with the preparations. It stops at the Tagliamento. It contains 18 portraits of generals, a panorama of the Plezzo basin and a good map. When the Germans entered Vienna in 1938 they made him a Prussian General of Infantry. He died soon afterwards.

LUDENDORFF: " My War Memoirs 1914–18 ". By General Erich Ludendorff. (English translation: Hutchinson.)

PENGOV: " Die Wahrheit über die Piave Schlacht ". By Major-General Pengov. (Mühlau bei Innsbruck: Im Selbstverlag des Verfassers.)

The author commanded an Austrian division, and gives a doleful account of the Austrian army in June 1918 from within.

PIAVE: " La Battaglia del Piave ".

Issued by Comando Supremo in 1920. An official account of the battle in 61 pages and with very good maps. Translated by Mary Prichard-Agnetti as " The Battle of the Piave (15th–23rd June 1918) ". (Hodder & Stoughton.)

SALANDRA: " Italy and the Great War. From Neutrality to Intervention ". By Antonio Salandra. (Edwin Arnold.)

The author (1853–1921) became Prime Minister of Italy on the death of Giolitti in March 1914, and remained in office until June 1916, the heavy losses of the Italians in the Austrian Trentino offensive being the occasion of his fall. He represented Italy at the Versailles Peace Conference. He is the man who coined the phrase " Sacro egoismo per " l'Italia ". His book attempts to explain Italy's policy before her entry into the War.

TOSTI: " La Guerra Italo-Austriaca 1915–1918 ". By Captain A. Tosti. (Milan: Edizion " Alpes ".)

A summary in 330 pages of the war between Italy and Austria in relation to the principal events in the other theatres of war. The author was given access to the official records, but makes no attempt at analysis or criticism.

TRANSPORTATION: " Transportation on the Western Front 1914–18 ". By Colonel A. M. Henniker. (H.M. Stationery Office.)

The official volume on the subject.

VIGANO: " La Nostra Guerra ". By General Vigano. (Florence: Le Monnier.)

The author, a former Minister of War, besides quoting conversations and opinions, provides a " contribution to the general history of the War ", which is a useful commentary as regards its conduct.

LIST OF BOOKS

VILLARI: " The War on the Italian Front ". By Luigi Villari. (Cobden-Sanderson.)
    The author, an Italian officer, son of a well-known historian, served alongside the British at Salonica. His book gives a far from impartial account of the military operations of the Italians in Italy and elsewhere, and makes great claims for the services rendered by Italy to the common cause, with many picturesque details.

VITTORIO VENETO: " Report of the Comando Supremo on the Battle of Vittorio Veneto ". Translated into English and printed by the Italian General Staff. 38 foolscap pages with 3 situation maps. (Undated.) Received 10th February 1919 by the British Chief Liaison Officer.
    This is a glorification of the Italian army with headings: " the valiant First Army ", " the unconquerable Third Army ", " the tenacious Fourth Army ", " the brave Sixth Army ", " the unyielding Seventh Army ", " the most gallant Eighth Army ", " the trusted Ninth Army ", " the audacious Tenth Army ", " the iron Twelfth Army " and " the vigilant and proud Cavalry Corps ".

WAR IN THE AIR: " The War in the Air ". By H. A. Jones. (Clarendon Press.)
    The Official History of the part played by the Royal Flying Corps and Royal Air Force.

WENDT: " Der italienische Kriegsschauplatz in europäischen Konflikten ". By Hermann Wendt. (Berlin, 1936, Junker und Dunnhaupt.)
    The author of this account of the military relations between Germany and Italy was *Dozent* in Tübingen University. He had access to all official documents and his volume is issued by the Military Historical Section of the Friedrich-Wilhelm University, Berlin. It contains a history of Italy as a theatre of war, and is particularly illuminating as regards the negotiations between the Italian Government and the Central Powers before she entered the war against them in 1915.

Note: " 1918 ", Vols. I, II or III signifies " The Official History of the Great War, Military Operations France and Belgium ".

A number of other books have been made use of but are not specifically quoted :
" The Fifth Division in the Great War ". By Br.-General Hussey and Major Inman.

LIST OF BOOKS   xxiii

"The Seventh Division". By C. T. Atkinson.
"The Defeat of Austria as seen by the Seventh Division". By Rev. E. C. Crosse, D.S.O., M.C. (late Senior Chaplain, C. of E., 7th Division.)
"The 23rd Division 1914–1918". By Lieut.-Colonel H. R. Sandilands.
"The 48th Division Signals in the Great War". By F. W. Dopson.
"Outline of the War History of the 240th Brigade R.F.A." By F. S. Gedye.
"War Record of the 1/5th Battalion R. Warwickshire Regiment". By C. E. Carrington.
"History of the 1/6th Battalion R. Warwickshire". (Author not named.)
"The Gloucestershire Regiment in the War 1914–18". By E. Wyrall.
"The Worcestershire Regiment in the Great War". By Major H. Fitz M. Stacke.
"The Oxfordshire and Buckinghamshire L.I. Chronicle 1917–18". By Lieut.-Colonel A. F. Mockler-Ferryman.
"War Record of the 1/4th Oxfordshire & Buckinghamshire L.I." By Major P. Pickford.
"The First Buckinghamshire Battalion 1914–19". By Captain P. L. Wright.
"The War Service of the 1/4th R. Berkshire Regiment". By C. R. M. F. Cruttwell.

Articles

"Some Tactical and Strategic Considerations of the Italian Campaign in 1917–1918". By Field-Marshal the Earl of Cavan. (*Army Quarterly*, October 1920.)
"A Fragment from the Last War". By Field-Marshal the Earl of Cavan. (*Army Quarterly*, November 1942.)
"A Summary of the Campaign in Italy and an Account of the Battle of Vittorio Veneto". By Major-General Hon. J. F. Gathorne-Hardy. (*Army Quarterly*, October 1921.)
"The Defence of the Cesuna Re-Entrant, 15th June 1918". By Captain C. E. Carrington. (*Army Quarterly*, July 1927.)
"Our Artillery in Italy". By Major A. G. Rolleston. (*Journal of the Royal Artillery*, July 1921.)

CALENDAR OF PRINCIPAL EVENTS

1914
AUGUST
3rd ... Italy declares neutrality.
4th ... Italy denounces the Triple Alliance.

1915
APRIL
22nd ... Battles of Ypres 1915 (First gas attack) begin.
25th ... Allied forces land at the Dardanelles.
26th ... Italy adheres to the Pact of London.
MAY
1st ... Austro-German Gorlice–Tarnow offensive against Russia begins.
9th ... French offensive in Artois begins.
23rd ... ITALY DECLARES WAR ON AUSTRIA-HUNGARY.
24th ... ITALIAN FORCES CROSS AUSTRIAN FRONTIER, MIDNIGHT 24TH/25TH.
26th ... Italian Government announce blockade of Austrian coast.
JUNE
3rd ... Przemysl retaken by Austro-Hungarians.
29th ... FIRST BATTLE OF THE ISONZO begins ; ends 7th July.
JULY
18th ... SECOND BATTLE OF THE ISONZO begins ; ends 10th August.
AUGUST
6th ... Suvla landing at Dardanelles.
SEPTEMBER
22nd ... Bulgarian Government order general mobilization.
25th ... Allied autumn offensive (Loos, Artois, Champagne) begins ; ends 15th October.
28th ... Battle of Kut.
OCTOBER
5th ... French and British troops land at Salonika.
6th ... Austro-German invasion of Serbia begins.
15th ... Great Britain declares state of war with Bulgaria.
18th ... THIRD BATTLE OF THE ISONZO begins ; ends 3rd November.
NOVEMBER
10th ... FOURTH BATTLE OF THE ISONZO begins ; ends 16th December.
30th ... Serbian retreat through Albania begins.

PRINCIPAL EVENTS

1915
DECEMBER
7th ... Siege of Kut begins.
15th ... Last Allied forces withdrawn from Macedonia into Greece.
20th ... Evacuation of Suvla and Anzac completed.

1916
JANUARY
8th ... Evacuation of Gallipoli Peninsula completed.
FEBRUARY
10th ... Remnant of Serbian Army concentrated in Corfu.
15th ... FIFTH BATTLE OF THE ISONZO begins; ends 17th March.
21st ... Attack on Verdun begins.
27th ... Durazzo captured by Austrian forces.
MARCH
18th ... Battle of Lake Naroch (Russia) begins; ends 30th April.
APRIL
29th ... Kut capitulates.
MAY
14th ... AUSTRIAN TRENTINO OFFENSIVE begins; ends 3rd June.
JUNE
4th ... Brusilov offensive begins; ends 17th August.
16th ... ITALIAN COUNTER-OFFENSIVE IN TRENTINO begins; ends 7th July.
JULY
1st ... Battles of the Somme 1916 begin; end 18th November.
AUGUST
6th ... SIXTH BATTLE OF THE ISONZO (Gorizia) begins; ends 17th August.
12th ... Italian troops join Allies at Salonika.
27th ... Rumania declares war on Germany.
Italy declares war on Germany.
29th ... Hindenburg succeeds Falkenhayn as Chief of General Staff.
SEPTEMBER
2nd ... German and Bulgarian forces invade the Dobrudja (Rumania).
14th ... SEVENTH BATTLE OF THE ISONZO begins; ends 18th.
26th ... Austro-German invasion of Rumania from north begins.

PRINCIPAL EVENTS

1916
OCTOBER
5th ... Battle of the Cerna and Monastir begins; Monastir captured by Allies 19th November.
9th ... EIGHTH BATTLE OF THE ISONZO begins; ends 12th.
31st ... NINTH BATTLE OF THE ISONZO begins; ends 4th November.

NOVEMBER
21st ... Emperor Franz Joseph of Austria dies.

DECEMBER
6th ... Bukharest capitulates to the Germans.
7th ... Mr. Lloyd George succeeds Mr. Asquith as British Prime Minister.
12th ... General Nivelle succeeds General Joffre as Commander-in-Chief of French Armies of the North and North-East.

1917
MARCH
11th ... Allied offensive in Macedonia begins; ends 23rd.
15th ... Nicholas II of Russia abdicates.
17th ... German retreat to the Hindenburg Line begins.
26th ... First Battle of Gaza.

APRIL
6th ... U.S.A. declare war on Germany.
9th ... Battle of Arras 1917 begins; ends 4th May.
16th ... Nivelle offensive begins; stopped 20th.
17th ... Second Battle of Gaza begins; ends 19th.

MAY
12th ... TENTH BATTLE OF THE ISONZO begins; ends 8th June.
15th ... General Pétain succeeds General Nivelle.

JUNE
7th ... Battle of Messines begins; ends 14th.
29th ... Kerenski offensive begins on Eastern Front (see 18th July).

JULY
18th ... German counter-offensive on Eastern Front begins; ends 28th.
31st ... Battles of Ypres 1917 begin; end 10th November.

AUGUST
17th ... ELEVENTH BATTLE OF THE ISONZO begins; ends 12th September.

SEPTEMBER
1st ... German offensive at Riga begins; ends 5th.

PRINCIPAL EVENTS

1917

OCTOBER
- 24th ... TWELFTH BATTLE OF THE ISONZO (CAPORETTO) begins.
- 27th ... Third Battle of Gaza begins; ends 7th November.
- 31st ... Italian Armies behind the Tagliamento. French force begins detrainment in Italy (4 divisions completed by 12th November, 6 by 23rd November).

NOVEMBER
- 1st ... British force begins detrainment in Italy (2 divisions completed by 16th November, 4 by the 25th).
- 3rd ... Italian Armies behind the Piave.
- 5th ... Rapallo Conference. Supreme War Council initiated. Lieut.-General Lord Cavan arrives at Pavia.
- 9th ... General Diaz succeeds General Cadorna.
- 13th ... General Sir Herbert Plumer arrives in Mantua.
- 16th ... M. Clemenceau becomes French Premier.
- 20th ... Battle of Cambrai 1917 begins; German counter-attack 30th November; ends 3rd December.
- 27th ... Members of Supreme War Council appointed.

DECEMBER
- 2nd ... Suspension of hostilities between Russia and Germany.
- 6th ... Suspension of hostilities between Rumania and Central Powers.
- 11th ... General Sir E. Allenby enters Jerusalem.

1918

JANUARY
- 8th ... President Wilson in message to Congress lays down his "Fourteen Points".

FEBRUARY
- 9th ... Peace of Brest-Litovsk between Ukraine and the Central Powers signed; Russia refuses to sign and Central Powers resume hostilities on 18th.

MARCH
- 3rd ... Peace of Brest-Litovsk signed.
- 21st ... German offensive on Western Front begins against Amiens; ends 5th April (see 9th April).
- 26th ... General Foch appointed to co-ordinate operations on Western Front.

APRIL
- 9th ... Second Act of German offensive on Western front towards Hazebrouck begins with Battle of the Lys; ends 29th.

PRINCIPAL EVENTS

1918

APRIL
14th ... General Foch appointed Commander-in-Chief of the Armies in France.

MAY
27th ... Third German offensive, across the Aisne, begins; ends 6th June.

JUNE
9th ... Fourth German offensive, Battle of the Matz, begins; ends 14th.
15th ... BATTLES OF THE PIAVE AND ASIAGO begin; end 24th and 16th.
30th ... American infantry regiment arrives in Italy.

JULY
6th ... French and Italian forces begin offensive in Albania; checked 22nd.
15th ... Fifth German offensive, in Champagne, begins; ends 18th.
18th ... French offensive against Soissons salient begins (Second Battle of the Marne) ends 7th August.

AUGUST
8th ... British offensive on Western Front begins and, the French, Americans and Belgians joining in, continues to the end.

SEPTEMBER
15th ... Final offensive in Macedonia begins.
18th ... Final offensive in Palestine begins.
27th ... Bulgaria asks for Armistice.
30th ... Armistice with Bulgaria signed.

OCTOBER
4th ... German and Austrian Governments send Notes to President Wilson proposing an Armistice.
14th ... Durazzo retaken by Italians.
President Wilson replies to Germany re military conditions of armistice and insists on dealing only with a democratic Government.
Turkey proposes Armistice to President Wilson.
16th ... EMPEROR KARL ISSUES MANIFESTO proclaiming a Federal State.
21st ... Czecho-Slovaks declare independence.
24th ... BATTLE OF VITTORIO VENETO begins: British cross the Piave and capture Papadopoli Island.
27th ... AUSTRIA ASKS ITALY FOR AN ARMISTICE.
Battle of Vittorio Veneto resumed.
29th ... Forcing of the Monticano.

PRINCIPAL EVENTS

1918
OCTOBER
30th ... Armistice between Turkey and Entente Powers signed at Mudros.
The Livenza reached.
31st ... Revolutions in Vienna and Budapest.
Austrian Armistice Commission received at the Comando Supremo.
NOVEMBER
1st ... Advance from the Livenza begins.
Advance from Asiago begins.
2nd ... The Hungarian Government order their Nationals to lay down arms.
3rd ... The Tagliamento reached.
The Austrians announce Armistice.
Headquarters of Austrian III Corps in Trent capitulates to British.
Armistice signed at Villa Giusti.
4th ... Armistice takes effect at 3 p.m.

No. 1.—30th October, 1918. Pontoon bridges over the Piave at Maserada.

No. 2. 2nd May, 1918. Entrance to Val d'Assa.

CHAPTER I

Preliminary

The Triple Alliance and Italy's Neutrality

At the outbreak of war in 1914 Italy was still a member of the Triple Alliance. When, in 1882, the secret Treaty of Alliance between Germany, Austria-Hungary and Italy, which was directed against France (the only Power named in it), had been drawn up,[1] it was expressly declared by all three Powers that its provisions " cannot, as previously " agreed, in any case be regarded as being directed against " England ". A previous Treaty of Alliance between Austria-Hungary and Germany, ratified in 1879, had secured military assistance between these Powers in the case of unprovoked hostilities by Russia.

The original Treaty of the Triple Alliance, when about to expire in 1887, was prolonged and developed by separate Treaties made by Italy with Germany and Austria-Hungary, in which the Balkans and other parts of the Orient were mentioned. These instruments, due to expire in 1892, were renewed with slight additions in 1891, 1902 and 1912 (when North Africa received mention).

In 1902, however, the Italian Government, in return for a secret Franco-Italian understanding which allowed Italy a free hand in Tripoli, had declared that the Triple Alliance was not directed against France. This declaration was followed later in the year by a secret Franco-Italian exchange of Notes whereby each Power promised neutrality in a war in which the other was engaged as a result of direct or indirect aggression. In 1909 Italy and Russia also reached agreement with regard to the " European East ".

The course of events in Europe after 1900, with the change in the alignment of the major Powers, and particularly the annexation in 1908 of Bosnia and Herzegovina by Austria-

---

[1] The important Articles are given in a Note at end of Chapter. The text and translation of the whole Treaty and of the others mentioned below will be found in " The Secret Treaties of Austria-Hungary 1879–1914 ", by Dr. A. F. Pripram and A. C. Coolridge (Oxford University Press).

Hungary, had made it almost certain that, in the event of a general war, Italy would not be found on the side of the Central Powers.

From the very birth of the Triple Alliance the German Great General Staff—and the Austro-Hungarian General Staff soon arrived at the same conclusion—never counted upon help from the Italians, but nevertheless it did not neglect to use its prestige to try to bluff them into covenanting to send it.[1]

General Field-Marshal von Moltke, uncle of the man of 1914, Chief of the German General Staff when the Alliance was signed, regarded military assistance from Italy as "uncertain and, in any case, only eventual", that is, would only be given if it suited Italy's own interests. General Colonel Graf Schlieffen, his second successor (1890–1904), in drafting and revising the plans for German aggression in France, Belgium and Holland, assumed that Italy, through fear of a French invasion of Piedmont and of coastal landings, would not allow any troops to leave her soil, nor would she herself attack; so that even the two French corps stationed on the Savoy frontier would not be held for very long. He doubted whether the French troops "de couverture" on that frontier would be maintained there for any length of time, and described as "an illusion the idea that Italy "could do anything of appreciable value" for Germany: the Germans "must expect to deal with the whole of the "French forces without any deduction for the Alpine "frontier".

Plans for Italy's Military Aid to Germany against France

Nevertheless, projects for the despatch of Italian troops to the Upper Rhine "had been repeatedly brought forward "for discussion by the Italians. They had also suggested "the violation of Swiss neutrality", so that their contingent could be railed direct to the Rhine instead of travelling by a roundabout route through Austria and Bavaria; but "this was not accepted by Germany".

---

[1] The account of the military relations of Germany and Italy which follows is founded on the German "Wendt" (See Book List) and the Italian "Alberti", whose texts agree.

THE TRIPLE ALLIANCE 3

General-Colonel von Moltke, Schlieffen's successor in 1905, also placed little reliance on Italian aid. He instructed his representative at a conference in 1907 to be very careful what he said, as " he suspected, in view of the behaviour of " the Italians at previous meetings, that Rome insidiously " wanted to obtain some information about the German " plan of operations (about which the Italians, had, naturally, " been told nothing) ".

A long pause in the conversations then ensued ; but they were resumed in 1912, at the instance of Italy, when the Italian war on Turkey in Africa was coming to a successful close and General Pollio, a pro-German, had become Chief of the General Staff. Pollio suggested indirect help in case of a Franco-German war by an attack on the French Savoy frontier, and direct help by sending troops to the Rhine, followed by a landing in Provence after command of the sea had been obtained : the Savoy and Provence forces could then combine and undertake an offensive up the Rhone in strength. Pollio declined the German suggestion that troops might be sent to help Austria-Hungary against Russia should a *casus foederis* arise, which was the whole essence of the original treaty from the German point of view.

More than ever sceptical of Italy's good faith, and in view of her age-long dislike of Austria and evidently increasing sympathy with France, General von Moltke did not make any change in his plans on the strength of Pollio's offer.

At the beginning of August 1913, Austria informed Germany and Italy that she might have to take action against Serbia. This had the result that a few days later, on 9th August, Signor Giolitti, the Italian Premier, directed the Minister of Foreign Affairs " to reply clearly that we do " not consider such eventual action as defensive and there- " fore do not believe a *casus foederis* will arise ".

At the close of the ensuing German Imperial manœuvres in September, a meeting of the German, Austrian and Italian Chiefs of the General Staff was held under the presidency of the German Emperor. Kaiser Wilhelm tried to extract a definite promise from General Pollio that in case of war with France, Italy would send an Army to the Rhine. Pollio pointed out that in view of her commitments in Tripoli, if Italy sent five corps[1] to Germany, only three

---

[1] It would therefore appear that this was the contribution asked for.

regular corps would be left for the defence of the Alps and the coasts of the peninsula. Moltke then argued that Italy had a superabundance of cavalry and might send a couple of cavalry divisions, as a political gesture, leaving the question of the despatch of an Army to be treated as a strategic matter on the basis that the *Triplice* was a single State fighting for its existence.

On his return home, General Pollio, after rendering a lengthy report, received permission from the Italian Government to study the question of direct assistance to Germany.

On 11th February 1914, Pollio informed General von Moltke that the Italian Government had decided in the event of war to send three corps and two cavalry divisions to Germany's assistance and had selected General Zuccari to command the force.[1] In March this officer visited Berlin to discuss details, and railway time tables for the movement of his troops were worked out in co-operation with a German Commission of which Colonel Tappen (Chief of the Operations Section of the Great General Staff) was a member. This combined planning, however, was treated as a military arrangement between the two General Staffs and did not commit their governments.

General von Moltke must still have remained sceptical; for on 13th March he wrote to General Conrad von Hötzendorf, the Austrian Chief of the General Staff, that he was acting "as if no Italian assistance at all was to be "expected". The two German speaking Chiefs of Staff then proceeded to discuss the case of Italy joining the *Entente*! As a result of their talk Conrad had a plan for an offensive campaign against Italy prepared; but he did not expect, he said, that it would ever be necessary to apply it, for a victorious German campaign against France would have the effect of keeping Italy neutral. He added, " she " will perhaps seek to associate herself with the successful " side in order to get some profit of another's success in " winning the war ". Little importance was attached by the Germans to her action; for should she come in on their side the French Alpine frontier defences were strong and could be effectively held by small numbers, and Italian forces, if any did leave Italy, could not possibly start for some time after German mobilization had been completed.

---

[1] The Italian General Staff's plans for the movement are given in Cadorna II (see Book List).

Italy's Plans against Austria-Hungary

For her part Italy had little confidence in the good faith of her chosen Allies. The Official History of the Italian Army in the Great War[1] contains a resumé of the plans of campaign against Austria-Hungary from 1882, the date of the Treaty of the Triple Alliance, before which there is no record of a definite plan.

These plans were of a defensive nature against Austria-Hungary; nothing was said in them with regard to other possible enemies.

Austria's entanglement with Serbia and the probable entry of Russia into the war gave Italy's problem a totally different aspect, and General Cadorna, who, in July 1914 on General Pollio's death, had become Chief of the General Staff, put forward a definitely offensive plan with the main attack across the Isonzo towards Trieste, and with the Trentino as a secondary objective.

The Outbreak of War; The Pact of London

At the outbreak of war, on 3rd August the day on which Germany declared war on France, Italy proclaimed her neutrality on the ground that the action of Austria-Hungary against Serbia, taken without consulting her, was a violation of Article VII of the renewed Treaty of 1912.[2] Later it was announced that the *casus foederis* did not arise for Italy in a war in which Great Britain was on the opposing side. On the advice of Berlin, Austria-Hungary agreed to Italy's interpretation of her obligations.[3] The Italian Army indeed, after its exertions in Tripolitania in 1912, was by no means ready to take the field, as the following chapter will show.

The steps by which public opinion and diplomatic action brought Italy into the war fall outside the scope of this history.

The policy of Italy, as defined by her Prime Minister, Signor Salandra, was one of *sacro egoismo*; but it would be

---

[1] I.O.A. ii., Chapter 1, from which the following paragraphs are derived.

[2] "The clash of interests between the two Allies in the Balkanic Peninsula, where they were engaged alongside Russia in an open struggle for predominance", had been a cause of friction for some time, Italy having her eyes on Albania. See "Italy's Foreign and Colonial Policy, 1914–37", by M. H. H. Macartney and P. Cremona, pp. 14–19.

[3] Salandra, p. 219.

unfair not to give some weight to the strength of the feeling in Italy in favour of the ideals for which the Entente Powers were fighting. None the less, the actual terms upon which Italy entered the War were a matter of hard bargaining, and they were put forward only after some negotiation with the Germans and Austrians and failure to obtain from them the promise, still less the immediate occupation, as demanded, of coveted territory in the Trentino and in the Trieste area; and they were put forward at a time when Italy felt confident that the Central Powers would be defeated.

After preliminary soundings, on 4th March 1915, the Marchese Imperiali, the Italian Ambassador, read over to Sir Edward Grey, the Secretary for Foreign Affairs, a memorandum of the conditions on which Italy was prepared to enter the War on the side of the Entente. They seemed to the British Cabinet to be " considerable ", and in some cases " excessive ". Some opposition came from the Russian Minister for Foreign Affairs. Agreement, however, was reached, and the Secret Treaty of London was signed by the Entente Powers and Italy on 26th April 1915. On 3rd May the Italian Ambassador in Vienna received instructions to hand to the Austrian Government a statement, already some days in his possession, formally breaking off the negotiations in progress and denouncing the Treaty of the Triple Alliance. On 23rd May the same Ambassador presented in Vienna the Italian declaration of war on Austria-Hungary. Next day Germany severed diplomatic relations with Italy; but not until 28th August 1916, the day after Rumania's declaration of war on Austria-Hungary, did Italy formally declare war on Germany.

The terms of the Treaty or Pact of London were as follows:[1]

Italy undertook to employ all her resources in pursuing the War in common with France, Great Britain and Russia against all their enemies (Article 2) and agreed to take the field at the earliest possible date, in any case within one month. The minimum of the Russian military forces to be employed against Austria-Hungary in order to prevent this Power from concentrating all her efforts against Italy was to be settled immediately by a convention (Article 1), and the fleets of France and Great Britain were to give their active

---

[1] For the text see Appendix VIII.

and continuous aid to Italy until the Austro-Hungarian fleet should have been destroyed, or peace concluded (Article 3).

Articles 4, 5, 6, 7 and 8 enumerated the territories which Italy would obtain in the Treaty of Peace, among them were the Trentino, Cisalpine Tirol, Trieste, all Istria, Dalmatia, Valona, and the islands of the Dodecanese ; but by Article 7 a right was reserved to the Allies to dispose of part of Albanian territory. If the Turkish Empire were broken up, a share in the neighbourhood of Adalia (south-west corner of Asia Minor), was reserved to Italy (Article 9). She was to succeed to the rights of the Sultan in Libya. If France and Great Britain increased their colonial domains in Africa at Germany's expense, Italy might claim territorial compensation, notably in the settlement of the frontiers of her African colonies (Article 13).

Italy was to receive a share of the eventual war indemnity and a loan to her of at least £50,000,000 was to be facilitated in the London market (Articles 11 and 14).

NOTE

Treaty of the Triple Alliance 1882

Article II

In case Italy, without direct provocation on her part, should be attacked by France for any reason whatsoever, the two other High Contracting Parties shall be bound to lend help and assistance with all their forces to the Party attacked.

This same obligation shall devolve upon Italy in case of any aggression without direct provocation by France against Germany.[1]

Article III

If one, or two, of the High Contracting Parties, without direct provocation on their part, should chance to be attacked and to

---

[1] It was in the endeavour to make this article effective that Germany in August 1914, falsely asserted that she had received " direct provocation " from France in that—before declaration of war—French troops had crossed the German frontier, even attacked German posts ; and aircraft, had also crossed, even dropped bombs on Nuremberg. (See the G.O.A. Vol. I p. 105).

Similarly, the Austrians, falsely, claimed that on 27th July " Serbian troops had fired from Danube steamers on the troops near Temesvar ". (See No. 10855 of the collection of the official papers of the Austro-Hungarian Ministry of Foreign Affairs, published under the title of " Oesterreich-Ungarns Aussen Politik 1908–1914 ").

be engaged in a war with two or more Great Powers non-signatory to the present Treaty, the *casus foederis* will arise simultaneously for all the High Contracting Parties.

Article IV

In case a Great Power non-signatory to the present Treaty should threaten the security of the states of one of the High Contracting Parties, and the threatened Party should find itself forced on that account to make war against it, the two others bind themselves to observe towards their Ally a benevolent neutrality. Each of them reserves to itself, in this case, the right to take part in the war, if it should see fit, to make common cause with its Ally.

CHAPTER II

FROM THE OPENING OF HOSTILITIES UNTIL THE END OF 1916[1]
(End-paper, Frontispiece, Sketch 1)

State of the Italian Army

The Italian army had gained useful experience, including experience in war flying and air bombing, in the Libyan War, in which troops in numbers up to nearly a hundred thousand had been employed. Owing, however, to the opposition of the Left, the government had not replaced the material and stores which had been used up in the campaign.[2] Immediately after the proclamation of neutrality, therefore, " the Ministry of War set itself the task of reorganizing the " army, replenishing the magazines and providing new " artillery ".[3] But the country was short of money and of means of manufacture. In regard to men, as a result of the Libyan War, there were still four classes with the colours in April 1915, instead of the normal peace strength of two, the number of effectives amounting to 14,000 officers and 284,000 men. At the outbreak of hostilities between the other Great Powers, Italy had called up two more older classes, and by May 1915 the total with the colours had risen to 23,039 officers, 852,217 soldiers and 9,163 civilians. They were organized in 14 corps, 35 infantry divisions, 1 Bersagliere (rifle) division, 4 cavalry divisions and 2 Alpine groups, and deployed as follows :[4]

In the Isonzo Sector : The Third and Second Armies (14 divisions in all) ;

---

[1] The facts as regards the operations are taken from A.O.A. for the whole period, from I.O.A. as far as it goes, that is until the end of 1916 ; and after that date from Cadorna, Capella, Caviglia, the German Monograph, etc.
[2] There had been 34 aircraft, besides dirigibles, in Libya, with 40 in Italy as reserve. In May 1915 Italy had available 5 dirigibles and 58 aircraft, organized in 12 flights (*squadriglie*).
[3] Villari, p. 22.
[4] See End-paper and Frontispiece.

in the Carnia Sector :   Alpine Groups ;[1]
in the Trentino Sector,
  from the upper Piave
  to the Swiss frontier :   The Fourth and First Armies
                                   (14 divisions in all) ;
in reserve :   Three corps (7 divisions).

THE THEATRE OF WAR

Vis-à-vis to Austria-Hungary, Italy's topographical position was weak. The lie of their common frontier, fixed in 1866 after the Prussian-Italian War against Austria-Hungary, and the shape of her territory with regard to that frontier were both strategicly and tactically most unfavourable to Italy.[2] The Venetian provinces, east of the Adige and the Trentino (the southern part of the Austrian Tirol) formed a huge bulge, enclosed on the north and east by Austria-Hungary and bounded on the south by the sea. Strategicly, therefore, these provinces were liable to be cut off by a successful Austrian offensive from the direction of the Trentino (as was attempted in 1916). On the other hand, an Italian commander, with a reserve in Venetia and his forces facing the two danger fronts, the Isonzo on the east and the Trentino on the west, would be on interior lines and able to reinforce one front at the expense of the other. Tactically, the common frontier of 375 miles, guarded along its whole length, except the six miles near the sea, by the massive rampart of the Alps on the north and by their rugged outliers on the east, was regarded as totally unfit in its central portion for the operations of large forces.[3] At the two ends, in the east the Isonzo area, though difficult, offered possibilities ; in the west, nine routes led from the Venetian plain into the Trentino. But in both these sectors the Austrians held the crest, and everywhere looked down on their Italian opponents.

In the east a spur of the main Alpine chain running south-east, called the Julian Alps, extending to beyond Tolmino, broadens out towards the Adriatic into limestone hills and plateaux. In this last sector, inside Austrian territory in

---

[1] 19 battalions, 1 cavalry squadron, 8 batteries, etc.
[2] See End-paper.
[3] The edge of the mountainous region, which rises sharply from the Italian plains, is shown on Sketches 4 and 5 by a brown line.

1914, parallel to the frontier, flowed the Isonzo river, unimportant of itself as a military obstacle, although running in a deep and rocky valley. East of the river the arid limestone uplands sloping gently westwards are deeply cut into a tangle of ridges and valleys. Here the denuded plateaux, known to fame as the Bainsizza and the Carso, the wooded Selva di Ternova lying back between them, form enormous natural fortresses, towering two thousand feet or more over the surrounding lowlands. The Bainsizza is described as " not flat, but traversed by ridges which rise " to a considerable height above the general level ", and the Carso is depicted as " a howling wilderness of stones sharp " as knives ".

If Italy took the offensive against Austria anywhere except along the coastal corridor leading to Trieste—and this was effectively flanked and enfiladed from the higher ground— she would have to attack uphill against a natural fortress.

The Opposing Austro-Hungarian Forces

During the months of Italian neutrality the Austrian frontier had been held, against possible inroads, by local militia, gradually strengthened by *Landsturm* and Reserve-men until the force amounted to over 120 battalions. In February 1915 these were partly organized into divisions :

> The Isonzo (sometimes called the Julian) front was then held by two divisions;
> the Trentino front by another two ;
> the Carnia Sector, between them, by a group containing more than the strength of a division ($14\frac{1}{2}$ battalions, etc.).

General Rohr, who was in command of the defence forces, was promised seven more divisions ; but this number, owing to events elsewhere, was early in April 1915 reduced to three and a half ; and of these, one was earmarked for the Trentino and one for Pola, the great naval port 70 miles south of Trieste. Arrangements had been made by Field Marshal Conrad von Hötzendorf, the Austrian Chief of the General Staff, for a combined full-dress offensive against the Russians, now known as the Battle of Gorlice-Tarnow of 1st May 1915. Although at least twenty divisions (ten of them German) were considered necessary by Conrad to hold the attack of the 35 Italian divisions, after a joint German-

Austrian Conference on 24th April, it was decided to let the offensive against Russia proceed, with 13 Austrian and 9 German divisions (Austrian *Third* and *Fourth Armies*, with the German *Eleventh* between them), and send help to the Italian front as soon as possible. Meanwhile General Rohr was to do his best to hold in check the Italian attack which seemed probable in the Isonzo area. The Archduke Eugen was appointed to command the troops against Italy. On 11th May one Austrian division was sent to the Isonzo from Serbia, and on 21st May, the Gorlice-Tarnow offensive having succeeded beyond all hopes, the Austrian *VII Corps* (3 divisions), earlier in reserve of the Austrian *Third Army* in Galicia, was entrained for the same front. Then rumours of the Pact of London reached Vienna, and in consequence eight or more divisions (3 from Galicia and 5 from the Balkans, where they were replaced by 3 German) were placed under orders to concentrate by 5th June around Marburg (in Styria, about 200 miles north-east of Trieste, with rail communication to that city), to form a new *Fifth Army*, under General Boroevic von Bojna Svetosar, on the Isonzo front, General Rohr taking over the Carnia group and General Dankl the Trentino. General von Falkenhayn, the German Chief of the General Staff, was more interested in an invasion of Serbia (which took place in October, for the purpose of transporting munitions to the Turks on the Gallipoli peninsula) than in operations against Italy. He did no more than send the *Alpine Corps* (actually the strength of a division, 13 battalions, 11 machine-gun companies and 9 batteries) to the Southern Tirol to make sure that Bavarian territory was not molested; but it was not to cross the Italian frontier. Unable to persuade the Germans to give him help, Conrad, much against his will, was forced into the defensive. When, on 23rd May, Italy declared war on Austria-Hungary, Boroevic had seven divisions on the Isonzo front, sufficient to delay the enemy, as the defences of the sector had been well prepared, with plenty of shelters excavated in the rock. Should, however, the Italians break through, Conrad was quite ready with a plan to deal with them on their exit from the mountain region with a force of 20 divisions which could meantime have been assembled in and east of the valley of the Save.[1]

---

[1] Some 40 miles from the Isonzo.

FIRST AND SECOND BATTLES OF THE ISONZO

THE FIRST FOUR BATTLES OF THE ISONZO[1]

The initial movements of the Italians, though described in their official history as the "First Offensive Bound", 24th May–16th June, were cautious without any attempt at surprise, and did no more than drive in the Austrian outposts and bring the Third and Second Armies, under Lieut.-General the Duke of Aosta and Lieut.-General Frugoni, in contact with the Austrian front line. General Cadorna, the Chief of the Italian General Staff, certain that the War would be a long one, preferred to go slow until Italy's resources in men and material had been further organized. Nevertheless, he took the offensive and maintained it for two years—except for an Austrian offensive in the Trentino in May 1916—until the rout of Caporetto. Throughout the campaigns the Italian objective was Trieste, and the ground rather than the Austrians was the enemy to be overcome.

In the "First Battle of the Isonzo", 23rd June–7th July 1915, the objectives were the Carso and Gorizia, with Tolmino as subsidiary. After the preliminary gaining contact, it was a trench-warfare battle, without a great preliminary bombardment, the Austrians holding a single line and relying on their fortifications. The Italians, with little result, lost 14,947 men (1,916 killed) ;[2] the Austrians, 9,958. After a pause for heavy artillery reinforcements, during which the Austrians were reinforced by two divisions, the struggle was resumed as the "Second Battle of the Isonzo", 18th July–3rd August 1915 ; it was brought to an end for lack of ammunition and guns, and want of aircraft and experienced observers, without much progress, at a cost of 41,866 (6,287 killed) ; in the slightly longer period 15th June –15th August, but mostly in the battle, the Austrians lost 46,640, including 12,290 missing. The Austrian maps show no change in the trace of the main front position in these two battles.

General Cadorna, on 20th July, informed Br.-General Delmé Radcliffe, the head of the British Military Mission, that he would continue to hammer as long as it could be done without unnecessary risk, or, as General Porro put it, until the Austro-Hungarians and Germans appeared in such

---

[1] See Sketch 1, which shows the progress made.
[2] In all the battles, the proportion of wounded to killed is exceptionally high, in this case about $5\frac{1}{4}$ to 1. Probably many were injured by fragments of rock.

14 THIRD AND FOURTH BATTLES OF THE ISONZO

force as to make a defensive attitude necessary. Already 27 generals had been removed from their commands.[1]

From the beginning of August until the middle of October only minor actions took place on all the fronts, the Italians meantime making every effort to train troops and repair losses ; whilst heavy guns were drawn from the Navy and the fortresses. The "Third Battle of the Isonzo", 18th October–4th November 1915, in which 11 Austrian divisions opposed 25 Italian with 1,200 guns instead of 212 as in the First Battle, had Gorizia as the objective. The plan was attacks on both wings on the Carso and at Plava, followed by one in the centre. The gain of ground was small, and the Italian casualties were 67,008 (10,733 killed, 11,985 missing).

After a week's pause for reorganization fighting was continued, to which the name of the " Fourth Battle of the " Isonzo ", 10th November–2nd December 1915, has been given. It produced no better results than the Third Battle. The Italian casualties are put at 48,967 (7,498 dead). The Austrians in the last two battles had lost a total of 71,691 men (25,865 dead and missing).

The balance of the fighting in the seven months of 1915 was not satisfactory to Italy : she had suffered on all fronts casualties amounting to about 250,000, and had gained no advantage either tactical or strategic. She had certainly drawn a dozen Austrian divisions to her frontier, but this had not interfered either with the great drive of the Central Powers into Russia to a north-south line 250 miles east of Warsaw, or with the subjugation of Serbia (October–November), which brought about as a corollary, the evacuation of the Gallipoli peninsula (begun on 19th December).

ALLIED PLANS FOR 1916 AND THE FIFTH ISONZO BATTLE

On 6th December 1915, at the suggestion of General Joffre, an inter-Allied Military Conference assembled at Chantilly, his headquarters, to consider plans for 1916.[2] It was

---

[1] The wholesale removal of officers (*siluramento*, torpedoing, is the Italian word) continued, and by October 1917 (Battle of Caporetto), 217 generals, 255 colonels and 335 battalion commanders had been relieved. Vigano, p. 97.

[2] For a fuller account of this conference see " 1916 " Vol I, pp. 4–10.

FIFTH BATTLE OF THE ISONZO

unanimously agreed by the delegates, Italy being represented by General Porro, Sub-Chief of the General Staff, that in 1916 Great Britain, France, Italy and Russia should attack as nearly simultaneously as might be with their maximum forces on their respective fronts, and that it was "very "desirable that this maximum effort should materialize at "a date as soon as possible after the end of March". Thus it was that the "Fifth Battle of the Isonzo", 11th–15th March, came about,[1] but on account of the German attack on Verdun (21st February) a fortnight earlier than the date originally suggested by General Joffre.

The weather was very unfavourable for an offensive, with snow falling on the higher ground, and rain and fog prevailing on the lower. The first two days were devoted to artillery bombardment. No tangible results accrued from the assault of two Armies, only small gains at three places were secured, "the same old three places" says the Austrian account, where slight advances had already been made, two opposite the Carso and the third at Plava. A gesture of co-operation with the Allies having, however, been executed, the battle was stopped on the fifth day. Although both the Third and Second Armies attacked, only the casualties of the former are given : 83 officers and 1,799 men. The Austrians suffered 485 killed and 1,500 wounded.[2]

Italian Requests for Heavy Artillery

From the Italian point of view the battle was described as a small effort designed to show the solidarity of the Allies and prevent the enemy from withdrawing troops and material from the Italian front : "the Italian Army could not advance "victoriously on the Carso or elsewhere until it had been "able to increase its resources in heavy artillery"[3] Whilst

---

[1] These are the dates of the battle given in I.O.A. ; A.O.A. says 11th–16th March.

[2] A.O.A. iv gives only half of p. 171 to this battle, and as regards the Italian Second Army says, " the attacks ordered had no success ". It makes the general remark that the giving of the name " Fifth Battle of " the Isonzo " was " an attempt by the enemy to pretend there had been " a serious battle ".

On 24th February the Italian Chief of the General Staff had told the British liaison officer that he hoped to make an attack on the Trentino, if artillery were available, at the same time as the Isonzo operation, or at any rate to drive in the Austrian advanced troops ; but nothing came of this scheme.

[3] I.O.A. iii (i), p. 180.

the fifth battle was in progress, on 12th March, at a second conference at Chantilly, General Porro called the attention of the Allied representatives to the necessity of augmenting the Italian artillery. General Cadorna also took up the question at a succeeding conference in Paris (27th—28th March 1916), when he said that, although Italy " had in-"creased her own means of production, she had not yet the "quantity of artillery which corresponded to her require-"ments ". But France and Great Britain, with the struggles at Verdun (which had begun on 21st February and went on until 16th December) and the Battles of the Somme (1st July–18th November) in prospect, were unable to offer help immediately, and it was not until April 1917 that any heavy guns were sent to Italy, as will be related in due course. When on 31st May, in the midst of the Austrian attack about to be described, Cadorna asked that his request might be reconsidered and some mobile heavy artillery sent at once, if only until the attack had been defeated, no heavy guns could be provided ; but his request for machine guns could be complied with, and henceforward about 250 pieces a month were sent to Italy, and from October about 500 tons of brass strip metal for the manufacture of cartridges. Italy, on her part, from September 1915 onwards sent large numbers of her obsolete Vetterli rifles with ammunition to Russia.[1]

The Austrian Trentino Offensive[2]

The Chiefs of the General Staffs of the Central Powers had also met in December 1915 to settle plans for 1916. The Serbians having been " liquidated " and the Russians driven back far enough, it was hoped, to prevent any interference on their part Conrad proposed to Falkenhayn to settle next with another of the weaker foes, Italy. The German commander had other views : he wanted to return to the Western Front and, by a startling success, to bring France, reported to be seething with defeatism, to capitulation. Unable to agree, the two Chiefs went their separate ways, the one to Verdun and the other to the Trentino.[3]

---

[1] See Note on " Financial loans to Italy " at end of Chapter.
[2] See Frontispiece.
[3] For a fuller account see " 1916 " Vol. I, pp. 52–5.

AUSTRIAN TRENTINO OFFENSIVE, 1916

Conrad set about increasing the Tirol Defence Command, under General Dankl, to form an *Eleventh Army*, sending to it five divisions from the now easier Russian front, and four from the Isonzo front. He further proposed to bring another Army, the *Third*, from Serbia, under General Kövess, to exploit the expected success of the *Eleventh*.

The concentration of these troops, with 60 heavy batteries, in the narrow valley of the Adige, north and south of Trent, in winter when avalanches as well as snow would be encountered, presented very serious difficulties. Far more complicated was their deployment in the Southern Trentino, east of the river; for all supplies had to pass through the bottleneck of Trent, whence one single line and one narrow-gauge line ran south. By 10th April, however, the *Eleventh Army* (8 divisions) had been concentrated, and the *Third* (7 divisions) was beginning to assemble, both Armies and the local defence troops being under the direct command of the Archduke Eugen, with Major-General Alfred Krauss as Chief of the Staff.

Conrad had hoped to attack in April, but weather conditions forced a postponement, and finally 15th May was made Zero Day, a diversion operation attack being carried out with some success in the Monfalcone sector of the Isonzo front on the previous day.

The attack did not come as a surprise to the Italians. The first reports of Austrian concentration in the Tirol were recorded in the early days of March, and all through April accurate information of the arrival of more men and material continued to come in. Cadorna, however, was inclined to regard a large-scale offensive from the Trentino as unlikely, and the Austrian preparations as a blind to distract attention from an attack elsewhere.

The Trentino front was held by the small Italian First Army (4 divisions), and its defences were regarded as poor—five lines had been prepared, but from lack of artillery and machine guns only the first two were armed. Early in April, therefore, Cadorna, notwithstanding his disbelief, reinforced the First Army by two divisions, to be held in reserve, guns and extra infantry; he also warned two more divisions in G.H.Q. reserve to be prepared to go to the assistance of the First Army, but the reserve was short both of ammunition and machine guns.

The Austrian *Eleventh* and *Third Armies*, after a short,

intensive bombardment, attacked on 15th May side by side on a 21-mile frontage east of the Adige, gradually extending eastward until this frontage was nearly doubled. Although the attack was not a surprise, its vigour certainly was. In the first five days the enemy advanced three to five miles, in places breaking through the Italian third line, but in general being brought to a stand before it. In the next nine days (20th–28th May) advance was made only in the centre; in the next 13 days (29th May–10th June), ground was won on the left (east) on the Asiago plateau, towards which side the battle front had been extended. During 11th to 18th June a final attempt was made to push down the valley of the Astico at the junction of the *Eleventh* and *Third Armies*. The general advance made by 10th June was from 12 miles on the left in the Asiago direction to about nine miles on the right near Mount Pasubio. The Austrians had not managed to debouch from the mountains. They were to go no farther. On 4th June, on the Eastern Front, General Brusilov, in response to Italian cries to Russia for help, had begun his offensive between the Carpathian mountains and the Pripet marshes towards Lemberg,[1] with the troops he had in the line. On a 50-mile front the Austrians were in flight. Conrad was now forced to beg Falkenhayn for help. At a conference between them on 8th June it was decided to stop the Tirol offensive and recall first $1\frac{1}{2}$ divisions and then $2\frac{1}{2}$ more.

As early as 25th May Cadorna had begun assembling reserves in the area Padua–Bassano–Vicenza, to form a Fifth Army, with a view to counter-attacking the Austrians as they emerged from the mountains, and he appealed to the Allies for the loan of mobile heavy artillery until the Austrians were defeated. The British proposed to send 32 horsedrawn obsolete 5-inch howitzers; but even this offer was soon withdrawn. By 2nd June, however, the Italian " Supreme Command felt certain that the Austrian effort " was nearly exhausted ", and an opportunity had come to use the Fifth Army for a counter-offensive. By that date this Army consisted of four corps (10 divisions),[2] and a

---

[1] The principal penetration was towards Luck, by which name the battle is known to the Austrians. For the Brusilov operation see " 1916 " Vol. I, pp. 55–6 : he captured 450,000 prisoners.

[2] Only one division and one corps headquarters were withdrawn from the Gorizia front. Some troops came from Libya.

AUSTRIAN TRENTINO OFFENSIVE, 1916

cavalry division, and two days later a fifth corps arrived. On 16th June, the very day on which Archduke Eugen ordered his Armies to revert to the pure defensive, the Italian counter-offensive was delivered: from the east, north of the Asiago plateau (sometimes marked Setti Comuni): and from the south, west of the plateau. The Austrians, by retiring, evaded the trap, and the Italians recovered about half the lost ground. On 9th July, however, their offensive was stopped, Cadorna not being prepared to push forward at all costs, and preferring to withdraw all divisions not required for the defence of the sector to take part in another Isonzo battle. Desultory fighting continued on the Trentino front until the 29th, and then ceased. The Austrians had been able to draw off without great loss, owing to their hold on the defiles leading north from the Asiago plateau.

The Trentino operations had cost the Italians 35,000 dead, 45,000 prisoners and 206,000 sick and wounded, and from 1st January to 1st July 1916 the total casualties suffered by the Italian Army had amounted to 56,680 dead in battle or by disease; 136,860 wounded and missing [*sic*], and 275,190 sick: total 524,760; but the total effective loss—owing to missing, wounded and sick rejoining—was only 203,298, less than half this total. Over 800,000 men having been called to the colours in the same period, the Army nevertheless was stronger than it had ever been.[1]

THE SIXTH BATTLE OF THE ISONZO (BATTLE OF GORIZIA)[2]
6TH–17TH AUGUST 1916

General Cadorna, in spite of the failures in 1915 to make any appreciable advance, was determined to persevere. He hoped, with the superior means in men and guns now becoming available, to be able to break the Isonzo front, and to that end he had continued preparations throughout the winter months. On 14th March 1916, as the Fifth Battle of the Isonzo, initiated as a gesture to please the Allies, was being brought to its futile close, he issued orders to the Third Army for the resumption, probably in June, of the attack on a front

---

[1] The Austrian casualties cannot be found, only the statement that in the two months June and July the strength of the Army fell by 346,000 men; but this figure includes the heavy losses in the Brusilov offensive (A.O.A. iv, p. 724). The Italian account does not give the number of prisoners taken.

[2] See Sketch 1.

of about ten miles from the Vipacco northwards, "with a "concentration of the maximum force against the entrenched "camp of Gorizia ".[1] The Austrian attack from the Trentino brought the Isonzo preparations to a stop, as the additional men and material intended for employment on the Julian front had to be transported westwards to reinforce the First Army, or were organized into a reserve Army to support it. On 2nd June, however, General Cadorna, having come to the conclusion that the Austrian effort in the Trentino was slackening, and that Conrad had withdrawn about 70,000 men from the Isonzo for the Trentino, informed his Armies that he proposed to proceed with the Isonzo operation. He confirmed this on the 16th, adding that as the means available were now more limited than originally expected the objective should be no more than the right bank of the Isonzo near Gorizia (which is on the left bank), as a starting line for future operations, whilst the forces on the Trentino front would stand on the defensive and prevent the enemy from using his position there as a jumping-off place for a renewal of his dangerous attack.

The success of the Gorizia operation " depended on the " secrecy and celerity " with which divisions and guns could be shifted back from the Trentino to the Julian front. The Italians, as already pointed out, were on interior lines, and could transport their men by several direct lines of railways whilst the Austrians, on exterior lines, were dependent on a long and circuitous route between the two theatres. The Italian movement of 12 divisions, a cavalry division, 132 heavy batteries and 37 trench mortar batteries, was entirely successful; for on the day of battle the 22 divisions of the Third (9 divisions) and Second (7 divisions and 2 Alpine Groups) Armies and the reserve behind the Second Army (6 divisions), with 624 medium and 62 heavy guns, found themselves opposed by only 9 of the Austrian *Fifth Army* (one in reserve), with 131 medium and 16 heavy guns, " not " enough defenders to stem a determined attack ", as the Austrian Official Account says. It was not the three-fold superiority usually judged necessary for a victorious offensive when the foes are otherwise well matched; but actually where the inner flanks of the Third and Second Armies made the main advance on the 8-mile frontage about Gorizia,

---

[1] I.O.A. iii (iii), p. 13.

their superiority was more than 10 divisions to 2, as two Austrian divisions held from the Vipacco as far as Plava.

The main attack at Gorizia, after diversions to the north and south, was begun at 4 p.m. on 6th August by the ten divisions of the three centre corps, after nine hours' bombardment. By the 8th the Isonzo had been crossed, the hills nearby secured and Gorizia captured, and the Austrian second position at the foot of the hills east of Gorizia reached. On the 7th General Cadorna, seeing the possibility of further success, ordered the necessary re-distribution of the heavy artillery. The second phase of the battle (10th–17th August) was not so successful; the right of the Third Army, however, after securing a footing on the Carso up to the gap called the Carso valley, came up into line between Monfalcone and the Vipacco. Then, the Austrians having been reinforced by three divisions and four brigades,[1] the defence stiffened, little more progress was made, and, although the writers of the Austrian Official Account think that, had Cadorna persevered, he might have broken through,[2] he decided to suspend operations at 6 p.m. on the 17th, without trying to expel the Austrians from the Tolmino bridgehead as planned.

The Italian casualties are put at 1,759 officers and 49,473 other ranks (12,128 missing), and the Austrian at 807 officers and 41,028. The number of prisoners is not mentioned by either side.

The Italians had gained possession of a strip of ground 15 miles wide and 3 miles deep, including a footing on the Carso and a bridgehead at Gorizia. In combination with the serious defeat of the Austrians on the Galician front, not to mention the difficulties of the Germans on the Somme, where the "material battle" was in full swing, and the consequent turn of the tide at Verdun, the moral effect on Italy and the Central Powers was very great, one result being that on 29th August the German High Command was transferred from Falkenhayn to Hindenburg-Ludendorff. On this same date Italy declared war on Germany. Rumania had done so two days earlier.

---

[1] Two divisions from the Russian front, the rest from the Trentino.
[2] Italian writers think that had General Capello (VI Corps of the Second Army) been given the reserves he asked for to exploit his initial success immediately in the sector Gorizia–Salcana, a decisive victory might have been achieved.

THE ITALIAN OFFENSIVE, 1916

THE AUTUMN OFFENSIVE 14TH SEPTEMBER TO 4TH NOVEMBER 1916

THE SEVENTH, EIGHTH AND NINTH BATTLES OF THE ISONZO

The three actions, officially called the Seventh, the Eighth and the Ninth Battles of the Isonzo, each lasting only three or four days (14th–17th September, 10th–12th October and 1st–4th November) were actually three stages of a single battle, with pauses for regrouping between them. Cadorna's purpose was to enlarge the Gorizia bridgehead, as the passages of the Isonzo were still liable to bombardment. The objectives indicated were a line on the Carso about six miles beyond the Carso Valley for the Third Army, and the Selva di Ternova for the Second Army, with the wooded San Marco hills as a preliminary objective. The artillery to hand being considered insufficient to carry out both operations at once, and the Carso attack being the easier, it was undertaken on 14th September after a month's preparation. The Second Army contributed a demonstration, and the Fourth Army, on the left of the Second, made an inroad from the Cadore to seize Toblach (48 miles north of Belluno), a great road and valley junction, an operation which completely failed.

The Third Army bombardment by 432 heavy and medium guns and 558 trench mortars, on a front of a little more than six miles, was distributed over eight days. Some ground was then gained by the infantry; but, on account of bad weather—the Austrians say on account of their counter-attacks—the action was suspended on the 17th. It was not renewed until 10th October, in this case after a 20 hours' bombardment, when the left corps of the Second Army co-operated with the Third Army by an attack against San Marco. Only a little more ground was gained on the Carso, and the battle was again suspended on the third day. In the final phase on 1st November two corps of the Second Army attacked east of Gorizia and two corps of the Third Army tried to push forward on the Carso. The results were very small and on the fourth day the operations were brought to an end on account of heavy losses, exhaustion of the troops and bad weather. The Italian casualties in the three actions amounted to a total of about 9,000 killed, 43,000 wounded and 23,500 missing, total 75,500; against this 21,500 prisoners had been captured. The Austrians lost about 63,000 (only round figures are given). Their official account sums up that " the success of the Italians " bore no relation to the mighty expenditure in men and "material which it cost," and that the failure to achieve more was due " mainly to the caution of the Italian Supreme " Command, who would not venture to throw in the last " reserves which might have secured victory".

NOTE

FINANCIAL LOANS TO ITALY

Large loans were made to Italy by the British Treasury : in round figures, *in cash*, in 1915–16, £49,000,000 ; in 1916–17, £98,000,000 ; in 1917–18, £112,000,000 ; in 1918–19, £110,000,000 ; and in 1919–20, £19,000,000 ; total £388,000,000 ; and in *Treasury Bills*, between 1915 and 1919, £411,840,000, with a total in 1926 of £610,840,000.

Against the above advances £22,200,000 Italian gold was deposited with Great Britain in 1915. Between 1920 and 1925 Italy refunded in cash £2,500,000.

In January 1926, the Treasury advances and gold deposit were funded, 1926–88, the total of the proposed payments being only £276,750,000. Repayments amounting to £23,812,500 were made by Italy up to 1931, when they ceased. Under the agreement the Italian gold advance of £22,200,000 was to be repaid over the period 1928–87, and up to 1931, £812,500 had been repaid, leaving £21,387,500 unpaid.

CHAPTER III

THE YEAR 1917 UNTIL THE EVE OF THE BATTLE OF CAPORETTO

(Frontispiece; Sketches 1, 2)

PLANS FOR 1917

During the course of 1916, no change had been made in the general principles for the conduct of operations agreed on at the Inter-Allied Military Conference held at Chantilly in December 1915. A similar conference, again under the presidency of General Joffre, was held on 15th and 16th November 1916 with much the same results as before.[1] The conclusions were:

(1) During the winter the operations actually in progress on each front should if possible be continued;

(2) the Allies should be ready to undertake combined offensives any time after the first fortnight in February 1917;

(3) as soon as the Armies were ready to attack the commanders-in-chief should act as circumstances required;

(4) if circumstances permitted, a date for the combined attack should be fixed by common accord.

A political conference, at which the French and British Prime Ministers (M. Briand and Mr. Asquith), the British Secretary of State for War (Mr. Lloyd George) and Russian and Italian delegates were present, was held in Paris simultaneously with the military conference. No change in the military policy was made at it, though some members were anxious that the forces at Salonika should be increased to about a million men for an advance through the Balkans into Austria.[2] Lack of sufficient shipping facilities and

---

[1] See " 1916 " Vol. II, pp. 530–3, where a fuller account of the conference will be found.

[2] Advocated by Mr. Lloyd George from the 1st January 1915 onward. See his " War Memoirs ", pp. 374, 392 and 431. He had suggested that the British contingent should be 600,000 men made up of 400,000 Territorials and 200,000 Regulars.

the nature of the communications in the Balkan theatre were, however, shown by the experts to be insuperable obstacles to the employment of a large force in the Salonika theatre.

Assistance to Italy Discussed

The month of December brought very important changes: General Joffre was superseded by General Nivelle, a man of magnificent promises with a recipe for winning the war, and Mr. Asquith was displaced by Mr. Lloyd George as British Prime Minister. Within a month of the latter event, at the instance of Mr. Lloyd George, an Inter-Allied Conference was held in Rome on 5th, 6th and 7th January 1917 for "a frank discussion of the whole military and political "situation", and the British Prime Minister laid before the assembly a memorandum "designed definitely to raise "important issues as to Allied strategy".[1]

The memorandum first discussed the Balkans, with regard to which it was admitted that "the grave shipping situation "provides an overwhelming argument against the dispatch "of further British divisions to Salonika", and it suggested that Italy might send a reinforcement of two divisions to that theatre.[2] It then turned to the Italian front with the introduction that "we can put the Germans out of action "just as well on the Italian as on the Western Front"— an oft-repeated phrase of General Wilson. The proposal was made that both in the contingency of the Italians having to stand on the defensive to meet an attack and of their mounting an attack for an offensive, which it was hoped would be the case, they should be largely reinforced by

---

[1] This memorandum (War Cabinet Secret G.106), reproduced in Mr. Lloyd George's "War Memoirs", is described by Field-Marshal Sir Henry Wilson in his diary as "an amazing document, written without [Sir William] Robertson's [the C.I.G.S.'s] knowledge or approval". Wilson was in London in November–December 1916 waiting orders, given whilst Mr. Lloyd George was still at the War Office, to accompany Lord Milner's Mission to Russia (28th January–2nd March 1917), and went to the Rome conference with Mr. Lloyd George.

Among others present at the Conference were General Lyautey, (the new French Minister of War), General Cadorna, General Sarrail (French Commander-in-Chief at Salonika), Lord Milner, Sir William Robertson, Sir Maurice Hankey, and General Sir George (Field-Marshal Lord) Milne (British G.O.C.-in-C. Salonika).

[2] The Balkan part of the Conference is given in "Macedonia", Vol. I, pp. 230–1.

French and British artillery : it was judged that Italy had more than sufficient infantry, and had failed of complete success from " lack of sufficient artillery, and more especially " heavy artillery and heavy artillery ammunition ".

The memorandum made the useful suggestion that orders should be given " to our respective General Staffs " to work out in full detail the arrangements and time-tables for the rapid transfer of artillery from the Western to the Italian front.

In the debate which followed Mr. Lloyd George pointed out that an Italian offensive would bring relief to the tension in the Balkans : that the Austrians were the weakest enemy and offered the weakest spot : that a successful advance from the Isonzo would lead to the enemy's " vitals " and " that if Austria were beaten Germany would be beaten too", being only " formidable so long as she could command an " unbroken Austria ". Had this advice been followed there might have been a great clash in Italy ; for the two great strategists in the enemy's ranks, Field-Marshal Conrad, the Austrian, and Colonel Wetzell (Ludendorff's Chief of the Operations Section), the German, were both advocating a German-Austrian offensive against Italy at this time.[1]

The French delegates at the Conference were, however, opposed to any scheme for a combined operation on the Italian front, whose mountainous nature presented special difficulties, for the good reason that France was already committed to the Nivelle plan for a great offensive on the Western Front with British collaboration. They stated, however, that General Nivelle had already sent Colonel Payot (Direction de l'Arrière) and Colonel Hellé (General Staff) to Italy to discuss the question of support in case of need and to plan its transport by train. Some heavy guns might, they said, be spared for three months, that is until April ; but this was of no use to General Cadorna, for no important operations were possible in the Italian theatre until that month. He made a request for the assistance for an offensive of three hundred heavy guns and eight French and British divisions.[2] As no promise could be made and there being little chance of such large forces being forthcoming, he became according to Sir Maurice Hankey

---

[1] See Note at end of Chapter.
[2] This estimate he subsequently raised to 400 guns and 10 divisions. Villari, p. 104.

"very lukewarm" in the matter. Finally the question of assistance to Italy was referred by the conference to the military advisers of the various governments.

GENERAL CADORNA'S VIEWS AND THE VISITS TO HIM OF GENERALS NIVELLE AND ROBERTSON

One reason for General Cadorna's unwillingness to undertake a great offensive was apprehension of a strong German attack against Italy, which, as just mentioned, had indeed been studied by Ludendorff. Forces freed by the collapse of Rumania were obviously available; for Bukarest had capitulated on 6th December 1916 and the Dobrudja had been evacuated by the Russians and Rumanians on 6th January. Not only did the Italian C.G.S. fear an offensive from the Tirol, where indeed it was known that some preparations were being made by German staff officers, possibly with intent to deceive, but he also professed to have evidence of a contemplated invasion via Switzerland. On 1st February, therefore, in the midst of his other preoccupations, General Nivelle in person paid a two-day visit to the Comando Supremo at Udine. He examined with General Cadorna the possibility of a German invasion through Switzerland, which he did not by any means wholly discount. He suggested, however, that weather conditions in the mountains would protect the Italian left until the month of May: meanwhile he trusted that in accordance with the Chantilly agreement the Italians would launch an attack on the Isonzo front contemporaneously with Franco-British offensives on the Western Front, about the beginning of April.[1] General Cadorna was doubtful whether he could be ready by the 1st April.[2]

At an Anglo-French-Italian Conference held at St. Jean de Maurienne in Savoy on 19th February, mainly to discuss Italy's claim to a large share of Asia Minor should the Turkish Empire break up, Mr. Lloyd George pointed out plainly to Baron Sonnino that Italy's effort was practically confined to a defence of her frontier against greatly inferior enemy forces, and that she was doing nothing to support the war against Turkey.

---

[1] The British Arras offensive was launched on 9th April, the Nivelle offensive on the Aisne, on 16th April.

[2] F.O.A. v. (i), p. 195.

At the end of March General Sir William Robertson, on the invitation of General Cadorna, paid a visit to the Italian front, and General Weygand joined the party to represent the French. The C.I.G.S. found the administration arrangements were good, but did not conceive a high opinion of the Italian defences, which were of pre-war pattern and without depth; there was, he learnt, no system of co-operation between the artillery and infantry in attack, in fact the relations between the two arms seemed strained; the creeping barrage was unknown; and signal communications at the front were elementary. He came to the conclusion that an occasion might easily arise when the Italians even in defence would require help in infantry as well as in heavy guns. His views were communicated to the French Government, and as a result General Foch, then without a command but specially employed, was sent to Italy. On 8th April he and General Cadorna came to an agreement with regard to the general lines of the eventual action of French forces in Italy and the areas of detrainment. The transport by train had already been settled. Simultaneously General Weygand, Foch's former Chief of Staff, went to Switzerland to concert measures in the event of a German inroad, and the entry of French and Italian troops for the purpose of co-operation in such a case was agreed on.

BRIG.-GENERAL CROWE'S MISSION

In December 1916, after the second Chantilly Conference, French G.Q.G. had initiated an examination of the best means of effecting a transfer of forces between the Western and Italian fronts. Sea passage and march by stages had been considered, but an all-rail route was evidently the safest and quickest. General Robertson on his return home on 5th April despatched Br.-General J. H. V. Crowe, General Staff,[1] to make a preliminary study of the communications and to plan tentative arrangements with officers of the Italian Supreme Command for the possible transfer of a force of six British divisions with their own services (about 120,000 men and 26,000 animals in all) by

---

[1] He had commanded the artillery in East Africa 1915–6 and had been selected to be Chief of the General Staff to General Sir Horace Smith-Dorrien who on account of a break-down in health did not exercise command in East Africa.

ANGLO-ITALIAN CONVENTION. MAY, 1917

rail to the Italian theatre. On his way to Italy he visited G.H.Q. to consult the Transportation authorities, in touch with Colonel Payot, in order to find out what arrangements had been made for the move of French troops. On 20th April the C.I.G.S. himself went to Paris for a conference with the French Minister of War at which "the bases of the "initial organization of the relief force" to be sent to Italy were settled.[1]

As a result of Br.-General Crowe's visit to Italy, on 7th May an Anglo-Italian Convention was signed by him and on behalf of the Italians by General Porro, the Deputy Chief of the General Staff, and the Intendant General S. Lombardi.[2] This provided for the concentration of the six British divisions in certain areas, their conveyance to these areas from the frontier, by train or motor bus; billeting facilities; a base at Arquata (on the Scrivia about 40 miles north of Genoa); port facilities and cold storage at Genoa; lines of communication, *haltes repas*, advanced depôts, supplies, hospital accommodation, postal and telegraph services, maps, interpreters, liaison officers, military and civil jurisdiction and other details.[3]

A railway route, the "Taranto (or Overland) route", from Cherbourg through France to Modane (Mont Cenis),[4] and thence along the east coast of Italy, with six trains per day, for the supply of Egypt and Salonika, was already organized and working;[5] and by this it was possible to send heavy artillery to the Italians, but it was inadequate for the transportation and supply of an Army.

The French military authorities, however, were prepared, for the purposes of the scheme, and as an essential preliminary to any detailed agreement with the Italian authorities, to provide 62 trains a day, using both the Modane and the Riviera routes. Of these, 28 would be through trains to the concentration areas in Italy, and the remaining 34 would convey the troops to frontier railway stations in France,

---

[1] F.O.A. vi (ii), p. 296, says that the "Président du War Committee" (*sic*) was also present, but attempts to discover who this was have failed. Mr. Lloyd George was at a conference in Paris on 4th May, but it did not touch on Italian affairs.

[2] The text is given in Appendix IX.

[3] The French proposed to send 4 divisions with heavy and mountain artillery and 8 or 10 air squadrons "at least". F.O.A. vi (ii), p. 296.

[4] The other railway route was by the Riviera, with Ventimiglia as the frontier station. See Sketch 2.

[5] See "Transportation" pp. 287–292.

whence they would have to march across the frontier mountains to Italian entraining stations. The Modane route was the shorter, about 800 miles, while the Riviera route via Etaples, the Rhone valley and Ventimiglia was nearly 1,200.[1]

PROJECTS FOR TRANSPORT OF TROOPS TO ITALY

To complete the work, therefore, on 21st June after conferences of the various departments concerned had been held at the War Office, Br.-General Crowe was sent to Italy again, with a mission of 4 officers (G.S., Q., R.E. and Medical)[2] and 6 other ranks, to reconnoitre the five transfrontier march routes.[3] A French officer and an Italian officer were attached to the mission in order to give any information and help found necessary, and the Italian authorities, through the good offices of the chief liaison officer, Br.-General Delmé-Radcliffe, supplied the necessary transport and gave every possible assistance.

Two schemes of movement were prepared, in one of which the infantry and dismounted units accompanied by their first line transport and part of the second line marched over the frontier; in the other, the mounted branches, artillery and transport also did so. The reports were rendered on 5th July. They included general descriptions of the routes; the state, grades, obstacles and telegraph communications of the roads; detraining stations (with plans); billeting facilities; camping and bivouac grounds; water supply; sanitation requirements; sign posts and notice boards. Advanced parties were provided for, and priority of movement fixed. The medical report drew attention to the effect on marching powers of hill climbing,

---

[1] A technical description of the two routes will be found in "Transportation," pp. 297-302.
[2] The medical officer was Colonel S. L. Cummins.
[3] See Sketch 2. The 5 march routes were :—

		Number of trains arriving per day at detraining station.
Bourg St. Maurice–Aosta (highest point 7,038 ft.)	55 miles (4 marches) ...	8
Modane–Susa	40 miles (3 marches) ...	6
Briançon–Pinerolo (highest point 6,678 ft.) ...	55 miles (4 marches) ...	6
Nice–Cuneo (Tenda) ...	37·5 miles (3 marches) ...	8
Ventimiglia–Savona ...	68·75 miles (4 marches) ...	6

reduced atmosphere pressure, the lower temperature at night in the mountains, prevailing diseases, the provision of sanitary apparatus and the disposal of sick. Appendices went into the question of the units of the ancillary services required for an Army headquarters, for corps headquarters and for Lines of Communication ; the strength of advanced parties ; the supplies and other items which the Italian army would furnish ; and other work, including arrangements for monetary exchange, which that army was prepared to undertake. The Italian authorities supplied railway time-tables for the concentration. Modifications were interpolated in case French troops should be sent either before or with the British. The Commander-in-Chief of the British Armies in France and Belgium was kept informed by the C.I.G.S. of the arrangements projected and he was requested to select an Army staff. All therefore was prepared for a rapid transfer of troops.

Loan of Heavy Batteries to Italy

As a result of General Robertson's visit ten newly raised 6-inch howitzer batteries (40 howitzers) in two groups under Br.-General P. D. Hamilton—the total number of batteries of this kind with the British Armies in France at this time was only 152—were sent from Aldershot to Italy on 7th April and went to the Carso sector.[1] It may be added here that they were reinforced in July by another group and three batteries,[2] and the French then " despatched a dozen " heavy batteries towards Italy ".[3] In August, one 9.2-inch howitzer arrived. At first this howitzer was attached to the 101st H.A. Group ; later on (in October) it was transferred to XCIV H.A. Group.

---

[1] The XCIV Heavy Artillery Group under Lieut-Colonel C. N. Buzzard, of the 302nd, 307th, 315th, 316th and 317th Batteries.
The XCV Heavy Artillery Group under Lieut-Colonel A. H. Moberly, of the 304th, 314th, 320th, 322nd and 334th Batteries.
Both detrained at Palmanova (15 miles south of Udine) and were attached to the Italian 2nd Heavy Artillery *Raggruppamenta* (collection of groups), XI Corps, Third Army. The batteries were commanded by Regular majors and mostly had Regular captains.
The XCIV went into action just south of the junction of the Vipacco with the Isonzo, and the XCV farther south, also on the east bank of the Isonzo, south of Gradisca.

[2] The 101st H.A. Group of the 394th, 395th and 396th Batteries under Lieut.-Colonel J. A. Purefoy Robinson. The three new batteries, the 390th, 391st and 392nd, were attached to the XCV H.A. Group.

[3] F.O.A. v (ii), p. 277   It is not stated how far they went.

The Tenth Battle of the Isonzo[1]
12th May–5th June

It was not until 12th April, that is not until after the British Arras offensive had begun, and General Cadorna's apprehensions of an attack from the Tirol had more or less subsided, that he gave orders for an Isonzo offensive. It was not, however, to begin until 7th May, and as the time approached bad weather compelled a postponement of five days. Thus the Italian attack did not take place for more than three weeks after the Nivelle offensive had opened on 16th April, by which time it was clear that the French effort had definitely failed to bring about the results promised. In the meantime General Cadorna had reorganized the command on the Isonzo front in order to give his most pushful and successful general an opportunity. The left corps of the Third Army and the three right corps of the Second Army were placed, as the "Gorizia Zone Command," under General Capello, whose VI Corps had captured Gorizia in the previous year. General Piacentino's Second Army was thereby reduced to only one corps, to which the Carnia Force was added as a XII Corps. Of the total Italian forces, now 59 divisions, 28 were to attack and 10 were kept in general reserve in Friuli.

Again, as it happened, there were two separate battles, on the right and left, as in the centre in the Gorizia sector of Capello's zone "there was not a step forward". According to Cadorna's plan, after a two days' bombardment Capello's Army (12 divisions, 528 heavy guns, 67 trench mortar batteries) was to attack at 12 noon on the 14th at the close of a final heavy burst of fire. It was to secure at least the hills east of Gorizia and the hammer-head of the Bainsizza, known as the Monte Kuk–Vodice ridge, the left of the Third Army protecting its right. When the Austrian reserves had been attracted northwards by the attack, the Third Army (16 divisions, 530 heavy guns and 63 trench mortar batteries) under the Duke of Aosta was to make the decisive attack over the Carso.[2]

This manœuvre was so far successful that of the four divisions in the Austrian reserve (behind the southern wing

---

[1] See Sketch 1.

[2] The figures for the guns are from Villari; the *Revista di Artigleria e Genio*, October 1933, gave the guns of the Third Army as 47 super-heavy, 733 heavy and 584 trench mortars.

of the Austrian *Fifth Army*) two were sent to Monte Kuk and a third went half-way there. Opposed to Capello in the first place were 5 divisions (3 around Gorizia), and to the Third Army 6 divisions.[1] Part of the Monte Kuk ridge was captured in the first onslaught, and then for a week the Italians repulsed all Austrian counter-attacks; but the Gorizia attack was, as mentioned, a complete failure. On 23rd May the Third Army delivered its blow according to plan, after 6 hours' bombardment; but on account of shortage of ammunition and the failure at Gorizia it advanced only between the sea and the Vipacco, and gained only some 2,000 to 4,000 yards of ground on the right.

On the 28th, General Boroevic, delivered a prepared counter-offensive against the Third Army, without, however, much result, and desultory fighting continued for several days. But alarmed for the safety of Trieste, Austrian G.H.Q. sent Boroevic three more divisions from the Russian front, and thus reinforced, on 4th June he made another counter-offensive on the southern flank with three of the old divisions. It regained part of the ground lost on the Carso, and led to the capture of many thousand Italians " the best part of 27,000 ". With this, however, the battle ended, for neither side could afford any further loss of life and expenditure of ammunition.

The casualties in the three weeks' fighting had been heavy: the Italian amounted to 36,000 killed, 96,000 wounded and 25,000 prisoners;[2] the Austrian were 7,300 killed, 45,000 wounded and 23,400 prisoners. The large number of Italian prisoners, mostly from the southernmost sector, was ascribed by General Cadorna as to some extent due to revolutionary and pacifist propaganda;[3] the appeal for peace in the Pope's Encyclical of 15th August is said to have raised false hopes in many serious minds.

The Battle of Ortigara. 10th June

An incident known as the Battle of Ortigara, occurred in the Trentino sector in June which is remarkable for the

---

[1] A.O.A. vi, p. 181, puts the opposing " front fighters " as 165,000 Austrians against 280,000 Italians; guns 1,400 against 2,200.
[2] A.O.A. vi, p. 181, says 27,000.
[3] The narrative attached to the war diary of the British XCIV Heavy Artillery Group (Carso) for August 1917 has the remark " mutinies occurred " apparently in some regiments ".

heavy casualties incurred. On the 10th, after thorough preparations, two Italian divisions attacked the Austrian flank north of Asiago[1] in order to turn the enemy out of a strong line of defence which as a possible jumping-off place menaced the rear of the Italians to the eastward in Cadore and Carnia. The Austrians counter-attacked; the Italians made a second attempt, and were again counter-attacked and lost all their gains. The affair ended on 29th June. The Austrian account speaks of the Italian effort as a complete failure (*Miserfolg*), the Italians call it "a most unfortunate episode"; artillery support had been lacking owing to unfavourable weather. They lost about 950 officers and 22,000 other ranks, many being Alpini, their best troops; the Austrian official totals are given exactly as 251 and 8,577.

The Eleventh Battle of the Isonzo (The Bainsizza)[2]

At the commencement of the Russian summer offensive of 29th June, associated with the name of Kerenski, then in power, although General Brusilov was the actual commander in the field, General Cadorna was informed of the coming British offensive (the Third Battle of Ypres, 31st July). He had already decided to resume operations in accordance with his agreement and had six new divisions and additional heavy artillery with which so to do. He proceeded to abolish the Gorizia Zone Command, promoted General Capello to the command of the Second Army, and reconstructed it on a front from the Vipacco to Plezzo (10 miles north of Tolmino) with a strength of 17 divisions, 6 brigades, 850 heavy guns and 960 trench mortars. A special force of 4 divisions and 150 heavy guns (VIII Corps) was detailed to hold the Gorizia bridgehead. The Third Army was also increased to 18 divisions, 700 heavy guns and 800 trench mortars. The Austrian force, eighteen divisions, opposite to these two Armies was only one division stronger than it had been at the Tenth Battle; for although four more divisions had arrived three tired ones had been transferred to the Russian front; no more reinforcements could be provided and the force in the Trentino was reduced to "only a thin "screen".

---

[1] See Frontispiece.
[2] See Sketch 1.

ELEVENTH BATTLE OF THE ISONZO. 35
AUGUST, 1917

At the London Conference of 7th and 8th August Baron Sonnino, the Italian Foreign Minister, demanded the loan of 400 heavy guns for the offensive in prospect. It did not seem that this would be possible; in fact the C.I.G.S. told the War Cabinet on 27th August that the guns would have to be withdrawn from the Flanders battle and the offensive there would have to be stopped: the best help to Italy would be given by continuing the offensive of Ypres. It was not until a further conference at Amiens on 7th September, that General Pétain now commanding the French Armies of the North and North-East, received orders from the Government to send guns, as will be mentioned later.[1]

Cadorna's directive, issued on this occasion instead of orders so as to leave the Army commanders greater freedom, gave to the Third Army the Carso and Trieste as objectives, and to the Second Army, the Selva di Ternova, but it was to take the Bainsizza first. To prevent any misunderstanding it was laid down that the force in the Gorizia bridgehead was not to attack à fond, but rather to wait an opportunity which the attacks on either side of it might bring. A diversion was to be made against the Austrian bridgehead south of Tolmino. General Capello took advantage of the liberty accorded to him and decided to put in his main attack flankwise between Plava and Selo, although this involved crossing the gorge of the Isonzo in the face of the enemy.

After a bombardment of the enemy's whole front from the sea to Tolmino, which began at 6 a.m. on 18th August, on the night of the 18th/19th, though many of the bridges thrown were broken, the leading echelons of five Italian divisions (two corps), opposed by the outposts of two and a half divisions, forced the passage of the Isonzo, on the 8-mile frontage selected by General Capello. According to the Austrian official account it was " the most violent of the " Italian attacks ". The corps to the north and south then joined in ; but the diversion at the Tolmino bridgehead on the left was a complete failure, and the Third Army on the right accomplished " very little progress ", though supported by gun fire from the sea, and nearly all the ground which it gained it soon lost to counter-attack. On the 22nd Cadorna

---

[1] F.O.A. v (ii), p. 279.

stopped the operations of the Third Army and sent troops and guns from it to the Second Army. The narrative of the battle rendered by Lieut.-Colonel C. N. Buzzard (XCIV Heavy Artillery Group) goes far to explain the failure of the Italians here and elsewhere. He says that the characteristics of the attacks were :

" (1) Almost entire lack of information supplied to " the Heavy Artillery. We were never told which way " the infantry would attack, the hours named were " never adhered to.

" (2) Fire was lifted far too soon : infantry had no " support in passing over four or five hundred yards of " open and difficult ground. We could have kept on " firing until the infantry was 200 yards from objectives.

" (3) Austrian prisoners say that during our bombard- " ment all their men were in caverns, and they hardly " lost any ; the trenches were quite wrecked : no shells " can touch their caverns.

" (4) The remarkable thing is that with such utter " lack of co-operation between artillery and infantry, " the Italian infantry ever take any of their objectives. " The artillery preparation is good, a large number of " the infantry are quite heroic ; but to advance behind " a proper creeping barrage is unheard of."

The Austrian Retreat

The troops of the Second Army continued their success on the 20th, and on the 21st broke through the enemy line near Auzza on a two-thousand-yard front, so that, it is admitted the Austrians grew shaky (*wankend*). They tried " elastic " yielding " and then a foot-by-foot defence, "a fight to " gain time for an orderly retreat " ;[1] but still had to fall back. On the next day General Boroevic was visited by the Austrian Emperor and General Arz, his Chief of the General Staff. The latter informed Boroevic that a plan for a great relieving attack from the Tolmino–Caporetto front was projected : he required fifteen divisions : now that the Russians were collapsing after the German counter-offensive against the Kerenski advance, he could provide eight and hoped to borrow six more from the Germans. Boroevič, influenced by this, and the desire to get his men out of range

---

[1] A.O.A. vi, p. 455.

AUSTRIAN RETIREMENT. AUGUST, 1917

of the Italian heavy guns in position on the west bank of the Isonzo, decided on a withdrawal from the front of the Bainsizza to a line roughly northward from Salcana. This plan was approved of by the Archduke Eugen, commanding the South-West Front, and by Arz, and at 9 a.m. on the 23rd orders were issued for the retirement to be begun on the night of the 23rd/24th, and Boroevic was prepared to go back farther if necessary.[1]

The sight of fires and the sound of demolitions gave the Italians notice of the withdrawal and a pursuit was ordered ; but progress across the naturally broken and now shell stricken surface of the Bainsizza, with roads destroyed and water lacking, was slow. It being useless to attack the new line, against which the infantry had " bumped", without bringing forward the heavy artillery, on the 29th, the Comando Supremo ordered the suspension of the offensive, except of the operation to capture the pivot of Monte San Gabriele[2] and of a final effort to break through the defences north and east of Gorizia.

General Cadorno announced, however, that his offensive would be resumed towards the end of September. It was at this crisis that the French Government, judging that a little extra pressure might induce the Austrian Emperor to bring to a head the peace proposals which he had secretly initiated on 31st March, and that the campaign in Flanders in progress would secure the French front from attack, authorized General Pétain to send nine artillery groups (of 2 batteries each) of medium calibre to Italy.[3]

The situation at Gorizia did not change ; at the pivot of Monte San Gabriele fighting continued until 13th September, when it died out ; but the hill, after changing hands remained in possession of the Austrians.

---

[1] Krafft, Chief of the Staff of the attacking German-Austrian troops at Caporetto, says that the Austrians were driven from their last prepared position and forced back into a wild mountainous region, where a new position could only be slowly developed by blasting : that they could not face another offensive where they lay and must go forward or back.

[2] At the western apex of the Selva di Ternova, near Gorizia.

[3] F.O.A. v (ii), p. 1132. They detrained on 10th September ; one part was employed near Gorizia and the other near Plava. This, it is said, made a total of 140 French heavy guns.

ELEVENTH BATTLE OF THE ISONZO.
AUGUST, 1917

RESULTS OF THE BATTLE

The Italians had lost about 40,000 killed, 108,000 wounded and 18,000 prisoners, the Austrians 10,000 dead, more than 45,000 wounded and roughly 30,000 missing (the Italians took 29,000 prisoners). Both sides claimed a victory; Ludendorff considered that the Italians were successful. They had certainly gained ground on the Bainsizza, but the Austrians still held securely the pillars of Monte San Gabriele and the Tolmino bridgehead on the flanks of the advance. The First Quartermaster-General—who it must be remembered, consistently depreciated the assistance given by the Austrians both on the Russian and Italian fronts—judged that "their losses on the Carso Plateau [he "does not mention the Bainsizza] had been so heavy and "they were so shaken that the responsible military and "political authorities of the Dual Monarchy were convinced "that they would not be able to stand a continuation of the "battle and a twelfth attack on the Isonzo".[1]

NOTE
AUSTRIAN-GERMAN CONSIDERATION OF A CAMPAIGN AGAINST ITALY AT THE BEGINNING OF 1917[2]

At the end of 1916 when the Germans had lost the initiative on the Western Front as a result of the fighting at Verdun and on the Somme, Conrad, the Austro-Hungarian Chief of the General Staff, counselled the military defeat of Italy by a double attack from the Tirol and on the Isonzo as the best the Central Powers could do to regain it. On 20th December 1916 Lieut.-Colonel Wetzell,[3] Ludendorff's strategist, gave the same advice in a lengthy appreciation, saying that an Italian campaign was "the only operation, which if successful, would immediately "benefit the Western Front". If the French, he said, sent aid to the Italians, it would weaken the Western Front, and if only the line of the Adige were reached, it would shorten the Austrian front and free troops for use either in the East or the West: should no Franco-British help be forthcoming the main Italian forces could be liquidated, Upper Italy occupied and France threatened from the Alpine front. Ludendorff in view of the

---
[1] Ludendorff, p. 482.
[2] Extracted mainly from Wendt.
[3] For Wetzell's excellent advice as regards the 1918 campaign, not followed by Ludendorff, see "1918" Vol. I pp. 139 and 141 and Appendix 20, where his appreciation is given in full.

ammunition shortage and of the probable continuation of the Allied offensive (as General Joffre intended) rejected Wetzell's plan.

On 23rd January 1917 at a Conference with the German High Command, Conrad who could not believe that unrestricted U-Boat warfare (announced 31st January) without a victory on land would bring the war to an end, again advocated a combined double attack on Italy. Going into details he proposed a main attack from the Tirol, preceded by another from the Isonzo front at the most a week before. The place he selected for the latter was the Caporetto sector. The German Supreme Command had already determined on the retreat on the Western Front to the Hindenburg Line, and informed him that only after the repulse of the expected (Nivelle) offensive in the West, would it be able to discuss the next situation. On 28th February the young Austrian Kaiser removed Conrad (aged 65) from his high appointment as Chief of the General Staff, giving him command of the Tirol front, and replaced him by General Arz von Straussenburg (aged 60), a successful division and corps commander[*]; but Conrad's Caporetto plan was not forgotten.

CHAPTER IV

TWELFTH BATTLE OF THE ISONZO

THE BATTLE OF CAPORETTO[1]
(Frontispiece, Sketches 1, 3, 4)

CADORNA ABANDONS THE OFFENSIVE

Early in September, 1917, the Secretary of State for War, Lord Derby, the Adjutant General of the Forces, Lieut.-General Sir Nevil Macready, and the Director of Military Operations, Major-General F. B. Maurice, travelled to Italy, and on the 11th took part in a conference at Udine with General Cadorna and General Porro. The main question discussed was the loan of more heavy guns to Italy. Though no promise could be made, the Italian C.G.S. was told that all the guns which could be spared, and it was hoped that this would not be less than 40 batteries, would be sent; but as the British were short of trained personnel it was suggested that Italian gunners, either in whole or part, might be provided. It was mentioned that although, in view of an offensive in Palestine, it would be necessary to send 6 batteries of 6-inch howitzers to Egypt, they would be returned by April, and General Cadorna agreed that he could spare them by the third week in October. He then asked for field guns. If he had the artillery, he said, he could form twenty more divisions, and in any case more field artillery would be valuable, as he must be prepared to act on the defensive if seventy to eighty divisions, freed by the collapse of Russia, were sent against Italy. This was the first hint of what was in his mind. He was told that Great Britain could not supply field artillery, but that the French would be asked to do so. He declined the offer of tanks, as he thought that there would be no possibility of using them in view of the natural difficulties of the country in which the fighting was taking place. Some suggestions for improvement of accommodation and roads at the port

---

[1] Caporetto is the Italian name. In Germany it is known as Karfreit, the German name for this place; in Austria, as Flitsch (Plezzo).

of Taranto, where men and material were being embarked for Egypt and Salonika, concluded the business of the meeting.

Cadorna Abandons Offensive

There were good reasons for General Cadorna's mention of a possible defensive attitude. On 14th September the German-Swiss frontier was closed and rumours of the concentration of Austrian, even German, divisions in the Trentino[1] began to reach the Comando Supremo, always very sensitive to danger from that quarter. An operation—a raid on a large scale—in the Brenta valley towards Trent, however, on the night of 18th/19th September, made by a Bersagliere division specially brought from the Isonzo for the purpose, discovered nothing unusual, although it captured a hundred prisoners. To the British and French General Staffs it seemed clear that, in view of the limited Austrian railway facilities for bringing up troops, no great operation could be conducted from the Trentino before the snows of winter set in and made movement impossible.[2]

General Cadorna, though he still left $12\frac{1}{2}$ divisions in the Trentino (facing about 7 divisions and many local troops) seems to have come to the same conclusion ; at any rate, on 18th September he wrote to the commanders of the Second and Third Armies :[3]

"The continued increase of the opposing forces on the "Julian front makes it probable that the enemy proposes "to launch a serious attack there very soon, and a violent "one considering the huge forces he can bring from the "Russian front.

"In view of the above and of the situation as regards "reinforcements and ammunition, I have decided to "abandon all projects for offensive operations and con-"centrate all efforts on preparation for a defence to the "last " ; and he directed the two Armies to set about the redistribution of their artillery for this purpose.

---

[1] See Frontispiece.

[2] A counter-attack from the Trentino was considered by the Austrians about the end of July. It was judged to be the most effective ; but at least 12 divisions trained in mountain warfare were required, and even with German assistance it would be hard to find them : railway communication too was by a single line and the deployment, as in the spring of 1916, would be slow. A.O.A. vi, pp. 493–4.

[3] Cadorna II, p. 112.

On 20th September he informed the French and British Missions, to whom it came as a surprise (for they thought preparations for an offensive were in hand), that he was compelled to give up temporarily any idea of an offensive, in order to economize ammunition. The Allied Missions were not alone in their disillusion; for the senior British heavy artillery officer serving with the Italians records the "stupefaction" of his Italian comrades that Cadorna did not go on after his great Bainsizza success. Officially General Cadorna gave as his reasons "the recent steady "concentration of enemy artillery and troops on the Italian "front and the increasingly serious and menacing situation "in Russia". Going into detail, he said[1] that the capture, essential to further progress, of Monte Hermada on the Carso, San Marco opposite Gorizia, and Monte San Gabriele on the Selva di Ternova would cost 150,000 men and entail the expenditure of about two million rounds of heavy gun ammunition—and the monthly production did not reach 600,000. He also adduced to the British Mission as factors which had influenced him: heavy losses, shortage of trained officers, lack of reinforcements, general repugnance to the rigours of an autumn campaign, and Socialist, Communist and peace propaganda.[2] He feared, he said, that the chances of success of the spring offensive might be imperilled by an autumn attack: it seemed certain to him that the Austrian High Command was preparing a counter-offensive: about fifteen Austrian divisions had disappeared from the Russian front: the departure of six German divisions for the Trentino seemed imminent:[3] further, some sixty Austrian battalions were being moved northward from the Carso to the Bainsizza: so that sector seemed the probable theatre of the great counter-offensive: it was the sector of the Second Army that was menaced. To meet the threat, the Comando Supremo reorganized the Third and Second Armies, so that the latter had 25 divisions and the former only 9, with 7 divisions in general reserve behind them.

---

[1] See Sketch 3.
[2] On 8th September the Italian Foreign Minister told the British Ambassador that "the next two months are critical for Italy on account "of the demands for peace".
[3] They were the six for Caporetto; but they were sent through Innsbruck in the northern Tirol for the purpose of deceiving the Italian Intelligence, and Kaiser Karl and the German plenipotentiary, General von Cramon, also went ostentatiously to Bolzano in the Tirol (Cramon, p. 128).

ENEMY INTENTIONS. OCTOBER, 1917   43

With the campaign of Third Ypres in progress and the Battle of Malmaison (23rd October) in preparation, the British and French Governments, on hearing of General Cadorna's plans, decided on 25th September to recall the heavy batteries lent to Italy solely for offensive operations,[1] and they did so simultaneously as an indication of solidarity; but at their conference at Boulogne on the 29th, at which Monsieur Painlevé and Mr. Lloyd George, the two prime ministers, were present, the Italian situation was not mentioned: the extension of the British front was the subject of discussion.

Information of Enemy's Offensive

According to General Cadorna,[2] the sum of the information received up to 7th October showed that Austria-Hungary, having failed to achieve the longed-for peace by negotiation, intended to do so by a military operation, and that very soon, not waiting for the spring, as German agents in Switzerland spread rumours: how great a force would be employed and at what point, it was difficult to say precisely; but the official bulletin concluded with the words " probable offensive on the middle Isonzo with the " intention of recapturing the Bainsizza plateau either in all " or in part; local operations on the rest of the front, of a " diversionary nature in the Trentino. German co-operation " very limited ". By 6th October 43 enemy divisions had been identified on the whole front,[3] of which $8\frac{1}{4}$ were opposite to the Third Army and 18 to the Second. The German *Alpine Corps*, the German *12th Division* and two Austrian divisions were reported to be on the lines of communication.

The intelligence of the enemy offensive gradually became more precise, indicating many troops in the zone Kal (on the Bainsizza)—Tolmino, and the assembly of German troops in the valley of the Save near Krainburg (60 miles east of Caporetto).[4] On the 9th the official bulletin ex-

---

[1] All the French batteries were withdrawn, leaving on 5th October, and 2 out of the 3 British Groups, the XCIV remaining. The XCV Group left for Egypt on 17th October and the 101st Group for Mesopotamia on 15th October.
[2] Cadorna II, p. 120.
[3] See Sketch 3.
[4] See End-paper.

pressed the opinion that "the last week of October might "be accepted as the most probable date of the commence-"ment of the enemy offensive". On the 13th it summed up[1] that an enemy offensive from Monte Santo (hammerhead of the Bainsizza) and Tolmino was very probable and near at hand. There were certainly all the signs of an impending major attack: much movement on the lines of communication,[2] new battery positions, increase of artillery fire, increase of deserters, and additional screening of roads. On the 17th the increase of enemy forces opposite the left of the Second Army, particularly in the actual sector of attack, Tolmino–Plezzo, was reported; but this was attributed to an enemy intention to fall on the flank and rear of the Second Army if it continued to attack, an unfortunate misreading. On the 20th the enemy strength was put at $7\frac{1}{2}$ divisions (1 in second line) opposite to the Third Army; 19 (6 in second line) opposite to the Second, and $7\frac{1}{2}$ (2 in second line) opposite to the First Army in the Trentino. On this day a Czech officer who had deserted stated that in consequence of bad weather the attack would probably take place on the 26th, and that German troops would attack from Tolmino. Next day two Austrian officers of Rumanian nationality gave the details from orders issued that the offensive would extend from the sea to Plezzo, with the decisive attack in the sector Selo (south of Tolmino) —Plezzo, and from hearsay mentioned that a corps (whether German or Austrian they did not know) would attack from Plezzo, and a German *Alpine Corps* (of 3 divisions) from Tolmino, with 2 mountain brigades and the German *12th Division* in the space between the two corps: farther south, 2 German divisions (one of them the *200th*) would make an attack convergent with that of the *Alpine Corps*: three more German divisions were in reserve: the objective was the Colovrat ridge beyond the Isonzo: the offensive would begin with 4 hours' gas shelling of the artillery, followed by 90 minutes' heavy fire, largely with trench mortars, on the infantry lines: the date would probably

---

[1] See Sketch 3.
[2] Cadorna speaks of his airmen noticing much movement on the enemy distant lines of communication; but Krafft says that the 12 attacking divisions were successfully hidden as "Italian airmen never crossed the "crest of the Julian Alps". So far, the Italian intelligence reports made Tolmino the northern limit of the offensive, while it was in fact beyond Plezzo.

INFORMATION OF ENEMY. 20TH OCTOBER, 1917

be the 25th/26th but might be earlier. This information, as will be seen, was extraordinarily accurate; but naturally General Cadorna could not know this. A flank attack from the Tolmino–Plezzo sector would have to be made over difficult mountainous country, and he believed that the enemy effort would be limited to the recovery of the ground lost in the last few battles. No one expected the attack to extend northward of Tolmino. No special air reconnaissance, therefore, to verify or disprove that the enemy was massing near Plezzo was thought necessary; yet four Austro-Hungarian divisions were assembled one behind the other in the valley running northward of that place. The division on the left of the Second Army was uneasy and asked for more men. This was refused; but General Cadorna went up to Creda (4 miles west of Caporetto) on the 22nd, and judged it sufficient to send an extra brigade to Saga, where the Isonzo makes a sharp bend; it was unwise to thicken the front line any more.[1]

What his views were General Cadorna made clear in a telegram on 21st October to Major-General F. B. Maurice, the Director of Military Operations War Office, which was communicated to the War Cabinet. He informed him " that the attack was coming, and that he was confident of " being able to meet it : owing to the very difficult country " on the Tolmino front, he was of opinion that an attack " there could be checked without difficulty and he was " holding that front in consequence lightly ".[2]

The change in the disposition of the Italian reserves, which were placed mainly behind the southern part of the front, showed that he continued to hold these views. On 24th October he had 4 divisions west of Palmanova (10 miles west of Gradisca) behind the centre of the Third Army, and 3 divisions around Cividale (2 north and 1 south) behind the centre of the Second Army.[3] On 3rd October, however, an order had been drafted placing a reserve of 6 divisions in the angle of the Tagliamento, west of Gemona,[4] which was exactly the right place, as it happened; but the order was not issued.

That an attack was imminent—and against the Second

---

[1] Vigano, p. 143.
[2] Quoted from the D.M.O's statement to the War Cabinet.
[3] Cadorna II, p. 132. Their exact position is not stated.
[4] For these places see Frontispiece.

Army—was beyond question ;[1] but Cadorna and Capello (Second Army) differed in their views as to how it should be met. The former gave appropriate orders for a defensive attitude, with local counter-attacks ; the latter favoured an offensive-defensive action, with a counter-attack on a large scale from the Bainsizza north-westward against the enemy's left flank in the Vrh valley, and he placed his three second line corps near the Isonzo north-west of Gorizia, around Plava–Monte Kuk, and south of Caporetto. Unluckily, on 4th October General Capello had to take to his bed, and on the 20th, by medical advice, he went away to Padua for convalescence and change, and his command was taken over by General Montuori (II Corps).[2] On hearing of the imminence of the attack, however, though still suffering from fever, he returned on the night of the 23rd. It may be added that on the 25th, after dictating the orders for the retreat, he was compelled to go on the sick list again.[3]

The Italian Defences

The Italian position[4] had nominally three systems of defence : the front zone, the position of resistance and the Army line ; but this last, and an occasional fourth (an

---

[1] The report, dated 21st October 1917, of the head of the British Mission, Br.-General C. Delmé-Radcliffe, to the D.M.O. leaves this in no doubt. It begins " The reports received recently indicate with increasing insistence, " the arrival of considerable German forces at Laibach [see End-paper] " and about the lines of communication. The indications further show " that the German forces are being directed towards the Upper Isonzo, " that is into the area north of Tolmino ". He continued that it was assumed that the German troops were being kept from contact with the Italians until the moment for action, but some were said to be wearing Austrian uniforms. " It is also known that the German artillery and " trench mortars have been considerably augmented. Other German " technical troops have been reported, and a few days ago the body of a " German soldier, of the *3rd Pioneer Battalion*, was fished out of the Isonzo " about Doblar [3 miles below Tolmino]. The German Alpine troops in " the Trentino are reported to be on their way to the Isonzo front [correct]. " A considerable reinforcement of German aeroplanes has been received " by the Austrians. . . . One of the most significant indications of an " impending offensive is the number of deserters who come over from the " Austrian lines. . . . There appears to be no doubt that the Germans " and Austrians attach considerable importance to hopes that an outbreak " of internal troubles in Italy will coincide with this intended offensive ".

[2] He later in March 1918 received command of the Sixth Army.

[3] Capello II, p. 243.

[4] For its order of battle see Appendix IV and for its distribution see Sketch 3.

ITALIAN DEFENCES. OCTOBER, 1917

earlier held line), were out of date and had not been kept in repair. In the corps upon which the brunt of the German attack fell, the XXVII (Kal on the Bainsizza— 9 miles south of Tolmino) under General Cavaciocchi had a good first and a poor second line, and the IV, under General Badoglio,[1] on the left (as far as Monte Rombon in the Julian Alps north of Plezzo) had a weak first line and a stronger second. Owing to the short time which had elapsed since the last Italian advance, neither line had adequate dugouts.

Cadorna's Orders

General Cadorna's tactical orders for the defence, issued on 10th October, were appropriate :[2]

(1) The defence of the advanced line was to be left to small forces depending on barrages and interdiction fire[3] of the artillery and machine guns, and on the organization of flanking fire. It was definitely ordered that the XXVII Corps (Second Army) should withdraw the greater part of its troops to the right (west) bank of the Isonzo.

(2) Only the most mobile of the medium guns of the XXVII Corps were to remain on the Bainsizza, and preparations were to be made to withdraw these.

(3) The artillery was to concentrate its attention on very violent counter-preparation fire, so as to disorganize and annihilate the attack before it could be launched.

(4) As the enemy was wont to launch his infantry after a very short fire preparation, both artillery and infantry were to be specially vigilant and in constant readiness.

These orders were only partially carried out : more than half of the infantry of XXVII Corps was caught on the east bank of the Isonzo, much of the artillery was still there ; owing to mist and to communications being cut, the counter-fire was very slight ; and far too many of the infantry

---

[1] The later Marshal. Born in 1871, he was a colonel of artillery in 1915. At the battle of Gorizia he commanded an infantry regiment and later a mixed force, and was then rapidly promoted, receiving a corps in May 1917.

[2] Cadorna II, p. 130–1.

[3] Interdiction fire : to deny the use of certain areas to the enemy.

battalions were up in the front line, in the Second Army 231 out of 353 battalions;[1] and it was known in London that the Italian gas mask gave little or no protection against the principal gases used by the enemy.[2]

THE AUSTRO-HUNGARIAN PLAN[3]

It has been seen that when on 23rd/24th August the Italian attack in the Eleventh Battle of the Isonzo forced a withdrawal on the Austrians, their High Command had already decided to restore the situation by a counter-offensive against the Italian northern flank, and to do so before winter arrived. On the Isonzo front 21 Austro-Hungarian divisions were opposed by 40 Italian,[4] and it was judged that at least 20 more were required to make an offensive possible. Kaiser Karl wished the attack to be wholly an Austrian affair; three divisions were actually on the way from the Russian front; he asked the Germans to relieve others in order to make up the minimum number required. This Ludendorff, in an interview with the Chief of the Austrian Operation Section on 29th August, declined to do, as he wished to settle with the Russians and Rumanians,[5] and he " also doubted, in view of the fighting " in progress in Flanders, whether he could free sufficient " forces ".[6]

At Hindenburg's suggestion, however, a German representative, Lieut.-General Krafft von Dellmensingen, a Bavarian with much experience in mountain warfare,[7] was sent to the Isonzo to investigate the possibilities of an operation.

---

[1] Villari, p. 147.
The British Fifth Army on 21st March 1918 had 37 battalions in the front zone and 73 behind it. " 1918 " Vol. I, p. 130.

[2] British tests showed that phosgene and chloropicrine (1 part in 1,000 of air) came through at first breath; and against mustard gas and Blue Cross the mask gave no protection whatever.

[3] The plan is discussed at length in A.O.A. vi, pp. 493–505, in the German Monograph and in Cramon, p. 126–9.
For the order of battle, see Appendix VI.

[4] By count in October, it was 22 to 42.

[5] The Riga operation was due to begin on 1st September and the Battle of Marasesti 120 miles N.N.W. of Bukarest by which the Germans hoped to drive the Rumanian-Russians over the Sereth into Moldavia was in progress.

[6] A.O.A. vi, p. 496.

[7] He was Chief of the Staff of the *Sixth Army* in Alsace-Lorraine in 1914; had commanded the *Alpine Corps* in the Rumanian campaign; and was in 1917 Chief of the Staff in Duke Albrecht of Wurttemberg's Group of Armies in the Vosges sector.

ENEMY PLAN. SEPTEMBER, 1917

On 1st September Kaiser Wilhelm wrote to Kaiser Karl that his strategic reserve (6 divisions), after its defeat of the Kerenski offensive, was engaged at Riga, and might at any moment be needed in defence in Flanders: to relieve Austrian divisions in the East " might lead to serious danger " to our combined conduct of the war " : if the general situation allowed, if the Riga affair were successful, and if weather permitted " an Isonzo offensive might come into " the picture and be carried out by the troops of our two " armies in common ". An attack from Tolmino, with Cividale as the objective, was suggested. A week later Lieut.-General Krafft von Dellmensingen returned from his reconnaissances. He recommended an Isonzo offensive, although, " in view of the circumambient (*obwaltend*) " difficulties, success lies only just on the border of " possibility ".

The Battle of Riga having terminated on 5th September in an unqualified success, the German Supreme Command agreed to send 6 divisions (2 from the Kerenski battle, 2 from Rumania, and 2 from Alsace-Lorraine), and a number of *Jäger* and *Sturm* battalions, which would be formed into a *Jäger Division*, with the necessary Army troops, artillery, trench mortars and air force, as the *Fourteenth Army*,[1] under the commander of the *Sixth Army*, General Otto von Below.[2] On 10th September a plan was agreed on between the two Supreme Commands, and orders were sent two days later to the Archduke Eugen, commanding the South-West Front. With the forces thus added to his two *Isonzo Armies* he was, on a day between the 10th and 20th October, to assume the offensive " in order to throw " the Italians over the frontier, and, if possible, over the " Tagliamento ".

---

[1] This was to be the third time in 1917 that 6 German divisions of the General Reserve were to turn the scale and bring victory : the first was against Kerenski, and the second at Riga.
The *Fourteenth Army* (see Sketch 3, where a distinction between German and Austrian divisions is made) consisted of the Corps of Krauss (an Austrian), Stein (a German), Berrer (a German), Scotti (an Austrian). South of it were the *Second* and *First Armies of the Isonzo*.
[2] Below was born in 1857. In 1914 he was G.O.C. of the *I Reserve Corps*, on the Eastern Front, and in November was promoted to command the *Eighth Army* there. From October 1916 to April 1917 he commanded in Macedonia, and then went to the Western Front to take over the *Sixth Army*, *vice* General von Falkenhausen, superseded for the loss of Vimy Ridge and the Battles of Arras 1917.

In particular, the German *Fourteenth Army*, issuing from the Tolmino bridgehead, received as its first task " to take the massif of the Jessa [Colovrat] and thus break through "the Italian front " ; Krauss's corps, on its right, made up of three of the best Austrian divisions and the German *Jäger Division*, was charged with protecting the right flank and issuing from the Plezzo basin, where the Isonzo gorge widens out, to make for Caporetto–Bergogna ; and the *Second Isonzo Army* was to join in on the left. The two Armies were then to reach the line Mt. Sabotino (north of Gorizia)—Cividale, whilst the *First Isonzo Army* (nearest the sea), " by energetic action, hindered the enemy from " sending troops against the direction of the main blow ".

To deceive the Italians a number of extra wireless stations were installed in the Trentino, and appropriate misleading orders were passed round, false troop movements were frequently made and small probing attacks carried out.

The main difficulty was to assemble the attacking troops and then make seven marches to the places of deployment undetected. Krauss's corps was assembled in the valley of the Drave[1] west of Klagenfurt and the bulk of the *Fourteenth Army* in the valley of the Save, around Laibach and Krainburg. However, as Lieut.-General von Krafft points out, it is easier to hide troops in hilly country than on a plain, and the Julian Alps, with summits around 6,500 feet, provided a screen which the Italian airmen never crossed. South of these mountains the features of the country are large, but the sides of the valleys are steep, sometimes precipitous. Roads and communications had to be improved ; but all the roads were narrow, and the troops were moved to the front by march on the block system of a single-line railway, with suitable crossing places and pre-arranged signals. The three hundred batteries were got up during the month of preparations at night, and mostly by hand, the infantry helping ; they were then left camouflaged, watched only by sentries. The infantry also moved by night, with no more than their first line transport, and they assisted in carrying up ammunition to the batteries. In spite of bad weather and constant rain after 10th October, here, as at Passchendaele, men and material were got into position unhindered by the enemy. That the troops were not entirely

---

[1] See End-paper on which the railways available are shown.

undetected, as claimed, is proved by the accurate information General Cadorna obtained, as already narrated.

The artillery registered during the last six days of the approach marches, the *Isonzo Armies* already in position firing heavily to disguise the process.

THE FIRST DAY OF BATTLE: 24TH OCTOBER[1]

24th October was selected as Zero Day, and General von Below's last order contained the following instructions :—

"The ruling principle for any offensive in the mountains is the conquest and holding of the crests, in order to get to the next objective by these landbridges. Even roundabout ways on the crests are to be preferred to the crossing of valleys and deep gorges, as the latter course takes longer time and entails greater exertions. The valleys are to be used for the rapid bringing up of closed reserves, the field artillery and supply units. Every column on the heights must move forward without hesitation ; by so doing opportunities will arise to help a neighbour who cannot get on, by swinging round in rear of the enemy opposing him."

At 2 a.m. on the 24th the German artillery opened fire with gas shell on the identified Italian batteries and on the garrison of the forward trenches. This fire was continued until 4.30 a.m., when a pause of two hours was made. The Italian guns had at once replied, but their fire soon grew weaker and did little harm to the waiting enemy infantry. Light rain had begun early, but then turned to a heavy downfall with snow storms on the heights and mist in the valleys. Visibility even when day dawned was very poor. At 6.30 a.m. the bombardment was resumed with high-explosive and at 7 a.m. the trench mortars joined in, and right down the line to the sea a general bombardment with guns of every calibre was opened ; at 8 a.m. the German infantry of the *Fourteenth Army* assaulted from the Tolmino bridgehead, and Krauss's corps advanced in the Plezzo basin one hour later. The *Second Isonzo Army* began to move a little before the main assault.

---

[1] See Sketch 3.

All, for once, went according to the German plan, but not quite according to time-table, as considerable confusion arose among the oncoming troops and transport behind the leading units. When in the early light and mist and rain, Stein's and Krauss's men broke out from the sally ports of Tolmino and Plezzo they found all resistance already overcome by the gas and the bombardment. At Tolmino after the *Alpine Corps*[1] had cleared the way, the German *12th Division* (Stein's corps) turned north to roll up the Italian line, and hardly encountered anyone; Krauss's men, who disregarding Below's advice moved along the valleys, are said to have been held back by the fire of their own artillery rather than by the enemy. The " pincers " had done their work : a 15-mile gap had been nipped out of the Italian front and, in the absence of anything of the nature of battle-police to stop fugitives, the four divisions of the Italian IV Corps which had held this sector disappeared, involving the left division of the XXVII Corps in their flight. By nightfall Stein's men were on the west bank of the Isonzo and at the foot of the Colovrat, whilst the head of Krauss's corps was at Saga.

The Italian VII Corps, in reserve, behind the gap, whose rôle was to counter-attack, had been afraid to do so in the mist and had taken up a defensive position in the Army Line on the Colovrat heights.

The next pair of Austro-German corps, Berrer's and Scotti's, their divisions issuing in turn from the southern part of the Tolmino bridgehead, had been given as objective the heights on the west bank of the Isonzo opposite them. They met with considerable resistance, but the former actually reached Mt. Jessa, at the eastern end of the Colovrat, which it dominates ; the latter corps reached Globocek, on the summit of the heights, but was turned back.

To strengthen the new Italian line, at 7 p.m. two divisions of the General Reserve were sent to Globocek, and others to the left to Bergogna and Nimis (9 miles north of Udine) to fill the gap between the Second Army and the Carnia Group, and to protect G.H.Q. and the lines of communication. The Comando Supremo also ordered 2 divisions from

---

[1] Really only a division of 11 battalions, 218 guns, etc. It belonged to Stein's corps.

the Third Army and 2 from the Trentino to the support of the Second Army.[1]

Further south again, the *Second Isonzo Army* on the Bainsizza failed to make any progress against the rest of the Italian XXVII Corps and XXIV Corps, and General Caviglia commanding the latter, who had taken over control of the XXVII Corps also, proposed to throw back a left flank to oppose the turning force ; but at 9 p.m. when information of the disaster became definite General Cadorna ordered these troops and the II Corps to abandon the front line on the Bainsizza and fall back during the night, swinging on the right, to the line Mt. Santo, Vrh, Globocek and join the VII Corps.[2]

At 6 p.m. General Cadorna had instructed the commander of the Carnia Zone to occupy Monte Maggiore (16 miles north of Udine, 1,619 metres high) with all speed, and heard three hours later that this had already been done. He proposed to make this mountain the left pivot of a wheel back to various lines of defence which he had already discussed with General Capello. These he put on paper at 11 p.m. The three lines were :[3]

(1) Monte Maggiore–Monte Stol–Monte Matajur–Colovrat–Monte Jessa.

(2) Monte Maggiore–Monte Lupia–Matajur–Globocek

(3) Monte Maggiore–Monte Carnizza–Monte Corada (north-west of Plava).

The third position nearly marks the line where the mountain region dips into the plain of Friuli.

He also ordered the commanders of both the Third and Second Armies to take measures, " with the utmost speed " and the maximum secrecy ", to put the line of the Tagliamento in a state of defence with local labour, for, he said, to save these Armies and their immense amount of material, the collection of two years and more, it might be necessary to fall back.

---

[1] Cadorna II, pp. 177–180, gives the orders he issued on the 24th, with, in most cases, the times.

[2] No situation maps are available for the night of 24th/25th October, nor for the two following nights. The first one, in the German Monograph, gives " the line as reached on the 27th ". This with the other lines taken from A.O.A. and Caviglia are reproduced on Sketch 4.

[3] They are shown on Sketch 4, taken from the sketch in Caviglia, p. 160 ; the places mentioned are marked on Sketch 3.

In view of the danger from the north, General Capello had ordered three divisions from the reserve to block the upper valley of the Natisone. These, with the divisions at Bergogna and Nimis would, he hoped, fill the gap between the Colovrat and Monte Maggiore and at least gain time for a retreat. To deal with the new situation he moved his own headquarters northward from Cormons to Cividale, and at 5 p.m. he appointed General Montuori to take charge of the left wing composed of the IV Corps (what remained of it) and the VII Corps.

THE SECOND DAY: 25TH OCTOBER

The weather improved on the 25th, the sun came out and warmed the troops, who were wet to the skin after a night passed in the open. In spite of entire lack of heavy artillery support and of little field artillery support, with only mountain guns and trench mortars, and in spite of the difficulties of the ground—attacks which, as at Monte Stol for instance, necessitated dropping all kit and clambering with the hands—the Austro-Germans made good progress. Stein's and Krauss's groups got into touch, and by evening had secured the Colovrat and some 30,000 prisoners. The whole of the Italian new line of defence, Globocek–Monte Maggiore, was in their possession, except the last-named place and Monte Matajur (at the western end of the Colovrat) —and this hill was about to be assaulted. Kusak's corps of the *Second Isonzo Army* had pushed down the Isonzo valley well below Auzza, driving southward the Italians who were leaving the Bainsizza, where the bulk of the XXIV and II Corps still remained, and outflanking those on the heights south of Globocek. Some air fighting took place in the Colovrat area, of which the Italians got the worse.

Early in the morning General Cadorna warned the Third Army to send back the less mobile of its heavy and medium artillery behind the Piave, and the rest west of the Carso Valley; to prepare a line in that valley to cover a retreat; and to be ready to begin a retirement to and behind the Tagliamento. The commander of the Carnia Zone troops (now called the XII Corps) was also warned of a possible retreat of the Second and Third Armies.

During the morning General Capello came to the Comando Supremo to discuss the situation verbally with General

Cadorna. Finally, he said, and put in writing, "the "situation is very grave : the left wing of the Army staved "in (*sfondata*) : the front line seriously notched : the "situation on the Bainsizza is impossible to maintain." He declared that it was imperative to break contact with the enemy under protection of strong rear guards and to retire at least behind the Torre (east of Udine), better still behind the Tagliamento. "A decision," he said, "must be given "as quickly as possible." General Cadorna seemed to agree and gave instructions to prepare orders for retreat.

General Capello then went back to Cividale and, after dictating the orders, felt compelled to return to the sick list ; and General Montuori took over command of the Second Army again. For easier control, the VIII Corps, on the right, was transferred to the Third Army and the other corps were divided into two wings, the VI, II and XXIV Corps under General Ferrara ; the XXVII, VII and débris of the IV under General Etna ; while what could be assembled in reserve was put under General Sagramoso.

At 8.30 p.m., when the orders for retreat were ready to go out, General Cadorna, wishing to make sure that retirement was absolutely necessary, put the question to the new commander of the Second Army. General Montuori, after consulting his corps commanders, replied " it is possible to " prolong resistance on the line of defence " ; in consequence Cadorna withheld his orders. The corps commanders can hardly have been aware of the progress made by the enemy during the day ; the valleys may have been blocked, but he was coming along " the tops ". The disorder spread by fugitives on the lines of communication does not seem to have been considered. General von Krafft[1] comments upon the day that the Italians had " thrown in their reserves "against the *Fourteenth Army* piecemeal and without plan " far to the north. This led the Army Command to hope " that the enemy would not contrive an orderly reconstruc- " tion of a strong front ".

The Third Day : 26th October

Both the Austrian Official Account and the German Monograph head the narrative of the 26th with the words

---

[1] German Monograph i, p. 113.

"The completion of the break-through". The door was in fact open for exploitation. The day was fine and there was again some air fighting near the Colovrat, in which the Italians lost 15 and the enemy 4 machines. The Austro-German right, Krauss's and Stein's groups, the former reinforced by two good divisions, continued to press on. The Army orders to them were to reach what was the third position of the Italian left flank. This they did, and more, driving the Italians before them, Krauss gaining possession of the pivot Monte Maggiore and breaking through the entire line between it and Monte Carnizza, whilst Stein got to within 5 miles of Cividale. Berrer's and Scotti's groups took Globocek and pushed up to the Italian third line on Monte Corada. The *Second Isonzo Army* reached the enemy second defence line on the Bainsizza, the Italians withdrawing over the Isonzo near Plava and northward. The *First Isonzo Army* reported that the enemy was beginning to withdraw before it on the front from Gorizia to the sea.

The confusion behind the Italian front already gave the appearance of disaster: depôts, stores and hutments had been set on fire and were burning; ammunition dumps exploded from time to time; roads and mountain paths were blocked with vehicles and with the transport of refugees, and bodies of troops were interpolated in these columns; control of traffic and march discipline were entirely lacking and pillage was flourishing unrepressed. Even on the Austro-German side, owing to the rapidity of the advance and the absence of good roads, there were blocks and stoppages, but nothing like the confusion of flight.

Bad news upon bad news came to the Comando Supremo during the morning, and about midday General Cadorna issued a directive to the commanders of the Third and Second Armies, the Carnia Group (XII Corps) and the Fourth Army on its left for retirement to the Tagliamento under strong rear guards, with the line of the Torre as "the first line of halt"; but the directive was to be kept secret and not to be acted on until he gave an order. This order he did not intend to give until the position of Monte Maggiore had been lost "for the distance of this mountain "from the bridges of the Tagliamento at Cornino and "Pinzano[1] is only half as great as the road which the right

---

[1] For these places see Sketch 4.

" wing of the Second Army and the whole of the Third
" Army have to traverse from the front line to the bridges
" at Codroipo and Latisana ".

News of the loss of Monte Maggiore arrived soon after midnight.[1] At 1.30 a.m. General Cadorna, through the French Mission, informed General Foch of the gravity of the situation[2] and at 2.30 a.m. on the 27th the Comando Supremo issued by wire a long retirement order. In the afternoon it moved its headquarters back from Udine to Treviso.

How far the morale of the Italian army, composed as it was of varying elements drawn from the hardy north and the easily excitable south, had been weakened by heavy losses and undermined by pacifist, defeatist, and Socialist propaganda must remain a matter for speculation. Of the immediate cause there is little doubt; it was, as General Cadorna told the head of the British Military Mission on the fatal 26th October : " a panic started in the IV Corps as " the result of the gas attack and the isolation of troops on " the mountains, which spread through the Second Army ". The reserves were ill-distributed to restore such a situation, and no attempt was made to fill the original breach made in the northern front.

---

[1] According to Krauss, p. 54, the position was taken " just after the " beginning of dusk ", say after 8 p.m., the Italians having commenced retirement earlier.

[2] F.O.A. vi (ii), p. 114, fn. 1.

CHAPTER V

AFTER CAPORETTO

THE RETREAT TO THE TAGLIAMENTO
(Sketches 2, 4)

ORGANIZATION OF BRITISH ASSISTANCE

Late on 24th October, through the British Mission, the Italian Government begged for help. Relying on an earlier statement of General Cadorna to the C.I.G.S., that he could hold on for five weeks until assistance could reach him, the authorities in London were not alarmed. On the 25th, too, they saw no reason to take action, as the information received from the Chief Liaison Officer in Italy, and duly reported to the War Cabinet by the Director of Military Operations, was that " a heavy bombardment by the enemy " commenced at 2 a.m. on the 24th instant. Shortly " afterwards the weather broke, after which only desultory " firing took place. No infantry attack is reported by the " Italians, but one is mentioned in the German wireless " message ". On the 26th, however, the day on which the final phase of the " Battles of Ypres 1917 ", officially known as the " Second Battle of Passchendaele " was begun, after further information had arrived from Colonel Delmé-Radcliffe, Mr. Lloyd George, without calling a meeting o. the War Cabinet, directed Sir William Robertson, as a preliminary measure, to send two divisions from France to Italy as quickly as possible.

Instructions to that effect were telegraphed to Sir Douglas Haig, with the addition:

" The French are sending four divisions. Please make " arrangements with the French authorities for movement by " rail. A corps commander for the two divisions will be " required. . . . Br.-General Crowe[1] will accompany the " divisions as my [C.I.G.S.'s] representative for the time " being. He will reach your headquarters to-morrow."

---

[1] He had made the reconnaissances for the movement in May. See p. 28.

At 11.15 p.m. on the 27th orders were sent out from G.H.Q. to the Armies. The Commander-in-Chief in France and Belgium had been desired to select " a good man " as corps commander, and a later telegram emphasized the importance of selecting two good divisions. His choice fell upon Lieut.-General the Earl of Cavan, commanding the XIV Corps, and the 23rd and 41st Divisions, commanded by Major-Generals Sir J. M. Babington and S. T. B. Lawford.[1]

No. 28 and No. 34 Squadrons, Royal Flying Corps, under the 51st Wing (Lieut.-Colonel R. P. Mills), were also placed under orders for Italy.

As the XIV Corps and the two divisions did not complete detraining in Italy until 16th November, and did not reach their position in the line until 25th November, the account of their move and that of the subsequent reinforcements sent to Italy will for the moment be postponed and the events of the interval dealt with.

Organization of French Assistance

It has been mentioned that in the early hours of 27th October, the Italian Chief of the General Staff, in reply to a message from General Foch enquiring if help was wanted and stating that if so it would be forthcoming, informed him of the gravity of the situation. By that time, however, the French Government had already decided to send four divisions to Italy. They selected the staff of the Tenth Army, under General Duchêne, and the staff of the XXXI Corps under General Rozée d'Infreville, with the 46th, 47th, 64th and 65th Divisions. Seven groups of French heavy artillery were still in Italy but on their way back to France; they were now to be left to cover the bridges of the Tagliamento, and six more groups were to be sent to join them.

Telegrams passed on the 27th between Generals Robertson and Foch with regard to the help to be sent to Italy. The former pointed out that Sir Douglas Haig could not spare very much, as " for three months all the British divisions

---

[1] The XIV Corps was in the left sector of the Fifth Army, and was relieved by the XIX Corps headquarters. The 23rd Division had been engaged in the Battle of the Menin Road Ridge, 20th–24th September, and had lost 82 officers and 2,218 other ranks. The 41st Division had been in the same battle 20th–22nd September. Both were actually in the line of the X Corps.

"had been engaged offensively", and he doubted whether much need be sent. General Foch replied: "It is incon-"testable that General Cadorna has all that is necessary in "material, troops and lines of resistance to stop the enemy, "if he knows how to make use of them; but events, not the "dictates of reason, dominate the situation".

Administrative and Transport Arrangements

Next day, whilst continuing all preparations for the despatch of the XIV Corps, Sir Douglas Haig protested to the C.I.G.S. that the operations in Flanders might be jeopardized by the withdrawal of troops; but he was informed in reply that he must be prepared to send more divisions and more heavy artillery. On the 28th, too, the Army Council, at a meeting at which Lord Cavan was present, made arrangements for the despatch of supplies to Arquata,[1] the British base in Italy selected by Br.-General Crowe in anticipation of the arrival of the divisions, and they fixed the number of units for the lines of communication. These units are here enumerated, as the list gives some idea of the magnitude of the task of shifting even a small army. They were one A.S.C. base depôt, one base mechanical transport depôt, one auxiliary petrol company, one central requisition office, one base pay unit, one base post office, one advanced medical stores depôt, one motor ambulance convoy, two sanitary sections, two casualty clearing stations, one general hospital, one stationary hospital, one base supply depôt, one field butchery, one field bakery, one L. of C. supply company, one veterinary hospital, one base depôt veterinary stores, one chief ordnance officer and base establishment, two companies Army Ordnance Corps, one base provision office, and one ordnance mobile workshop.

Major-General W. H. Grey was appointed Director-General of Transportation, and Br.-General J. A. Strick, Base Commandant. Both these officers were at the time employed on the Mediterranean Lines of Communication (Cherbourg–Taranto).

The transport of the British troops to Italy was discussed at a meeting held at French G.Q.G. at Compiègne on the 29th, under the chairmanship of Colonel Payot, Aide

---

[1] See Sketch 2.

Major-Général, representing the Directeur des Transports Militaires aux Armées, at which Br.-General G. S. Clive and Br.-General C. R. Woodroffe, of the British Mission at G.Q.G. and Colonel C. L. Magniac, Deputy Director-General of Transportation, were present. They had as their guide Br.-General Crowe's report.[1] The British representatives were desirous: first, that the movement should begin as soon as possible, so that their divisions should arrive simultaneously with the French, and, secondly, that it should be carried out entirely by train. Colonel Payot raised objections on the ground that it would be better to allow the transport vehicles of the fighting echelons of the French troops to proceed by both rail routes (via Ventimiglia and Modane) until it was completed; the southern line with 24 trains every 24 hours could then be handed over to the British, the remaining French troops continuing to use the northern route: this would result in the arrival of the British troops at their destinations before the complete detrainment of the French. As regards the second point, the French, he said, were actually using eight trains on the southern route and six on the northern, which did not cross the frontier, and the troops carried by them had to march over the frontier mountains; it would seem, in the general interest, that the British should conform to this system, which would mean that 4 of the 24 trains per day would stop at Nice and 4 at Ventimiglia, the troops then marching by road to Tenda and Savona, respectively, where they would entrain in Italian rolling stock; for these marches the French would provide motor lorries to carry rations and tents until the British vehicles arrived; if these proposals were accepted the British troops could begin entraining on the southern line on 6th November, also continuing to have the use of two trains a day on the northern line allotted to them for the Mediterranean L. of C.

The French proposals were accepted, and later approved by G.H.Q. and by the War Office. Four days later, however, it having been ascertained that motor transport could not be used on the Nice–Tenda route,[2] and as horse transport

---

[1] See Chapter III and Sketch 2.
[2] Br.-General Crowe's report mentioned steep ascents and descents and that "the road in places follows a series of short zig-zags with very steep turns at either end".

in sufficient quantity to carry tents and rations could not be found, it was decided not to use that route. The French Transportation service, was, therefore, informed that the four trains a day stopping at Nice would not be required, and were at the disposal of the French, subject to three days' notice if the British at any time desired to make use of them. The divisional artilleries (less ammunition columns), corps cavalry regiment and cyclist battalion, would be able to march by the Ventimiglia–Savona route along the coast.

The two Prime Ministers, Monsieur Painlevé and Mr. Lloyd George, had already decided to go to Italy; but it was settled that General Foch and Sir William Robertson should precede them, and these officers left for General Cadorna's headquarters on the 29th. At a meeting of the War Cabinet on that day, the Director of Military Operations explained the situation as far as it was known:[1] the break-in at Tolmino and Plezzo, the flight of the IV Corps and the spread of the panic. He said, however, that the Italians had good defensive positions behind their present front, but that whether these positions would be held would necessarily depend on whether the Italians would put up a fight: General Cadorna had indicated that his intention was to hold the line of the Tagliamento (on which, a little time before the war, two bridgeheads at Latisana and Codroipo had been organized with permanent works, and a line of forts covering Pinzano built; but in the autumn of 1915 the armament of these defences had been handed over to the field army). In conclusion the D.M.O. said that the Italian Third Army was not being heavily pressed and was retiring in good order: and the advance of the Austro-Germans was unlikely to be rapid, there being only one railhead, Tolmino, which for the moment they could use.

The Italian Retreat[2]
27th October

In the orders for retirement the Comando Supremo allotted the very few bridges which there were over the

---

[1] See Sketch 4.
[2] See Sketches 3 and 4.
The movements of the Carnia Group (XII Corps) and the Fourth Army on the north of the Second Army are not referred to in the text until they become of importance. These formations retired *pari passu* with the Second Army, and on the 28th the right of the Carnia Group established contact again with this Army.

THE ITALIAN RETREAT

Tagliamento in the zones of the Third and Second Armies:

To the Third Army:

At Latisana: stone bridge and railway bridge;

At Madrisio (5 miles north of Latisana, where there are two wide branches of the river): a permanent floating bridge;

At Codroipo: permanent footbridge, railway bridge, and stone bridge (called Delizia).

To the Second Army:

At Bonzicco: a trestle bridge (partly carried away by flood on the 27th);

At Pinzano: stone bridge and permanent footbridge to the north;

At Cornino: railway bridge.

Thus the Second Army was ill provided, and to reach the Pinzano–Cornino bridges its right wing would have to make a flank march across the enemy's front. Orders were given to construct two bridges of boats north of the Codroipo group, but floods made this impossible. The Tagliamento, it must be remembered, is a torrent rather than a river; its bed is of great width, as much as 3,000 yards and more in the Friuli plain, stony and traversed by many branches, fordable in ordinary weather, but after heavy rain raging torrents carrying all before them; below Madrisio the river narrows into a single channel, about 250 yards wide.

During the 27th the Second Army, under cover of rear guards left on the third line of defence, retired behind the Torre, and General Montuori indicated to his corps the sectors they were to occupy behind the Tagliamento. To strengthen the left of the Second Army the Comando Supremo directed to the Pinzano sector two divisions under General di Giorgio from the general reserve.

On the same day the Third Army began its retreat. To this Army, and the British heavy artillery with it, the order to retire came as a complete surprise. Transport and infantry marched off first, leaving the artillery in action; but the heavy guns were gradually pulled out, until at 6 p.m. only one of the British guns was in action; the field artillery remained a little longer. The British batteries, making for Latisana on the Tagliamento, retired via Gradisca and Palmanova, which latter place was reached early on the 28th. Rain fell throughout the night of the 27th/28th, but the roads were lighted up by the flames of burning houses and of petrol and supply dumps. Systematic destruction was carried out by the Third Army, so that the air was full of the roar of fires, the crackle of blazing woodwork, the crash of falling houses, with every now and then the explosion of ammunition.[1] The Third Army marched off in good order, but there was little attempt at traffic control, and the columns were seriously impeded by the stream of refugees with slow-moving wagons drawn by oxen, as well as by the breakdown of motor vehicles, so that blocks were frequent. No interference, however, came from the enemy.

Retirement had not been foreseen and there was lack of orders. Such orders as were issued were constantly changed, no information was given, the transport available was wholly insufficient, and "the sole idea seems to have been " to get away as quickly as possible, without regard to " stores, material or anything else ".[2]

In the Second Army, the right (VI, II, XXIV and right wing of the XXVII[3]) swung back, pivoting on the western outskirts of Gorizia, with the left in Cividale. It was towards this town that the only serious enemy pressure was directed, so that the centre of the Second Army, now composed of the VII Corps, formerly in reserve, and the reserve divisions of General di Giorgio, organized as the XXVIII Corps, with the left wing of the XXVII Corps, fell back to the Torre in considerable haste, the Germans capturing a number of Italians sitting round bivouac fires, without any outposts. A wedge was thus driven between the two wings of the Second Army.[4] On the northern wing, always the dangerous one strategicly, complete confusion prevailed ; not only inhabitants but many of the soldiery were in flight, and the formed bodies of troops had to push their way through as best they could, nothing being fixed as to the order of their going.

---

[1] A good description of the scene will be found in " With the British " Guns in Italy ", by Right Hon. Hugh Dalton, then an artillery subaltern.
[2] Report of a senior British officer to the British Military Mission.
[3] General Caviglia of the XXIV Corps had taken over command of this right wing of the XXVII Corps in the absence of its G.O.C. with the left wing.
[4] Most accounts henceforward speak of the right, centre and left wings of the Second Army, the last being composed of only the much broken left of the XXVII Corps and the IV Corps. As this centre and left kept together, they are henceforward called the left wing.

28TH OCTOBER

On the 28th the Austro-German pressure was not very heavy, but the line of the VII Corps (Second Army) on the Torre was broken by a small party of Germans, then the breach was widened and disaster ensued. The Second Army had orders to hold the line on the Torre until the evening of the 29th in order to give time for the Third Army to get clear and to save material The river was in flood, but at 4 a.m. on the 28th the advanced guard of Berrer's *200th Division* got across at Beivars (a village three miles north-east of Udine), where it was fordable, and, working southwards, enlarged the breach and entered Udine. There a division of Scotti's corps joined it. General Berrer, who had pushed ahead in a motor car, was shot dead at the entrance of the town ; but by his thrust, the Second Army had been definitely broken into two parts : the right wing was still on the line Gorizia (exclusive) to Buttrio (5 miles south-east of Udine), whilst the southern flank of the left wing was swung back to Fagagna, about eight miles from the Torre, and its northern was in confusion. The main road from Udine via Codroipo to the Tagliamento was thus exposed to the enemy unless the right wing of the Second Army could manage to cover it, and of this there seemed little chance, as during the night, after the bridge near Codroipo became tight wedged by traffic, the road for 12 miles east of it became one solid obstacle of vehicles.

Much is written after all retreats of the confusion and panics and the loosening of the bonds of discipline, the throwing away of arms, the headlong flight of crowds of soldiers, and plundering. Panics are very catching ; such incidents undoubtedly occur on a major or minor scale during retirements and are seen of many and reported ; but little is said of the units and bodies of brave men who remain, even move up to the front, counter-attack and do all they can to delay the enemy, for they are seen by fewer spectators. Where they stand and in what strength is not even known to the staffs concerned. The nature of the retirement of the Italian Second Army after the first collapse near Caporetto has been to a large extent misunderstood. Great trouble there was, but the uninterrupted flight must be attributed to the failure of the higher staffs to issue appropriate orders, to see that such orders as were issued were obeyed, to ensure traffic control, particularly at the bridges, and to have supplies dumped at the roadside and properly issued.

That the Germans did not accomplish more is ascribed to the Torre being in flood, the bridges broken and to the half-starved and tired troops succumbing to the temptations of the food and drink they found in abundance in the villages.

Meantime, by 10.30 a.m., all the Third Army was across the Isonzo without much interruption from the *Isonzo Armies* under General Boroevic.

29TH OCTOBER

By the original agreement with the Austrian Supreme Command, the German *Fourteenth Army* was not to go farther than the Tagliamento; but during the evening of the 28th General von Below issued orders for the seizure of the bridges over that river before they could be destroyed. On Ludendorff's enquiry during the 29th as to how far it was intended to go—for, on account of the strained conditions on the Western Front, he wanted five German divisions back—he was informed by the High Command of the South-West Front that it was intended to carry the offensive over the Tagliamento and obtain a shorter front and, as the *Fourteenth Army* was leading, German divisions could not be given up until the river had been crossed. General von Arz, too, the Austrian Chief of the General Staff, telegraphed to Hindenburg that it would be best " to let the operations continue to the Piave ".

The German *Fourteenth Army*, in consequence, directed the corps of Hofacker (*vice* Berrer, killed) and of Scotti on Codroipo, Bonzicco and Pinzano. The *Alpine Corps* was ordered to send a detachment in lorries to make a *coup de main* on the bridge at Bonzicco; but, the lorries not being forthcoming, nothing was done. Some of the infantry of the German *200th Division* actually reached the Bonzicco bridge, only to find fifty yards of it carried away by flood. The *Alpine Corps* and *Jäger Division* had no cavalry; but each of the other German divisions had a whole cavalry regiment; why these five regiments were not at the front in a pursuit has never been explained. The fact seems to be that the success of the Austro-Germans was much greater than they expected, and the necessary measures for full exploitation had not been prepared.

THE ITALIAN RETREAT. 29TH OCTOBER

In general, on the 29th the left wing of the Second Army, in great disorder, covered by the 2nd Cavalry Division and cyclist battalions, reached the Tagliamento at Pinzano and Cornino, and the Third Army, covered by the VIII Corps, the 1st Cavalry Division and cyclists, was for the most part across the Tagliamento. By midnight of the 29th/30th, all the British guns had crossed the road bridge at Latisana or were a mile or two east of the town, but much equipment and ammunition had been lost or destroyed.

It was the right wing of the Second Army which was in most danger. It had retired during the night covered by the XXIV Corps, but it had to protect its own left flank, the left flank of the Third Army, and cover Codroipo and the three bridges there. The two main roads from Palmanova and Udine converged on the bottle-neck of Codroipo, and a mass of artillery and transport of both the Third and Second Armies was moving down them and getting blocked in the town, so that as each unit came along it simply abandoned its transport, adding it to the tail of the block, and the men struggled through as best they could. Enemy aircraft machine-gunned and dropped bombs on the roads, but from so great a height that little damage was done, though some confusion was caused. Hasty endeavours were made by General Ferrera (commanding the right wing of the Second Army) to man the permanent bridgehead, and to gain time for evacuation. The rear guard of the XXIV Corps, too, remained out in position at Pozzuolo (5 miles south of Udine) and southward. It proved comparatively easy to hold off the Austro-Germans; the corps of Hofacker and Scotti had in the morning moved out from Udine and southward, but, having failed to take by surprise the bridges over the Tagliamento, Hofacker in the afternoon ordered any attempt to capture them by force of arms to be abandoned: he had other plans. Little, therefore, was accomplished, except to discover that the bridge of Bonzicco was unusable. The mountain troops were not at their best on the Friuli plain, and, owing to the confusion and blocks on the roads on the German side, little artillery was up to support them. All that is claimed for the day is that the German advance "sensibly interfered with General Cadorna's "plans",[1] which is only partly true.

---

[1] A.O.A. vi, p. 576.

30th October: Loss of Codroipo

On 30th October the Codroipo area was the focus of interest. The Third Army pursued its way with little interference from the *First Isonzo Army*, though a few bombs and the arrival of some Italian cavalry at a rapid pace, who were mistaken for Germans, caused confusion and a panic at Latisana. In the north the Pinzano bridgehead continued to hold off the corps of Krauss and Stein, which had been directed to cross there. At Codroipo the scene was very different: it was one of inextricable confusion. Making for the bridges beyond the town were the greater part of 350,000 stragglers and 400,000 refugees.[1] Many soldiers left the ranks in search of food; for General Cavigilia says briefly, "during the retirement from the "Isonzo and the Tagliamento, the Intendance services of "the Second Army did not function". The roads were blocked with traffic, three, even four, deep; and all the fields around right up to the river were covered with innumerable vehicles, guns, ammunition wagons, motor lorries bogged in the mud and abandoned, and in many cases, according to German photographs, piled one on top of the other.

At midnight of the 29th/30th General Ferrera had assembled his corps commanders at a village about ten miles south of Udine, and informed them that the Pozzuolo position must be held to cover Codroipo; southward the VIII Corps of the Third Army was responsible: an inner defence line would be provided by the forts of the bridgehead. Unfortunately, owing to frequent changes of command during the 28th and 29th, little had been done as regards the dismantled forts except to tell off four thousand men of various units, not an organized body, for their defence. Change of orders, friction and bad staff work on the part of the Germans was to contribute to save the Italians from complete disaster.

In the afternoon of the 29th General Hofacker, who was at the front, had come to the conclusion that a good opportunity offered to cut off the greater part of the Third Army and the survivors of the right wing of the Second Army. His orders for the 30th therefore directed his corps, then between Udine and Bonzicco, to wheel southward on

---

[1] Cadorna II, p. 202.

Latisana, and he persuaded Scotti's corps on his left near Udine to conform. Lieut.-General Krafft von Dellmensingen, Chief of the Staff of the German *Fourteenth Army* who came up to Udine, was informed and appeared to agree. But shortly before midnight General von Below from his advanced headquarters at Cividale, after announcing that there were only weak Italian detachments in front of the *Fourteenth Army* and that the Italian Third Army had apparently not yet crossed the Tagliamento, sent out orders that " the pursuit will be continued until the Italian army " is annihilated ". With this object in view, he directed the corps of Krauss, Stein and Hofacker against the sectors included between the Alpine foothills and a point below Codroipo. Scotti, reinforced by a German division from Hofacker's corps was to march via Pozzuolo in the general direction of Latisana. Thus General von Below, without regard to the *Second Isonzo Army*, for the line Udine–Pozzo (3 miles north of Codroipo) was the German southern boundary, sent his troops, as Hofacker had done, across its front, ignoring too, it is admitted by Krafft, that the Italian rear parties were " farther eastward than supposed."[1]

These German orders led, during the 30th, to collisions, delays and recriminations.

Hofacker, it being impossible to communicate in time with the *Fourteenth Army*, as all wire communications were down and wireless was interrupted by bad weather, was at first inclined to disobey Below's orders ; but he finally despatched his two divisions southward in the direction of the Codroipo bridges, his *26th Division* thus being sent between Codroipo and the river, where there was no organized defence. On the appearance about 1 p.m. of a few Germans, the three Codroipo bridges were blown up without regard to the Italians still on the east bank, so that the *26th Division* captured 12,000 prisoners and immense booty. Meantime, the Italian XXIV Corps, on the Pozzuolo position, held off Hofacker's other division and Scotti's Austrian divisions until the close of the day. Then, marching by night, three divisions of this corps crossed the Tagliamento unhindered at Madrisio, and the rest did so at Latisana, where General Caviglia states that the

---

[1] German Monograph ii, p. 88.

bridges and streets were found empty and deserted. All the troops were across by 7 a.m. on the 31st.

Thus none of the passages of the Tagliamento had been secured by the Austro-Germans and the destruction of the bridges had not been prevented. The improvised part of Below's operation, undertaken with insufficient forces for a decisive success, had met with unexpected opposition, and had not achieved the hoped for results ; but according to German and Austrian accounts 60,000 prisoners had been taken and a great part of the equipment of the Second and Third Italian Armies captured.

31st October: The Italians on the Tagliamento

" On 31st October 1917 the greater part of the [Italian] " army, badly knocked about and diminished in numbers, " found itself behind the Tagliamento ".[1] Bridgeheads were still held at Latisana (but during the day the garrison was reduced from 10 to 4 brigades and during the night these 4 followed the others across the Tagliamento) and at Pinzano, and in the north the Carnia Group and the Fourth Army were aligned behind the upper, west-east, course of the river opposite the Austrian *Tenth Army*. General Cadorna, feeling that the halt on the Tagliamento could only be temporary, but, he hoped, " long enough to rest " and reorganize the units ",[2] ordered all the artillery of the Second and Third Armies, not strictly necessary for the defence of the river, to be withdrawn as speedily as possible behind the Piave.[3] Nowhere did the Austro-Germans cross the Tagliamento, in spite of orders from the higher staffs. The confusion, owing to part of the *Fourteenth Army* trying to cross the front of the *Second Isonzo Army* and remaining in its area, increased. The G.O.C. of the right corps of the latter Army appeared at Below's advanced headquarters, at 5 p.m. and stated that he meant to push through by force if necessary and take command of all German troops in his allotted " strip ", and the Austrian divisional commanders at the front said the same.

---

[1] Caviglia, p. 227.
[2] Cadorna II, p. 204.
[3] Tosti, p. 241.

Below's evening order of the 30th had directed Krauss and Stein to force a passage at Cornino and Pinzano, Hofacker was to continue his operations at Codroipo, Scotti was to pursue in the direction of Latisana. All attempts to secure a passage failed ; no pontoons had been brought up, the strongest swimmers could not get across, and the western side was defended by machine guns and a few field guns. Some slight successes, however, were won at the two bridgeheads. The *Second Isonzo Army* began to reach Codroipo, and Scotti's corps delayed by this Army crossing its route, arrived at Madrisio, where the bridges were under water, without interference from the Italians. The *First Isonzo Army* occupied Latisana.

Arrival of Generals Foch and Robertson

General Foch arrived at the Comando Supremo in Treviso on the 30th and General Robertson reached there next day. General Cadorna could not say whether the Italian Armies would stand on the Tagliamento : " the Second Army has " been so badly shaken at Caporetto that its power of " resistance seems for the moment to be compromised, and " it is probable that a retirement to the Piave will be " necessary ".[1]

General Foch's first telegram to Paris was : " The Com- " mander-in-Chief of the Italian Army has directed that " resistance shall be offered on the Tagliamento, but without, " however, appearing to place much reliance on this ; he " already has his eyes turned towards the Piave. We will " endeavour to prolong the resistance on the Tagliamento " and if possible render it definite ".[2]

Cadorna's first idea was that the French contingent should concentrate at Bassano,[3] detraining at Vicenza, and the British concentrate at Brescia (west of Lake Garda) so

---

[1] Foch : Mémoires, ii p. xxxvi. It has been stated that Cadorna, fearing envelopment from the Trentino, decided to fall back on the Adige and that Foch thereupon said " c'est sur le Piave qu'il faut résister ". From the Mémoires ii, p. xxxvii, it appears that these words were said not on 30th October nor to Cadorna, but on 1st November to the Italian Prime Minister, Orlando. Cadorna, however, states (II, p. 263) that the Adige line had been considered and preparation made for inundations on its course.

[2] F.O.A. vi (i), p. 95.

[3] See Frontispiece.

as to be in a position to secure the Italian retirement to the Piave and to guard against an attack from the Trentino. The Comando Supremo was greatly in fear of an offensive on one side or other of Lake Garda, and the Third Army had already been warned to be prepared to send a corps of two divisions back to Brescia and another of three divisions to the Vicenza–Bassano area.

General Cadorna, however, soon changed his mind and proposed to General Foch that the Allied contingents, or at least the French divisions, should be pushed up to the Piave to hold the Montello position,[1] so that when the Armies fell back to that river, the Third Army would be on their right flank and the Fourth Army on their left, the Second Army going into reserve. With this disposition General Foch agreed; but the orders had hardly been communicated to General Duchêne, before General Cadorna asked that two divisions might be sent to Brescia, as he was uneasy about a concentration of German troops reported at Bolzano (Tirol). To this the French again agreed; but to prevent the dispersal of their force it was settled that whilst two divisions went to the north-east of Brescia, the other two should detrain and remain at Verona instead of proceeding to the Piave.

After Generals Foch and Robertson had met on the 31st they proceeded together to inform the Italian commander of their views. They were of accord that the twenty divisions asked for by him were not necessary; the Italian Armies, they felt, were not beaten, only one in fact had been attacked; provided that order was re-established, the Armies were of quite sufficient fighting value to permit the line of the Tagliamento being disputed without Allied assistance, and to offer resistance on the Piave and in the Trentino. To prevent any misunderstanding they handed a joint note to General Cadorna which recorded these views and added:

> "The Allied Forces can in Italy serve only as a
> "complement (*appoint*) to the Italian army. This

---

[1] The Montello, frequently mentioned in this narrative, is a commanding rounded hill of oval shape which rises isolated from the surrounding plain and overlooks the Piave. It is roughly seven miles long from east to west with a maximum of four miles in breadth and about 800 feet above the river bed; but its generally convex form is broken by a number of large circular depressions as much as a hundred yards across and 50 to 60 feet deep, and it was covered by vineyards, patches of cultivation and copses.

"army remains responsible for the defence of its country, whose fate depends, for that matter, on the conduct and behaviour of the Italian army.

"The defence of Italy thus foreshadowed can be achieved provided that the Italian High Command

"(a) adopts a plan of defence and sticks to it;

"(b) ensures that the important points of the lines of defence (Tagliamento and Piave) are held before the Armies fall back on them by troops commanded by energetic chiefs;

"(c) reunites its troops behind the lines of defence either to occupy the line or to reorganize".

In reporting to London, General Robertson said that there was great confusion and lack of grip of the situation at Italian headquarters, and General Foch suggested to the French Government that it might be advantageous to redouble the attacks on the Western Front, particularly in Alsace, and to act so as to assist the Italian Trentino front.[1]

---

[1] F.O.A. v (ii), p. 1143.

CHAPTER VI

THE RETREAT FROM THE TAGLIAMENTO TO THE PIAVE[1]
1st–10th NOVEMBER 1917
(Sketch 4)

THE HALT ON THE TAGLIAMENTO: VISIT OF GENERALS FOCH AND ROBERTSON

On 1st November the Italian Armies were established behind the Tagliamento without having been greatly pressed by the enemy in the last stage of the retirement; but on the morning of that day the Austrian *50th Division* (Krauss's corps) and the German *12th Division* (Stein's corps) assaulted the Pinzano–Cornino bridgehead, and, the two bridges at the former place having been blown up prematurely, the Italian brigade in the bridgehead was captured.

Reports of the speedy arrival of French and British troops in Italy having reached Ludendorff's ears, he began to grow nervous, and on this day recommended to the Austrian Supreme Command that " the continuation of the march " from the Tagliamento to the Livenza, should have the " character of a closed up forward movement, from which " deployment into battle could be carried out." As usual, he entered into details quite outside his province, and ended by saying that it was highly desirable that the German divisions in Italy should be relieved by Austrian troops of the Isonzo Armies. The Austrian Supreme Command, in response, informed him it had directed that bridgeheads should be formed on the Tagliamento, but added " the " immediate object of our operations in Venetia is to reach " the Piave line ".

The retirement had greatly improved the Italian situation; besides affording time to reorganize, it had brought the Third Army and the Fourth Army (including the XII Corps) closer to each other, and thus allowed of the frontage of the shrunken Second Army being reduced. Unfortunately,

---
[1] See Sketch 4.

HALT ON THE TAGLIAMENTO. 1st NOVEMBER

the weakest troops were on the endangered northern flank.[1] The Third Army could be relied on; the Duke of Aosta assured General Foch, who visited him on the 1st, of the good order and spirit of his troops. The appreciation formed by Generals Foch and Robertson seemed to be confirmed; so they felt able to report that " the situation " of the Italian army continues to develop without surprise " and without difficulties; entirely withdrawn behind the " Tagliamento, it is being reorganized and reconstituted ". General Robertson, who travelled back to Rome, followed in the evening by General Foch, saw Baron Sonnino, the Minister for Foreign Affairs, who told him that energetic measures were being taken : that the civil population had behaved much better than he had expected : and that he was satisfied the country could be held together provided no further great disaster occurred. Sir Rennell Rodd, the British Ambassador, also considered the temper of Italy satisfactory. General Foch later saw the Prime Minister, Signor Orlando,[2] and other Ministers. He impressed on them the necessity for watching the morale of the troops, of ensuring close relations between the Government and the Comando Supremo, and of free and open communication with the Allies. He stressed that the situation, though grave, was not desperate, provided that the headquarter staffs displayed energy.

THE AUSTRIAN–GERMAN BREAK INTO THE TAGLIAMENTO FRONT

This confidence was soon to be shaken. The Austro-Germans having failed on 1st and 2nd November in frontal attacks against the passages of the Tagliamento, General von Below had decided to try other means. Invoking the co-operation of the Austrian *Tenth Army* on his right, at

---

[1] South of Codroipo were troops which had hardly fought : the Third Army and right wing of the Second. Opposite that place and northwards were the XXIV Corps, XXVII Corps and VII Corps (once reserve in the north), which had borne the brunt of the later fighting ; then came di Giorgio's corps as far as Cornino ; next the remains of the IV Corps (from Caporetto), holding 6 miles of the torrent bank with the mountains behind them ; and then the XII Corps, round the angle of the Tagliamento in the mountains.

[2] He had on the 29th succeeded Signor Boselli, who had resigned on 25th October.

whose disposal he placed General Krauss with a corps of two divisions, he determined once again to turn the Italian line from the north, this time via Tolmezzo, with Longarone on the upper Piave, as objective. Here, and not in the Trentino, was the Italian danger. On the night of 2nd/3rd November, however, the Austrian *55th Division* (Krauss's corps) forced a passage by the partly damaged railway bridge at Cornino.[1] A little later the German *12th Division* (Stein's corps) repaired and rushed the permanent footbridge near Pinzano, and, the flood having somewhat subsided, forded the river a little farther south. Di Giorgio's special corps fought on for some twenty-four hours, but, failing to stem the inroads, retired behind the next river line, that of the torrent Meduna. According to German accounts, what remained of the old Second Army simply dissolved and " ran for home, threw their arms away, tore off their badges " of rank, many soldiers put on civilian clothes and, forming " themselves into bands, plundered the peasantry ".[2]

In order to save time, General Below at once abandoned the Tolmezzo plan of a turning movement to revert to a direct pursuit, always maintaining a strong right wing; and he fixed the north-south line Longarone-Vittorio Veneto-Tezze as the next objective, and withdrew five divisions, under Scotti, into reserve.

The High Command of the South-West Front ordered a general concentric advance. The *Tenth Army* was to march south-westwards, with its left on the line Longarone-Belluno-Feltre towards the Asiago plateau. The two *Isonzo Armies* were to press westwards with their northern flank on the line of the railway Codroipo-Sacile-Conegliano. The Group of Armies of Field-Marshal Conrad, who was now commanding in the Tirol and on the front as far east as Carnia (exclusive), having under him the *Eleventh Army* and numerous frontier guards, approximately ten divisions, was to attack southwards against the Asiago front about 10th November.

The capture of the Pinzano-Cornino area had broken the Tagliamento line where it entered the mountains, and there-

---

[1] Nearly a mile long. Only the western span was damaged when the Italians blew up the bridge on the 30th. This was repaired under an artillery barrage, and the bridge was carried by a bayonet and hand-grenade charge, the defenders not having put up any wire or other obstacle.
[2] German Monograph i, p. 173.

fore compromised the XII Corps (late Carnia Zone), whose line of retirement from the upper Tagliamento lay through Paludea (3 miles north-west of Pinzano). Two of its three divisions which marched south and might have taken the Austrians in flank, were cut off in the mountains by Krauss's corps and driven towards the Austrian *Tenth Army*, so that over ten thousand were captured during the 4th and 5th November; the third division escaped westward and, as will be seen, helped to cover the retreat of the Fourth Army.

CADORNA ORDERS A RETREAT TO THE PIAVE

During the afternoon of the 3rd, General Cadorna informed the Italian Prime Minister of the full gravity of the situation, and left no doubt of his opinion of the morale of the Second Army: " 180,000 prisoners, 400,000 stragglers, a mass of " morally unnerved (*sfibrata*) humanity ". He proposed, if he could get the Third and Fourth Armies back in good order to the Piave, to play his last card on that river and await a decisive battle; for, he said, a further retirement to the lower Adige or to the Mincio,[1] to which the First Army would have to conform, would mean sacrificing most of the artillery and destroy what remained of the fighting powers of the army.[2]

The line which it was intended to occupy extended behind the Piave from the sea to the elbow which the river makes round the Montello, and then turned north-westward to Monte Grappa, to meet the First Army line on the Brenta. To have held the river line as far north as Feltre, its course being then south-westward, would have exposed the defenders of this sector to an easy turning movement. Both the Montello and Monte Grappa were important pivots in the line; they had been fortified after the Trentino offensive in 1916, and an immense entrenched camp had been organized east of Treviso as a support to the Piave line. The Piave itself is a considerable military obstacle, a wide river subject to floods and passable only at the bridges. Ten miles above the Montello it is nearly a mile wide, but near that place it narrows to about 275 yards, then it divides into a number of branches, first with sandbanks and lower down with

---

[1] For these rivers, see Frontispiece.
[2] Caviglia's "Piave," pp. 215-18, where Cadorna's letter is printed at length.

islands covered with brushwood also between them; at Nervesa the width is 660 to 880 yards, but at the big island (Papadopoli) five miles below, it is 2½ miles.

The Third Army was allotted the sector from the sea to a bridge just south of Nervesa; the Fourth Army had the rest of the front, as the Second Army was to be withdrawn into reserve. The total frontage was more than a hundred miles shorter than it had been on the Isonzo, roughly 120 miles against 250.

The retirement of the Third and Second Armies across the Venetian plain presented no special difficulties as, besides the Tagliamento itself, the river lines of the Meduna, the Cellina and the Livenza were available for rear guards to hold, and the enemy had neither bridging trains nor cavalry. The Fourth Army (General di Robilant), however, extended east and west in the mountains on the upper course of the Tagliamento, with its right about twelve miles east of Pieve di Cadore, was in a dangerous position; for to escape it must file down the upper valley of the Piave past Longarone and Belluno. Moreover it had instructions not to uncover Belluno until the troops of the Second Army had passed the meridian of Vittorio Veneto—later it was told to take measures for its own safety without regard to the Second Army. To make matters worse, its commander, having held the same line successfully for two years, had failed to carry out General Cadorna's order, given thirty-six hours earlier, to bring his advanced troops back to the main position, behind the crest of the Carnic Alps.

All preparations had been made for a retreat of the Third and Second Armies from the Tagliamento; the heavy and medium guns had already been sent back behind the Piave, but it was not until the afternoon of 4th November, when General Cadorna received news that Paludea had been lost by the Second Army, that he ordered the movement to take place that night, material and non-combatants being sent off during the day.[1] The Second Army, having farther to go, was to make the march in three stages, the Third Army in two stages, starting at 6 p.m. and 10 p.m., respectively.

The retirement was to be covered by a system of rear guards, all of which, together with the Cavalry Corps of

---

[1] The details are in Cadorna II, pp. 235-7.

four divisions,[1] were placed under the commander of the Third Army, the Duke of Aosta, with instructions to halt on each of three successive named lines until further orders. Except in the north, where the enemy had crossed the Tagliamento and some fighting around Paludea was still in progress, the Italian Armies were able to march off without interference.

The Rapallo Conference[2]

Two weeks earlier, on 14th October, Mr. Lloyd George had suggested to the French Government the desirability of establishing " a permanent staff of military officers " to study the War as a whole, not merely from the point of view of one particular national army, and to advise the Allied Governments as to strategy. On 30th October, when Monsieur Painlevé was visiting London in connection with the assistance to be given to Italy, the question of a Supreme War Council was opened for discussion by Mr. Lloyd George, and a preliminary organization agreed on. The Italian dilemma offered an occasion to introduce and settle the matter with the other Allies; so it was arranged that a conference should be held in Italy, at Rapallo, on the coast 15 miles east of Genoa, nominally to discuss what military assistance should be given to Italy. To this place travelled Mr. Lloyd George and General Smuts, accompanied by Lieut.-General Sir Henry Wilson, already selected as the British military member of the proposed new organization. Monsieur Painlevé and the French representatives travelled on 3rd November, and Generals Foch and Robertson were summoned from Rome to attend.

At a preliminary meeting of the French and British representatives on the evening of the 4th a plan of action for despatching assistance was agreed upon. A proposal put forward by General Pétain was mentioned and at once dropped. In a mood of pessimism he had informed the British Prime Minister that he considered the Italian position to be extremely serious and expressed doubts as to whether the Italian army existed any longer: " if it did

---

[1] The 3rd and 4th Cavalry Divisions had been brought up from Lombardy, where they had been keeping order.
[2] This is dealt with at greater length in " 1918 " Vol. I, p. 29, *et seq.*

"exist, it was probably only in the shape of individual units, "and not as an army". The French and British must take charge, he said, like the Germans had taken charge of the Austrians. He therefore proposed a division of the Western Front between himself and Sir Douglas Haig, the British C.-in-C. taking command of all the Allied troops from the Channel to about Verdun and the French C.-in-C. from this point southwards to the Adriatic, thus including the Italian front and the Franco-Swiss frontier. It was judged unlikely by the two Prime Ministers that the Italians could accept this, and that in any case it was not good policy.

At the first session of the conference at 8 p.m. on 5th November, Signor Orlando, Baron Sonnino, Minister of Foreign Affairs, and General Alfieri, Minister of War, with General Porro, the Deputy Chief of the General Staff, who represented Italy, depicted the situation as very serious, the retreat from the Tagliamento having been ordered and begun. They urged that fifteen British and French divisions should be sent in order to enable the line of the Piave to be held. General Porro assured the Conference that nine German divisions had taken part in the original attack at Caporetto, and that twelve or fifteen more had subsequently left the Western Front for Italy. Both Generals Foch and Robertson pointed out the unlikelihood of such a concentration, the latter stating on the authority of his Director of Military Intelligence, correctly as is now known (except for the omission of the extemporized *Jäger Division*), that there were only six German divisions on the Italian front. They therefore considered a total of eight Allied divisions would be sufficient assistance.[1] Mr. Lloyd George promised to send two more divisions forthwith, and more if necessary,[2] as did also Monsieur Painlevé ; and Italy was assured that she could depend upon the Allies to help her.

The French and British had agreed at their preliminary meeting, on the advice of their Chiefs of the General Staff, that the removal of General Cadorna from command and the reorganization of the Italian High Command were of

---

[1] The British record says " eight ", the French " twelve ". The latter number appears to have been agreed on later, in accordance with a report from General Foch dated 13th November, six French and six British divisions.

[2] G.H.Q. were warned on the 7th to send two more.

prime importance. When Mr. Lloyd George, supported by Monsieur Painlevé, pressed for these changes, the Conference was informed that the matter was under consideration. Seizing the opportunity offered by the divergence of opinion on the strength of the German forces in Italy, Monsieur Painlevé put forward the proposal for the creation of a Supreme War Council as a co-ordinating body with power to ensure effective unity. This was at once agreed to by all three Powers, and the fifth session of the Conference, on 7th November, was converted into the first session of the Supreme War Council, better known as the Versailles Council.[1]

Diaz Succeeds Cadorna

On the night of 7th November most of the Allied representatives travelled from Rapallo to Peschiera (at the southern end of Lake Garda), where a meeting was held on the morning of the 8th, presided over by H.M. the King of Italy. Mr. Lloyd George laid before him, in somewhat strong terms, the views of the Conference on the unsatisfactory state of the Italian High Command and the necessity for a change. The King, in reply, said that, although he did not agree in every respect with the criticisms to which General Cadorna had been subjected, it had already been decided to replace him. On the 9th, General Diaz[2] took over from General Cadorna, and, to strengthen the High Command, General Giardino, the former Minister of War and General Badoglio, commander of the IV Corps, were appointed his deputies.

General Cadorna was appointed the Italian Military

---

[1] How the Council functioned and how on 26th March 1918 General Foch was appointed Generalissimo are related in " 1918 " Vol. I.

[2] Armando Diaz, born December 1861, died February 1928, came of a family of Spanish origin. Artilleryman and Staff College graduate, he commanded an infantry regiment in the 1912 Libyan Campaign. He then became secretary to General Pollio, Chief of the General Staff, and on his death in July 1914 served his successor, General Cadorna, as head of the Operations Section for about a year, then obtaining command of a division, and in May 1917 of the XXIII Corps in the Third Army. The Duke of Aosta, commanding that Army, had been suggested as Cadorna's successor, but he was a cousin of the King, and for dynastic reasons it was considered that he should not be appointed Chief of the General Staff or given the chief command ; for, in theory, the King was Commander-in-Chief.

Representative with the Supreme War Council.[1] As their first task the Military Representatives were instructed to report immediately on the present situation on the Italian Front. In consultation with Italian G.H.Q., they were to examine into the present state of affairs and, on a general review of the military situation in all theatres, to advise as to the amount and nature of assistance to be given by the British and French Governments, and as to the manner in which this assistance should be applied. Their report was not handed in until 21st December and is given later.[2]

Foch and Wilson Remain in Italy

Before leaving Italy, however, the French and British Prime Ministers, in view of the urgency of the situation, agreed that Generals Foch and Wilson should be given complete discretion to move the six Allied divisions already in or on their way to Italy to wherever best use could be made of them. Thereupon Lieut.-General Wilson proceeded to Verona to visit General Duchêne, commanding the French contingent, and then went on to Padua, where the Italian Comando Supremo was now established, whither Generals Foch and Weygand had also travelled. On the morning of the 9th General Wilson and these two officers had an interview with General Diaz. The new Italian Chief of the General Staff had only just arrived and had not had time to acquaint himself with many of the details of the situation; but he declared his intention of holding the line of the Piave, on which the Italian Armies had just established themselves, and promised to countermand the orders which General Cadorna had given for the Italian Fourth and First Armies to abandon their positions on the hills about the Upper Piave. At a meeting next day it was decided that the French and British divisions should concentrate near Vicenza. General Robertson then returned to London, and in a short time General Wilson left for Versailles; but General Foch remained in Italy to watch events, in particular to judge whether Allied help was required on the

---

[1] General Weygand was the French representative, Sir Henry Wilson, the British; in December General Tasker H. Bliss joined as the U.S.A. representative.
[2] See pp. 120-21; also " 1918 " Vol. I, pp. 57-9.

Piave line, his policy being to let the Italians if possible restore the situation by their own efforts.

THE RETREAT FROM THE TAGLIAMENTO[1]

To take the Third and Second Armies first: on 5th November the main bodies, after a good night march, reached the Livenza; but the rear guard of the Second was hustled off the Cellina, its floods having subsided, by the advanced guards of the *55th* and *50th Divisions* of Krauss's corps.[2] The other Austro-Germans were delayed by having to bridge the Tagliamento and by the collapse of Krauss's bridge at Cornino. On the 6th all the Italian rear guards maintained themselves on the Livenza, the cavalry delaying Stein's corps, which was advancing in two columns; the main bodies continued their march to the Piave, which they began to cross on the 7th, the rear guards falling back under pressure to the Monticano. That line they continued to hold on the 8th, crossing the Piave on the morning of the 9th. All the bridges over that river were blown up at mid-day, about the same time as General Diaz took command.

Of the three corps of the Fourth Army, the left and centre, the XVIII and IX, got away without interference and occupied the new position on the Monte Grappa front; but the right, the I Corps, fell into trouble, being chased by Krauss's corps making for the line Vittorio Veneto–Longarone, the only one which exhibited energy in the pursuit. On the 5th, the day on which Krauss's left wing drove the rear guards of the Second Army from the Cellina, the Italian I Corps had not reached Pieve di Cadore, and the Austrian *22nd* and *Edelweiss Divisions,* his right wing, with several tracks at their disposal, the best *via* Barcis, converging on Longarone, were as near to that place as were the Italians. A difference of opinion then arose between Generals von Below and Krauss; the former insisted on the Barcis mountain route by mule tracks to the Piave being taken, and the latter preferred the routes on the edge of the plain *via* Vittorio Veneto, which was reached on the 8th. Finally, the *50th Division* went straight on to the Piave below Feltre, and the *55th* northwards to Belluno, both places

---
[1] Map 30 in A.O.A. vi shows the movements of both sides in detail.
[2] It now contained the *22nd, Edelweiss, 55th* and *50th Divisions.*

being reached on the 10th. The other pair of Krauss's divisions, after driving in the flank guard of the Italian Fourth Army, reached Longarone on the 9th; but finding the bridge down it turned north, and thus cut off the rearguard of the Fourth Army, formed by a division of the I Corps, capturing about ten thousand men and seventeen guns. The Austrian *Tenth Army*, which by Conrad's orders had begun the pursuit on the 5th, had already taken another ten thousand men and ninety-seven guns in following up the I Corps. The rest of the Fourth Army got clear, thanks to the bridges near Feltre and Belluno being wrecked after they had crossed them.

The Italians on the Piave

Thus the 10th November found the Italian Armies on the Piave position, the Third Army, with eight divisions, faced by two *Isonzo Armies*, numbering 19 divisions; the Fourth Army, with seven divisions, faced by the *Fourteenth Army*, numbering 15 divisions; whilst, west of Lake Garda, was the III Corps of two divisions, faced by three divisions. But the pursuing Austro-Germans were very short of heavy guns, and of all kinds of gun ammunition, in fact, had only enough for one battle-day. It had not been possible to restore much of the railways, railheads were sixty miles behind the front line in the south and ninety miles in the north, and the number of motor and horsed columns was wholly insufficient to work such long distances.

The British heavy artillery from the Isonzo was sent into position in a sector on the right bank of the Piave, east of Treviso. Each battery made up a complete section, the others going back to Ferrara by train to refit, and for the rest of the month harassing fire on roads and destructive fire on houses were carried out, the enemy replying with field guns and 5.9-inch howitzers.

By the same date, the 10th, four French divisions had completed detrainment in Italy and were concentrating: two divisions about Brescia,[1] one division between Lake Garda and Mantua (18 miles south of Verona), and one division about Verona. The British were on their way, but had not yet begun to detrain.

---

[1] See Frontispiece.

ON THE PIAVE. 10TH NOVEMBER

In spite of the enemy's numerical superiority it was hoped to hold the Piave position; for the third time the danger lay on the northern flank, where Krauss's corps, thrust in front of the slow-moving *Tenth Army*, was marching towards the Monte Grappa position, and the eastern wing of Conrad's Group of Armies also seemed about to take action.

On reaching the Piave the Austro-German commanders on the spot quickly had realized from the heavy fire and the sight of entrenchments that the Italians meant to make a determined stand there, and they knew that Allied help, estimated at as much as twenty divisions, was on its way to Italy. Though success obviously depended on speed, no orders came from the High Command; the Austrian Kaiser and his Chief of the Staff were from 5th to 18th November in Trieste carrying out inspections of troops, and the visit of the German Kaiser and the King of Bulgaria to the theatre of war was wasting the time of the High Command of the South-West Front. On the 11th, however, the Archduke Eugen issued directions that attempts should be made to cross the Piave, the lower course being mentioned as the least difficult to reach. To assist this, Krauss's corps—the *Tenth Army*, in difficulties about transport in the mountains, standing fast—was to attack between the Piave and the Brenta, that is against the Monte Grappa sector, whilst, as already arranged, the *Eleventh Army* of Conrad's Group of Armies was to move against the Asiago plateau.

THE ASIAGO PLATEAU

Hindenburg-Ludendorff, apparently under the idea that the Italians would go back to the Brenta, the Bacchiglione or the Adige, and regardless of weather conditions in the mountains, but in the hope that action in Italy would cause the Allies to send more troops there from the Western Front, now wished a force to be sent from the Trentino, either east or west of Lake Garda, towards Verona, to prevent further Italian retirement. They suggested its spearhead should be the *Alpine Corps* and the *Jäger Division*, now in reserve, with the *195th Division*, specially trained in mountain warfare, from France.

On 10th November, Conrad's *Eleventh Army* had already begun an offensive with five divisions towards Asiago.

Fighting ensued without result, except that the Austrians reduced the width of No Man's Land and established themselves in the ruins of Asiago, and it was brought to an end on the 16th on account of heavy losses and the breakdown of supply in consequence of winter conditions.

The Comando Supremo was, however, very upset and anxious about the situation, and on 18th November informed General Plumer, who had arrived on the 13th, that the Asiago plateau had been heavily gas-shelled and that the Italians would have to retire from the mountains or at least from the Brenta valley if they were attacked. General Plumer calmed down his informants and said that he would send up one of his General Staff officers to report. This officer was driven in a car into the front line in the Brenta valley in full view of the Austrians on the cliffs overlooking the river; but there was hardly a shot fired either here or on the Asiago plateau. The Italian troops seemed to be in good shape, but nervous, too many of them looking over their shoulders to see if their neighbours were going to run away. A determined attack would have had every chance of success.

On the main front Papadopoli island was occupied by the Austrian *28th Division* on the 10th; but attempts to force passages of the Piave gained only one small success on the night of the 12th/13th, when small parties, amounting in all to three battalions, crossed by boats and seized the 30-foot high embankment on the west bank of the river at Zenson, 15 miles from its mouth, where there is a loop, and held it as a bridgehead, overlooking all the flat country around. A mass attack was planned for the 16th, and on the night of the 15th/16th four battalions of the German *117th Division* succeeded in crossing at the railway bridge below Nervesa; but those who were not killed were taken prisoner. All other attempts failed, and their repetition, and any action to enlarge the little Zenson bridgehead, were forbidden.

THE MONTE GRAPPA OFFENSIVE 13TH NOVEMBER

The offensive against the Monte Grappa section, defended by one division of the Italian IX Corps and two of the XVIII of the Fourth Army, was a more serious affair.

AUSTRIAN OFFENSIVE. 13TH NOVEMBER

Krauss attacked on the 13th with four divisions, very weak after all the previous fighting. A long struggle ensued, unnecessary to describe, but it had the effect that it was to this sector rather than to the Piave the eyes of the French and British commanders in Italy were directed.

CHAPTER VII

THE ARRIVAL OF THE BRITISH AND FRENCH DIVISIONS
(Sketches 2, 5)

THE MOVE OF THE XIV CORPS TO ITALY

On 28th October G.H.Q. France issued orders that advanced parties, consisting of 8 officers and 13 other ranks from the XIV Corps staff and troops, and 8 officers and 14 other ranks each from the 23rd and 41st Divisions, should reach Paris in time to catch the evening mail train for Italy on the 30th. The Quartermaster-General and the Director General of Transportation also sent advanced parties of a total of 21 officers and 48 other ranks. These parties were instructed to report to the British Mission with the Comando Supremo.[1]

On 1st November warning orders were given to the units that they would entrain shortly, and about midday on 6th November—when the Italians were falling back from the Tagliamento to the Piave—the entrainment of the Base units was begun at Rouen, of the corps troops and the 23rd Division at stations at and near St. Omer, and on the next day that of the two squadrons of the Royal Flying Corps.

Twenty-four trains a day were provided; but some of these had to be used for the carriage of ammunition, supplies and other stores to stock the advanced depôts in Italy; even after these had been filled, from four to five train loads per day were required to keep them full. Supply columns and ammunition sub-parks (M.T.) went to Italy by road.[2]

---

[1] For the British Order of Battle in Italy in November 1917, see Appendix I.
[2] See Sketch 2.
An account of the march of the Supply Column of the 48th Division from Auchel (7 miles W.S.W. of Béthune) to Cologna Veneta (18 miles south-west of Verona) is given in the *Royal Army Service Corps Quarterly* for April 1921. The route lay through Lyons, Cannes, Ventimiglia, Genoa, Arquata and Mantua. The distance of 1,118 miles took the 65 motor vehicles 16 marching days, with one day's halt.

The entrainment of the last units of the 23rd Division was completed on the 11th, that of the 41st was begun on the same day and finished on the 13th, each division requiring 59 trains. That of the corps troops, the two Army brigades of field artillery, six batteries of 6-inch howitzers,[1] and various medical, veterinary and remount units then began. By 17th November the entrainment of the XIV Corps, its two divisions, the R.F.C. units, and Base and Line of Communication units was completed. The trains proceeded by the Riviera route, the journey taking four to seven days; halts were made for meals, washing and exercise; the mere sight of the beauties of the south of France and western Italy after months spent in Flanders acted, it is said, like a tonic on the tired men. On arrival at Ventimiglia, whence there was only a single line to Savona, the field artillery, both divisional and Army, was detrained and it carried out the next part of the journey by march along the coastal road, the 74 miles taking 5 days to cover.

Lord Cavan in Italy

Lieut.-General Lord Cavan, with a small staff,[2] had left France for Italy on 2nd November, and he arrived at Pavia at 10 a.m. on the 5th, ahead of his troops. He then motored to Padua, where he was received by the King of Italy, and later met General Piccione, head of the Operations Branch, and Br.-General Delmé-Radcliffe, head of the British Mission. Next day he went to the Comando Supremo at Treviso and had a long interview with General Cadorna. The Italian C.G.S. was obviously disappointed at the proposed concentration of the British force being placed so far back, in the area[3] Pavia — Mortara — Milan — Lodi, which had been fixed by the General Staff, War Office, on 2nd November. He explained that in his opinion the fate of Italy was in the balance and that close active support by both French and

---

[1] Five batteries of the XCIV Heavy Artillery Group were already in Italy. For the Italian campaign the 60-pdr. battery was restored to each division. These batteries had been taken away in 1915 and treated as part of the heavy artillery commands.

[2] The B.G.G.S., and the Prince of Wales as A.D.C., accompanied him. B.G.G.S., Br.-General Hon. J. F. Gathorne-Hardy; D.A. & Q.M.G., Br.-General H. L. Alexander; C.R.A., Br.-General A. E. Wardrop; C.H.A., Br.-General T. R. C. Hudson; C.E., Br.-General C. S. Wilson.

[3] See Sketch 2, where the area is marked " 3 ".

British troops was necessary to save Italy to the Allies. Lord Cavan agreed provisionally, subject to the consent of the War Cabinet, which was given next day, to advance his concentration to an area about Mantua on the west bank of the Mincio, as it would be covered from the north by the French concentration near Lake Garda. With this General Cadorna seemed pleased and satisfied. Lord Cavan also had a satisfactory interview with General Duchêne, the two commanders agreeing to act in close concert in all eventualities.

The impression left on Lord Cavan's mind by his visit to the Comando Supremo, as he reported, was that the Italian débâcle, although it may to some extent have been due to treachery and disinclination to fight, was largely the result of faulty dispositions and bad orders. He had passed on the road many thousands of men of the Second Army marching westwards: on the whole, they were of fine physique and did not appear to be as demoralized as might have been expected.[1] All information available in the British Mission pointed to the conclusion that the retirement of the other Italian Armies to the Piave was in process of completion in good or fair order, and there seemed no reason to suppose that the line of the Piave could not be held against any Austrian-German attack. The weakness of the Italians lay, he thought, in the considerable shortage of artillery, an unfortunate circumstance when the infantry to be covered was somewhat shaken: there was further the possibility of a breakdown of the transport service owing to the under-feeding and over-loading of the horses and mules. As long as the Piave could be held, he summed up, the situation, though serious, was not desperate: but if this river was forced, there would be few, if any, reserves for counter-attack or for manning back lines until the Second Army was re-formed, and this might take a month: the forcing of the Piave line might therefore entail the entire breakdown of Italian resistance: if the enemy made a vigorous offensive the critical time on the Piave line would be between the 15th and 22nd November, and as the concentration of the British troops would probably not be completed until the 20th, no assistance could be expected of them during that period.

---

[1] See, however, below on this point (p. 100).

CONCENTRATION AREAS. NOVEMBER

Decision as to the Area of Concentration

After establishing himself in Mantua—where the rest of his Staff joined him on the 11th—Lord Cavan went on 9th November to Padua to see Sir Henry Wilson in the latter's capacity as one of the Military Representatives of the Versailles Council. The Comando Supremo had been pressing General Wilson for a more forward detrainment and concentration of the British force; but Lord Cavan was averse to any alteration in the place of concentration of the leading division, the 23rd; if the situation hardened he was agreeable, however, to the 41st Division being detrained further forward, where the 23rd could join it by march. He impressed upon Sir Henry Wilson that he could not consent to any concentration east of the Mincio unless it appeared reasonably probable—and the Italian Armies had not yet completed crossing the Piave—that the river line could be held long enough to allow the two British divisions to complete their concentration unmolested. At General Wilson's suggestion it was settled that small parties, each of one officer and six other ranks, should be sent to the different Italian Armies as soon as possible, in order to give ocular demonstration that British infantry had arrived in Italy.

On the following day, the 10th, the XIV Corps issued orders for the concentration of the two divisions in the Mantua area, west of the Mincio. The leading troops of the 23rd Division began detraining on the 11th, and those of the 41st on the 16th; the completion of the operation and of the concentration took five days more. Detrainment was a nightmare. Under the stress of a continuous mass of French and British troops arriving, Italian railway organization completely broke down; trains were run into any siding—often without any unloading platforms—that happened to be vacant at any station, and the occupants told to detrain. Officers who knew not a word of Italian—one interpreter per battalion arrived in due course—tore round the country trying to collect scattered units and to concentrate them by brigade groups. The utmost good will prevailed, however, and both publicly and privately the British troops were received with enthusiasm and expressions of joy and gratitude.

There was only one misunderstanding: the Italian women greeted the British in the Italian fashion by extending the arm with the hand cupped towards themselves, and then moving the fingers backwards and forwards. This the British soldier took to be a " come hither " signal and consequently suffered a few rebuffs before he realized it was merely the Italian method of waving!

The question of the areas of concentration of the British contingent was, however, not settled. On the morning of the 11th a long discussion took place between Generals Diaz, Foch and Wilson.[1] The new Italian C.G.S. insisted on the vital necessity of French divisions taking over as soon as possible the line of the Piave from Nervesa[2] to a point 12 miles above, that is around the Montello : otherwise he could not be responsible for that sector of the line and if the Montello, the angle of the front and the connecting link between the Piave and mountain sectors, was lost, the whole line was lost. General Foch declined to comply, his reason being that he wished the French troops to be properly concentrated and then moved forward into the fighting line as complete divisions, and not sent forward prematurely and piecemeal on roads blocked with troops in retreat, or to be mixed up with Italian troops already in occupation of the sector.[3] General Diaz then read a telegram from the Italian Prime Minister urging that Allied troops should be moved up, and stating that the impression was gaining ground that the Allies were hanging back. After a long and heated discussion, General Foch yielded so far as to agree that the four French divisions should be brought forward to the Vicenza area.

On the next day (the 12th), whilst the detrainment was in progress, Lord Cavan received a letter from Sir Henry Wilson conveying to him the decision made at his meeting with Generals Diaz and Foch. It was that, whilst the French force advanced to a position with its right on Vicenza (inclusive), the British XIV Corps should join up on its right, behind the Bacchiglione river, with its own right at Montegalda : once there, it could be considered how best to help the Italians : with the Vicenza position in view, the detraining stations of the British divisions were to be as close to the Bacchiglione as the military situation permitted. Lord Cavan made no change in the detrainment programme,

---

[1] Reported by Sir Henry Wilson to the C.I.G.S. at 2.10 p.m.
[2] See Sketch 5.
[3] Mémoires, p. xl.

and preparations were made for the two divisions to march from the Mantua area to the new line.

Arrival of General Sir Herbert Plumer

On the evening of the 13th General Sir Herbert Plumer arrived in Mantua and took over command of the British troops in Italy. When the Prime Minister had decided at the Rapallo Conference to send two more divisions to Italy, Sir Douglas Haig had on the same day been warned of the decision by the General Staff, War Office, by telegram, and he was directed to arrange with the French as to the movement of the divisions and to report when it could begin. He was further informed that General Plumer was to proceed to Italy to command the British forces there and report on the situation for the information of the Government with special regard to any further desirable and necessary reinforcements. It was added that General Plumer might like to be accompanied by Major-General Harington, his chief General Staff officer, and such others of his Staff as could be arranged ; for it was considered most important that he should be able to get to work at once with a Staff to which he was accustomed. General Plumer was to proceed to Paris to meet the C.I.G.S. on his return from Rapallo on the 9th or 10th. The day was later changed to the 11th.

General Plumer was by no means anxious to leave the command of the Second Army ;[1] among other reasons, his troops, after a series of successes, were on the point of reaching Passchendaele.

General Sir Henry Rawlinson, commanding the Fourth Army, then employed in the Flanders coastal area, was directed to relieve General Plumer in the Second Army, and the two Army commanders were told to arrange between themselves for the relief by the Fourth Army Staff of such members of General Plumer's Staff as he wished to take

---

[1] He wrote, " I do not want to go in the least. . . . I simply loathe " leaving the Second Army, and feel very depressed ". " Plumer of Messines ", p. 134.

with him. He decided to take all his principal Staff officers.[1] Handing over command at 6 p.m. on 9th November, General Plumer next day attended a conference with Sir Douglas Haig and Sir William Robertson at St. Pol. The C.I.G.S. explained the general situation and stated that the War Cabinet directed that every effort should be made to save Italy from further invasion. He then handed to General Plumer his formal instructions.[2] The most important points in these were that he, like Field-Marshal Sir John French on the Western Front in 1914, was to regard himself as an independent commander, but, in order to co-operate effectively, he was to conform to the wishes of the Italian Commander-in-Chief in respect of the disposition and employment of his troops and to give all assistance in his power; but if at any time he was requested to carry out an operation which in his opinion would unduly endanger the safety of his troops, he was to make suitable representations to Italian General Headquarters and, if necessary, refer to the Chief of the Imperial General Staff for the instructions of the War Cabinet. He was to report on the situation as soon as possible and indicate the amount and nature of the reinforcements which he considered to be required.

In Paris, on the 11th, General Plumer saw the Prime Minister and the French Prime Minister, Monsieur Painlevé.[3] He found Mr. Lloyd George was "only too anxious to take "as many troops from the Western Front as he could wish".[4] Sir Henry Wilson's reports of the 10th to the C.I.G.S. had been gloomy; he had expressed the opinion that the Italians were not in a condition to withstand any determined attack on the Piave or elsewhere: he had urged General Diaz to prepare other lines in rear: if the Piave were lost in the next few days there would be little chance of stopping the enemy before the Adige.

---

[1] M.G.G.S., Major-General C. H. Harington; D.A.G., Major-General W. G. B. Western; D.Q.M.G., Major-General A. A. Chichester; G.O.C.R.A., Major-General C. R. Buckle; Chief Engineer, Major-General F. M. Glubb.
  The Administrative Staff did not at once proceed to Italy, and the XIV Corps Administrative Staff carried on for all troops until its arrival on 6th December.
[2] These are given in full in Appendix X.
[3] He gave way on the 16th to Monsieur Georges Clemenceau.
[4] "Plumer of Messines," p. 135. The author, the late General Sir Charles Harington, was present at the meeting.

After the situation had been discussed, General Plumer, as already mentioned, left for Italy and arrived at British Headquarters in Mantua on the 13th. After taking over from Lord Cavan, who reverted to the command of the XIV Corps, he visited General Duchêne. He then proceeded to Padua and was received by the King of Italy, and met General Diaz, General Foch, General Weygand and Sir Henry Wilson. At a meeting on the 14th it was agreed that the 23rd and 41st Divisions should move forward to the Vicenza line as soon as the Comando Supremo was able to give road and billeting area facilities, which, at the earliest, would be 19th November: the next two divisions, of whose despatch they had been informed, would be detrained farther forward. General Weygand left next day for Versailles.

General Plumer established his headquarters temporarily in Padua;[1] he dispensed with the presence there of Br.-General Crowe as representative of the C.I.G.S., saying that if he disagreed with him it would be unpleasant, and if he agreed with him there was no point in his being there; it was therefore arranged that Br.-General Crowe should act as liaison officer, returning to England and travelling to Italy as required.

GENERAL PLUMER'S FIRST REPORT

In reporting by telegram on the evening of the 14th, after his meeting with Generals Diaz, Foch and Wilson, General Plumer said that he had seen Sir Henry Wilson's reports—presumably those of the 10th and 11th already mentioned—and considered that " the situation in general is tactically " such that there would be no cause for anticipating more " than local loss of ground, if it were not for the probability " that one or two local reverses would mean a general " abandonment of the line now held ": further developments in the situation might occur before the Allied divisions could reach the Vicenza Line about the 24th or 25th, " but if the Italians can hold their present [Piave] line " until we and the French are on the Vicenza Line, we " should be able to hold that for some time, cover any

---

[1] He moved them back to Legnano, as nearer Mantua, on the 20th, but returned to Padua on the 30th.

"retirement of the Italians if one is made, and possibly "deliver a counter-stroke".

General Plumer advised that two more divisions should join the first four, and that a cavalry brigade should follow ; he did not ask for any more heavy artillery.

Move of the XI Corps to Italy

On 8th November, in accordance with the instructions formulated at Rapallo, Sir Douglas Haig had selected the 7th Division (Major-General T. H. Shoubridge) from the X Corps of the Second Army, and the 48th (1st South Midland) Division (Major-General R. Fanshawe) from the XVIII Corps of the Fifth Army, as the second pair of divisions to be transferred to Italy.[1] Additional Army and corps troops and additional units for the Lines of Communication were also detailed. The Fourteenth Wing of the R.F.C. with Nos. 5, 42, 45 and 66 Squadrons, under Lieut.-Colonel P. B. Joubert de la Ferté was also placed under orders for transfer to Italy, and, to administer the increased air detachment there, a VII Brigade headquarters was formed under Br.-General T. I. Webb-Bowen.[2]

A meeting was held at French G.Q.G. at Compiègne on 8th November to discuss the transport of these additional British troops. Colonel Payot again represented the French Direction de l'Arrière and the British officers were Major-General P. A. M. Nash, the D.G.T., and Br.-General C. R. Woodroffe of the British Mission. No conclusions could be arrived at until it was known whether additional French troops were to be sent to Italy : if no more were to go, then four or five more trains could be allotted to the British every day from about 10th November. On the same day, in accordance with the instructions of his Government, General Pétain selected the XII Corps (23rd and 24th Divisions) under General Nourrisson, then resting, to go to Italy, and it began entraining on the 11th. On the previous day, however, Colonel Payot definitely allotted to the British six trains a day by the Modane route in addition to the trains by the Riviera route.

---

[1] Both divisions had been engaged in the Flanders campaign : in the battles of Polygon Wood 1st–3rd October : of Broodseinde 4th October : and of Poelcappelle 9th October. The 7th Division had been further engaged in the Second Battle of Passchendaele, 26th–29th October.

[2] " War in the Air " vi, pp. 275 *et seq*.

XIV AND XI CORPS. NOVEMBER 97

The 7th Division began entraining in the St. Pol area on the 17th, directly after the original two divisions finished, and its last train left at midnight 20th/21st. The 48th Division entrained on the St. Pol–Arras line between the 21st and 24th and the Line of Communication troops on the 25th/26th. Between the 17th and 21st two more Army field artillery brigades were sent by the Riviera rail and road route.

On the 15th the XI Corps headquarters (Lieut.-General Sir Richard Haking) from the First Army were warned to be prepared to move to Italy. They were relieved by the XV Corps and began entraining at Lillers on the 23rd.

In response to General Plumer's recommendation of 14th November, the 5th Division (Major-General R. B. Stephens) and the 21st Division (Major-General D. M. G. Campbell) both of the X Corps of the Second Army were warned on the 22nd to proceed to Italy.[1] The 5th Division began entraining near St. Pol on 27th November; but on the afternoon of 1st December the operation was suspended, as the railways were required for troops which were being sent to the Battle of Cambrai 1917, where the advance had come to an end and a German counter-attack was in progress.[2] The entrainment was resumed on 10th December and completed on the 12th. On account of the situation at Cambrai, by decision of the War Cabinet, the despatch of the 21st Division was cancelled on 4th December.[3]

The total number of trains used for the transfer of British troops from France to Italy up to 31st December 1917 was 715, made up approximately of 442 troop trains, 102 supply trains, 102 ammunition trains, 32 for Ordnance stores, 28 for engineer stores and 9 miscellaneous.

Arrival of the French Contingent

The following is the time-table of the movement of the French troops :[4]

---

[1] Both had been engaged in October in the same actions as the 48th Division.
[2] The date of the German counter-attack is 30th November–3rd December.
[3] The 2nd and 47th also received warning orders to be ready to go to Italy, but were diverted to Cambrai.
[4] From F.O.A. vi (i), p. 94. For the Order of Battle see Appendix III.

31st October :		commencement of the detrainment of the XXXI Corps (65th and 64th Divisions) under General Rozeé d'Infreville
5th November :		completion of the detrainment of the above, commencement of the detrainment of the 47th Division
6th	,,	commencement of the detrainment of the 46th Division
10th	,,	completion of the detrainment of the 47th Division
12th	,,	completion of the detrainment of the 46th Division
20th	,,	commencement of the detrainment of the XII Corps (23rd and 24th Divisions) under General Nourrisson
22nd	,,	completion of above

Inter-Allied Consultations

On 16th November, the day on which the two enemy offensives against the Monte Grappa and the Asiago sectors mentioned in the previous chapter were brought to an end, and before the 23rd and 41st Divisions left the Mantua area for the Vicenza Line, Sir Herbert Plumer after consultation with Generals Foch and Wilson (who left next day for Versailles) put forward to the Comando Supremo a recommendation that the British and French, respectively, should take over these sectors, that under their command the Italian troops, used to the mountains and suitably equipped, should hold the mountain defences and that British and French troops should be in the foothills behind them. General Diaz, though pleased at the offer, considered that the difficulties of equipping British and French troops for such service and employing them even in the foothills in winter, would be very great, and asked that assistance might be given in some other way. It was therefore agreed that the Allied troops should concentrate on the Vicenza Line as arranged, and this done the Italian C.G.S. should say, taking into account how the situation had developed, in what way he wished to utilize the Anglo-French forces.

Appointment of General Fayolle

When on 8th November the French, on the advice of General Foch, had decided to send two more divisions, to make a total of six, General Fayolle, commanding the Group of Armies of the Centre was appointed to the command of the French contingent. General Foch was anxious " if possible to unite the two Armies, French and British, " sent beyond the Alps under the same command ".[1] As long as he himself remained in Italy this union was tacitly in operation, but he was bound soon to return to his duties in Paris as C.G.S. He tried to persuade General Robertson that General Fayolle should be placed in supreme command of the two contingents, but met with a blank refusal on the grounds that it was impossible to place such a brilliant commander as General Plumer in a subordinate position; and besides he was already provided with a letter of service which conferred on him complete independence.

Advance of the XIV Corps[2]

In a letter dated 14th November the head of the British Mission gave the XIV Corps the details of the roads and billeting areas which would be available for the British force in its advance to the Vicenza area. Two roads (1) Mantua–Legnago, allotted to the 23rd Division, and (2) Isola della Scala–Lonigo, allotted to the 41st Division, were defined, with an area for billeting along them of an average width of two or three miles. The usual reconnaissances were carried out, and the distances by the two roads found to be 45 and 64 miles respectively. It was settled that the marches should begin on the 19th and the western boundary of the new area reached on the 23rd. In fine weather, though it was rather cold with frost at night, both divisions started to time, less the artillery delayed by having to march from Ventimiglia to Savona, less one infantry brigade of the 41st Division and other units which had not arrived, and hampered by the transport being insufficient.[3] Both were covered by advanced guards for which the Corps Cyclist Battalion and No. 12 Motor

---

[1] F.O.A. vi (i), p. 23.
[2] See Sketch 5.
[3] This matter is discussed in Chapter IX below.

Machine Gun Battery were available. The French contingent, called the Tenth Army after the XII Corps began detraining on 20th December, was also on the move for the Vicenza area. During the march of the XIV Corps inconvenience was caused by the presence of Italian troops in billets which the British expected to occupy; but with good feeling on both sides, any difficulties which arose were overcome at the expense of a little discomfort.

The following is an extract from the letter of an Italian officer transmitted by the British Ambassador in Rome to the Secretary of State for Foreign Affairs. Speaking of the British troops, the writer says: " They are marvellous. I " am not speaking of their discipline, which is perfect, but " of the singular delicacy of feeling which distinguishes " officers and soldiers. When they leave a billet which they " have occupied not a chair is out of its proper place. Their " cleanliness is so great that you would not find a straw on " the ground. So also with their camps, where hundreds of " wagons and quadrupeds have stopped; they do not " leave any trace of their passage. No one even takes a " glass of water without leave."

The corps commander felt moved to congratulate his divisions on their good march discipline (which includes picking up waste paper and leaving no trace), the smartness of the transport and the fine spirit of the men in spite of fatigue.

Not the least of the tasks of the Allies was that performed by the police and traffic controls in clearing a way through the columns of weary Italian soldiers who were passing westward along the roads by which the British were moving forward. It was a most depressing sight: the men on foot straggled along in parties or at best in a rough column, mostly without arms and lacking anything of the nature of march discipline; sullen and apathetic, and above all dog-tired and hungry—groups were seen devouring the raw flesh of oxen which had fallen by the way. The officers came along in carriages in the intervals, the seniors in victorias and phaetons, the juniors in pony carts, some of them playing cards. The impression left on the British who saw these melancholy processions was that such troops would never put up a fight again. Time was to show that this impression was completely wrong.

THE ALLIES TAKE OVER. NOVEMBER 101

Anglo-French Troops Ordered into the Line

Up to 16th November the Austrians had made little progress in the Monte Grappa sector; but on the 17th they opened a violent attack against Monte Tomba at its eastern end near the Piave. This was broken up by Italian artillery fire; but General von Below himself then took charge and ordered an attack in the centre which overlooked Monte Tomba. This was launched on the 22nd and again failed; but with the aid of flame-projectors Monte Tomba was taken. A general attack on the whole front from the Piave to the Brenta was then ordered and continued through the 23rd, 24th and 25th; but it was only a half-hearted effort, as the Austrians were on very short rations, and not only without winter clothing but in rags; and they were everywhere held.

On the 22nd a conference took place between Generals Diaz, Foch and Plumer, at which it was agreed that French and British troops should advance beyond the Vicenza Line in order to be within supporting distance of the Italians, and then should take over from the right of the Italian Fourth Army the sectors of the line including the Montello and Monte Tomba. This was then put in writing and signed by Generals Foch and Plumer.

Accordingly, General Plumer directed that the XIV Corps should continue its march on the 24th to positions on both banks of the Brenta between Padua and Cittadella, about 25 miles from the front, and be prepared to take over at an early date the front line on the Piave from Nervesa 7 miles northward to Rivasecca.

The roads were reconnoitred, and by corps orders the 23rd Division was to start at 3 a.m. on the 24th to occupy the new area, and the 41st Division to march at 10.30 a.m. to occupy the area the 23rd had vacated. It was then discovered that the Italians could not clear the area east of the Brenta in sufficient time to permit of British and French troops crossing the river on the 24th and that they must not do so before 5 a.m. on the 25th. Fresh orders therefore were issued.

By the evening of the 25th, however, the area assigned on the Brenta had been reached, with the 41st and 23rd Divisions side by side, and the French XXXI Corps on their left. Next day General Plumer directed the XIV Corps, moving forward on the 28th, to relieve the Italian I Corps (Fourth Army) on the line of the Piave between Nervesa and Ciano (which is 1¼ miles below Rivasecca) where it would be in touch with the French, and officers were sent to the sector to make the usual reconnaissances.

During 26th and 27th November, therefore, the troops of the XIV Corps halted on the positions they had reached on the Brenta, and the artillery and the 123rd Brigade were able to catch up and rejoin, so that both divisions were now complete. Between the 22nd and the 27th, the 7th Division detrained west of the Adige in an area between Legnago and Isola della Scala as reserve to the XIV Corps, and on the 25th, by corps order, began moving to an area about ten miles deep, with its front on the Bacchiglione between Montegalda and Longare. The corps cavalry regiment and four batteries of heavy artillery also arrived. The XI Corps was on the point of entraining in France. The French had the XXXI Corps (4 divisions) up alongside the British, with the 24th Division of the XII Corps at Peschiera (southern end of Lake Garda) and the 23rd at Vicenza.

The End of the Caporetto Offensive

On 23rd November General Foch, feeling that all was well, left Italy to return to his duties as Chief of the General Staff in Paris, leaving General Fayolle, who had arrived on the 21st, in command of the French contingent.

In the eyes of the Allies the departure of General Foch marked the close of the great Caporetto offensive; but it was not until 2nd December that it was officially brought to an end on the Piave front by the Austro-Germans when the little Zenson bridgehead on the Piave was evacuated. Three of the German divisions were ordered back to Germany via Feltre and Trent: the other four, including the *Alpine Corps* and the *Jäger Division*, were to remain in Italy for the present.

The total Italian casualties in the campaign had been 265,000 prisoners, 10,000 killed, and 30,000 wounded, besides a large number of stragglers scattered about the country; in material 3,152 guns, 1,732 trench mortars, 3,000 machine guns and immense quantities of stores and supplies had been lost.[1]

---

[1] Villari, p. 172.

The total Austrian-German losses have not been disclosed.[1]

The reorganization of the Italian army was rapid. On 17th December 1917, Br.-General Delmé-Radcliffe reported, for the information of the War Cabinet, that the class of recruits called up in 1917 was being incorporated in the field Armies, and that the total strength of the Italian army (including 110,000 in Albania and Macedonia), 1,769,700 on 5th November, was 1,859,500 on 1st December : the next class would be called up between 1st January and 1st April, and was expected to produce 250,000 men : the position as regards rifles and machine guns was satisfactory owing to French and British assistance : by the end of the year 51 divisions would each have 10 batteries of field artillery : the supply of heavy howitzers and guns was being delayed by the manufacture of sights, fillings and spare parts falling behind the programme.

---

[1] Occasional items only are given in the German Monograph, e.g., that in the Monte Grappa fighting between 17th and 27th November the *Jäger Division* lost 33 officers and 1,173 men, and that some battalions were down to 200 men. The sick list was very high.

CHAPTER VIII

THE BRITISH ENTER THE LINE
(Sketch 5)

THE MONTELLO POSITION[1]

The Italians had not adopted defence in depth or the latest form of entrenchments. The Montello position consisted of three lines of well—revetted trenches parallel to the river bank, along which ran a road, with numerous conspicuous machine-gun emplacements and shelters of the 1914 pattern rather than shell-proof dug-outs. The forward trench was generally dug in the sand and shingle along the bank of the Piave; but in places the river was bordered by steep cliffs and there the trench ran at their foot, exposed to fire but with a good deal of cover from view afforded by trees and scrub.

Behind the front position was the flat top of the Montello, broken by small summits and narrow wooded clefts, and with the depressions already mentioned, which gave good cover for howitzers; twenty unmetalled narrow roads bordered by hedges ran across it from north to south. The river, with a bed about 800 yards wide at this point, flowed not as one stream, but, like the Tagliamento, was split into as many as ten different channels with sandbanks or islands between them; the waterways except after rain or snow were seldom more than 4 feet deep with the top of the bank 6 feet higher than the surface of the water; but the current ran very strong and, the water being icy-cold, fording or swimming was not a light matter. Attempts were made by the Austro-Germans to cross in boats and on rafts, but, as already mentioned, few had been successful.

A thousand to two thousand yards away stretched the Austrian position. Opposite to the Montello were wooded foothills, at first lower than that hill, but gradually rising, so that from four miles or more away the enemy had an uninterrupted view of the lines and back areas on the western side of the Piave. Below Nervesa the country was dead

---
[1] See Sketch 5.

THE PIAVE COUNTRY

flat on both sides of the river; here view was restricted by rows of mulberry trees with vines between them; but the roads, which ran on embankments on account of floods, were clearly visible and had to be screened. Except for these restrictions of view the Montello gave the most perfect observation over the enemy's side of the Piave. In early December, however, no appearance of life could be observed there, rarely was a gun heard, and not a shell hole was to be seen.

The XIV Corps takes over the Montello Sector

On the 28th the 41st and 23rd Divisions began their march north-eastwards from the Brenta to the Montello sector, the one via Camposampiero and Volpago, the other via Castelfranco and Montebelluna. They halted on the evening of the 29th some ten miles from the front. The routes and times were carefully selected and adhered to, as the Italian XXV Corps was crossing the lines of march from north to south on the 29th, yet some delays ensued. The 7th Division on this day began to move forward from the Adige to the Brenta. The country was flat, the roads frozen hard and the weather dry, so that marching conditions were excellent; extra kit and two blankets per man had to be carried, so transport in the form of slow-moving ox-wagons was hired where possible.

Opposite to the sector to be taken over were the Austrian *13th Division* and the German *12th Division* of Stein's group; but early in December Stein's group was replaced partly by Scotti's (Austrian) group and partly by Hofacker's (German) group, and then the German *117th Division* and the Austrian *13th* faced the British.

The relief of the Italian I Corps was carried out division by division as follows: The infantry of the 41st Division relieved the Italian 1st Division between 30th November and the morning of 2nd December, and then the infantry of the 23rd Division began the relief of the Italian 70th Division, completing it by the morning of the 4th, on which day at 10 a.m. Lieut.-General Lord Cavan took over command of the sector, with headquarters at Fanzolo, 4 miles north-east of Castelfranco, General Duchêne's headquarters. Each division put two brigades into the front position, and each of these brigades put two battalions into the line, with one in support and one in reserve. On completion of each divisional relief, the artillery of the division began to take over, beginning in the afternoon and completing the operation in three days. During the period of the relief a certain amount of enemy artillery registration was in progress, but no casualties were suffered.

The French began the relief of the Italians on the left of the British sector on 3rd December and placed the 65th and 47th Divisions in the line,[1] with an Italian brigade (under the French XXXI Corps) on the right next to the British.

The British were received by all ranks with the greatest cordiality and hospitality and it was a new and pleasant experience for battalions and companies to take over undamaged houses as headquarters, and to find barrels of wine among the trench stores.

Communication with the Italians presented some difficulty as few British officers or men could speak their language; very few Italian officers too could speak English and few anything approaching perfect French; but in the ranks the number of Italian soldiers who had picked up English in the United States was remarkable, and they served as unofficial interpreters. Another difficulty experienced in co-operating with the Italians was their habit of closing down all business from 12 to 3 p.m. every day for the midday meal and rest, a habit continued even when the war was not going too well for them; as the Austrians knocked off at 11.30 a.m. for a couple of hours, the cause did not suffer. As noon approached Italian officers very obviously became uneasy and wanted to stop any work in hand.

The two divisional headquarters were established at Selva and Montebelluna respectively. The 7th Division in reserve came up to an area around Vedelago, east of Castel Franco.

Much work remained to be done to strengthen and deepen the defences, both on the improvement and wiring of existing trenches and by digging new trenches. A reserve line to the front position was dug by the infantry along the northern side of the Montello plateau and a new line was constructed across the middle of it. The Italian method of holding the front had been to put nearly every man and machine gun into the front line with really no supports and reserve,

---

[1] The position of the other four French divisions is shown on Sketch 5.

which entailed heavy losses during bombardment, and in any case an unnecessary strain on the men. Every endeavour was therefore made to organize the British sector as a model with the purpose of demonstrating to the Italians how few men need be kept in the front line.

Much labour was devoted to the formation of strongpoints on the plateau and to the construction of shell-proof dugouts and emplacements for machine guns and trench mortars, and work on them was continued night and day by the engineers and pioneers. The soil was easy and did not require much revetting. The ground was, in fact, in every way favourable; and as timber for pit props was plentiful, galleries were easily made for headquarters and offices by tunnelling into the steep sides of one of the circular depressions or into the back of one of the small ridges. The similarity of the depressions made differentiation and choice of nomenclature difficult; but this was overcome by the adoption of such names as Sidebottom, Longbottom, Shufflebottom, and in the invention of others in which much ingenuity was displayed. In the river gravel on the extreme left tunnelling was not practicable and there ferro-concrete was used. In places the concreted banks offered excellent protection for machine guns; but any attempt to interfere with them drew down the wrath of the Italians, who knew the terrific force of water which the banks had to withstand when the Piave was in spate.

When some progress had been made General Plumer invited General Diaz to visit the British sector on the plea that an inspection by him as Allied Commander-in-Chief would greatly please the troops and give them confidence. The Italian commander was highly flattered and agreed to come. After his visit it was noticed that the Italians on either side of the British set about improving their very simple defences, which previously they had never troubled about.

General Plumer's main idea—as it had been General Foch's—was to set the Italians on their own feet again, and return to France at the earliest possible moment, and his diplomatic handling of them, as in the above instance, and his studied endeavour to show them that he regarded them as equals were no doubt the source of the immense confidence they came to place in him and of the restoration of their confidence in themselves.

It was in the end found impossible to break the higher Italian Staffs of their habit of making constant changes in orders, and of considering that an order issued was an order obeyed. Nor was it possible to induce them to issue clear instructions for the allotment of roads, and for such details as the synchronization of watches, a practice unknown to them. In the result, whenever British troops marched there were invariably collisions and crossings with Italian troops. Fortunately as one officer wrote, " the enemy's " aircraft were not interested ".

Artillery of the XIV Corps

After the divisional reliefs, eighteen Italian heavy batteries (reduced to fifteen on 20th December) and three Italian mountain batteries remained in the line under the XIV Corps, so that on 31st December the total of the artillery defending the corps sector was 204 field and mountain guns and 104 heavy guns, the former organized under the two divisions, and the latter in four groups, the 24th, 80th, Italian 64th and Italian 71st.[1]

Air Support

The XIV Corps had the support of five aeroplane squadrons, the 28th, 34th, 42nd (which arrived on 12th and 14th November and 7th December respectively), the 66th (which arrived on 28th November), and the 45th (which arrived on 21st December), that is two fighter and three corps squadrons. On 30th December No. 4 Balloon Wing with two balloon companies, for artillery observation, arrived at Padua. The

---

[1] 18 pdrs.. 144 ; 4.5-inch howitzers, 48 ; mountain guns, 12 ; 6-inch howitzers, 3 5; 60-pdrs., 12; Italian 149-mm. guns, 24; 149 mm. howitzers, 36.

The 41st Division had in addition to its own two brigades of field artillery, the LXXII Army Brigade R.F.A. and the three Italian mountain batteries ; the 23rd Division had in addition to its own two brigades R.F.A., the XIV Army Brigade R.H.A.

The 24th H.A. Group contained the 105th, 172nd, 229th and 247th Siege Batteries of 6-inch howitzers and the 1/1st Warwickshire 60-pdr. Battery.

The 80th H.A. Group contained the 137th, 176th, 181st and 289th Siege Batteries of 6-inch howitzers and the 90th Heavy Battery of 60-pdrs.

None of these heavy batteries belonged to the groups sent to Italy in April and July. The XCIV Heavy Artillery Group was refitting after its losses of equipment in the Caporetto retreat.

AIR OPERATIONS. DECEMBER

French provided seven "escadrilles." The air situation when the French and British appeared on the scene was unsatisfactory.[1] The victories gained over the Italian ground forces, and the constant success of the Austrian and German aircraft over the Italian fliers had made the enemy pilots aggressively confident and accustomed to do as they liked in the air. This state of affairs was gradually changed; they then became more cautious and did not attack the British except in retaliation. Thus after a German airfield near Conegliano had been twice bombed, German fliers made a low level attack on the airfield at Istrana (on the railway between Treviso and Castelfranco)[2]—doing little damage and losing 6 machines. On 25th December the R.F.C. raided the headquarters of an Austrian flying squadron and next day in retaliation 25 Austrian planes, the pilots emboldened by Christmas libations, bombed Istrana airfield again, but lost 11, shot down, without a British casualty.

When the British arrived in Italy they were informed that there was a sort of general understanding with the Austrians that towns were not to be bombed. This understanding was rudely shaken when the Germans sent to Italy two squadrons of night bombers which they flew from captured Italian airfields. The German night fliers chiefly directed their operations against the towns of Treviso, Bassano, Castelfranco, Vicenza and Padua and on the 29th damaged General Plumer's offices in Padua. There was no defence, as the Italian A.A. batteries, though they went into action when enemy aeroplanes were signalled, ceased fire when the first bombs were dropped, and reopened fire only after the enemy machines had left. By January, however, " air " superiority definitely passed to the Allied air services ",[3] but enemy night bombing continued. How it was reduced will be related in due course.

---

[1] The enemy air forces were distributed to corps. Counting by Austrian companies (German *Abteilungen*) containing 6 to 9 aeroplanes, the number allotted were Krauss 5; Stein 2; Hofacker 2; Scotti 1; and the others 1 or 2 (German Monograph).
The Italian figures are not available, but at the end of 1916, the Italian Second Army possessed only 9 *squadreglie* (8 reconnaissance 1 fighter) " about sixty machines " (I.O.A. i, p. 42).
[2] Other airfields in use were Limbraga (2 miles north of Treviso), Grosso (7 miles east of Vicenza) and Villalta (6 miles E.N.E. of Vicenza).
[3] " War in the Air " vi, p. 278–9.

The Group Plan of Defence

During the progress of reliefs on 4th and 5th December, the Austrians again attacked north-east of Asiago and drove the Italians out of a salient known as the Melette massif, which had a front of nearly five miles, and was three miles deep. As snow was late in falling and the passes were still open, it was to be expected that further attacks would be made with the object of reaching the plain of Lombardy, which begins near Bassano, before the coldest part of the winter set in. Arrangements were therefore made for the close co-operation of the French and British reserves with the Italians in case of necessity. On 7th December, General Plumer met General Fayolle, and they discussed proposals for the grouping of French, British and Italian troops under fixed commands in order to ensure that the passes from the mountains were blocked, and that the enemy was driven back at once should he force his way to the plain.

The proposals for grouping, solely for tactical not for administrative purposes, which they laid before General Diaz next day were:

(1) Right Group under the Duke of Aosta: Italian Third Army.

(2) Centre Group under General Sir Herbert Plumer: the French XXXI Corps (French 47th and 65th Divisions and one Italian Alpine brigade); the British XIV Corps (British 23rd and 41st Divisions); reserves: the British 7th Division and one Italian corps.

Artillery: mountain guns 48, field guns 368, heavy guns 294.

(3) Left Group under General Duchêne[1]: the French XII Corps (French 23rd, 24th and 46th Divisions); the British XI Corps (British 48th Division and French 64th Division); reserves: the British 5th Division and one Italian corps.

Artillery: mountain guns 36, field guns 428, heavy guns 230.

General Diaz accepted the proposals in principle, and directed that the necessary staff arrangements and troop movements should be carried out. He decided, however,

---

[1] General Duchêne returned to the Western Front to command the Sixth Army, and on 17th December was succeeded by General Maistre, who vacated command of the Sixth Army.

GROUPS FORMED. 8TH DECEMBER

that the moment at which the Grouping Plan should come into force as regards command must be settled by the Comando Supremo when the necessary moves had been completed. He enquired if the British and French troops were prepared to operate in the mountains : but both Allied commanders said that this would be impracticable without special clothing and equipment, which could not be provided in time.

In accordance with the plan, at 10 p.m. that night, General Plumer ordered the following to take place :

> The 7th Division, in reserve in the Vedelago area, to move on the 10th eight miles north-westward to the Altivole area.
>
> The 48th Division, which was strung out on the road on both sides of the Brenta, to move on the 10th north-westward to an area around Tezze (5 miles north-west of Cittadella), and to be prepared to move farther north on the 11th or 12th to Marostica, the date depending on the clearance of the area by the French 46th Division.
>
> The artillery of the 5th Division, then assembling with its head on the Bacchiglione, to move forward as soon as possible to the west bank of the Brenta, east of Cadusano.
>
> The XI Corps to report as soon as its first infantry brigade had arrived and was ready to move.

General Diaz's Indecision

On the 9th, the very next day after the conference, General Diaz seems to have taken a gloomy view of the situation. He informed General Plumer that the Italians could hold on no longer to the Monte Grappa sector and must retire towards Rome to the neck of the peninsula where a narrow front offered itself. This information was repeated several times, apparently in expectation of a reply. The British commander, thus forced to speak, merely said that he should continue to hold the Montello. General Diaz then explained again at great length, suggesting that what he had said could not have been understood ; for if the British stayed behind they would be isolated and cut off. General Plumer replied that he understood perfectly, but saw no reason to retire. Then the Italian general said that he would not retire either.

Arrival of the XI Corps

The XI Corps staff[1] and corps troops had detrained at Mantua and Camposampiero, respectively, between 1st and 5th December, and Lieut.-General Haking's corps headquarters were opened in Mantua on 1st December, moving via Padua to Camposampiero on the 6th. The 48th Division had detrained between 27th November and 1st December at the stations on the Este–Verona line between Este and Isola della Scala, amid the usual confusion experienced in Italy. On 29th November the division was ordered to concentrate east of the Adige around Cologna Veneta. Thence, on 1st December, it began moving north-eastward and on the night of the 4th its head had reached the Brenta west of Camposampiero. On the 5th it moved forward again to an area with the head at Castelfranco and the rear at Camisano, where it remained until it left on the 10th for its place under the Grouping Plan around Tezze.

The other division allotted to the XI Corps was the 5th, and its advanced party arrived at Legnago on 1st December. The units of the division arrived between the 2nd and the morning of the 7th, detraining on the line between Este and Legnago and concentrating in the western portion of the Vicenza area. Then owing to the suspension of entrainment in France entailed by the Battle of Cambrai 1917, no more trains arrived until the evening of the 15th. But on the 6th the two infantry brigades and artillery which had arrived, by Lieut.-General Haking's order, marched to the eastern end of the Vicenza area west of the Bacchiglione river. Here they remained until the 17th, when under the Grouping Plan they moved into the triangular area east of the Brenta marked by Padua (exclusive)–Camposampiero–Cittadella, just vacated by the 48th Division. The remainder of the division began to arrive from France on the evening of the 15th, and by the evening of the 17th all the trains had come through except two which had been held up by an accident to a French troop train, and these appeared on

---

[1] B.G.G.S., Br.-General J. E. S. Brind ; D.A. & Q.M.G., Br.-General A.F.U. Green ; C.R.A., Br.-General E. W. Alexander ; C.H.A., Br.-General R. H. F. McCulloch ; C.E., Br.-General H. J. M. Marshall.

the 20th. Detrainment was carried out at two stations just short of Cittadella, actually in the area allotted to the division, where it remained the whole of December.

General Plumer's Report of 14th December 1917

General Plumer kept his two corps commanders informed of the general situation, and of the Grouping Plan and of the areas the groups would occupy in the event of the plan coming into force. The Centre Group, under himself, was to support the Italian Fourth Army to hold the line of the Piave ; the Left Group was to support the Italian First Army, the French XII Corps being on the west bank of the Astico, and the British XI Corps between the Astico and the Brenta (with the British 48th Division about Marostica with advanced troops on the roads descending from the Asiago plateau) in touch with the French 64th Division astride the Brenta. The Anglo-French forces, General Plumer said, were not to interfere with the responsibility of the Italian First and Fourth Armies for the defence of the line : their mission, in the case that the front between the Astico and the Piave was broken, was to block the exits from the mountains and, in conjunction with the Italian troops, drive the enemy back.

General Plumer made a second report by telegram to the Chief of the Imperial General Staff on 14th December. As regards the general situation during the past month, he said : until the British and French troops had arrived in sufficient force to be a material factor, the situation was certainly critical. The Italian commanders and troops were only just beginning to recover from the shock of their enforced retreat. They had halted mainly because the pressure of pursuit had abated ; but they believed this abatement was only temporary and they had little confidence in themselves or each other. A further serious pressure would probably have caused another retirement, and this would have involved the loss of Venice and of the Venetian provinces. As the days went by and no serious attack was made on them the Italians recovered confidence ; but they were desperately anxious to relieve some of their troops from the front line and, owing to want of proper organization, they were unable to do this systematically themselves. The troops were told, however, that British and French troops were coming to their assistance and would afford them the relief they looked for. . . . As soon as more troops had arrived an offer was made to take over sectors of the front line and this was eagerly accepted by the Italians. It was important that there should be no delay in carrying this into effect, as reports were being sedulously put about to the effect that the Allied troops had come to consume the supplies in the country, but had no intention of taking any part in the fighting. . . . As soon as the French troops and our own were in the line the general atmosphere brightened. There was less talk of retirement, and good progress was made with the defences on the Piave which would now suffice to meet even a serious attack, and in other sectors of the line works were undertaken and arrangements made with a view to confining any loss of ground to the particular locality and avoiding anything like a general retirement.

General Plumer then went on to mention the attacks made on the Italian positions between the Piave and the Astico, and the measures taken by the Allied commanders (as described above) to prevent the enemy from penetrating into the plains should the Italian positions in the mountains be broken through : meanwhile, the season was getting late and most of the mountain roads would soon be blocked by snow, making the enemy attacks here extremely difficult. He ended the report with the words, " I think the general " situation, while not altogether free from anxiety, is " distinctly hopeful ".[1]

INSTRUCTIONS OF THE SUPREME WAR COUNCIL

On 8th December the following instructions as to the policy in view had been issued to the Military Representa-

---

[1] One of the senior officers on General Plumer's staff wrote that in this report his chief had " dealt tenderly with the Italians. The impression " we received, from what he told us, was that their army was demoralized, " that they were all for falling back to a position from which they could " defend Rome, that they were already moving back some artillery to " this position, and that the only way in which they could be kept on their " present front was to tell them that the French and British intended to " remain on the Piave if the Italian Armies did retreat ".

GENERAL POLICY. 8TH DECEMBER

tives for study by the Supreme War Council and by them were transmitted to the various headquarters:[1]

(1) A definite and co-ordinated system of defence to be prepared from the North Sea to the Adriatic.

(2) Every possible means to be utilized for strengthening the front with a view to:

(*a*) Providing the maximum reserve.

(*b*) Resting and training the troops (this does not preclude such minor forms of active defence as any commander-in-chief may consider necessary for maintaining the offensive spirit of his troops).

(3) In order to be in a position to meet attack and subsequently to be able to conduct attack, the greatest possible development of rail and sea communication along the front North Sea to Adriatic is essential.[2]

(4) Co-ordinated development to the utmost of the manufacture of war material is of the utmost importance.

(5) The study of lines of defence in France and in Italy, including a study of the Swiss problem. The lines of defence in Italy must be agreed on ".[3]

THE CLOSING DAYS OF 1917

The 41st and 23rd Divisions enjoyed, in comparison with the conditions of the Western Front, a fairly quiet time; the Austro-Germans on the Piave having stopped their advance were at work preparing their *Dauerstellung* (permanent position) for the winter. There was only one day, 8th December, of real shelling on the scale of the Western Front and that was when the German *12th Division*, about to be withdrawn to return to Germany, fired off all its ammunition. The killed and wounded of the 23rd Division, up to 31st December, numbered only 121 and those of the 41st Division, 158. The British artillery soon became active with bombardments and counter-battering, and every endeavour was made by example to infuse an offensive spirit

---

[1] Why the Secretariat did not issue the instructions to the Chiefs of the General Staff is not known.

[2] This is the English official translation. The French is " il est essentiel " de donner le plus grand développement possible aux communications de terre et de mer, Mer du nord à l'Adriatique ".

[3] Other paragraphs dealt with the Balkans, Palestine and Mesopotamia.

into the Italians. The enemy's reply was not serious; but on 11th December his artillery fire on the flanks of the Montello increased and seemed to indicate an attack. Just before dusk Austrian troops were reported to be massing opposite the Italian brigade on the left of the 23rd Division; but after the British artillery had searched the locality, nothing materialized. On the 12th and 19th night-patrols explored the islands and channels, even crossed to the enemy's side, capturing a prisoner on the second occasion.

On the other hand, snow being late in falling, the enemy attacks, large and small, against the Monte Grappa and Asiago fronts continued throughout the month. On the 11th the Austrians advanced east of the Brenta and by the 18th had captured Monte Asolone ($2\frac{1}{2}$ miles west of Monte Grappa and about a thousand feet below it) which dominated part of the main road to Monte Grappa. Next day the Italians could do no more than recover the southern slopes of the mountain.

The loss of Monte Asolone created a dangerous situation, and talk of a retirement was renewed by the Comando Supremo. Lieut.-Colonel W. W. Pitt-Taylor of the XIV Corps General Staff and Captain M. B. Heywood of the Army General Staff were sent by General Plumer to investigate the situation on the spot. They went round the line and as the younger officer's report says were "duly depressed." The maps given them by the Italian corps were quite inaccurate; the front trenches were blasted out of the rock, and shallow; the machine guns were mounted on "pulpits" on the parapets; communication trenches did not exist, and the wire was close to the parapets. To crown all, there were far too many men, "at least 70 per cent. too many", in the front line and all the machine guns were there; the reserve brigades were down in the valleys miles away. The flimsy telpherage lines[1] were used only for badly wounded and urgent supplies; most of the men in the trenches were very young, thinly clad and feeling the cold intensely, and they had been left in the line for a long period without relief. Many of them were weeping and some had ice on their faces: the conducting officer said that three or four of them were frozen to death nightly. As winter was coming on fast and conditions in the Austrian

---

[1] Wire rope-ways known to the army as "telerifica" for "*teleferiche*".

ranks, higher in the mountains and with an Alpine hinterland behind them, were much worse and quite as haphazard as regards defences, the situation was not so perilous as it appeared at first sight, and as events proved.

On the 23rd the Austrians again attacked in the Asiago sector, exploiting the earlier Monte Melette success, and captured Monte Melage, an advance of two miles. The situation was critical for some hours: but it was restored by a counter-attack which retook the mountain. On Christmas Day the Italians still further improved their position here. No other Austrian attacks were attempted during the remainder of 1917; but to close the year, on 30th December, the French 47th (Chasseur) Division in the Monte Grappa sector, by a well-organized operation at 4.5 p.m. after a five hours' bombardment, recaptured Monte Tomba at the cost of only 249 killed and wounded, the Austrians leaving over 500 dead on the field and 1,564 prisoners in the hands of the French.

Whilst this fighting was in progress on the mountain front the Anglo-French commanders, in collaboration with the Comando Supremo, were elaborating plans for the construction of rear lines of defence to be held if the enemy should break through.[1] General Plumer's plan for the Centre Group was that the line of the Piave should continue to be held up to Pederobba, near the left of the French sector, but that a defensive line, to form a rallying position for the Italian Fourth Army and a jumping-off place for counter-attack, should be dug from Pederobba running south-westwards behind the Monte Grappa defences just clear of the foot of the mountains, towards Bassano, east of which place it would join the Left Group line. Should the Fourth Army retire, it was to occupy the left sector of the new position and come under General Plumer's command, but such troops as were not required for manning it would continue their withdrawal southwards to the Castelfranco–Cittadella railway. The right sector would be held by the French 65th Division and the British 7th Division, which were in reserve behind it, and a counter-attack to drive the enemy back into the mountains was to be launched as early as possible.

Behind the Pederobba–Bassano line, another line, starting

---

[1] See the lines on Sketch 5.

four miles below Pederobba via Asolo to join the first near Bassano, was to be dug. A division of the work was made between the three Allies, and it was arranged that the 7th Division should furnish working parties for the British portion in the eastern half. Major-General F. M. Glubb, General Plumer's Chief Engineer, was made responsible for the general lay-out of both lines, and for the co-ordination of the portions constructed by the French and Italian forces. Work was begun on 17th December.

In the Left Group, under the French Tenth Army, in which if the plan came into force Lieut.-General Haking with his own 5th and 48th Divisions and the French 64th Division, under his command, would operate, the Pederobba–Bassano line was continued westward to the Astico, behind the Asiago defences. The troops available for this line were the French 64th Division, the British 48th Division, and an Italian division under the British XI Corps, and under the French XII Corps, its own 23rd and 24th Divisions. The British 5th Division would be in general reserve under the French Tenth Army. The main difficulty in working out the schemes was that the Italian staffs were, as already mentioned, unaccustomed to allot roads and billeting areas, and it took a long time to persuade them of the necessity of this.

In addition to the lines above mentioned the Comando Supremo arranged for the construction of another line behind them. This ran westward from a point on the Piave $4\frac{1}{2}$ miles south of Nervesa. By the end of the year good progress had been made on all these lines.

In spite of entrenching and work on the defences and training, there was much leisure ; whilst the sun shone all was well, but in the shade and directly night fell it was bitterly cold ; so football, trying to keep warm and picking up sufficient Italian for bargaining, were the order of the day. Soon a " bobbery pack " and concerts were got going, and even a theatre was extemporized. Vermouth, drunk in tumblers, was found even more cheering than strong ale. The British soldier, accommodated in dry house-billets even in the front line, although most of the rooms were comfortless, stone chambers without stove or fireplaces and the cooking with oil was an abomination, decided that this was better than the mud of Flanders from which he had come and that it was "a very good war ".

Cold was the real enemy ; especially in the last days of the year, when the weather deteriorated, the dry cold ceased, and rain and snow fell. The army allowance of coal was sufficient only for cooking, and local fuel was terribly short and commanded prohibitive prices ; coal in Padua cost £28 a ton, while even wood cost £18. Staff officers had to work in great coats and gloves, and all ranks on going to bed instead of undressing put on all the clothes they possessed.

Italy's Shortage of Coal and Foodstuffs

There are no coalfields in Italy, her imports of coal before the war had been very nearly a million tons a month ; but after the outbreak of hostilities in 1914 the amount she could obtain gradually diminished, as France lost some of her coalfields, and export from England was affected by the shortage of shipping. Supplies were, however, continued by France and England, though they could ill spare them, mainly to enable Italy to manufacture munitions, and Italy had lent France 100,000 men for labour in return. In the four-month period July-October 1917 the total received had averaged 508,000 tons, but the total for December was expected to be no more than 300,000 tons, with 350,000 tons in prospect for January 1918.

As a result of the shortage of coal, only a third of the pre-war trains were running on the railways, goods traffic except for the Armies had come to an end, gas supply had been stopped in all except eight cities, and central heating in all public and private buildings, even hospitals, had ceased. On 23rd December 1917 the Italian Prime Minister addressed a private letter to Mr. Lloyd George in which, after giving these particulars, he said that Italy's minimum requirement was 690,000 tons a month for the following purposes : 200,000 for munition factories, 70,000 for light and power, 60,000 for the navy, 240,000 for the State railways—to a large extent for military traffic—and 120,000 tons for steamship companies, for food supply companies, railways other than State and tramways.

France being unable to give much help, arrangements were made in England, by order of the War Cabinet, to comply with the request of Signor Orlando and in addition a strategic reserve of 150,000 tons was to be gradually accumulated in Italy. After the Allied successes in Italy, in order to supply the recovered provinces, on the advice of Inter-Allied Transportation Council, the monthly supply was in November 1918 increased from 690,000 to 800,000 tons, endeavour being made to carry the whole of the coal for Italy by sea in order to relieve the railways between France and Italy.

Signor Orlando had also drawn attention to the food crisis in Italy. His statement was that Italy required 750,000 tons of cereals for the quarter September-November and she had received only 370,000. By the invasion after Caporetto she had lost over 400,000 tons but few consumers, as the population of the invaded territory had escaped to the Italian lines: and food riots were threatening. Here again transportation was the difficulty: Great Britain was already providing 110,000 ships' tonnage, but the Italian Minister asked that this might be raised to 220,000. This request also was complied with, although it interfered with the transport of U.S.A. troops to Europe.

Reports of the Military Representatives of the Supreme War Council

The account of the year 1917 will be closed by giving the reports, dated 21st and 25th December, of the Military Representatives of the Supreme War Council, after their visit to the front, which had been called for on 6th November at the first sitting of the Council.[1]

In their Joint Note No. 3 of 21st December[2] the military Representatives, General Weygand, General Sir Henry Wilson and Marshal L. Cadorna advised that no more men or guns should be sent from the Western Front to Italy.

In their Joint Note No. 6 of 25th December, the Military Representatives gave their opinion that:

    1. The situation appeared to be restored on the Italian front. During the last six weeks the Italian army had shown very considerable powers of resistance, which ought to be sufficient to hold, with the help of the Allied forces, the line Piave–Grappa–Asiago.

---

[1] See p. 82.
[2] The various Joint Notes are given in " 1918 " Vol. I, pp. 57–9.

GENERAL SITUATION. 25TH DECEMBER

2. It did not at the present moment appear possible, or desirable, to take the offensive in Italy. The duty of the Allied forces was to maintain a defensive of the utmost tenacity with the object of preserving the line which they then occupied, which protected the port of Venice. With this object the line should be strengthened with every engineering device and with successive and mutually supporting lines behind it so that the ground could be defended inch by inch. As a measure of precaution, the works undertaken behind the Bacchiglione and on the Mincio–Po line should be hurried on without delay.

3. The Allied reinforcements were sufficient in the existing situation of the Italian front. In any event, the general situation at the present would not allow them to be increased.

4. The re-organization and training of the Italian army should be pushed forward with the utmost despatch to meet any eventuality that might arise on the Italian front, as well as to facilitate the withdrawal of all or part of the Anglo-French forces in Italy at the earliest possible date.

In conclusion the military representatives said that they would continue closely to watch the Italian situation and would communicate any views that any change in this situation might suggest.

CHAPTER IX

BEHIND THE FRONT
(Sketches 2, 5)

Administration, Schools, Signals, Intelligence

The situation of the small body of British troops co-operating with Allies in a friendly country, partly but not entirely detached from the British Armies in France and Belgium and for some matters communicating direct with the War Office, being peculiar, the special arrangements made deserve notice. The order followed in the account of them here is first the items of the Adjutant-General's, Chief Engineer's, and Quartermaster-General's branches and then the Lines of Communication, Schools, Signals and Intelligence.

Reinforcements and Postings

By the authority of a War Office letter dated 22nd November 1917 all personnel required for the British Force in Italy was demanded direct from the War Office. The Base Depôt for Reinforcements for Italy still remained in France; reinforcements were posted to units by the D.A.G. 3rd Echelon in Rouen and then sent on to the Base Depôt for Italy at Arquata.[1] Thence they were at first sent direct to units, but later were consigned to the Corps Reinforcement Camps near Torreglia (9 miles south-west of Padua)[2] when these were established in January. Postings of officers were at first carried out under the orders of the Adjutant-General in France, but before the end of December this procedure had ceased and demands were submitted direct from Italy to the War Office, and postings were ordered by the D.A.G., Italy.

Prisoners of War

It was decided by the War Office that prisoners of war taken in Italy should be sent to France.

---
[1] See Sketch 2.
[2] See Sketch 5.

Medical

Surgeon-General F. R. Newland, the Director of Medical Services, Italy, arrived at Milan on 1st November and selected Genoa as the site of the first General Hospital in Italy. No. 11 General Hospital began to arrive there on 11th November, and on the same day the first Casualty Clearing Station was established at Canneto (20 miles west of Mantua). Between 14th and 21st November, Surgeon-General Sir W. Babtie, Inspector of Medical Services at the War Office, made a reconnaissance in company with the D.M.S., Italy, and it was decided, on the understanding that six ambulance trains would be available, that three General and four Stationary Hospitals should be allotted to Italy, also a Convalescent Depôt, if possible, on the Riviera. Base hospitals in Italy were to evacuate cases to Marseilles, where they would be taken over by the Director-General of Medical Services, France. For this purpose, two General and one Stationary Hospital were established in Marseilles. The Base Hospitals on arrival were posted, one to Genoa, two to Bordighera (on the Italian Riviera), and one to Cremona (40 miles west of Mantua).[1] Five Casualty Clearing Stations arrived in Italy during November.

Engineer Services

R.E. stores, except such as could be obtained locally in Italy, were supplied from France. A Base Depôt was formed at Arquata and an Advanced R.E. Base at Padua. Each corps had an R.E. Park in its area ; but the requirements of units were, in some cases, met by the Italian Intendenza (which dealt with supply of all kinds). The Chief Engineer, Major-General F. M. Glubb, was made responsible for the construction and maintenance of roads in the British areas, the Italian authorities undertaking to provide the labour. He worked through the Italian Intendenza's representative at G.H.Q. Italy ; but an Italian liaison officer was sent to the Chief Engineer of each of the corps. When the XIV Corps took over the Montello sector of the front, the Italian military labour (about 5,000 men) working on the roads was left in the area under the orders of the XIV Corps. It was arranged with the Comando Supremo that the water supply

---

[1] See Sketch 2.

in the British areas should remain in the hands of the Italian engineers, who carried out the necessary work under the supervision of the British Chief Engineer and the Director of Medical Services. Cholera being endemic in Northern Italy, a good water supply was essential. A catchment area in an isolated position behind the line was therefore selected and guarded, and from it water was piped forward to the trenches and rearward to the reserve area.

Ordnance

Ordnance stores were at once received at the Base from France in sufficient quantities; but as it took time to get them by rail from Arquata to the front, a small advanced depôt was formed at Padua. Clothing and equipment for mountain warfare for about a thousand men were obtained from the Italians in case British troops should be required to hold the line in the mountains. This was all that the Italians could spare, as they were themselves short of mountain equipment. For use in operations in the snow, 4,000 white suits were obtained from the Italian Government.

To enable repairs to guns to be carried out, an Ordnance Mobile Workshop (medium) was established at Padua. Additional machinery was demanded from France and the Medium was later expanded to a Heavy Workshop.

Ammunition

All ammunition for Italy was sent by train from France. The Base Depôt for ammunition was at first established at Ovada (22 miles north-west of Genoa),[1] but during December it was moved to Rivalta Scrivia (quite close to Arquata). The G.H.Q. Railhead and Ammunition Depôt was at San Georgio delle Portiche (4 miles south-west of Camposampiero).[2]

The reserves held in Italy were:

13-pdr. A.A.	3,000 rounds per gun
18-pdr.	3,000 ,, ,,
4.5-inch how.	2,500 ,, ,,
60-pdr.	2,050 ,, ,,
6-inch how.	1,400 ,, ,,
9.2-inch how.	600 ,, ,,

[1] See Sketch 2.
[2] See Sketch 5.

Of 3-inch Stokes-mortar shells, S.A.A., grenades, fireworks, etc., a total of three months' estimated expenditure was maintained.

Supplies

By a War Office letter dated 22nd November, to G.H.Q., France, all aircraft, ammunition, stores and supplies for the British Forces in Italy were to be demanded from G.H.Q., France, except oats, meat and flour, which came from England by sea to Genoa and were to be demanded from the War Office.

During the concentration in Italy of the first two divisions in November, the receipt of adequate quantities from France, owing to railway congestion, was uncertain, so the arrangements made by Br.-General Crowe to supply the troops with Italian rations were adopted. Throughout November the supply trains often arrived three days late and frequent call had to be made on the Italian supply depôts at Mantua and Padua. From the beginning of December, however, matters began to improve and the system of supply became normal. This system[1] was that a " section pack train ", complete with bread, meat, groceries and fuel was sent up every day from the advanced supply depôt to the railhead of the division concerned. There it was handed over to the divisional supply column (M.T.), which carried it to the divisional refilling point. Before the end of November reserve supplies for three weeks had been built up at the Base at Arquata, and for one week at the Advanced Supply Depôt at Legnago. Hay and petrol, too, were gradually accumulated. By the end of December there were 200,000 gallons of petrol in the country and a reserve of 26 days of hay.[2] Coal and coke were unobtainable in Italy and supplies of these arrived by sea at Spezia. Early in the campaign 8,000 tons of coal arrived there, and this was enough to last throughout hostilities. Meanwhile, firewood for the bare necessities of cooking was purchased locally. Potatoes were difficult to obtain, but onions and oranges could be bought in large quantities and were issued to the troops. Field

---

[1] It is described at length in " 1916 " Vol. I, pp. 99–105, and the Postal Service on pp. 125–9.

[2] Hay was at first brought from France. Later it was bought more cheaply in Italy.

bakeries were originally established at the Base at Arquata, but later the greater part of them was moved forward into the two corps areas.

Transportation

The Director-General of Transportation was Major-General W. H. Grey, who was already, as previously mentioned, in Italy in charge of the transport of British troops and stores through Italy to the Mediterranean. On 1st November he took over the appointment of D.G.T. to the British Forces in Italy in addition to his previous duties. The transport of the fighting troops during their moves to the front after detrainment presented difficulties, for the motor transport units did not arrive till after the infantry, artillery and engineer units. This difficulty was met to some extent by the use of " en cas mobiles ", i.e., supply trains containing imperishable rations which were moved along the railway parallel to the line of advance of the troops, and from which the rations could be drawn by horse transport. Further it had been arranged by Br.-General Crowe's Mission that the Italian authorities should supply five hundred Fiat lorries, and these were available; [1] but drivers could not be supplied for them, and only a few could be engaged locally. Drivers were therefore obtained by calling on infantry units, as they detrained, to produce men who had had previous experience as M.T. drivers.[2] The local purchase of 40 Italian cars was also carried out. Two Fiat companies of motor transport were then organized, one of 80 lorries for the XI Corps and one of 70 lorries for the XIV Corps. By these means the fighting units were able to march forward towards the Piave and to be supplied immediately on concentration. Fiat lorries were also obtained for the siege batteries, and a number of light Fiat lorries for work in the mountains, these having more climbing power than the British 3-ton lorry. The Base Motor Transport Depôt was at Arquata, and an advanced depôt was established at Cremona (40 miles west of Mantua).

---

[1] The Fiat Company was holding a large number of lorries built for Russia, but not sent there owing to the Revolution.

[2] A few months earlier M.T. drivers of high medical category in France had been transferred to infantry. Thus most infantry units contained a proportion of experienced drivers.

After the original movement of troops was completed about one train a day per division was required for normal maintenance, apart from the Cherbourg–Taranto service. The makeshift arrangements for the feeding and convenience of the troops travelling by rail routes were organized into a system by which twenty permanent British " haltes repas " were established by the beginning of 1918, divided into three groups under the Base commandants at Cherbourg and Marseilles and by the Commandant Paris Area. At each station the following personnel and accommodation were provided :

>1 n.c.o., 2 men as police and orderlies, and 2 men for sanitary duties, with living accommodation and a small store room.
>
>Latrine accommodation for 12 officers, 4 warrant officers and 60 other ranks.
>
>Ablution arrangements for about double the above numbers.
>
>Arrangements for boiling about 165 gallons of water.
>
>An incinerator.

Remounts

Two remount squadrons arrived from France in the last week of November. A third squadron was despatched from France later. One Remount Depôt of two squadrons was formed at Cremona and one of one squadron at Pavia.

Veterinary

A veterinary hospital was established near Voghera (40 miles north of Genoa), where the worst cases were sent by special sick-horse trains. Another more advanced veterinary hospital was established at Cremona.

Canteens

Canteens were opened at the Base at Arquata and at Ventimiglia station. Advanced canteens were established for the XIV Corps at Istrana, for the XI Corps at Carmignano (south-west of Cittadella) and for the training area at Torreglia.

Lines of Communication and Base

Major-General Grey, the D.G.T. also performed the duties of Inspector-General of Communications in Italy, till 16th November 1917 when Lieutenant-General Sir H. M. Lawson was ordered to take up this appointment. The new I.G.C. left London on the 17th and reported to General Plumer at Legnago on the 21st. On 28th November, he established his headquarters provisionally at Mantua, but on 19th December moved to Tortona (35 miles north of Genoa),[1] so as to be nearer to the Base. The duties of the I.G.C. and his staff extended not only to the communications between the Base in Italy and General Plumer's force, but also to the "overland" line through Italy to Taranto.

Training and Schools of Instruction

A G.H.Q. training area, accommodating up to an infantry brigade, was obtained from the Italian authorities, with headquarters at Torreglia (9 miles south-west of Padua). A central school was established at Praglia monastery (near Torreglia) and was opened in January 1918, largely in the hope of instilling good doctrine and practice into the Italian army. It consisted of:

(a) An Army Wing for the training of prospective commanders and platoon sergeants, with a course of 30 working days.

(b) A Corps Wing: XI and XIV Corps Schools for the training of platoon commanders and junior n.c.os., including general and specialist training, with a course of 30 working days.

(c) Corps Gas Schools to give five days' training to officers and other ranks who had passed through the courses (a) and (b); and to provide periodical courses for senior officers and selected n.c.os.

(d) XI and XIV Corps Reinforcement Camps for the further training of men not considered fit to take their places in their units.

The following schools were also established in towns and villages close to Torreglia, and opened in January 1918:

(e) A Musketry School for the training of officers and n.c.os. as instructors, with a course of 18 working days.

---
[1] See Sketch 2.

SCHOOLS

(*f*) A Scouting, Observation and Sniping School, with a course of 18 working days.

(*g*) A Signal School and Depôt for the instruction of novices and the further instruction of signal personnel, the courses lasting about ten weeks.

(*h*) An Artillery School and Depôt was opened in February for the training of battery officers and n.c.os. as instructors. A Trench Mortar School was also opened in February.

(*i*) A Mule Pack Train Demonstration School.

(*j*) A Camouflage Works, Depôt and School.

Exchanges were to be made with the Allies, French and Italian officers attending courses at all the above schools, and British officers those at French and Italian schools.

Signal

The Italian telegraph and telephone system was found to be thoroughly disorganized. The postal officials had " a playful habit of collecting cipher telegrams until there " was a nice package and then sending it by post ". A telephone call on 13th November from Mantua to Padua, only 160 miles away, took 10 hours to get through and was very indistinct.

On the arrival, on 21st November, of Colonel A. B. R. Hildebrand, Deputy-Director of Signals, Second Army, at General Plumer's headquarters at Legnago, he found that no telephonic communication was in existence from that place. On the 22nd arrangements were made with the Comando Supremo which permitted telephone lines to be installed, connecting with the civil exchange, to Padua and Mantua, and by the 24th, the 34th Motor Airline Section had established a line between Legnago and XIV Corps headquarters at Lonigo. On 30th November, G.H.Q. Italy moved from Legnago to Padua, and on 1st December a telegraph line was laid from that place to the new XIV Corps headquarters at Fanzolo (near Castelfranco). On 2nd December the former Second Army Signal Company arrived at Padua from France. By 5th December communication was established with the XI Corps, whose headquarters were beginning to arrive at Camposampiero. By 10th December communication had been established with the Italian Third and

Fourth Armies and the French Tenth Army and the French XXXI Corps. For the Royal Flying Corps, the VII Brigade was connected with G.H.Q., and the two aerodromes at Grossa (8 miles east of Vicenza) and Istrana with the XIV Corps. Communication with the Base at Arquata by the Italian lines had been difficult; so on 23rd November a daily despatch-rider service was organized between Legnago and Arquata. The building of two lines was begun on 12th December to provide telephonic communication from Padua to the Base, and they were finally established by the 27th.

Intelligence

The organization of Intelligence work in Italy presented certain difficulties; for a start had to be made from the beginning and in a strange country in which there was practically no control of the civil population, no censorship and no counter-espionage organization, and in which Italian and French systems were already functioning. By the means of many conferences and interviews these difficulties were gradually overcome and by the end of December the Intelligence Branch at G.H.Q. Italy, under Lieut.-Colonel C. H. Mitchell, was in full working order and giving satisfactory results. The closest touch was maintained with the Italian Intelligence Section through the British Mission with the Comando Supremo.

CHAPTER X

THE FIRST QUARTER OF 1918, UNTIL GENERAL SIR HERBERT PLUMER'S RECALL TO FRANCE
(Sketches 5, 6)

GENERAL SITUATION AND AIR ACTIVITY

Except for the beginning of the reduction of the French and British forces in Italy, the period from 1st January to 10th March 1918, on which day General Sir Herbert Plumer handed over command to Lieut.-General Lord Cavan to return to the Western Front, was uneventful. The British troops were not engaged in any operations of importance. They took over a little more of the line, the XI Corps coming up on the right of the XIV; the usual shelling, patrolling and small raids were carried out, and certain preparations were made for other action.

Owing to the swift current of the Piave, its many channels and the icy coldness of its water, patrolling was limited to the islands. The parties, hauled across in boats by men stripped to the buff and well rubbed with oil, wore felt or straw shoes to obviate noise in crossing shingle, and generally were camouflaged. Occasionally Austrians were encountered and miniature battles ensued—and prisoners were captured. Raids on the enemy's shore were difficult, as the eastern channel of the river was the widest and deepest. After 1st March the Piave became impassable for a time, owing to heavy rain.

If an Austrian battery became more than usually troublesome it was hunted by the British counter-batteries until, change position as it might, it was knocked out of existence.

The Italians, as will be seen, only engaged in some minor enterprises. Yet the Austrians complained that " the pause " in hostilities, so necessary for the elaboration of the " defences and for the much desired repose of the troops, " was right soon brought to an end "[1]. In particular, they were much alarmed by the building of about twenty foot-bridges to the islands in a 2,000-yard reach of the Piave in

---

[1] A.O.A. vii, p. 180.

the British sector; so much so that the German divisions about to leave Italy were retained on the Tagliamento in case a strong attack were made.[1]

A new Italian Fifth Army of three corps was formed in place of the disgraced Second Army, mostly of new units, but retaining old corps names, the II, XII (of the Carnia Zone) and XIV, each of two divisions.[2]

Owing to frequent enemy night bombings of Padua, it was decided that all Allied headquarters should move out of the town, and on 16th January British G.H.Q. were shifted to Noventa (3 miles east of Padua). At night enemy bombs were often dropped on the front position, but they were unaimed, and did little damage except to spoil sleep.[3] Otherwise British air superiority was retained, and 28 enemy machines were shot down in January for the loss of 4. As a reply to the night bombing, an offensive against the enemy aerodromes was undertaken by the R.F.C.[4] The first attack, in the early morning of 19th February from 200 feet, was so successful that four machines from each of the five squadrons were set aside for this purpose. The Italians bombed the naval port of Pola and the railway yards at Innsbruck, Trent, Bolzano and smaller places.

General Plumer's Report of 13th January 1918

On 13th January General Plumer made the third of his periodical reports to the Chief of the Imperial General Staff. In the last few days, he said, there had been a fall of snow, not sufficient to render operations in the mountains impossible, but enough to make them increasingly difficult and to lessen the probability of any offensive on a large scale on the mountain front being attempted by the enemy in the immediate future: as the snow hardened there would probably be local actions on both sides so as to regain

---

[1] For the departure from the front of the German divisions, see Note I at end of Chapter. The last had left by mid-March.

[2] The II Corps went to the Western Front at the end of March, and the Fifth Army was broken up, and a Sixth Army formed.
See Note II at end of Chapter.

[3] According to A.O.A. vii, p. 183, the Austro-German raids were directed against the railway centres of Castelfranco, Treviso and Mestre (junction north-west of Venice), the Italian aerodromes and the Arsenal at Venice where on 26th February 200 bombs were dropped, but no military damage done, as some failed to explode.

[4] " War in the Air " vi, p. 279.

PLUMER'S REPORT. 13TH JANUARY

the power of initiative, and the Italians had several in preparation. The recapture of Monte Tomba by the French on 30th December had, he thought, encouraged the Italian commanders by showing them how a well-organized attack could be successfully made with comparatively few casualties: the positions, which the British troops occupied, with the Piave on their front, precluded any such minor offensive operations on their part, but small raids had been successfully carried out.

As regards defences, he said that work was being continued on the rear lines in the foothills south of the mountains: these defences were being constructed in depth so as to illustrate the principles which from experience on the Western Front had been found most effective: Italian commanders, whose troops had been detailed to occupy these positions, had agreed as to the advantages they had over their own system of single defensive lines into which every man and every machine gun were crowded: the sector of the front line held by the XIV Corps had also been organized so as to bring prominently into notice the value of defence in depth.

As regards artillery, all British batteries not required for the defence of the British sector were being used to assist the Italians,[1] and a mobile reserve was being formed which could be moved to different parts of the line to co-operate with Italian artillery: it was hoped to effect some improvement in the Italian counter-battery work, which was far from satisfactory.

The Royal Flying Corps, he wrote, had set a fine example, and had on many occasions rendered help to the Italians: the Italians had plenty of A.A. guns and searchlights, but lacked co-ordination of their resources: they were being helped to get a good system which should prove of value in defence of their towns.

General Plumer continued, that he had arranged that British commanders and staff officers should constantly

---

[1] The XV H.A. Group with 2½ siege batteries was transferred to the Italian First Army on 6th January, and assistance was given to the Italian VIII Corps (Third Army) in counter-battery work by the XI Corps Artillery from 10th January onwards.

The XCIV H.A. Group which had been with the Italian Third Army, after refitting, joined the British XI Corps at Cittadella in early December and on 7th January was sent to the Italian Fourth Army in the Asiago sector.

visit the Italian lines to discuss matters with Italian commanders and staffs, and they had been very well received and had seized opportunities of throwing out suggestions as to the defensive arrangements : the different schools of instruction were beginning to function, and British, French and Italian officers were to go to each others' courses : all British general staff publications about the lessons learnt in France were being translated into Italian : the Italian gas masks having been found not to be proof against all gases, 800,000 British gas masks had been asked for, of which 300,000 had been received.

The worst defect of the Italian army, General Plumer considered, was the small amount of attention given by its commanders to the serious training of the troops and their failure to appreciate the necessity for it : it was obviously a matter of vital importance, and he hoped to persuade the Italian commanders to realize it : in all such matters it was necessary to proceed very quietly and cautiously : the Italians, although they deplored the behaviour of their Second Army, did not consider that much was wrong with the remainder of their forces, and, though they were willing to profit by the experience of their Allies, any attempt to force foreign methods on them would result in nothing being done : instructions had been issued to all British officers that they were to be most careful to avoid any appearance of superiority or of imparting instruction : everything was to be done by illustration and demonstration.

General Plumer's Report of 20th January 1918

In addition to his periodical report, General Plumer considered that it might be useful to lay before the C.I.G.S. his views as to the standard of fighting efficiency which the Italian troops might reasonably be expected to attain under present conditions in about three months' time. The substance of a report rendered on 20th January is as follows :

Of the five Italian Armies[1] only three were in the line, the Third on the Lower Piave and the Fourth and First in the mountains on the left of the sectors held by the British and French. The Fourth and First were the only

---

[1] See Sketch 6

Armies which had been seriously engaged more or less continuously, and their losses had been heavy: it might be reckoned that in these two Armies eleven brigades had suffered very heavy casualties and had been withdrawn, and that eleven others had had considerable casualties but had returned to the line: a large proportion, too, of the crack units, the Bersaglieri regiments and Alpini battalions, had suffered heavy losses: the severity of the climate in the mountains had caused and would continue to cause considerable wastage, and altogether a large proportion of the infantry of these two Armies required a period of rest, reorganization and training before they should be called on to take part in any extensive operations: the Third Army had improved lately, and had the possibilities of making still more rapid improvement in the next two or three months.

The Second Army, the one responsible for the retreat in October, he said, had not been engaged since: one or two of its divisions had been reorganized and had returned to the front sectors: they were believed to have regained confidence, but experience alone could show the standard of their fighting efficiency; the Fifth Army, newly organized and composed for the most part of new formations, must be considered for the present an unknown quantity.

General Plumer's conclusions were: "If then, as seems "possible, the fighting on the front for the next two or "three months should be limited to minor local actions, "the opportunity should enable the First and Fourth "Armies to recuperate and become efficient, the Third "Army make really good progress, and the Second and "Fifth be sufficiently advanced to be gradually available "as supports and reinforcements." This, however, could only be accomplished if the higher commanders devoted the next two or three months to really strenuous training of their troops: the vital necessity of this they did not seem to realize.

General Plumer's opinion of the staff work of the Italian army was that: "The Italian staff officers are exceedingly "easy to work with, and try in every way to help; but "their knowledge of staff work is so theoretical that they "do not understand the practical difficulties of their orders. "Paper is the ruling factor, and they agree to things and "issue orders which cannot be carried out, and this has "been the chief defect in their operations. All staffs are inclined to think that once an order is issued it is as good as done, which is far from being the case, and staff officers do not go out to see that the orders are being carried out.[1] They are generally speaking not active and do not visit the front line enough. I think in this respect they have been much impressed by the frequent visits of British commanders and staffs, and that this will have a good effect. There is a lack of co-operation between the General Staff and the other branches. The General Staff, Artillery, Engineers and Flying Corps are all separate branches, so is their Intelligence".

The artillery was, he thought, the weakest part of the Italian army, and its want of co-operation with the infantry was responsible for some of the recent failures. The infantry for their part, had little confidence in their artillery. Individual batteries could shoot, but there was a lack of knowledge and energy on the part of the higher commanders. Organization was defective and application of fire poor, while counter-battery work was hardly carried out at all. On the other hand, the Austrian artillery had made considerable improvement lately, due probably to instruction received from the Germans, and the Italian artillery might find its task more difficult in forthcoming operations. General Plumer considered the Italian engineers as probably the finest in Europe in the actual details of their work; but as a military organization they were very backward: what lacked was the higher training of the officers, who seemed almost entirely ignorant of war conditions and failed to apply their technical knowledge to any practical military purpose.

The efficiency of the infantry varied: he had seen very much of different units: the greater proportion of the rank and file were excellent material, and the spirit and morale of the majority of the battalions was good in spite of the very trying and strenuous time which many had experienced, but they also lacked training and had not much confidence in their officers: very few of the officers had been trained to look after their men or to study the responsibilities of leadership, but many were gallant fighters and staunch under fire: the infantry brigades and battalions were much behindhand in higher tactical training.

---

[1] This was also a German failing.

In conclusion, General Plumer wrote : "All that I think can be expected at the end of three months is a force of fairly good, if somewhat uneven, infantry, capable of making a brilliant attack or a stubborn defence for a time, but incapable of anything but the simplest manœuvres and uncertain if called upon for any sustained or prolonged effort either in attack or defence ; the infantry will have for its support artillery which will almost certainly be inferior in tactics and fire effect to what is opposed to it, and the conduct of operations will be by commanders and staff with too little practical experience and training to be able to make up for any deficiencies or shortcomings on the part of the troops ".

A report on the Italian army by General Fayolle, dated 26th December 1917, which reached the War Office a month later, more than confirmed all that General Plumer had written.[1] Fortunately the Italian Armies were to have five months in which to train and reorganize before they had to meet a great attack.

The Breaking Up of the Grouping for Defence[2]

The fall of snow in the mountains about the time that General Plumer was writing his report of 13th January was heavy, rendering impossible an enemy attack there on a large scale. No object therefore seemed to exist for maintaining the Group Plan in being ; for it entailed keeping considerable British and French forces in reserve to meet enemy attacks which were unlikely to materialize in the next few months. On 14th January 1918, therefore, General Plumer visited General Fayolle and suggested that the Groups should be broken up and that the British XI Corps might take over part of the front line. The French general concurred in this, and proposals in writing were put forward to the Comando Supremo. On 17th January General Diaz agreed to the breaking up of the Groups, subject to arrangements being made for their revival at short notice if required. He also agreed to the XI Corps relieving the Italian VIII Corps (Third Army) in the Arcade sector on the right of the

---

[1] See Note III at end of Chapter.
[2] See Chapter VIII.

XIV Corps.[1] On 19th January a conference was held with the French and Italian Headquarters Staffs, and orders were then issued for the necessary movements of Allied troops to begin on the 22nd. To ensure the revival of the Groups should the necessity arise, General Plumer ordered that the reserve division of the XI Corps should be ready to return at short notice to the area on the Brenta, then occupied by the 48th Division, and that the reserve division of the XIV Corps should be prepared to occupy the central sector of the northernmost of the rear defence lines.

The XI Corps Takes Over the Arcade Sector on the Piave[1]

On 17th January warning was received by the XI Corps from G.H.Q. that the corps would shortly be required to relieve the Italian VIII Corps in the Arcade sector on the Piave from the right of the XIV Corps to a point five miles below. Lieut.-General Haking thereupon paid a visit to General Caviglia, the Italian corps commander, at his headquarters at Merlengo (4 miles N.N.W. of Treviso), and discussed the details of the relief. The usual reconnaissances of a new sector were then carried out.

In the Arcade sector the width of the Piave river bed varied from about 800 yards on the left to about 2,000 yards in the greater part of the right half. As in the Montello sector, the river ran in several channels of varying depth, with islands or sandbanks between them. The sector was a quiet one, the width of the Piave preventing any effective sniping or machine-gun fire, and enemy shelling was not heavy. The soil was loose and shingly, and required more revetting than that of the Montello sector.

In accordance with G.H.Q. orders, it was settled that the 5th Division should begin its march from its area south of Cittadella to the new sector on 22nd January and relieve the Italian 48th and 58th Divisions, infantry reliefs being completed by the 27th. The artillery reliefs were to begin on the 27th and to be completed by 6 a.m. on the 30th. The 48th Division was to move into an area west of Treviso, being clear of its present location on the Brenta north-west of Cittadella by 25th January, and be in reserve. The

---

[1] See Sketch 5.

XI Corps Heavy Artillery and the Corps Cavalry Regiment were to be in the new corps area by the 26th. Work on the rear lines of defence was to cease for the time being.

The march to the new area was considerably hampered by a sudden thaw which set in on the 19th and made the roads very muddy, and in some cases impassable. Routes originally allotted had to be changed, and the troops often did not reach their billets till after dark. By the evening of the 23rd the two leading brigades of the 5th Division (the 95th and 13th) arrived in areas about two miles south of Arcade. Here they remained on the 24th and 25th, taking over the front line on the nights of the 25th/26th and 26th/27th. The 15th Brigade was in reserve. Divisional headquarters were established at Villerba (5 miles south of Nervesa and 4 miles behind the front line). The field artillery relief was completed by the morning of the 29th and the heavy artillery relief by the morning of the 30th.

The following Italian artillery came under the orders of the G.O.C. XI Corps on completion of relief:

>Headquarters 49th Group of Siege Artillery; 131st Group (3 batteries of 148-mm. guns; 101st Battery (152-mm. on railway mountings).

The XI Corps headquarters were established at Merlengo (5 miles north-west of Treviso) at 10 a.m. on the 27th.

The 48th Division began its move from the Tezze area on 22nd January, its infantry reached the reserve division area west of Treviso by the 28th, and its field artillery by the 30th.

Italian Winter Operations

Three operations were undertaken by the Italians during January. Two were begun on the 14th. The first of these was to improve the bridgehead held beyond the river Sile (sometimes called the Old Piave, west of the present course) near the mouth of the Piave. After an initial failure, the attack succeeded and the Austrians decided to abandon a projected counter-attack.

The second operation on the 14th was an attempt by two divisions to recover Monte Asolone (10 miles north of Bassano)[1] and adjoining heights. Here the Austrians held

---

[1] For this place see Sketch 7.

the summit in uncompleted defences and the Italians the southern slopes.[1] The summit was gained in the first rush, and four hundred prisoners were captured, but the Austrians counter-attacked and, after two days' hard fighting, drove the Italians off their conquest.

The third operation, which was begun on 27th January, was more successful. The attack was again made by two divisions on the Asiago plateau, with a col east of the village as objective. It was reached on the 27th, but an Austrian counter-attack retook the western heights on the 28th. These, however, were recovered on the 29th and the whole objective remained in Italian hands. The Italian casualties in the three days' fighting are reported as 5,240. About 2,600 Austrian prisoners were taken.[2] The British 302nd and 307th Siege Batteries and half the 317th under the XV Heavy Artillery Group (XI Corps) took part in this action, and the Royal Flying Corps co-operated.

After these three operations, except for isolated encounters in No Man's Land, no further fighting worth mentioning took place on the front between the sea and the Astico until the end of March. West of that river, at Monte Pasubio,[3] where mining operations in the solid rock had been carried on, at 3 a.m. on 13th March, using 110,000 lb. of ecrasite, the Austrians blew the whole salient of the Italian position into the air.

Projected Operations by the 5th Division

A fourth operation, a continuation of the first, was planned by the Italian Third Army, and in it the British were to play a part. It was proposed to attack from the Sile bridgehead, which had been extended in January, in order to drive the Austrians over the estuary of the Piave and farther from Venice. For the purpose of assisting the Third Army by drawing attention from the lower Piave and attracting reserves, the British were asked to send a force across the river in their sector on the day of attack, establish a bridgehead and hold it for forty-eight hours, at the expiration of

---

[1] See p. 116.
[2] The total Austrian losses are not given in A.O.A. Four divisions took part and their losses were " very heavy "; but the losses of only one, 1,547, are mentioned, and a claim to 810 prisoners is made.
[3] For this place see Sketch 7.

which time the force could be withdrawn. On 11th February General Plumer went to the Comando Supremo to discuss the proposal, and it was decided that the operation should be carried out by the XI Corps in the reach below Nervesa. One brigade was to be employed and Lieut.-General Haking selected the 5th Division to supply the troops.

According to a plan prepared by him and Major-General Stephens, the passage was to be forced at two points: at the broken Priula railway bridge in the centre of the Xl Corps sector, using gangways and boards, and at the island of Lucca (1 mile below Nervesa), where 12 bridges were to be laid by the engineers, covered by infantry who would cross by boat. Under a rolling barrage, the brigade was to reach and entrench a position about a mile from the river. At the same time, another brigade was to simulate an attempt at crossing on the right of the real attack, using smoke and dummies, and if this met with success a battalion was to cross and raid the Austrians. Working at night, the engineers drove in piles at the site of the bridges; but although the heads of the piles were driven well below the surface of the water, they showed in aerial photographs, and were spotted by the Austrians.

Very strong artillery support was organized: the C.R.A. 5th Division, Br.-General A. H. Hussey, having under his command 37 batteries of field artillery and 6 of trench mortars; the C.R.A. XI Corps, Br.-General E. W. Alexander, having 101 heavy guns; and the Italian XI Corps, on the right, promising the assistance of 15 batteries. The R.F.C. was to co-operate.

The troops were practised in water work on the river at Treviso, and a party of seamen from H.M.S. *Earl of Peterborough* and some gondoliers from Venice arrived to help in the crossing.

This well-planned operation was not, however, to take place. Zero was fixed for the night of 5th/6th March; but from the 1st onwards rain fell and by the night of the 3rd/4th the river had risen 4 feet and several of the piers of the projected bridges had been washed away. On the 4th, therefore, the Italians decided to abandon the whole operation, to the relief of the G.O.C.'s and Staffs of the XI Corps and the 5th Division, who felt that little profit or advantage could be gained by a large-scale raid of the nature indicated.

NOTE I

REORGANIZATION OF THE AUSTRO-GERMAN FORCES IN ITALY

When the Austrian-German Army settled down for the winter, a reorganization of the commands and redistribution of the front were taken in hand, as " during the autumn offensive there had " been found to be too many higher commands, and the opera-" tion had suffered thereby ".[1] As a result, the South-West Command (which included all the troops operating against Italy), under the Archduke Eugen, was abolished; the two *Isonzo Armies* under General Freiherr von Boroevic, were amalgamated into one under General Freiherr von Wurm; and Boroevic, promoted to Field-Marshal, took command of the new *Isonzo Army* and the German *Fourteenth Army*, renamed the Austrian *Sixth Army* and the Archduke Joseph put in command of it, as an Army Group. The German General von Below had left for the Western Front, and only the *117th Division* of the German contingent remained at the front, the *200th Division*, *Alpine Corps* and *Jäger Division* being in reserve and awaiting entrainment.

Thus the forces engaged against Italy were the *Isonzo Army* and *Sixth Army* in Field-Marshal von Boroevic's Group, and the *Eleventh* and *Tenth Armies* in Field-Marshal von Conrad's Group. The two Army Groups depended directly on the Austrian Supreme Command under Kaiser Karl, the dividing line between them running a little east of Monte Grappa.

To avoid German claims to a share, the captured Venetian province was administered not as occupied territory but as a Lines of Communication area.

NOTE II

THE REORGANIZATION OF THE ITALIAN ARMY

By the Caporetto disaster the Italian army had shrunk to about 700,000 men under arms: 400,000 in the First Army, untouched by the disaster, and 300,000 in the Third and Fourth Armies, somewhat shaken. The Second Army and XII Corps (Carnia), numbering about 300,000, had become a disorderly mass. Plenty of recruits were available in the depôts and the 1899 and 1900 classes ready to fill the ranks; after allowing for unfit, exemptions and postponements, each of these years produced about 400,000 men.

---

[1] A.O.A. vii, p. 177.

REORGANIZATION OF THE ITALIAN ARMY

Of the Second Army the VI, XXV, XXVIII and XXX Corps were assembled in an area between Vicenza and Verona, but at the beginning of December 1917 the two former were sent to the Monte Grappa front. Its II, XII and XIV Corps, which had been reduced to mere skeletons, were reorganized under the new Fifth Army, south of the Po, for the most part with French guns and rifles, and became available for service in the middle of February 1918.

The IV, VII and XXIV Corps were not reconstructed.

Supernumerary infantrymen were formed into march brigades in a camp at Castelfranco.

The whole of the Second Army artillery was reorganized. The very numerous personnel were collected in a large instructional camp near Bologna, where they received new equipment, mostly of French and British origin.

In the reorganization were included 50 infantry brigades with 104 regiments and 47 independent battalions ; 812 machine-gun companies ; 22 field artillery regiments with 188 batteries ; 50 mountain batteries, 60 heavy field batteries, 91 siege batteries ; 23 engineer battalions, etc. By the end of February, that is in under four months, the reorganization had been completed.

After the disaster the Italian army possessed 62 heavy, 1,534 medium and 2,390 light guns ; on 15th April it already had 104, 2,466 and 3,301, of which 11·7 per cent were of French and British origin. Only the construction of aircraft was behind the programme time.

NOTE III

SUMMARY OF A REPORT ON THE SITUATION OF THE ITALIAN ARMY BY GENERAL FAYOLLE, 26TH DECEMBER 1917

I. Effectives

Including the standing army under arms at the moment when war was declared, 4,350,000 officers and men have been enrolled since the beginning of the war. Of this number 2,840,000 are still under arms, 2,010,000 being in the war zone. After deduction of men in hospital and in reorganization camps, and the troops in Macedonia and Albania, there remain about 1,600,000 of all ranks capable of being used at once on the Italian front.

II. Organization

The Italian forces are grouped in 5 Armies (3 in the line, 1 in reserve and 1 composed of units in course of reorganization).

Excluding the forces in Macedonia and Albania, there are 22 army corps, containing 50 divisions (6 of which are re-forming).

III. Command and Staffs

The Staffs are energetic, but suffer from two defects :—
  (1) Lack of organizing capacity ;
  (2) inability to adapt themselves to the circumstances of the present war.

The resulting bad effects are :

1. The necessity of keeping formations intact is not recognized. Troops are frequently detached, without sufficient reason, from divisions and even from brigades. One result is inefficiency in command, and imperfect liaison between infantry and artillery.

2. There is no proper system of reliefs. Troops are left in dangerous sectors continuously until they are thoroughly worn out.

3. The defence is not sufficiently distributed in depth. This is manifested in two manners. In the first place, there is a lack of defensive works behind the front, especially in those parts of it where movement has recently taken place. In the second, troops are massed in the front line in excessive numbers, with insufficient reserves behind.

4. Artillery defence is not properly understood. There is imperfect liaison with the infantry ; batteries are pushed too far forward, so that a slight enemy advance entails heavy loss in material ; and not enough counter-battery work is done.

5. The infantry do not understand the principles of the counter-attack. Their immediate local counter-attacks tend to be delivered too late (or not at all, owing to lack of reserves), and their delayed methodical counter-offensives too hastily.

IV. Morale

In spite of the above defects in organization the spirit of the men is good, and they are capable of good results if better handled.

The morale of the different Armies varies considerably. The Third Army (from the sea to Nervesa) was not badly shaken by the autumn retreat, and recovered itself quickly. It lives in comparative comfort behind a formidable obstacle. The Command is energetically taking up the question of training.

The Fourth Army (from Monte Tomba to the Brenta) was greatly exhausted after the retreat, but recovered to a considerable extent after the part of its front had been taken over by the British and French. Recently on the whole, it has fought well, though some units did badly. Training is not possible for this Army, all its energy is needed for maintaining its positions on the Grappa.

The First Army (from the Brenta to Lake Garda) was hardly at all affected by the autumn retreat. Nevertheless, it has done very badly on certain occasions. The troops massed on the

Asiago plateau, with no regular system of reliefs, have suffered considerable hardships which have no doubt impaired their power of resistance. No measures have been taken to organize training.

The III Corps (West of Lake Garda) has enjoyed complete rest in strong positions, and is in good heart.

To sum up, the Armies in the line are practically complete in effectives and equipment. Their morale has risen considerably since the retreat, aided by the arrival of Allied troops, and is now good in the quiet sectors, though it can scarcely be relied upon to resist an attack. Training has been neglected.

Reserve Armies

The Second Army has two corps ready for the line, and one which should be ready by 1st January.* Here, too, training has been almost entirely neglected.

The Fifth Army is being reconstituted near Parma. Its commander is seriously engaged with the problems of training.

V. Measures to be taken to complete the reorganization of the Italian army

We can employ three methods:
- Advice,
- Example,
- Penetration.

Advice must be given in the most tactful manner, as the Italians take offence readily. It has already produced results, but only to a limited extent.

Example. The schools of the French Tenth Army are in course of formation. But even if Italian officers attend these schools regularly, the results will only reach the Italian army at second hand.

Penetration. This is the best method of all. A number of tactful and experienced French officers should be attached to the Italian army. To make this measure more acceptable the French army might receive Italian officers in exchange.

VI. Summary of Conclusions

The Italian army possesses adequate resources in personnel and material. But it is imperfectly trained in the methods of present-day warfare, and its morale, though good, is unstable. It is strong enough to hold its present front, but a collapse is not impossible. Such a collapse would have to be made good by the Franco-British forces, and in the most favourable circumstances it will probably not be possible, within a measurable period of time, to leave the Italian army unsupported.

---

* Note. Now ready, 26th January 1918.

CHAPTER XI

WITHDRAWAL OF PART OF THE BRITISH AND FRENCH TROOPS FROM ITALY
(Sketches 2, 5)

THE RETURN OF THE BRITISH TROOPS FROM ITALY ENVISAGED

The inactivity of the Austro-German troops in Italy after mid-December 1917, and the gradual withdrawal of the German contingent were not entirely due to the advent of winter. Ever since a conference on 11th November 1917 on future operations, the German General Staff had been preparing a great blow against the Western Front to end the War, with forces augmented by the collapse of Russia. " By the end of December it was known [in London and " Paris] that at least ten and probably fifteen divisions " had already been transferred from the East to the West, " in addition to drafts, totalling about 80,000 of selected " officers and men ".[1] On 4th January 1918 information was received from a high neutral source that Germany had decided to play her last card in a formidable offensive in France. On 7th January the Intelligence Summary stated " the impression derived from all sources of information is " that the offensive along the whole Italian front is sus- " pended ; German troops are being withdrawn, and from " all sides the information is that they are destined for " the Western Front ".

As early as 19th January 1918 the General Staff in London was in communication with the General Staff at G.H.Q. France in regard to " the best position of the British reserve " divisions in Italy with a view to their being brought to " France in case of emergency ". Turin and Alessandria had been suggested as suitable,[2] and the C.I.G.S. wanted to know from the D.G.T. in France :

---

[1] " 1918 " Vol. I, p. 49. The details of the German plan and the accurate information gathered with regard to it will be found in that volume.

[2] See Sketch 2.

(1) How long it would take, without interference with the normal supply of the French and British troops in Italy, to move two divisions to Amiens, using (*a*) the Modane route only, (*b*) the Riviera route only, and (*c*) both routes simultaneously ;

(2) How long it would take to move these two divisions to Amiens from places in France close to the Italian frontier and convenient for moving them back to the neighbourhood of Padua.

The calculations made by the Acting Director-General of Transportation, Br.-General S. D'A. Crookshank, showed that the times of the railway journeys under (1) would be :

Turin via Modane to Amiens, 50 hours.
Turin via Ventimiglia to Amiens, 80 hours.
Alessandria via Modane to Amiens, 56 hours.
Alessandria via Ventimiglia to Amiens, 75 hours.

Assuming that 12 trains a day were available by Modane and 16 via Ventimiglia, a division requiring 59 trains :

(*a*) Via Modane, the Turin division would complete detrainment in 183 hours.
Via Modane, the Alessandria division would complete detrainment in 307 hours.
(*b*) Via Ventimiglia, the Turin division would complete detrainment in 183½ hours.
Via Ventimiglia, the Alessandria division would complete detrainment in 266 hours.
(*c*) Using both routes at once the Turin division would complete detrainment via Modane in 183 hours, and the Alessandria division via Ventimiglia in 177½ hours.

In the situation contemplated in heading (2), it was considered essential by the D.G.T. to concentrate one division in the neighbourhood of Lyons and the other near Marseilles, whence both divisions could be detrained in the Amiens area by the end of 135 hours. To get them back to Padua from Lyons and Marseilles would require 173 and 147½ hours respectively.

Discussions in the British War Cabinet and the Decision to Recall Two Divisions

The question of the withdrawal of some of the British troops from Italy was first considered by the War Cabinet at a meeting held on 15th February 1918. The Chief of the Imperial General Staff (Sir William Robertson[1]) read an urgent message which he had received from General Foch, now President of the Allied " Executive War Board ", in control of the General Reserve newly formed at Versailles.[2] This letter pointed out that in a comparison of the numbers of the opposing forces on the Western and Italian Fronts, the enemy possessed a superiority of force on the former, and the Allies on the latter,[3] and expressed the opinion that it was essential that part of the Allied forces now in Italy should be brought back without delay to the Western Front. As the British reserves in France were smaller than the French reserves, and, apparently, the British front more immediately menaced, General Foch suggested that two British divisions might be brought back at once from Italy to France, followed by two French divisions. In view of the changed importance of the two fronts, General Fayolle had been recalled to France on the 14th to command the Group of Armies of Reserve, and his duties in Italy had been taken over by General Maistre. General Foch asked to be informed by telegram of General Robertson's views, and of the earliest date at which the British divisions could begin their movement.

General Robertson told the War Cabinet that personally he agreed with the French Chief of the General Staff that the British divisions in Italy ought to be brought back to the Western Front, but that it was a question, he considered,

---

[1] He was superseded on the 18th by General Sir Henry Wilson. See " 1918 " Vol. I, p. 88.

[2] This Executive War Board was set up at a meeting of the Supreme War Council on 2nd February 1918. It consisted of the Military Representatives of Great Britain, Italy and the United States, with General Foch as President. It was hoped to collect a General Reserve of British, French and Italian divisions ; but this never materialized. See " 1918 " Vol. I, pp. 77 *et seq.*

[3] On 1st March the Italians had 53 divisions against, according to Intelligence Reports, 41 Austrian and 3 German (all of which had left by mid-March) ; on the Western Front, 104 French divisions, 12 Belgian, 4 American and 57 British, that is 177, confronted 180 German divisions (increased by 15th March to 192, and later to 203). " 1918 " Vol. I, pp. 6, 15, 84.

which should be dealt with by the Allied Executive War Board in control of the General Reserve.

The Secretary of State for War (Lord Derby) strongly urged that the divisions should be brought back. The point of danger, he said, was now on the Western Front, not on the Italian Front, and the British and French Governments would be quite within their rights in recalling the divisions.

On the other hand, it was pointed out that the question of the recall of divisions from Italy was closely connected with that of the employment of Italian troops on the Western Front, the study of which had been remitted by the Supreme War Council to the Executive War Board in control of the General Reserve : it was very desirable to secure as many Italian divisions as possible for the Western Front, and, if the British divisions were suddenly withdrawn from Italy, the Italian Government might well become nervous and decline to part with any divisions at all.

A suggestion was also made that the British divisions might be used as a lever to induce the Italian Government to begin the sending of divisions to France. For example, they might be informed that unless they sent, say, four Italian divisions to the Western Front, Great Britain would be compelled to withdraw two divisions from Italy. It was pointed out, however, that Sir Douglas Haig might prefer to have two British rather than four Italian divisions.

The War Cabinet also had before it the opinion of Major-General Harington (Chief General Staff officer to General Plumer), who had attended its meeting on 13th February to make a statement as to the situation on the Italian front. He had then said that the task which the British troops in Italy were now doing with five divisions could be equally well performed by three, though he was unaware what numbers would be required for a proposed offensive. He also stated that, in his opinion, the Italians could spare ten good divisions for the Western Front, as they now had 688 battalions on their own front.

The War Cabinet, therefore, decided at its meeting on 15th February :

" 1. That the Chief of the Imperial General Staff
" should ascertain from Field-Marshal Sir Douglas Haig
" whether he would prefer to be reinforced by two
" British or by four Italian divisions from the Italian
" front.

"2. That in the event of a reply by the Field-Marshal that he would prefer two British divisions, the following action should be taken :

"(a) The Chief of the Imperial General Staff should send orders to the General Officer Commanding the British Expeditionary Force in Italy to send two British divisions at once to the Western Front, and that the Chief of the Imperial General Staff should also notify the Secretary of State for Foreign Affairs.

"(b) The Secretary of State for Foreign Affairs should at once notify the Italian Government of this step. In communicating with the Italian Government he should inform them of the fact that the enemy, while greatly inferior to the Allies on the Italian Front, had now achieved a superiority of force on the Western Front ; and should add that the action now taken was consistent with the principles which had long governed the distribution of forces between the British and French sections of the Western Front, where the reinforcements had always been distributed in accordance with the strategic exigencies of the moment ".

With regard to paragraph 1 of the above decision, the C.I.G.S. telephoned to Sir Douglas Haig at 6.15 p.m. on 15th February, and received an answer from him that he would prefer two British divisions. Action was therefore taken to carry out the orders of the War Cabinet in paragraph 2 of its decision.

General Plumer, therefore, received instructions on 18th February to send two divisions back to France, and on the 19th further instructions to hand over command to Lieut.-General Lord Cavan and return to France himself with the bulk of his headquarters and with the XI Corps headquarters. When this was notified by the British commander to the Comando Supremo, General Diaz replied that he had so far received no intimation from his own Government, and that until he did receive orders from them he could take no action, that is could provide no facilities for movement. It was not till 22nd February that information reached him from the Italian Government of the proposed reduction of the British troops. On the evening of that day General Plumer issued orders to the XIV Corps that the 41st and 7th Divisions would proceed to France as soon as possible, and were to be relieved in the line by the 23rd and 48th Divisions respectively. The 41st Division was to entrain first.

Protests by the Italian Government

The decision to withdraw British troops did not pass without protest from the Italian Government. At a meeting on 21st February the War Cabinet had before it a telegram from Signor Orlando, the Italian Prime Minister, to the Italian Ambassador in London, in which surprise was expressed at the decision to withdraw two British divisions from the Italian Front and at the procedure followed in arriving at this decision, which appeared to be in contradiction to the recent deliberations at Versailles. According to these deliberations, the question of the destination of Allied divisions from the Italian front was to be intimately connected with the constitution of the General Reserve, and this had to be decided by the Supreme War Council on the advice of the Executive War Board for the Control of the General Reserve. Signor Orlando also called attention to the almost inevitable conclusion of peace with Rumania and the consequent release of more Austrian battalions, which would be thrown against the Italian front. The new Chief of the Imperial General Staff, Sir Henry Wilson, said that he had some sympathy with Signor Orlando's complaint as to the procedure which had been followed; as his predecessor had suggested, the matter ought to have been considered at Versailles: he himself would not have advised the War Cabinet to bring back the two divisions at the present moment. Lord Derby, expressed the hope that the War Cabinet would make no change in the decision to which it had come: he had on the previous day telegraphed to the Italian Minister of War, pointing out that there was now a preponderance of divisions against the Allies on the Western Front.

The War Cabinet thereupon decided that the Chief of the Imperial General Staff should draft a suitable reply to be sent to Signor Orlando by the Secretary of State for Foreign Affairs on behalf of the Prime Minister.

The matter was again referred to at a meeting of the War Cabinet on 22nd February, when Sir Henry Wilson said that he had received a telegram from General Plumer, dated the 21st instant, which stated that General Diaz was rather perturbed about the withdrawal of two British divisions from Italy. He reported that a telegram had already been sent to General Alfieri, the Italian Minister of War, expressing regret for the manner in which these two divisions had been ordered away from Italy, and informing him that they would form part of the Allied General Reserve in France : he thought that this statement would satisfy General Diaz and therefore had drafted no letter to him.

A further discussion took place at a meeting of the War Cabinet on 1st March 1918. General Smuts recounted a conversation which he had had with Baron Sonnino, the Italian Foreign Minister, in Rome, during which the latter had expressed strong dissatisfaction with the forthcoming removal of the two British divisions from Italy. Baron Sonnino had given it as his opinion that Italy could be kept in the War to the end, but that this removal of British divisions was not the way to help her to do so : if any troops were to go they should be French rather than British, because the British were so popular and their presence had exercised so good an effect on the Italian morale ; Austrian divisions were pouring in on the Italian front and he could not help feeling anxious ; while it was true that the German divisions had gone away, peace with the Ukraine on the other hand had released numbers of Austrian troops ; if a big attack came and the Italians failed, they would say that the English had deserted them, and the blame would be put on the British Government.

The Chief of the Imperial General Staff pointed out that, while the Italians asserted that eight or nine Austrian divisions had arrived in the Trentino, the British and French Intelligence reports mentioned only two additional Austrian divisions on that front : these rumours and apprehensions always came from Rome, not from General Diaz ; while it was quite possible that Germany might attack Italy, the attack could not come till the snows had melted. With reference to the removal of British divisions from Italy, General Wilson informed the War Cabinet that he had approached General Foch on the subject, and that General Foch had admitted that the initiative had come from him personally and for the reason that the Executive War Board at Versailles had not yet got into working order ; General Foch had confessed, too, that the Italians had not been consulted, either through Versailles or directly. General Wilson added that one of the two British divisions was starting to return to France that day (1st March) and the second would follow.

The War Cabinet then decided that :

" (1) The Chief of the Imperial General Staff should " refer the following questions to the Executive Com- " mittee at Versailles for the Control of the General " Reserve :

" (a) The question of whether the second British " division should be moved from the Italian front.

" (b) The question of whether, and, if so of how " many, Italian divisions should be brought.[1]

" (2) The Secretary of State for Foreign Affairs " should inform the Italian Government of this " decision ".

The transfer to France of the 41st Division was allowed to proceed, but the question of the transfer of a second division was held in abeyance. The War Cabinet thus delayed the execution of its original decision, taken on 15th February, to bring two British divisions back to France at once.

Departure of the 41st Division and the XI Corps and Reorganization of the British Force in Italy

The 41st Division had been relieved by the 7th Division in the right sub-sector of the Montello front on 19th January, and, after nearly a month in reserve, had on 18th February taken over the left sub-sector of the line from the 23rd Division. On the receipt of the G.H.Q. orders of 22nd February, the XIV Corps at once sent out instructions for relief of the 41st Division by the 23rd Division, to begin on the 24th. The relief of the infantry was completed by the 27th, and between 1st and 3rd March the 41st Division (less artillery) entrained for France at Padua, Camposampiero, and three smaller stations. It detrained in France in the Doullens–Mondicourt area between 6th and 8th March. The artillery, which had been relieved in the line later, joined the division there between the 10th and 13th.

---

[1] " Brought to the Western Front " presumably.

The relief of the 7th Division by the 48th Division was completed by the morning of 2nd March. Its entrainment for France was begun on 4th March and some units were already in their seats in the train when a telegram was received from G.H.Q., in consequence of the decision of the War Cabinet to delay its departure, just in time to prevent the trains starting. The division remained in its entrainment area till 7th March, when it began a move to another area on the Bacchiglione, nine or ten miles south-east of Vicenza. On the 24th, G.H.Q. received orders from the War Office that the 5th Division, not the 7th, was to go back to France, and the 7th Division remained in Italy for the rest of the War.

The first intimation that the XI Corps headquarters were to return to France was contained in a telegram from G.H.Q. Italy, received by the corps at 11.45 p.m. on 24th February. By this order, the 48th Division was to be transferred to the XIV Corps to relieve the 7th Division in the line, and the 5th Division was also to come under the XIV Corps at a date to be notified later.

On 9th March the XI Corps transferred the following troops to the XIV Corps: LXXVI and 175th Army Brigades R.F.A., XV, XCIV and 104th Brigades R.G.A., 290th A.T. Company R.E., No. 42 Squadron R.F.C., No. 20 Balloon Company, 36th Motor Ambulance Convoy, 75th Sanitary Section.

The XI Corps headquarters and all other corps troops entrained at Treviso and Padua on 10th and 11th March, detrained in France at Aire on the 14th and 15th, and moved to Lieut.-General Haking's old headquarters at Hinges on the 16th.

The 48th Division began the relief of the 7th Division in the right sub-sector of the Montello sector on 27th February and completed it by the morning of 2nd March, coming under the XIV Corps at noon on 28th February. The division held this sub-sector till relieved by the Italian 58th Division between 14th and 16th March.

The 5th Division, as already related, was holding the Arcade sector and was under orders to take part in an operation in conjunction with the Italian Third Army. It was not therefore till this operation was cancelled that the transfer of the division to the XIV Corps took place at 2 p.m. on 9th March. On 6th March an order had been

RELIEFS. MARCH

issued by XI Corps warning the 5th Division that it would be relieved by the Italian 48th Division. On 16th March the relief began and was completed by the morning of the 18th. The division then moved back to an area south-west of Treviso and on 24th March received orders to be prepared to move to France at short notice.[1]

The VII Brigade headquarters R.F.C., 51st Wing headquarters, 4th Balloon Wing headquarters, No. 42 Squadron and No. 20 Balloon Company also left Italy for France in March. There then remained 14th Wing and Nos. 28, 34, 45 and 66 Squadrons and No. 9 Balloon Company.

Departure of General Plumer

General Plumer left Italy on 10th March, handing over the command of all British troops in Italy to Lord Cavan at 2 p.m. on that day. He returned to his old headquarters at Cassel and on 17th March took over command of the Second Army again. His services in Italy were so highly appreciated by the Italian Government that they had made a request through the British Embassy that he should be allowed to remain in Italy. This matter was brought before the War Cabinet on 5th March by the Secretary of State for Foreign Affairs (Mr. Balfour), when the Secretary of State for War made the statement that he had been urged by Sir Douglas Haig to recall General Plumer to command an Army in France. In consequence, the War Cabinet decided that while recognizing the very valuable services which General Plumer was rendering in Italy, in view of the very serious events expected on the Western Front, they could not refuse Sir Douglas Haig's request.

Final Decision of the War Cabinet and the Reduction of the British Force

At the meeting on 22nd March, that is the day after the opening of the great German offensive, the Chief of the Imperial General Staff produced a telegram which he had

---

[1] Orders were received from the War Office by G.H.Q., Italy on the 23rd to send the 5th Division and the four Army Brigades R.F.A. to France. These brigades (XIV R.H.A. and LXXII, LXXVI, and 175th R.F.A.) left for France at 24 hours' notice on the 25th. No heavy artillery was sent back from Italy to France.

received from General Rawlinson,[1] stating that he (General Rawlinson), General Foch and General Bliss (U.S.A.) all considered that an opportune moment had arrived to transfer two Italian, two French divisions and one more British division from Italy to France: General Giardino, who had succeeded General Cadorna as Military Representative at Versailles on 11th February, was of opinion that the two Italian divisions should be transferred at once, and that the question of the transfer of the British and French divisions could be considered at a later date.[2] Monsieur Clemenceau, the telegram continued, had advised the transfer of all five divisions. The C.I.G.S. therefore advised the War Cabinet that the two Italian divisions should be brought to France at once, followed by the two French, and finally by the British division: his object in bringing the Italian divisions first was to avoid a controversy with the Italian Government: these divisions could relieve two British or French divisions in the line in France. The War Cabinet accepted the advice of the C.I.G.S.,[3] and instructed the C.I.G.S. to notify the Supreme War Council to that effect.

Reduction of the French Force

Instead of two, three French divisions, the 46th, 64th and 65th, began to leave Italy, the first two on 24th March and the third on the 26th. General Maistre, too, returned to France to command a new Tenth Army there and General Graziani (XII Corps)[4] became commander of all the French troops in Italy.

---

[1] General Sir Henry Rawlinson had succeeded General Wilson as Military Representative in the Supreme War Council after handing back the command of the Second (temporarily renamed the Fourth) Army to General Plumer on 17th March.

[2] This telegram evidently refers to a meeting of the Executive War Board for the Control of the General Reserve held at Turin on 20th March. The Supreme War Council account of this meeting says that General Diaz, as well as General Giardino, considered that only the two Italian divisions should move at once. General Diaz had been consulted by the Committee before its meeting.

[3] In view of the serious situation on the Western Front the British and French divisions left Italy before the Italian divisions, which did not entrain until April and then went to the French Fifth Army near Reims. See "1918" Vol. III, p. 231, 233.

[4] Although he bore an Italian name he was a Frenchman.

REDUCTIONS ACHIEVED. APRIL

The second British division, the 5th, began its entrainment on 1st April and its concentration near Doullens was completed on 9th April.

Thus there were left in Italy a French and a British corps, each of three divisions, in the line on the Montello–Monte Grappa front.

Between 18th–27th April the Italian II Corps, under General Albricci, with the 3rd and 8th Divisions, arrived in France.[1]

---

[1] Mention of its operations will be found in "1918" Vol. III. It had been involved in the Second Army in the Caporetto disaster, but had withdrawn in good order.

CHAPTER XII

THE MOVE OF THE FRENCH AND BRITISH CONTINGENTS TO THE ASIAGO PLATEAU
(Map I ; Frontispiece, Sketches 6, 7)

GENERAL FAYOLLE'S PROPOSALS FOR AN ALLIED OFFENSIVE FROM THE ASIAGO PLATEAU

Towards the end of December 1917, as soon as the situation in Italy seemed stabilized, General Fayolle, the French Commander-in-Chief, had begun to consider what offensive action would be possible as soon as the melting of the snow in the mountain sectors permitted operations. On 2nd February, shortly before his recall, he was in a position to submit a plan to General Foch.

In his proposals he at once put aside any idea of reconquering Friuli by an attack across the Piave. He rejected it not on account of the tactical difficulties which it presented, which he did not regard as serious, but because every step of an advance across the Venetian plain would be exposed to flank attack from the mountain regions, of which the enemy was in possession.[1] General Fayolle therefore proposed to take the offensive northwards on the Asiago plateau in the general direction of Trent, with the transverse railway line Levico–Primolana in the valley of the Upper Brenta called Val Sugana, which the Austrians could use as a " ligne de rocade ", as first objective.[2] They would at any rate be prevented from descending on to the Plain of Lombardy if this line were in Allied hands. He planned that the attack should be carried out by three groupments of forces : on the right, one of 5 British and 2 Italian divisions, under General Plumer, would attack Primolana by the valley of the Brenta ; in the centre, one of 4 French and 6 Italian divisions, under General Maistre (who was shortly to succeed General Fayolle), would attack

---

[1] See End-paper for the railways, Sketch 6 for the situation and Sketch 7 for the Austrian plan.

[2] Primolana (east of Trent, Sketch 7) and Feltre (End paper) were the Austrian railheads on this front.

FRENCH OFFENSIVE PROPOSALS. FEBRUARY

Levico by the valley of the Astico; and on the left, one of 2 French and 6 Italian divisions, under an Italian commander, would take Rovereto as its objective via the valley of the Adige.

The Comando Supremo approved of the scheme when informed of it, and agreed to the attack being carried out in the spring, but with the important alteration that it should be entrusted to the newly formed Italian Sixth Army, under General Montuori. This was composed of two Italian corps and was to be reinforced by a French corps and a British corps; and subsidiary attacks were to be undertaken on other parts of the front. It was then settled between Generals Diaz, Maistre and Plumer on 28th February that Italian troops should take over all the Piave front and release the French and British divisions, which should be transferred to the Asiago sector as soon as possible. Whether the attack would be launched or not was, by the desire of General Foch, to depend on the nature of the expected German offensive in France; if it was a serious one, the attack would not take place.

The Italian Modifications of General Fayolle's Proposals

The Redistribution of Italian Armies

These discussions with the Comando Supremo on future operations had begun whilst General Plumer was still in command of British troops in Italy, and on 21st February Major-General Harington, his Chief General Staff Officer had a conversation on the subject with General Badoglio, the senior of General Diaz's two deputies. The Italians looked on the Asiago sector as a dangerous part of their front; in the Sette Communi[1] the Austrian line was within ten miles of the plains; by an advance of only three miles the enemy would overlook the plains, and a break-through there would threaten the flank of the whole Italian line to the east. In agreeing, therefore, to the French plan of an offensive in this

---

[1] The area (see Map I) bounded on east and north by the Brenta, on the west by the Astico and on the south by the southern edge of the Asiago plateau is called the Sette Communi (the seven communes of which Asiago is one).

sector, General Diaz hoped to free the Italian front from the dread of this possibility.

General Badoglio informed Major-General Harington that, in preparation for this offensive, General Diaz intended to make a redistribution of his troops and commands as follows :

(a) To constitute a Seventh Army on the left, composed of the III Corps (already there) and the XIV Corps, under General Tassoni, on the front from the Stelvio Pass on the Swiss frontier eastwards to Lake Garda.

(b) To the south of Lake Garda would be the Fifth Army in reserve, consisting of the II and XII Corps.

(c) The First Army would extend from Lake Garda only to the western edge of the Asiago Plateau.

(d) The Sixth Army was to be brought in to take over the front of the three former right corps of the First Army, between the western edge of the Asiago Plateau and Col Moschin about 3 miles east of the Brenta.[1]

(e) The Fourth Army would continue to hold its present front between Col Moschin and Monte Tomba.

(f) The Second Army would be brought up to relieve the French and British troops on the front which they held near the Piave.

(g) From the old British right to the sea the Third Army would remain as before.

Before any offensive on the Asiago Plateau[2] was begun, it would be necessary to retake Monte Asolone on the Fourth Army front, three miles east of the Brenta.

It was expected, said General Badoglio, that the relief of the British and French divisions on the Piave might be begun by the middle of March, and that they might be in their new positions facing the Asiago Plateau by the end of that month. By the beginning of May ammunition and other stores should have been accumulated and other preparations for the offensive completed.

He considered it very important to take the offensive with all possible vigour. The enemy's offensive should be anticipated, and there was every reason for confidence in the success of energetic action by the combined Allied forces.

---

[1] This re-arrangement was carried out by 2nd March.
[2] It is called indifferently the Asiago Plateau and the Plateau of the Sette Communi.

The Plan of Operations

In March the detailed scheme of the proposed offensive operations on the lines proposed by General Fayolle was received from the Italian Sixth Army, in which the British troops were now to serve. The offensive was directed towards the valley of the Upper Brenta, with the same objective as before, but it was to be on a reduced scale and two intermediate objectives were given.

It was now to be carried out by seventeen divisions instead of twenty-five, eight in front line and nine in second line, with the Italian XX Corps on the right, the French XII Corps in the centre and the British XIV Corps on the left, that is the British were on the left instead of on the right, and the left was directed not up the valley of the Upper Adige, but halfway between the Astico and its eastern tributary.[1] Deficiencies in the number of divisions in the French and British corps were to be made up by the attachment of Italian divisions, three to the British XIV Corps and two to the French XII Corps.

Defensive flanks were to be formed, particularly on the left, where in the forward area of the main attack a defensive flank would face a strongly held enemy line in the Vezzena district.[2]

The advance contemplated by the Sixth Army from the Allied line near Asiago to the Val Sugana was about thirteen miles and the country is mountainous. In Lord Cavan's opinion the proposal for an offensive was deserving of every encouragement, as it ought to meet with considerable success and would raise the Italian morale; but he regarded the scheme as too ambitious and would prefer that the objective should be limited to the first intermediate objective through Monte Melette and Monte Erio,[3] and he informed the C.I.G.S. accordingly. In any case, the move of the British and French contingents to the Asiago district was sanctioned by their governments.

The French and British Troops Remaining in Italy

When Lieut.-General Lord Cavan took over command of the British troops in Italy from General Plumer on

---

[1] Its name cannot be found on any available map. Its lower valley is marked Val d'Assa.
[2] Midway between Asiago and Trent. See Map IV.
[3] See Map I.

10th March 1918, there remained under him four divisions, but one of these—the 5th—began entraining for France, as already noticed, on 1st April. This left the following troops in Italy, organized as the XIV Corps, 7th, 23rd and 48th Divisions,[1] five brigades of heavy artillery, and four squadrons and one balloon company R.F.C. under 14th Wing.[2]

On 10th March the distribution of the XIV Corps was:[3]

    48th Division (vice 41st) holding the right sub-sector of the Montello sector, soon to be relieved by the Italian 58th Division.

    23rd Division holding the left sub-sector of the Montello sector, under orders to be relieved by the Italian 51st Division, beginning on the 11th.

    7th Division (less artillery) in reserve in an area on the Bacchiglione, eight to ten miles south-east of Vicenza. Its artillery was still in the line in the Montello sector, where it was relieved on the night of the 18th/19th by the artillery of the 48th Division; it then marched to an area north-west of Padua.

The French divisions remaining were the 23rd, 24th and 47th, organized as the XII Corps under General Graziani, but on the 7th April the 47th Division left for France.

Relief of the British in the Montello Sector

On 12th March 1918 the XIV Corps[4] issued a warning order that the corps would towards the end of March take over a part of the front on the Asiago Plateau from the Italian XXVI Corps: the sector would be divided into two divisional sub-sectors: in the first instance, the 23rd Division would take over the entire front, but after a few days the 7th Division (if it remained in Italy) would relieve the 23rd Division in the left sub-sector.

Staffs and commands of all divisions were directed to reconnoitre the new front, especially with the view of taking the offensive there, and before taking over the new line to pay particular attention to training in mountain

---

[1] The strengths of these divisions—establishment, 18,825—were: 7th Division, 12,117; 23rd Division, 13,054; 48th Division, 11,302.

[2] Details of the troops and of the Line of Communication troops are given in the Order of Battle for 15th June 1918 in Appendix No. II.

[3] See Sketch 5.

[4] On 18th April the XIV Corps headquarters received the designation of G.H.Q., British Forces in Italy.

warfare. The importance of directing fire on distant objectives by visual observation was emphasized ; for in France, where the ground was usually flat, this had been to some extent neglected. Attention was also called to the importance of visual signalling.

The 23rd Division was relieved in the left sub-sector of the Montello sector by the Italian 51st Division between 11th and 14th March. After relief, the field artillery and infantry in brigade groups marched by stages to an area east and north-east of Vicenza, and the whole division was concentrated there by the 16th.

The 48th Division (less artillery) was relieved in the right sub-sector of the Montello sector by the Italian 58th Division between 14th and 16th March. After relief the division was concentrated in an area west of Treviso, and on the 17th began to move to an area on the Brenta between Cittadella and Padua where all units (less artillery) had arrived by the 23rd. The artillery of the division was not relieved by the Italian 58th Division artillery until the night of the 21st/22nd, and joined the rest of the division on the 24th.

During the halt in the plains, as the weather in the mountains was still very cold and likely to continue to be so for some weeks,[1] the following equipment was issued, to be held as trench stores :

	Per Division	Per Corps Heavy Artillery
Fur sleeping bags	2,000	100
Short fur boots	2,000	50
Hoods, fur or cloth	5,000	1,000
Ice grips (crampons), pairs	5,000	1,000
Alpenstocks	5,000	500
Hose tops	10,000	2,000
Hot food containers	150	50
Ice axes	100	20
Coloured glasses	1,000	100
Goggles, stonebreaker's	1,000	400

The fur sleeping bags, short fur boots and hoods were for men in exposed positions, such as front line trenches and observation posts. The hose tops were to be turned up at night for the " shorts " to be tucked into them. On a division being relieved in the line all sleeping bags, fur

---

[1] Fresh snow fell at times during April. Even on 5th June snow fell and lay 6 inches deep at Monte Carriola, 5 miles S.S.W. of Asiago, and froze hard on top at night ; it soon melted in the sun, and such weather did not last long at that time of year.

boots, hoods and hose tops which had been used were returned to the Ordnance to be cleaned and disinfected before re-issue.

The Occupation of the Asiago Position

On 19th March, G.H.Q. (XIV Corps) issued orders to the 23rd Division to relieve the Italian 11th Division and part of the Italian 12th Division in the line :[1] details were to be settled direct between 23rd Division and Italian XXVI Corps : the field artillery relief was to be completed by 25th March : the infantry relief was to be carried out between 26th and 28th March : all moves, including those of the field artillery, would be carried out by motor lorry.

The relief of the field artillery in the Asiago sector was carried out before that of the infantry. By an order of the C.R.A. XIV Corps, dated 21st March, the field artillery of the 23rd Division was to take over the right sub-sector of the new sector, and the field artillery of the 7th Division the left sub-sector. The relief was carried out on the nights 22nd/23rd, 23rd/24th and 24th/25th. The dismounted portion of the 23rd Division artillery was moved by lorry from Vicenza to take over the line, one section of each battery making the relief on each of the three nights. The guns were towed up the mountains by lorries ;[2] the wagon lines remained some way below on the mountain side and were never moved up to the plateau. The gun positions taken over were all approached by very steep slopes and hidden among trees, so that the guns had to be hauled in position by hand, and in many cases had to be dismounted and the various parts of gun and carriage carried up separately. The 7th Division artillery was similarly moved up to the line from the Padua area by lorry and took over the left sub-sector of the new line. At 10 a.m. on 25th March the C.R.A. 23rd Division assumed command of the field artillery of the whole sector, until the G.O.C. 7th Division should arrive.

The orders of the 23rd Division for the infantry relief were issued on 22nd March. There were 240 lorries available for each brigade group, and 65 additional lorries for divisional

---

[1] See Map I.
[2] Lorries took 2½ hours, horses pulling guns or wagons 6 hours, infantry using short cuts 5 hours.

headquarters, the machine gun company, and the pioneer battalion. The lorries were provided half by British XIV Corps and half by Italian Sixth Army, and were organized under brigade arrangements into sections of 10 lorries each. Each lorry took 15 men with their kits, and they were despatched with intervals of 200 yards between sections and 400 yards between units.

The move forward towards the line began on 26th March; on the 27th the 68th Brigade took over the left sub-sector of the line from the Italian 12th Division; on the 28th the 70th Brigade took over the right sub-sector from the Italian 11th Division, and the 69th Brigade moved into the Granezza area (4 miles south of Asiago) as divisional reserve. At 12 noon on 29th March the G.O.C. 23rd Division took over from the Italian XXVI Corps, with headquarters at Lonedo (9 miles south of Asiago).

The XIV Corps had on its right the French XII Corps which had taken over the line here on 24th March, and on its left the Italian 12th Division of the X Corps, the right of the Italian First Army.

On 22nd March G.H.Q. issued orders for the 7th Division to take over the left sub-sector of the Asiago sector from the 23rd Division on the 30th and 31st. Lorries were provided as in the case of the 23rd Division. On the 27th the brigade groups began to move northwards from the Vicenza area towards the new line. On the 30th the 91st Brigade took over the right of the new sub-sector and on the 31st the 22nd Brigade took over the left, and divisional headquarters were established at Monte Carriola (5 miles S.S.W. of Asiago). The 20th Brigade was in reserve in the Camisino area (3 miles south of Monte Carriola). The 48th Division went to the reserve area, known as Trissimo,[1] in the Agno valley at the foot of the mountains 10 miles west of Vicenza.

While the British troops were moving to the Asiago sector patrols were kept in the air over both its old and its new sectors to prevent enemy air observers from discovering the movements.[2]

---

[1] Marked on Sketch 5.
[2] The move of the R.F.C. to the new area had begun on 10th March, for which see Sketch 5, when No. 66 Squadron moved to Casa Piazza (6 miles W.S.W. of Cittadella). On the 17th No. 45 Squadron flew to Grossa (7 miles east of Vicenza); on the 26th Headquarters 14th Wing moved to Sarcedo (10 miles north of Vicenza); on the 30th No. 34 Squadron moved to Villaverla (7½ miles north of Vicenza). No. 28 Squadron remained at Grossa, which was within easy flying distance of both sectors.

On 2nd April the 48th Division by order of G.H.Q. began to move westward from its area on the Brenta, and on the 3rd arrived in its new area west of Vicenza as corps reserve.

Thus by 3rd April the British Forces in Italy were holding the Asiago sector with two divisions in the line and one in reserve ; and by that time the whole of the British heavy artillery in Italy had joined them, and there were in addition in the Asiago sector under them 37 Italian heavy batteries.

The heavy artillery in Italy when Lieut.-General Lord Cavan took over command from General Plumer consisted of the XV, XXIV, LXXX, XCIV and 104th Brigades R.G.A. When the 23rd Division was relieved in the left sub-sector of the Montello sector by the Italian 51st Division, the LXXX Brigade remained in the line under the Italian XXVII Corps. Similarly when the 48th Division was relieved in the right sub-sector by the Italian 58th Division the XXIV, XCIV and 104th Brigades remained in the line under the Italian VIII Corps, which now took over this part of the front. The XV Brigade had been temporarily lent to the Italians since 6th January and was in action between the Brenta and Asiago ; between 21st and 23rd March it was pulled out from its positions and marched to the Asiago sector where it went into action on 31st March under British G.H.Q. The other four brigades still in the Montello sector were pulled out between 26th and 29th March and marched to the Thienne area behind the Asiago sector. The XCIV Brigade began to go into action on the 31st and part of the XXIV and LXXX Brigades in the first few days of April. The 104th Brigade and the rest of the XXIV and LXXX Brigades remained in reserve.

CHAPTER XIII

THE ASIAGO SECTOR
MARCH TO MID-JUNE 1918
(Map I ; End-paper)

Description of the Asiago Sector and the British Position

The new sector occupied by the British contingent, with two divisions in front line and one in reserve, was in the mountain area of the Italian front.[1] The boundary of this area with the Plain of Lombardy lay about twelve miles behind the front trenches. Starting from the plain, at a level of 350 feet, the ground rises rapidly, cut and broken by the valleys of many small streams, and in eight to nine miles of steep ascent reaches a line of summits—Monte Corno (4,560 feet), Cima di Fonte (4,980 feet) and Monte Brusabo (4,950 feet)—the site of the British reserve line, sometimes called "The Marginal Line". So rapidly does the ground rise—its general slope being 1 in 10—that the roads mount by a series of zig zags and hairpin bends.[2]

From the line of summits the ground drops gradually down for three miles to the so-called Asiago plateau, a kind of step in the ascent of the Alps, and actually a shallow basin, which has a general level of about 3,300 feet. This downhill slope is not an even incline, but a confusion of rugged pine-clad hills and valleys, bare rock where there are no trees, with spurs projecting towards Asiago ; the only large open spaces were one around the village of Cesuna and a clearing on the slopes of M. Kaberlaba. The roads in this area wind through flat or gently sloping valleys, occasionally of noticeable width.

At the bottom of the long, wooded slope, on the southern boundary of the Asiago plateau, was the new British front line. The plateau itself, which the Austrian line crossed, measures some seven miles from east to west and three miles

---

[1] The End-paper shows the general lie of the ground ; Map I presents it in detail.
[2] More is said below as regards communications.

from north to south, and consists of undulating, cultivated ground, freely sprinkled with villages of cottages and wooden huts, with the little war-battered town of Asiago, in which the only substantial buildings were a church and the barracks of an Alpini battalion, situated about the left centre, inside the Austrian lines.

The Ghelpac, which ran from east to west along the middle of No Man's Land, is at first an insignificant watercourse in a shallow bed, but it deepens as it runs westward, becoming a very serious obstacle on the extreme left. In the Italian sector on the left of the British, this stream runs in an impassable ravine, so that, combined with the Val d'Assa gorge, no danger existed of the British position being turned from that flank.

On the north the plateau is bounded by another range of summits, including Monte Longara and Monte Mosciagh, of 5,000 feet altitude, about three miles away, and the ground then gradually rises to the old frontier, over 6,000 feet above sea-level, falling from it down to the Val Sugana in the valley of the upper Brenta, beyond which lie the High Alps. The tactical importance of the plateau lay in the fact that it was the only part of the whole mountain front where the comparative flatness of the ground permitted of the ordinary methods of attack being used. To the east of the plateau rise rugged heights of about 4,500 feet, overlooking the north-south course of the Brenta, nearly four hundred feet below. At the western end the plateau narrows towards the ravine of the Val d'Assa. Here the opposing trenches faced each other across the impassable gorge, 2,000 feet deep. Elsewhere No Man's Land was at its narrowest half a mile wide, and for a great part of the front was quite a mile wide.

When British troops took over the sector, orders were given for the establishment of an outpost line five hundred to a thousand yards beyond the front line, and by 10th April a number of posts had been established about five hundred yards out in accidents of the ground, covered by loose wire; for to blast the rock or make concrete shelters would have attracted notice. For observation over No Man's Land a few hillocks were occupied during the day.

The grave disadvantage of the Asiago position was its lack of depth; from the front line to the reserve line on the first line of summits was barely three miles. If the British were driven back towards this line artillery support became impossible, as the ground behind it dropped sharply to the plain. Field gun support even to the existing front lines was difficult, as the batteries, perforce, were on higher ground, driven to new conditions of large angles of depression to reach their targets, and in the right sub-sector the low trajectory of the field gun could not clear the trees, and lanes had to be cut by sawing off the heads of the pines. To hide these embrasures, two or three saplings were lashed horizontally across the upper part of the gap, but the flash of discharge was still visible, so registration was usually carried out by lone guns on the flanks. Eventually the British copied the Italian procedure of using reduced charges with improvised range tables. The howitzers, on the other hand, could find tolerable positions, though the rocky ground entailed hard work to make level platforms, and rock drills were in demand and in constant use. Regular intervals between guns could not be arranged, and the dispersion involved often handicapped control.

The British front line ran, as already mentioned, along the southern edge of the plateau, with a background of wooded spurs which trend towards Asiago rising to a height of 400 to 500 feet above the little valleys lying between them. It was not completely exposed to enemy observation, as the dense pine woods provided concealment in the greater part of the right division's sector; in much of the left division's area, however, no such cover from view existed, and movement was perilous during daylight. In compensation, most of the left division had a good field of fire, although three patches of wood extending into No Man's Land—one as much as a thousand yards— offered covered approaches to the enemy, whereas the view to the front of the right division was much restricted by irregularities of the surface of No Man's Land. From the higher ground in their possession both divisions could get good observation over the Austrian front and support lines and the approaches to them, with the result that the enemy was forced to restrict all movement to the hours of darkness.

The front trench, as taken over from the Italians, was of the deep, narrow type, with a high fire-step, laid out in bold zig zags, without traverses, partly dug in the earth, partly blasted in the rock. It was not well sited to be held by posts as the British held it, as its trace often prevented mutual support. The second line, about eight hundred yards behind the first, on the slope of the hills and almost entirely in the woods, was of the same type, but most of it blasted in the rock. The dug-outs, as found, were of poor construction and provided wholly insufficient accommodation, and except for a few caves there was no shell-proof cover whatever. Communication trenches did not exist, being judged unnecessary in the wooded sector, and of little value on the steep, exposed slopes elsewhere. The only thing of the nature of a switch to limit penetration was formed by some belts of wire running obliquely to the front between the lines, with occasionally a short length of trench behind them.

Communications

All signal communication had to be above ground, as it was not possible, except at great expense of time, to bury cables in the rocky ground ; so runners and visual signalling were largely employed.

The railway communication with the Asiago sector was the branch line from Vicenza through Thiene to Rochette.[1] The line is broad gauge, double up to Thiene and single beyond this. From Rochette there was a narrow-gauge rack and pinion railway to Asiago, which could be used at night for the first 7½ miles to Campiello.[2]

There were three good mountain roads available for communication from the foot of the mountains into the Asiago sector. All three could be used for two-way traffic by lorries :

>   (1) A permanent road to Granezza and beyond to the front line at the right boundary of the sector. This road continues on through Asiago to the enemy's railhead at Levico, and so to Trent ;
>
>   (2) a war road through the left division headquarters at Monte Carriola to the front line near the right boundary of the left division ;
>
>   (3) a war road through Caltrano to the left of the front line, following the route of the rack and pinion railway, partly in the Italian area.

These roads were well constructed, but the many hairpin bends gave trouble. In summer the surface was excellent,

---
[1] See End-paper.
[2] See Map I.

but in winter it became covered with ice, snow or very slippery mud, and vehicles had to be driven with the greatest care; for a skid did not involve a simple case of ditching, but a drop of several hundred feet. It was found impracticable to use the ordinary 3-ton type of lorry on any of these roads; in many places, in fact, these vehicles could not pass each other with safety, and the radius of the hairpin bends was so small that, owing to insufficient steering lock, lorries could not get round the bends without " tacking ". Another difficulty, which applied to all British-made motor vehicles, was that the radiators, made for the climate of Northern Europe, became overheated in the semi-tropical summer of Italy. By the " Crowe Convention ",[1] three hundred 30-cwt. Fiat lorries and two hundred Fiat 2-ton lorries had been handed over to the British. Of these, the 30 cwt. lorries were found far the best for mountain work, and they became the standard vehicles for such use. The 2-ton lorries were not so reliable and, requiring constant repair, threw a heavy strain on the workshops; but as Italian transport was very short owing to losses at Caporetto, these vehicles were kept in service till the end of the war.

Touring cars of British make suffered from the same defects as the lorries when used in the mountains, and they were replaced as far as possible by Italian cars. For this purpose, eighteen 35-h.p. Lancia cars were provided. For ambulance duty, sufficient " M.Y." type Talbots were collected, and they proved satisfactory for mountain work.

Mule tracks were numerous in the mountains, and were the only means of communication to many places. Colonel W. S. Swabey, the Director of Transport, converted an auxiliary horse-transport company into a pack-mule company by exchanging the heavy draught horses for the mules of the divisional ammunition column and obtaining local saddles. Some pack-mules were handed over to units and used by the artillery to carry ammunition; the remainder were kept as a pool in the hands of the officer commanding the divisional train for use as required. The total number of animals maintained in the mountains was limited to 1,500 per division, on account of the shortage of water (see below). In the ascent of about four thousand feet from the plain to the top of the first line of summits, the infantry usually

---

[1] See p. 29.

followed the mule tracks, the roads being reserved for artillery and transport. In any case the continual zig-zagging of the road made the distance covered so much longer that the ascent by mule tracks was preferred as quicker and easier.

Another means of communication with the Asiago sector was the wire ropeways, the " teleferiche ", to the top of the first ascent from the plain. They consisted of an endless steel cable supported on up-ended girders every two or three hundred yards, with small flat trucks suspended from the cable at intervals of about a hundred feet, and the cable was worked by electric power from terminal stations at the foot of the mountains. Passengers were occasionally carried, but it was not a comfortable means of transport. The following " teleferiche " existed :

1. On the right, capacity 8 to 9 tons per hour. This was shared between the British and French, and had two extensions to Granezza. Capacity of each, 2 tons 15 cwts. per hour.

2. In the right centre ; under construction when British troops took over.

3. In the left sector, not fit for use when the British troops took over, as the road access required improvement ; but it was in use later.

4. On the left, capacity 15 cwts. per hour. Not suitable for artillery ammunition as access for wheels was poor.

The " teleferiche " were not found suitable for supplies, as delays occurred owing to the constant breakdowns of the motive machinery. Also it was found difficult to load rations on the flat trucks, and they sometimes fell off. After a week's trial it was decided to use the rope-ways for sending up ammunition only, and for this purpose they were of great service.

Method of Supply[1]

The railhead for supplies for the right division was at Villaverla (8 miles N.N.W. of Vicenza). From railhead

---

[1] A good account of the Austrian system of supply on the mountain front is given in "Intendanzdienst im Gebirgskriege" by General-Intendant F. Glingenbrunner. It is worth noting that in winter snow was used for cooking and drinking in lieu of water, with a dash of lemon to hide the taste.

the divisional train's lorries carried supplies to the foot of the mountains six miles away. Thence first-line transport took the loads to the transport lines at Granezza on light general service wagons, carrying 1,000 lbs. and drawn by four mules. It was found that the best arrangement for this part of the journey was to keep half the mules in the plain and half in the mountains, changing the animals at a half-way point. The necessity for the mules spending alternate nights in the heat of the plains and the cold of the mountains was thus avoided. From the transport lines most of the units could be reached by wheeled vehicles which, using the cover of the woods, could pass unobserved; but some could only be served by pack animals after dark.

The railhead for supplies for the left division was at Chiuppano (2 miles east of Rochette) at the foot of the mountains. Supplies for troops of the division billeted in the plain were taken off here, and the remainder sent on, still by broad-gauge line, to Rochette, where they were transferred to trucks of the narrow-gauge rack and pinion railway and taken up to Campiello after dark. This place is situated in a steep valley five or six hundred yards wide, and was three miles behind the front line; there they were off-loaded without delay to enable the train to return to Rochette before daylight; for parts of this line and Rochette itself were under direct enemy observation. From Campiello first-line transport carried the supplies to units as soon as it was light in the morning. The roads from Campiello to unit headquarters were good, but could be made very unpleasant by enemy shelling.

Water in the Asiago sector was very scarce. There were some ponds fit for watering animals, but they dried up in summer; at that season the supply of water for the troops and animals was pumped by pipe-line from the Astico river. Various reservoirs, tanks and standpipes were provided, catchment tanks were constructed by the R.E., and the supply was usually adequate; but, owing to the danger of the pipe-line being cut by shell-fire, care was taken to husband water, and it was rationed at a gallon a man per day for all purposes.

The number of animals kept in the mountains was strictly limited, and all the wagon lines of the artillery were, as already mentioned, several miles behind the batteries.

Housing, Canteens and Recreation

In the front line, dug-outs were few and gave very insufficient cover against shell-fire. Fortunately the Austrian artillery was usually inactive, although its heavy shells, especially an occasional 17-inch, did considerable damage when they did come over. The accommodation immediately in rear of the front line was poor, and consisted of tin or wooden shelters built into the sides of the ridges. When the snow melted the accumulated filth of three years was unveiled around and even under the huts, and, as it could not be buried in the rocky ground, it had to be burnt. In the Granezza valley, on the main Asiago road, hidden from the enemy's direct observation, were crowded together the headquarters of the right division, the reserve brigade, a field company R.E., most of the first-line transport of the division, part of its divisional ammunition column, in addition to ammunition and ration dumps. There were also a football ground, a wooden church, and a wooden theatre. The valley was shelled occasionally, but never heavily bombarded till the battle of 15th June. At M. Carriola, the other divisional headquarters, conditions were similar.

The reserve division in the Trissino area had good billets in four large villages and the smaller hamlets between them, and a theatre at Arzignano (a silk industry town of 12,000 inhabitants). Here the weather was so hot even in May that the troops wore khaki drill shorts and Egyptian helmets, and training was done in the early morning and evening. Football could be played in the few fields left free of vines; but the country was so closely cultivated that no good training area was available.

Expeditionary Force Canteen depôts were established at Thiene and Calvene (3 miles south of Granezza, at the foot of the mountains), and Y.M.C.A. huts or tents were available at Thiene, Calvene, Granezza and M. Carriola. Some of the Italian recreation rooms, soldiers' clubs and refreshment shelters were also taken over. Baths were established at Granezza and M. Carriola in the mountains and at Fara (5 miles south of Granezza) and Calvene in the plain.

A rest station for British troops was organized in German-owned and abandoned villas and hotels at Sirmione on the southern shore of Lake Garda, and here, far from the turmoil of war, officers, N.C.O.s and men could idle their time away in bathing, fishing and taking trips by motor launch, with open-air concerts and a theatre to amuse them in the evening. The place was of special value, there being no possibility of home leave. The men staying there were under no description of discipline. Leave was also granted to visit Rome, Florence, Naples, Pompeii and Venice, where arrangements were made to show the sights to the visiting troops.

Schools of Instruction

When the British troops moved from the Piave to the Asiago sector, the schools of instruction remained in the Torreglia area, near Padua. On 29th May information was received that the Italians proposed no longer to send officers and N.C.O.s to British schools. The reasons given were :

(a) The need for all officers to be with their units in the coming time of stress ;

(b) The fact that, being trained on somewhat different lines to what they were accustomed, officers and N.C.O.s emerged with a lessened faith in their own training and an incomplete knowledge of the British ;

(c) The intention of starting in the future a large training centre of their own.

Lord Cavan deplored this decision and approached General Badoglio on the subject ; but he met with no more success than was represented by a suggestion that the question might be reconsidered in two months.

Discussions on Policy: Offence or Defence

The Italian Sixth Army's scheme for an offensive from the Asiago sector was published before the departure of the second pair of French divisions on 28th March and 7th April, leaving only two under General Graziani in Italy. On 12th April, the day on which Field-Marshal Sir Douglas Haig issued his " Backs to the Wall " Order of the Day, the C.I.G.S. telegraphed to Lord Cavan, expressing doubts as to the expediency of carrying out the proposed offensive in view of the departure from Italy of the two French divisions and of the serious situation on the Western Front, where the second act of the German offensive, the Battle of the

Lys, in the Hazebrouck sector, had begun on 9th April. There was, he said, a great shortage of men, and we were unable to maintain the strength of our divisions in France: unless there were strong reasons for the offensive in Italy, any such extra drain on our resources should be avoided. There would, however, be no objection, he thought, if, in Lord Cavan's view, the plan could be carried out at small cost, and the situation so improved thereby as to lead in the long run to economy of men : but under all other conditions the offensive should be postponed.

Lord Cavan had come to the conclusion that a limited offensive was advisable for three reasons : first, to deepen the zone between the front line in the mountains and the edge of the plains; secondly, to anticipate a possible Austrian offensive; and, thirdly, to raise the morale of the Italian Army. Before replying, however, he decided to consult the Comando Supremo, and on 15th April he wrote that he had seen General Diaz, who entirely agreed with General Wilson as to the absolute necessity of economizing men in the present situation, and had therefore decided to postpone the offensive for the moment ; but, in two cases, the Comando Supremo still intended to attack on the Asiago plateau : first, if the Austrians sent strong reinforcements to France; and, secondly, as a counter-offensive if the Austrians attacked in Italy elsewhere than on the plateau.

The situation, therefore, for the moment, said Lord Cavan, was that the Allied troops in Italy were acting on the defensive but were ready to take advantage of any favourable chance of an attack on the enemy which would not be costly in men.

On the same day Lord Cavan held a conference with his divisional commanders, and impressed on them that, though they were not to slacken their efforts as regards preparations for the offensive, those for the defensive were from now onward to have precedence.

On 30th April Lord Cavan received information that the French High Command had ordered General Graziani to press for the proposed offensive.[1] This divergence of views between the French authorities and the C.I.G.S. put Lord Cavan in a difficult position.

---

[1] The French had lost Mont Kemmel on 25th April, and a great German success in Flanders seemed probable.

AN OFFENSIVE PROPOSED. MAY 177

A hankering after an offensive was apparently still in the mind of the Comando Supremo ; for General Montuori, at a conference of his corps commanders held on 1st May, told them that the elements of doubt had to a considerable extent disappeared and that the offensive might be considered as highly probable. As a result of this conference, the Italian 11th Division, which was to be attached to the British Forces for the offensive, was placed under the British Commander-in-Chief for training.

On 10th May Lord Cavan again wrote to the C.I.G.S. on the subject of the uncertainties of the situation. He considered that an offensive in Italy would gain no more than a local advantage, and he did not agree with the French view that a success in Italy would ease the situation in France ; the attitude of the Comando Supremo seemed on the whole to accept the British view, but it was hoping for great results from Czech propaganda in Austria, and was determined to launch an attack at short notice if it thought the moment suitable. Lord Cavan ended this letter with the words :

" As a result, I am faced with two difficulties :

" (a) My inclination now is to suggest a course " contrary to that being pressed for by the French " commander ;

" (b) My troops are being kept in a constant state of " tension ; reliefs become difficult,[1] and the necessary " preparations for offensive conflict with the labour " demands for defensive work.

" I write this letter solely so that you may be fully " informed of the situation now facing the British " troops in this country."

DECISION TO LAUNCH AN OFFENSIVE

By 15th May the uncertainties of the situation had disappeared, the great German effort in Flanders had died away, and Lord Cavan wrote on that date to the C.I.G.S. that the offensive of the Sixth Army had now been decided upon, and that he was to see General Montuori on the

---

[1] The relief of a division in the mountainous country, with few roads, took five days.

following day. At the conference on the 16th, corps commanders were told by General Montuori to be ready by 31st May to launch an attack on whatever day the Comando Supremo should decide.

A warning order had been issued on the 15th by British G.H.Q. giving full details of the attack. It was to be carried out in two stages :

> First Stage, to the northern edge of the Asiago plateau and the edge of the woods on the rising ground beyond; this meant for the British an advance of about three thousand yards on the right, and half that distance on the left.
>
> Second Stage, to the line of summits Monte Longara–Monte Mosciagh, about three miles farther.

Both stages were to be carried through in one day by, from right to left, the British 23rd and 7th Divisions and the Italian 11th Division. In reserve, under British G.H.Q., were to be the British 48th and the Italian 57th and 60th Divisions. The 12th Division of the Italian First Army was to cover the left flank of the 11th Division and eventually establish a defensive flank.

On 25th May the orders for the offensive still held good, but there had been rumours of an impending Austrian attack, and Lord Cavan ends a letter of this date with the words : " my fear is that the dread of an Austrian offensive " may paralyse the preparations for our offensive ".

British Ground and Air Activity in April and May

The change in policy had naturally a disturbing effect on the labours of the British troops : a defensive policy meant that time and labour would be chiefly spent on reorganizing and strengthening the forward defences, reconnoitring, and making rear defences, instead of heavy aggressive raiding, destructive shoots, moving batteries forward, the formation of dumps and construction of passages to the front; it meant that aggressive action would be reduced to raids for identifications, and that, in particular, the artillery would be less active. Actually a great deal of work was done to improve the switches and at least begin strongpoints as pivots of support to counter-attacks, though little more could be accomplished in constructing the strongpoints in the short time available than to wire in portions of trenches and deposit ammunition and stores in them, and to select O.P.s and strengthen dug-outs.

When the British troops first took over the Asiago sector at the end of March, when an offensive seemed likely, active patrolling of No Man's Land was begun and many raids were carried out. The earliest of these was made by a patrol of the 11/Sherwood Foresters (23rd Division), which took three prisoners on the night of 30th/31st March. On 7th April a fighting patrol of the 1/R. Welch Fusiliers (7th Division) entered the enemy's trenches, killed or wounded 17 of the enemy and brought back a wounded prisoner. On 8th April a patrol of the 8/York & Lancaster (23rd Division) also took two prisoners. On the 16th the 2/R. Warwickshire (7th Division) raided the enemy trenches and took a prisoner, eight enemy dead being counted. On the night of 17th/18th April the 7th Division made two raids: at 10 p.m. two companies of the 1/South Staffordshire attacked a strongpoint and surrounded it, killing about twenty of the enemy and taking 22 prisoners. At 4 a.m. a party of the 20/Manchester entered the enemy's front line, killing or severely wounding at least twelve of the enemy, with a loss to itself of six.

After this, all without retaliation, in deference to the defensive policy, the raids were smaller and less deep. On the night of 22nd/23rd April strong patrols of the 7th Division went out to clear No Man's Land of enemy posts, and capture prisoners. The right brigade had no encounters, but the 2/1st H.A.C., the right battalion of the left brigade, met with strong opposition from posts in front of the enemy's front line. The posts were taken, however, and held against counter-attack. On the 29th, at 11 p.m., one company of the 6/R. Warwickshire (48th Division) made a raid opposite the extreme right; some of the objectives were reached and a prisoner taken; but such a heavy artillery barrage was put down that fifty casualties were suffered.

On the early morning of 3rd May the 1/R. Welch Fusiliers (7th Division) raided trenches on the left, and captured an officer and two men. At 10.45 p.m. on the 4th the 8/Devonshire (7th Division) raided and took four prisoners.

On the early morning of 15th May the 2/Border Regiment (7th Division) raided enemy trenches on the left, south of the main line, and took five prisoners, including an officer.

On the night of 1st/2nd June, the 11/Northumberland Fusiliers (23rd Division) raided three houses in front of the Austrian line on the right, killed at least ten of the enemy and took two prisoners. On the night of 8th/9th June the 8/Green Howards (23rd Division) raided a group of houses in front of the enemy trenches in the centre. The enemy was on the alert, and put up a very strong resistance. In spite of this, two out of the three objectives were reached, several of the enemy were killed and eleven prisoners taken. On the same night the 1/1st Buckinghamshire (48th Division) raided trenches on the left of the 8/Green Howards, took a prisoner and inflicted casualties.

The R.A.F. units in the Asiago sector were also busy. The weather in April was for the most part stormy and unfavourable for observation, but the conditions improved in May and there was a notable increase in air activity. One of the biggest operations was carried out on the morning of 30th May, when 35 Sopwith Camels from Nos. 28, 45 and 66 Squadrons dropped a ton of bombs and fired 9,000 rounds of ammunition on enemy hutments in the sector north of the Val d'Assa. The attacks were made from under five hundred feet. In June enemy air reconnaissances increased, and to prevent these, a double system of patrols was instituted, a close patrol zone extending about two and a half miles to the front, and the second zone, beyond the first, covering another five miles. The increase in enemy air activity was marked on the Piave front, and during May and June constant reconnaissances were made by the R.A.F. to report on road and rail activity behind the enemy's immediate front. In the Asiago sector nothing unusual was discovered, for the Austrian Command had taken great precautions to conceal their preparations: attacking divisions were kept well behind the lines, and were only sent forward on the morning of the attack.

The Austrian account of the period " Beginning of April " to Beginning of June 1918 " records : " Air fighting " greatly increased in liveliness. Whilst at night when " there was good moonlight both sides did damage with " bombs, by day British low-flying fighters, in particular, " were unpleasantly attentive. Troops at training, railway

"stations crowded with trains, supply columns unsuspi-
"ciously wandering on the road, even single motor cars,
"were the targets of their attacks, which often occasioned
"heavy losses". Successful Italian attacks on airfields are
then mentioned.

During May, on the 9th/10th, 21st, 25th/26th and 26th/27th the Italians carried out four successful minor operations. The first three were in the mountains to drive the enemy off good observation posts, and the fourth was undertaken to extend the Sile bridgehead. Against this last the Austrians used the *1st Cavalry Division*, on foot, to stem the rout of the *28th Reserve Division*, and it lost no less than 15 officers and 1,671 other ranks.[1] The prisoners taken on these four occasions amounted to 93, 51, 870 and 450, respectively, and the Italians were greatly elated. The Austrians make no claim to any successes.

Between the occupation of the Asiago sector and the Battle of Asiago the following reliefs took place :

On 23rd April the 48th Division relieved the 23rd Division in the right sub-sector. On 19th May the 23rd Division again took over the right sub-sector from the 48th Division. On 31st May the 48th Division relieved the 7th Division in the left sub-sector.

In May, soon after sun-helmets had been issued, a great epidemic of influenza, as in other parts of the world, raged among the British troops in Italy. The attack usually lasted three days and recovery was quick ; but the disease was so widespread that as many as thirty per cent. of the strength of a division might be out of action when it was at its worst. "Gargling" was the prescribed prophylactic. The epidemic continued into June, but by 1st July Lord Cavan was able to report that the influenza had practically vanished.

The Offensive Postponed

Lord Cavan's foreboding, recorded earlier, that the Comando Supremo would abandon the offensive, soon proved to be justified. On 27th May he found himself obliged to write to the Chief of the Imperial General Staff :
" There has been a kaleidoscopic change in the Italian

---

[1] A.O.A. VII, p. 210.

"situation in the last 24 hours, and I cannot deny that I am disappointed at the attitude adopted. The Italians received, two or three days ago, through a Czech deserter, information of an impending Austrian offensive on the Lower Piave". On the previous night, Lord Cavan continued, he had attended a conference at which General Montuori had made it clear that the information was considered accurate; the Italian Army commander also stated that there was news of the approaching arrival of ten German divisions on the Austrian front, though he admitted that the evidence as to the number was not yet conclusive. Lord Cavan was not yet prepared to accept the information in full without confirmation; he was more than sceptical about the report of German reinforcements—and rightly, as on 27th May the Germans began their third great offensive of 1918, on the Aisne front. However, the fact remained that the Italian High Command did accept the information, and were unwilling to commit their reserves to a limited offensive in the mountains, where movement is necessarily slow, if a really large Austrian offensive was imminent on the Piave. In the result, the Asiago offensive was definitely postponed, and the withdrawal of the Italian guns and men intended for it was at once begun. Thus, it could not now be undertaken at short notice.

In a second letter on the same day Lord Cavan wrote that there were certain slight corroborative signs that the information given by the Czech deserter who was, it seemed, an officer, was accurate. On the 29th he wrote that information obtained from prisoners and documents captured in the Italian operation on the Sile river on the night of the 26th/27th did undoubtedly point to an Austrian concentration behind the Lower Piave. It appeared that the Austrian *Fifth Army*[1] had been reinforced by four or five divisions; but there was no confirmation of the presence of German divisions. Lord Cavan considered that the prospects of an Austrian offensive were increasing, and that it was likely to be a "pincer" movement: astride the Brenta and across the Lower Piave.

Lord Cavan's next letter to the C.I.G.S. was written five days later, on 3rd June, when he said that reports from both prisoners and deserters constantly referred to an approaching

---

[1] The Austrian *Fifth Army* (late *Isonzo*) now faced the Italian Third Army on the Piave from the sea to near the Montello.

SIGNS OF ENEMY OFFENSIVE. JUNE 183

Austrian offensive on the Lower Piave; British air reconnaissances reported an increase in aerodrome accommodation in areas east of the Piave.

On 7th June signs of a coming Austrian attack on the Lower Piave were on the increase, and Lord Cavan was fairly convinced that it would be made in the not far distant future. Whether the attack would extend to the mountainous district of the Brenta valley was less clear. Prisoners captured in this district by the French and Italians did not corroborate previous reports of an imminent attack there. On the other hand, seven deserters came over to the French on the night of the 9th/10th, stating that they did so because an attack was imminent.

On 9th June, the Battle of the Matz, the fourth of the German offensives on the Western Front in 1918, was begun, and Monsieur Clemenceau inquired of General Foch, since 3rd April charged with the strategic direction of operations on the Western Front, whether he approved of the Italian inaction. This question had the result that on 12th June General Foch despatched a letter to General Diaz in which he remarked that the Austrian offensive expected at the beginning of June not having materialized, the absence of it might be interpreted either as a renunciation of the project, or as an indication of hesitation on the part of the Austrian High Command; possibly the sole object of the enemy's preparation had been to parry an Italian attack; or again to deceive the Allies and induce them to maintain larger forces than necessary in Italy to the detriment of the Western Front. In any case, the Generalissimo said that the best way to deal with an enemy whose acts showed uncertainty was to attack vigorously.[1]

Italian Plans for Minor Offensives

Comando Supremo were meanwhile making plans for a series of minor offensives along the front to disturb the enemy's plans and, if possible, ascertain his intentions. In reference to these plans Lord Cavan met General Badoglio at Sixth Army headquarters on 7th June, and discussed the Sixth Army's part in the operations. On the 10th the Italian plan was received at British G.H.Q. Five small operations

---

[1] F.O.A. vi (ii), p. 353-4.

at different points on the front were proposed. In the Sixth Army the British were to advance on 18th June to the southern edge of the Val d'Assa and the southern exits of Asiago, in combination with a French attack on Monte Sisemol (3 miles east of Asiago) and an Italian attack, on the right of the French, on Stoccareddo.

On 11th June, however, another sudden change of plan occurred. When at 10 a.m., Lord Cavan attended a hastily summoned conference at the Comando Supremo, General Diaz stated that information had been received from an Italian officer, who had been dropped from an aeroplane behind the enemy's line, that the Austrian troops in position for an attack on the Piave were marching eastwards (*sic*) towards the Tagliamento, and thence probably either to the Brenta or the Trentino : increased signs of an offensive astride the Brenta had also been noticed. On this evidence, General Diaz falsely assumed that the enemy's proposed attack across the Lower Piave had been abandoned, and he considered that the enemy should be struck while his reserves were still moving. To effect this, he proposed an attack from the French sector—against what he looked on as the weakest part of the Austrian line—to drive a wedge up the Val di Nos (east of Monte Sisemol), and then to enlarge the gap thus made both eastwards and westwards. At the same time, there being a possibility of this plan being forestalled by a hostile attack, he laid down that no movement of artillery from its present defensive positions should take place.

At 4 p.m. Lord Cavan went to see General Graziani, commanding the French Forces in Italy, and found that he was generally in favour of the above proposal, provided that his flanks were duly protected. Lord Cavan then went on to attend a conference at Sixth Army headquarters. Here General Montuori suggested that, immediately after the French attack near Monte Sisemol and a British attack over the Ghelpac on the 18th, the French should push forward to the northern edge of the Bosco di Gallio ($1\frac{1}{2}$ miles north-east of Asiago) and the British should capture Monte Catz ($1\frac{1}{2}$ miles north of Asiago). It will be remembered that on 27th May, when the Asiago offensive was definitely postponed, the three Italian divisions and guns attached to the British for this offensive had been withdrawn ; with only his own three British divisions under his command, Lord

Cavan considered that the advance to Monte Catz was impossible. After hearing his reasoned argument, General Montuori accepted this view and decided that, unless overruled by the Comando Supremo, the Anglo-French attack on the 18th should be limited to the objectives originally decided on, namely, Monte Sisemol, southern exits of Asiago, southern edge of Val d'Assa. On the 14th, British G.H.Q. received official notification from the Sixth Army that this limitation of the attack was agreed to by the Comando Supremo. In the event, all these Allied offensives were forestalled by the Austrian attack on 15th June.

Proposed Anglo-Italian Army

In April 1918 a proposal for an Anglo-Italian Army under a British commander was made in London.

On 2nd April 1918 Lord Cavan received a secret letter, dated 29th March, from the C.I.G.S. (Sir Henry Wilson) which discussed the question of an Anglo-Italian Army in Italy under a British commander. In his reply, Lord Cavan expressed the opinion that any such proposal would be treading on dangerous ground, owing to international jealousies. He thought that it would be very difficult to push through, and was not convinced that it would be possible to push it through at all. On 8th April the C.I.G.S. telegraphed a more definite plan : " Do you think a proposal
" as follows would be entertained by the Italians, viz., to
" form an Army under you of three corps, each of two
" Italian divisions and one British division ? I will put it
" forward if you think it would be entertained ". On 9th April Lord Cavan replied : " I do not think any proposal
" of reorganization should be made to the Italians till after
" offensive or some definite change of plan occurs. Mean-
" while will consult [Delmé] Radcliffe ".

On 10th April Lord Cavan wrote to the C.I.G.S. :

" I had a talk with Br.-General Delmé-Radcliffe last
" night on the subject of the possible formation of an
" Army of three corps, each corps to contain a British
" division. We agreed that it was quite impossible to
" propose any reorganization *now*, as all General Diaz's
" dispositions for meeting an attack or for taking the
" offensive are made. . . . I think that if the enemy

"attacks in the course of the next three weeks and we were successful in repulsing such attacks, the suggestion that I command an Army would, of course, carry more weight. At the same time I feel obliged to repeat my opinion that the question is one of great difficulty which may, if not most carefully handled, lead to misunderstanding and very probably will not be entertained by Comando Supremo".

On 28th April Lord Cavan wrote again to the C.I.G.S. as follows:

"After careful consideration I am of opinion that the difficulties in front of us are so great that it would be advisable to drop the proposal altogether. There are not sufficient divisions in Italy to justify the formation of a new Army. Therefore, if the plan were adopted, one of the existing Army commanders would have to be removed".

After discussing the difficulties which the removal of an Italian Army commander would entail, Lord Cavan went on to say:

"Before moving in the matter, I consider the French attitude should be ascertained, as we do not wish to disturb the excellent relations which at present exist between us. I hope it may never be thought that the suggestion originated with me".

When Lord Cavan wrote this letter he did not know that General Diaz was already aware of the proposal and looked upon it favourably. On 30th April the information was given to him by Br.-General Delmé-Radcliffe. Lord Cavan then wrote a further letter on the subject to the C.I.G.S., and the proposals then seem to have been dropped for the time being, as there are no more letters on the subject till October when, as will be seen, Lord Cavan was given an Army command by the Comando Supremo of its own volition.

CHAPTER XIV

THE AUSTRIAN PLANS FOR AN OFFENSIVE IN 1918[1]
(Sketch 7)

First Proposals

As soon as the prospects of the conclusion of peace by the Central Powers with Russia and Rumania became definite,[2] the Austrian High Command began to consider how best it might employ the divisions which would be freed by the cessation of hostilities on the Eastern Front. On 30th January 1918, before any sort of conclusion had been reached, Field-Marshal Conrad von Hötzendorf (commanding the *Trentino Group of Armies*) put forward a memorandum pointing out that the front between the Adige and the Piave was the decisive one,[3] and that every available man and gun should be employed there, if only to prevent the enemy from taking the offensive in that important sector; he maintained that the Italians dare not attempt to advance eastward across the Piave until they had created more elbow room in the north. General Diaz held the same views on that point, as we know.[4]

The Austrian High Command, established at Baden, near Vienna, was not at the moment ready to give a decision. Notwithstanding this, Conrad informed the Austrian *Eleventh Army* (General-Colonel Graf Scheuchenstuel)[5] that he had an attack between the Astico and the Piave in mind; and in the middle of February he wrote again to the High Command, giving his calculations, according to which he would require for this attack eighteen divisions in front line, and seven in second line: any other troops remaining should be employed to throw the Italians over the Sile (the old course of the Piave and west of that river), and roll up the Piave front northwards. He emphasized the possibilities

---
[1] Extracted from A.O.A. vii, pp. 186–211.
[2] The actual treaties were not signed until 3rd and 5th March, 1918, respectively.
[3] See Sketch 7.
[4] See p. 92.
[5] See Appendix VII for Austro-Hungarian Order of Battle.

of such a " pincer " attack; but again argued that the northern attack was the more important, as it would come down on the flank of the enemy's communications, whilst the Sile attack would only drive him back along them.

Field-Marshal Boroevic (commanding the *Piave Group of Armies*), on the other hand, had no offensive plans. He was in favour of letting the Germans finish the war on the Western Front, and of keeping the Austro-Hungarian army intact.

Gradually the idea of a decisive attack against Italy began to take form at Baden, and on 8th March the Operations Branch, under Lieut.-Colonel Ritter von Schilhawsky, put forward an appreciation on the basis that Austria would have 44 divisions against 72 Italian and Allied divisions, but that, in consequence of the impending German offensive (of 21st March) on the Western Front, the number of British and French divisions in Italy would soon be reduced. In discussing the best place for attack, the appreciation rejected the western and southern Trentino fronts altogether, and also the sector between the Astico and Asiago (included in Conrad's plan), as too difficult because the Italians had been fortifying it for over two years. The Operations Branch, favoured an attack on either side of the Brenta with the greater weight on the eastern bank; but it pointed out that in the M. Grappa area the Italians again had the advantage of defences elaborated in the course of two years.

In the sector of the *Sixth* (late *Fourteenth*) *Army*, a crossing of the Piave was regarded as having but indifferent prospects of success, on account of the strength of Monte Tomba and the Montello, and the exposure of the wide, pebbly bed of the river to enemy fire: Papadopoli Island appeared to offer the best place for attack, as the Piave in that reach was narrower, though deeper, with little water in it in summer.

In conclusion, a " pincer " attack from north and east simultaneously, as in Conrad's memorandum, was recommended, and, if all the available artillery was concentrated, it offered, it was thought, every chance of success.

The High Command's Plan

After the German offensive of 21st March had been launched, the Austrian High Command decided to go ahead with an offensive, and on the 23rd instructed Field-Marshal Conrad that he should proceed with the Asiago–Piave attack, as the main offensive, on both sides of the Brenta, with the "Bacchiglione area" as objective: he would be " powerfully supported by guns and trench-mortars (prin- " cipally gas shell) ", and should reach the foot of the mountains as soon as possible and force the Italians to abandon the Piave line. He was later on the same day ordered, at an appropriate time and in suitable force, to make an attack west of Lake Garda in the Tonale Pass area, " in " order to occupy important stretches of the Italian realm, " to threaten Lombardy, particularly Milan, and to shorten " our front ".[1]

Five days later, on 28th March, Field-Marshal Boroevic was informed of the orders sent to Conrad, and instructed that the *XV Corps*, the right of the *Sixth Army* (General-Colonel Archduke Joseph), should co-operate in the attack of the *Eleventh Army*. " The main attack [he was told] " will be between the Astico and the Piave, it will be " accompanied by a thrust of the *Isonzo Army* (General-" Colonel Freiherr von Wurm), against Treviso." In the distribution of forces from the Eastern Front, Conrad was to receive 5 divisions and 1 cavalry division, 3 mountain artillery regiments, etc., and a number of heavy Austrian batteries from the Western Front ; Boroevic was to receive 5 cavalry divisions, 4 field artillery brigades, etc. The transport of these reinforcements was to begin on 8th April and was expected to take fifty days. It later became known to Conrad and Boroevic that a general reserve of 4 divisions would be held between Belluno and Vittorio Veneto.[2]

Discussions

Conrad, on 1st April, pointed out that he required for the High Command's scheme 31 divisions and 3 cavalry divisions, allowing only 2 divisions, in addition to the

---

[1] Thus A.O.A. Arz p. 266, however, says that the reason for sending the 2 divisions west of Lake Garda was that " the Italians had recently " reinforced the troops on the western frontier of the Tirol ; this increased " the standing danger of an enemy inroad over the Tonale Pass, and " threatened the railway Bolzano-Trent, the life line of the defence of " the Tirol ". This seems evident, as a glance at the Frontispiece will show.

[2] For these places see the End-paper.

garrison (2 divisions and 2 independent brigades, etc.), for the Tonale enterprise ; thus, even after the reinforcements from the East had arrived, he would be 11 divisions and a cavalry division short. He deprecated the use of large forces on the Piave, as the attack there could only be a "secondary operation". In the end, he obtained 3 of the cavalry divisions earmarked for Boroevic.

In the latter's plan the *Isonzo Army* was to cross the Piave in the Papadopoli sector, with 2 divisions attacking lower down, and the *Sixth Army* (less *XV Corps*, which was allotted to assist Conrad) was to co-operate, "passing along "the southern foot of the Montello". Boroevic naturally objected to 3 cavalry divisions being taken from him for Conrad, and to 4 divisions being allotted to the general reserve, remarking that "reserves in being are worthless, "only those on the field are of value" : he required a minimum of 23 to 24 divisions, and had calculated on having $30\frac{1}{2}$: under the conditions of re-distribution, he would now have nothing with which to meet an emergency, which he characterized as "regrettable", as he considered the Piave offensive was the decisive affair. Each of the two commanders of the Groups of Armies not unnaturally held his operation to be the vital one, whilst the High Command now looked on the offensive as a "pincer" attack in which both thrusts were of perfectly equal value. So General Arz von Straussenburg allotted $23\frac{1}{2}$ divisions to each, the 4 divisions in the general reserve being included in the *Piave Group* ; for in view of the difficulties of transportation on the mountain front, no more troops could be effectively moved and supplied there. It was pointed out by the Archduke Joseph that to make both attacks of the same strength was unwise ; for one reason alone that if both were successful their inner flanks would collide, and an accumulation of force would thus occur where it would be of no value. If either of the two thrusts was made very strong, he said, it would as it penetrated ease the task of the other. General von Arz therefore decided to make the Piave attack the main one ; but it seems that Kaiser Karl favoured Conrad's bolder plan, and the result was a compromise.

Both field-marshals contested the final decision given on 21st April, both complaining of lack of reserves. Boroevic wrote on 9th May : "for an attack from two fronts the "necessary forces must not only be available but be corre-

"spondingly grouped. If the forces are not available, the "attack should be abandoned; for no one can foresee the "troubles which will ensue if an attack is made with insuffi- "cient forces. In my opinion, the forces on the South-West "[the Italian] front are sufficient, but they are wrongly "grouped".

The High Command, however, stuck to its plan, but reinforced Conrad further with 1 division and 3 field artillery brigades, and Boroevic with 1 division and 2 field artillery brigades "from the Hinterland"; as one division of the former's group and one infantry brigade of the latter's had to be broken up to bring other formations to reasonable strength, the gain was not great.

At the end of April, after Ludendorff's two offensives against the British had failed to bring about a decision, and "Italian troops had appeared in the Argonne, while the "British and French troops who went to Italy the previous "autumn had stayed there",[1] Ludendorff appealed to the Austrians for action of some sort.

Final Modifications

One change was made in the plan: Field-Marshal-Lieutenant Goiginger, the commander of the *XXIV Corps (Sixth Army)*, which was to skirt the southern edge of the Montello, protested that to do this was impossible with the enemy in possession of the hill, and he pointed out that to seize the hill was not difficult, as once over the Piave the attackers would be in dead ground as regards artillery fire. He desired, therefore, to gain possession of the Montello and move down to its southern edge and then accompany the main attack. The High Command replied on 1st June by ordering the Montello operation to be abandoned, and the *Sixth Army* to stand fast in its trenches, sending to the *Isonzo Army* all troops not required to hold its line. The 15th June having been fixed as Zero Day, Boroevic pointed out that there was little time left to transfer guns and bridging apparatus, etc., from the *Sixth Army*, and that the possession of the Montello was indispensable for the success of the *Isonzo Army*. After a little discussion, the plan of the *XXIV Corps*, to take the Montello, was allowed to stand.

---

[1] Ludendorff ii, p. 609.

The point that Conrad's attack would encounter the French and British contingents does not appear to have been touched on; in the statement of strengths in the Operations Branch's appreciation of 8th March it was assumed most of these divisions would have been withdrawn to France. Conrad in his detailed plan recognized, however, that " the centre of gravity lay on the Sette Comuni [Asiago] " plateau ", and he specially brought the *XIII Corps* headquarters (General Csanady) from the Adige sector to take command there, exchanging them with the *XXI*.

The *III Corps* of 5 divisions of the *Eleventh Army*, which was faced by the French 24th and the British 23rd Divisions was " on the first day to reach the southern edge of the " woods which extended from Asiago "; the attainment of this was regarded as all-important for the success of the *Eleventh Army*; " east of the Brenta any advance depended " on the rapid capture of Monte Grappa "; further progress, it was said, would depend on the action of the Allies; but the various stages forecast, with the left (eastern) wing leading in order to assist the *Isonzo Army*, are shown on the sketch;[1] that Army intended, with three corps on a narrow front, to make its main thrust towards Treviso.

Strategically, the plan was excellent, but the conception of " arm-chair " strategists; for the Austrians had neither the material means, nor the numbers to carry it out with any chance of success, and the ground both on the Piave and on the mountain front was against them.

Little care was exercised to prevent information of the offensive reaching the Italians: there was a constant stream of deserters; actually, shortly before the attack three Austrian officers entered the British lines, accompanied by their servants carrying their portmanteaux. Apart from this source of leakage, overhearing of the Austrian field telephone provided detailed information, so that the most minute particulars of the bombardment and assault across the Piave were in the hands of the Comando Supremo before 15th June.[2]

The Austrian account sums up as regards numbers: " altogether the Italian Army, including the French and " British reinforcements, totalled 725 battalions, about 100

---

[1] Sketch 7.
[2] General the Hon. Sir J. F. Gathorne-Hardy, *Army Quarterly*, October, 1921.

" squadrons, 7,550 guns and 524 aircraft. Against this force,
" the Austro-Hungarian South-West Front sent 642
" battalions, about 8,700 machine guns, 73 half-regiments
" of cavalry, 53 squadrons, 6,833 guns and 280 aircraft."

NOTE

The Opposing Forces

The following Tables give the Total Forces available
to the Austrian and Italian Commanders on the
Italian Front

AUSTRIAN TROOPS ON ITALIAN FRONT ON 15TH JUNE 1918

Armies	Inf. Divs.	Cav. Divs.	Artillery			
			Mountain & Field Guns	Medium & Heavy Guns	A.A. Guns	Total Guns
Tenth	7 (a)	—	1,021	269	70	1,360
Eleventh	21	3	2,256	573	106	2,935
Sixth	3	2	556	142	70	768
Isonzo	12 (b)	2	1,302	352	116	1,770
G.H.Q. Reserve	4	1	—	—	—	—
Totals	47	8	5,135	1,336	362	6,833

(a) Counting two independent brigades as one division.
(b) Plus one *Landsturm* regiment, not included in a division in the XVI Corps.

ALLIED TROOPS ON ITALIAN FRONT ON 15TH JUNE 1918

Armies	Inf. Divs.	Cav. Divs.	Artillery
			guns
Seventh	6	—	2,339
First	9	—	
Sixth	10	—	1,214
Fourth	8	—	881
Eighth	4	—	744
Third	7	—	1,273
Ninth (c)	10	4	567
(G.H.Q. Reserve)			
A.A. Guns	—	—	524
Totals	54	4	7,542 (d)

(c) G.H.Q. Reserve was administered by Ninth Army, but its troops could only be used by order of G.H.Q.
(d) Of the total of 7,542 guns, 3,478 were mountain and field guns, 3,540 were medium and heavy guns, 524 were anti-aircraft guns.

CHAPTER XV

THE BATTLE OF ASIAGO, 15TH-16TH JUNE 1918[1]
(Map I; Sketches 7, 8)

Situation on the Morning of 15th June 1918
Influenza; The Opposing Forces

The Austrian plan[2] produced four attacks. First, on 13th June, came an attack by part of the Archduke Peter Ferdinand's Group against the Tonale Pass; then, on 15th June, two attacks from north to south between the Adige and the Piave by the *Eleventh Army*, with the centres of gravity at Asiago and Monte Grappa; and, fourthly, also on the 15th, an attack from east to west by the *Isonzo Army* (extended on the right by a corps of the *Sixth Army*), across the Piave, from the Montello (inclusive) to the sea, with the centre of gravity at Papadopoli Island.

It may be said at once that the Tonale offensive, carried out by 2 divisions, was a complete failure: " the enterprise, " from which important gain of ground and the holding of " strong enemy forces was expected, collapsed on the first " day ".[3] The attack immediately east of the Brenta in the Monte Grappa sector had small success. There 5 Austrian divisions attacked 7 Italian. A little ground, as much as a mile at one place, was gained, but nearly all of it was lost by counter-attack, and the Austrians made no further effort to advance.[4]

In the Asiago offensive, ground was won from the Italians and, temporarily for a few hours until regained by counter-attack, from the British. It is with this last action that

---

[1] For the Italian and British Orders of Battle see Appendices V and II.
  The official name of this engagement is " The Fighting on the Asiago " Plateau ", but the battle-honour " Piave " was awarded for it. The Italian nomenclature, " The Third Battle of the Piave ", includes the operations on the river and in the mountains. The Austrian Official Account calls the battle, " The Last Attack of the Austro-Hungarian Army ". It has seemed best to call it by the name by which it is known to the British troops who took part in it, more than thirty miles away from the nearest point of the Piave.
[2] See Sketch 7.
[3] See A.O.A. viii, p. 232.
[4] On Map I the western half, and on Map II the eastern half of the final gain is shown.

BRITISH DISPOSITIONS. 15TH JUNE   195

this chapter is mainly concerned.[1] The Piave offensive met with initial success, but the weight behind the blow proved insufficient to carry it through—something more will be said about it later.[2]

The British front on 15th June was held by the 23rd Division (New Army) and the 48th (1st South Midland T.F.) Division, each with a frontage of about four thousand yards. Both divisional commanders were officers of considerable experience, Major-General Sir J. M. Babington having commanded the 23rd Division since 18th September 1914, and Major-General R. Fanshawe, the 48th Division since 31st May 1915; so that both had fought at the Somme and at Third Ypres. The 7th Division (Major-General T. H. Shoubridge, in command since April 1917) was resting in the Trissino area, on the edge of the plains, some twenty-five miles from the front, with 2 battalions of the 91st Brigade in the mountains to provide working parties to assist the heavy artillery, and the two other battalions close up at the foot of the mountains. All 3 divisions were short of reinforcements and, in addition, both front-line divisions were suffering from the influenza epidemic and were very considerably below establishment. The 48th, which had come back into the line on 31st May, was weaker than the 23rd, which had returned twelve days earlier and had largely got over the trouble. Some 800 cases were admitted to hospital on the 13th and 14th, and 1,500 had already been evacuated, although light cases were not sent away. Of the headquarters staff at one time, only Major-General Fanshawe and the Intelligence Officer were at duty, and G.H.Q. had to send up staff officers to help. Two of the three infantry brigadiers were away, and 6 of the 12 infantry battalions were on 15th June commanded by majors.[3]

---

[1] See Map I for the battleground as a whole and Sketch 8 for the details of the British sector.
[2] See Chapter XVI.
[3] The figures of the actual fighting strengths are not available. In the 144th Brigade the average company strength of the 4 battalions, instead of 250, was, 1/4th Gloucestershire, 70; 1/6th Gloucestershire, 75; 1/7th Worcestershire, 65; 1/8th Worcestershire, 85. The average battalion fighting strength of the 48th Division was 491; but these strengths were still further reduced by men still with their units but affected by influenza (48th Division, p. 70).
The 1/5th Gloucestershire of the 145th Brigade had a strength of about 400, and was so weak that the brigadier had hesitated whether or no it

Continued at foot of next page

H

The 24 infantry battalions of the 2 divisions were distributed in depth, as will be seen from the map.[1] Eight were in front line (an average of 1,145 yards per battalion) ; 6 were in or near the second line ; 3, with the engineer field companies and the pioneer battalions, were near the two divisional headquarters at Granezza and Carriola ;[2] 4 were in the reserve line ; and 3, on account of lack of accommodation, at the foot of the mountains.[3] The doctrine of defence taught at the schools, for the benefit of the Italians, was that the front line should not be held too strongly, and that any trench lost should be recovered by counter-attack ; and the counter-attack had been rehearsed by each battalion as, in turn, it went into brigade reserve.

G.H.Q. were at Lonedo, $4\frac{1}{2}$ miles south of Granezza, and connected to it by the best of the zig-zag roads and by telephone line.

In view of the offensive arranged for 18th June, the artillery of the 7th (the resting) Division had been brought up into the line on the 12th and 13th,[4] so that the front had the support of the artillery of 3 divisions, that is 6 brigades, each of three 18-pdr. batteries and one 4.5 inch howitzer battery.[5] The guns were mostly in the woods behind the ridge marked by M. Torle–M. Kaberlaba–M. Magnaboschi, and behind M. Lemerle ; but, in view of the projected offensive, a number of batteries, all those of the 7th Division, had been pushed forward, and some, as will be seen in the narrative of the battle, were as close as a hundred yards to the front line.[6]

Continued from previous page

should take its turn in the line ; the 1/6th and 1/7th Warwickshire, with " fighting strengths " of 379 and 380 respectively, were not in the line.

The 5/R. Sussex (pioneers), with a strength of 900, in camp south of M. Carriola, numbered on the day of battle barely 300 (inclusive of sick awaiting evacuation) as a result of the influenza epidemic.

[1] Map I.

[2] Here used instead of its official name, " Monte Carriola Camp ".

[3] The French had 4 battalions on their short frontage of 3,300 yards, and their supports and reserves were closer up. See Map I. The French dispositions are taken from F.O.A. vi (ii), Carte 23.

[4] One battery, recalled from the G.H.Q. School, did not come into action until the 16th.

[5] C.R.A. 7th Division, Br.-General H. C. Stanley-Clarke ; C.R.A. 23rd Division, Br.-General Sir D. Arbuthnot ; C.R.A. 48th Division, Br.-General W. Strong.

[6] One battery of the XXXV Brigade R.F.A. had not completed its pits, and the guns were not up.

BRITISH DISPOSITIONS. 15TH JUNE

The heavy artillery consisted of 5 British brigades R.G.A. (the XV, XXIV, LXXX, XCIV and 104th), a total of 25 batteries.[1] Under Br.-General T. R. C. Hudson, commanding it, were also three Italian *Raggruppamenti* (the 41st, 42nd and 68th), with a total of 19 batteries, and 8 batteries of heavy mortars. All batteries of heavy artillery in reserve had been brought up between the nights of the 11th/12th and 14th/15th and others moved forward in readiness for the offensive. Of the total 44 batteries, 21 (the XV and XCIV Brigades, and the Italian 41st and half of the 68th) were detailed for counter-battering, leaving 23 and the 8 Italian mortar batteries for bombardment.

In view, too, of the offensive, a number of dumps of ammunition, stores and supplies had been formed near the front, some even half across No Man's Land. The main artillery dump was at Handley Cross, a cross-roads east of " Magnaboschi ", a collection of huts near Monte Magnaboschi and therefore called by its name.

The general nature of the British sector has already been described.[2] It remains only to point out that, starting from the right, the front line ran for over two thousand yards just inside the pine woods, at the foot of the slope, then crossed a clearing of about a thousand yards, and for the last five hundred yards of the 23rd Division's sector, was in the woods again. In the 48th Division's sector it ran for about a mile through the woods, which in places extended well into No Man's Land, emerging into treeless but broken country and following the south side of the Ghelpac ravine, the last thousand yards being again in woods.

Opposite the 2 British divisions were arrayed 5 Austro-Hungarian divisions.[3] An observant British officer who

---

[1] Twenty had four 6-inch howitzers ; 4, four 60-pdrs. and 1 a 9.2-inch howitzer.

[2] See Chapter XIII.

[3] According to A.O.A. vii, Map XV.

For the Order of Battle of the Austrian *Eleventh Army*, see Appendix VII. From east to west : in front line were *38th Honved Division, 52nd Division* and *6th Division*. In second line were *74th Honved* and *28th Divisions*. Opposite the French were *16th Division* and one regiment of *42nd Honved Division*, with *5th Division* in second line. It appears, however, that some of the *16th Division* and of *42nd Honved* drifted westward in the mist towards the British right front, perhaps to get the shelter of the woods, just as on the British front itself many Austrians from the 68th Brigade front drifted over open ground to the woods on the 145th Brigade front ; prisoners from these formations were captured. The Italians on the left of the British, where their X Corps was faced by a cavalry division, were not attacked.

was taken prisoner stated subsequently that the Austro-Hungarians were not badly clad and certainly not half-starved, as has since been put forward as excuse for defeat. "They were excited, and some of them seemed, not drunk " but having drink taken, which probably accounts for the " stories of the confusion in their ranks. The support " troops assembled in the ravines just behind the Austrian " front line seemed to be definitely inferior and unused to " shell-fire; they ducked whenever one of 'ours' came " within four hundred yards of them ".

Warnings of an Enemy Offensive

" On 13th and 14th June the Italian Intelligence received " [what it believed to be] precise information of the im-" pending Austrian attack : on the 13th the hour and the " duration of the preparatory bombardment were still " doubtful, but on the 14th both one and the other became " precise ".[1]

The Armies were at once informed. On the morning of the 14th Lord Cavan summoned his divisional commanders to a conference and told them that the attack would take place next day, that the information was very precise, and according to it the British front was expected to be outside the western limit of the infantry attack, which would end with the French area:[2] meantime, the offensive for which all were preparing was, for the present, "off".

The information was passed on at divisional conferences held in the afternoon, with the warning that, though the Austrian infantry might not attack, the bombardment, which would probably include gas shelling, would be likely to extend to the British sector. The Defence Scheme was then reviewed. That night all slept in their clothes, hoping for the best and expecting the worst.

Local confirmation of the impending assault was not lacking. At nightfall an Austrian deserter came over and said there would be an attack at dawn ; and at 1.30 a.m. a patrol of the 1/4th Oxford & Buckinghamshire L.I., on the right of the 48th Division, captured an Hungarian

---

[1] Caviglia's Piave, p. 67.
[2] The Austrians had attacked this sector, then held by Italians, on 10th November 1917 without success. See pp. 85-86.

prisoner, who by signs indicated that an attack would begin with bombardment at 3 a.m. On the other hand, patrols farther west met no one, and the front seemed exceptionally quiet.

The Enemy Bombardment

At 3 a.m., just as it was getting light, the bombardment, with gas, shrapnel and H.E., even armour-piercing shell, opened from every calibre of gun against the whole British front system, battery positions, divisional and brigade headquarters and other centres, including the ammunition dump at Handley Cross, which caught fire, and the explosions of its shells seriously hampered the movement of reinforcements to the 48th Division front. Some enemy shells cleared the mountains altogether and fell on the plain. The first that Major-Generals Babington and Fanshawe knew of the storm at hand was the falling of 8-inch shells around their headquarters. It was at first thought to be merely a demonstration. It was the subsequent opinion of artillerymen that the bombardment was " unregistered " and not a success. It is now known that a number of the Austrian batteries had advanced into position only a few hours before the bombardment opened and had had no opportunity to register. The Austrian fire was certainly very dispersed, and it had neither the volume nor the accuracy that the troops had been accustomed to on the Western Front in 1917. On the other hand, the noise was increased by reverberation in the mountains, and the heavy shells threw masses of rock in all directions and brought down trees on the heads of the defenders. Respirators had to be worn at times ; but the gas was so disguised by the smell of burning pines that it was difficult to detect. All forward telephone cables were soon cut one by one ; a shell put the wireless station of the right brigade of the 48th Division out of action ; and soon after the Austrian assault the power-buzzers in use to connect battalion headquarters to the brigades ceased to work ; but wireless from divisional headquarters to the left brigade continued to function all day. At 3.20 a.m. G.H.Q. telephoned to the divisions to withdraw their outposts, and informed the artillery that " counter-preparation " (meaning no doubt the " defensive " barrage ") could start within the outpost line at 5 a.m., thus giving the outposts about two hours to come in. These messages got through, and the outposts were withdrawn, but in place of them piquets and a few well-placed machine guns were left out beyond the wire.[1]

At 3.30 a.m. Br.-General A. E. Wardrop, in command of all the artillery, ordered counter-preparation beyond the outpost line,[2] and at 5 a.m. the defensive barrage. Conditions for observation could hardly have been worse, as at first there was a thick ground mist which reduced visibility to nearly nothing; it cleared a little during the day, but never disappeared altogether; so runners, and cyclists when possible, became the main means of communication even for the artillery.

Battery commanders, therefore, had to a great extent to act on their own initiative, and as the day went on took advantage of opportunities whenever there was a temporary break in the mist; when no observation was possible they fired on S.O.S. lines or against pre-arranged targets. On the whole, "it was a great day for the counter-battery "groups",[3] for concealed positions were few on the Asiago plateau, and daylight when it came revealed enemy batteries in the open, which were quickly put out of action by the 6-inch howitzers. In the early part of the day the ground mist and low cloud prevented regular air observation, but in the occasional breaks the R.A.F. was able to give a few useful targets. In the afternoon the weather for flying became so bad in the mountains that the three squadrons were diverted to help the Italians on the Piave, which the Austrians were crossing and where flying conditions were better.

The Beginning of the Infantry Assault

At 4 a.m., there being still doubt of the enemy's intention to assault, but none of the seriousness of the bombardment,

---

[1] There was evidently some misunderstanding at G.H.Q. It had been decided at a conference in April that the outposts must be withdrawn before a "defensive barrage" was put down. The action of the artillery at this period was divided into two stages: first, "counter-preparation" which included counter-battery work, and bombardment concentrated on the enemy's probable areas of assembly; and, secondly, the "defence barrage", that is the dropping of a curtain of fire close in front of the front line when the enemy advanced from his assembly areas to assault.

[2] The French, who expected an infantry attack, began their counter-battering at 11.45 p.m. on the 14th.

[3] See *The Journal of the Royal Artillery*, July 1921, p. 149.

THE AUSTRIAN ASSAULT. 15TH JUNE 201

G.H.Q. telegraphed to the 7th Division, in reserve, ordering it to be ready to move at two hours' notice from 5 a.m. Then, at 7 a.m., the Austrian infantry was seen to be close on the wire, cutting it with heavy shears and pushing in the equivalent of Bangalore torpedoes; against the wooded salients of the front, they used flame-projectors.[1]

The Battle of Asiago was a battalion commanders' and soldiers' battle, and not only a battle in the clouds and mist like Chattanooga, but also a battle in the woods. What happened, therefore, can only be pieced together, and the exact relation in time of events, even in adjoining battalion sectors, is not always certain. In outline, from right to left of the mountain front, its features were that between the Piave and the Brenta in the area containing M. Tomba, M. Grappa and M. Asolone[2] the Austrians gained no ground whatever from the Italian Fourth Army, except a small salient, about a mile wide and seven hundred yards deep, in the woods near the Brenta. West of that river they broke in on the whole front of the Italian XIII Corps between the gorge of the Brenta and the French sector, to a depth varying from a mile to two miles on a frontage of $3\frac{1}{2}$ miles. Against the French, whose front line, except a short piece on the extreme left, was in the open, nothing was accomplished. It is claimed by the Austrian official history that the curious salient, called Capitello Pennar,[3] was captured, but this had been evacuated previously in accordance with the defence scheme, and the French were able to bring effective assistance to the Italians, on their right, who had been driven back. In the front of the British 23rd Division, the enemy penetrated the extreme flanks, but by 2 p.m. the right of the line had been re-established by a counter-attack, and the left was recovered somewhat later; the rest of the division held its line. The front of the 48th Division was broken into at several places, one at the junction with the 23rd Division, with the general result that the right battalion was driven back two hundred yards, and the centre battalion, the weak 1/5 Gloucestershire, gave ground at one point about a thousand yards. Part of the lost ground was recovered by a counter-attack beginning

---

[1] After the action 15 of these weapons were found, with a few British dead who had been burnt to death.
[2] See Sketch 7.
[3] See Sketch 8.

at 2 p.m., and the whole of the rest by another counter-attack at 4.30 a.m. on the 16th. Disheartened at the failure to break through, the Austrians had earlier abandoned the contest. The details of the conflict follow.

The Assault on the 23rd Division
It Holds Its Ground

The 23rd Division had the 70th and 68th Brigades (Br.-Generals H. Gordon and C. D. V. Cary-Barnard) in the line, the former with the 11/Sherwood Foresters and 9/York & Lancaster in the front trenches and the 8/York & Lancaster in support in the second line; and the latter with the 13/Durham L.I., the 12/Durham L.I. and the 11/Northumberland Fusiliers, in the front line, finding their own supports. They were supported by their own artillery, the 102nd and 103rd Brigades R.F.A., and by the XXII Brigade R.F.A. of the 7th Division. Both infantry brigade headquarters were behind the second line, and each brigade had one battalion, the 8/K.O.Y.L.I. and the 10/Northumberland Fusiliers, respectively, in reserve, some half a mile in rear of headquarters. The machine-gun companies and brigade trench-mortar companies were distributed in and behind the two lines.

The Austrian assault on the 23rd Division by 4½ regiments[1] struck the left about 7 a.m. and the right about a quarter of an hour later. The French 108th Regiment, next to the British, held its own successfully, and the 9/York & Lancaster, the second battalion from the right, brought the enemy to a standstill by gun, rifle and machine-gun fire a hundred yards from its line, and held its position intact throughout the day. The Sherwood Foresters, on the right, whose line ran north-east and south-west, near the edge of the woods, were enfiladed by gun-fire from the north-east; all the officers of the right company and many men became casualties, and the enemy succeeded in taking about a hundred and fifty yards of the front trench, and then gradually advanced to the long knoll, known as the S. Sisto ridge, about five hundred yards to the south. Here a company in support held a thousand yards of trench with four posts, between two of which, about 8.30 a.m., the

---

[1] *Nos. 24, 21* and *22 Honved,* the *26th* and half the *6th.*

Austrians penetrated. Lieut.-Colonel C. E. Hudson, commanding the battalion, at his headquarters at the south foot of the knoll, on learning this, at once formed his headquarters party and a few Italian trench-mortar gunners for counter-attack and, leading them himself, drove the enemy off the knoll. He then went forward with five men to the front line and, revolver in hand, called on the Austrians there to surrender, which some of them at once did by putting their hands up. As an Austrian officer came forward to surrender, one of his men threw a bomb, killing him and severely wounding Lieut.-Colonel Hudson; but, rolling over into a trench, the latter continued to give instructions for the counter-attack to go on and recover the whole of the lost trenches. Meantime, Br.-General Gordon had ordered up a company of the 8/K.O.Y.L.I., his reserve, to reinforce the Sherwood Foresters, and about 1 p.m. it attacked along the trenches by bombing and, after some fighting, retook all that had been lost, capturing about a hundred prisoners and six machine guns, so that by 2 p.m. the front of the 70th Brigade was again intact; and it remained so.[1]

The three battalions of the 68th Brigade in the front line were supported by the 103rd Brigade R.F.A., which had one gun destroyed and three put out of action by the bombardment. They had an open field of fire in front of them, and when, in the poor visibility, the Austrians came into sight, they brought them to a halt by gun, rifle and machine-gun fire, and, in spite of the enemy's gallantry, only ten men succeeded in reaching the front line and these were either killed or captured. By 9.45 a.m., the enemy had abandoned attempts to advance, and except on the left no further attacks took place, though movement in No Man's Land, where many enemy troops were sheltering in broken ground, often gave good targets for rifle, machine-gun and artillery.

From the first, here and elsewhere, the Austrian infantry had little direct support from artillery after the bombardment ceased at 7 a.m.; but shelling of the second line and rearward establishments continued, and in the afternoon the Cesuna Switch received attention.

On the left flank of the 68th Brigade where the 11/Northumberland Fusiliers stood, the enemy had at-

---

[1] Lieut.-Colonel C. E. Hudson, D.S.O., M.C., was awarded the V.C. for his "high courage and determination", which saved a serious situation.

tacked strongly, and at the same time had fallen on the right of the adjoining battalion, the 1/4th Oxford L.I. of the 48th Division. There about 8 a.m. he had broken through. The Northumberland promptly formed a defensive flank towards the Boscon Switch, and sent out patrols[1] to gather information and keep the Austrians at a distance. After some hard fighting, they succeeded in preventing the enemy from exploiting his success eastward. One company of the 10/Northumberland Fusiliers, in brigade reserve, with three machine guns and two companies of the 8/York & Lancaster of the 69th Brigade from the second line, were sent during the morning to reinforce this flank. Thus reinforced, the 11/Northumberland Fusiliers, which suffered 104 casualties, a fifth of its strength, held its ground.

The Assault on the 48th Division. A Pocket Made in its Front

The 48th Division, supported by its own 240th and 241st Brigades, R.F.A. and the XXXV Brigade of the 7th Division, was better prepared to meet the attack than the 23rd Division ; for, thanks to the warning obtained from the Hungarian prisoner, some of its rearward units had been brought up into their battle positions. It had the 145th Brigade (Lieut.-Colonel L. L. C. Reynolds, 1/1st Buckinghamshire, in temporary command) and the 143rd Brigade (Br.-General G. C. Sladen) in the line. The former had put two battalions

---

[1] The leader of one of these patrols 2nd Lieut. John Scott Youll, was awarded the V.C. The full citation is :

"For most conspicuous bravery and devotion to duty during enemy "attacks when in command of a patrol, which came under the hostile "barrage. Sending his men back to safety, he remained to observe the "situation. Unable subsequently to rejoin his company, 2nd Lieut. Youll "reported to a neighbouring unit, and when the enemy attacked he "maintained his position with several men of different units until the "troops on his left had given way and an enemy machine gun had opened "fire from behind him. He rushed the gun and, having killed most of "the team, opened fire on the enemy with the captured gun, inflicting "heavy casualties. Then, finding that the enemy had gained a footing "in a portion of the front line, he organized and carried out with a few "men three separate counter-attacks. On each occasion he drove back "the enemy, but was unable to maintain his position by reason of reverse "fire. Throughout the fighting his complete disregard of personal safety "and very gallant leading set a magnificent example to all".

He was killed in action on 27th October 1918 at the crossing of the Piave, at the age of 20.

1/4th Oxford L.I. and 1/5th Gloucestershire (Lieut.-Colonel A. J. N. Bartlett and Major N. H. Waller) into the front position, and since 4 a.m. the 1/1st Buckinghamshire (Major P. A. Hall) had been in its battle position in Lemerle Switch and Polderhoek Trench. Brigade headquarters were at the south side of M. Lemerle, and the fourth battalion, 1/4th R. Berkshire, was in brigade reserve at Carriola. In the 143rd Brigade, one battalion the 1/5th R. Warwickshire (Major E. A. M. Blindloss) held the whole of the front position, about 2,500 yards, with the 1/6th and 1/8th R. Warwickshire (Lieut.-Colonel W. M. Pryor and Major P. H. Whitehouse) in brigade reserve, 5,000 and 3,000 yards behind respectively, at M. Pau and M. del Busibollo; but at 4.45 a.m. Br.-General Sladen ordered the 1/8th to its battle position in the Cesuna Switch and the 1/6th to come forward to his headquarters, a mile south-west of Cesuna. The 1/7th R. Warwickshire (Lieut.-Colonel J. M. Knox) was in divisional reserve at Handley Cross.

When, about 7 a.m., the Austrians attacked,[1] after hand-to-hand fighting in the mist, they broke through the front of the 48th Division at four places by sheer weight of numbers, which are generally decisive in wood fighting. These places were: one on the right flank of the 1/4th Oxford L.I., at its junction with the 23rd Division, and three on the front of the 1/5th Gloucestershire: at its junction with the 1/4th Oxford L.I., on its right front, and on its left flank near the junction with the 1/5th R. Warwickshire.

The first news of the assault reached 48th Division headquarters by means of the 143rd Brigade wireless at 8 a.m. There was little that the divisional commander could do, as all other means of communication, except by runners, had failed, and the woods between his headquarters and the front were under continuous shell fire. From the look-out over the battlefield the noise of fighting could be heard below but nothing seen. Major-General Fanshawe was sure that all units knew the parts they should play, and by sending up officers to the brigade headquarters, he learnt as much as they knew of the situation, and then despatched to them such reinforcements as he could. Eventually, he was able

---

[1] Six and a half regiments: half *6th*, *12th*, *74th*, *27th*, *17th*, *127th* and *81st*. No less than 7 battalions were identified on the front of the 1/4th Oxford L.I.

to order a counter-attack with artillery support. The headquarters of the 145th Brigade, on the southern side of M. Lemerle, where there were also the headquarters of several artillery units, and of the 1/1st Buckinghamshire and of 3 of its companies, came in for a long bombardment, and their members had to take cover in a cave.

By 9 a.m. the 1/4th Oxford L.I., with 3 companies in the front position, hard pressed on both flanks, had been forced to abandon the front trench, and the 35th (H.) Battery of the XXII Brigade (7th Division) and A/102[1] (23rd Division, but in the 48th Division area) only a hundred yards behind the front, were lost, but later recovered undamaged. Major D. R. C. Hartley, M.C., of the former battery, after shooting the leading Austrian with his revolver, with the aid of some of his n.c.os. armed with rifles, and others, from a hundred yards' range, prevented the pits being occupied. The guns of the 104th and 105th Batteries (XXII Brigade), also close up, were withdrawn in time, their pits being used as machine-gun posts. The Oxfordshire occupied a line some hundred and fifty to two hundred yards back, round Hill 1021 (near Pelly Cross), with the right thrown southwards and the left at a bridge over the Asiago light railway. Here, with the help of occasional counter-attacks led by the head-quarters company, they held on. Although about midday Austrians appeared behind the left, their further progress southwards was stopped by the 1/1st Buckinghamshire in the Lemerle Switch. A further withdrawal of the left was then made from the railway bridge to a small ridge in the neighbourhood of battalion headquarters, which was in a sunken road five hundred yards behind the front line.

The battalion now held a semi-circular line, the left of it manned by clerks, cooks, orderlies, servants and everyone who could use a rifle. Both flanks were open, as connection could not be gained with the 11/Northumberland Fusiliers on the right, or with the 1/1st Buckinghamshire, in Lemerle Switch, behind the left. To fill the former gap, Major-General Fanshawe instructed the C.R.E., Lieut.-Colonel E. Briggs to send up the 477th Field Company R.E. to Boscon Switch, with instructions to get in touch with the left of the 23rd Division; but it did not succeed in doing so, as that

---

[1] That is " A " Battery of the 102nd Brigade.

flank was refused. About noon a leading company of the 1/4th R. Berkshire, sent off from brigade reserve at 8.40 a.m., reinforced the Oxfordshire, and the battalion retained its position for the rest of the day, in spite of the enemy having brought up machine guns to within two hundred yards.[1]

The first break in the 48th Division's front had occurred on the extreme left of the 1/5th Gloucestershire, which was wholly in the woods and on a slight ridge.[2] Here two posts had been obliterated by the bombardment and a gap left, and about 7.30 a.m. the Austrians were found to be advancing in large numbers through this entry, sweeping into the valley behind the battalion, and cutting all communications with the front.

The left company (D) was overwhelmed—as was also its western neighbour, the right company of the 1/5th R. Warwickshire—although one post at least held out till midday—and soon the enemy appeared on the front and flanks of the support company, which had a line of Lewis gun posts strung out along a track about five hundred yards behind the front. This line was gradually overcome, although a battery of heavy trench mortars did tremendous havoc among the bunched enemy, and the survivors of the two companies of the Gloucestershire, only 3 officers and 37 other ranks strong, dropped back southward to the Cesuna Switch. There they found a company of the 1/5th R. Warwickshire in posts supported by two 4.5-inch howitzers of D/240 in pits, which they helped the gunners to pull out so that they could fire over open sights. By this means they checked the enemy's further advance until their position was enfiladed from the left by a machine gun in Guardiana. This was knocked out by a gun of the 12th Battery (XXXV Brigade) of the 7th Division, which, covered by a detachment with rifles led by Major C. Jardine, had been man-handled down the woody slope of M. Lemerle to stop the enemy's advance in the open ground around Cesuna, and, reinforced by the brigade headquarters party under Lieut.-Colonel H. Oldham, had succeeded in doing so.

---

[1] The day's fighting cost the 1/4th Oxfordshire L.J. 6 officers and 42 other ranks killed, 2 and 92 wounded and 34 missing. Total 176, out of 552 (less influenza cases) with the battalion.

[2] It had A, B (lately outpost) and D Companies in front line, and C in support.

Meantime, a little after 10 a.m., the right company (A) of the 1/5th Gloucestershire, and the outpost company (B) which had come in unhindered, their right already broken by the attack which struck the left of the 1/4th Oxford L.I., were driven out of the trenches by a strong attack by large numbers of Austrians who had crowded into the woods; the survivors retired up-hill to the Lemerle Switch, but some of B Company were collected in the Cesuna Switch. Pressure on the battalion now declined as a result, it is believed, of the Austrians discovering rum and other supplies in the quartermaster's stores at battalion headquarters.[1]

Next on the west, where the 1/5th R. Warwickshire was holding the whole front of the 143rd Brigade with D and B Companies in the front trenches and the other two in support, D was overpowered, as already noticed, at the same time as the left of the 1/5th Gloucestershire, for it was impossible to cover with fire the slope in front, strewn with broken rock and shrub, which ran down to the Ghelpac. The field batteries, ready for the offensive about a hundred yards behind the front, were also overrun. The left company, however, whose field of fire was less obstructed and whose view in fact commanded nearly the whole valley of the Ghelpac, had no difficulty in maintaining its position, and did considerable execution among the enemy by dropping Stokes mortar bombs into Ghelpac ravine and the gulleys and steep approaches from it. Its security was assured by the G.O.C. of the Italian 12th Division, on its left, offering assistance in any form, in particular suggesting that he should take over eight hundred yards of the extreme left. The offer was accepted, and it enabled more men of the company to be held ready for counter-attack. In trying to discover and report the situation of D Company, Major E. A. M. Blindloss, the acting commanding officer whose headquarters were behind this company, and his intelligence officer, were killed, and the adjutant taken prisoner. In this critical situation, the regimental sergeant-major, R. Townley, took command of battalion headquarters. With a party of thirteen men, pioneers, cooks and orderlies, he made a stubborn defence among the headquarter huts and held

---

[1] The 1/5th Gloucestershire lost on this day: killed 4 officers and 24 other ranks; wounded 7 and 64; missing 6 and 114; well over 50 per cent. of its strength.

the Austrian attack for six hours until relief came from the brigade reserve.[1] The left company also continued to stand fast, and was able to inflict heavy losses upon the Austrian supports and carriers crossing No Man's Land. The two support companies, ignorant of the situation and, owing to the casualties among the regimental staff, receiving no orders, organized the defence of the Cesuna Switch, and made this side of the Austrian penetration safe.

The Situation of the 48th Division About Midday

Thus the situation as midday approached was, that, on the right, the 1/4th Oxford L.I., on a semi-circular front was standing fast, not in touch with the 23rd Division on the right, which had formed a defensive flank facing west, so that what had been the junction of the two divisions had become two sides of a gap, into which the enemy did not care to press. On the west of this gap, were the 477th Field Company R.E. and then the 1/1st Buckinghamshire and the bulk of the remnants of the 1/5th Gloucestershire in the Lemerle Switch and its continuation, Polygon Trench. Between these troops and the garrison of the Cesuna Switch (most of the 1/5th R. Warwickshire, and a few of the 1/5th Gloucestershire) was another gap—in which ran the rack railway—and beyond this was a company of the 1/6th R. Warwickshire—sent up as the result of a very useful reconnaissance made by Captain H. A. Linfoot of that battalion—serving to connect with the left company of the 1/5th R. Warwickshire, still in the line. But, hidden as the troops were by the pine woods and mist, the exact situation was not known either to the enemy's command or to the headquarters of the 48th Division; both knew that the Austrian troops were advancing towards Lemerle Switch and Polygon Trench, but neither knew that about noon, or soon after, all Austrian attempts to push on had come to an end, although opposed by only small scattered parties.[2]

---

[1] R.S.M. Townley was awarded the D.C.M.
[2] Actually, according to A.O.A. vii, p. 244, it was learnt afterwards that about midday No. 74 Infantry Regiment (52nd Division), opposite the 1/4th Oxford L.I. " retired in panic ", No. 26 (of the same division), opposite the left of the 23rd Division, " flinched (gewankt) and took the " neighbouring portions of the 38th Honved Division with it ".

About 8.30 a.m. Major-General Fanshawe had heard by wireless from the 143rd Brigade that the Austrians had taken a large portion of the front line and that they were pushing on through the woods against Lemerle Switch and Polygon Trench. He thereupon warned Lieut.-Colonel F. M. Tomkinson (1/7th Worcestershire), commanding the 144th Brigade, the reserve, and took the first steps to fill the gaps which he guessed must exist. He ordered Lieut.-Colonel Tomkinson to bring up by lorry his two rearmost battalions, the 1/4th Gloucestershire (Major E. Shellard) and the 1/7th Worcestershire (Major J. P. Bate), which were at the foot of the mountains.

Lord Cavan, too, at 10 a.m., ordered the 7th Division to have the two battalions of the 91st Brigade at the foot of the hills (two were already in the mountains with the heavy artillery) ready to embus at short notice, move into hills and concentrate at a house near Cima di Fonte, midway between and a little to the south of Granezza and Carriola, the two divisional headquarters.

The Afternoon Counter-Attacks

The information of the enemy's advance having been confirmed by a personal reconnaissance made by the brigade-major of the 143rd Brigade, at 9.30 a.m., Major-General Fanshawe took the next step by ordering the 1/7th R. Warwickshire of the 143rd Brigade, held in divisional reserve at Magnaboschi—where the Handley Cross ammunition dump was in a state of explosion—to counter-attack, drive the enemy back and then hold the southern end of the Cesuna Switch. The order reached it at 10 a.m. This counter-attack was part of the divisional defence scheme and had been practised by the 1/7th R. Warwickshire. By now two companies of the 1/4th R. Berkshire (Lieut.-Colonel A. B. Lloyd Baker), the reserve of the 145th Brigade, were occupying Oxford Trench covering brigade headquarters, and the 474th Field Company R.E. and the 5/R. Sussex (pioneers) were covering divisional headquarters, in what was called in the Defence Scheme the "Red Line".

As another step, to close the gaps, a third company of the Berkshire had already been sent forward to reinforce the 1/4th Oxford L.I. on the right, and the fourth was now ordered to assist the 477th Field Company R.E. to close the gap between the Oxfordshire and the Lemerle Switch, thus completing the line on the right of the Austrian pocket.

When, about midday, the 1/7th R. Warwickshire, moving to make its counter-attack, reached Polygon Trench, Lieut.-Colonel J. M. Knox found that the gap between this trench and the Cesuna Switch was defended only by the guns (now two; a third was used to enfilade a ride on the right), and by the rifle party of the 12th Battery, firing at the enemy's advanced troops at a range of only five or six hundred yards, themselves under machine-gun fire. Learning that two small groups of houses, called Clo and Guardiana, near the light railway were in the enemy's hands, he determined first to make the defensive position secure and then retake these two localities. He filled the gap between Polygon Trench and the Cesuna Switch, gaining touch with the troops on either side, and the fire of his companies, at once opened, seems to have been the determining factor in quenching any desire of the Austrians to press farther. Lieut.-Colonel Knox then made preparations to go forward in counter-attack.

Whilst these were going on, Major-General Fanshawe again sent for the commander of the 144th Brigade, and when he arrived, about 12.20 p.m., told him that little more information had come in and that the situation was still obscure. Lieut.-Colonel Tomkinson suggested that if he went personally to the headquarters of the 145th Brigade, with which all communication was cut, he was confident that Lieut.-Colonel Reynolds, the acting brigade commander, would have an accurate idea of the position on his front and flanks. This proved to be the case, and on Lieut-Colonel Tomkinson's return in a little over an hour, orders were given him to attack westward from Cesuna Switch with two battalions and drive the enemy out of the ground he had captured. Lieut.-Colonel Tomkinson had under his hand only one battalion, the 1/6th Gloucestershire (Lieut.-Colonel H. Schomberg), which had reached Magnaboschi about 12.30 p.m., in spite of the exploding ammunition dump; of the other battalions of the 144th Brigade the 1/8th Worcestershire (Lieut.-Colonel H. T. Clarke) was still in reserve a thousand yards behind divisional headquarters; and the 1/7th Worcestershire and 1/4th Gloucestershire on their way up from the plain—the former arrived at Carriola at 2 p.m. and the latter at 5 p.m. Lieut.-Colonel Tomkinson therefore issued orders for the 1/6th Gloucestershire, with the 1/7th Worcestershire in support, to attack from Magnaboschi, but not until 6 p.m.

To return to the 143rd Brigade: at 2 p.m. the 1/7th R. Warwickshire from the southern end of Cesuna Switch, led by Lieut.-Colonel Knox in person with two platoons, and covered by three guns of the 12th Battery, which by now had been got into position (one gun manned mostly by officers of D/240, which had been overrun), attacked and took Clo and Guardiana. Resistance came mainly from machine guns, and this was again the case when the battalion pushed on astride the switch to within five hundred yards of the old front line. Lieut.-Colonel Knox then heard from an officer of the 1/6th Gloucestershire, sent by Lieut.-Colonel Tomkinson to get in touch with the 143rd Brigade, that the Gloucestershire were coming into the attack at 6 p.m. from Magnaboschi. Lieut.-Colonel Knox, therefore, decided to hold his position until they should arrive. Machine-gun fire and sniping were troublesome, but most of the enemy's riflemen were stalked.[1]

During the afternoon Lord Cavan came up to the 48th Division headquarters to see if he could be helpful; his presence was encouraging, and he did not interfere with the arrangements which had been made.

The orders received by the 1/6th Gloucestershire for the 6 p.m. attack were to pass through the south-eastern part of Cesuna Switch between Polygon Trench and Guardino, gaining touch with the 145th and 143rd Brigades on the right and left, clear the enemy from the pocket he had occupied and re-establish the front line. It was therefore arranged between the commanding officers of the 1/7th R. Warwickshire and 1/6th Gloucestershire, as their object was the same, that two companies of the Gloucestershire should join in the attack on the right of the Warwickshire. It was realized that it would be better to put in all four companies, but anxiety about the gap on the right led to two being kept behind the flank.

The troops moved in what was almost "artillery formation", lines of small groups of men, followed by echelons of increasingly large bodies, each battalion on a front of two companies. Met by machine-gun and rifle fire,

---

[1] Lieut.-Colonel J. M. Knox, D.S.O. and bar, was killed at S. Sisto by a shell on 23rd September 1918.

the general progress made was not much more than a hundred and fifty yards. The right Gloucester company got farther, almost to the 1/4th Oxford L.I., on the right of the divisional line ; but it failed to gain touch with that battalion, and, being counter-attacked in front and on both flanks, had to fall back on its battalion. By now the 1/7th Worcestershire, in support, had come up—under considerable artillery fire despite counter-battery work—and with its co-operation on the right the attack was renewed at 8 p.m. with the second pair of the 1/6th Gloucestershire companies still in support. The 1/6th R. Warwickshire was still in 143rd Brigade reserve at M. Pau, near brigade headquarters, and the 1/4th Gloucestershire brought up from Carriola to Magnaboschi in divisional reserve.

With a complete absence of enemy artillery fire, an advance eastwards of about three hundred yards was made by the three counter-attacking battalions. It drove the enemy riflemen on to their supports ; but then, again, it was stopped by machine-gun fire, the light khaki of the British showing up amid the pines more than the Austrian gray. An attempt by a party of the 1/6th R. Warwickshire, on the left of the counter-attack, to retake Perghele failed under heavy rifle and machine-gun fire. About 9.30 p.m. touch was obtained by a patrol of the 1/7th Worcestershire with the 1/4th Oxford L.I. on the right, about three hundred yards south-west of Pelly Cross. Thence a line, though not continuous, ran westwards, held by the 1/7th Worcestershire and the 1/6th Gloucestershire to near the Cesuna–Canove road, where the 1/7th R. Warwickshire joined on and, mixed with the 1/8th and 1/5th R. Warwickshire, held the Cesuna Switch. Linfoot's company of the 1/6th R. Warwickshire and the original left company of the 1/5th R. Warwickshire continued the line north-westwards.

The 4.30 a.m. Counter-Attack on the 16th

At 9.30 p.m., the three battalion commanders who had been engaged in the counter-attack met and decided to hold the line they had gained and to continue the attack in the morning ; but until midnight fighting continued in the woods, and now and then ground was gained. From

11 p.m. onwards, however, the enemy almost uninterruptedly kept his numerous machine guns firing, as though to create a defensive belt; this made movement difficult, but, being directed high and into the pines at large, caused comparatively few casualties.

About 9.30 p.m., also, reports reached Major-General Fanshawe that the evening counter-attack had not made much progress, and that the gap on the left of the 1/4th Oxford L.I. and the two companies of the 1/4th R. Berkshire with it, was still open. After seeing Lieut.-Colonel Tomkinson (144th Brigade) and approving of his plan to close this gap by sending up the 1/8th Worcestershire, the last battalion of his brigade, which was waiting south of divisional headquarters, Major-General Fanshawe gave verbal orders for a combined attack at 4.30 a.m. by all three brigades with the object of regaining the front line. The written confirmation did not reach the 143rd and 145th Brigades until about 2.15 a.m., but then found everything ready. The 1/8th Worcestershire had moved up at 1 a.m. to its forming-up line in front of the Lemerle Switch, the 1/1st Buckinghamshire, reinforced by the 477th Field Company R.E., continuing to hold this trench as local reserve. Movement was greatly hampered by the many trees brought down on the paths by the bombardment, but the attack took place punctually at 4.30 a.m. in the grey light of dawn, three battalions of the 144th Brigade being in the centre between the 145th and 143rd Brigades. Artillery, machine-gun and heavy trench-mortar support was arranged for; but, artillery support in wood-fighting being difficult, the enemy's back areas were the principal target for the guns. Full use was made of the regimental Lewis guns.

On the right the 1/4th Oxford L.I., with two companies of the 1/4th R. Berkshire (the other two were in brigade reserve), and the right company of the 1/8th Worcestershire, re-occupied its original front line against slight resistance by 5.45 a.m.[1] The left company of the 1/8th Worcestershire, with the 1/6th Gloucestershire (part of the battered 1/5th with it), 1/7th Worcestershire and 1/7th R. Warwickshire (parts of the 1/8th and 1/5th with it), met with much

---

[1] The history of the "First Buckinghamshire Battalion 1914–1918" states (p. 112) that a message was found on the body of a dead Austrian officer, timed 2.50 a.m., ordering a complete withdrawal to the original line.

THE END. 16TH JUNE

opposition from machine guns and snipers, as did also the 1/6th R. Warwickshire, on the left, where the left company of the 1/5th R. Warwickshire was still in position. About 7 a.m. Major-General Fanshawe made an inspection of the front on foot and in a second combined effort at 7.30, in three-quarters of an hour, the whole of the divisional front line was re-occupied, many prisoners being taken and many dead and wounded found on the ground.

ACTION AFTER THE BATTLE

Patrols were at once sent out along the whole divisional front and the outpost line was re-occupied, the guns lost in the enemy's first rush being recovered. His front line near Canove and near Ambrosini was then raided by a mixed detachment of the 1/5th and 1/6th R. Warwickshire, under Lieut.-Colonel Pryor (1/6th); little resistance was offered and prisoners surrendered freely.

On hearing that a patrol had occupied Ambrosini, Lord Cavan, at 3.15 p.m., gave orders to both divisions that, as it appeared probable that the enemy was largely demoralized and ready to surrender, strong patrols should be sent out as soon as they could be organized to occupy the objective line given for the attack which had been proposed for the 18th, that is the enemy's front line from Cima Tre Pezzi on the west to Ave on the east, from which point it ran back to the British front line near San Sisto: the present front line was to remain the line of resistance: if strong resistance was encountered, likely to cause considerable casualties, as the Italian troops on the flanks were not going to advance, the patrols were not to proceed too far. Both Lord Cavan and General Graziani, the French commander, pressed hard to be allowed to pursue, and ever after maintained that an opportunity for an outstanding success had been lost; but the official reply from the Comando Supremo was that General Diaz had no reserves available, as they were required on the Montello.[1] In the event, the Austrians, who had brought up the divisions in second line, opened fire on the patrols and offered strong resistance. The raiding parties had already been withdrawn from Canove and Ambrosini on account of the difficulty of supplying them across a wide

---

[1] An account of the Battle of the Piave is given in the next Chapter.

open No Man's Land, so the 23rd and 48th Divisions reverted to holding the old front line and outpost line as before.

The night of the 16th/17th passed quietly. The 91st Brigade of the 7th Division, which by the evening of the 15th had concentrated in the neighbourhood of the eastern end of the " Red Line ", six miles south of Asiago, was retained there. It was not employed except to send one battalion to Monte Pau as reserve to the 48th Division.

As far as British troops (less the R.A.F.) were concerned, their participation in the Battle of the Piave, officially fought between the dates of the 15th and 24th June, began and ended with the Battle of Asiago on the 15th and 16th, and by that time the other attacks of the Group of Armies under Field-Marshal Conrad von Hötzendorf at Tonale and east of the Brenta had also completely failed.

The casualties of the 48th Division on the 15th and 16th June were 922, of which 206 belonged to the artillery. The division took prisoner 25 officers, 515 other ranks and 188 wounded ; it buried 576 Austrians. The losses of the 23rd Division totalled 556, and it captured 230 unwounded and 127 wounded prisoners.[1]

In the period immediately after the Austrian attack much work had to be done in repairing the damage caused by the bombardment and in improving the defences. Active patrolling was continued, and some raids were carried out, of which the most important were made on the night of the 21st/22nd by the 69th Brigade, which had relieved the 70th in the right brigade sector of the 23rd Division. One company of the 10/Duke of Wellington's entered the enemy's front line at Ave, killed at least fifty and took 31 prisoners, suffering 21 casualties itself. A hundred men of the 11/West Yorkshire raided Sec (to the east of Ave), and, after sharp hand-to-hand fighting, annihilated the garrison of that part of the trench. This raiding party had 8 men wounded, 4 of them from bayonet wounds.

Some idea still persisted of carrying out the Allied offensive which had been planned before the Austrian attack took

---

[1] The total losses of the Austrian *Eleventh Army* are given in Note at end of Chapter.

place. On 23rd June, Lord Cavan visited the Italian Sixth Army headquarters, and was informed by General Montuori that, in the event of the enemy withdrawing troops from the front opposite the Sixth Army (Asiago area), he might decide to attack; and if the enemy attacked again and were defeated the Sixth Army was to be prepared to pursue him. Accordingly, Lord Cavan issued orders at 9.30 p.m. on the 23rd that, should either of the above situations occur, the two divisions in the line were to be prepared to attack at very short notice, with the enemy front line as objective.

REFLECTIONS

Many factors had militated against the British in the Asiago fight. The mist, as usual, favoured the attack up to a certain point; the troops were all ready for and distributed in view of an offensive on the 18th, and had been told that the enemy assault would not extend as far as their sector. Thus it was that the French, who expected attack, began counter-battery work at 11.45 p.m. on the 14th, whilst the British did not do so until nearly four hours later, after the Austrian bombardment was under way. Influenza had taken its toll, particularly of the 48th Division: not only were the infantry companies very weak, but all its General Staff officers were on the sick list. The British had no experience of mountain warfare in Europe; they had a definite doctrine in defence which all officers understood—and in the end it worked successfully at comparatively small cost. Had the line been more strongly held, in the Italian fashion, there might have been no break-in; but the British, accustomed to German, not Austrian, bombardments, preferred to stick to their own methods: occupy the front position thinly and rely on counter-attack and, if that failed, on a prepared counter-offensive. The French who had more men to the yard (800 yards to a battalion as against the British 1,145) completely repelled the assault by fire alone. This is not conclusive, as the French—and the British 23rd Division next them—were attacked partly by Hungarian *Honved* troops, inferior *Landwehr*, who desisted, even panicked, after a few casualties. The Austrian Official Account also speaks contemptuously of the *16th Division*, composed of Hungarians and Rumanians, which attacked the French. The front held by Italian troops was broken at three places, two first-class Austrian divisions, the *Edelweiss* (E.D.W.) and the *18th*, being engaged on the front where the biggest success was obtained, and the gains were held; so it may be argued that to man the front line strongly was not an infallible policy against Austrians.

The enemy bombardment, both of the front line and back areas, of the 48th Division seems to have had greater effect than elsewhere; the explosion of the ammunition dump near the road communications of that division was a serious handicap throughout the morning of the 15th; and the destruction of the headquarters of the 145th Brigade, with its wireless station, brought also a break in the signal communication which lasted throughout. In any case, the attacker's guns, firing from the Asiago plateau, had a distinct advantage over the guns of the defence emplaced in pine woods on the forward slopes of a hill; on the other hand, having to attack up the hill checked the enemy's infantry.

British officers who were present think that had the Austrians pressed their attack with determination they would have penetrated far deeper without much difficulty; but at the vital moment no fresh impulse was given to the battle by any echelon of command, and, that impulse failing, "the diminishing force of the offensive" brought the usual result. The difference of the Austrian and British leading was very marked: when the enemy's advance came to its first standstill, there it stayed; when the British counter-attack at 2 p.m. failed to progress it was renewed at 6 and 8 p.m., and when these achieved little more than to provoke a fierce fire-fight, counter-attack was tried for the fourth time at 4.30 a.m., and was then entirely successful. The triumph of the leading is the more remarkable as the Austrians were certainly more accustomed to wood fighting than the British, and, as a German author[1] has written: "Thick woods are very apt to make men feel lost and "bewildered, particularly when shots from an invisible hand "come whistling through the branches. Wood fighting, "owing to the danger of missing one's way and losing direc- "tion, and the length of time a good sniper can carry on "without being detected, is one of the least desirable forms "of warfare, especially when troops unaccustomed to woods "are pitted against trained sharpshooters".

---

[1] Professor E. Banse, Professor of Military Science in Brunswick 1933, in "Raum und Volk im Weltkriege", p. 36.

NOTE

THE AUSTRIAN ACCOUNT OF THE BATTLE OF ASIAGO[1]
(Map I ; Sketch 7)

Very little detail about the infantry attack can be found in the Austrian official account, as it is written from an Army point of view. It does, however, mention that the right flank of the *52nd Division* and the left flank of the *6th Division* achieved a notable success at first, breaking into the British position to a depth of a kilometre after hard fighting. The rest is strangely inaccurate : later, it says the attackers came on excellently masked posts, well wired, and about 10 a.m. the advance had come to a halt.

"About midday the picture suddenly changed. One Job's " messenger followed another, and in the evening the Army " commander had to report that, on account of overwhelming " counter-attacks, the *52nd Division* [opposite the left brigade " of the 23rd Division and the 1/4th Oxford L.I. of the 48th " Division] was driven back to its starting place. Whereupon " General Martiny [the *III Corps* commander] had withdrawn " the *6th Division* [opposite the 48th's centre and left], and sent " up the *28th Division* to reinforce them. Further, in the *XIII* " *Corps* [east of the *III*], the *38th Honved Division* [opposite the " right of the 23rd Division], and apparently also the *16th* " *Division* [opposite the French] had been driven back, whilst " the eastern wing of the *42nd Honved Division* [opposite the " Italian XIII Corps] was probably still in position on Monte " Nosa [well inside the Italian lines] ". Orders were then issued for the divisions to hold on where they were : " There could be " no idea of renewing the attack. The reports which came in " during the course of the night from subordinate leaders made " the condition of the beaten troops (*von Rückschlag getroffene*) " appear serious, even critical ".

Later reports gave a different but still a wrong impression, and the historians comment on " the fatal errors in the battle " messages ". " The initial success did not last. The regiments " which had got somewhat mixed up in the wood fighting were " at once strongly attacked. The first counter-attacks were " repelled by the *6th* and *52nd Divisions*, as also by the *38th* " *Honved* and the *16th Divisions*. But between 2 p.m. and 3 " p.m., after a very effective preparation by very numerous and " unweakened artillery, the British and French proceeded to a " powerful counter-attack—as far as can be gathered from

---

[1] For the Order of Battle of the Austrian *Eleventh Army* see Appendix VII.

" imperfect and fragmentary reports—the *16th* and *52nd Divisions*
" were the first to be compelled to give way ".

Such very erroneous accounts indicate the confusion on the Austrian side and in some measure the magnitude of the defeat.

The casualties of the Austrian *Eleventh Army*, 14th to 25th June are given as a whole, without subdivision by corps or divisions, as killed 5,692, wounded 32,901, sick 14,117, missing 10,370, total 63,080, whilst the two Armies engaged on the Piave lost a total of 79,470.

" On General-Colonel Arz [Chief of the General Staff] the news
" of the lack of success of the *Eleventh Army*, particularly of the
" *XIII Corps* at Asiago, had a crushing effect from which he
" never recovered, as he had pinned his faith on the success of
" the northern attack ". [A.O.A., iv, p. 276].

CHAPTER XVI

THE BATTLE OF THE PIAVE
15TH–24TH JUNE 1918
(Map II; Sketch 7)

The Initial Situation

The battle of the Piave was begun simultaneously with the Battle of Asiago, and was fought by Field-Marshal Boroevic's Group of Armies consisting of the *Sixth Army* (General-Colonel Archduke Joseph) and the *Isonzo Army* (General-Colonel Freiherr von Wurm). Of longer duration than the battles of Conrad von Hötzendorf's Group of Armies in the mountains, it seemed at one time to have prospect of success. It is of special interest as indicating to some extent the comparative value of Italian and Austrian troops in battle unaided by their powerful Allies.

In the plan finally approved[1] the *XXIV Corps* (Field-Marshal-Lieutenant Goiginger)[2] of the *Sixth Army* was to attack the Montello on a 3-mile frontage, crossing the Piave north of Nervesa, and the *Isonzo Army* was to cross lower down between Spresiano and S. Dona on a 20-mile frontage. On the four miles between these two attacks, that is between Nervesa and Spresiano, no action was intended.

The opposing forces and their distribution can be seen on the map. It will be noticed that the Italian 58th Division, holding the Montello, had also to cover a wide frontage along the river bank, a total of 8 miles (half of which was not attacked). It had 3 divisions opposed to it, and lower down the Piave 4 Italian divisions were attacked by 9 Austrian. Of reserves, not counting mounted cavalry, the Austrians had 7 divisions (4 G.H.Q.) readily available; the Italians had 11 (8 G.H.Q.), and others from the mountain front could be railed to the Piave by the Italians more quickly than by the Austrians, who would be forced to use a circuitous route.

---
[1] See Map II.
[2] This rank was equivalent to Lieut-General.

222 BATTLE OF THE PIAVE

By the day of battle the Italian defences consisted of a number of lines, none of them, however, well developed in depth. In addition to First and Second Systems, each of several trenches, there was a Third System, which, starting from the Sile, included special defences around Treviso and then swung westward behind the mountain front. Next came lines behind the Marzena (on which lies Castelfranco) and the Brenta; then an elaborate system running from the coast near Venice,[1] covering Padua and Vicenza, and finally two further lines, one running in front of Verona and the other in front of Mantua, both resting their right on a great inundation reaching from the sea westward to Legnago. There were in fact so many continuous trench lines and so many belts of barbed wire behind the front that the bringing up of reinforcements was seriously impeded and delayed.

The Opening Phase on 15th June—The Montello

At 3 a.m. the Austrian bombardment opened; it included lacrymatory gas to neutralize the Italian artillery and was modelled on the German bombardment of 21st March 1918, but with one gun every 16 metres instead of every 9 metres. The Italians did not at once reply, reserving their fire for the passage of the infantry.[2] The bombardment effected very little, as the exact position of the Italian batteries and rear lines was not accurately known owing to lack of aircraft and balloons, and in the flat country (that is excluding the Montello) covered with high crops and vineyards, flash spotting was useless. The river, however, was in the early morning enveloped in thick fog, and this combined with the smoke of bursting shells and artificial smoke soon filled the whole valley and enabled the Austrian infantry to cross by boats and pontoons—dragging them round or over the gravel banks—almost unharmed. Later the weather was dull and sultry, and towards evening it rained.

The instructions for the passage of the river were that the battalions after landing should keep close to the western bank, ready to assault when the bombardment ceased at

---

[1] For the places mentioned in this paragraph see Sketch 5.
[2] Caviglia, p. 73, says " our artillery was slow in intervening ". A.O.A. VII, p. 261, says " only towards 5 a.m. did enemy artillery fire begin, " but mortar and machine-gun fire from the shore positions was active "the whole time ".

7.40 a.m. in the Montello sector and at 7.30 a.m. lower down. Then, after a slight pause, they were to go forward under a creeping barrage, and two bridges were to be constructed in each divisional sector.

In the Montello sector, the bed of the river averaged 800 yards in width; the many channels were mostly 6 feet to 10 feet deep, in which the stream had a velocity of a little over 60 feet a minute. The assault battalions of three divisions of the *XXIV Corps* engaged—the *II Corps* on its right contributing artillery fire—actually reached the front Italian trenches close to the bank undetected, between 6.15 a.m. on the left and 7.15 a.m. on the right, although the shore was heavily wired, and they went forward punctually at zero hour. They had 37-mm. and 75-mm. mountain guns allotted to them; but as these guns had been brought up too close to the river in order to be ready at hand, many were knocked out by the Italian counter-preparation. Supporting troops soon followed across the river; by the early afternoon the *XXIV Corps* had advanced two miles or more and secured the eastern end of the Montello. For a long time, however, the situation was critical as Italian artillery fire and British bombing frustrated the construction and maintenance of bridges. It has already been mentioned that in the afternoon the weather in the mountains had become so bad, that the British R.A.F. in the Asiago sector had been diverted to the Piave front. First, about 1 p.m., nine "Camels" of No. 45 Squadron arrived, each carrying four 20-lb. bombs, which they dropped on the ferry pontoons in the Montello sector, hitting two. It being evident that the Austrians were crossing in large numbers, it was decided to employ all available aircraft to help the Italians, and by 4 p.m. thirty-three were in action.[1] Two pontoon bridges had been constructed in the Montello reach; the one upstream was bombed by No. 66 Squadron from about fifty feet and broken in two places and its pontoons broke away and, caught by the strong current, dashed against the lower bridge and carried it away also. This air success, as far as can be judged, wrecked the Austrian hopes. If, as planned, they had gained possession of the Montello, the Piave front would probably have collapsed. To add to the enemy disaster, about 6 p.m. the

---

[1] See " War in the Air " vi, p. 283 *et seq.*

British airmen caught a mass of Austrian troops in boats, and bombed and machine-gunned them. The Italian reserve division of the VIII Corps, the 48th, too, had been brought up to hold the embankment of the railway which runs from Nervesa to Montebelluna. Thus hampered and engaged, and as even by 3.30 a.m. on the 16th only one bridge had been repaired, the Austrian efforts to pass men and material over and widen the front on the left by crossing at Nervesa and on the railway bridge, were unsuccessful. Italian resistance on the hill also stiffened, as the reserve brigades of the 48th Division and the 51st Division on the left came up, and a counter-attack brought to an end for the day any further gain of ground by the Austrians.

The Opening Phase on the Lower Piave

In front of the *Isonzo Army* the Piave, as far as the railway bridge at Ponte di Piave ran in several channels, but below that point formed a single stream. Although the Austrian outposts were in possession of Papadopoli island and the channels between it and the western bank were at the time fordable in places, only a few parties of the 3 divisions of the *XVI Corps*, mainly in boats, succeeded in crossing the river. They held on for a few hours, but, after the one footbridge constructed had been destroyed, they were overwhelmed by a counter-attack. The Austrian attack had failed with very heavy casualties—one division lost 1,915 men, another 1,200, mostly in the unsuccessful attempts to cross and on Papadopoli island—and was not renewed. The failure was attributed by the corps commander to "the misapprehension of relation between the "effect of artillery fire and the time necessary to overcome "obstacles." But the Austrian artillery fire, being ill-directed, had occasioned hardly any losses.

The *IV Corps* attacked with two Hungarian *Honved* divisions. The advanced troops crossed the Piave and took the Italian first line and part of the second of the First System, although here, as elsewhere, on the lower Piave, artillery fire directed on the eastern bank contributed powerfully to hold the Austrians back. But in the late afternoon, being bombed from the air, the two bridges smashed and the corps commander, who had come up to the

THE LOWER PIAVE. 15TH JUNE

front, severely wounded, they were driven right back to the river's bank with their centre broken.

In the *VII Corps* (4 divisions, one in reserve), two and a half battalions on the extreme right managed to cross the river and get in touch with the *IV Corps;* but below this for a stretch of about a mile athwart the Oderzo-Treviso railway all attempts to cross failed. In the left centre a brigade of infantry of the *24th Division*, and part of the *9th Cavalry Division* made the passage of the river successfully, advanced about three-quarters of a mile, captured 2,400 men, and secured Zenson ; but the extreme left of the corps failed to cross.

The *XXIII Corps* (3 divisions in line but only 2 attacking) met with considerable success. In thick fog, the two divisions crossed without much difficulty and then pressed on towards their objective, Meolo, so that a small bridgehead, 3 miles wide and $2\frac{1}{2}$ miles deep, was secured. The third division (dismounted cavalry), holding a long frontage in marshy ground, did not take part in the general attack, but one regiment crossed the Piave after driving out a small Italian bridgehead established on the Austrian side.

Result of the First Day

On the whole, it was considered at Austrian G.H.Q. that sufficient crossings of the Piave had been made to cover the construction of bridges and give good hopes of further progress. The Comando Supremo was equally satisfied: " the front on the Asiago plateau had been held nearly " integrally; the advance of the enemy in the Grappa " sector had been arrested; the powerful thrusts of the " enemy in the sector of the Montello, on the lower Piave, " at Ponte di Piave and S. Dona di Piave had been tenaci- " ously opposed "; one division each (33rd, 13th, 50th) from the XXV, XXVI, and XXX Corps, in general reserve, had been moved nearer to the front, so as to be in a position to assist the Eighth and Third Armies, which seemed to be the most seriously menaced; reserves from the Seventh and First Armies, on the extreme left opposite Conrad's Group of Armies, were warned to be ready to be railed eastward. Later on, the 50th and 13th Divisions were allotted to the Eighth Army to restore the situation on the

Montello, and the 33rd Division to the Third Army; other divisions of the XXV and XXVI Corps and the 4th Cavalry Division (back at Legnago) were ordered to move closer to the lower Piave, and two divisions were entrained from the Lake Garda sector towards the area Padua–Treviso. No suggestion is recorded that an attempt should be made at once to drive the Austrians from their precarious footing on the western bank of the Piave.

16TH JUNE: A WASTED DAY

The 16th June was a wasted day for the Austrians: a few reinforcements were passed over the Piave, a little ground was won at one place and lost in another.

Field-Marshal von Boroevic issued no orders for the 16th. Having given his two Army commanders their objectives, he considered that the measures to be adopted should be left to their judgment. At midday, however, he placed the *41st Division* from the G.H.Q. reserve at the disposal of the *Sixth Army*, and later the *35th Division*. British bombing of the crossings continued throughout the day, about two tons of 20-lb. bombs being dropped. The Archduke Joseph decided, contrary to the wishes of G.H.Q. as it turned out later, to abandon the design of occupying the whole of the Montello, and directed the *XXIV Corps*, whose commander wanted to go on, to confine itself to reaching a line only just slightly ahead; but it was to endeavour to pass the rest of its troops, particularly guns, over the Piave. Bridges, however, were lacking. The one bridge restored at 3.30 a.m. was at 10 a.m. struck by a bomb; and attempts made during the night of the 15th/16th to build another failed under Italian gun-fire. Passages by boats and pontoons still remained the only means, and heavy rain fell during the day and " mightily swelled " the Piave. It is mentioned that 2 mountain batteries, 4 " accompanying " batteries, and a cyclist battalion, besides infantry, managed to cross to the Montello, but that only a wholly insufficient quantity of ammunition and supplies could be shipped over. In order to protect the bridge construction, " after long discussion " between the *XXIV Corps*, the *Sixth Army* and the *Group of Armies Command*, the *XVI Corps* (now standing fast) was ordered to send 16 batteries to the *XXIV* to counter-battery the Italian artillery; and all available machine-gun companies and A.A. batteries were collected to deal with the aircraft which were bombing the passage of the river. "It was very lucky for the *XXIV Corps* on the "16th [says the Austrian Official Account] that the Italians "did not undertake any large counter-attacks". The Italian Official Account of the battle states that 2 fresh divisions, the 13th and 50th from the general reserve, did counter-attack, "but at evening the resulting situation was "almost (*pressochè*) unchanged". It is perhaps significant that in the two days of battle on the Montello the Austrian *XXIV Corps* had brought in as prisoners 194 officers and 6,600 men.

General-Colonel Wurm's orders to the *Isonzo Army* for the 16th were that the *XXIII Corps*, on the left, reinforced by the one division in Army reserve (*57th*), should advance to the Meola stream; the *VII Corps* should advance to the same line to help the *IV Corps*, which should at least maintain its precarious footing on the west bank, even if it could not advance; the *XVI Corps* at Papadopoli island was not to repeat its attempts to cross the Piave, but support the *Sixth Army* with its artillery, as already mentioned, and be ready to advance if pressure by that Army caused the Italians to fall back—which did not happen.

Very little did happen to alter the situation, although bridges were available for the *Isonzo Army*, only one pontoon bridge in the *XXIII Corps* sector being lost by air attack about 9.45 a.m. The attack of the *XXIII Corps* was put off until the 17th, as the reinforcing division, which did not arrive until evening, would not be available before then, and this postponement affected the *VII Corps*. Meantime, the Italian XXVIII Corps attacked the bridgehead north of the Venice–Latisana railway, drove the defenders back a kilometre and destroyed by fire two trestle footbridges they had built. One of the two divisions of the *IV Corps* managed to bring nearly all its infantry and one mountain battery over the Piave; the other was less successful; but at 2 p.m. both divisions attacked north-west and westwards, and pushed on about fourteen hundred yards from the river, capturing the village of Saletto in the centre, but failing to hold Candelu on the right, each division taking about seven hundred prisoners.

It became clear to General Diaz that the Austrian

mountain attacks had failed and that he was free to bring all reserves to the Piave front, first to stop the enemy advance and then to proceed to a planned counter-offensive. In the evening he ordered additional artillery to the Third Army holding the right half of the Piave front, and to the Eighth Army holding the left half, he sent two more divisions of the general reserve and one of the two " assault divisions ", by lorry, from the Padua area. Field-Marshal Boroevic, for his part, reported that he could hold the bridgeheads with his present force, and that with 7 fresh divisions he could proceed to a new offensive, provided the mountain front remained active.

The 17th June: The Austrians Enlarge Their Bridgeheads

The 17th June was a day of heavy rain, which turned the Piave into a swirling torrent, with disastrous results later to the Austrian communications across the river, although clouds and rain impeded low-flying attacks. As regards the Montello sector, where the Austrian *XXIV Corps* had now the support of part of the *41st Division* on the left near Nervesa, the Italian Official Account sums up the fighting as " a dogged (*accanita*) struggle, with many episodes through-" out the day ". Actually, the Austrians made a limited attack to improve their position, and, although they did not retain all the ground won during the day, they made gains on both sides of their original salient, so that the two flanks rested on the Piave.

On the lower Piave also the Austrians improved their position and the *VII Corps* joined its bridgehead to that of the *XXIII*. On the left, the *XXIII Corps*, now reinforced on the right by the *57th Division*, ordered all 3 divisions to attack at 10 a.m. after a short fire preparation. The right and centre divisions obeyed, but immediately ran into the fire of machine guns well hidden amid the vineyards and cultivation, and could make only slow progress. The left division, which had passed a lively night under artillery fire and had repelled several counter-attacks, did not advance until 2.30 p.m.; then, after a thorough artillery preparation, it gained a mile and a half of ground, although it did not reach its objective, the Meola river. Thus at nightfall the bridgehead of the corps had been considerably enlarged.

AUSTRIAN BRIDGEHEADS ENLARGED. 229
17TH JUNE

The *VII Corps*, like the left division of the *XXIII*, had an uneasy night. During the 17th its right division stood fast : the other two in front line, reinforced by part of the corps reserve division, had a long day of battle which did not end until midnight ; but they gained ground, joined up with the *XXIII Corps* on the left, and took prisoner 89 officers and 2,932 men.

The two Hungarian divisions of the *IV Corps* also had heavy fighting. They managed to join up their two small footings on the western bank ; but they lost all their gains in a counter-attack made by the Italian XI Corps about 5 p.m.

The Italian account of the day is that the Third Army, reinforced by the 1st Assault Division, was in the afternoon to carry out an energetic counter-attack " south-eastwards " against the Austrian salient pointing towards Meolo ", that is against the Austrian *XXIII Corps;* but of the three corps of the Army, two, the XXVIII and XXIII, were only " to make minor blows in co-operation with tne principal " counter-attack " ; the main operation therefore was left to the XI Corps, and this corps, it has just been seen, advanced eastwards against the Austrian *IV Corps*. The Italian account continues, " the intended action was " prevented by a heavy enemy attack launched from Zenson " and Gonfa [a little above S. Dona] ".

It had been planned that the Austrian *XVI Corps* should launch a night attack from Papadopoli island ; " but during " the night of the 17th/18th and on the 18th itself, the " high-water on the Piave inflicted serious hurt (*Unheil*) on " the bridges of the *Isonzo Army* ". Not only did the rise of water stop the night attack of the *XVI Corps*, but floating débris of the destroyed bridges of the *Sixth Army* tore through the trestles and supports of the built-up bridges of the *IV Corps*, so that it was judged advisable to dismantle the pontoon bridges in order to save them from destruction, and to depend on ferrying ; it was found that a round journey across and back in a pontoon required $4\frac{1}{2}$ hours. Medical dressings and some supplies were dropped from aircraft. One of the bridges of the *VII Corps* was flooded over, and no sooner was it rebuilt than it was smashed up by floating timber. A similar fate overtook the bridge of the *XXIII Corps* at S. Dona, and of the 7 bridges over the Sile, 5 were swept away.

General Diaz, in the evening, gave orders for more reinforcements to be brought up. All the divisions of the XXX, XXVI and XXV Corps, in general reserve, having been allotted to the front line corps, the XXII Corps, at Castelfranco was moved towards Treviso, and one division each from the three Armies of the left wing, the Seventh, Ninth and First, were brought up by rail to take the place of the XXII Corps in general reserve. The instructions sent to the Third Army were that it should react energetically to any enemy progress. On the other side, Field-Marshal Boroevic was not yet prepared to break off the battle, and reiterated his order for the *XXIII Corps* to reach the Meola river.

18TH JUNE: LITTLE CHANGE IN THE SITUATION

The 18th June was cloudy and wet, but towards evening the rain ceased and the Piave began to fall. In the Montello sector the commander of the *XXIV Corps* had intended to renew the offensive; but conditions prevented this. All the bridges were down—as a British airman reported—except two at S. Dona, and most of the signal communications cut; no reinforcements and none of the much needed artillery could be got across the Piave—only 85 light guns had so far been taken over; the supply of food and ammunition was failing; wounded and prisoners could not be evacuated; and the troops were thoroughly exhausted. Nevertheless, such attacks as the Italians made were beaten off. These attacks are not mentioned in the Italian accounts available: the official story says: "the enemy "continued to hammer at the southern sector of the "Montello, gaining a little ground towards the Nervesa "railway bridge". In the evening, the situation being considered critical, the *Sixth Army* informed Field-Marshal Boroevic that the bridgehead must either be reinforced by 3 divisions and 4 artillery brigades (of 2 regiments each) or evacuated.

On the lower Piave the Austrians slightly improved their position. The left of the *XXIII Corps* nearly reached the Meola, but was then driven back to about its starting line by a counter-attack of the 1st Assault Division, attached to the Italian XXVIII Corps, which, in turn, was stopped by the attack of 3 Austrian battalions. The right of the

XXIII Corps succeeded in advancing and filling the re-entrant south of Campolungo. This corps brought in during the day as prisoners, 170 officers and 6,489 men. It was obvious, however, that a serious advance was impossible without the immediate assistance of numerous reinforcements.

The *VII Corps* had orders to hold what it had gained, to improve its defences and to bring its artillery (still on the east bank) closer to the river; but the right division, discovering by patrols that opposition was weak, made a mile advance on a $2\frac{1}{2}$-mile frontage, one regiment alone taking 1,200 prisoners. Next to it, the *IV Corps* made vain endeavours to enlarge its bridgehead; the left took the village of San Bartolomeo; the right took Candelu, but was driven out again. The corps was in fact exhausted, and heavy losses in officers had made command difficult. Otherwise, on the whole, the Austrians had the best of the fighting on the 18th, in spite of inferiority of numbers and the serious handicap imposed by the swollen Piave and the inadequacy of artillery support.

Austrian Discussion on the Continuation of the Battle

F.M.-Lt. Goiginger (*XXIV Corps*) pointed out to the *Sixth Army* the supreme importance of further operations for maintaining hold on the Montello: the position gained could not be considered sufficiently deep to afford protection to the bridges over the Piave from artillery fire: the conveyance across the river of troops, food, ammunition and stores could not be guaranteed unless the front was pushed forward about $3\frac{1}{2}$ miles to a line through Spresiano: from this line a decisive thrust might be made towards Castelfranco, which, in his opinion, would render both the enemy's mountain and Piave fronts untenable. Field-Marshal Boroevic, however, was of the opinion that the Austrian line on the far bank of the Piave must be pushed forward on the lower Piave as well as from the Montello, and he reported to Austrian G.H.Q. on the 18th by telegram that not only should the bridgehead of the *Sixth Army* be extended to the Spresiano line and run thence to the southern end of Papadopoli Island, but that of the *Isonzo Army* also should be pushed forward to the Meola stream. Laying stress on the urgent need of an immediate decision, as the opportunity if lost now could never be regained, he did not believe that a continuation of the battle was hopeless, provided reinforcements and an increased supply of bridging material and other equipment could be sent.

The moment was not propitious, as on the 16th General-Colonel Arz had received a request from Ludendorff for 6 good divisions—not Czech—and "particularly plenty of "artillery", for the Western Front. Whether this would be possible depended on the issue of the fighting in Italy. The operations of Field-Marshal Conrad's Group of Armies having failed, Kaiser Karl had visited him in Botzen on the 17th to discuss the causes of the collapse and whilst there Field-Marshal Boroevic's telegram arrived. At 5 p.m. on the 18th, therefore, he left in the headquarters train for Spilimbergo, 15 miles west of Udine, where, shortly after arrival early on the 19th, he received Field-Marshal Boroevic in audience. By this time the commander of the Isonzo front was opposed to the continuation of the battle. He made it clear that it would scarcely be possible to keep the troops supplied with sufficient ammunition and rations for more than a few days, and he considered further loss of life useless; even should the *Isonzo Army* reach the Meola, the situation would hardly be improved. His arguments were all in vain, the Kaiser replying, "But Conrad "wants it [continuation of the Piave offensive]". Even a dispatch from Hindenburg to the German plenipotentiary at Austrian G.H.Q., Major-General von Cramon, when brought to his notice, carried no weight; although in it was urged that the Austrian offensive had no prospect of success and should be abandoned, and the request for the transfer of 6 divisions to the Western Front was repeated. Kaiser Karl merely asked Boroevic what he proposed to do. The reply was: "Attack of the *Sixth Army* [westwards] via "Asolo [near M. Gressa] on Bassano, with protection of the "south flank by the *Isonzo Army* towards Treviso". At a later conference at 6 p.m. Major-General Waldstätten, Deputy Chief of the General Staff, stated that neither of the two Armies of Boroevic's Group could engage in further fighting on the western bank of the Piave with the means now at its disposal. The Chief of the Quartermaster's Department then depicted the desperate state of food supply, not only in the Army but in the Homeland, and the Head of the Arms and Ammunition Department declared

AUSTRIANS PROPOSE WITHDRAWAL. 233
19TH JUNE

that, although he had sufficient ammunition for the moment, the output was falling owing to the under-nourishment of the workers and the decrease in the coal output. According to many, the physical condition of the troops was poor owing to bad and insufficient food, to lack of clothing and boots, and to there having been little time for training and rest.[1] Field-Marshal Boroevic then made the formal proposal to withdraw both Armies of his Group behind the Piave, and to hold on to the Italian territory already gained: operations could be resumed when the material conditions had improved.

Kaiser Karl would not give the necessary order, nor would he do so at another conference at midday on the 20th. Boroevic had therefore to consider the continuation of the battle. He requested and obtained sanction for the 3 divisions held in G.H.Q. reserve—he already had the fourth—to be placed at his disposal, intending to allot them to the *Sixth Army*. As this exhausted the G.H.Q. reserve in the Piave area, except for one cavalry division, orders were sent to the Minister of War to dispatch 21 divisions, then in the Homeland, to Venice, and to Fied-Marshal Conrad to detail 3 divisions for transfer by rail to the *Isonzo Army* and asking him to do what he could to prevent the Italians from withdrawing troops from the mountain front. Subsequently, Kaiser Karl motored to visit the commander of the *Sixth Army*, the Archduke Joseph, at Vittorio Veneto, and heard from him, as he already knew, that in his opinion the Montello should be evacuated or reinforced. The Archduke specially wished to avoid a withdrawal imposed by the enemy, which might result in a disaster. The Kaiser then travelled on to *XXIV Corps* headquarters at Conegliano (9 miles north-east of Nervesa). He found F.M.-Lt. Goiginger greatly elated by the repulse, to be related later, of a heavy Italian counter-attack and full of confidence; he guaranteed to the Kaiser that he could hold the Montello bridgehead and enlarge it if given reinforcements and antiaircraft weapons to protect the bridges and a rope-way. To the Kaiser's question as to an abandonment of the Montello, he replied that it would be a more difficult operation than the storming of it.

---

[1] Pengov, p. 25.

Kaiser Karl then visited the headquarters of the *Isonzo Army*. This Army had failed to improve its position during the 19th and 20th; far from reaching the Meola, it was in fact farther from the river on the evening of the 20th than it had been on the 18th; and it had lost by counter-attack the small gains made during the 20th. General-Colonel Wurm is stated to have said that his Army was incapable of continuing the offensive without fresh forces, that it was quite possible to hold the bridgehead, but a defensive behind the Piave would be very much safer.

THE ITALIAN DECISION TO TAKE THE COUNTER-OFFENSIVE

On the other side, General Diaz had on the 18th come to the conclusion that the time had arrived for a counter-offensive to drive the Austrians back across the Piave. He chose the Montello as the first objective; for there the enemy had penetrated to some depth on to high ground which commanded the battle area, and had almost thrust a wedge between the Italian Armies holding the line of the Piave and those on the mountain front. The Eighth Army (General Pennella), consisting of the VIII and XXVII Corps, was directed to carry out the operation. As both divisions (48th and 58th) of the VIII Corps had already been heavily engaged on the Montello, the Army was reinforced by 2 corps from G.H.Q. reserve: the XXX (one of whose divisions, the 50th, had already reinforced the XXVII Corps on the 16th) and the XXII Corps, brought up from Castelfranco. This gave General Pennella 8 more divisions (4 quite fresh), and a considerable force of artillery.

The Italian bombardment opened at 2 p.m. on the 19th, and the infantry attack of the two fresh corps, on the extreme right and the extreme left of the Austrian position, followed at 3.30 p.m.

The fall in the waters of the Piave had allowed the Austrians to reconstruct three bridges and send over munitions, but the passage of reinforcements was, until evening when the ban was raised, forbidden by the *Sixth Army*. Nevertheless, the fragments of the three very tired divisions of the Austrian *XXIV Corps* held firm on the Montello, repelling repeated attacks, so that the Italians

ITALIAN COUNTER-OFFENSIVE. 19TH JUNE

gained very little ground except on the extreme right. There, towards evening, the 48th Division of the VIII Corps joined in the attack, and by an advance on a very narrow front up the river bank, took Nervesa. At 5 a.m. on the 20th the Italians renewed their attack, but with no better success, and the Austrians in one of their counter-attacks retook Nervesa. The Italian casualties having been heavy, at 2 p.m. General Pennella gave orders to cease attack, hold the position occupied and use all the artillery to bombard the Montello and the Austrian bridges.

The Austrian Decision to Withdraw across the Piave

This change of Italian tactics could not take effect at once and of course was unknown to Austrian G.H.Q., where, five hours later, at 7.16 p.m. on Kaiser Karl's return, the Chief of the General Staff issued to Field-Marshal Boroevic the order:

" The troops of your Group of Armies will be withdrawn " to the left bank of the Piave ".

At the same time Field-Marshal Conrad was informed that the order to send 3 divisions to the Piave was cancelled.

Soon after Kaiser Karl's decision was taken Field-Marshal Boroevic issued Group orders for the withdrawal across the Piave. The night of the 22nd/23rd was selected as Zero; all the field artillery, train and wounded, and any infantry not essential to the defence, were to be withdrawn on the night of the 21st/22nd; no movement was to be made in daylight; the troops were not to be informed until the last moment to ensure that no hint of the order to retire should reach the Italians through prisoners or deserters. It was a great advantage to the Austrians that the Italian order to stop the counter-offensive came at the very moment that the withdrawal was decided on. According to the Italian Official Account,[1] the Comando Supremo had come to the conclusion that the Italian troops, tired after six days of hard fighting, would be unlikely to succeed in a counter-offensive, and that the Austrians must in any case feel obliged to recross very soon; so that there was no reason for further expenditure of Italian blood. General Diaz,

---

Piave, p. 28.

therefore, decided to confine his counter-offensive to the recovery of the small gains of ground made by the enemy on the mountain front.[1] Except for an attack on the 21st by the Italian XXVIII Corps near the junction of the *XXIII* and *VII Corps*, where the Austrians held their ground; some feeble efforts against the flanks of the Montello on the night of the 21st/22nd, also repelled; and some pressure on the *XXIII Corps* on the 23rd, with some sporadic gun-fire and bombing, no interference came from the Italians. The Austrian engineers constructed a number of extra footbridges; not one of them was damaged, and only two bridges for wheeled traffic were hit, one near the Montello and the other in the *VII Corps* sector; and they were repaired.

The front of the Montello sector was held by the Austrians until after dark on the 22nd, and during the night the whole of the infantry, with the machine guns, retired in one bound without the Italians showing that they were aware of any movement. By 5 a.m. the *XXIV Corps* was in position on the eastern bank, having suffered only a few casualties from artillery fire and bombing whilst crossing the Piave. The first Italian patrols did not show themselves on the western bank until 6.45 a.m. As soon as the withdrawal became a certainty the Italian bombing squadrons turned out in force to harass the retreating troops, and the whole of the R.A.F. strength was employed to help, as many as fifty British aircraft being engaged at one time.

On the lower Piave, the *IV Corps* also withdrew on the night of the 22nd/23rd without interference. The *VII* and *XXIII* had been ordered to retire in two stages: on the night of the 22nd/23rd to any intermediate line and next night, across the Piave. The commander of the *VII Corps* thought this too risky, as when the Italians realized that the *IV Corps* was gone they might fall on the *VII* and *XXIII* with all their strength. General Schariczer, therefore, decided to carry out the whole withdrawal on the night of the 22nd/23rd, and succeeded in doing so undetected.

The *XXIII Corps* carried out the withdrawal in two stages, as ordered. The first stage, half-way to the river, was quite successfully achieved on the night of the 22nd/23rd; but at 5.30 p.m. on the 23rd the Italians, under

---

[1] See p. 215.

CASUALTIES

the impression that the Austrians intended to retain a bridgehead on the western bank opposite S. Dona, made an attack and, although it was repelled, they pressed the Austrian retirement in the evening closely and caused severe losses to the two rearguard brigades before the withdrawal was completed during the night.

CASUALTIES

The Italian Official Account does not give the total Italian casualties, but claims 24,475 prisoners and 70 guns. A private writer,[1] gives the following figures of killed, wounded and missing from 15th to 25th June :

Italian Third Army	43,085
„ Eighth Army	22,322
„ Fourth Army	14,152
„ Sixth Army	5,271
Total	84,830

The Austrian Official Account gives figures for casualties from the 14th to the 25th June :

Isonzo Army	51,900
Sixth Army (with *XV Corps*)	17,179
Total	69,079[2]

In addition, the Austrian sick amounted to 10,391. The prisoners "taken from the enemy during the June battle" amounted to about 50,000", mostly in the Piave fighting.

ACTION ON THE MOUNTAIN FRONT

On 23rd June, as soon as it became evident that the Austrian retirement across the Piave had taken place, the Comando Supremo instructed the Armies on the mountain front to take advantage of what was thought to be the beginning of the Austrian collapse. The Italian Fourth

---

Baj-Macario in "Giugno 1918", p. 404.

Baj-Macario gives the total for Boroevic's Group at 60,180, probably excluding the *XV Corps*.

Army, therefore ordered the 3 corps immediately east of the Brenta, that is the XVIII, VI and IX,[1] to attack and secure the Monte Grappa line of summits which overlook the plain. After a bombardment begun at midnight on the 23rd/24th the attack was made "in the morning hours". It completely failed, and the Italians on the Monte Grappa front resumed the defensive. The Italian corps of the Sixth Army (XX and XIII)[2] did not move until the 26th, when the XIII Corps attempted to recover the Col del Rosso, lost at the time of the Battle of Asiago. This also failed. Reinforced by Storm detachments, and after a day of "lively harassing fire", the attack was repeated at 3 a.m. on the 29th in heavy rain. Small gains were made; but at 10 a.m. on the 30th the Italians captured the Col del Rosso, and, as a result, the commander of the Austrian *VI Corps* ordered a retirement that night to the old line of 15th June. The order did not reach some units until the morning of 1st July, so that the retirement was not completed until the following night. Further attacks were made by the Italians west of Monte Grappa and east of the Brenta on 4th, 6th, 7th and 15th July, all without success.

The French and British troops in the Asiago sector were not called on for an offensive as they had lost no ground; but at 9.30 p.m. on the 23rd Lord Cavan issued orders to the two divisions in the line to be prepared to attack the Austrian front line at short notice. On 29th June, however, instructions were received from the Italian Sixth Army to cancel all preparations for attack, and on the same day a letter from the Comando Supremo announced that it had been decided to abandon for the moment all intention to proceed to a general offensive.

Italian Advance from the Sile (Old Piave) to the Piave[3]

A further action, however, requires notice: In the retreat after Caporetto the Italian Third Army had crossed the Piave below S. Dona and taken position behind the old course of the river, generally known as the Sile. General Diaz now judged that advantage might be taken of the

---
[1] See Map II.
[2] See Map I.
[3] See Map II.

probable disorganization of the Austro-Hungarian forces to undertake a small offensive to recover the ground between the two waterways, a wilderness of bush intersected by numerous canals. Some change in the Austrian garrison had been made by the *XXIII Corps*, the cavalry division being relieved by parts of two divisions amounting to $18\frac{1}{2}$ battalions, with 292 guns. The attack was made pincer-wise on the morning of 2nd July at 3 a.m. by the 4th Division (XXIII Corps) on the right and the 54th Division, from the First Army, on the left. Assisted by bombardment and bombing, the Italians experienced no difficulty in crossing the river under cover of artificial smoke, and on the left, at least, took the enemy by surprise, capturing a thousand prisoners. Confused fighting followed, and at 4.20 p.m. on the 5th, in order to avoid further losses, General-Colonel Wurm ordered the island to be evacuated during the night. The retirement was carried out in good order " without any interference by the enemy worth " mention ".

Reflections on the Austrian Offensive

The great Austro-Hungarian offensive in Venetia, entered on with all available forces, and with full confidence that it would result in a victory as complete as Caporetto, ended in a failure which was little better than a defeat. Whether events would have turned out differently if there had been a German spearhead, or if General Krauss who had so successfully led the corps on the Austro-German right flank at Caporetto and in the pursuit, had been present in high command, is a matter for speculation; for, in June 1918, through professional jealousy, he was in exile, so to say, with the troops of occupation in the Ukraine.

The strategic plan was a compromise. Field-Marshals Conrad and Boroevic enjoyed equally high reputations in the Austrian army, and they advocated different plans, both excellent theoretically. Conrad's advance from the mountains in a direction well behind the Piave front naturally offered great possibilities, but the communications were indifferent, whereas an offensive across the Piave would have taken in flank the defenders of the mountain front, and had the advantage of excellent railway communications in the Venetian plain for supply. Both strategists ignored the natural difficulties of the ground. Conrad's offensive was forced to take place not only in mountains, but also in mountains covered by thick woods in which artillery could not destroy machine-gun nests, or wire, by bombardment—in fact, bombardment, by bringing down trees, added to the obstacles to a rapid advance. Boroevic's attack had in front of it an indestructible water obstacle, not even a clear one, but interspaced with gravel banks and small islands, the many arms entailing more bridging equipment and requiring more time to bridge than a single stream of the same total width.

As a result of the difference in the views of the commanders of the two Groups of Armies, the total available troops were divided equally between them, so that neither had sufficient weight to break through. With the forces on both sides so nearly equal and the Italians being able to reinforce one wing at the expense of the other more quickly, such a division was courting disaster in spite of the superior morale of the Austrians. The plan suggested by Major-General Waldstätten, the Deputy Chief of the General Staff, for an offensive between the eastern edge of the Montello and the Brenta, would, with the weight of the attack on the eastern wing, seem to have offered the best prospect. Boroevic's plan might well have succeeded had the *XXIV Corps* after capturing the eastern end of the Montello—which the Italians should never have lost—been able to push south from it in force. The Tonale diversion was the waste of two divisions badly needed elsewhere.

The writers of the Austrian Official Account offer many reasons, besides the rise of the Piave in flood, for the lack of success : the effective bombing of the bridges leading to the Montello by the R.A.F. is not included amongst them. The Austrian gas was, it is said, ineffective because it had deteriorated by keeping, and the Italians were now, as they had not been at Caporetto, " equipped with the excellent " English gas mask ". Secondly, the ground west of the Piave was entirely covered with vineyards and cultivation, offering good cover and a ready-made obstacle for the defence, and, being flat, hampered artillery observation. Thirdly, sufficient bridging equipment was lacking. Fourthly, as the time for the offensive approached and the Piave was found to be higher than normal in summer, Zero could not be postponed, on account of the shortage of rations. It has transpired that supply was so difficult in the mountain sector that Conrad relied on capturing Italian dumps to feed his men.

Probably the best plan of all for the Austrians would have been, as originally proposed by Boroevic, to stand fast and let the Germans finish the War.

In that case, however, Kaiser Karl could hardly have refused to comply with Ludendorff's request for 6 Austrian divisions to be sent to the Western Front, which he was unwilling to grant; after the Battle of the Piave he had to let two go.

The outcome of the failure of the offensive proved disastrous. Desertion both to the enemy and back to the Homeland reached high figures, leave men did not return, and bands of marauders began to infest the lines of communication and the countryside. Influenza and malaria took heavy toll of the underfed and exhausted men. Demands for a scapegoat arose both in Austria and in Hungary, and on 14th July Kaiser Karl removed Field-Marshal Conrad—not a *persona grata* at Court—from his command. The best strategist on the side of the Central Powers, who had held office as Chief of the General Staff, virtually Commander-in-Chief, longer than any of his friends and rivals of the other contending Powers (Joffre, French, Moltke, Grand Duke Nicholas, Cadorna, Falkenhayn, Nivelle, Pétain), Conrad had had little luck as a commander, and, like Benedek in 1866, was sacrificed for the continuance of the Hapsburg dynasty.

CHAPTER XVII

PRELIMINARY DISCUSSIONS ON AN ITALIAN OFFENSIVE

Generals Foch and Diaz[1]

After the conclusion of the Battle of the Piave and the retirement of the Austrians to the eastern side of the river, the Comando Supremo considered, and decided against, an immediate counter-offensive. Tired after six days' fighting and without previous preparations for attack, it was thought unlikely that the Italian troops would succeed in forcing and exploiting a passage of the Piave, when the Austrian effort, methodically prepared, had resulted in failure. General Diaz therefore decided to limit his operations to retaking the small pieces of ground on the mountain front which the Austrians had won, and, as already mentioned, to making an advance on the extreme right of the Italian front between the old (Sile) and the new courses of the Piave.

On 1st July General Foch was invested with the power of "co-ordinating the action of the Allied Armies" in Italy as well as on the Western Front, with advisory, but not executive, power in Italy. This was all that could be achieved by the Supreme War Council, owing to the position of King Victor Emmanuel as titular Commander-in-Chief of his army. General Foch could make recommendations to General Diaz, and was able to send troops and material to help him—subject, of course, to the veto of the Supreme War Council—but could not give him orders.

The Supreme War Council afforded the Generalissimo the fullest support; their Military Representatives investigated what material resources could be spared to Italy and examined what operations might be undertaken by the Austrians; the Chief of the Imperial General Staff kept the British War Cabinet informed of the happenings in the

---

[1] A full account of General Foch's endeavours to persuade the Italian Chief of the General Staff to take the offensive will be found in F.O.A. vi (ii), pp. 362–9 and vii (ii), pp. 355–8.

FOCH ADVISES OFFENSIVE. 27TH JUNE

Italian theatre; but correspondence with the Italian headquarters was left to General Foch.

The Generalissimo did not agree with the Italian decision to be satisfied with minor operations, and even before his appointment as co-ordinator begged General Diaz to exploit the victory he had gained over the war-weary, ill-fed, ill-equipped and disintegrating forces of the Hapsburg Empire, " as he was anxious that the impending general offensive on " the Western Front [which began on 18th July with the " Second Battle of the Marne][1] should be accompanied by " an Italian offensive ". He therefore continued to press for action.

On 27th June he wrote to General Diaz that the Germans were engaged in a series of offensives on the Western Front and would not be able to send troops to Italy: the danger therefore of a large scale offensive by the Austrians, reinforced by Germans, was remote: on the other hand, the Allies in the present situation could not spare the reinforcements for Italy necessary for a large-scale Italian offensive: but it was important to exploit the recent Italian victory, even by a limited offensive: an advance on the Piave front was not advisable against the well-organized defence of the Austrians, and with a wide river to cross at the outset of the attack. General Foch, therefore, recommended an offensive on the mountain front to gain enough ground there to be useful for future operations. He considered that the eventual objective of the Italians should be the Feltre–Trent road and the Trentino region,[2] the possession of which he thought was indispensable for a further attack to the east and across the Piave. As a preliminary, he suggested that an attack should be made as soon as possible on the Asiago plateau to gain possession of Monte Lisser and Monte Melette (respectively, 9 miles north-east and 5 miles north by east of Asiago).

General Diaz was not convinced that the Germans would not send troops to reinforce the Austrians in Italy with a view to a large-scale attack. Except for this, he agreed with General Foch's programme, but he asked for time to reorganize his troops and to make preparations before undertaking such important operations: his resources in

---

[1] See " 1918 " Vol. III, p. 228, *et seq.*
[2] See Frontispiece.

man-power were not great, and he hoped that American troops might be sent to Italy.[1]

General Foch was not satisfied with this answer, and wrote again on 13th July, insisting on the necessity of the Italian army undertaking offensive operations. This letter was brought to General Diaz by Colonel Girard, the French chief liaison officer; but the Italian Chief of the General Staff was still pre-occupied with the reorganization of his forces and would not give Colonel Girard any definite date on which he could begin offensive operations. On 6th August Maréchal Foch[2] repeated his insistence on the urgent necessity for an attack by the Italian army without loss of time, and for a continuance of this attack as long as the season was favourable. In this letter the Maréchal informed General Diaz that he was now able to satisfy requests which the latter had made, and could send him the 75 light tanks and the 40,000 rounds of artillery ammunition for which he had asked.

On 13th August General Diaz replied that the preparations for the offensive against the Asiago plateau had already begun and should be completed about 10th September, after which date it should be possible to attack. This did not seem very hopeful, for information previously given to the Entente General Staffs by the Italians, as Sir Henry Wilson (C.I.G.S.) told the War Cabinet on 20th September, was to the effect that this date was " too late for operations " on the Italian front owing to the shortness of daylight, " snow and other climatic conditions ". As an excuse for inaction, the Italian Chief of the General Staff said that he was short of transport, and could not carry out the offensive without more lorries. These he had already demanded from Marechal Foch, but had been refused; and on 17th August the Maréchal repeated that the lorries could not be spared from France.

Signor Nitti, the Italian Finance Minister, at a conference in Downing Street on 24th July, also tried to obtain material assistance from Great Britain, on the grounds that recent operations had made large inroads on the Italian resources. He also alleged, like General Diaz, that the Austrians were

---

[1] On 25th July the American 332nd Infantry Regiment of the recently arrived 83rd Division was sent by rail from France. The difficulty of finding shipping across the Atlantic prevented more from being sent.

[2] General Foch was promoted Maréchal de France on 6th August 1918.

in superior force in Italy—71 divisions against 57 of the Allies; but Major-General Sir George Macdonogh, the Director of Military Intelligence, pointed out that according to his calculations the Austro-Hungarians, omitting the 2 divisions on the Western Front, had only 76 divisions altogether, of which 14 were in Russia, 3 in Albania and 1 in the Homeland, that the total in Italy was 58 or 59,[1] with 1,770 heavy guns against the Italian 3,136, and about 4,000 field guns on each side. From statistics produced, too, the inference was drawn that the supply of gun ammunition in Italy was ample. Nevertheless, Signor Nitti begged that American divisions might be sent to Italy, as she had no reserves with which to meet an emergency, and had called up all classes of recruits up to the 1900 levy; and he persisted that the Austrian gun superiority amounted to no less than 3,000. Mr. Lloyd George pointed out that among practical things the improvements of railway communications with Italy required attention, so that if the Germans again attacked there the Allies could reinforce rapidly; and it was pointed out by the British Transportation expert, Major-General Nash, that the capacity of the Modane route could be increased 50 per cent. by improvements which would take two or three months to effect. It was arranged that Italian tank crews should be trained in England.

At the end of August General Diaz went to Paris and had interviews with Maréchal Foch, who received him very cordially, but was not able to persuade him to hasten the Italian offensive. The Italian Chief of the General Staff did not believe that the Austrian army was in a state of disorganization or that there was any great prospect of a revolt of the Slav elements in that army. Given the necessity for a large-scale offensive in the following year, he did not wish to compromise the efficiency of the Italian army by an attack in the current year, especially at a time when no help could be obtained from Allied forces. The Maréchal, while still adhering to his opinion that an attack should be made as quickly as possible, had to be satisfied

---

[1] According to A.O.A. vii, p. 438 and Appendix 32, 55 infantry and 5 cavalry divisions in Italy; 5 cavalry divisions, 8 divisions and 4 brigades in Russia-Balkans; 1 cavalry division, 2 divisions and 1 brigade in Albania; 4 divisions on the Western Front, and 1 in the Homeland. Total, $72\frac{1}{2}$ divisions and 11 cavalry divisions.

with the Itâlian army assuming an "aggressive attitude", ready to take advantage of any favourable opportunity.[1]

The personal interviews had, however, this effect: that General Diaz, on his return, addressed a circular to the Army commanders asking for their views on a possible large-scale offensive in the autumn.[2] This elicited from the Third Army a suggestion for an attack across the Piave at the junction of the two Austrian Groups of Armies; it was elaborated by the Comando Supremo, and, though judged hazardous by General Diaz, was eventually accepted by him.

General Diaz's cautious attitude had been supported by Signor Orlando, the Italian Prime Minister, who wrote to Maréchal Foch on 24th September, on the eve, as it happened, of the final great offensive of 26th September on the Western Front. His view was that an Italian offensive would be exposed to serious danger from an enemy counter-offensive at a time when Italian reserve of manpower had been exhausted, so that, after an autumn battle, Italy might not have the numbers necessary for operations in the spring of 1919; for an immediate offensive a reinforcement of 10 Allied divisions would be required on the Italian front. However, Signor Orlando continued, the Italian Government would take the decision to attack if Maréchal Foch would assume entire responsibility for operations in Italy. To this the Maréchal replied that he still adhered to his opinion that an Italian offensive should be launched without delay: as to the suggestion that he should be responsible for this offensive, he could not, as Commander-in-Chief of the Allied Armies, make a detailed study of an operation which affected only a small part of them, nor was it possible to send Allied divisions from the Western Front to Italy, for all there were engaged in fighting. Maréchal Foch concluded his reply with the words: "There "is no war without risks. The question to-day is to know "if, with the breakdown in morale and the disorganization "of the Austrian army, the Italian Command is ready to "run these risks".

The Maréchal's reply seems to have helped to dissipate the hesitations of the Italian Government and the Comando Supremo. It may be that the request on 27th September

---

[1] Baldini, pp. 164-5.
[2] Villari, p. 248.

ITALY AGREES TO ACTION. 1st OCTOBER

of Bulgaria for an Armistice influenced them. Certainly the successes of the Allies all along the line on the Western Front 26th-28th September had some effect on General Diaz. In any case on 1st October Signor Orlando informed Maréchal Foch that he and General Diaz had now agreed to take the offensive as soon as possible. According to the French Official Account, the Austrian and German proposal for an armistice addressed to President Wilson on 4th October had the effect of hastening the Italian preparations; for the Italian Government and the Comando Supremo began to be haunted by a fear that hostilities might cease before they had obtained even a modest victory.

Generals Lord Cavan and Diaz

After the defeat of the Austrians in the Battle of the Piave, Lord Cavan and General Graziani, the French commander, both hoped that General Diaz would take the offensive quickly whilst the Austrian army might be presumed to be in a shaken condition. General Diaz, however, as stated above, decided otherwise.

On 29th July Lord Cavan had an interview with General Badoglio, the Deputy Chief of the Italian General Staff, who was ardently in favour of an offensive; but with no help forthcoming from France, with only 51,000 men available for drafts after replacing the losses incurred in June, and with, as he imagined, inferiority in numbers of five or six divisions, he did not consider an offensive possible.

During August a limited offensive in the mountains, including the Asiago plateau, was under consideration by the Comando Supremo;[1] but by September no date had been fixed for this attack, and Lord Cavan was much disappointed to see the favourable season for mountain warfare passing away with nothing done. In the early days of September, General Diaz was in Paris, in conference with Maréchal Foch, but returned to his headquarters in Italy on the 7th. Lord Cavan had an interview with him on the 9th and spoke frankly. He felt it his duty to say that, in his opinion, the opportunity of successfully attacking in

---

[1] This proposal is dealt with in more detail in Chapter XVIII.

the mountains became less favourable with every day's delay for three reasons :

(1) The shortening day, necessitating an attack extending beyond one day and consequent loss of surprise, with higher casualties ;

(2) The daily strengthening of the enemy's line ;

(3) The loss of morale in our own troops caused by perpetual postponement : they had been " toeing " the line " to start since April.

To this, General Diaz replied : " I must visualize the " situation as a whole. The Austrians have more divisions " than I have, they are fighting with stubborn tenacity, " and to take an offensive just for the sake of doing so would " be a waste of life. I think that if in the course of the next " week, or even sooner, Maréchal Foch were to break through " the Hindenburg Line and take Cambrai or St. Quentin, " or both, the Germans would be bound to call on the " Austrians for help. If that situation arose, I should " attack at once at all costs, and it is for this that I want to " be ready ".[1]

Lord Cavan agreed with this view, and was much struck with General Diaz's evident desire to do all he could to help, while very naturally guarding his country's interests. General Diaz asked Lord Cavan—who was going to London —to impress on the Chief of the Imperial General Staff the important fact that the Austrians were not ready to fall down and be trampled on : they had shown good fighting qualities on several occasions since their defeat in June.

Later in September General Diaz became alarmed that an Austrian attack from the M. Grappa sector might roll up the whole line along the Piave, and ordered the commander of the Eighth Army, Lieut.-General Caviglia, to be prepared to counter-attack.[2] Nevertheless, as the month of September passed, by various signs and silences it was guessed at British headquarters that something was afoot— the first orders for concentration with a view to an offensive were, it will be seen, issued by General Diaz on 26th September. On 3rd October Br.-General Gathorne-Hardy, Lord Cavan's Chief of Staff, reported that a senior officer of

---

[1] The " Hindenburg Line " was broken through by the British Fourth Army on 29th September. St. Quentin was taken by the French on 3rd October, and Cambrai by the British on 9th October.

[2] Caviglia II, p. 102.

ACTION ORDERED. 6TH OCTOBER

Maréchal Foch's staff had for the past few days been impressing the necessity of offensive action on the part of Italy, and General Badoglio asked him to recall Lord Cavan from London, as he proposed to ask him to wire urgently to G.H.Q. France for some Inglis bridges, and he asked that the British should collect all bridging material they could in their area at Treviso.

No definite orders for an offensive were, however, received from Comando Supremo till 6th October, when General Diaz asked Lord Cavan to accept at once the command of a "Mobile Army of Reserve" (later called the Tenth Army), to be formed of the British 7th and 23rd Divisions and of the Italian XI Corps of 2 divisions: the British 48th Division would remain in the Asiago sector, under the Italian XII Corps, also one French division; this retention of the 2 divisions was intended to prevent the Austrians discovering that French and British troops had been withdrawn for employment on another front, and these would eventually rejoin their sister divisions on the Piave. Lord Cavan asked General Diaz for a definite statement that he meant to take the offensive at an early date. This assurance was given unequivocally, and Lord Cavan then accepted the offered command.

NOTE

THE AUSTRIAN PLANS AFTER THE BATTLE OF THE PIAVE[1]

In spite of ill-success in the battle and the increasing economic and internal political difficulties in the Homeland, the Austro-Hungarian High Command continued to cherish hopes that it might be possible to launch another offensive, at any rate in the late autumn, if only to ensure that the initiative was not left entirely to the enemy. A conference was held at G.H.Q. Baden on 2nd July, between the Deputy Chief of the General Staff, Major-General Waldstätten, and the Chiefs of Staff of the two Army Groups (Conrad's and Boroevic's) at which it was agreed that before anything else, the tired and hungry troops must have rest, and that "all further plans are dependent on the measure " of the material resources which can be furnished to the Armies ". Sixty divisions (55 infantry and 5 cavalry) only were available for the Italian fronts: "their equipment, with heavy artillery, "ammunition, machine guns, modern trench mortars, and

---

[1] See A.O.A. vii, p. 437 *et seq.*

"particularly aircraft, required to be considerably increased". It was also agreed that the only front which could be attacked with any hope of success was between the Montello and the Brenta.

From mid-July onwards the Allied raiding and patrol activity convinced the High Command that an offensive was impending, and Field-Marshal Boroevic forecast that it would come[1] from the upper Piave eastward towards the line Vittorio Veneto–Belluno (13 miles north of Vittorio). Plans for the Montello–Brenta attack were, however, prepared and discussed on 3rd August: 13 divisions (8 in first line) were to attack between the Montello and Pederobba (9 miles above the Montello on the Piave) and 11 divisions (8 in first line) between the Piave and the Brenta; but all depended on German help. In the middle of August—that is shortly after Ludendorff's "Black Day" of 8th August, the German communiqué having "caused great alarm in Vienna"[2]—General-Colonel Arz went to a conference at Spa with Hindenburg–Ludendorff; he had to confess that the Austrian army no longer possessed the material means for such a great operation, and that the Dual Monarchy was short of food, coal and raw material—he did not add that the Austrian army on the Italian front was in August 198,000 men short and the artillery so short of officers that it was ceasing to be serviceable;[3] nor that the army on the Piave had 33,000 cases of malaria in August.[4] Hindenburg–Ludendorff left him in no doubt that Austria could no longer count on the assistance of German troops; they wanted to know how many Austrian divisions could be sent to the Western Front, as so far only 2 had arrived. The heading of the last section of the Austrian Official Account of this period sums up the situation. It is: "Fettered to the Defensive".

The defeat of Germany on the Western Front, which made it impossible for her to send help to her Allies, brought about their collapse. On 4th October, Austria associated herself with Germany in an appeal to President Wilson for an armistice.

---

[1] See End-paper.
[2] Ludendorff ii, p. 685.
[3] A.O.A. vii, p. 45.
[4] A.O.A. vii, p. 465.

CHAPTER XVIII

THE FRONT DURING THE LONG PAUSE IN THE OPERATIONS 25TH JUNE—24TH OCTOBER
(Map II; Sketch 9)

Trench Warfare on the Asiago Front

During the four months between the close of the Battle of the Piave on 24th June and the opening of the final offensive on 24th October, whilst the Allied Armies on the Western Front, starting with the British offensive on 8th August, Ludendorff's "Black Day," were continuously engaged in driving the Germans from one prepared position and river line to another, no operational event of outstanding importance took place on the front in Italy. The Austrians had lost the initiative which they had seized on 15th June, the Italians declined to take advantage of the temporary confusion and demoralization in the Austrian ranks on the battle fronts, and a period of trench warfare ensued both on the Piave and in the mountains. On this latter front, according to the Austrian Official History,[1] the activity was confined almost exclusively to the French and British sectors where, on the Asiago plateau, besides numerous local actions, " daily bursts of artillery fire never allowed the front to " rest. Time after time enemy airmen crossed over the " mountains, swooped over the valleys of the Adige and the " Sugana and dropped bombs." The account goes on to say that in July the average number of Allied shells per day which fell on the Asiago plateau was 14,165 against 5,730 Austrian, whilst to the east, between the Brenta and Monte Grappa (exclusive), the number was 5,581 against 4,273.

The French Official Account speaks only of " actions by " small forces, offensive patrols and surprise thrusts. In " the Asiago sector the French forces carried out some minor " operations with particular success." The Austrians regarded the activity on the Asiago plateau as preparation for a subsidiary and possibly, later, a decisive attack.

---

[1] E.g. Vol. vii, p. 441, *et seq.*

Some desperate fighting took place amid the snow and glaciers of the Tonale Pass region in the west, where, as on 13th June, the Austrian local forces failed to obtain any success.

On the Piave front the Italians were more or less active, although " July was markedly quiet "; harassing artillery fire and bursts of fire, including gas, were employed by both sides, and the Italians carried out " isolated, occasionally "strong patrol enterprises on the islands and across the "river, with the deployment of much air activity ", and they consolidated their recapture of the ground between the old (Sile) and new courses of the Piave. These operations, which in September included building footbridges in the Piave and all the *simulacra* of attack, were from early August sufficient to lead the Austrians to expect an offensive at any moment.

In more ways than one it was the British front on the Asiago plateau that provided most interest.

July

At the beginning of July the British front was held by the 23rd Division (Major-General Sir J. M. Babington) and the 7th Division (Major-General T. H. Shoubridge), but on the 23rd the 48th Division (Major-General Sir H. B. Walker who had taken over command on 4th July) relieved the 23rd Division (less artillery, all of which remained in action). Each division had two brigades in the front position. In accordance with the policy laid down by the Comando Supremo, the month was mainly devoted to improving the defences, the Italians lending 3 engineer companies to assist the British. A piquet line of resistance was begun, and by the end of July had been completed and occupied in the 7th Division area, but it was not so far forward in the right sector owing to loss of time during relief of the 23rd Division. The enemy showed little activity except during the last week of the month, when his artillery fired a little more than usual. The weather was hot, with frequent thunderstorms, which hindered flying. In spite of this handicap, the R.A.F. destroyed 76 enemy aircraft and drove 3 more out of control, all for the loss of 4.

A number of raids were carried out; some of these will be mentioned in order to show the ascendency achieved on the ground over the Austro-Hungarians. On the night of 1st/2nd July the 11/West Yorkshire (23rd Division) raided Sec, and, at the cost of one man wounded, killed 15 and captured 43 all ranks. On the two following nights, raids were carried out by the 7th Division. In the first of these the 22/Manchester had trenches in the Canove salient as objective; at least 12 of the enemy were killed and 7 captured for the loss of one man missing and one wounded. On the second night a raid against trenches slightly farther west made by the 2/1st H.A.C. cost one killed and 15 wounded, but accounted for 29 killed and 3 captured. In four raids on the 15th/16th and following nights by the 10/Northumberland Fusiliers (23rd Division), 21/Manchester (7th), 9/Green Howards (23rd) and 2/Border Regiment (7th), 140 Austrians were killed, 56 brought in as prisoners, at a cost of only 10 killed and a few wounded and missing.

On 4th July Lord Cavan ordered that, except in the case of an S.O.S., the British artillery should be completely silent for three days from midnight of 6th/7th July (a period later extended to 4 a.m. on the 10th). The purposes of this silence were to mystify the enemy, to give some, but not complete rest to the R.F.A. which, since 15th June, had been overworked, to save ammunition, and to afford the sound-ranging and flash-spotting sections a clear field to locate new Austrian battery positions. The results were considered highly satisfactory: 8 new batteries were discovered, the enemy showed signs of nervousness and was evidently puzzled, as throughout the three nights he fired bursts of shell and did not cease to discharge Very lights.[1]

At 8 a.m. on the 11th the Italian 12th Division (X Corps) on the left of the British, took over a thousand yards of the frontage of the 7th Division. Five days later Lord Cavan assumed command of the Italian Sixth Army during the absence of General Montuori.

---

[1] Listening sets intercepted the following messages on the 7th: " 8.15. " Hello Fratze, please, situation unaltered. Enemy behaviour extra-" ordinary. Quite quiet. Aircraft activity ". " 9.10 Hello Erza. " Enemy extraordinarily quiet. Nothing observed except individual " movement ".

August

A Multiple Raid

Between the 13th and the 19th, the 23rd Division (less artillery) relieved the 7th (less artillery, which remained in action). In spite of raids, the enemy during August, in so far as his infantry was concerned, maintained a continuously passive attitude on the British and French fronts, only breaking it to retire on those fronts to a back position in circumstances to be related. As a result, too, of counter-battery work in this sector, he also withdrew his artillery, so that many Austrian batteries fired from positions beyond the range of the British 6-inch howitzer, and in consequence the forward areas suffered more than before from shelling. Hostile aircraft increasingly endeavoured to avoid combat, but nevertheless 66 were destroyed for the loss of 4.

On 2nd August Lord Cavan, being at Comando Supremo to discuss general policy, took the opportunity to mention the subject of the employment of the British troops during the winter months. He pointed out to General Badoglio, in the absence of General Diaz, that, except for the period when they were marching from the Montello to the Asiago plateau, his troops had been continuously in the line since their arrival in Italy in November 1917, and that it would be highly beneficial if they could have December and January free for combined training in an area, say, west of Lake Garda, where the ground was suitable for the purpose: that if this were impossible they ought to be sent back to the Montello, as he did not think they should be converted for the winter into Alpini without being given the special equipment and put through the special training required to keep them fit and well. He also had in mind the question of leave; this was important, as six thousand men had not had any leave for eighteen months or more; for it was impossible whilst in the line to spare more than eight hundred a week, which meant, allowing for the journeys, that over three thousand would be away at one time: if the troops were taken out of the line he should ask for facilities to send sixteen hundred away at a time, and try to clear off arrears.

General Badoglio informed him that the Comando Supremo intended to relieve the French and British troops on the Asiago plateau, the date depending upon the decision arrived at with regard to an offensive, and to give them five or six weeks for rest and training, if possible : it was hoped to double the allotment of leave trains : when the British troops went into the line again it would probably be on the Montello. These answers were satisfactory to Lord Cavan, who in reporting to the Chief of the Imperial General Staff made the suggestion—which was accepted— that ". . . contingent on our maintaining a passive rôle " throughout the winter . . ." his three divisions should be relieved gradually by divisions from the Western Front, which would be the better for a change and for a comparatively quiet winter in a healthy area : he would feel regret at parting with the divisions now under his command, but this would be outweighed by the benefit the transfer would confer on the army at large.

By 5th August evidence had accumulated which went to show that the Austrians intended to withdraw their line on the French and British fronts to the north of Asiago. Work was seen in progress on a line to the north-west of the town between Bosco and Camporovere. A captured senior officer gave as a reason for this move the heavy losses opposite the British sector and the persistent raids and artillery fire. Further evidence was afforded by the fact that during 1st–4th August the enemy registered his own front line, and a deserter volunteered the information that the withdrawal would take place on the 10th. Information reached the British that, as a preliminary to retirement, the Austrians would attempt to raid the British lines on the night of the 4th/5th. Arrangements were therefore made by the British for the advanced groups to show red lights instead of the usual S.O.S. signal on the approach of the enemy. Before the Austrian patrols were seen they themselves by mere coincidence happened to send up red lights, with the result that the British barrage fell on them, and they decamped, leaving 14 killed and 50 wounded on the ground.

On the evening of the 5th General Montuori (Sixth Army), having returned, held a conference at which Generals Lord Cavan and Graziani (commanding the French) were present, to meet General Badoglio. It was at first suggested that the French and British should attack, the first objective being the line of hills about three miles north of Asiago and the second, as the attack swung westward, the line marked by M. Longara–M. Catz–M. Rasta–Canove, which included the new Austrian line then under construction; but this should be not later than the 10th, the expected date of the enemy retirement. Lord Cavan asked for a few hours' reflection and the conference then adjourned. When it re-assembled later in the night General Badoglio put forward as an argument for action that it was important to give the Austrians some sort of push so that it might be claimed that the retirement was forced upon them and was not voluntary. Lord Cavan expressed his willingness to make the attack in order that the opportunity should not be lost, but pointed out that he would only be able to get two-thirds of his artillery into position in the few days available; that as the process of supply to the new position through Asiago would be expensive in material and life he did not think it desirable for the troops to stay on it for more than a week, when the advance should be continued against M. Mosciagh (north-east of M. Rasta) with a simultaneous advance against M. Erio (3 miles west of M. Rasta), as this summit commanded the greater part of the Asiago plateau.

Considerable discussion took place, and it was eventually decided to organize two raids—that is the attackers after reaching their objective and inflicting casualties and damage, would return to their own lines. One raid was to be carried out by the British on the night of the 8th/9th and the other by the French on the following night, in each case supported by all the Allied guns which could help. Further, on conclusion of the raids, preparations were at once to be begun for a large-scale operation in case the Versailles Supreme Council should sanction it.

In view of his limited man-power, Lord Cavan considered that this was the correct solution of the problem: should the enemy retire as forecast, the difficulty of advancing the guns for a large offensive must be overcome by pushing forward the batteries singly to carefully camouflaged positions and by their remaining silent until the day of action.

The British action comprised eight simultaneous raids,[1] which covered the greater part of the British front, and were carried out by a total of twenty-two companies drawn from all four brigades, 143rd, 144th, 91st, 22nd, in the front position and the 20th (the 7th Division's reserve brigade).

---

[1] See Sketch 9.

The eight raiding parties were furnished respectively from right to left by the 1/5th R. Warwickshire (2 companies), 1/7th R. Warwickshire (4 companies), 1/8th Worcestershire (3 companies), 1/6th Gloucestershire (3 companies), 1/R. Welch Fusiliers (2 companies), 1/South Staffordshire (4 companies), 20/Manchester (2 companies), 2/Border Regiment (2 companies). The night was dark and moonless, and the parties were led by guides into No Man's Land to forming-up lines about four hundred yards from the enemy's defences. The artillery barrage, which opened at midnight, was the signal for the infantry to advance, and it was effectively swelled by French and Italian guns; the twenty-two known enemy battery positions were counter-batteried with gas shell with complete success, and M. Ambrosini, on the left flank, was kept under machine-gun fire by the 7th Division Machine Gun Battalion until the raid was over. Some wire-cutting had been done, but, in order not to excite suspicion, not on an extensive scale; in places the obstacle was still thick, notably in front of Canove, but even here there were gaps. In the 7th Division sector two searchlights were used to light up the area of the objectives: experiments had shown that if the beam was directed sufficiently high, the downward glow enabled the attackers to see without being seen, and that the best results were obtained by directing the beam immediately above the point to be raided. The men of the 48th Division carried green lights, to be exhibited in the enemy's lines, it having been observed that the Austrians fired red lights from points attacked and green lights from those not being attacked.

Forming-up was achieved without drawing fire, and only occasional bursts of machine-gun fire from Canove indicated nervousness rather than vigilance on the part of the enemy.

The raids were entirely successful. There was little resistance in the front trench, more among the concrete dug-outs and emplacements in the support line, whilst half an hour before withdrawal at 2 a.m. some attempts at counter-attack were made, but easily disposed of by rifle-fire. The raiders, under an excellent artillery barrage which continued until 3 a.m., returned practically undisturbed; a bonfire was lighted on M. Lemerle as signal for withdrawal, and is said to have been of great help in the smoke and mist in guiding the parties back to their own lines.

The Austrians lost heavily in killed and wounded, and 8 officers and 347 other ranks were carried away prisoners. The total British casualties were 204, including slightly wounded, and all the wounded were brought back. The physique, health and general appearance of the prisoners was excellent; they showed no signs of malnutrition; their clothing was only fair, but their boots were strong and made of excellent leather; all of which seems to dispose of one of the excuses made for the poor fighting qualities exhibited by the Austro-Hungarians in 1918.

The French made their raid on the 9th/10th, with one battalion against M. Sisemol, "clearing the Austrian "trenches and capturing 241 prisoners, with very small "(*infime*) loss";[1] the British 143rd Brigade, next to the French, raided at the same time, but took no prisoners.

The enemy retirement was made a week later to a position called the *Winterstellung*, "which enclosed Asiago on the "north in a half-circle", because, as the Austrian Official Account states, "the strength of the divisions in the con- "tinuously shelled and repeatedly attacked lines south of "the Asiago was being slowly consumed", nearly a thousand men having been lost on the plateau in the previous week. "Only strong security posts remained in the old trenches, "which were to fall back if the enemy attacked in force"[2], that is they were left as a "false front", and this was not discovered for some time.

In spite of British activity in Italy and the great successes in August on the Western Front, Lord Cavan found it necessary to point out to the Chief of the Imperial General Staff that, to judge from the Italian newspapers, the war everywhere was being fought entirely by the French, Americans and Italians, and the prestige of the Empire was likely to suffer: that there was a lack of propaganda, and at very small expense it could be arranged that accounts of the exploits of the British Navy and Army appeared regularly in the Italian Press. No steps were taken to remedy this state of affairs.

The month of August was closed by two considerable raids against the enemy security posts in the old trenches. On

---

[1] F.O.A. vii (ii), p. 354.
[2] A.O.A. vii, p. 462. The line on Sketch 9 is taken from Maps 31 and 34 in that volume.

the 26th/27th the 1/Buckinghamshire Battalion and the 1/4th R. Berkshire of the 48th Division, with powerful artillery support, raided the enemy trenches east of Ave. They killed many Austrians and brought back 210 prisoners, their casualties amounting to 169 killed, wounded and missing. In the 23rd Division, which had relieved the 7th, on the same day, the 10/Duke of Wellington's attacked the post near Vaister, killed about eighty men and captured 65 at a cost of 56 casualties. In both cases the enemy was found prepared and at first offered resistance.

Towards the end of August the weather began to break and a period of rain and fog set in. By this time the British area was well organized and well provided with shelters, so that no great hardships were suffered. It was uncertainty as to what would happen next which troubled the troops. More than rumours were afloat of an offensive into the Alps beyond Asiago ; for large dumps of ammunition, reserve rations and forage were in course of formation in the most forward positions possible, pack transport was being re-allotted to units, and tables issued showing what each unit was to carry, and how. Certain senior officers only were informed that an offensive had been planned to take place in September, launched on a front of about forty miles from the Montello to Lake Garda, for the conquest of the Trentino. Such an offensive, in view of the mountainous country ahead and its few roads which could easily be blocked, was not in favour with the subordinate staffs. One divisional account speaks of the plan as "fantastic and "contrary to the elements of common sense". From the point of view of the higher leading there did not seem to be enough depth behind the front to organize a great offensive—and what ground there was was uphill and thickly wooded. As camouflage, a rumour was set about that, in consequence of British successes on the Western Front, the Austrians were about to retire and that the preparations were for a pursuit ; but this did not tend to deceive anyone.

The defeat of the German Armies had indeed a great effect in Austria. Lieut.-General von Cramon, German Military Plenipotentiary with the Austrian High Command, records :[1]

---

[1] Cramon, p. 174.

"The turn of events in the West [8th August 1918] had a crushing (*niederschmetternd*) effect in Austria. The belief that Germany's power could work miracles was so deeply rooted and so widely spread, that the exposure of the delusion was a thorough knock-down blow. Even the Kaiser [Karl] was deeply affected. He had me summoned to an audience, and told me that the disaster on the Piave had not produced such an impression on his people as the turn of events in the West".

September

Reduction and Partial Relief of the British Contingent

September was a month of many changes, and no British raids of importance were carried out, except on the 10th when, at 4 a.m. under a heavy barrage, the whole battalion of the 1/4th Oxford L.I. (48th Division) raided the enemy line at Sec on a front of a thousand yards. A demonstration was at the same time made against Ave. Everything went according to plan. The casualties were only ten. One officer and 37 men were brought back prisoner.[1] On the 6th it became known that the projected offensive might be abandoned, and on the 8th, to everyone's relief, that it had been definitely abandoned. On the 9th, the War Office, by telegram, ordered the reduction of the infantry brigades from 4 to 3 battalions, as had been carried out in January-February 1918 on the Western Front on the recommendation of a Cabinet Committee, "not one of whose members was a soldier",[2] against the protest of the Army Council. The 9 battalions thus rendered surplus were to be sent to the Western Front and the remaining battalions brought up to 900 strong from the reinforcements pool.

The battalions selected to remain were:

7th Division: 9/Devonshire, 20/ and 21/Manchester.

23rd Division: 9/Green Howards, 11/Sherwood Foresters, 13/Durham L.I.

48th Division: 1/8th R. Warwickshire, 1/5th Gloucestershire, 1/8th Worcestershire.

---

[1] The French on the 23rd, using two companies, took 105 prisoners near M. Sisemol.

[2] See "1918" Vol. I, p. 51.

The entrainment of the others for France was begun on the 13th and completed on the 14th, where they served to reconstitute the 25th Division.

The remainder of the 7th Division, which was out of the line and in the rest area near Trissino, was expecting to follow the 9 battalions as soon as the tired division from France, which was to replace it under the scheme suggested by Lord Cavan, should have arrived. Its divisional artillery, which had remained in the line when the infantry and engineers had come out, was brought down to the plains. Advanced parties were later detailed and despatched to France to take over the transport of the 47th (2nd London) Division, which had been nominated to exchange with the 7th, in order to save train space; but these parties had hardly arrived in France before it became known that they were returning, and that the advanced parties of the 47th, which had started, had been recalled by the Supreme War Council. This was the more puzzling to the 7th Division, as Lord Cavan, before leaving for a visit to England on the 11th, had visited its headquarters to say farewell to Major-General Shoubridge and his staff. It was hard to keep pace with the repeated changes of instructions. On the one hand, it was felt necessary to keep a sufficient reserve of material on hand for a possible offensive; on the other, it had to be borne in mind that the troops might be withdrawn at short notice, with little time to clear all British material and stores from the area.

The reduction of the infantry strength by a quarter, and the prospect of a tired division, selected on ground of its exhaustion[1] and difficulty of maintaining its numbers (the 47th (London) was a 1st Line Territorial Division whose county was also furnishing the 56th, 58th and 60th Divisions), with its infantry strength approximately no more than 6,200, taking the place of the fairly fresh and up-to-establishment 7th Division raised the problem of the holding of the line on the Asiago plateau. It was also stated that, owing to the pressure on the railways, the division could not leave before the 25th. The agreement that the British should maintain their position until mid-October required modification.

---

[1] The 47th had fought in the Battles of St. Quentin, Bapaume and the Ancre in the V Corps (Third Army) in March, and the battles of Albert and Second Bapaume in the III Corps (Fourth Army) in August and September.

During the absence of Lord Cavan, Major-General Sir H. A. Walker communicated with the Chief of the Imperial General Staff to enquire whether it was desired that the Comando Supremo should be approached with a view to the relief by Italian of the British divisions gradually, in the order they were required to go to France, and to the shortening of the British front on the plateau. He was directed to do so, and through Brig.-General Hon. J. F. Gathorne-Hardy, the chief General Staff officer, entered into communication with General Badoglio (Deputy-Chief of the General Staff) and General Montuori (Sixth Army). He found that the Comando Supremo recognized the claims of the Western Front, but was most anxious to interpolate British battalions on the Piave, and it was arranged (17th September) that the 23rd Division should be relieved by an Italian division, so that it might proceed to France in due course—it was relieved by the Italian 20th Division, command passing at midday on the 27th, and was then concentrated in the Vicenza area. As the 7th Division was in reserve, this left only the 48th Division in the line at Asiago; similarly the French 24th Division was left in the line at Asiago, and the 23rd went to a rest area near Vicenza.

On the 29th Lord Cavan, who was still in England, appealed to the C.I.G.S., who was on a visit to France, that more should be done to co-operate with the Italians, who had declared themselves ready to seize a favourable opportunity to take the offensive, than to provide three tired divisions from France which would hardly arrive in time to form a reserve and would be practically useless in the mountains, owing to their lack of experience in pack work, rock drilling, the difficulties of movement at high altitudes and of exploiting success in such regions. The move of the divisions to France was then postponed indefinitely, and the Comando Supremo informed that the British troops now in Italy would be available if required.

October

In October the only raids recorded are : one made by the whole 1/6th R. Warwickshire battalion against Ave, when, at a cost of 3 killed and 25 wounded, 4 Austrian officers and 146 other ranks were brought back prisoner. A second by the 1/7th R. Warwickshire against Sec was expected to make an equally large bag ; but only a small garrison was encountered, of which 32 were captured. The French, about the same time, raided M. Sisemol and took over three hundred prisoners.

With a view to an offensive, all troops were engaged in preparations—an account of which will be given in the next chapter. The French 24th Division and British 48th Division remained on the Asiago front; but on 9th October, General Diaz, in fulfilment of his promise, formed two new Armies, which incorporated the rest of the French and British contingents:

Tenth Army, under General Lord Cavan, consisting of the:
British XIV Corps (re-formed) and corps troops (7th and 23rd Divisions);
Italian XI Corps (23rd and 37th Divisions).

Twelfth Army, under General Graziani:
French 23rd Division and corps troops of the French XII Corps;
Italian I Corps (24th and 70th Divisions);
Italian 52nd Alpine Division.

On 11th October, British G.H.Q. left Lonedo for the Piave front, and the 48th Division came for tactical purposes under the Italian XII Corps, but was told that it would shortly rejoin the rest of the British forces and that it should push on with the evacuation of reserve stores and equipment from the plateau. On the 19th, however, Major-General Walker received sudden orders from General Pennella (XII Corps) to take part in an attack, in co-operation with the French, in four days' time. General Odry, the commander of the French 24th Division, announced plainly that his artillery would take part, but not an infantryman would leave the trenches. Reference was therefore made to Lord Cavan, with the result that the orders were cancelled on the 21st; but a series of raids were ordered by the Italian Sixth Army for the night of the 23rd/24th, the eve of the Battle of Vittorio Veneto, as they would be of assistance in protecting the flank of the Italian Army engaged against the M. Grappa sector in the main battle.

The British raid was made by the 1/4th Gloucestershire, which attacked Ave and eastwards of it and brought in 6 officers and 223 other ranks with the loss of 4 wounded. The French, on the right, secured 761, and the Italians on the left, 14.

CHAPTER XIX

THE BATTLE OF VITTORIO VENETO
24TH OCTOBER—4TH NOVEMBER 1918

THE CONQUEST OF PAPADOPOLI ISLAND 23RD/24TH OCTOBER
(Map III : Sketches 10, 11)

THE OPPOSING FORCES

On 12th October General Diaz held a conference of his Army commanders at his headquarters near Padua, at which the chief of the British Military Mission, Br.-General C. Delmé-Radcliffe, was also present.[1]

The disposition of the Italian forces, after the two new Armies, the Tenth and Twelfth, had been interpolated on the 14th, was to be :[2]

Third Army (Duke of Aosta), 4 divisions, along the Piave, on the right, as throughout the War ;

Tenth Army (General Lord Cavan), 4 divisions (the British XIV Corps and Italian XI Corps, each of 2 divisions)[3], along the Piave ;

Eighth Army (General Caviglia), 14 divisions, around the Montello ;

Twelfth Army (General Graziani), 4 divisions, at the junction of the Piave and Mountain Fronts, containing 1 French division ;

Fourth Army (General Giardino), 9 divisions, on the M. Grappa front ;

Sixth Army (General Montuori), 6 divisions, on the Asiago front, containing 1 French and 1 British division ;

First Army (General Pecori-Giraldi), 5 divisions, astride the Adige valley; the left on Lake Garda ;

Seventh Army (General Tassoni), 4 divisions, Lake Garda northwards to the Swiss frontier ;

---

[1] His notes, as well as the accounts in Vittorio Veneto, Villari, Caviglia II, etc., have been drawn on. See Sketch 11, which is taken from Map 1 in Vittorio Veneto and Map 31 in A.O.A. vii.

[2] The number of divisions is from Villari ; it differs slightly from Appendix V. See Sketch 10.

[3] It was mentioned at the Conference that in certain circumstances, which arose, the Italian XVIII Corps in reserve in the Eighth Army area might be transferred to the Tenth Army.

Ninth Army (General Morrone), 6 divisions, in general reserve, plus one unallotted Czecho-Slovak division and 1 American infantry regiment, behind the Twelfth and Fourth Armies;

Cavalry Corps (Count of Turin), 4 cavalry divisions, south of the Ninth Army, north of Padua.

Opposite them were the two Austrian Groups of Armies of Field-Marshal Boroevic and the Archduke Joseph (his *Sixth Army* was now under General Fürst Schönburg-Hartenstein), the boundary between them being the Cismon, a tributary of the Brenta, which, as it happened, coincided with the boundary between the Italian Fourth and Sixth Armies. Thus the Italian right wing, Third, Tenth and Eighth Armies (22 divisions and 4 cavalry divisions) were faced by the Austrian *Isonzo* and *Sixth Armies* (14½ and 7½ divisions respectively and 3 cavalry divisions[1]); the right centre, the Twelfth and Fourth Armies (13 divisions), was faced by the *Belluno Group* (12 divisions); the left centre, the Sixth Army (6 divisions), by the *Eleventh Army* (9 divisions and 2 cavalry divisions); and the left wing, the First and Seventh Armies (9 divisions), by the *Tenth Army* (9 divisions and one cavalry division).[2]

Thus the total numbers, 56 Allied divisions with 4 cavalry divisions against 55 divisions with 6 cavalry divisions, were, as near as may be, equal. But, as pointed out before, the Allied Armies were on "interior lines" with good railway communications, so that General Diaz could shift troops from the mountain to the river front and *vice versa* far more quickly than the Austrians, who had to use a circuitous route.[3]

The total guns, according to the Italians, was 7,700 against 6,030 estimated Austrian;[4] of the latter number about

---

[1] One of them, the *Reitende Schützen Division*, we should call mounted infantry.

[2] The number of Austrian divisions, 52, is taken from the Order of Battle in A.O.A. vii, Beilage 32, and, with 3 in general reserve, makes a total of 55 divisions and 6 cavalry divisions, of which 6 divisions and 1 cavalry division were back between the Livenza and the Tagliamento behind Boroevic's Group of Armies, 3 divisions near Belluno, and one in the Val Sugana. Vittorio Veneto (p. 14) puts the Austrian total at 63½ divisions, "of which at the beginning of the battle 39½ were in the front line, 13¼ in the second line, and 10¼ in reserve".

[3] See End-paper: via Trent, the valley of the Drave, Villach and Udine.

[4] Villari, p. 252; the Austrians say they had 6,145 (A.O.A. VII, Beilage 32).

eighteen hundred were heavy guns, half the Italian total of that calibre.[1]

A large amount of bridging material was collected, including 20 Italian service bridging trains; 5,000 yards of "tubular foot bridging", to be supported on boats; regulation heavy pontoons and trestles for another five thousand yards; and hundreds of barges and boats brought from the lakes and waterways. In view of the current of the Piave, two anchors were provided for every one normally used. For the repair of damaged permanent bridges, 700,000 cubic feet of timber, with ironwork and accessories, were concentrated in the area south of Treviso.

To the British XIV Corps were attached the 477th Field Company R.E. and bridging material of the 48th Division, the 18th Pontieri Company and 50 Italian sailors, and the 4th and 5th Bridging Trains from France.

General Diaz's Plan

The fundamental idea of General Diaz's plan[2] was, by a decisive break-through across the Piave to separate the Austrian Armies on the river front from those in the Trentino, and then by an enveloping movement westwards to roll up the mountain front. "This would necessarily "cause the complete yielding of the enemy's front in the "[Venetian] plain", because if by the break-through Vittorio Veneto was reached, the enemy's railway communications to the Piave would be severed.

The operation was to be carried out in two phases. In the first, the main blow would not be aimed at the junction of the river and mountain fronts, but at the junction of the *Isonzo Army* and the *Sixth Army*.

The Tenth and Eighth Armies were to force the Piave in the sector Papadopoli island[3]–the Montello, judged to be the weakest part of the enemy front, and advance, the Eighth Army northwards to the line Sacile–Vittorio Veneto and

---

[1] The total air force is not mentioned in the Austrian Order of Battle, and the Italian is not available. Little is said about the air, the weather being unfavourable, except that a British account says that Treviso was bombed on the night of the 22nd/23rd whilst the XIV Corps was concentrated there, without effect.

[2] Vittorio Veneto, p. 11. See Sketch 10.

[3] The full name is Grave di Papadopoli. "Grave" here means a shingle beach or bank ("Lido" being a sand beach).

the Tenth Army, protecting the Eighth Army's right, to the line of the Livenza between Portobuffole and Sacile. Thus it was hoped to cut the communications of the *Sixth Army*, all of which passed through Sacile and Vittorio Veneto, and perhaps succeed in cutting it off completely. Part of the Twelfth Army was to support the left of the Eighth, and part attack up the Piave valley in the direction of Feltre, thus menacing the right flank of the *Sixth Army*, and tending to isolate it. For this first phase of the operations the co-ordination of the movements of the three Armies was entrusted to General Caviglia, commanding the Eighth Army.

Besides the main operation, the Fourth Army, on the left of the Twelfth, was to support the latter's advance by attacking northward in the M. Grappa sector, with its left on the Brenta. The Sixth Army, on the left again, was to be ready to repulse any enemy offensive on the Asiago plateau, and to take part in any general advance northward if opportunity should offer. The Third Army, on the right, was to advance eastward over the Piave as soon as the Tenth Army had secured the passage of the river.

In the second phase of the operations the main effort was to be against the mountain sector, an advance from the east being combined with an attack northwards. From Vittorio Veneto the Eighth Army was to turn north-westward towards Belluno (on the upper Piave) and then northwards, up the Piave and Agorda valleys; the Twelfth and Fourth Armies were to push northwards on the left of the Eighth to Feltre. The centre of the Austrian Armies thus broken, the Trentino front would be cut off and, threatened with envelopment and disaster, must fall back.

Circumstances brought about a very different form of operation to that planned.

CONCENTRATION FOR BATTLE

The orders of the Comando Supremo for the concentration for the offensive of additional heavy artillery, supplies and bridging material, were issued on 26th September, and by 10th October sixteen hundred guns and five hundred trench mortars, with a million and a half rounds of gun ammunition had been transferred from other parts of the line and from reserve to the battle-front, to which also

21 divisions, including 1 French and 2 British, were shifted, moving chiefly by night.

Placed in command of the Tenth Army, Lord Cavan had on 11th October formed an advanced headquarters at Villa Marcello (6 miles south of Treviso). There, on the 14th he was joined by the remainder of the Army headquarters.[1]

Lieut.-General Sir J. M. Babington assumed command of the XIV Corps, now composed of the 7th and 23rd Divisions, and was succeeded in command of the 23rd Division by Major-General H. F. Thuillier.[2] The corps headquarters[3] assembled at Dosson (2½ miles south of Treviso).

The 7th Division was at the beginning of October in reserve in the Trissino area. During 5th–7th October it marched eastward to an area north-west of Vicenza, and during the 12th–14th, in bad weather, was moved by rail and concentrated south of Treviso. A severe epidemic of influenza broke out and soon affected the whole of the XIV Corps, but tended to disappear as soon as the troops left billets and bivouacked in cold and wet in the fields and vineyards.

The 23rd Division, as already mentioned,[4] had been relieved in the Asiago sector between 24th and 27th September, and was also billeted in an area north-west of Vicenza. On the arrival there of the 7th Division, it took the latter's place at Trissino, but during the 14th–16th followed the 7th Division by rail, and also concentrated south of Treviso.

During this period of concentration of the XIV Corps,[5] the Italian XI Corps (23rd and 37th Divisions) was holding a 9-mile sector of the Piave front from opposite Ponte di Piave to Palazzon near Spresiano; on the 16th the Tenth Army ordered the XIV Corps to relieve the XI Corps in the northern

---

[1] Chief General Staff Officer, Major-General Hon. J. F. Gathorne-Hardy; D.A. & Q.M.G., Major-General H. L. Alexander; C.R.A., Major-General W. H. Kay; C.E., Major-General C. S. Wilson.

For discipline and administrative purposes the Italian XI Corps, which, with the XIV Corps, made up the Tenth Army, remained directly under the Italian Third.

[2] Previously G.O.C. 15th Division, Director of Gas Services, G.H.Q., and head of the Chemical Warfare Department, Ministry of Munitions.

[3] B.G.G.S., Br.-General W. W. Pitt-Taylor; D.A. & Q.M.G., Br.-General C. Ogston; C.R.A., Br.-General E. S. Hoare-Nairne; C.H.A., Br.-General T. R. C. Hudson; C.E., Br.-General E. Barnardiston.

[4] See p. 262.

[5] See Map III.

half of its line between Salettuol and Palazzon, both inclusive. The 7th Division was detailed to take over the front, with a brigade of the 23rd attached for the purpose of occupying the left half of the front. All reconnoitring and taking-over officers were put into Italian uniforms, and all British troops likely to be seen were to wear Italian great coats and helmets, and it was arranged that no British guns should open fire before Zero, unless this was necessary to repel an attack. The British air force, the Fourteenth Wing, with the 28th, 34th, 66th and 139th Squadrons and the 3rd and 7th Kite Balloon Sections, remained in the Asiago sector until a general move to the Treviso area was made on 22nd October; but although (high flying) Bristol fighters might be used, no R.E. 8's (low flying artillery planes) were to appear over the Piave front before the battle.

The 7th Division Takes Over a Piave Front

The 22nd Brigade (Br.-General J. McC. Steele) relieved the Italians in the whole sector between the 18th and 20th, on which latter day the command passed to the 7th Division, with headquarters near Lancenigo station (3 miles north of Treviso). The position, on low-lying flat ground, was found to consist of three lines, the first at the water's edge, all with small low dug-outs, or rather shelters; but there was a complete absence of suitable observation posts. On the 22nd the 69th Brigade (Br.-General A. B. Beauman) of the 23rd Division took over the left sub-sector from the 22nd Brigade, and on that day XIV Corps headquarters moved to Villa Margherita ($1\frac{1}{2}$ miles north of Treviso).

It had originally been intended to begin the offensive on 16th October; but heavy rain and a consequent rise in the level of the Piave caused a postponement, and, the weather continuing to worsen, on the 18th it was evident that this postponement must be prolonged for about a week. The delay brought the advantage that it became possible to carry out the transfer of four hundred more guns from the western sectors of the front, and the Comando Supremo decided to use them to reinforce the Fourth Army (M. Grappa) sector; and this Army, whose original rôle was merely to support the Twelfth, on its right, was now ordered to push home its attack in the hope of drawing the enemy reserves. General Diaz had always been anxious about the M. Grappa front, where a successful advance by the Austrians would separate his river and mountain fronts, and offer all the advantages he himself hoped to gain by a similar operation ; an attack there would in any case serve as a diversion. As the transfer of the additional artillery would be finished by the 23rd, October 24th was made Z Day.

Lord Cavan's Instructions to the Tenth Army

On 14th October, immediately after taking over command of the Tenth Army, Lord Cavan held a conference with his British and Italian corps and divisional commanders, at which he explained General Diaz's plan and the part the Tenth Army was to play in the operations. The corps commanders were given a 1 : 100,000 map showing the general lines of an offensive across the Piave and were asked to send in their proposals. Lieut.-General Babington suggested the advisability of occupying Papadopoli previous to the general advance, and this was accepted.

After all proposals had been discussed, on the 20th the Tenth Army issued preliminary instructions, with one map showing the enemy's defences and the various objective lines, and another the barrages. At a date to be communicated later the Italian XI and British XIV Corps were to force the passage of the Piave and advance rapidly some twelve miles to the Livenza. The enemy defences consisted of two " battle belts " or " zones ", designed German fashion for defence in depth, formed of lines of trenches with mutually supporting centres of resistance in and behind them on points of tactical advantage. The first zone, about 2,200 yards deep, with its front on the river embankment and with outpost trenches on the Grave di Papadopoli and other islands, was called the *Kaiserzone* (Emperor's Zone). The second, described as " behind the Monticano " (a stream which runs from Vittorio Veneto to join the Livenza), and known as the *Königzone* (King's Zone) was about six miles from the Piave.[1] Owing to bad

---

[1] This second position had been begun only at the end of June (Berndt p. 64).

weather no recent air-photographs of the Papadopoli area were available, but this was remedied, as on the 22nd the whole XIV Corps area was covered by the R.A.F., and during the night five thousand prints were made and issued to formations.

It was calculated by the Comando Supremo that on the Papadopoli front the enemy could use 350 guns against the 800 Allied guns in position—in the subsequent action, the proportion seemed reversed.

The passage of the Piave and the advance beyond it were to be made as a continuous operation, but in two phases:

    (i) the capture of Papadopoli island, and

    (ii) the advance from this island on to and beyond the left (eastern) bank.

In the first place, both corps of the Tenth Army were to attempt to gain a footing on Papadopoli by surprise. The general plan would be to push troops across the river channels to the island under cover of darkness by means of ferry boats and footbridges. Artillery fire was not to be opened unless the crossing was opposed, in which case barrages should be put down, under corps arrangements, sufficient to secure the capture of the island.

In the second phase, the general bombardment of the defences on the front of the Tenth Army was to begin at 11.30 p.m. (23rd); at an hour which would be notified later, shortly before dawn, the passage of the river on the far side of Papadopoli island would be made. One thing was clear, that Cavan's Tenth Army was to be the spearhead in the crossing of the lower Piave. Lord Cavan's instructions pointed out that as the Third Army on the right was not to cross the Piave until the Tenth Army had gained the passages, the XI Corps, which would be attacking on the right of the XIV Corps, must take measures to protect its right flank, and, similarly, though part of the Eighth Army on the left of the Tenth Army was to advance on the first day of attack, the XIV Corps must be prepared to guard its left flank. On the rest of the front of attack the bombardment was to open at 5 a.m. on the 24th, and the assault would follow the next day at 6.45 a.m., or perhaps earlier; seven bridges for the Eighth Army were to be thrown between the destroyed Priula bridges and the Montello, and one, near Pederobba, for the Twelfth Army; the bridging would be preceded by a crossing in boats.

The Preparations to Seize Papadopoli Island[1]

According to the final plan of the XIV Corps, on the night of 23rd/24th October the 7th Division was to occupy the northern part of Papadopoli island down to a fixed line opposite Salettuol. At the same time, the Italian XI Corps was to occupy two islands on its front, Caserta and Maggiore, and, if time permitted, to push troops on to the lower end of Papadopoli up to the Salettuol line before the general attack about dawn on the 24th. For the seizure of his part of the island, Major-General Shoubridge was to put one brigade over by boat or fording; then bridges were to be built and the other two brigades would cross.

Patrols of the 7th Division had spent the previous nights trying in vain to find any place where the river was fordable; no complete crossing to the island had, however, been discovered, nor had the patrols set foot on it. From a reconnaissance made on the morning of the 23rd, two places appeared suitable for crossing: one using the island of Veneto as a stepping stone, and the other higher up, from the island of Cosenza. The latter was too exposed to view and fire for the construction of a pontoon bridge, but the island was already connected with the right bank by two footbridges, and it would be possible, during the hours of darkness, to get troops across from it to the north-west end of the Grave di Papadopoli in boats, and probably by a footbridge. This end of the Grave, which was called the Lido, appeared to be unoccupied by the Austrians—for, although they had constructed trenches there, owing to a rise in the river these had been evacuated and not reoccupied when the river fell. A landing on the Lido would enable the enemy defences to be taken in flank and rolled up. It was therefore decided to adopt this plan for the capture of the island.

A bridge for use by wheeled vehicles for the further operations against the enemy positions beyond the Piave would, however, also be a necessity. When Papadopoli had been captured it would be possible to construct a pontoon bridge to the island at or near the small island of Veneto, where it would be screened from direct enemy view by the trees and undergrowth on Papadopoli. The

---

[1] See Sketch 11.

bridging and crossing operations at this site and at Cosenza would meet with considerable difficulties from the rapid current in the river channels and the liability of the river to rise at short notice. When Papadopoli had been occupied the problem of crossing the channels of the river lying between that island and the further bank of the river would still remain to be solved.

The general nature of the Piave river, its islands, shingle banks, many channels, varying depth and rapid current, has already been described;[1] so only the portion of it which confronted Lord Cavan's XIV Corps requires closer description. The streams between the island of Papadopoli and the right bank of the river, at the time, formed the main channel, with a total width from shore to shore of about 280 to 780 yards. The island, flat and very little above high-water level, with a shore of river sand and gravel, was some four miles long, with an average breadth of over a mile. Its exact extent is variable, as the streams around it, which themselves vary their channels, are frequently dried up, when the adjacent islets and banks become part of the island.[2] At the date of the attack the branch which separated the island from the left bank was broken by many shingle banks and islands, and fordable nearly everywhere, so that Papadopoli was almost part of the eastern bank, with which, in any case, it was connected by a number of footbridges at its lower end. The upper portion of the island was river sand and gravel, with patches of marsh, the centre was covered with scrub, and in it was a fosse, three feet deep, a former water channel; only the southern, and higher, portion had been inhabited, as the ruins of twelve small houses showed, and was cultivated and planted with vines and maize.

The Austrian defences consisted of two main lines of shallow trenches—the water-level would not permit much depth—with good wire hidden by long grass and rushes, and plenty of machine-gun posts, trench-mortar emplacements and little barrow-like shelters scattered about behind them. The first line was close to the water's end, the second followed roughly the line of the fosse. The garrison was

---

[1] See pp. 77–8, 104.
[2] No two of the several available maps of the island and the channels were found to agree. The latest Italian 1 : 10,000, dated 25th September 1918, did not show the islands at the Lido end as found on 23rd October.

thought to consist of 3 companies, but it was subsequently ascertained that there were on the island at the outset 8, the outposts of 3 regiments of the *7th Division*, subsequently reinforced to 15.[1]

PASSAGE OF THE PIAVE BY THE 22ND BRIGADE[2]

The British operation was entrusted to the 22nd Brigade of the 7th Division, at 10 p.m. on the 22nd, and Br.-General J. McC. Steele selected the 2/1st H.A.C., with 2 machine-gun sections, to make the landing with 2 companies in first line, and 1 in support, and 3 companies of the 1/R. Welch Fusiliers were to follow in reserve. All companies were to consist of a hundred other ranks, and Lieut.-Colonel R. N. O'Connor (H.A.C.)[3] was placed in charge of the operations on the island. For the crossing, Italian shallow flat-bottomed boats or, rather, scows, pointed at the ends, each capable of holding 12 men standing up, were provided. Each was to carry 7 men and be manoeuvred by two Italian pontoneers of the 18th *Pontieri*, who by means of punt poles kept the boat at the proper angle to the current so that the stream carried it across. Some days had been spent by the 7th Division in practising with this type of boat on the much slower flowing Sile near Treviso—even there with disastrous results, for the navigation of a torrent is a special art, and in the hands of a tyro such a boat usually spins round and, if not washed ashore, capsizes. As no more than 12 boats could be procured, only about eighty men could be carried on each trip, and the process was bound to be slow.

---

[1] From south to north the *37th*, *38th* and *132nd Regiments* of the *7th* (*Hungarian*) *Division*. The island was divided into 3 sectors in which they had, respectively, 4, 2, and 2 companies, with similar numbers in support behind the river embankment, the rest of the three regiments being about 2 miles back in reserve, with a fourth regiment behind them. See " Letzter Kampf und Ende der 29 Division ", by Field-Marshal-Lieutenant Ritter von Berndt. The *29th* and *7th Division* formed the *XVI Corps*, of which Berndt was in temporary command. He states that owing to sickness the *7th Division* had only two-thirds of its establishment, and that the attack came as a complete surprise, it not being known that the British were in the line : the only good news he received was that the Italians on either side were unable to cross the river.

[2] The report rendered by the 2/1st H.A.C., with 4 situation maps, is particularly full, and a vivid and detailed account of the landing, based on it, will be found in " The Defeat of Austria as Seen by the 7th Division ", by its senior chaplain (C. of E.), the Rev. Canon E. C. Crosse, D.S.O., M.C.

[3] Lieut.-General Sir Richard Nugent O'Connor, K.C.B., D.S.O., M.C.

When at 5 p.m. on the 23rd the companies of the H.A.C. paraded at their billets at Maserada, two miles south of the place of embarkation, the sky was cloudy and the moon, half full, was obscured. At 7 p.m., when it was dark, the first boat, carrying an officer and 3 other ranks and the Italian officer in charge of the boatmen, set out from Cosenza island to reconnoitre. They returned in twenty minutes to report that there were three main streams to be crossed, separated by banks of sand and shingle, round the end of which the boats must be hauled—the noise of the stream over the shingle being sufficient to drown any sound: the first stream was about seventy yards wide, with a swift current and unfordable; the second was about fifty yards wide with even a swifter current, also unfordable; the third was about a hundred yards wide, but only two or three feet deep and fordable.

At 8.15 p.m. the first two platoons, detailed to form a bridgehead, started to cross; two boats were swept down stream, but the other ten landed safely about a hundred yards below the point of embarkation, and the small party of the H.A.C. at once pushed inland. Entering the trenches it found them manned by only a few posts, and within fifteen minutes 12 Hungarians were on their way to the beach as prisoners, the rest of the garrison having been bayoneted. The remainder of the company and a second company had now to cross to sweep down the defences; but at 8.45 p.m., before the other two platoons of the leading company could cross, an Austrian S.O.S. went up at the lower end of the island—due, no doubt, to the Italian 37th Division's attempt to reach Maggiore island—and the Austrian artillery opened on that part of Papadopoli. A few minutes later S.O.S. signals were fired from the Lido end, an artillery barrage came down on the embarkation beach, and machine-gun bullets began to spatter around. Then a searchlight to the north opened and continued to sweep the western bank, being generally followed by artillery fire on the targets illuminated. To add to the anxiety of the leaders, the moon broke from the clouds, so that from the embarkation beach the men and boats could be distinguished landing on the opposite shore. There were a fair number of casualties, but no boat was hit, and the crossing was continued.

Simultaneously with the ferry crossing two footbridges

were constructed across the unfordable channels at a point about four hundred yards farther upstream by the remainder of the Italian *Pontiere* Company, assisted by the 101st Field Company R.E. of the 23rd Division. These bridges were made of boats similar to those used for ferrying, spaced 20 feet apart and connected by special strong duckboarding. Directly the bridges were complete, the remainder of the two battalions of the 7th Division crossed by them. Since the site of the bridges was completely exposed to enemy view and machine-gun fire they were dismantled before dawn and the equipment hidden in the undergrowth on the shore for the day; they had therefore to be reconstructed each night during the ensuing crossing operations.

BRITISH PORTION OF PAPADOPOLI ISLAND SECURED

About 11 p.m., as soon as all of the first two companies of the H.A.C. had landed and formed up facing south-east, they started to advance down the island. Rain began to fall heavily and a thick ground mist formed; but guided by the trenches, in which they found only small posts, the right company and part of the left one pressed straight on. The Hungarians, taken by surprise by the flank attack, offered little resistance, so that by 1 a.m. most of the two companies had reached their objective, opposite Salettuol, and there hung on. The left platoon and the support company, by a mistake, drifted to the left until they came opposite Francia island, but recovered direction, and, "winkling out" the garrison of a strongpoint (3 officers and 60 men) on the way, rejoined the leaders, and completed the H.A.C. line. All then set about clearing the front and completing the line across the western half of the island, feeling more secure as a company of the 1/R. Welch Fusiliers had come up, with instructions from Lieut.-Colonel O'Connor to protect the left rear of the H.A.C., prevent enemy reinforcements crossing to the island, and clear up "pockets" within the perimeter which had been captured. Three companies of the Fusiliers had begun to embark at 9.45 p.m., and completed the crossing, partly by boat without mishap, and partly by the footbridges, by 1 a.m. To connect with them, battalion headquarters and one platoon of the H.A.C. advanced north-westwards across the island. In so doing they surprised and took prisoner 8 Hungarian officers and about two hundred other ranks, only two posts offering any real resistance. The R. Welch Fusiliers took up position in support on the left of the H.A.C. with one company holding the eastern shore as a defensive flank; the enemy shelling fell, however, on the western shore. Later a company of the 11/West Yorkshire (23rd Division) arrived and took post on the left, having been ferried across from Cosenza island as soon as the 22nd Brigade had cleared the northern end of Papadopoli.

Thus by 5 a.m. (24th) the objective had been everywhere reached and secured at small cost in casualties; about 330 Hungarians had been captured; and, in spite of the difficulties of the passage and the beach being under fire, the wounded had been evacuated, and bully beef and biscuits brought over; but communication with the right bank was only by messenger; for rain had silenced the power buzzers, no cable could be laid, and mist and rain made visual signalling intermittent.

Nothing could be heard or seen on Papadopoli of the Italian 37th Division. It was known that 6 battalions had crossed on to Caserta island by a footbridge; but "they "failed to cross over to the Isola Maggiore, on account of "enemy fire and the great depth of water".[1] In fact the Italians made no attempt to force the passage of the Piave until their liaison officer with the 7th Division had reported that the British troops were on the Grave de Papadopoli.

The Main Attack is Postponed

At 5.30 a.m. on the 24th the Italians opened a lively bombardment by guns and trench mortars on the enemy front, which died down about midday.[2] Except for Austrian shelling of Papadopoli, little happened on the 24th: about a hundred more prisoners were rounded up; but the Hungarians at the lower end of the island kept quiet, and

---

[1] Villari, p. 259. A.O.A. says they were stopped by the rifle fire of the *37th Hungarian Regiment*.

[2] Thus A.O.A. vii, p. 614, which says the fire covered "the whole "front of the *Sixth Army* and the northern wing of the *Isonzo Army*": that might correspond to the Italian Tenth and Eighth Armies, but it is expressly stated on the next page that the fire on the Papadopoli front was not above normal, and as no Italian artillery fire is reported in British accounts, except slight retaliation, and no British artillery was to open until the main attack, the bombardment mentioned by the Austrian Official account must have been fired by the Eighth Army.

no counter-attack took place, as the commander of the *Isonzo Army* regarded the landing as " a local diversion " attack " designed to assist the operations in the M. Grappa sector, which began on the 24th.

Rain fell heavily throughout the day of the 24th and was still falling when at dusk the crossing of troops from Cosenza to Papadopoli was resumed. The main assault on the enemy position on the other bank of the river having been fixed for the next morning at 6.45 a.m., it was the intention of the 7th and 23rd Divisions to send across to the island that night all the troops selected to carry out the assault. The 7th Division planned to send over first the remaining (fourth) companies of the H.A.C. and R. Welch Fusiliers, and the remaining two machine-gun sections, to complete the garrison of Papadopoli, and then the 20th and 91st Brigades. The 23rd Division intended to send over the remainder of the 69th Brigade, of which one company each of the 11/West Yorkshire and 8/Green Howards had already crossed, followed by the 68th Brigade.

The above units began to cross by boats at dusk. The river was rising rapidly, the current increasing, and the passages took considerably longer than on the previous night. The construction of the footbridges was also found to be impracticable in view of the condition of the river, and it became obvious that the assaulting brigades would not be able to get into position during the night. When the companies of the H.A.C. and the R. Welch Fusiliers, and the machine-gun sections, had crossed, and one company of the 8/Green Howards of the 23rd Division had followed them, an order was received from XIV Corps to stop the operation. General Diaz had decided to postpone the general attack fixed for the following morning on account of the state of the Piave.

The situation of the British troops now marooned on Papadopoli, namely the 22nd Brigade of the 7th Division, and the companies of the 11/West Yorkshire and 8/Green Howards of the 23rd Division, was an unhappy one. They were wet through, under shell fire, and their only cover was shallow holes dug by their portable intrenching implements, since picks and shovels had not been carried. Fortunately the enemy fire was directed principally on the former Austrian defence trenches which the old soldiers of the 7th Division were careful to avoid.

The 22nd Brigade Captures the Rest of the Island

Rain ceased on the morning of the 25th; the Hungarians, for reasons best known to themselves, still remained quiescent. Plans to advance the left that evening were made by Lieut.-Colonel O'Connor; but before any action had been taken, the brigade-major of the 22nd Brigade arrived with an order that the remainder of the island was to be captured, so that the Italian 37th Division could cross from Maggiore island and form up on Papadopoli for further attack. Major-General Shoubridge himself went to 22nd Brigade headquarters on the beach and, 16 boats (the extra ones begged by Lord Cavan from the Duke of Aosta, Third Army) now being available, ordered the rest of the brigade, that is brigade headquarters and the third battalion, the 2/R. Warwickshire, to cross to the island. Br.-General Steele crossed by boat in the afternoon—at the second attempt—one boatman being wounded and the other, jumping overboard, drowned, at the first attempt, when the general had the lining of his helmet torn by a bullet. After dark, the river having begun to fall, crossing of troops from Cosenza island was resumed, by the boat ferry and by the footbridges as soon as they could be re-erected. In order to screen the operation from the enemy, the beam of the Austrian searchlight on the opposite bank was blanketed by a beam of light established by the 3rd Italian Searchlight Company (attached to the 23rd Division) from a point on the river bank some 500 yards upstream. This threw its beam parallel to, and in front of, the scene of the crossing, and formed a perfect screen. The 2/R. Warwickshire and the headquarters 22nd Brigade (7th Division) were then transferred to the island of Papadopoli, and in addition the headquarters and 2 more companies of the 8/Green Howards (69th Brigade, 23rd Division). The latter, together with the company of this battalion which had already crossed, took up a position at the northern end of the island facing towards the enemy bank of the river and finding what little cover they could in rough scrub and shallow excavations.

The operation to clear the island was fixed to start at 9.30 p.m., with a plan on the same lines as in the original advance, that is the right was to thrust along the defences whilst the left covered that flank and the rear. As time for reorganization and for preparation was short, the attack was again made by the 2/1st H.A.C., in lieu of the R. Welch Fusiliers, first selected, who were now to support the attack under instructions from Lieut.-Colonel O'Connor; the 2/R. Warwickshire, on arrival, was to take over the front on the northern side of the island.

From 9 p.m. to 10.30 p.m. the enemy's artillery shelled the occupied part of the island, as if he expected attack; but this did not cause any alteration in the plan.

There was sufficient moonlight to aid movement, and for the first half-mile no resistance was encountered; then it stiffened, and under exceptionally heavy machine-gun fire progress became slow; but the island was cleared. By 5.15 a.m. a hundred and thirty prisoners had been taken, and the 2/R. Warwickshire had relieved the 1/R. Welch Fusiliers in the northern part of the island, so that the 22nd Brigade was strung out, the H.A.C. from abreast of the southern end of Maggiore along the southern and eastern shores past the Austrian bridges;[1] then came a company of the R. Welch Fusiliers, with the rest in support behind the left and then, later, the Warwickshire. After a short enemy bombardment at 5.30 a.m., two determined counter-attacks developed: the principal one, on the H.A.C., from the bridges, and the other on the company of the Welch Fusiliers, across the fordable channel.[2] The Hungarians were successful in so far as they gained a small footing near their bridges, but from this they were expelled by the H.A.C., fifty being killed, 110 taken prisoner, and the rest escaping. By 9 a.m. the whole of the island was in British possession, and from this small holding the great Piave bridgehead was soon to be built up. The rain now stopped and the British were no longer alone; for at dawn the advanced guard of the Italian 37th Division had landed, having crossed over from Maggiore island, and by 8 a.m. it had taken over the right company front of the H.A.C. There was spasmodic artillery fire during the 26th after 8 a.m., but the Austrians made no further attempt to

---

[1] For these, see Sketch 11.
[2] The counter-attacks were made by " 4 hastily thrown together companies [units not stated] ", A.O.A. vii, p. 614; and it is admitted that " they were brought to a stop ".

recover Papadopoli,[1] and at dusk the attacking troops of the 23rd Division began their passage to the island.

Construction of Pontoon Bridges

The site selected for the pontoon bridge was just below the tail end of the island of Veneto, about 300 yards above Salettuol. The whole problem presented to the engineers of providing bridges for wheeled traffic across the Piave to Papadopoli, and from that island to the far bank, was one of extraordinary difficulty. The distance from the near bank to the island was about 550 yards, but the depths varied, and in some parts were shoals or sandbanks uncovered by water. The main stream, which mainly flowed close to the near bank, was about 250 yards wide to the nearest shoal. The portion from the further edge of Papadopoli to the Bund, which marked the left bank of the river bed and was the enemy's front line of defence, was approximately 2,000 yards in width. It was composed partly of dry gravelly banks and partly of water channels of varying depth. It was probable that for regular wheeled traffic some of the latter would have to be bridged; but how many and of what width was not at this time known; it was therefore uncertain whether the pontoon equipment of the XIV Corps would suffice to fill all the gaps. The design of the British equipment was ill-suited to the 8–10-knot currents of the Piave and it was doubtful whether the pontoons would ride at anchor in it. The Italian 18th *Pontiere* Company, attached to the XIV Corps, had, however, a certain number of Italian pontoons, bigger than the British, having a high bow which enabled them to ride easily in the waters of the swift Alpine rivers. Another serious difficulty was that the field companies, R.E., had had little or no training in pontooning, having been mainly engaged throughout the war in trench warfare, and neither officers nor men had any experience of how to get pontoons into position, or lay out anchors in such a rapid current, and they had no motor launches to assist them.

The operation of constructing the bridge was under the

---

[1] A.O.A. vii, p. 614, says that the Austrians were much disturbed by the appearance of British and French troops on the Piave, and that the local corps commander decided to keep his reserve brigade for the main attack, now expected.

command of Lieut.-Colonel W. A. FitzG. Kerrich, C.R.E. of the 7th Division, who had at his disposal for the work the three field companies of the 7th Division, the 128th Field Company of the 23rd Division, with all the pontoons of that division, and an Army Troops company, R.E. He had also the 18th Italian *Pontiere* Company, less the portion of it required for ferrying troops and constructing the footbridges at Cosenza island. The *pontieri* were excellent workers, many of them specially enlisted watermen, skilled at boat work in rapid waters.

On the night of the 24th/25th the 54th Field Company, with great difficulty owing to the rise of the river, got a cable 250 yards long across the main stream and laid twelve kedged anchors. On the evening of the 25th the *Pontiere* Company placed four Italian pontoons in position in bridge. On the 26th, the whole of Papadopoli being in Allied hands, work on the bridge could be carried on by day, and this was facilitated by mist which obscured the site from distant view and also from the air, lifting only for an hour about 1 p.m., so that the enemy remained unaware of the existence of the bridge, or at least did not fire on it. The engineers put into position ahead of the Italian pontoons three bays of Weldon trestles and continued the bridge in shallower and slacker water with ten British pontoons. It became obvious, however, that the bridge would not be finished to the island before nightfall, so about half of it was completed as a footbridge of duckboards on wooden trestles. This enabled the troops of the 20th and 91st Brigades of the 7th Division to cross during the night of the 26th/27th and to get into their positions for the assault of the Austrian main line the next morning.

Thus, without any help from the Italian 37th Division, the very hazardous operation of seizing an island in a torrential river had been brought to a completely successful end with small casualties (the H.A.C. lost in all 92) ; but it could not have been achieved without the aid of the Italian boatmen and without the cover of the providential mist.

The Monte Grappa Fighting[1]

To complete the story of this period before the main attack across the Piave, it must be recorded that the attack

---
[1] See Sketch 10.

MONTE GRAPPA. 24TH OCTOBER

by the Italian Fourth Army, supported on the right by the I Corps of the Twelfth Army, in the M. Grappa sector, had no success. " By the end of the first day [24th] the " Italians had captured eighteen hundred prisoners and " machine guns, but their losses had been heavy and the " territorial gains very slight ".[1] On the 25th some summits on the edge of No Man's Land were gained, but only two were retained, and, " in view of the heavy losses of " the Grappa Army, General Giardino decided to suspend " operations in order to give his men a rest and time to " consolidate ". On the 26th, however, " furious fighting " still continued " and some ground was won ; " but the " Austrians could still sting, and by what proved to be their " last offensive effort recaptured the lost positions ".[2]

The Austrians remained in possession of their front here until the night of the 30th/31st October, when events on the Piave forced them to leave the Grappa sector. Italian accounts claim that the attack prevented the enemy from shifting reserves from the M. Grappa to the Piave front ; but there was no means of transferring them except by road. The 3 divisions in reserve near Belluno would have had a 30 miles' march by mountain roads to reach Vittorio Veneto.

On the Asiago front it was not until 1st November that the Allied troops began to attack, as will be related in due course.

---

[1] The quotations here are taken from Villari and Vittorio Veneto. A.O.A. vii, p. 600, says " by the evening of the first day the attack was " completely shattered ".

[2] A.O.A. vii, p. 602–3, speaks of " fruitless attacks " by the Italians. It states that by 5 p.m. " all lost positions were again fully in possession " of the brave defenders ", and adds that the Italians had lost nearly 35,000 men, and the outcome of the 3 days' fighting was " equivalent to " a defeat ", and greatly raised the spirits of the Austro-Hungarian army.

CHAPTER XX

THE BATTLE OF VITTORIO VENETO (*continued*)

THE PASSAGE OF THE PIAVE

27TH OCTOBER 1918
(Maps III, V ; Sketches 11, 12)[1]

On the afternoon of the 26th, the weather having turned fine and the waters of the Piave continuing to subside, General Diaz, at 6 p.m., issued orders to the Tenth, Eighth and Twelfth Armies to take in hand the postponed operations for the passage of the river, the general bombardment opening at 10.30 p.m.

The Twelfth and Eighth Armies

On the left, in the Twelfth Army, under the French general Graziani and containing the French 23rd Division, two companies of the French 107th Regiment crossed the Piave in boats at 6 p.m. to cover the construction of two bridges, by which the right wing of the Army, the XII Corps, was to cross. The boats for one of the bridges were carried away by the current ; but by 1.40 a.m. (27th) the other bridge had been completed, and by 2.30 a.m. 3 French battalions were across and were followed by $2\frac{1}{2}$ Alpini battalions. By this time the Austrians had awakened and taken the bridge under gun-fire, and about 6 a.m., just as a second French regiment of 3 battalions was about to cross, it was hit and the boats broke away. A storm having arisen farther north about 3 a.m. and brought increase of water into the Piave, it proved impossible to repair the damage during daylight. Nevertheless, the 5 battalions already over the river took the offensive, enlarged the bridgehead until it was pushed about two thousand yards

---

[1] Sketch 12 shows the campaign on the whole front in Italy ; Map III gives the Battle of Vittorio Veneto as a whole ; Map V gives the advance of the British XIV Corps in greater detail.

ITALIAN EIGHTH ARMY FAILS. 27TH OCTOBER

from the shore, and repulsed several counter-attacks. The situation was, however, very critical, as so little ground had been gained and connection with the west bank was broken. At night the repair of the bridge was undertaken with improvised material, the pontoon train ordered up not being able to reach the spot owing to the roads being blocked with traffic.

The Italian I Corps, the left wing of the Twelfth Army, on the western bank of the Piave alongside the Fourth Army in the Grappa area, made a little progress northwards on the 27th; the Fourth Army itself could make none.

The Italian Eighth Army, next on the south, was to throw seven bridges; it was able to make only two in the left centre, where parts of the 1st Division " d'assalto " crossed at Falzè, and forced the *41st Honved Division* and the *12th Mounted Rifle Division* to wheel back behind a stream, the Saligo, at right angles to the Piave, so that these divisions faced west.[1] The 57th Division secured a tiny holding three miles to the westward of Falzè; but sufficient ground was not gained at either place to free bridging operations from observed and destructive artillery fire. All other attempts to cross failed, and the two bridges which had been constructed were soon broken. Thus the Eighth Army, which was cast to play the principal part in the battle, was not in a position to do so.

The following summary of the situation is given by General Caviglia, the commander of the Eighth Army:

" During the night of the 27th/28th the [Italian] pon-
" toneers made prodigious efforts to re-establish the
" bridges, and here and there they succeeded; but by
" morning there was not even a footbridge behind the
" troops huddled together on the left bank except at the
" Grave di Papadopoli[2]".

The situation at Falzè, however, met with an unexpected improvement during the night (27th/28th); for the Austrian *25th Division*, on the west of the landing, instead of counter-attacking the isolated invaders, fearing for its exposed flank, wheeled back, thus, as it were, opening the second half of a folding door to admit the Italians.

---

[1] The Austrian accounts call the bridgehead here Saligo; the Italians call it Sernaglia.
[2] Caviglia I, p. 149.

THE TENTH ARMY. PREPARATIONS FOR THE ASSAULT

The branches of the Piave which ran between Papadopoli island and the eastern bank varied in number from two to six; all were fordable, but in places waist-deep, with a swift current, as much as ten knots an hour. Although bridging was unnecessary, the task before the Tenth Army, of which the British XIV Corps was the left wing, was formidable. The main Austrian line was the embankment of stones and gravel, overgrown with grass, known as the Bund, built to contain the river when in flood. It resembled a miniature railway-embankment, about ten feet high, six feet wide at the top, with sides sloping at 60 deg.; at curves of the river it was reinforced with concrete. Its weak point, discovered after it had been captured, was that the machine guns mounted on it could not be depressed sufficiently to be effective when the attackers were within eighty yards. In front of it were two strong belts of wire in good condition. To reach it from the front line on the island, south of Francia island, the attackers had first to cross a stretch of about a thousand yards of sand and gravel, the last two hundred without a bush or tree; secondly, the branches of the Piave, separated by gravel shoals, without a scrap of cover except such shelter as the three-foot bank of the river afforded after it had been crossed; thirdly, a stretch, twenty to two hundred yards wide of scrub and trees between the river and the Bund, not only wired but also scarred by the remains of trenches, snipers' posts and machine-gun emplacements. So secure did the Austrians consider the Bund, backed as it was by a good shooting artillery, so confident were they that this could destroy any bridges which were thrown, that at only a few places had they cut fire-steps and made machine-gun emplacements in it. Immediately behind it, instead of a support line, were only concrete "dug-outs", not contrived for use as machine-gun nests.[1]

The Bund availed the enemy little: for it was found possible to place guns on the extreme left of the XIV Corps area, which completely enfiladed it behind, on top and in front, so that it afforded no protection to troops immediately behind it.

---

[1] According to Berndt, p. 189, a second line behind the great embankment, though marked on the map, had not been begun; not until August was any attempt made to organize a battle zone and a rear zone in accordance with the German manual on the defensive battle.

ORDERS FOR THE ATTACK

Lord Cavan had issued orders to the Italian XI and British XIV Corps for the main operation at 1 p.m. on the 24th, after the successful occupation of Papadopoli. He gave five objectives, three of them to be reached by the 27th, the first being the Bund, and he fixed 6.45 a.m. as Zero.[1] As the field artillery on the western bank—roughly five hundred yards from the river—could not cover the advance beyond the third objective, divisions were ordered not to leave that objective without orders from the corps.

Owing to language difficulties, Lord Cavan had some doubt as to his intentions being clearly understood by his Italian coadjutors and neighbours. He therefore invited General Paolini (XI Corps) and General Basso (XVIII Corps) to meet him at a look-out which he had caused to be built by his engineers in a high tree. From this point of vantage, speaking in simple French, he showed them the exact lines on which he wished them to direct their advance after crossing the river.

The attack was to be made, from left to right, by the British 23rd and 7th Divisions (XIV Corps), and the Italian 37th Division (XI Corps), followed by the Italian 23rd Division.

Every man was to carry an iron ration and one day's complete hard ration.[2] The delay on the 25th and 26th had enabled two days' supply for the XIV Corps to be collected on the river bank at Maserada and Lovadina (2 miles north-west of Maserada).

The artillery available for the XIV Corps made a total of 19 field and mountain batteries, 37 heavy batteries and 27 trench-mortar batteries, none too much for a 3,800-yard front :

> 7th Division (C.R.A., Br.-General S. C. Stanley-Clarke), XXII and XXXV Brigades R.F.A. and three trench-mortar batteries.
>
> 23rd Division (C.R.A., Br.-General J. Byron), 102nd and 103rd Brigades, R.F.A. and three trench-mortar batteries.

---

[1] The objectives are shown on Map V, except the fifth which was the Monticano river.

[2] The infantry carried, besides, one extra bandolier of s.a.a., one Mills grenade per 3 men, and wirecutters. The ration for the 28th was brought over by carrying parties.

VITTORIO VENETO

Three Italian mountain batteries;
XV and XCIV Brigades R.G.A. (a total of nine heavy batteries);[1]
Nine groups of Italian heavy guns (a total of 28 batteries);
Three groups, each of 4 batteries, of Italian trench mortars;
Three groups of Italian heavy trench mortars (a total of 9 batteries).

Divisions were to arrange their own machine-gun barrages, and it was notified that contact aircraft would fly over the front at zero hour, 9 a.m., 11 a.m. and 12.30 p.m.

It has already been mentioned that in order to conceal the presence of British artillery until the last moment, none of the batteries had been used in the conquest of Papadopoli island; fire was to be opened—as at Cambrai a year earlier—without previous registration, on observations made by the 6th Field Survey Company R.E., and this was done with conspicuous success, although the batteries did not move into position until dusk.

One brigade of the 7th Division and advanced troops of the 23rd and 37th (Italian) Divisions were already on Papadopoli island. The crossing of the rest of the 23rd Division, begun about 6.30 p.m. (26th) in darkness, was made by the two existing footbridges to Cosenza island, and thence by boat ferry, until footbridges were completed across the two channels between Cosenza and Papadopoli by the 101st Field Company R.E. and Italian *pontieri*. This was done by 10.30 p.m., and an hour later the heavy artillery opened fire and the field artillery began cutting the wire of the Bund. By 3.30 a.m. (27th) the whole of the 68th and 69th Brigades, detailed for the attack, had crossed on to the island, with the exception of two companies of the 10/Northumberland Fusiliers, retained by the 68th Brigade as reserve. The Austrian searchlight, which might have disclosed the large assemblies of troops at the crossings was again blanketed and there was no interference from the enemy until after the British bombardment opened, when in the counter-bombardment a few shells fell in the neighbourhood of the bridges without doing any damage.

---

[1] The other 3 brigades of British heavy artillery were with the 48th Division in the Asiago sector.

THE BRITISH ASSAULT. 27TH OCTOBER

On arrival of the troops they were guided to their assembly places on the east side of the island, where they dug in, using their entrenching implements, as no picks and shovels were carried. All were in position by 3.30 a.m. The 20th and 91st Brigades of the 7th Division crossed under similar conditions, alternating battalions, by the Salettuol bridge, in single file, only one small stream, fifteen yards wide, having to be waded, and they were in a position by midnight. Its *pontiere* having bridged the main stream, the rest of the Italian 37th Division now crossed to the island, using Caserta and Maggiore islands as stepping stones.

Under enemy artillery fire, shrapnel and fragments of shell dropping all over the island, but occasioning extremely few losses, and drenched about 5 a.m. by a heavy rainstorm, the infantry waited until 5.30 a.m., at which hour they began to creep forward in order to be as close as possible to the edge of the stream at zero hour, thus reducing the thousand yards' No Man's Land on the island to about two hundred. At the same hour (5.30 a.m.) news was received at divisional headquarters that the bridging arrangements of the Italian 58th Division, on the left of the XIV Corps, had broken down and it would be unable to take part in the attack.

Zero had been chosen that it might be just getting light as the troops started. At 6.25 a.m., twenty minutes before Zero, the field artillery dropped a very accurate but thin barrage—only 1 gun to about seventy-five yards—on the edge of the river, and at zero hour this barrage—with a percentage of smoke-shell in it to mark its position—began to creep forward. It was timed to advance 15 yards a minute, with halts on each of the objectives, before finally at Zero plus 5 hours 17 minutes, settling for the day in front of the third objective. The two 4.5-inch howitzer batteries of the 23rd Division fired respectively a smoke and a creeping barrage; and two batteries of Italian heavy artillery fired a standing enfilade barrage in order to protect the left flank.

By zero hour rain had ceased and a slight mist lay on the water.

THE ASSAULT OF THE 7TH AND 23RD DIVISIONS

On the exposed wing, the left, the 23rd Division (Major-

General H. F. Thuillier)[1] had the 68th Brigade (Br.-General C. D. V. Cary-Barnard) and the 69th Brigade (Br.-General A. B. Beauman) in the line, the former with the 11/Northumberland Fusiliers on the left, with a left flank guard provided by 2 companies of its sister battalion, the 10th, and the 12/Durham L.I. on the right ; this flank guard, it had been hoped, would only be necessary in the first stage of the advance, as the Italian 58th Division, starting at a distance of 5,000 yards from the 23rd Division, was to make a converging attack ; but as the Italians had failed to cross the river, additional flank protection had to be provided and the 8/K.O.Y.L.I. of the reserve brigade (70th) was sent up to reinforce the 68th Brigade and assist Br.-General Cary-Barnard in protecting his left, which presently would be completely in the air. The 69th Brigade used the 10/Duke of Wellington's and 8/Green Howards, but one company of the 11/West Yorkshire was interpolated in the centre between them ; otherwise each battalion had 3 companies in line and 1 in support, arranged not in waves, but broken into a platoon artillery formation. Each brigade had attached to it a machine-gun company, one mobile (pack) 6-inch trench-mortar battery, and a section of a field company R.E.; the rest of the engineers were employed on bridging work. The water channels were crossed by sections, mostly by the men linking arms, and dragging their feet along the bottom ; for in places to lift one foot meant that the other would be swept away : some men were actually washed off their feet and a few drowned. As the barrage lifted off the Bund the whole line rushed forward. Machine-gun fire was heavy, and amongst others Lieut.-Colonel A. A. St. Hill of the Northumberland was killed. The bombardment had not destroyed much of the wire, but this was thin in places, where the men could trample it down, and there were sortie gaps in it, whilst other gaps were cut by hand under Lewis-gun covering fire to keep Austrian heads down. Through these gaps platoons passed and then extended again right and left, and the bayonet did the rest. It was reported that no Austrian had his bayonet fixed ; many surrendered, others ran.

In spite of resistance, in which the 11/Northumberland Fusiliers, on the left of the line, lost all its senior officers,

---

[1] The strength of the 23rd Division was 380 officers and 9,931 other ranks. In April, with 12 battalions, it had been 593 and 13,647.

THE BRITISH ASSAULT. 27TH OCTOBER

so that it was led by a lieutenant, soon after 7 a.m. the whole Bund on the front of the 23rd Division was in its possession.

The 7th Division (Major-General T. H. Shoubridge) had the 91st Brigade (Br.-General R. T. Pelly) on the left, and the 20th Brigade (Br.-General H. C. R. Green) on the right, retaining one in reserve like the 23rd Division. They each put only 1 battalion in the front line, instead of 2 as the 23rd Division had done, the 22/Manchester and the 2/Gordon Highlanders, respectively; the 1/South Staffordshire and 8/Devonshire were in support, and the 2/Queen's and 2/Border Regiment in reserve. The first line was thus weaker than in the 23rd Division, and the resistance offered seems to have been somewhat stouter; in any case the support companies and battalions had to be brought up before the wire was passed; but, under conditions similar to those in the 23rd Division, the Bund was captured up to time.

At this stage 9 aircraft of the R.A.F., in patrols of 3, began attacking the enemy kite balloons, and very soon brought down 3. Enemy machines were very active all day, in particular attacking the bridges and the troops crowded near them, and engaging the aircraft co-operating with the artillery. On the British side, besides reports of progress, a number of low-flying attacks were made; an attempt was also made to hit a bridge over the Monticano near Vazzolo.

That the Italians on the left had not crossed the Piave was not the only misfortune. On the right nothing could be seen of the Italian 37th Division, and at the moment of the first success, when the British divisions were over the river and on the Bund, a message was received by Lieut.-General Babington from General Paolini to say that his corps (XI) had failed to cross the river, and that he intended bringing the barrage back for a fresh attack. Thus the British spearhead was left without support on either flank. Lieut.-General Babington could do no more than request General Paolini not, at any rate, to fire the new barrage within a thousand yards of the right boundary of the XIV Corps, as the Austrians were on the run and he meant to go on with or without the Italians. Soon there was better news: first to the effect that a number of Paolini's men had crossed the river and that it was not now proposed to bring back the barrage; and, secondly, that General

Diaz had placed the XVIII Corps (General Basso), consisting of the 33rd Division (General Sanna) and the 56th Division (General Vigliani), the reserve of the Eighth Army, under Lord Cavan, and that it would arrive in his Army's area, that evening to cross by the British bridges during the night.

Advance to the Second and Third Objectives

At 7.10 a.m. the advance was successfully continued to the second and third objectives, over dead-flat ground, but broken by cultivation, sparsely covered with withered vines and patches of high grass and scrub, and dotted with the remains of villages. The barrage was timed to move at 15 yards a minute with a halt on the second objective. In the advance the main resistance was experienced on the exposed flanks, the enemy troops in the centre, having met the British on Papadopoli island and on the Bund, were not prepared to stand. In the 23rd Division, the flank guard of the 68th Brigade had stiff fighting against enemy machine guns, and as the 7th Division was lagging a little behind, the 69th Brigade on the right also had for a short time its right flank exposed; nevertheless the second objective, a trench line found to be quite well wired, was taken by 8.10 a.m.

The 7th Division had been delayed by the resistance of Austrian strongpoints. The 20th Brigade with the 2/Gordons still leading, and the 91st Brigade with the 1/South Staffordshire now leading, had to deal with three villages, Cimadalma, Vendrame and S. Michele, all reduced to ruins by the bombardment, but well prepared for defence, with field guns in the intervals between them. The final resistance came from 8 machine guns and a number of snipers; it took time to liquidate them, and the Gordons, having an exposed right flank, lost their commanding officer, Lieut.-Colonel H. A. Ross, and 5 other officers killed. But many prisoners were taken and the second objective was reached by both brigades before the barrage moved on again.

There was still no sign on the right of the Italian 37th Division; a company of the 8/Devonshire (20th Brigade) was therefore sent down the Bund to look for it, and, finding the 281st Regiment about half a mile away, assisted it to get on.

In the next advance at 9.30 a.m. of the 23rd Division, in the same formation as before, the Borgo Malanotte, a fair-sized house with an outbuilding, standing in a garden, on the right front, offered strong resistance; but it was captured by the company of the 10/Duke of Wellington's which was in the front line of the 69th Brigade, and the third objective, a road covered by short lengths of trench and wired in places, was reached by both brigades about noon. At 1 p.m. the enemy counter-attacked against Borgo Malanotte and, ammunition running short, gained a footing; but the garrison being reinforced from the brigade reserve by a company of the 11/West Yorkshire, the buildings were recaptured about 4 p.m., most of the enemy being killed or taken prisoner. The position of the 23rd Division in front and on the right, where the 7th Division was up, was secure. On the left, however, owing to the failure of the Italian VIII Corps to cross the Piave, there was a good deal of machine-gun and trench-mortar fire, and the rest of the 10/Northumberland Fusiliers had been sent up to reinforce the 2 companies already engaged. Later, the three 18-pdr. batteries of the 103rd Brigade R.F.A. were switched over to supplement the howitzer batteries already covering the flank, and by evening most of the enemy machine guns had been silenced. The situation was much improved by the arrival in the evening of the leading brigade of the Italian 56th Division (XVIII Corps, now under Lord Cavan), which had crossed the Piave by the British bridge at Salettuol, and in the early morning (28th) it relieved the 10/Northumberland Fusiliers, left flank guard of the 68th Brigade, the relief being completed by 6.30 a.m. The 10th then relieved the 11/Northumberland Fusiliers.

The 7th Division in the advance from the second to the third objective had the 1/South Staffordshire, 22/Manchester and 2/Gordons leading, with the 8/Devonshire guarding the right flank. It was confronted this time not with ruined villages, but by a large number of isolated farms almost all untouched by shell fire, mostly turned into strongpoints by the employment of concrete and timber, and well garrisoned and containing two or three machine guns. Their reduction took time, as a separate attack on each had to be organized. The usual procedure, the assault party having been deployed, was to open fire of Lewis guns and rifles, and under cover of this parties were to work round the flanks of the buildings and rush them from the rear with bomb and bayonet. On the other hand, the village of Tezze, on the left at the junction with the 23rd Division, was cleared after a little desultory skirmishing. Thus in the course of the afternoon the third objective was secured, assistance being given by two batteries of the XXII Brigade R.F.A., which, crossing early by the bridge at Salettuol now available for wheeled traffic, came into action on Papadopoli island about 2.30 p.m. An Italian mountain battery also crossed, and 3 mobile trench mortars were brought over. The Italian 37th Division not being up on the right of the 7th Division, the 8/Devonshire bent back a flank a mile to establish touch.

As a result of the day's operation, which had terminated in the successful occupation of the set objectives, the number of prisoners who had passed through the corps cages had been :

    7th Division, 1,690 (90 officers)
    23rd Division, 1,830 (31 officers).

The 7th Division had captured 25 guns ; the 23rd, 29 guns.

The Tenth Army, under Lord Cavan, or rather one should say the British XIV Corps, was the only formation which achieved complete success on the 27th : the passage of the Piave had been forced and an advance of over 3,000 yards made from the further bank. Detailed as flank guard to the Italian Eighth Army, the XIV Corps had become the spearhead of the attack.

Completion of Bridging Operations

The line of the third objective was near the extreme limit of range up to which the field artillery could cover the advance from its original positions on the right bank of the Piave. It became therefore of urgent importance to complete the bridge at Salettuol for wheeled traffic, in order to permit of the artillery advancing to more forward firing positions north of the river. This urgency became greater when it was decided to pass troops of the Italian XVIII Corps across the river for operations on the left flank of the 23rd Division. On the 27th, therefore, the engineers, under Lieut.-Colonel Kerrich, had completed the bridge to Papadopoli by substituting pontoon bays for the half of the bridge which on the 26th had been built as a trestle footbridge. This work was finished by midday. The 101st Field Company R.E. (23rd Division) was this day

THE BRITISH ASSAULT

added to the companies under Lieut.-Colonel Kerrich, and, thus reinforced, they also bridged the channels between the island and the far bank of the river. As soon as the pontoon communication was through, the bridges were taken into use for the passage of artillery and transport of both the 7th and 23rd Divisions. It has already been mentioned that on the night of the 27th/28th the Italian 56th Division (XVIII Corps) began to cross by the Salettuol bridge. On the same night a brigade of the Italian 33rd Division (also of the XVIII Corps) began to cross the river by the Cosenza footbridges, which were once more reconstructed for this purpose, with a view to co-operation in the movement of the 56th Division. On this night also a second pair of footbridges were constructed across the two channels to the Lido (the northern tip of Papadopoli) alongside the two which had been used on the preceding nights, and from this time these bridges remained permanently on the site.

When the infantry of the XIV Corps was moving towards the third objective, which was the extreme limit of fire of the field artillery from the right bank of the Piave, the bridging of the river to permit the crossing of artillery and other wheeled traffic was well in hand. From Cosenza island, now in the 23rd Division sector, a footbridge was completed to the left bank of the river on the night of the 27th/28th, and this was duplicated on the 29th; but for wheeled traffic both divisions had to look to the bridge at Salettuol in the 7th Division area. Two field companies of the 23rd Division engineers were sent to assist the 7th Division, and attempts to convert the footbridge at Salettuol into a medium bridge (in which the pontoons would be closer together) on the 27th were successful.

On the 29th a bridge for wheeled traffic was built from Papadopoli island to the mainland near Cimadalma, and then duplicated.

THE AUSTRIAN ACCOUNT

The Austrian account of the British feat of arms seems of sufficient interest to be included in the narrative.[1]

---

[1] A.O.A. VII, p. 619–20. The Order of Battle of the Austrian divisions facing the XIV Corps from right to left was *29th, 7th* and *64th*. The infantry regiments of the *7th Division* were the *37th, 68th* and *132nd*.

"Against the northern flank of the *Isonzo Army*, after a
"short bombardment, the attack of the troops of the
"British XIV Corps already on Papadopoli island took
"place between 7 and 8 a.m. on the 27th. The Hungarians
"and Southern Slavs of the *7th Division* could not stand up
"to it. Part of the *68th Regiment*, which was in reserve,
"refused to go into the fight and left the battlefield of its
"own accord. The appearance of the British created
"universal terror (*löste einen Massenschreck*). The beaten
"regiments of the *7th Division* fled north-eastwards. The
"artillery left the infantry in the lurch and went back to
"the 'King's Zone' on the Monticano river. What
"remained of the *68th Regiment* withdrew on Rai and S. Polo,
"the survivors of the *132nd Regiment* fled even behind the
"Monticano. Part of the *92nd Regiment*, of the *29th
"Division*, on the right (north) bank was involved in the
"retreat, and the *29th Division* itself, after a short fight
"[against the 23rd Division] had to withdraw its left and
"centre from the banks of the Piave to the Piavesella".

On the left (east) bank, too, *No. 6 Regiment* and its relief, *No. 19 Regiment*, of the *64th Honved Division*, were also swept away (by the 7th Division).

The Austrian account goes on to say that directly the British had seized the Bund it was decided by Field-Marshal-Lieutenant Berndt, the local corps commander, to make a counter-attack with his reserves, a brigade and a regiment, to drive them back on to Papadopoli island, and the commander of the *Isonzo Army* ordered up two divisions of his reserve to the Monticano. The *201st Honved Brigade* and *No. 137 Regiment* did attack Borgo Malanotte, close by Tezze, independently; but as the commander of the *137th Regiment* and his staff were captured by the British it was leaderless, and after a good fight had to retire. The *Honved* brigade was "stopped by heavy losses before it got as far "as Tezze".

CHAPTER XXI

THE BATTLE OF VITTORIO VENETO
(*continued*)

THE FORCING OF THE MONTICANO
28TH-29TH OCTOBER
(Maps III, V ; Sketch 12)

28TH OCTOBER
THE EXPANSION OF THE PIAVE BRIDGEHEADS

THE ORDERS OF THE TENTH ARMY

On the 28th all 3 bridgeheads, the British at Papadopoli, the Italian near Sernaglia, and the French near Pederobba, were expanded.

The orders of the Tenth Army, issued at 1.25 p.m. on 27th October, began with the words, " The attack of the " Tenth Army has met with considerable success, and it will " be continued to-morrow, the 28th inst ". A general bombardment from the whole front of the Tenth Army was to begin at 5 a.m. (28th), and the rate of advance of the barrage for the attack was to be 100 metres in 6 minutes.

The Italian 56th Division (XVIII Corps)[1] was to attack at 9 a.m., with the object of extending the left of the XIV Corps about three thousand yards. The Italian 33rd Division was then to come up on the left of the 56th.

At 12.30 p.m. the whole Tenth Army was to advance with the objectives, beginning on the left :

The XVIII Corps from a point on the Piave due east of Nervesa, north-eastward past the northern edge of S. Lucia, thence eastward to C. Milanese (2,000 yards east of S. Lucia) ;

the XIV Corps, pivoting on its right at a road junction a mile east of Tezze, to wheel up to C. Milanese—this line was about a thousand yards ahead of the original fourth objective ;

---
[1] One brigade of this division, by order of XIV Corps had crossed the Piave, on the night of the 27th/28th, and taken over duty as left flank guard of the British 23rd Division.

the XI Corps, to advance to a line from the above road junction, running eastwards through Rai to Tempio, and thence southward to the Piave.

The Fourteenth Wing R.A.F. was to arrange to watch the front of the XVIII Corps, as well as that of the XIV Corps.

The headquarters of the XVIII and XIV Corps were to be together at Villa Margherita ($1\frac{1}{2}$ miles north of Treviso).

Trouble at the Bridges

During the night of the 27th/28th the one road, from Maserada and beyond, leading to the Salettuol bridge, just wide enough for a double line of vehicles, was terribly congested, although no less than a hundred men of the 7th Division were employed on traffic control, and whilst the road was blocked by infantry of the Italian XVIII Corps marching up—and its transport ordered to be left behind— it was bombed by the Austrians, and the Italians lost some fifty killed and many wounded. The bridge was not hit either by bomb or shell, although it was under constant artillery fire. The following morning, however, it was broken by the current, 1 pontoon and 3 trestles being carried away. Efforts to repair the bridge failed, and the Italian 18th *Pontiere* Company having been summoned, it was by 7 p.m. rebuilt thirty yards downstream, and a second passage over the main stream was completed by building a bridge from Veneto island (to which a bridge existed) to Papadopoli. As a result of the bridging troubles, rations and ammunition had to be taken over to the troops on the 27th and 28th on mules, with not a few mishaps, and wounded—though the task of carrying a loaded stretcher across the small arms of the Piave in flood was both arduous and dangerous—were carried back on stretchers either to collecting stations near the Bund or on the island, whence they were removed to an advanced dressing station near Maserada. After the 28th no damage was suffered by the bridges.

The Attack of the Italian XVIII Corps

In the XVIII Corps, now the left wing of Lord Cavan's Army, owing to congestion on the roads only the Como Brigade of the 56th Division, and one regiment of the

Bisagno Brigade of the 33rd Division, had been able to cross the Piave by the Cosenza footbridge on the night of the 27th/28th. Advancing at 9 a.m. under a barrage fired by the British 23rd Division artillery—Italian infantry officers said that although they had been fighting three years, it was the first proper barrage they had ever seen—the Como Brigade, which during the previous night had relieved the troops of the 68th Brigade holding the left flank of the 23rd Division, attacked in a westerly direction, and made a wheeling movement to the north, pivoting on the new left flank of the 68th Brigade. Before midday it had come into line with the latter in readiness to continue the advance on the left of the 23rd Division. The leading regiment of the Bisagno Brigade co-operated in this movement and came up on the left of the Como Brigade, and the second regiment of the brigade pushed up the left bank of the Piave to a point east of Nervesa, taking in flank the Austrian defences against which the Italian attack of the previous day had failed to develop. These manœuvres were very successful, and Lord Cavan in his report mentions the Como and Bisagno Brigades " for the splendid dash with which " they took up the attack with little opportunity for " previous reconnaissance. These brigades alone captured " about three thousand prisoners, 7 guns and over a hundred " and fifty machine guns ".[1] The Como Brigade, however, did not succeed in taking the whole objective, for at night its line ran south instead of north of S. Lucia. More important was the success of the second regiment of the Bisagno Brigade in pushing up the left (east) bank of the Piave ; for this enabled the VIII Corps (Eighth Army) at last to construct bridges at Ponte Priula during the ensuing night.

Advance of the British XIV Corps[2]

The orders of the XIV Corps were issued at 5.45 p.m. on 27th October. At zero hour (12.30 p.m.) a field artillery barrage was to come down two hundred yards in front of the left half of the line, and six minutes later move forward.

---

[1] From *29th Division* which, involved in the disaster of the previous day, when its left had been smashed by the British 23rd Division, had taken up a line from the Piave to the Piavesella.

[2] See Map V.

At 1 p.m., by which time the field artillery would have come to the limit of its range, it was to cease fire, and the advance of the infantry would then be protected by the heavy artillery only, to whose barrage, on account of the greater effect of the shells, it could not keep so close. On the right half of the corps front the range was already too great for the field artillery, and only heavy artillery could cover the advance.

The R.A.F. was to keep G.H.Q. informed of the progress of the advance ; in the event, however, the fighter pilots were mostly employed in bombing the Austrian columns in retreat on the main roads.

The Attack of the 23rd Division

The advance began at 12.30 p.m. The 68th Brigade attacked with the 10/Northumberland Fusiliers on the left and the 12/Durham L.I. on the right. After the field artillery barrage ceased at 1 p.m. the attack was continued by rushes, supported by the fire of machine guns from the upper storeys of buildings, of the mobile trench mortars attached to brigades, and, as long as the captured ammunition lasted, of captured Austrian guns manned by trench-mortar gunners.[1] The attack went well, and reached its objective—Vazzola–S. Lucia—between 3 and 4 p.m. The opposition from enemy rear guards of the divisions defeated on the previous day was not very serious, but stronger on the left than on the right. Some difficulty was found by the left battalion in consolidating the line, for it was under close machine-gun fire, especially from the left flank, where the troops of the Italian XVIII Corps had failed quite to reach the objective and had left S. Lucia in enemy hands.

In the 69th Brigade, the 11/West Yorkshire passed through the 10/Duke of Wellington's on the left, and the 8/Green Howards continued the attack on the right. Lieut.-Colonel H. H. Hudson of the West Yorkshire was wounded, but the brigade met with little opposition and reached the objective about 3 p.m. At 12.30 p.m. the XIV Corps issued orders to both divisions to push forward rapidly, as the enemy showed signs of retiring ; these reached brigades between 4 and

---

[1] It was remarked that very few dumps of ammunition or anything else were found, which seems to indicate that preparations had already been made by Field-Marshal Boroevic to evacuate Venetia.

5.15 p.m. As there was no contact with the enemy, Br.-General Beauman (69th Brigade) on this order reaching him, asked divisional headquarters to stop the artillery fire covering his front, and ordered the 11/West Yorkshire to send a strong patrol to Suffrata, and the 8/Green Howards another to Vazzolo. These objectives were reached before dark, and the brigadier then directed both battalions to push forward one company to seize the bridges over the Monticano beyond the two villages which they had occupied. The 11/West Yorkshire company reached the crossing of the river, but found the enemy holding the farther bank in force. In the dark the Green Howards' company mistook a bridge over a canal eight hundred yards short of the Monticano for its objective. It duly formed a bridgehead and the mistake was not discovered till the next day.

In the 68th Brigade, at night a company of the 12/Durham L.I. pushed on a mile beyond the objective to Marena, and sent a patrol to hold the near bank of the Monticano north-east of Marena.

The 23rd Division had thus established itself a mile or a mile and a half beyond the original fourth objective, and had in two places pushed forward patrols to the near bank of the Monticano, behind which it was known the Austrians meant to stand. Close touch had been maintained with the 7th Division on the right, but all contact had been lost with the Italian 56th Division on the left, and indeed was not re-established on this flank until the Livenza was reached on the 31st.[1]

The Attack of the 7th Division

The advance of the 7th Division was not covered by any regular barrage; but two batteries of the XXII Brigade R.F.A. from Papadopoli island, which had forded the Piave to the left bank in the early morning on the 28th, gave good support, one battery to each infantry brigade.

The 91st Brigade, as a brigade group with a battery R.F.A., an Italian mountain battery, a troop of Yeomanry and a platoon of cyclists attached, advanced with the

---

[1] For most conspicuous bravery and initiative, Private W. Wood (10/Northumberland Fusiliers), whose action with his Lewis gun caused first 140 enemy to surrender and, later, 163 more, received the V.C.

1/South Staffordshire on the left and the 22/Manchester on the right. In the 20th Brigade, the 2/Border Regiment covered the whole front of the brigade. Opposition was slight and the objective was reached without difficulty, although single guns concealed in standing crops gave some trouble by firing a few rounds at close range before they could be surrounded and captured.

In the afternoon, in accordance with the XIV Corps orders issued at 12.30 p.m., the 7th Division arranged for the advance to be continued at night by both brigades to the Vazzolo–Rai road (the original fourth objective), and for patrols to be sent forward to the Monticano river. In the 91st Brigade the 2/Queen's took over the right of the front line from the 22/Manchester at dusk and advanced about midnight, with the Staffordshire still on its left, reaching the objective with little opposition by 4 a.m. on the 29th. In the 20th Brigade, the 2/Border Regiment also reached this further objective during the night. A strong patrol of two platoons was sent forward to the bridge over the Monticano half a mile north of Visna and took up a position covering it. At dawn (29th) the enemy blew up the bridge, and then several hundred of his troops still south of the river collected at Visna, finding an enemy between them and home, attacked and surrounded the patrol and captured it.

Thus the 7th Division, like the 23rd, by the early morning of the 29th was well beyond its objective, and was in touch on the left with the 23rd Division near Vazzolo, and on the right with the Italian 37th Division at Rai.

The Attack of the Italian XI Corps

The Italian XI Corps had on the 28th to extend the front of the XIV Corps about four thousand yards to the right, to Tempio, and thence form a right defensive flank back to the Piave. Strong resistance was offered on this flank and the Austrians counter-attacked. After special artillery preparation another effort was made by the XI Corps when Roncadella and Ormelle villages, in the middle of the flank, were captured, but not Tempio, touch with the British being gained two miles to the north-west, at Rai. South of Roncadella no progress was made.

ITALIAN FLANKING ARMIES. 28TH OCTOBER

Thus by early morning of the 29th,[1] the Tenth Army line ran, from left to right, from the Piave opposite Nervesa, south of S. Lucia, in front of Marena, Suffrata, Vazzolo, Rai, Ormelle and Roncadella, to the Piave, and the enemy seemed prepared to defend the line of the Monticano (the *Königstellung*).

THE ARMIES OTHER THAN THE TENTH ARMY

The Third Army, on the right of Lord Cavan's Army, did not move on the 28th.

On the left, in the Eighth Army, the VIII Corps, nearest to the British, was unable to begin bridging the Piave until darkness fell. The XXII Corps, next on the left, managed to put another division over the river to reinforce the parts of two divisions already in the Sernaglia bridgehead; the XXVII Corps, owing to its bridges being broken, could do no more than send over one battalion by boat. After a long artillery battle a slight advance was made in the afternoon by these detachments into the "folding doors" opened by the Austrians, and two villages, about two thousand yards from the river, Sernaglia and Mariago, were secured; but some of the Italian subordinate generals, unhappy about the situation and fearing a counter-attack, proposed a withdrawal.[2]

In the XII Corps, the right wing of the Twelfth Army, towards 5 a.m. the French, after many attempts, succeeded in repairing one bridge, and the French 138th Regiment crossed rapidly to reinforce the 5 battalions in the Pederobba bridgehead, followed by Alpini, until about 8 a.m., when the bridge was again broken by a shell. Ammunition and rations were, however, sent over by boat. By nightfall, the bridgehead was deepened to two thousand yards, by an attack of the 138th Regiment, with Alpini on the right, after an effective bombardment, the French capturing 18 guns and seven hundred prisoners at small loss.[3]

---

[1] See Map III.
[2] Villari, p. 264. The Austrians sent up the *34th Division* to counter-attack (see Note at end of Chapter); but three of its battalions mutinied, "and the rest of the troops of the division were in such a doubtful "(*bedenklich*) state that they could be used only to man the trenches".
[3] The guns were lost owing to lack of teams says A.O.A. The defence was made by 2 weak divisions, the *31st*, and the *20th Honved*.

The Italian I Corps, the left wing of the Twelfth Army, on the west bank of the Piave, made progress of about a mile northwards. The Fourth Army, alongside, confined itself chiefly to artillery bombardment and there was no change in the infantry situation. Farther west the Armies had not yet joined in the forward movement.

29TH OCTOBER

THE FORCING OF THE MONTICANO

THE ORDERS OF THE TENTH ARMY

On 29th October the three bridgeheads were further expanded, and were joined up; and the British success in forcing the Monticano brought about not only the retirement of the right wing of the Austrian *Isonzo Army*, but also that of the *Sixth Army*, on its right. Early in the morning of this day, by the Emperor's order, an Austrian *parlementaire* entered the Italian lines in the Adige valley to begin conversations to secure an armistice.[1]

Lord Cavan issued his orders for the 29th at 4.53 p.m. on the previous evening, supplemented by some additions sent out at 8.14 p.m. The advance of the Tenth Army was to be continued at 8.30 a.m. on its whole front. The objective was a line, about $2\frac{1}{2}$ miles ahead, beyond the Monticano, with flanks turned back, as neither the Italian Third Army on the right, nor the Italian VIII Corps (Eighth Army) on the left had yet crossed the Piave. The objective was allotted, from left to right, as follows:

    To the XVIII Corps: Marcatelli–Susegna–Conegliano –Cosniga (exclusive).

    To the XIV Corps: Cosniga–eastward to Codogne– southward as a flank to Fontanellette.

    To the XI Corps: Fontanellette (exclusive)–Tempio.

Second objectives, about two miles farther on, were also given; but as they were not attempted on the 29th, they are not included here.

Corps were to make their own artillery arrangements.

By the same Tenth Army order, issued at 4.53 p.m., the Italian 31st Division was transferred from the reserve of the XI Corps to the XIV Corps, and came into corps reserve.

---

[1] See Chapter XXV.

The Attack of the British XIV Corps[1]

The orders of the XIV Corps were issued at 9 p.m. on 28th October. On the left, touch was to be kept with the XVIII Corps by liaison posts at three named cross-roads. On the right, the 7th Division was to arrange direct with the Italian 37th Division to keep touch with the XI Corps. The advance of the 23rd Division was to be timed so that the heads of its columns should reach a road about $1\frac{1}{2}$ miles beyond the Monticano at 10.30 a.m. The left of the 7th Division was to conform to this movement. In the event of the enemy's resistance being slight, the corps mounted troops were to pass ahead of the infantry with, as their first objective, some villages about four miles beyond the Monticano. If the enemy offered resistance, the mounted troops were to seize tactical points and to hold them till the arrival of the infantry. As it turned out, the Austrians, having brought up considerable reserves in order to hold the line of the Monticano, the opposition was greater than expected, and the infantry objective, $2\frac{1}{2}$ miles beyond the river, was not reached until evening.

The country ahead was still flat and covered with vineyards and cultivation, but traversed by several deepish streams, the Bragnola, the Piavesella and the Favero, tributaries of the Monticano. That river itself was enclosed by artificial dykes about twenty feet high, which gave command over the surrounding country and were well prepared for defence. The stream was about fifteen yards wide, but quite shallow at the time and sluggish. Such bridges as existed were of wood and ran at the level of the top of the dykes.

The attack of the 23rd Division was to be supported by the 102nd Brigade R.F.A. and that of the 7th Division by the XXII Brigade, with 2 Italian mountain batteries. The guns did some good service in dealing with buildings, otherwise there was little artillery support for the attack, as the situation of the infantry was seldom sufficiently clear on this day for guns to be used with effect, ground observation from the flat countryside being impossible, and the Austrians had destroyed all possible O.Ps., including church towers.

The R.A.F. continued to bomb and machine-gun the

---

[1] See Map V.

roads behind the Austrian positions, as on the previous day —indeed, the Austrian Official History attributes the first break-in in the Monticano line to machine-gunning from the air.[1] Although the enemy made a stand on the Monticano and westward on the Conegliano line, observers reported that the roads were closer packed with retreating troops than on the 28th, and in the later British advance the tremendous execution done was evident, as the vicinity of the roads was littered with dead men and animals and broken vehicles. Only 3 machines were lost.

The attack of the XIV Corps was made, from left to right, by the 68th and 69th Brigades of the 23rd Division and the 91st and 20th Brigades of the 7th Division. The left and centre were a little over a mile from the river, but the right had farther to go. The Italians on both flanks were not up: they had not reached S. Lucia on the west, nor Tempio on the east, and the British, to cover their front, had to extend a thousand yards to the right to Fontanellette, originally in the Italian area.

Opposite the two British divisions of the XIV Corps was the *XVI Corps*, with the equivalent of quite three divisions, of which two were fresh : the left half of the fresh Austrian *10th Division*, the remnants of the *29th Division* (originally opposite the British left wing on the Piave), the fresh *26th Rifle Division* (astride the Vazzolo–Cimetta road), the *201st Landsturm Brigade*, and, on the east, the fresh *24th Division*, still on the southern side of the Monticano, and aligned behind the Piavesella, thus threatening the British flank.

In both divisions, after the first objective, roughly the Conegliano–Cimetta–Codogne road, had been reached, their third brigades, the 70th and the 22nd, were to come up and pass through to the second objective. The former, which was in divisional reserve on the right bank of the Piave, began at 6 a.m. (29th) to cross the river by the Cosenza footbridges ; it was accompanied by the divisional pioneer battalion (9/South Staffordshire). The 22nd Brigade, after the successful operation of the taking of Papadopoli, had remained on the island till 5 p.m. on the 28th, when it received orders from the division to cross to S. Michele, on the left bank of the Piave and, moving promptly, did so

---

[1] See Note at end of Chapter.

whilst some daylight still remained. The channels between the island and the left bank were deep, but the whole brigade got across safely by the methods used on the 27th, and by midnight was billeted or bivouacked in the ruins of S. Michele. The move forward was continued at 8.30 a.m. on the 29th.

It was hoped also to push the Italian 31st Division (General de Angelis), transferred from the XI Corps, ahead after the Monticano line had been gained. Its Caserta Brigade, containing the American 332nd Regiment, which had arrived in July, crossed the Piave on the morning of the 29th and came up behind the 20th Brigade on the right ; but, owing to the congestion at the bridges, the rest of the division did not cross until the morning of the 30th.

The British advance from the line gained on the previous evening began at 8.30 a.m. In accordance with corps orders, the corps Mounted Troops, under Lieut.-Colonel Sir C. B. Lowther, came up to pass through the infantry. One squadron of the Northamptonshire Yeomanry was at once sent on ahead by the 23rd Division to reconnoitre the bridge over the Monticano north-east of Vazzolo. Finding it held by the enemy, the leading troop promptly charged, captured a machine gun and prevented the enemy from blowing up the bridge. A line of machine-gun posts beyond the river prevented any farther advance by mounted troops; but the bridge was held by the dismounted squadron for nearly an hour till the arrival of the infantry of the 69th Brigade. At 10 a.m. the 8/Green Howards, the right battalion of the 69th Brigade, then passed through the Yeomanry at the bridge, and had some severe fighting before they made good the passage of the river.

About 9.30 a.m. the left battalion of the brigade, the 11/West Yorkshire, succeeded in forcing a crossing at C. Malta, and, after heavy fighting, captured C. Balle at noon. The battalion was constantly subjected to counter-attacks from the left flank, where the 68th Brigade had not yet crossed, and one company of the 10/Duke of Wellington's in reserve, was ordered up to form a defensive flank here.

In the 91st Brigade (7th Division), on the right of the 69th, the leading battalion, the 2/Queen's, nearest the river, began its advance by the Vazzolo–Cimetta road, apparently under the impression that the bridge over the Monticano on this road was held by troops of the 23rd Division, owing to a mistaken report to that effect circulated on the previous night. The Queen's soon came under fire from the far bank of the river, and 3 companies were eventually deployed. They secured the bridge for the troops of the 23rd Division on the left and after some pretty sharp opposition were then able to force a passage to the right of them, and to advance five hundred yards beyond the river.

Resistance then suddenly stiffened and touch could not be got with the 20th Brigade, on the right, where the enemy in the absence of the Italian XI Corps was by midday working round the flank between the 91st and 20th Brigades. The situation was relieved by the 22/Manchester, which was ordered to act as a right flank guard, and came up and waded across the Monticano on the right of the Queen's. In Cimetta, ahead of the Queen's, the enemy's resistance was still very obstinate, and at 12.50 p.m. Br.-General Pelly ordered his third battalion, the 1/South Staffordshire, to support them. Crossing the river by the Vazzolo bridge, and, after a preliminary bombardment by two guns of the 105th Battery R.F.A., this battalion reinforced the Queen's and the two battalions went forward together at 2.30 p.m., took Cimetta with 720 prisoners by 3.15 p.m., and gained touch on the left with the 23rd Division.

In the 20th Brigade, on the extreme right, the 2/Border Regiment covered its whole front, with Visna and Fontanellette to the east as objectives, in order to guard the right flank. Visna was found evacuated, and the left of the battalion reached the Monticano at C. Grison (north of Visna), recovering touch with the 91st Brigade, but in broad daylight was too small a body to force a passage. The right met with opposition at the river Piavesella, which was overcome by an attack covered by a battery of Italian mountain artillery, Fontanellette was then taken without much difficulty, and the Monticano beyond it reached about midday. The left of the battalion, at C. Grison, was going to force the passage of the river at 6.30 p.m., but at the last moment the attack was stopped by orders from the division, as it was considered that, in view of the successful crossing by the 91st Brigade, the enemy on the 20th Brigade front would be sure to retire during the night, and this proved to be the case.[1] To make connection

---

[1] See Note at end of Chapter.

THE PURSUIT. 29TH OCTOBER

with the 20th, the 91st Brigade formed a defensive right flank from the first objective back to the Monticano at C. Grison.

On the extreme left, in the 68th Brigade, the 10/Northumberland Fusiliers suffered from the disadvantage of having no troops on its outer flank, where the Italian 56th Division should have been ; and, in consequence, this battalion was held up at the Monticano till evening. The right of the 68th Brigade, the 12/Durham L.I., also met stiff opposition, and it was not till 1 p.m. that the right of the battalion forced the passage of the river at C. Balbi, the left being still held up. When news of the crossing of the river on his right reached Br.-General Cary-Barnard, he at once gave orders to the 11/Northumberland Fusiliers, in reserve, to cross behind the right of the Durham L.I. and to sweep westwards up the bank of the Monticano behind the enemy.

The 11/Northumberland Fusiliers, owing to heavy casualties on the 27th, was weak, and had been reorganized in 2 companies ; it crossed the Monticano at 2.30 p.m., and, in co-operation with the part of the 12/Durham L.I. which had already crossed, advanced westwards at 4.15 p.m., with its right on the little river Cervada. There was considerable resistance from machine guns in farmhouses and ditches ; but the attack was completely successful, and by 6.30 p.m. the 11th had cleared the enemy from the whole brigade front, thus enabling the 10/Northumberland Fusiliers, on the left, to cross the river. Touch on the left was not gained with the Italian XVIII Corps at Ramera, on the south side of the Monticano, south-east of Conegliano, until 4 a.m. (30th). The operations of the 68th Brigade this day had been greatly helped by the support of the 146th Italian Mountain Battery, whose personnel, having carried their guns and ammunition across the Piave, had dragged them forward by hand in support of the 68th Brigade throughout the operations to date.

After the 8/Green Howards (69th Brigade) had secured the bridge north-east of Vazzolo the battalion had continued its advance towards Cimetta, but met with strong opposition from the front and counter-attacks from the right, where the left of the 7th Division was not yet so far forward, and was finally held up at a stream five hundred yards south of

Cimetta. By this time the 70th Brigade had come up in accordance with plan and deployed in readiness to pass through the leading brigades of the 23rd Division. The 9/York & Lancaster, which was now behind the 8/Green Howards, was placed at the disposal of the 69th Brigade, and passed through the Green Howards about 3 p.m. The 7th Division troops on the right were by this time successfully attacking Cimetta, and the York & Lancaster, supported by the Green Howards, were able to advance to the first objective. The left of the 69th Brigade, the 11/West Yorkshire, with its left flank cleared by the successful attack of the 68th Brigade, was also able to advance and to reach the objective in touch with the Green Howards; the York & Lancaster now held the right flank of the 69th Brigade.[1]

Thus by evening both the 23rd and 7th Divisions had crossed the Monticano, except on the extreme right, and were in possession of the first objective. They had, without artillery bombardment and barrage, forced a strongly held line protected by an embanked river. The boldness of Lord Cavan in ordering such an attack notwithstanding the resistance offered to the British on Papadopoli island was fully justified. The casualties had not been heavy: 40 officers and 1,221 other ranks;[2] and the number of prisoners captured by the Tenth Army amounted to 345 officers and 11,002 other ranks. But after the long day's fighting the men were very tired. To make matters worse, owing to the congestion at the bridges, rations and ammunition had not come up except for the 23rd Division; but the erection of telpherage cables over the Piave—that is wire ropes carrying baskets below them—and other improvizations somewhat eased the situation there. It was not, however, until the evening of the 30th that 30-cwt. motor lorries and ambulances could cross the river, and until then the troops had to eke out what they carried on them by purchase of poultry, eggs and vegetables, all that the

---

[1] For conspicuous bravery and skilful leading on this day and on the 27th, Sergeant W. McNally, M.M. (8/Green Howards), received the V.C.

[2] 7th Division, 10 and 342; 23rd Division, 30 and 879. Only nine hundred reinforcements were available, but discharged influenza patients helped to make up the number, and next day the War Office agreed to send two thousand infantry to Italy at once, and a thousand more later.

country could offer.¹ Much of the delay in troops crossing the Piave and in the forwarding of supplies was due to the utter disregard by the Italians of traffic control—a characteristic already mentioned in the account of the retreat of the Third Army after Caporetto, and in the original march up of the British to the Montello. All thought of proceeding to the second objective had, therefore, to be abandoned, and the execution of the order to the 70th and 22nd Brigades to pass through the line was postponed to the following morning. To avoid a daylight relief, the leading battalions were moved up close behind the front line while it was still dark in the early morning of the 30th.

Meanwhile, during the 29th the Italian corps of Lord Cavan's Army on the right and left of the XIV Corps had been making efforts to come up.

The Italian XI Corps[2]

The principal task of the XI Corps, the right wing of Lord Cavan's Army, had been to guard the right flank. Its northern objective alongside the XIV Corps was only Tempio–Fontanellette (exclusive), less than two thousand yards in length. Evening found the Austrians still in possession of the former village; but the 7th Division had taken the latter and the Italian 37th Division had established touch with the British near it, and had pushed out the eastern flank of the corps, right down to the Piave, for about a mile. At 5 p.m. its 23rd (Bersagliere) Division was transferred to the Third Army, on its right, leaving General Paolini with only the 37th Division and the 11th Assault Detachment. This, however, was not of consequence, as the Italian Third Army was to begin crossing the Piave next day.

---

[1] The rations for the 30th were carried over by hand at the fords or footbridges; those for 31st October and 1st November were brought over by the first line transport, often double-horsed, which was augmented on 1st November by dumping the baggage on the east side of the river and using the wagons, again assisted by 30-cwt. Italian lorries where the distance demanded it. This remained the system, as no 3-ton lorries could cross the Piave bridges, or negotiate the stretches of shingle and fordable arms of the river.

[2] See Map III.

The Attack of the Italian XVIII Corps

Turning to the left wing of Lord Cavan's Army: by the early morning of the 29th the infantry of the two divisions of the XVIII Corps had crossed the Piave by the XIV Corps's bridges. The Bisagno Brigade of the 33rd Division, the left of the corps near the Piave, finding that the Austrians had disappeared,[1] instead of waiting till 8.30 a.m., the hour fixed by the Army, began to advance westwards at dawn in order to help the advance of the right of the VIII Corps, and reached Susegna (1½ miles west of S. Lucia) at 8 a.m. But the bulk of the 33rd Division continued to advance northwards, against weak resistance at first, without any change in orders when, at 10.35 a.m., the XVIII Corps reverted to the Eighth Army. Conegliano was found to be strongly defended;[2] resistance was overcome by a turning movement from the north; but it was not until the morning of the 30th that the town, five miles from the Piave, was finally taken.[3] Touch was kept during the day with the VIII Corps (Eighth Army) along the Susegna–Conegliano road.

The 56th Division, the right division of the XVIII Corps, advancing northwards, met with strong opposition; it reached the Monticano and gained touch with the 33rd Division, and with the British XIV Corps, as already mentioned, at 4 a.m. (30th).

The Italian Eighth Army

The advance of the left of the XVIII Corps on the 28th along the eastern bank of the Piave opposite Nervesa, under Lord Cavan's orders, had the effect of forcing the retirement of the Austrian batteries which had so far prevented the construction of bridges by the Eighth Army at Ponte Priula. For that Army the most important event of these days was the completion of these bridges by midnight of the 28th/29th, thus at last opening a passage for the advance

---

[1] Berndt, commanding opposite the Tenth Army, says that the rest of the story of the operations was merely a succession of retirements, the Austrians moving by night as far as possible to avoid attacks by aircraft.

[2] This place was in the new line of resistance to which the Austrian *Sixth Army* was retiring.

[3] The Italian Situation Map 3 in "Vittorio Veneto" shows the front line 2¼ miles short of Conegliano, and A.O.A. Map No. 33 puts the Austrian line a mile south of it. Both sides speak of fighting in the town, to which, apparently, a small Italian advanced party penetrated for a time.

THE PURSUIT. 29TH–30TH OCTOBER 313

of the VIII Corps, so that it could fill the gap between the Papadopoli and Sernaglia bridgeheads. Crossing the Piave in the early hours of the 29th, its 2 divisions, without any opposition, passed Susegna and came up on the left of the XVIII Corps on the Susegna–Conegliano road ; but General Diaz, dissatisfied with the leading of the VIII Corps, removed its commander.

On the left of the VIII Corps, the XXII and XXVII Corps from the Sernaglia bridgehead, after a bombardment which demoralized the already shaken Austrians, had no difficulty in coming up into general line, short of the new enemy position, which seems to have been reached only near Conegliano.

At night the VIII Corps sent forward a light column of Lancers and Bersaglieri cyclists to seize Vittorio Veneto, which they occupied on the early morning of the 30th. Italian accounts do not mention any opposition to the advance of this column, and the Austrian Official Account[1] states that the retreat through Vittorio Veneto was carried out quite uninterrupted by the enemy.

THE ITALIAN TWELFTH ARMY[2]

In the Twelfth Army, its right wing, the XII Corps, still had difficulty in maintaining communication across the Piave near Pederobba. The bridge had been repaired again by 6 a.m. (29th), and during the morning five Alpini battalions, the French 78th Regiment and some mountain batteries, as well as a brigade of Eighth Army troops, crossed the river. But by 1.20 p.m. enemy bombardment had become so heavy that it brought the use of the bridge to an end for the rest of the day. A telpherage rope stretched across the river was used to carry rations, and, by means of a submerged cable, telephone communication was established. Progress northwards of from two thousand to four thousand yards was made by the XII Corps.

The I Corps, the left corps of the Twelfth Army, was hampered by the ill-success of the Fourth Army on its left, and was only able to make a small advance of about a thousand yards with its right.

---

[1] A.O.A. vii, p. 658.
[2] See Sketch 12.

The Italian Fourth Army

The Fourth Army attacked again on the 29th in front of M. Grappa, but the Austrians made an obstinate resistance and the attacks met with no success.

NOTE

The Austrians on the 28th and 29th October
(Map III ; Sketch 12)

On the 27th Field-Marshal Boroevic had ordered up reserves to counter-attack the Papadopoli and Sernaglia bridgeheads—3 divisions, the *10th*, the *24th* and the *26th Rifle*, with the *8th Cavalry Division*, against Papadopoli, and the *34th Division* against Falzè. The proportion is significant. The first group got no farther than the river Monticano on the 28th, and the *34th* proved useless on account of refusal to obey orders. Trouble had occurred on the Trentino front some days earlier, on the 23rd, among the Hungarian and Southern Slav troops, as will be narrated later. Now it began in the Venetian theatre. The main cause was that, Bulgaria having concluded an armistice with the Allies on 30th September, and the Emperor Karl, having on 16th October, declared his Empire a Federal State, rumours had reached three contingents, the Hungarian, Czech and Southern Slav, that their now independent countries were being invaded and they wanted to hasten home to defend them.

At 9 a.m. on the 28th Field-Marshal Boroevic reported to the High Command, " The strength of the resistance offered by our " troops is conspicuously on the decrease, the more so as the " number of Polish, Hungarian, Czech, Slovak and Southern Slav " units, who, calling attention to the Emperor's manifesto, refuse " obedience, is increasing in a very marked degree, and means " fail to compel obedience ". Unless, he said, suitable political measures were taken, anarchy, and with it catastrophe for the Monarchy and army, would ensue.

On this day the High Command assembled an Armistice Commission at Trent to get in touch with the Comando Supremo, and obtain the terms of an armistice.[1]

In the evening Boroevic came to the conclusion that, the *IV* and *XVI Corps* of the *Isonzo Army* having been driven from the Piave by the British, and the *Sixth Army* holding on with difficulty, the only way to save his Armies, if the enemy advance could not be stopped, was to retire slowly, evacuating Venetia, to the Austrian frontier. It was decided, that the

---

[1] The armistice negotiations are dealt with in Chapter XXV.

right wing of the *Isonzo Army* should defend the line of the Monticano on the 29th, when the reinforcements had arrived, and that during the night (28th/29th), the *Sixth Army* should retire to the position in front of Conegliano and the adjacent hill country. By evening (29th), with breaches in these positions near Conegliano and where the *34th Division* had failed on the Sernaglia front; with a gap between the *Sixth Army* and the *Belluno Group* formed by the retreat eastward of that Army; with no reinforcements to stem the enemy's advance; with " mutinous reserves making for home ", Boroevic considered the situation " unequivocally hopeless " (*geradezu hoffnungslos*).

All hopes were concentrated on an early armistice; if the troops could hold their ground so much the better would the terms be.

The 29th October is called the decisive day by the Austrian official historians. The disastrous defeat on the Monticano of the *XVI Corps* of the *Isonzo Army*, opposite the British, where 3 fresh reinforcement divisions, the *10th*, the *24th* and the *26th Rifle*, were employed, was brought about by the *12th Rifle Regiment* (*26th Rifle Division*), whose infantry were Czech, panicking when machine-gunned from the air, a form of attack new to them, and taking the whole division with them. This let a wedge of British troops over, and it was easy for them to roll up the rest of the line, in spite of all reserves being thrown in, including parts of the *36th*, the *43rd Rifle* and the *44th Rifle Divisions*, from east of Conegliano. Only at Cimetta, where a West-Austrian *Landsturm* Brigade (*201st*) was engaged, did it come to serious fighting. " Towards evening," the commander of the *XVI Corps* gave orders for a retreat to the Livenza, and the remnants of the *IV Corps*, on its left, conformed.

The *Sixth Army* had been holding its own only with difficulty, and, fearing to be cut off from the Livenza when the *Isonzo Army* went back, also ordered a retreat. This caused the *Belluno Group*, which was still defending itself successfully against the Italian Fourth Army, to prepare for a retirement.

The Austrian Official Account (vii, p. 657–8) will now be quoted verbatim:

" On 29th October, in view of the confusion in the interior
" of the Monarchy and the increasing dissolution of the
" Army and Navy, the Imperial and Royal High Command
" had come to the conclusion that it was impossible to con-
" tinue the struggle. At evening, therefore, instructions
" were sent to Field-Marshal Boroevic from Baden to
" evacuate Venetia and to offer only such resistance as was
" necessary to the enemy who followed up. When this order
" reached Udine, the *Sixth Army* and the northern wing of

"the *Isonzo Army* were already in full retreat. After three
"days' heavy fighting, in order to withdraw the troops
"whose moral power of resistance was already much shaken
"from enemy pressure, these forces retired during the night
"of 29th/30th October on the edge of the mountains north
"of Vittorio, on Sacile, and behind the Livenza to beyond
"Brugnera in the south".

CHAPTER XXII

THE BATTLE OF VITTORIO VENETO (*continued*)

THE PURSUIT FROM THE MONTICANO TO THE LIVENZA

30TH–31ST OCTOBER 1918

(Maps III, V; Sketch 12)

30TH OCTOBER

All information brought in by airmen on the afternoon of 29th October pointed to a general Austrian retreat from the Piave front, and towards evening General Diaz ordered the Italian Third Army, on the right of the Tenth Army between it and the sea, to cross the Piave and join in the battle next day. It was about time, as Lord Cavan said in a telegram to the C.I.G.S., " as my Army front was " rapidly assuming the shape of an umbrella ". For the purpose of assisting the Third Army to cross the river, the Italian 23rd (Bersagliere) Division, taken from the XI Corps of Lord Cavan's command and already over the Piave, was to work down the river bank clearing the Austrians away, just as on the other flank of the Tenth Army, the 56th Division (XVIII Corps then under Lord Cavan) had on the previous day cleared the way for the VIII Corps to cross. Four of the Italian cavalry divisions were ordered to the front, and " the 1st Cavalry Division was thrown " forward between the Eighth and Tenth Armies, having " as its objective the Livenza north of Sacile, and, further on, " the Tagliamento ".[1]

THE XIV CORPS IN PURSUIT[2]

Lieut.-General Babington's XIV Corps, with the Italian XI Corps and XVIII Corps on either side, was to advance at 9 a.m. to the Livenza, 5 miles away on the right, but 9 on the left, from Portobuffole in the south up to Sacile and

[1] *Vittorio Veneto*, p. 22.
[2] See Map V.

3 miles beyond that town to Roncho and Col de Fer. In dividing the objective between his divisions, Lieut.-General Babington fixed an intermediate objective, about $3\frac{3}{4}$ miles ahead, passing through Gajarine and Orsago. For the day's operation the Italian 31st Division, hitherto in reserve, was to take over the right sector of the 7th Division, that is the 20th Brigade's frontage; this its Caserta Brigade did on the evening of the 29th; its second brigade, directed to Visna to guard the right flank, did not cross the Piave until the morning of the 30th. Thus the XIV Corps was to advance on a 3-division front. The American 332nd Regiment was kept in corps reserve; the Corps Mounted Troops, if opportunity offered, were to advance rapidly on Sacile and secure the bridge there.

The progress made on the 30th was not rapid. The troops were somewhat tired and many of the infantry were also footsore, as their boots after getting wet in crossing the Piave, and in some cases the Monticano, had dried hard; even a change of socks was out of the question; and without blankets the men slept ill; fortunately the weather, though cold, was fine.

The Corps Mounted Troops (Northamptonshire Yeomanry, 14th Cyclist Battalion and 12th Motor Machine-Gun Battery),[1] pushing on at speed, reached the outskirts of Sacile on the Livenza soon after noon. Entering the town they surprised some two or three thousand Austrians, who at first held up their hands; but later finding the British force was so small they took heart and attacked it. About 3 p.m. the mounted troops were skilfully withdrawn with casualties of 7 killed, 8 wounded and 2 missing; they also lost a couple of their machine guns, but carried off three hundred and fifty prisoners. They retired a short distance, keeping in touch with the enemy by scouts, to await the arrival of the infantry.

Both the 7th and 23rd Divisions now sent forward their reserve brigades. In the former, the 22nd Brigade, on the right, the victors of Papadopoli, passed through the line with the 1/R. Welch Fusiliers and 2/R. Warwickshire leading in extended order. The country ahead was a densely populated agricultural area, with numerous farms and

---

[1] The cyclists were 14 officers and 301 other ranks strong, less detachments of about 50 each with the 7th and 23rd Divisions.

villages, so some caution was necessary. The 91st Brigade followed in support and the 20th in reserve. Hardly any Austrians were encountered, and the few who were seen for the most part surrendered promptly. It was not until the advanced troops came within about a mile of the Livenza that they were received by a few shells, and a little rifle and machine-gun fire from the far bank, especially from Brugnera and Sacile. One man of the R. Welch Fusiliers was hit. He was the last man of the 7th Division to be killed in the war of 1914–18. The river was a hundred yards or more across, between high banks, deep and swift in places, and all the bridges, except one in Sacile (where the channel was only 40 yards), were down; the division still had only one brigade of field artillery with it (the second managed to get up next day); supplies had not arrived; the Italian 31st Division, on the right, was not abreast of the 7th Division, and was itself out of touch of the Italian XI Corps on its right. Major-General Shoubridge therefore decided most unwillingly to make a halt, for he had said to some of his troops on the previous day " You have only to march like Hell and you have won the War". The 23rd Division had farther to go to the Livenza than the 7th. Major-General Thuillier sent forward the 70th Brigade— under Br.-General H. Gordon, made into a brigade group by the attachment of two batteries of the 102nd Brigade R.F.A., an Italian mountain battery, two companies of the 23rd Machine-Gun Battalion, 3 mobile sections of 6-inch trench mortars and the 9/South Staffordshire (pioneers). The 68th and 69th Brigades were in reserve. The advance was led by the 9/York & Lancaster, the 8/K.O.Y.L.I. and the 8/York & Lancaster, in line.

No opposition was encountered, and the right of the line reached the intermediate objective, south-east of Gajarine, about 1.30 p.m., and the rest, having farther to go, later. Shortly after 3 p.m., when the advance had been resumed, Br.-General Gordon received information of the attack on the Corps Mounted Troops, said to have been made by a force of Austrian cavalry and infantry from the direction of Sacile and Roncho. The 9/York & Lancaster had by this time reached the Meschio, a branch of the Livenza which runs almost west to east, and, in the uncertainty of the situation, the battalion was ordered to hold the southern bank of the river from a little north of where the railway to Sacile crosses it westwards, and the other two battalions, as they came up, were to continue the line to Cordignano, thus refusing the left flank of the XIV Corps in ground just outside its boundary. This disposition was effected by 5.30 p.m., and touch obtained at Cordignano with the Italian cavalry. The mounted troops were then withdrawn behind the infantry.

Thus, the XIV Corps was halted for the night along the Livenza and Meschio, just short of Sacile. Nothing was seen of the enemy near the Meschio; but a patrol of the 9/York & Lancaster which reached the outskirts of Sacile reported the place strongly held. It looked as if the enemy meant to stand on the Livenza; all the afternoon the R.A.F. had been engaged against Austrian columns in dense masses retreating on the roads from Conegliano leading to Sacile and Vittorio, and news came that columns were leaving the lower Piave.

The Italian Armies[1]

On the right of Lord Cavan's Army only one division of the Third Army, next to it, got across the Piave on the 30th. A bombardment had been opened at 4 a.m., and two hours later 6 crossings were attempted, only 2 of which were successful: one near S. Dona di Piave (8 miles below Ponte di Piave), and the other at Solgareda (just below Ponte di Piave). The former was lost,[2] and at the latter no advance could be made, until the flank advance of the Italian 23rd Division from the left made itself felt about 1 p.m. when it captured Ponte di Piave. Thus, at night, the Tenth Army had still a long right flank between the Piave and the Livenza, held by the Italian 23rd and 53rd Divisions, near the Piave, the weak XI Corps still south of Oderzo, and the Italian 31st Division on the Monticano. No threat developed against it, for early on the 30th, almost as the Third Army's bombardment started, the 3 Austrian corps, the VII, XXIII and XXII, between the Papadopoli bridgehead and the sea, in fear of envelopment, had begun to retire to a position along a great drainage canal about four miles from the Piave, leaving only weak rear guards

---

[1] See Map III.
[2] There is no account of this; but no hold on the place is shown on the Italian situation maps.

behind; and after the Italian 23rd Division had secured Ponte di Piave, the rear guards withdrew, and the main bodies continued undisturbed their retirement to the Livenza.

On the left of Lord Cavan's Army, on the front of the Eighth Army,[1] as on the front of the Tenth Army, "the "enemy was everywhere retiring in haste, only offering a "little resistance at obligatory points of passage", and at night the heads of the Eighth Army's columns were on a line from the left of the British near Sacile to Vittorio Veneto, and thence south-westwards along the foot of the mountains. In the Twelfth Army the French 23rd Division and the Italian 52nd, on the east bank of the Piave, advanced about two thousand yards into the mountains; but on their left its I Corps and the Fourth Army remained held up: Italian authors claim that the Fourth Army detained 15 Austrian divisions, preventing their use at some other point of the front; but this does not seem to have been the case, as 12 Italian divisions confronted 12 Austrian.[2]

31st October: Halt on the Livenza

On the 31st the Austrian retreat on the whole front from the sea to the M. Grappa sector, inclusive, became general. The corps of Cavan's Army were halted on the Livenza, waiting not only for bridging material, but also for ammunition, now subject to added delay as the bridges over the Piave and the roads near them were required for the passage of the 4 Italian cavalry divisions. Sacile was captured, and the Army as a whole moved a little closer to the banks of the Livenza; the Italian Armies, the Italian Cavalry Corps included, advanced towards the river, and the Eighth and Twelfth Armies pushed farther on the roads into the mountains.

General Diaz's orders for the 31st directed the Third and Tenth Armies to close up to the Livenza and establish

---

[1] See Sketch 12.
[2] There were never more than 12 weak Austrian divisions in the *Army Group Belluno* (Sketch 10) to hold the front between the Piave and the Brenta, with 9 in front line, and these 9 were attacked by 9 Italian divisions, with 3 in corps reserve of the Fourth Army and I Corps of the Twelfth Army behind them.

For the Austrian action on 30th October, see Note at end of Chapter.

bridgeheads over it; the Eighth Army was to turn northwards, with Belluno as objective, in the hope of cutting off the retreat of the Austrians on the M. Grappa front; it was left to the cavalry to keep connection between the Tenth and Eighth Armies. The Twelfth and Fourth Armies were to continue to thrust northwards. The Comando Supremo also decided on the 30th[1] that the Sixth Army (in which was the British 48th Division) in the Asiago sector, should be launched to the attack; but it did not move forward until 1st November.[2]

The orders to the XIV Corps[3] were to close up to the Livenza when not already there and secure bridgeheads over it. The XI Corps was also to push on to the Livenza; it was delayed by the bridges over the Monticano being broken, and the greater part of it got no farther than Oderzo.

The 7th Division being already close up to the Livenza on its whole front, no operation except preparations for bridging took place; there was a certain amount of shell and other fire, and the places whence it came were engaged. The Italian 31st Division, on the right, reached the Livenza between Portobuffole and Brugnera, with the XI Corps on its right down to Motta.

Owing to the great destruction of the Italian service bridging equipment on the Piave, there was a scarcity of pontoons, and means had to be improvised, which accounts for some of the delay on the Livenza; but the slow arrival of reinforcements and gun ammunition was due not only to the congestion on the roads but also to the fact that, the floating bridges on the Piave lacked adequate support, so that heavy vehicles could pass over them only one at a time.

The 23rd Division had a more lively day than the 7th. At 9 a.m. the 70th Brigade sent forward its 3 battalions, the 9/York & Lancaster, 8/K.O.Y.L.I., and 8/York & Lancaster in line, each with one 18-pdr. battery of the 102nd Brigade attached. As the Italian Eighth Army, on the left, was to thrust northwards, the 70th Brigade was directed not to the Livenza but to maintain its refused flank and advance across the Meschio to the line of a small

---

[1] Vittorio Veneto, p. 25.
[2] See p. 330.
[3] Maps III and V.

stream marked by Sacile–Caneva. Almost immediately after starting, the right, the 9/York & Lancaster, came in contact with the Austrians holding Sacile railway station south-west of the town; but by 12 noon it had driven them off, captured five hundred prisoners and effected junction with the other 2 battalions of the brigade, which had gained the objective without opposition. The enemy now withdrawing across the Livenza, the right bank was occupied, much abandoned material being found, including 54 guns, and a junction effected with the 7th Division at the railway bridge, which was still passable by infantry.

At Sacile, an ancient town of high buildings and narrow streets (9,000 inhabitants in 1914), the Livenza makes a U-shape bend to the eastward; in this bend was the southern part of the town, thus divided by the river from the northern portion; one wooden bridge provided the only connection. There was another bridge just above the town, but both these bridges had been demolished, and the Austrians still held the far side of the river and continued to fire on the western part of the town. Appreciating that the enemy was on the run, the officer commanding the 9/York & Lancaster (Lieut.-Colonel S. D. Rumbold) requested, and was granted, permission to force the passage at Sacile and form a bridgehead. After a hostile battery had been silenced by the 18-pdrs. of the 102nd Brigade R.F.A., Stokes and 6-inch mortars were brought up and silenced the machine guns and rifles which, from the houses on the bank, commanded the road bridge over the Livenza; but when men of the 9/South Staffordshire (pioneers) set about improvising a footbridge, a machine gun opened fire from the tower on the opposite bank, wounded several men and made further work impossible. Br.-General J. Byron, the C.R.A. of the division, on being informed of the situation, personally ordered up an 18-pdr. gun to a point a thousand yards from the tower, on which it scored several direct hits. The first hit entered the window whence the machine gun was firing, and the gun and its operator were seen to fall out of the window on to the ground below. The pioneers resumed their work and quickly made a passage over the wreckage of the bridge. Three companies of the York & Lancaster crossed to the left bank and proceeded to clear the town. After some sharp street fighting, followed by some desultory shooting which continued into the dusk of the evening, the Austrian rear guard drew off. The last shots of the 23rd Division in the War, whose first battle had been at the Somme on 4th July 1916, had been fired.[1]

The Italian 31st Division (XIV Corps) reached the Livenza on the front Portobuffole-Brugnera during the morning, and the XI Corps from Oderzo moved up to Motta-Portobuffole.

Assured that all was going well, at 2 p.m. (31st October) the G.O.C. and staff of the XIV Corps left the Villa Margharita, near Treviso, crossed the Piave and established themselves at Vazzolo.

On the right of the Tenth Army, only the Italian 23rd Division (Italian XI Corps), the leading troops of the Third Army, reached the Livenza, much delayed by innumerable streams, and by inundations and other obstacles devised by the enemy in the low-lying country they had to traverse. They found all the bridges of the Livenza down, and enemy rear guards on the far bank. The Italian cavalry divisions also reached the Livenza, but only crossed at one place, Fiaschetti (2 miles north of Sacile), where at 3 p.m. the 2nd Cavalry Brigade surprised the bridge as the enemy was preparing to destroy it. Otherwise the Italian horsemen merely rode up to the British front line and then returned to rest well in the rear. Thus during the day only two bridgeheads, at Sacile and Fiaschetto, were secured.[2]

---

[1] The following appears in the Italian Official Account (Vittorio Veneto, p. 25) :
" A detachment of the Guide (19th) Light Cavalry Regiment attacked " Sacile, which was strongly defended and, with the assistance of British " infantry, took possession of it, after sharp house-to-house fighting ". Tosti (official summary), p. 316, omits the British altogether : it runs, " The regiment of Guides chased the enemy from Sacile after obstinate " house-to-house fighting ". That any Italian troops were present is not recorded in the British war diaries The G.O.C. 23rd Division and other British officers present in Sacile, report that they saw no Italian troops there. A body of Italian cavalry certainly made a dashing charge to capture a farm occupied by the headquarters of a British brigade in reserve.

The Austrian account A.O.A. vii, p. 665) is : " English cavalry " [Yeomanry] of Cavan's Army, which had in vain tried to cross the " Livenza at Sacile in the evening, pressed through Sacile after street " fighting with the last rear guards of the XXIV Corps ".

See the text below for the movements of the Italian cavalry.

[2] The Italian official account, Vittorio Veneto, p. 24, states :
" On the 31st the Cavalry Corps debouched into the plain beyond the " front of the Tenth Army ". This was not the case. To confirm British

Continued at foot of next page

THE AUSTRIAN RETIREMENT. 30TH OCTOBER

On the northern flank, the Austrian *Belluno Group*, having at last begun to retreat, the Eighth, Twelfth and Fourth Armies all made progress in the mountains towards Belluno and Feltre, the latter place being entered. General Diaz's plan to break the front of the Austrians had succeeded ; but their general retirement had prevented any large detachments being cut off ; this retirement, combined with political causes, was, however, rapidly bringing about the disintegration of the Austrian forces.

On the night of 31st October/1st November the Austrian *Eleventh Army*, in the Asiago sector, began a withdrawal. Leaving the Tenth Army on the Livenza, what happened in that western sector will be related in the next chapter.

NOTE

THE AUSTRIANS ON 30TH OCTOBER

On this day the Comando Supremo declined to receive the delegates of the Austrian Armistice Commission, on the grounds that they had not regularized full powers.[1]

The Austrian orders for the gradual evacuation of Venetia, with, as first stage, a retirement behind the Livenza, have already been noticed ; the *Belluno Group* was to carry out its withdrawal northwards on the 31st ; to complete the general retirement,

---

Continued from previous page

information, the Austrian Official Account, p. 699, states that 4 Italian cavalry divisions crossed the Livenza not on 31st October but on the morning of 1st November, and all the places which, according to both Italian and Austrian accounts, the Italian cavalry reached next day, S. Quirino, Sedrano, Aviano, etc., are north of the Tenth Army area, not east of it, where the Austrians were in possession until about midday on 1st November.

The only contacts with the enemy mentioned are at Sacile, Fiaschetti and Polcenigo (4 miles north of Sacile). No Italian cavalry was on the Tenth Army front. The following is taken from a report from British G.H.Q. to the Chief of the Imperial General Staff, dated 2nd November 1918 :

" I am not at all impressed with Italian cavalry in pursuit. Their " commanders are terribly lacking in dash. The country north of " Pordenone is ideal for cavalry and is their regular manoeuvre ground in " peace time. Yet they do not drive forward, but sit down before each " machine gun ".

The Austrian Official Account (vii, pp. 699–700) speaks of the ground beyond the Livenza as " a wide, meadow-covered plain, only broken by " a few brooks and small woods, ideal ground for cavalry action "—but the Italian cavalry did no more than " come near " the Austrian rear-guard positions.

[1] See p. 368.

orders were issued on the 30th to the western group of Armies (*Eleventh* and *Tenth*), now under Field-Marshal Krobatin, for withdrawal in three stages to the " 1917 Positions ",[1] held from June 1916 until the Caporetto period, which were to be reached by the night of 1st/2nd November.

THE AUSTRIANS ON THE 31ST OCTOBER

On the night of 30th/31st October the *Belluno Group* between the Piave and the Brenta, some seventy thousand men, began its retirement to a mountain position which was to be held until 2nd November, and at midnight the defenders of the line so long held against the Italian Fourth Army drew off, as the Austrian Official Account says, from " the bloodstained slopes of M. " Asolone, M. Pertica and M. Spinuccia ". The greater part of the artillery, about a thousand guns, had to be left behind ; " the retirement of the infantry was carried out unnoticed by " the enemy," but only to enter a line of communication area teeming with anarchy. " When, on the morning of 31st October, " the Austrian guns were silent, Italian patrols began to move " forward ". " By the evening of the 31st, the mass of the " *Belluno Group* had at the last moment escaped envelopment ", the Italians capturing no more than " bands of stragglers lying " exhausted, small rear guards, damaged guns and abandoned " equipment ".

On the Venetian plain orders were issued at 3.45 p.m. to the *Sixth Army* for retirement that night from the Livenza to behind the Meduna, and northwards, as a stage on the way to the Tagliamento, which was to be reached by the night of 3rd/4th November. " Great portions of the *Isonzo Army* were already " over the Livenza and making for the Tagliamento in one " bound ", covered by rear guards left on the Livenza.

---

[1] See Frontispiece.

CHAPTER XXIII

THE END OF THE WAR ON THE MOUNTAIN FRONT
(Map IV)

The Austrians Abandon Asiago

After the initial success in forcing the Piave on 28th October, although desperate resistance was still being offered in the M. Grappa sector (from which the Austrians did not retire until the night of the 30th/31st), there was every expectation on the Asiago front that the Austrians would begin a retirement, of which indeed prisoners had frequently spoken.[1] The enemy continued, however, as far as could be discovered by patrols, to hold his old, including the false, front. Suspicion, however, was aroused, and probing patrols were sent out on the nights of the 27th/28th and 28th/29th; but it was not until the night of the 29th/30th, when the 1st Buckinghamshire Battalion made a large-scale raid between Sec and Ave, that the old defence line was found completely deserted, except for a single man left to fire flares. Reconnaissance patrols of the battalion then searched Asiago and the localities between it and the front, and found them all abandoned and lifeless, but received fire from the hills beyond. French and Italian patrols on the right and left found a similar state of affairs. The false front had, in fact, been withdrawn during the previous evening (28th), and the enemy had gone back to the prepared *Winterstellung* position behind Asiago, marked by M. Catz–Bosco–Camporovere. A patrol centre was then established in the barracks in Asiago; but when, during the morning (30th), parties tried to approach the Austrian position, although they met no outposts they were received by machine-gun fire. They then worked along the south-western slopes of M. Catz, and had their first encounter with the enemy in Bosco, where they took 16 prisoners.

In view of the possibility of a general retreat on the mountain front, plans were prepared by the 48th Division

---
[1] See Map IV.

for an attack on the line M. Catz–Camporovere, and the brigades were warned.[1]

During this day and the next (31st) the Austrians exhibited a good deal of artillery activity, firing shells of all calibres, including gas, indiscriminately and wildly into the Allied areas; many fires, too, were seen and explosions heard, which seemed to indicate that a deep retreat was intended. During the 31st both the French and British pushed forward patrols, the British outpost line was advanced to pass through the northern outskirts of Asiago, and the French were abreast of it. At 9.30 p.m. on the 31st the British liaison officer with the French 24th Division telephoned that General Odry had directed him to say that, as far as he could make out, his raiding party against M. Sisemol had found the trenches unoccupied, that the final objectives of the party were Eck and Covola ($\frac{1}{4}$ mile south-east and south of Gallio), and that if the area examined was found unoccupied, he intended to attack M. Longara at 5 a.m. (1st November): he asked if the 48th Division would help by covering his left by artillery fire. Major-General Walker replied that if the French did attack he would also do so, whether his Italian corps commander, who could not make up his mind, approved or not, and that he would move against M. Mosciagh and M. Interrotto.

Warning orders were then issued by telephone to the 144th and 145th Brigades in the line and to the C.R.A., and permission was obtained from General Pennella to make the attack if the French did.[2]

The Attack on the Austrian Winterstellung

At 12.15 a.m. (1st November) the liaison officer with General Odry telephoned that Eck and Covola had been

---

[1] Vittorio Veneto, p. 25, says that on the 30th " it was decided that the " Sixth Army also, although its forces had already been reduced for the " benefit of the principal action, should be launched to the attack of the " front Portecche [not identified]—Stenfle [N.E. of M. Sisemol]— M. Mosciagh.

" This action, prepared for on the morning of the 31st by the storming " of the enemy's flank positions—Melaghetto [1$\frac{1}{2}$ miles east of M. Sisemol] " on the right and Canove on the left—was continued in the evening with " Levico and Caldonazzo as objectives ".

No such decision was made known to the French or British, and nothing happened until 1st November, and then only on their own initiative.

[2] The strength of the 144th Brigade on this date was reported as 109 officers and 2,420 other ranks.

found unoccupied and that the French would attack at 5 a.m. The British bombardment was opened at that hour, but, owing to the short notice and the distances involved, the infantry zero hour was made three-quarters of an hour later, and even then at least one battalion was only just in time, after having marched seven miles. The weather on this day and throughout the closing period of the war was fine, with cold nights.

The French 24th Division, using 2 regiments, had complete success; by 8 a.m. M. Longara had been captured, and the mopping up of the Austrian machine-gun posts was being taken in hand. General Odry then obtained permission to push on, and did so at 4.30 p.m. without artillery support when, though his men were hampered by the mountainous nature of the ground, the left pushed beyond M. Baldo and M. Cimon, but the right was not able to advance much beyond M. Longara.[1]

The 1st Buckinghamshire Battalion and the 1/4th R. Berkshire of the 145th Brigade (Br.-General G. W. Howard) and the 1/4th and 1/6th Gloucestershire of the 144th Brigade (Br.-General H. R. Done) moved forward at the appointed hour. The right of the British attack was entirely successful, but not without hard fighting at first. By 6.30 a.m., although the Austrian guns were served to the last, it had broken through the *Winterstellung* and had captured M. Catz, regarded as its key. Soon the troops were pushing along the ridge, and patrols eventually made touch with the French left at Caseta Zingarella (2½ miles north-east of M. Mosciagh). The captures amounted to about four hundred prisoners and 15 guns. The left brigade met with stiff resistance from troops among the rocks on the eastern and southern slopes of M. Interrotto, a dominating position with open ground to the south-west, where success would have given access to the southern end of the Val d'Assa, one of the few Austrian lines of retreat in the sector. The two Gloucestershire battalions were driven back, the one to and out of Bosco and the other into Camporovere. Assistance offered by the Italian 20th Division, on the left, by means of a frontal attack from the

---

[1] According to Vittorio Veneto, pp. 26–7, the Italian XIII Corps co-operated with the French 24th Division, which was used to exploit a breach made by the Italians.

F.O.A. vii (ii), p. 377, merely mentions Italians on the right " whose progress was slower ". The Italian front line at night was about three thousand yards behind the Franco-British junction posts.

south was declined by Major-General Walker, as such an operation in broad daylight must have resulted in heavy casualties.

At night the line of the 145th Brigade ran—with a gap—from the left of the French at M. Longara, westwards on to the northern slope of the M. Catz ridge, with 1½ companies of the Berkshire forward near M. Mosciagh, and south-west to "Sichestal" (a mile south-east of M. Mosciagh) ; whilst, separated from it by a step back of two thousand yards, the line of the 144th Brigade ran from Costa (on the southern slope of M. Catz) to Camporovere. To fill the gap should the enemy try to penetrate into it, the 1/4th Oxford L.I. and a company of the 1/4th R. Berkshire were held ready in Asiago.[1]

THE PURSUIT BEGINS

On the morning of 1st November, without informing at any rate the British, that an Austrian Armistice Commission had arrived at Italian headquarters on the previous evening after 3 days' negotiations,[2] orders were issued by Comando Supremo to all the Armies on the mountain front, the Sixth, the First and, beyond Lake Garda, the Seventh, " to push forward rapidly and energetically towards the " origins of the enemy's communications and strangle them".

---

[1] The account in A.O.A. vii, pp. 686–7, is as follows :
"The British 48th Division [actually 2 battalions of the 144th Brigade] "in the forenoon attacked M. Rasta [between M. Interrotto and "Camporovere], but was beaten off with heavy loss [the divisional losses "for the whole period 1st–5th November were only 162. See p. 345.] by "the K.u.K. *52nd Division*. West of the British, the Italian 20th "Division was prevented by the fire of the K.u.K. *6th Division* from "entering the Val d'Assa. Thus, while the *III Corps* maintained its "position, the thin line of the *XIII Corps*, on its left (east), was completely "broken through [by 2 battalions of the 145th Brigade]. The French "24th Division, in the Italian XIII Corps, started early to win M. Longara. "The battle-weary regiments of the *38th Honved Division* made very "slight (*gering*) resistance. . . . *Honved Regiment 24*, in divisional reserve, "refused to attack and retired of its own accord. . . . What of the *38th* "*Honved Division* was not captured or dispersed, hurried away in dis- "orderly and precipitate retreat. . . . Only the commander of the *75th* "*Honved Brigade*, with, in all, about a hundred men, remained north of "M. Longara.
"The break-through of the left wing of the *38th Honved Division* at "once brought the whole of the already wavering front of the *XIII Corps* "to breaking point ".
See Chapter XXV.

THE BRITISH PURSUIT. 1st NOVEMBER

The direction of pursuit[1] was Trent–Bolzano, the Sixth Army north-westwards, the First Army northwards up the valley of the Adige (it did not move until the night of the 1st/2nd[2]) and the Seventh Army north-eastwards from the Tonale Pass, down the upper valley of the Noce[3] (it did not move until the afternoon of the 2nd[4]). The Fourth Army, in the Grappa sector, was also ordered to move in the direction of Bolzano.

As early as noon (1st November) Major-General Walker had decided to exploit the success on the right of the 145th Brigade, in order to assist the 144th by turning the Interrotto position from the north; but, in view of the many enemy machine-gun posts, he further decided to wait until dawn on the 2nd to do so. He allotted the 1/7th Worcestershire, the reserve of the 144th Brigade, to the 145th for the purpose, and he concentrated the 143rd Brigade (Br.-General G. C. Sladen), his reserve, near Asiago. The Machine-Gun Battalion was distributed: 1 company to each brigade, with the fourth in reserve.

After receiving General Pennella's instructions to push on to Levico and Caldonazzo in the Val Sugana (upper valley of the Brenta) south-east of Trent, so as to block the retreat of any Austrians retiring by that route, Major-General Walker warned Br.-General Sladen that, as soon as the Interrotto situation permitted, his brigade, with a section of 18-pdrs., two 4.5-inch howitzers and "a half " company R.E." attached, would be required to move up the Val d'Assa as advanced guard. Reconnaissances were carried out, and at dusk the 1/6th R. Warwickshire was moved up into Asiago, the 1/5th and 1/7th remaining at S. Sisto, a mile and a half to the south. Later in the evening, Br.-General Sladen obtained permission from the division to carry out a right turning movement by the Val Portule with 1 battalion, whilst the rest of the brigade would march by the Val d'Assa.

---

[1] See End-paper. For the orders to the rest of the front see Chapter XXIV.
[2] Vittorio Veneto, p. 28.
[3] The Noce eventually turns south and joins the Adige above Trent.
[4] Vittorio Veneto, p. 29. Its attached map (No. 3) shows no advance on the 2nd, only on the 3rd.

2ND NOVEMBER: ENTRY INTO THE VAL D'ASSA

At dawn (2nd November) the 1/7th Worcestershire and the 1/4th Oxford L.I. attacked M. Mosciagh, also M. Dorbellele, a summit quite close to it, and by 7.30 a.m. were in possession of both of them, thus taking the M. Interrotto position in reverse and forcing the Austrians to decamp. The 144th Brigade at the same time advanced again against the trench covering M. Interrotto, which it found evacuated, and by 8.45 a.m. was on the top of the ridge. An hour later Major-General Walker issued orders for the advanced guard (Sladen's 143rd Brigade) to get on the move and give the enemy no rest, whilst the remainder of the division concentrated, ready to follow: but the two brigades R.F.A. were to leave half their guns behind.

The turning battalion, the 1/6th R. Warwickshire, had already left Asiago whilst the 145th Brigade was attacking and, moving by the south-east side of M. Catz and north of M. Mosciagh, started for the Val Portule, capturing en route an Austrian battery at breakfast. At 10 a.m. the main body of the 143rd Brigade, the 1/7th R. Warwickshire, which had reached Asiago at 7.30 a.m., leading, entered the Val d'Assa by the road from Camporovere, the 145th Brigade being responsible for piqueting the heights on the right, and the Italian 20th Division for those on the left.

In compliance with these instructions, the 1/4th Oxford L.I. was ordered to occupy M. Meatta ($1\frac{1}{4}$ miles north-west of M. Mosciagh), where—in the clouds—it found and put to flight a garrison of about a hundred Austrians. Otherwise, except for the finding of much abandoned material, the operation was carried out without incident. The Italians on the left followed a road along the heights from M. Erio to M. Verena, where the Val d'Assa turns westward.

The entrance to the Val d'Assa is a gloomy, heavily wooded gorge, with sides so high and steep that the sun shines into it only for a few hours each day. The road is cut as a ledge in the flank of the mountains on the eastern side, so that it has sheer slopes on the right and a drop of some thousand feet down to the torrent of the Assa on the left, and movement for vehicles off the road is impossible. From the Val Portule (3 miles up from Camporovere) the gorge widens, and the mountains on each side are less precipitous; the road ascends nearly fifteen hundred feet

THE BRITISH PURSUIT. 2ND NOVEMBER

in eight miles to Vezzena. About a mile and a half beyond this place the valley opens out into a grassy tableland, the Altipiano di Lavarone. This crossed, the road descends 3,200 feet to Caldonazzo in the Val Sugana.

A mile north of Camporovere and onward the road was in good condition, and wide enough for two-way traffic, but in No Man's Land and around Asiago it was badly damaged by British shelling; there, however, early on 1st November, the 474th and 475th Field Companies R.E.[1] and a company of the 1/5th R. Sussex (pioneers) had been set to work to clear, repair and widen it for wheeled traffic, and, following up the column, they continued their labours, on which the supply of the force depended, throughout the succeeding days. They were most efficiently aided by an Italian road-making detachment sent up by the Sixth Army.

A mountain road of this character might easily have been rendered impassable: but only at one point, a thousand yards short of Porrecche d'Avanti, had the Austrians "blown a landslide across it"; this did not stop infantry or pack animals, but held up limbered wagons and guns for about two hours.

THE AUSTRIAN FRONTIER CROSSED

In spite of some resistance by isolated machine-gun teams and the occasional fire of super-heavy Italian guns in position behind Asiago, the advanced guard pressed steadily forward. By 1 p.m. the main guard had reached the Val Portule, 3 miles from Camporovere, where a well-equipped Austrian hutted camp was found, and the 1/6th R. Warwickshire, the turning force, rejoined without having encountered resistance, but with fifty prisoners. It was then ordered to occupy M. Porrecche and Porrecche d'Avanti, whilst the 1/7th pushed on rapidly to reach and block the Val Sugana, the 1/5th marching in rear in the centre of the road. By 3 p.m. Porrecche d'Avanti, 3 miles farther on, was passed after a short fight, covered by two 18-pdr. guns, against parties of riflemen and machine guns, which, although the fire was at close range, caused only one casualty, and the guns with the riflemen were taken by outflanking. The

---

[1] The third company, the 477th, was with the XIV Corps on the Piave front.

145th Brigade (less 1 company still on M. Meatta) was by now concentrated in the Val Portule—where divisional headquarters were established at 5 p.m.—with the 144th Brigade just north of it in the Val d'Assa. It had been left to the discretion of the G.O.C. advanced guard whether he should continue on to Vezzena or not, and he decided to go on. At Osteria del Termine, 1⅓ miles beyond Porrecche d'Avanti, at dusk, the 143rd Brigade crossed the Austrian frontier, being the first British troops to enter the territories of the Central Powers, and after mopping up some more isolated machine-gun posts, halted for the night at some hutments short of Vezzena, where the artillery of the advanced guard rejoined it. The outpost company of the 1/7th R. Warwickshire was fired on during the night, and its patrols found the enemy was holding a line of trenches—an earlier built defensive position—two thousand yards east of Vezzena in considerable strength. Later information was received from the Sixth Army, that the Austrian *Edelweiss Division* was holding the defences, constructed in 1917, around M. Rovere for a final stand.[1] It was indeed the last place for a stand, as less than two miles beyond Vezzena the road begins to descend by sharp turns and hair-pin bends to the Val Sugana. Some three thousand prisoners had been gathered in during the day, and several hundred guns in their positions on the hills round Asiago, over a hundred guns parked together near Osteria del Termine, and much material had been found abandoned. Every sign, indeed, of a hurried and disorganized retreat was apparent: wagons, lorries and guns ditched by the roadside, horses still harnessed to their carts lying across the road, dead or dying; even a well-stocked canteen and a cask of brandy were found: and, no doubt in order to travel lightly, the Austrians had thrown away gas masks, helmets, packs, haversacks and even rifles.

The French 24th Division, having served as spearhead, by order of the Italian XIII Corps did not advance on 2nd November, and at noon a light column of the Italian 14th Division passed through its outposts by Campomulo to take over the duty of covering the right of the 48th

---

[1] In Austrian accounts this position is generally called the Lavarone Plateau Position; this plateau lies just south-west of Rovere. The front line of trenches ran on the crest of a spur from Bosco Varanga, due south, past the east side of Vezzena, and thence south-west.

GENERAL ADVANCE. 2ND NOVEMBER

Division. The French then went into reserve and returned to their cantonments. They had in the two days captured six hundred prisoners and more than two hundred guns.

The light column of the Italian 14th Division, following the track westward across the mountains from Campomulo, was reported in the evening to have reached Bocchetta di Portule, and the Italian 20th Division, on the left, was reported to be at Bosco Posellaro, not quite two miles south-east of Vezzena; but neither of them established touch with the 48th Division nor gave sign of being in its neighbourhood. From all parts of the front came news this night that the Austrian retreat was being followed up, including the information that the Italian 21st Division, the left wing of the Fourth Army (on the right of the Sixth), moving up the valley of the Brenta, was about four miles beyond Grigno, thus cutting off the retreat of any Austrians by the Asiago–Campomulo high road which runs to Grigno, whilst the spearhead of the First Army, on the left of the Sixth, working up the valley of the Adige, was close to Rovereto (abreast of Asiago), which was occupied at 1 a.m. (3rd November).[1]

DIFFICULTIES OF SUPPLY

In this advance through the mountains supply was the great anxiety, and as early as 1st November a scheme had been prepared and issued to the 48th Division. Railhead was at Villaverla, 6 miles from the foot of the mountains and ten miles south of Granezza.[2] Thence, previous to the advance, rations were drawn in bulk by the divisional train (motorized) and taken to the foot of the mountains. There they were split up and taken by the light Fiat lorries of the first-line transport in two stages to Granezza (where 3 days' reserve rations were normally kept). From this centre they were delivered to units by horsed wagons and pack animals. On 1st November the lorries available for supply work were twenty-two 3-ton and 16 Fiats. These being considered insufficient, application was made to the Italian XII Corps for 50 extra Fiat lorries. At first some

---

[1] This agrees with Map 3, in Vittorio Veneto, showing the daily advances, on which, however, the head of the British advance is not shown at Vezzena, nor, indeed, quite even as far as M. Porrecche d'Avanti.

[2] See Map I.

difficulty arose, but as it was made clear that the division could not be fed and consequently could not advance without them, on 2nd November 23 lorries appeared, and by the 3rd all 50 were at Granezza (though never more than 40 were in a serviceable condition), and they worked forward from that place. At Asiago, too, a S.A.A. and grenade dump and a drinking water-point had been formed on the 2nd, and next day that place became lorry-head. Early on the 3rd, 4 Fiat lorries, loaded with 120,000 rounds of S.A.A. were sent forward and got through right up to the advanced guard, and the divisional dump at Asiago was moved forward to Val Portule.

3RD NOVEMBER : THE AUSTRIANS PREMATURELY ANNOUNCE AN ARMISTICE

On the 3rd, the 48th Division, the field artillery still with only half their guns, moved forward with the orders, issued at 6 p.m. on the previous evening, to gain the high ground (M. Rovere)[1] overlooking the Val Sugana : if this was successfully achieved, Caldonazzo and Levico were to be captured and the Val Sugana blocked : it was stated for information that " the enemy resistance has been very " weak and there is every sign of a rapid retreat ", and that after M. Verena had been passed " no touch has been " obtained with Italian column [14th Division] on the right ", nor with that (20th Division) on the left.

Resistance from the M. Rovere position being expected, the advanced guard, the 143rd Brigade as before, was reinforced by a tractor-drawn section of 6-inch howitzers, and the reserve machine-gun company, and strengthened by the increase of the field artillery from a section to a brigade (4 batteries).

The outpost battalion, the 1/7th R. Warwickshire, as advanced guard of the 143rd Brigade, moved off in the dark at 4.30 a.m. The 144th and 145th Brigades followed in due course, leaving the Val Portule at 3.15 a.m. and 4.30 a.m. respectively. Major-General Walker fully realized the risks he was taking by pushing into the mountains whilst depending for ammunition and food on a single road, which by a change of weather, already due, might be blocked by

---

[1] See Map IV.

snow. He was uncertain, too, of the support which he might expect from the Italian columns on his flanks—it was not until noon that men of the Italian 20th Division were seen moving in extended order down the slopes of M. Campo, south of Osteria del Termine. In view, however, of the evident demoralization of the Austrians and the importance of keeping them on the run, he felt that risks were justified.

Some resistance was encountered by the 1/7th R. Warwickshire near Vezzena and from Bosco Varanga, on the heights on the north of the road ; but it was soon evident that the enemy had no intention of making a protracted defence, and parties of ten and twenty, advancing carrying torches and firing coloured lights, began to surrender. At the former place, where a well-placed fort on a hill to the north, large enough to hold a couple of battalions, covered the defile, Austrian troops were drawn up across the road, and their divisional commander who had come up insisted through an interpreter that an armistice had been signed.[1] Br.-General Sladen gave him ten minutes to surrender or be shot down, and bluffed him into capitulation by means of parties sent out to the flanks. The garrison of the fort at first refused to come out, but capitulated when threatened by the officer who carried the white flag with bombardment by non-existent guns. The whole area as the advanced guard went on was covered with parties of sullen Austrians, unable to fight and unwilling to surrender, but quickly compelled to do so. By 8 a.m. all opposition, except a little long-range rifle fire, had been overcome or had ceased. The 144th Brigade, coming up to Vezzena, found the 1/7th R. Warwickshire embarrassed by having to guard so many prisoners and lent to the 143rd Brigade the 1/4th Gloucestershire, which remained thus attached until 4th November, and so enabled the latter brigade to push on.

In Vezzena itself, which had been the headquarters of the Austrian *III Corps*, were over two hundred huts and many dumps containing, it was first reported, enough food and fodder to last two divisions for several weeks : then it appeared there was nothing eatable by humans left ;

---

[1] In the " Manual of Military Law " 1914 Edition, p. 275, para. 272, it was laid down : " No one is bound to believe a notification by the enemy " that an armistice has been concluded ".

but later search revealed great quantities of flour, potatoes, sugar and tea.[1]

In view of the assertion that an armistice had been signed, an Austrian party with a white flag was permitted to pass through the line to communicate with divisional headquarters, which had moved forward to Osteria del Termine, and there, about 9 a.m., an Austrian general, Ritter von Romer,[2] and other officers appeared and protested against any further advance of the British, stating that an armistice had been signed at 3 a.m. that morning. No information having been received to that effect, the Austrians were firmly but courteously told that the advance must continue.

Terms Offered to the Austrians

As soon as the parley was over, Major-General Walker sent his G.S.O. 1, Lieut.-Colonel H. C. L. Howard, and an Intelligence officer by car to the headquarters of the Austrian *III Corps* in Trent. The British officers were cheered the whole way as they drove through the retreating Austrian troops. They carried the following terms, drawn up by Major-General Walker, he at the time being out of touch with the Italian forces on his right and left, and not in communication (it was not restored until 3 p.m.) with the Italian XII Corps or the Sixth Army :

---

[1] The Austrian account (A.O.A. vii, p. 738) is that the commanders and troops of the *III Corps* were standing fast, in the belief—like those in the Piave theatre—on information which reached them between 2 a.m. and 4 a.m., that an armistice had been arranged. Having at the same time been ordered to retire to Caldonazzo and Levico, they were waiting to march off as soon as the road was clear of the *XIV Corps*, coming up from the front between the *III Corps* and the Adige valley. Then, " at " 6 a.m.; infantry of the British 48th Division appeared on Lavarone " plateau. The British overran the rear guards of the *III Corps*, disarmed " the unsuspecting *Infantry Regiment No. 127* and, soon after, parts of " *Infantry Regiments Nos. 27, 42* and *74* ".

An account of how the mistake about the armistice arose and the collapse of the Austro-Hungarian Army will be found in Chapter XXV.

[2] His name does not appear among those of the brigade, divisional, corps or Army commanders in the Austrian Order of Battle of 15th October, the last issued. A.O.A. says merely that *parlementaires* were sent by the *III Corps* (General-Colonel Martigny von Malastow).

SURRENDER TERMS. 3rd NOVEMBER.

Osteria del Termine
9.35 hours,
3rd November, 1918

" (1) In response to the Austrian *parlementaires*, the G.O.C. 48th Division states that the British forces have received no order to suspend hostilities, and that in accordance with orders, he has given orders for his troops to occupy Levico, Pergine and Trent. He demands the unconditional surrender of hostile troops in the above area and an assurance that no action will be taken against the troops of the Entente.

" (2) He will hold General Romer as hostage whilst the occupation of the above area is carried out.

" (3) He demands that food be provided for all British troops in the above area.

" (4) He sends his chief of staff with this demand to the H.Q. Austrian *Eleventh Army* [to which the *III Corps* belonged], Levico.

" (5) He reserves to himself the right to take such steps as will ensure the control of the troops and civilians in the above area and the prevention of the removal of enemy troops from the Austrian front."

At the same time the brigades were informed that " the " armistice announced by the enemy is not yet acknow- " ledged by us ", and were ordered to push on via Caldonazzo to Pergine and Levico and Trent, with full military precautions, taking steps on arrival in any locality to devise measures to control the civil inhabitants, to prevent withdrawal of enemy troops, and to requisition food supplies for their own troops. The 145th Brigade was detailed to provide two companies to keep guard over the evacuation of enemy prisoners to Asiago. By later orders from the Italian XII Corps, Pergine and Trent were allotted to the Italians and the vicinity of Levico was then given as its destination to the 143rd Brigade, and that of Caldonazzo to the other two brigades.

The two British officers sent by Major-General Walker

arrived in Trent between 1 and 2 p.m.[1] and were received by General-Colonel Martigny (*III Corps*), as representative of General-Colonel Graf Scheuchenstuel (*Eleventh Army*), who had departed at 3 a.m. for Bolzano, after putting him in charge of the retirement. According to the Austrian account, unconditional surrender was refused, but it was added " the road to Levico, Pergine and Trent was open to " the British ". The British record is that " the terms were " accepted [they certainly were signed and took effect] with " the reservation that food could probably not be supplied, " as supply trains had been pillaged by Austrian troops ". Actually, the reservation was not of importance, as on this day, with lorryhead at Asiago, 6 British Fiat lorries carried rations, also mail, spare socks and rum to the advanced guard brigade, and first-line transport took similar supplies to the others. Little food was found in the Austrian depôts round Trent, as, owing to the breakdown of the enemy supply system, most of it had been consumed or looted ; plenty of oats and forage, however, was still on hand.

Pursuit Down into the Val Sugana

Disposal of Prisoners

Meanwhile the advanced guard, the 1/5th R. Warwickshire now leading, after sending back more prisoners, had continued on, making for the one-way zigzag road down three thousand feet to Caldonazzo, and passing dumps of stores and ammunition blazing fiercely by the way.

From the crest of the ridge retiring columns could be seen converging on Levico on all the roads.[2] Small parties of the Warwickshire dashed ahead, sliding down the steep slope

---

[1] The first Italians (of the First Army), in armoured cars, appeared in Trent " shortly after 3 p.m. " The times are taken from A.O.A. vii, p. 739. Vittorio Veneto, in its anxiety to show that Italians reached Trent first, on its situation map No 2 puts the British not as far forward on the 3rd as Vezzena, reached on the previous day.

[2] Map 34 in A.O.A. vii for 3rd November shows 4 divisions (*6th, 18th, 52nd* and *53rd*) and the *6th Cavalry Division* retiring in front of the British 48th Division and converging on Levico and Caldonazzo, with the *19th* and *Jäger Divisions*, north of them, towards Trent, and fragments of the *39th Division* (Hungarian) at Levico ; otherwise nothing in the Val Sugana. The prisoners on the Trentino front came from the above-named 8 divisions. On the left of the British, the *Edelweiss Corps* (*XIV*) is shown holding back the Italian X Corps, with the *XXI Corps*, on its left, abreast of it in the valley of the Adige, beginning to retire.

by hill tracks between the bends to pounce upon the heavily laden Austrians. As soon as the leading platoons, now almost running, approached the railway sidings at Caldonazzo, some three or four hundred small transport wagons were seen trying to get away along the roads to Lavarone, Pergine and Levico; a platoon was at once sent down each road at the double, and the majority of the transport was captured. Lieut.-Colonel W. C. C. Gell organized a mounted patrol on riding horses thus taken, and put men into some of the wagons in order to push on and hustle the retreating foe, and the other battalions as they reached the valley dealt with armed Austrians, amounting to at least a battalion and persuaded them to surrender. The section of 6-inch howitzers with the advanced guard had attempted to follow down the zigzag but, as it took half an hour to negotiate each hair-pin bend, it blocked the road until, fortunately, two recesses were found by a staff officer into which the howitzers could be squeezed so that traffic could pass them.

In Caldonazzo, a straggling village of 2,000 inhabitants but with extensive hutments, which had been the railhead of the Austrian *Eleventh Army*, was accumulated an enormous quantity of stores; and over two hundred guns were found by the vanguard prepared for demolition by a slab of guncotton in breach and muzzle, and connected up by fuze; in the ordnance sheds were over five thousand machine guns and a million rifles; and in the station were three loaded trains, and in one truck two cases containing Zeiss field glasses, which were distributed to the officers; but no resistance was offered. There were also huge parks of transport of all kinds, and a fair supply of forage, but hardly any food except a little flour: the Austrians had commandeered everything, so that the inhabitants had eventually to be supplied from Army stores. It was impossible to guard the large area involved, and, amid scenes of utter confusion, crowds of Austrians were looting the dumps of material, and seizing such little food as there was, mostly tins of sardines which had gone bad. A little firing took place in the streets, but this was quickly brought to an end, and the inhabitants flocked out of their houses to greet their liberators.

The mounted patrol, under Lieut.-Colonel Gell himself, capturing another transport column en route, pushed on to

Levico, a summer resort, of about 6,000 inhabitants, on a very pretty lake, which was reached at 12.50 p.m. and found to be practically deserted; but in the course of the afternoon 6 Hungarian battalions arrived, retreating westwards up the Val Sugana before the Italian 14th Division and, finding the British between them and home, formally surrendered. Fortunately, the main body of the 1/5th R. Warwickshire (less a company temporarily left as prisoners' guard) soon appeared, carried by captured transport and followed by the artillery, as the number of prisoners had reached nearly six thousand. They were secured in Levico by piqueting all the exits.

The 1/6th R. Warwickshire and the 1/4th Gloucestershire, of the advanced guard, had meantime passed through Caldonazzo, making for Trent via Pergine; but soon General Pennella arrived on the scene and requested Br.-General Sladen to slow up the advance as the Italian troops could not go the pace, and they must be the first to enter Trent. The 2 British battalions were therefore ordered to halt for the night at Ischia, on the eastern shore of Lake Caldonazzo, two miles short of Pergine. At this moment a high-powered car arrived, and an oldish Austrian general descending from it, cried, " I surrender to the English, but not to the Italians ". It was the Duke of Braganza, a cavalry commander, who was much hurt when a sergeant was put beside the chauffeur to take him back to British headquarters.

Lieut.-Colonel W. M. Pryor (1/6th R. Warwickshire) went on to Pergine in a car, where he found 3 Austrian battalions; they at first claimed him as a prisoner and refused to lay down their arms on his summons, as they were, they said, retreating that evening; his men being tired out and not wishing to call upon them for another march, he let the Austrians be. The 145th and 144th Brigades went to Caldonazzo, after providing escorts for the earlier prisoners collected in a great mass on the Lavarone plateau, where " an open space of about a hundred acres appeared to be " absolutely packed with humanity moving about like a " swarm of ants ". At Caldonazzo, too, the divisional commander soon arrived, although his headquarters, with the 1/5th R. Sussex (pioneers) as guard, stayed at Vezzena.

To deal with the " bedlam " of prisoners, now well over 20,000 and more coming in, was the first problem, and a start was made on Lavarone plateau as early as 11 a.m. After the officers there had been divided from the men, all were informed that there was no food for them nearer than Granezza, 15 miles away downhill, and so their only chance of avoiding starvation lay in marching back quietly under escort. They seemed to accept their fate, and were marched off in parties of 500 at 20 minutes' interval, the officers, about six hundred, last. Each party was in charge of ten men of the 1/4th Oxford L.I. (145th Brigade), 2 companies of which had been detailed for the purpose, and by nightfall practically all Austrian troops near Vezzena had been evacuated, except four generals, who, with their attendants, were accommodated in a hut until next morning.

At Caldonazzo it was too late to do anything more than put a guard over the prisoners, and next morning, when the Italians began to appear, 14th Division from the east and parties of the 20th Division from the south-west, blocking the streets with their transport and commandeering every building, they were persuaded without much difficulty to take over charge of the prisoners both at Caldonazzo and Levico, and arrange for their feeding and evacuation.

4TH NOVEMBER: THE ARMISTICE TAKES EFFECT AT 3 P.M.

Divisional orders were issued on the evening of 3rd November for the march to be resumed on the following day at 10 a.m., the 143rd Brigade moving to Baselga di Pine (6½ miles north of Lake Caldonazzo) and the 144th and 145th Brigades to an area north of Pergine (2 miles north of Lake Caldonazzo), with divisional headquarters at Civezzano (5 miles north-west of the northern part of the lake).[1]

At 9.40 p.m. on the 3rd the following message (translated) was sent from the Comando Supremo to the Tenth Army.

> "To-morrow, 4th November, at 1500 hours Central European time, hostilities with the Austro–Hungarian forces on land, on sea, and in the air will cease.

---

[1] See inset on Map IV.

"At the moment of cessation of hostilities, our troops must halt on the line reached, whilst the enemy must withdraw at least 3 kilometres from that line. Armies will make the necessary measures to define exactly the line reached at 1500 hours by their respective troops. All hostile troops who still remain inside the line reached by us at that hour will be considered prisoners of war.

"In the event of a breach of these provisions on the part of the enemy strong reactionary measures are to be taken."

A corresponding message was received at 48th Division headquarters at Vezzena at 3 a.m. on the 4th and became known to all troops by about seven o'clock.

The marches ordered were carried out without sign of any enemy, except for the prisoners picked up by the way and for the roads being strewn with equipment, broken rifles and other arms, and dotted with the carcasses of horses. Orders were received from Italian XII Corps defining the line to be held at 3 p.m. This was a rough half-circle, with Baselga di Pine,[1] the halting place of the advanced guard, near its summit, and was defined as extending from C. Brada on the right to M. Calisio (3 miles N.N.E. of Trent) on the left. This the 143rd Brigade held by a piquet line. General Pennella, the Italian corps commander, fixed his headquarters at Pergine, in the British area, where an ammunition dump and hutments were, at evening, set on fire, lighting up the whole countryside. The Italian units in the British area flocked into Trent to celebrate the recovery of the city; but they left a guard over the prisoners at Caldonazzo. There, however, no organization of the Austrians into squads and parties had taken place and no supply arrangements had been made, so the prisoners were soon in a state of uproar, and the 48th Division was forced to resume charge.

The 145th Brigade (less the 1/4th Oxford L.I., which was providing prisoner guards) marched through Pergine to the villages of Madrano and Vigalzano; the 144th Brigade (less the 1/4th Gloucestershire, attached to the 143rd Brigade) was on its left, at first at Cire (an airfield, where

---

[1] See inset on Map IV.

THE FINAL SCENE. 4TH NOVEMBER

French aircraft with Italian pilots were landing); but after a long halt there, a move was made, 1½ miles northwards to Seregnano, where there were good billets.

The marches of 3rd and 4th November had been remarkably good considering that the altitude at the start was 3,100 feet, that the rise from the Asiago plateau to Vezzena was over fifteen hundred feet, and the drop down to Caldonazzo, three thousand feet; on the 3rd the main body, covered over twenty miles, and on the 4th (by 3 p.m.) over fifteen; and only one man fell out. The advanced guard marched farther. The nights were very cold and greatcoats were not carried by the men, but on pack horses with the Lewis guns, signalling and medical stores, and did not arrive at the front until the 6th.

Lorryhead had been moved forward from Asiago to Val Portule on the 3rd, and on the 4th supplies, with some delays owing to congestion on the zigzag road and elsewhere, came through to the troops, now seventy-five miles and more from railhead; but to ease the first-line transport, on the same day, 15 Fiat lorries were loaded up at Val Portule and sent forward to Caldonazzo. The 4 Austrian generals who had been taken prisoner before the Armistice hour were handed over to the Italians, but the *parlementaire* and his party who had appeared at Osteria del Termine on the morning of the 3rd were sent back to the Austrian lines. Twenty-nine escaped British prisoners, 28 belonging to the 48th Division, reached the British lines on the 4th.

The grand total of captures of the 48th Division during the three days, 2nd to 4th November was over twenty-two thousand unwounded and 365 sick and wounded prisoners, with 63 guns, 161 howitzers, besides a park at Caldonazzo of over two hundred guns, one 17-inch howitzer, a train loaded with field guns, and an uncounted number of abandoned guns in the neighbourhood of Vezzena.

The total casualties of the 48th Division for the period 1st to 5th November, probably all suffered in the first three days, were:

	Killed	Wounded	Missing
Officers	1	8	—
Other ranks ..	25	121	7

NOTE

LESSONS IN MOUNTAIN WARFARE

REPORT BY MAJOR-GENERAL SIR H. B. WALKER, COMMANDING 48TH DIVISION

I forward certain notes on the recent fighting in which this division took part.

Whilst there is nothing new among the lessons brought out, at the same time various points already known were particularly emphasized.

In Mountain Warfare :

Artillery. (a) (i) An artillery barrage cannot, owing to the configuration of the ground, be expected to have the same destructive effectiveness as in ordinary country ; it is very difficult to destroy hostile nests.

(ii) Long-range artillery positions must be selected a long time beforehand. It is almost impossible to get heavies forward ; in this case two 6-inch howitzers accompanied the advanced guard.

Flanks. (b) The preliminary piqueting of flank ground is emphasized.

Communications. (c) Failing unlimited cable, which cannot be expected, more dispatch riders are required. Journeys take so long that occasionally the available supply of dispatch riders becomes dangerously low.

Stokes Mortars. (d) Stokes Mortars drop out altogether, or at most only 2 mortars per battery can be got forward, with an at all adequate supply of ammunition.

Liaison. (e) More liaison personnel was required, as the division was working in an Italian corps, with an Italian division on one flank.

This point should have been legislated for by the higher formation.

As regards the other flank, so many people have now got a working knowledge of French, that the same difficulties did not arise.

Equipment. (f) The British equipment is not suitable for mountain warfare. Men's loads should be lightened, and difficulties arise in the carriage of greatcoats.

MOUNTAIN WARFARE

Transport. (g) In spite of the distance from the railhead to the most advanced troops (eventually 119 kms.), and the unsuitability of the British organization, troops were never without rations ; but it is doubtful if the system could have lasted long, it certainly could not have done so if the weather had broken, and snow fallen heavily.

More light lorries are required, and the G.S. wagon is very unsuitable on account of weight and lock.

Headquarters. (h) The necessity of headquarters moving to definite points was brought out, as the Italian XII Corps was frequently not in communication with the division. They moved without sending information as to their move.

That the position of the divisional report centre should be near the advanced guard was clearly brought out. If the flanks are secure, the whole work of the divisional commander lies in the problems which arise at the head of his command.

CHAPTER XXIV

THE BATTLE OF VITTORIO VENETO (concluded)

THE END OF THE WAR ON THE VENETIAN FRONT, 1st–4th NOVEMBER 1918

FROM THE LIVENZA TO THE TAGLIAMENTO
(Map V; Sketch 12)[1]

1st November: Halt on the Livenza

The orders issued by General Diaz on the morning of the 31st instructed Armies " to push rapidly and energetically " towards the bases of the enemy's communications and " strangle them, and at the same time to avoid as much as " possible frontal engagements outside the line of envelop- " ment ".[2] In the Venetian theatre the Third and Tenth Armies were ordered to the Tagliamento, the Cavalry Corps beyond it to the Isonzo, in order to forestall the enemy at the bridges; the Eighth Army was to advance well beyond the valley-junction of Belluno, throwing out a detachment to Toblach (40 miles due north of Belluno); the Twelfth Army, crowded out by its neighbours in the advance, was to assemble in the Feltre basin and await orders.[3]

The Tenth Army's orders stated that " the enemy is " retiring along the whole Italian front; the pursuit is to be " pressed vigorously towards the Tagliamento ". In conformity with these instructions, the XIV Corps ordered that: (1) the divisions should advance no farther than sufficient to cover the construction of bridges, (2) that the advance should be continued on the 2nd, and (3) that the Italian 31st Division would take over about one and a half miles more of the 7th Division's front, to one kilometre north of Francenigo, relieving it before the advance on the 2nd; but the divisions were to form bridgeheads on their

---

[1] The Italian situation map on which Sketch 12 is based shows a considerable advance on 1st November. For this and succeeding days it seems to represent ground abandoned by the enemy rather than ground gained. Thus, the Tenth Army is shown at Pordenone, which was actually the limit of the advance, not on the 1st but on the 2nd.
[2] Vittorio Veneto, p. 26. See Map V.
[3] For the orders to the rest of the front see p. 330.

BRIDGE BUILDING. 1st NOVEMBER

present frontages, and the Italian 31st Division was made responsible for the bridgehead at Portobuffole. The Chief Engineer of the XIV Corps, Lieut.-Colonel E. H. Rooke (formerly C.R.E. 23rd Division), managed to send up 10 pontoons; they were eked out with 40 others captured from the Austrians, and 800 tons of seasoned timber, which with large quantities of iron straps, bolts and spikes, were found in Sacile.

About 2 p.m. on 1st November, when what little firing there had been during the morning had died down, 2 battalions of the 22nd Brigade (1/R. Welch Fusiliers and 2/R. Warwickshire) crossed the Livenza by pontoons and put out outposts to cover bridge building on the front from Brugnera (exclusive) to Sacile, with a view to the advance next day, when the 23rd Division would be in reserve, and the 7th Division in front line, with the Italian 31st Division on its right.

The bridges constructed on the 1st November were:

At Brugnera, 1 footbridge and 1 trestle bridge for light lorries, by the Italian 31st Division;

At Francenigo, 1 footbridge by the 7th Division;

At Cavolano, 1 footbridge and 1 medium pontoon bridge, by the 7th Division;

At Sacile, 1 bridge repaired to take 3-ton lorries by the 23rd Division, and 1 Inglis steel bridge thrown by the 285th Army Troops Company R.E.

Of the Italian Armies on 1st November[1] the leading units of the Third Army reached the Livenza, but only the 23rd Division, on the extreme left at Motta (on the western bank and evacuated by the Austrians), was able to cross the river, and it could make no headway; it was even counter-attacked. During the night of 1st/2nd November, the 45th Division crossed at S. Stino, 4 miles below Motta, as the main bodies of the *Isonzo Army* had begun to retire during the previous night to the Meduna, and the rear guards had drawn off as darkness fell, on 1st November.

The Italian cavalry, on the left of the Tenth Army, crossed the upper Livenza during the day, accompanied by armoured vehicles; but, according to the Italian situa-

---

[1] See Sketch 12.

tion map,[1] did not advance more than eight miles in the narrow strip between the Tenth Army and the foot of the mountains, being at night on the line Roveredo–Aviano.

Three divisions of the Eighth Army reached Belluno, but too late to catch the retreating Austrians of the *Belluno Group*. The Twelfth Army remained near Feltre.

2ND NOVEMBER : CROSSING OF THE LIVENZA

On 2nd November the leading brigade of the Italian 31st Division crossed at Brugnera,[2] and the 22nd and 20th Brigades of the 7th Division, which used the crossings at Cavalano and Sacile, resumed the advance in column at 9 a.m. followed by the rest of the division, and covered by the Yeomanry and Cyclists of the Corps Mounted Troops. The 23rd Division, in reserve, also crossed the Livenza, the 69th Brigade by the bridge at Cavolano, one and a half miles south of Sacile, and the remainder of the division at Sacile. A severe traffic jam occurred at the approach to the bridge in Sacile, caused by the action of 3 Italian divisions (2 infantry and 1 cavalry) invading the road by which the 23rd Division was approaching the town. On the wide straight road west of it all these formations were able to march abreast of the 23rd Division, who were on the right side of the road, but when the bottleneck formed by the narrow street leading to the bridge in Sacile was reached a scene of indescribable confusion ensued. Drastic measures had to be taken before the tangle could be straightened out and the march of the 23rd Division to the bridge resumed. After crossing the Livenza the 23rd Division billeted in the Porcia area, about five miles beyond the river.[3]

Absolutely no opposition was encountered in the advance, but the roads were found encumbered by the discarded impedimenta of a defeated army : abandoned guns and wagons, dead horses and dead men—good testimony to the effective bombing of the R.A.F. Everywhere, too, on the route was found evidence of demoralization : arms and equipment thrown by the roadside, looted shops, wanton damage to buildings and household goods ; but the Austrian

---

[1] Vittorio Veneto, Map 3.
[2] See Map V.
[3] Its strength was reported as 342 officers and 8,834 other ranks on this day.

engineers had not neglected to destroy the bridges over the Meduna. A line was occupied in the evening on the eastern side of Pordenone, nine miles from the Livenza, and about the same distance from the Tagliamento; it lay astride the Meduna, which was fordable in the British sector, although extra horses had to be used to get vehicles across, but required bridging in the sector of the Italian 31st Division.

The Third Army and XI Corps both crossed the Livenza, and at last came abreast of the XIV Corps. The points of two divisions (3rd and 4th) of the Cavalry Corps reached the Tagliamento—the places named being Bonzicco, Spilimbergo and Pinzano (5 miles north of Spilimbergo), all northward of the area of Lord Cavan's Army[1]—after running into Austrian rear guards.

3rd November: The Tagliamento Reached

The Austrians Assert Signature of Armistice

In the XIV Corps the orders for 3rd November were to push on to the Tagliamento and not give the enemy time to organize a stand behind it. The Corps Mounted Troops again covered the advance and kept contact with the Italian cavalry on the left. Again there was no opposition. The Yeomanry and the Cyclists reached the Tagliamento about 1 p.m. and found the river much like the Piave, its course divided by low islands and banks of shingle; it was nearly a mile wide, with eight branches, and the main stream ran under the far bank, which seemed to be absolutely lined with Austrians with whom Italian cavalry appeared to be fraternizing. The general commanding the latter requested the officer commanding the Corps Mounted Troops not to cross, and Lieut.-Colonel Sir C. B. Lowther deemed it best to comply. When during the afternoon the leading infantry, the H.A.C. and Gordons, arrived at the river, the forcing of a passage by their small force seemed out of the question without substantial artillery support, which was not available—indeed, no guns had come up, as all wheeled traffic had been delayed by the difficulties of crossing the Meduna until the engineers had built a pontoon bridge east of

---

[1] The 1st Cavalry Division halted near the Meduna on the night of the 2nd/3rd; the 2nd . . . was to follow the 3rd and 4th. (Vittorio Veneto, p. 30).

Pordenone. The Italian 31st Division was similarly delayed at Prato, and did not reach the Tagliamento until after dark.

The unexpected now happened, and events occurred similar to those taking place at the same moment on the Trentino front. The Italian general, Count Guicciardi, commanding the 3rd Cavalry Division, on the left of the 7th Division, sent Major-General Shoubridge a message asking him to be present at the surrender of the Austrian divisions on the east bank of the Tagliamento, whilst Br.-General H. C. R. Green (20th Brigade) was informed by an Italian cavalry commander that the Austrians had reported to him that an armistice had been signed and was already in force, making the Tagliamento the line of demarcation. Neither Major-General Shoubridge nor the Italian general had received any notification of this. When the former arrived at the partially restored bridge beyond Gradisca,[1] he was met by four Austrian *parlementaires*, who showed him a telegram saying that an armistice had been signed at 6 a.m. that morning, and said that an Italian general was negotiating. He told them that he knew nothing about an armistice and that unless the Italian general returned soon he should continue the advance, and in their hearing he ordered his artillery up. He declined to sign a paper presented to him purporting to give an account of the situation. A message now came from the Count of Turin, commanding the Cavalry Corps, to the effect that nothing was known about an armistice, and that the Italian cavalry were to resume the advance. Thereupon Major-General Shoubridge ordered the 20th Brigade to cross the river at Gradisca and form a bridgehead, which was done by 2 companies of the Gordons without opposition. On the British right the H.A.C. (22nd Brigade) had advanced on to a shingle bank more than half-way across the Tagliamento, likewise to be informed by Austrians that an armistice had been signed, but that any further advance would be resisted. Lieut.-Colonel O'Connor, judging the story quite probable, and not wishing to incur unnecessary casualties, suspended the attack, and reported to brigade headquarters; in the centre of the river the H.A.C. remained until nearly midnight, when orders from Br.-General Steele arrived directing the battalion to retire to the western bank and billet. The

---

[1] Earlier called the Bonzicco bridge. Bonzicco is on the eastern bank Gradisca, opposite on the western.

THE PURSUIT. 3RD NOVEMBER

parties of the American 332nd Regiment (Italian 31st Division), on the right of the 7th Division, which had pushed over the Tagliamento remained on the eastern bank.

What had occurred on the Italian cavalry front was as follows:

On the patrols of the 3rd Cavalry Division reaching Bonzicco in the morning of the 3rd, they found the bridge passable—in view of the armistice the Austrians had not destroyed it—and, as the enemy troops were waving white flags, they had crossed, to learn of the armistice and why fire had not been opened. About midday General Count Guicciardi came up and entered into discussion with an Austrian divisional commander, with the result that he withdrew his horsemen to the western bank—in the meantime one squadron was riding on to Udine unopposed. General Count Barratiere, commander of the 4th Cavalry Division, now arrived, and the two generals informed the Austrian commander that they had no information about the conclusion of an armistice, and they persuaded him into the surrender of the arms of his division and of an adjoining brigade, on the understanding that they would be restored if it turned out that an armistice had been arranged.

In the Third Army, advanced troops had in the early afternoon seized the bridges at Latisana (13 miles below Codroipo), without attempting to go farther.

Thus at night the pursuit ceased for the moment, with the greater part of both the Austrian *Isonzo Army* and the *Sixth Army* making their way back to the old frontier. Only the *II Corps*, the northernmost of the *Sixth Army*, in the Alpine foothills, making for Tolmezzo (at the bend of the Tagliamento, 23 miles north of Bonzicco) had, about midday, overheard a wireless message that the armistice did not take effect until 3 p.m. on the 4th; but, owing to breaks in the signal communication, it had been unable to make this known to other commands.

4TH NOVEMBER: PASSAGE OF THE TAGLIAMENTO

At 3 a.m. on 4th November, the XIV Corps received notice from the Tenth Army that an armistice had been signed but would not come into effect until 3 p.m., and that, meanwhile, all troops were to push on, the XIV Corps to a general line Villaorba–Meretto–Coseano, about six miles beyond the Tagliamento. The corps orders for an advance at 7.30 a.m. therefore held good, and soon after that hour the 1/R. Welch Fusiliers and 2/R. Warwickshire (22nd Brigade) and the 2/Border Regiment (20th Brigade) crossed the river, the last at the Gradisca bridge, and the two former, in attack formation, by wading waistdeep. The American 332nd Regiment was on the British right. Guns and machine guns were in position to fire a barrage, but it was not required. No opposition was offered, except by a single machine gun, which fired on the Americans and was quickly captured. Protests were made to Major-General Shoubridge by the Austrians at being expected to surrender when the armistice was about to come into force ; but nearly a whole division laid down its arms[1] and submitted to be marched into captivity under tiny escorts. Supply arrangements were now so well ahead that a day's rations of the 23rd Division could be spared to feed the prisoners.[2] After some delay to collect prisoners and to place guards over a vast accumulation of booty, the brigades of the 7th Division marched on to a selected line, the Corps Mounted Troops, who crossed the Tagliamento after the infantry, sending forward patrols to the Armistice line. Similar scenes were enacted elsewhere. Only by the Austrian *XXIV Corps*, at Germona, about eighteen miles above Gradisca on the Tagliamento, is any resistance recorded to have been offered, and all its divisions and detachments got clear. The Italian cavalry squadrons and armoured cars pushed on as much as thirty miles from the river, and as the Austrians did not fire had an easy task to disarm them.

Captures and Casualties

According to a report of the Comando Supremo, the total taken prisoner in the last 36 hours amounted to three hundred thousand men—the greater part of them came from the lines of communication says the Austrian account, which

---

[1] Apparently parts of the *41st* and *51st Honved Divisions*.
[2] The staff of the 23rd Division were specially thanked for " untiring " energy and skill by means of which they succeeded in maintaining the " supply of rations, ammunition and medical stores under circumstances " of exceptional difficulty caused by length of communications and the " insufficiency of the bridges in rear ".

BRITISH SHARE IN THE VICTORY

adds that there were not more than 260,000 combatants on the Italian front. Not less than five thousand guns, and an immense quantity of war material became booty. In the period 24th October to 4th November Lord Cavan's Army had taken 1,087 officers and 33,959 other ranks, and well over two hundred and forty guns, excluding many left in position and not counted. The share of the XIV Corps was 959 officers and 27,664 other ranks and 219 guns. In round figures, the Austrian account says 3 cavalry divisions and 16 divisions were destroyed, whilst 2 cavalry divisions and 35 divisions escaped captivity.

The British casualties in the period 24th October–4th November had been only a little over sixteen hundred.[1]

The prominent part taken by the British troops in the final battle has been ignored in Italian accounts, both official and unofficial, which have exaggerated their own share. But the Italian commanders recognised it. When in January 1919 Lord Cavan was leaving Italy, the Duke of Aosta (commander of the Third Army throughout) and others came to British headquarters to bid him farewell. The duke said "Goodbye "General. I am indeed sorry that you are leaving Italy. "Without the presence of you and your troops there would "have been no Vittorio Veneto".[2] Directly after the battle he had said to the British liaison officer with his Army headquarters, Lieut.-Colonel C. E. D. Bridge, R.A.: "If the British had not crossed the Piave, the Italians "would not have crossed the Piave. After the war other "things will be said".

BRITISH STRENGTH AND TOTAL CASUALTIES

Between November 1917 and December 1918 the average strength of the troops (excluding L. of C.) had been 78,477, with a maximum of 113,759 in January 1918 and a minimum in December 1918 of 60,192.

[1]

	Officers			Other Ranks			
	Killed	Wounded	Missing	Killed	Wounded	Missing	Total
7th Division	8	14	3	101	497	137	760
23rd Division	10	33	—	169	582	68	862

[2] See note on Vittorio Veneto in List of Books.

The battle casualties had been :

	Officers	Other Ranks	Total
Killed	90	1,140	1,230
Died of wounds	—	58	58
Missing	4	62	66
Prisoners of war	26	252	278
Died of disease or injury	26	733	759
	146	2,245	2,391
	Officers	Other Ranks	Total
Wounded who did not die	289	4,400	4,689
Sick or injured who did not die	3,290	47,262	50,552
	3,579	51,662	55,241

The total admitted to hospital was 56,453.

The total sick from influenza amounted to 11,514 of whom 481 died.

REFLECTIONS

In judging of Italy's effort, it should be recalled that in 1914 she had only recently emerged from war with Turkey in North Africa and her reserves of material were therefore seriously depleted, and that she possessed no mineral resources, neither iron nor coal, so that either the raw material for munitions, or the finished article had to be imported from abroad, and in the early days of the war the Allies could spare very little.

Operations in northern Italy were of a special nature, their direction being dictated and their extent limited by the topography of the theatre of war. The theatre, as already pointed out, consisted of two very distinct parts. In one of them, the mountain front, movement was limited to a few roads and passes, and in the other, the great plain, was hampered by broad rivers, or rather torrents, difficult to bridge with either service or extemporized material. To gain entry into Austria, the Italians had to fight uphill ; on the other hand, the shape of their frontier gave them the advantage of interior lines and enabled them, aided by good railways, to shift troops from the plains to the mountain front, and *vice versa,* far more quickly and easily than could their adversaries. Thus defence was more favoured than

REFLECTIONS

offence. On the map, the strategic advantage of the shape of the common frontier seemed to be with the Austrians; for if they could push south from the Trentino they would cut in behind the Italians standing on the Isonzo, the Tagliamento or the Piave. The difficulties, however, of the communications through the Trentino prevented any decisive blow being delivered from that direction. This became evident in Conrad von Hötzendorf's attempt in 1916, even before the Brusilov offensive forced him to desist. Similarly, the repeated Italian attempts to break into Austria from the Isonzo area achieved nothing decisive; but in this case it was lack of heavy artillery as much as anything which handicapped the attacker. The Germans chose the Isonzo area rather than the Trentino for their decisive attack, although in that sector the paucity of railheads was bound to slow down the operations.

Neither Italians nor Austrians were equipped with the up-to-date material used on the Western Front: not only was super-heavy artillery lacking, but the number of medium guns also was inadequate on the Italian side, even after loans from the French and the British Armies. Tanks did not appear at all; gas, except when employed by the Germans to make a breach at Caporetto, is never mentioned, and the Italian gas mask afforded little protection. Aircraft were few; such niceties as flash-spotting and sound-ranging were unheard of; and the field defences were of the pre-1914 text book type and in the lay-out of defences both sides depended on a strong front line. Defence in depth meant no more on the Italian side than one or two back lines of single trenches, and on the Austrian side a few not-shell-proof machine-gun posts in farms and villages, in feeble imitation of the German system, without *Eingreif* (super counter-attack) divisions in support.

The interesting features of the campaign were first the immense success, after months of indecisive fighting, achieved by the Central Powers when, in the Caporetto campaign, the Germans sent, to effect a break-through, seven divisions of their Central Reserve. Six of these divisions had earlier been employed to smash the "Kerenski" offensive, and then to win a decisive victory at Riga. Secondly was the equally great success gained by the Allies, when two French and three British divisions were used on the Piave and in the mountains as spearheads in the final phase. It must be admitted that the German aid to the Austrians was better timed than the Entente aid to the Italians, being calculated to prevent a disaster, not to repair one. In each case, both at Caporetto and the Grave di Papadopoli, " *Massenschreck* (wholesale terror)," nearly amounting to panic, overcame the defenders when they found that they were being assailed by fearless, hard-fighting troops.

Italian accounts have not rendered justice to the moral support and sound advice given to the Comando Supremo by Maréchal Foch, or to the vital assistance given by the French and British troops both in the mountains and on the plains. That assistance has usually been ignored,[1] for if a true account were given it could not be overlooked that the British were first across the Piave, and that they received the surrender of the Austrian forces in Trent before Italian troops arrived there ; and in both parts of the theatre the French were equally prominent in leading the way.

---

[1] No request was ever received from the Historical Section of the Italian General Staff for particulars of the British operations in Italy. With the French and German Historical Sections the British had throughout, until 1939, intimate exchange of information. An example of the Italian one-sided method of writing history has been given in pp. 324–25 when, as on other occasions, credit is taken for a British feat of arms.

CHAPTER XXV

HOW THE ARMISTICE CAME ABOUT[1]
(Map IV)

Early Austrian Efforts to Obtain Peace

The Armistice of Villa Giusti of 4th November 1918 was the climax of a long series of efforts made by the Austrian Government to get out of the War. The Austrian military situation in October was far from critical. It was indeed by no means so critical as that of the German Armies on the Western Front which, since 8th August, had been steadily driven back, suffering defeat on every line which they tried to hold, whether it was one of the multiple lines of the Hindenburg Position or of the Flanders Position, or the water lines of the Schelde, the Selle, or the Sambre Canal. The Austrians in the early days of October were holding a good line, not only behind the Piave, but also on the Mountain Front, where the few routes by which the Allies could advance—the upper valleys of the Piave, the Brenta, the Astico and the Adige (route to the Brenner Pass)—only led to the high Alps and could by demolitions be made nearly impregnable. The failure of the Austrians in June to defeat the Allies on the Piave and on the Asiago front was good evidence of the difficulty of the task which lay before their enemies.

Austria, however, had been in desperate need of peace for at least two years, on account not only of ill-success in the field and very heavy losses, on the Eastern Front particularly, but also on account of the interior economic situation and the war-weariness of a disillusioned, easy-going people.[2] When on 21st November 1916 the Emperor Franz Joseph died and was succeeded by his nephew, Karl, the young

---

[1] Besides the Austrian Official Account, and Villari (at some length), Arz and Caviglia, there are other authoritative narratives: Ratzenhofer's "Der Waffenstillstand von Villa Giusti", Alberti's "L'Italia e la Fine della Guerra Mondiale", Kerchnawe's "Zusammenbruch", Glaise-Horstenau's "Die Katastrophe".

[2] See Note at end of Chapter, on the Economic Conditions of Austria-Hungary.

Emperor set about measures to obtain at least an armistice. At first he was aided and abetted by the German Government, which, alarmed by the heavy losses at Verdun and on the Somme and the shadow of final defeat, saw a chance of permanently retaining some of its conquests. An attempt at negotiations in December 1916 through the President of the United States (then neutral) having failed, the Emperor, in April 1917, using Princes Sixt and Xavier of Parma-Bourbon, his brothers-in-law, as his agents, made secret overtures to the President of the French Republic. These leading to nothing, on 1st August 1917, on his urging, the Pope sent a Note to the belligerent governments, appealing for peace. As by this time the U.S.A. had entered the War, and to bring it to an end now would obviously have been to the advantage of Germany and her Allies, the appeal had no result. German promises of speedy victory, the Russian collapse, and the great German offensives of March-June 1918, then kept the Emperor Karl quiet for a time; but on 14th September 1918, when it was evident that the Berlin promises could not be redeemed—and the Austrian monarch told the German Kaiser that the defeats of the German Army had shaken his people far more than the disasters of their own troops—the Austrian Foreign Minister, Graf Burian, addressed a Note through the press to all the belligerent Powers, urging that an end should be brought by "understanding" to the "catastrophe of a suicidal conflict". This receiving no attention, the German Government, forced thereto by Ludendorff, addressed a Note from the Central Powers to President Wilson, with proposals for an armistice founded on his "Fourteen Points". In the certain hope of the success of this move, the Austrian Chief of the General Staff on the very next day, 5th October, assembled an armistice commission at Trent, under the presidency of General Weber Edler von Webenau.[1] With what ease the Austrian High Command expected to obtain terms and bring hostilities to an end is shown by the facts that the commission, as will appear, was not provided with a cipher or with rapid means of communication with General Headquarters.

On 9th October, when the reply of the President to the proposals of the 4th reached Vienna, in which he demanded

---

[1] A.O.A. vii, p. 577. He was commander of the *VI Corps*.

the evacuation of the occupied territories as evidence of good faith, the Austrian Emperor wished to send a *parlementaire* to the Comando Supremo at once in order to initiate armistice negotiations. He was dissuaded from so doing by Graf Burian; and Hindenburg, hearing of the proposal, sent a message through his liaison officer begging that before any steps were taken the result of the negotiations between Berlin and Washington should be awaited. Field-Marshal Boroevic, on the 11th, with a view to a possible evacuation of the Venetian provinces, gave orders to his (Piave) Group of Armies that all valuable war apparatus which could be spared should be sent back to the Homeland; but three days later, when this had been begun, the idea of evacuation was abandoned on the very good grounds that once the troops had their faces towards home, it would be difficult to induce them to halt on the frontier, and the Italians, who were obviously ready to strike, would quickly follow up and turn retirement into a rout. Further, the lack of transport made a rapid evacuation out of the question. Nevertheless, complete preparations for a retirement of the troops on the Piave were made, and on the 15th a written warning was sent to the Army commanders of the Boroevic Group and also to the Archduke Joseph, commanding the Group of Armies on the Mountain Front, directing them to be prepared to send homewards everything that could be spared (*alles entbehrliche*).

The Emperor Karl Proclaims his Empire a Federal State

President Wilson's tenth item in his " Fourteen Points " put forward in January 1918 had been " the freest possi-
" bility of the autonomous development of the peoples of
" Austria-Hungary "; so, with a view to propitiating him and at the same time taking a step which he had long judged desirable, the Emperor Karl, on 16th October, after a Crown Council on the previous day, issued a Manifesto to his peoples. Beginning with a reference to his efforts for peace from the moment he had ascended the throne, its most important pronouncements were:

"Austria, in accordance with the will of its peoples,
" will become a Federal State (*Bundesstaat*) in which

"each nationality will form its own state community on the territory on which it is settled.

"This reorganization, which in no wise affects the integrity of the territories of the Hungarian Holy Crown, is intended to secure independence to each of the single national States. It will at the same time protect the common interests. . . .

"I call upon the peoples, on whose self-determination the new *Reich* will be founded, to co-operate in the great work by forming national councils (*National-rathe*) which, drawn from the members of the [existing] *Reich* Parliaments of each nation, will serve to further the interests of the various nations in their relations to each other and to maintain communication with my Government".

A Special Order of the Day to the same effect was issued to the army and navy.

Disastrous Effects of the Emperor's Proclamation

The result of these proclamations was not to close the ranks and to consolidate the bonds of union, but to loosen them and to initiate and complete the disintegration of the Dual Monarchy. The Poles and Italians within its borders saw a way of escape from Austrian supremacy, and took steps to ensure advantage of it ; on the 19th the Ruthenians assembled a *Nationalrath* at Lemberg, and the Rumanians a similar council at Czernowitz, with a view to getting in touch, not with Vienna but with their brethren beyond the frontier ; the Czech Council at Prague protested against their kinsmen, the Slovaks, being left under Hungarian rule, and formed a government of their own, whose first act was to declare that an independent Czecho-Slovak State had come into existence. The Hungarians talked of a fully independent National State, with its own foreign policy and its own army ; the other peoples within the Magyar borders would have to be satisfied, they said, with a certain amount of autonomy. The leader of the Parliamentary opposition, Graf Karolyi, who on the 31st became Hungarian Prime Minister, called for the return of the Hungarian troops.

The High Command, fearing the disintegrating effect of the proclamations, at once sent General Staff officers to the more important National Councils in the hopes of persuading them to help in preventing the break-up of the army until the troops had returned home. On the 23rd the Emperor Karl made a personal appeal to the Pope through the Nuncio in Vienna to persuade the Italian Government to abstain from an offensive on humanitarian grounds; but the Italian offensive on the 24th made any such step abortive from the outset.

On the 25th the first unmistakable signs of trouble among the troops had become manifest. The units of the various contingents began to clamour for immediate return to their now separate native countries; but no active disobedience occurred until next day, when on the Mountain Front a Hungarian battalion (*27th Division* in the Asiago sector), ordered to take part in a counter-attack against M. Sisemol, declared that it would fight no more for Austria, and demanded to be sent home to Hungary; the other 2 battalions of the regiment made common cause and refused to leave camp; and another infantry regiment of the division, which was at rest, decided to leave the front when the mutinous regiment did so. A regiment of the *38th Honved Division*, at rest at Levico in the Val Sugana, refused to go up to the Asiago plateau, entrenched itself in the town and covered all the approaches with machine-gun fire.

Appeals to the troops and to the new rulers of Hungary proved of little avail. The Archduke Joseph—a pronounced pro-Hungarian—reported that there was no alternative but to send the *27th* and *38th Divisions* back to Hungary to be taught discipline and brought to their senses; he suggested that other Hungarian troops should be promised transport home as soon as the state of the railways permitted, and he implored the Emperor " without loss of time, to conclude " an armistice or peace, even at the cost of very hard " conditions, in order to save the army, at least, from total " collapse and to be in a position to maintain tranquillity " in the interior with its more reliable units ".

Meantime, the mutiny spread to other Hungarian units, and the *5th* and *16th Divisions* became affected;[1] 2 companies

---

[1] According to A.O.A. vii, Map 34, the one was at rest near Borgo in the Val Sugana, and the other at Bolzano.

of another division left their trenches near Asiago, and the rest of the battalion joined them; another battalion refused to go to the front; a third burnt its huts. The troops of the *11th Cavalry Division* and the *7th Division*, composed entirely of Hungarians, declined to fight. The news that the mutineers had remained unpunished and that the *27th Division* was on its way home, ran like wildfire along the front and reached the troops on the Piave, where Croats, Czechs and Serbians, Poles and minor nationalities—fifteen languages were officially recognized in the Austro-Hungarian Army—in various ways refused obedience. At least seven or eight divisions were reported to be untrustworthy.

The Emperor Karl Decides to ask for an Armistice

The stout fight put up by the Austrian troops on 24th October on the Grappa at first raised the hope that the situation was not as bad as depicted; but this hope soon faded, and on the 26th the Emperor Karl informed the Kaiser of his intention, within twenty-four hours, to ask for an armistice and conclude a separate peace, as internal order and the monarchical principle would be in grave risk if the struggle was not brought to an end. The Kaiser, by telegram, begged him to abstain from any action which would disclose a breach in the solidarity of the Alliance.

At 9 a.m. on 28th October, however, Field-Marshal Boroevic reported that the number of mutineers was increasing, and that means failed him to compel them to obedience and at 1 p.m. he was informed that the Austro-Hungarian Government had that day already requested from President Wilson a separate peace and an immediate armistice. To this the field-marshal replied that the morale of the army was not likely to be raised by the news of an early armistice, and that "nothing could stop the "avalanche-like nature of the crisis except fiery appeals "from the elected representatives of the new National "States". At 3.45 p.m. an order was sent by the High Command to the Armistice Commission in Trent, which had been dispersed on the renewal of fighting on the 24th, to get into touch with the Comando Supremo, but in the negotiations not to discuss any conditions which would allow

BREAK-UP OF THE DUAL MONARCHY. 365
29TH OCTOBER

the Italians to utilize the territories of Austria-Hungary for the continuation of military operations against Germany.

In the afternoon of the 29th, at the suggestion of Field-Marshal Boroevic, the Armistice Commission was instructed to notify the Comando Supremo that the Austrians would evacuate the Venetian provinces voluntarily, and at the same time let it be known that the country would be saved from devastation and ruin only if they were allowed to draw off unhindered. A wireless message to the same effect was directed by the field-marshal to the Comando Supremo.

As soon as the contents of the Emperor's Note to President Wilson became known, the National Councils of the Czechs and of the Jugoslavs proclaimed their secession from the Monarchy;[1] and an assembly at Agram of Croats, Slovenes and Serbs, after declaring themselves an independent Serbo-Croat National State, followed suit, and the whole of the national troops placed themselves at the disposal of the new Governments. In Cracow a "Liquidating Commission" notified the adherence of the whole of Galicia and the Polish part of Silesia to the resuscitated State of Poland; in the Bukovina and Siebenbürgen the Rumanians seized power with a view of joining their mother state.

Field-Marshal Boroevic's troops on the Piave front in Italian territory were being hustled back; but they were still offering resistance and in a position to destroy bridges over the many rivers and otherwise delay the Allied advance. On his part of the Mountain Front the position was less favourable, and his right wing, the *Belluno Group* of the *I, XV* and *XXVI Corps*, under Field-Marshal Ritter von Goglia, reported on the afternoon of the 29th that a retreat must be begun that night, and the *Eleventh Army* (in the Asiago sector) of Field-Marshal Freiherr von Krobatin's Group of Armies[2] was thereupon directed to go back to the positions of the autumn of 1917. But the higher commanders were under no illusion that once the troops were in motion it would be possible to get them to halt on this or any other line; the Chiefs of the Staffs of the two Groups

---
[1] A pro-Ally Czecho-Slovak division was already organized and in Italy.
[2] He had vacated command of the *Tenth Army*, on whose front on the 26th the Allied offensive had not yet started, to take over that of the *Mountain Group of Armies* from the Archduke Joseph, whose presence was required in Hungary to try to maintain order.

of Armies, of the *Belluno Group* and of the *Eleventh Army*, indeed, agreed that it would be better for the troops to surrender than be driven back into the Homeland in flight under enemy pressure.[1] On the evening of 30th October, however, orders were issued to Field-Marshal Krobatin's Group of Armies for a retreat in three stages to the 1917 position, which was to be reached on the night of 1st/2nd November. By the 30th, however, the "mass flight for home" had already begun, combined with some separation in the field into national groups of the various contingents; the non-German speaking troops were already wearing cockades or armbands of the national colours as sign of their new allegiance.

The Hungarian Government Decides to Lay Down Arms

Then came a real "stab in the back". At 5 a.m. on 2nd November a despatch of the new Hungarian Minister of War, Colonel Bela Linder, telephoned on by the High Command without instructions or comment, arrived at Balzano, Field-Marshal Krobatin's headquarters. It contained the following fatal words:

> "The internal condition of Hungary makes this country incapable of continuing the War. On the authority of a resolution of the Hungarian Government, I, as responsible Royal Hungarian Minister of War, order (*verfuge*) arms to be laid down".

At that very moment the defence of the Val Sugana from the Italians advancing westwards up the valley of the Brenta depended mainly upon the *38th Honved Division* at Levico, as most of the troops farther eastward in the valley were retiring northwards.

Field-Marshal Krobatin did not take any action on this order except to address a frantic appeal to the Emperor, urging that a one-sided surrender of the Hungarian troops would turn the prevailing anarchy into chaos: he saw no hope of salvation, except in an armistice with conditions, and if this could not be obtained, then the surrender of the whole army. No reply came to him during 2nd November, and meanwhile the nature of the despatch of the Hungarian Minister of War " leaked out all over the place " through

---

[1] A.O.A. vii, p. 677.

Hungarian telephonists who had transmitted it; it was already known, too, that the Emperor had permitted the troops of the interior to place themselves at the disposal of the National Councils; and a rumour spread that officers and men had been released from their oath of allegiance to the Emperor. Among the material results, particularly in the Val d'Assa and the valley of the Adige, up which the Allies were now pressing, were the plunder of supply dumps, and the reign of complete disorder at the railway stations in the valley of the Adige, where the railway personnel, terrified at the excesses of the troops, refused to deal with the overfilled trains, so that none ran except northward of Trent. During the day, Field-Marshal Krobatin repeatedly reported the hopeless condition of affairs; Field-Marshal Boroevic's troops, however were still holding the line of the Tagliamento with only Italian cavalry in contact; but, for reasons which are given below, it was not until 2 a.m. on 3rd November that any communication came from the High Command to the Trentino front, and then the message ran:

" Armistice conditions of the Entente accepted. All " hostilities on land and in the air are at once (*sofort*) " to be stopped. Details of the conditions will follow."

Delay in the Reception of the Austrian Armistice Commission

Before this final order was issued much had gone on behind the scenes. On the evening of 28th October the Austrian Armistice Commission had reassembled at Trent and, in obedience to orders, after drafting a letter from General Weber to the Comando Supremo asking that negotiations for an armistice might be immediately instituted—wireless was forbidden, as the message might be read and become public property—deputed one of its members, Captain Ruggera of the General Staff, to carry it to the Italian lines. At dawn on the 29th he approached the Italian front at Serravalle (25 miles south of Trent), bearing a white flag. He was taken to the headquarters of the Italian 26th Division in Avio, six miles farther on, whence the letter he carried was at once sent on by motor car to the Comando Supremo at Abano, near Padua, ninety miles away. The Italian reply to General Weber, when drafted, ran that "no kind of negotiation could be opened "with him, as the documents forwarded by him presented "no personal and regular full powers conferred on him by "the Royal and Imperial High Command".[1] It was not intended, the reply continued, "to negotiate with any "commission whatever, neither for an armistice nor for a "cessation of hostilities which aimed at an interruption of "the operations in progress. Nevertheless, the Italian High "Command would very gladly receive delegates who were "duly accredited with full powers for the purpose, and "would disclose to them the conditions which the Italian "High Command, with the approval of its own government "and in the fullest agreement with their Allies, will lay "down".

The reply from General Diaz reached Avio about 9 p.m., and an hour later was handed to Captain Ruggera. He at once declared that all the members of the Commission possessed the necessary full powers, and begged that he might be informed whether the Italian High Command would now receive the Commission and that the day, place and hour might be fixed. At 9.15 a.m. next day (30th October) he was told that General Diaz regretted that he could not accept the interference of Captain Ruggera in the matter: that the reply was addressed to General Weber, and that the Comando Supremo insisted on a regularized answer from General Weber, supported by the exhibition of the full powers conferred on him by the Austrian High Command. Captain Ruggera had therefore to return to Rovereto, fifteen miles from the Italian front line, where the members of the Commission were awaiting him.

A full report of the above proceedings from General Weber reached the Austrian High Command at Baden (13 miles south of Vienna) towards 3 p.m., and was soon after communicated to the commanders of the two Groups of Armies, with the addition: "It is the business of the commanders "to carry out a retirement in such a way as to offer the "necessary resistance on the most suitable positions, and to "slow up the advance of the enemy by extensive demoli-"tions". At the same time, about 4 p.m., General Weber was directed by a telegram on behalf of the Emperor, "to cross the enemy lines in person with the necessary

---

[1] A.O.A. vii, p. 709.

"members of the Commission to receive the conditions of "the Comando Supremo".

THE ENTENTE PREPARES ARMISTICE TERMS

On the afternoon of the same day (30th October) the Conference of Allied Premiers and the American President's representative, Colonel House, was assembled in Paris for the purpose of approving the proposed terms of the various armistices which had been, and might have to be, accorded, and Signor Orlando, the Italian Premier, reported to it that an approach had been attempted by an Austrian *parlementaire* to General Diaz, who had refused to treat except with a properly accredited envoy and until he himself had obtained instructions from his Government. Monsieur Clemenceau and Mr. Lloyd George were anxious that no rebuff should be experienced by Austria, as they wished her out of the way as a belligerent so that they would be in a stronger position to settle with Germany. The general terms of the armistice, drawn up by a committee of experts appointed on the 21st, were approved by the Premiers and Colonel House on the morning of the 31st, and formally approved by the Supreme War Council in the afternoon. The terms applied to all the Austro-Italian fronts.

The opening sentence was "Immediate cessation of hostilities" without any mention of the day or hour.[1] The principal conditions were :[2] the demobilization of the Austro-Hungarian army, its eventual reduction to a peace strength of 20 divisions, and the immediate withdrawal of all units operating on the front from Switzerland to the North Sea (that is Austrian divisions and heavy guns with the Germans on the Western Front) ; half the total material of the artillery to be handed over ; evacuation of all territory invaded during the War and withdrawal of all forces behind a fixed line within a space of time, both to be settled by the Allied commanders on the different fronts : free movement by the Allied armies by all roads, railways and waterways, in Austro-Hungarian territory : complete evacuation, within

---

[1] "The Manual of Military Law", 1914 Edition, p. 276, Article 278, gives the customary rule that "an armistice commences, unless another time is expressly mentioned, at the moment it is signed".

[2] The full terms of the protocol of the Armistice and the later attached details are in Appendix XI.

15 days, of all German troops not only from the Italian and Balkan fronts, but from all Austro-Hungarian territories: and in the naval clauses the delivery of a number of ships, and concentration, demobilization and disarmament of the remainder.

It was agreed at Versailles that General Diaz should act on behalf of the Allied Governments in receiving accredited representatives of the Austrian High Command and in communicating to them the terms, and the Italian Government were requested to act on behalf of the Supreme War Council in transmitting this decision and the terms to General Diaz.

Under direction of Signor Orlando, a summary ("*bozzo*", that is a sketch or rough outline) in Italian of the terms was telephoned to the Comando Supremo in the early morning of 1st November, and an officer was despatched with the full French text by train.

It may be added that at a meeting of the Premiers and Colonel House on 2nd November, after consultation with the military representatives, it was decided to give Austria until midnight 3rd/4th November to accept the terms.

THE AUSTRIAN ARMISTICE COMMISSION IS RECEIVED BY THE ITALIANS

On receipt of the Emperor's telegram of 4 p.m. of 30th October, General Weber prepared a Note for the Comando Supremo, with which he enclosed the full powers of the members of the Commission, and himself proceeded to the Italian outpost line, accompanied by Colonel Schneller of the General Staff and another officer. After being detained there for an hour and a quarter, he was permitted to go on to 26th Division headquarters at Avio, where at 7 a.m. next morning (31st October) orders arrived from General Diaz to assemble the whole Commission at Avio—where they arrived at noon—and bring the members to Padua. A German colonel, Baron Schäffer von Bernstein, who declared that he was deputed to be the delegate of the German O.H.L. at the armistice negotiations, was refused entry into the Italian lines, as the Austrian delegates had not mentioned the participation of a German representative.

At 3.30 p.m. the Austrian delegation left Avio by motor, arriving at the Villa Giusti, outside Padua, about 8 p.m.

There General Weber was informed that the first meeting with the Italian plenipotentiaries, under the presidency of Lieut.-General Badoglio, would take place at 10 a.m. next day (1st November). Thus, as the Austrian Official Account points out, " three full days had elapsed before the Austro-" Hungarian Armistice Commission succeeded in reaching " the Italian negotiators ". But, as it has been seen, a summary of the terms decided on was not telephoned from Paris to General Diaz until the early morning (between 1.50 and 6.15 a.m.) of 1st November; so the delay could not be laid to the blame of the Comando Supremo. In fact, at the first meeting General Badoglio had to tell the Austrian delegates that the full text could not be communicated to them until the officer bringing it arrived next day, and he could do no more than give them the Italian summary received by telephone. General Weber asked for certain explanations, but was informed that there was no question of discussion, and it was for the Commission to accept or decline the terms.

The Austrian Armistice Commission Refer the Terms to Vienna

Feeling that he was not justified in accepting such severe conditions, about 3 p.m. General Weber sent Colonel Schneller and another officer to Trent, whence they were to telegraph the terms to Baden, and report that " the " Commission did not feel authorized to accept the harsh " and unexpected terms, because points 2 and 4 of the " military conditions [total demobilization and handing over " of material, and free passage over Austrian territory] and " all the naval conditions were incompatible with the " honour of the army and navy ".

Meantime, General Weber, quite unconscious that during the morning of this day (1st November) General Diaz had ordered the four Armies of his left wing to join in the Vittorio Veneto offensive and push forward rapidly on Trent,[1] did his best to obtain a suspension of arms. He was informed by General Badoglio that " the cessation of " hostilities could take place only after the acceptance of " the conditions laid down " and that, as plenipotentiary of

---

[1] See p. 330.

the Versailles Supreme War Council he had only to carry out its wishes and might not engage in any kind of negotiation. This discussion General Weber reported to the High Command by sending an officer to telegraph it in full from Trent ; at the same time he suggested that, as no discussion was permitted, a complete set of counter-terms might be proposed. General Diaz, for his part, communicated with Versailles on 2nd November, suggesting that as the operations were going so well the terms might be amended in Austria's favour. He was told by Signor Orlando that the Allies had decided to give Austria until midnight 3rd/4th November to accept, and that any request from her representatives for alterations or modification must be considered as a refusal to accept.

At 5 p.m. the authoritative French text of the terms which had just arrived from Paris was handed to General Weber, and was found to agree with the summary in Italian already received, except in the matter of a few trifling clerical errors due to mistakes in telephoning. General Weber was also informed that the Allies had fixed a time limit for acceptance, that any armistice concluded at Padua applied to all Austrian fronts, and that negotiators would not be received on the Balkan or Rumanian fronts, and he was given "the protocol attached containing details and executive "clauses", in which it was stated that the Armistice would commence twenty-four hours after signature.

DIFFICULTIES OF COMMUNICATION

Now came bad news for General Weber. At 6 p.m. (2nd November), he was told that fighting was taking place in the Adige valley—in consequence of General Diaz's order of the 1st for the offensive of the 4 western Italian Armies— so that a courier service with Trent was no longer possible and that the return of the 3 officers sent there to telegraph to Vienna could not be counted on. He was permitted to use the wireless station in Padua ; but direct transmission to Vienna could not be established, so that air messages had to be sent via Pola and Budapest, whence they were telegraphed to Vienna.[1] At 5 p.m. he had received a cipher

---

[1] One message sent from Padua at 8.30 p.m. (2nd November) reached Baden at 12.4 p.m. (3rd November) ; another took from 2 a.m. to 5.10 a.m. and a third from 3 a.m. to 11.18 a.m.

message from the High Command, but could not decipher it, and had to ask that all telegrams should be sent *en clair*.

Reception of the Terms by the Austrian High Command

The Italian summary of the terms telegraphed from Trent about 6 p.m. (1st November) reached the High Command at Baden at 12.30 a.m. (1st/2nd November). The Emperor Karl was prepared to accept, but found himself in a dilemma over one point. Only three days earlier he had in a personal telegram promised the Kaiser, urged thereto by the German liaison officer at his headquarters, that he would never let the Italians march through the Tirol to attack Germany, and that he would himself lead his troops to prevent a passage by force of arms. On the other hand, he wished to avoid Austrian lands becoming a theatre of war. His Chief of the General Staff informed him that the military situation was so desperate that the terms must be accepted without demur; the new Hungarian Minister of War, Colonel Linder, after demanding on the telephone when and where the Hungarian troops would lay down their arms, had finally consented to their remaining in the line until the Austrian frontier was reached—and on this day (2nd November) British and Italian troops on the Mountain Front crossed it. It was discovered later that Hungarian telegraphists forwarded without delay Linder's instructions to the Hungarian troops, and managed to hold up the High Command's messages to the Groups of Armies, which told them to ignore the Hungarian Minister's instructions. In any case, Magyar co-operation could not be depended on. Linder actually defended his country's defection, finally saying " the Hungarian Government and people take over " the responsibility for laying down arms ".

The Emperor, in the hope of transferring the responsibility for surrender to other shoulders—as the German High Command managed to bring off—summoned to a conference representatives of those new States of his creation which were most concerned in the terms of the armistice. They met at 4 p.m. and finally declared that the " management " which had begun and carried on the War without consulting the people's representatives must bear full responsibility for its conclusion. General Arz left to go personally to the

German-Austrian Parliament (that is of the non-Hungarian parts of the Dual Monarchy), then sitting in Vienna, to influence them to approve of the acceptance of the terms.

One despairing message after another had come during the day from the Mountain and Belluno Fronts, from both Field-Marshals Krobatin and Goglia, reporting retirement, disorder and plundering, but nothing special from the Venetian front; also about 7 p.m. one came from Colonel Schneller of the Armistice Commission, waiting in Trent, who reported that the situation was so desperate—the British crossed the frontier in the Val d'Assa at dusk and the Italians in the Adige valley reached Rovereto that night— that " I consider it my duty, if no order comes, to leave here " [for Padua] and propose conclusion of the armistice on " the strength of the full powers of the Commission ". It was no good hesitating, he added, about the free passage of the Entente troops, for if not granted by the terms of the armistice, they would decide the matter by arms.

The Armistice Terms Accepted

A Crown Council had assembled at 9.15 p.m. (2nd November): it was only known that the hour and other details of the Armistice were " being studied ". About midnight, before the French text of the terms had been received, or the despatch from General Weber reporting that the time-limit for acceptance expired at midnight on the 3rd/4th, and that the armistice applied to all fronts and would take effect 24 hours after signature, a message was finally prepared. This was despatched to General Weber at 1.20 a.m. (3rd November) via Trent, in the hope that he might telegraph it on via the Italian 26th Division headquarters, and it was also sent on by wireless from Vienna, via Pola, to Padua to be delivered to General Weber. The acceptance of the terms was, the Austrian Official Account points out, based on the first words of the summary: " Immediate cessation of " hostilities by land, by sea and in the air ".

The message ran:

> " All Armistice conditions are accepted, without
> " prejudice to peace, if modification not obtainable
> " without loss of time. The Austro-Hungarian troops
> " have accordingly already received orders to stop
> " hostilities at once (*sofort*). It is presumed that

"Land Point 4 (a) and Water Point 4 (Right of
"Passage), are not to be so understood that the enemy
"armies can use the right of free movement for an
"attack on Germany. Although such action cannot
"be prevented, a suitable protest must be raised against
"it. It may be that this condition must be accepted;
"but attempt should first be made to delay the enemy's
"march at least as regards time ".

The Armistice terms having thus been accepted, towards 2 a.m. (3rd November) Major-General Waldstätten, the Chief of the Operations Section of the General Staff, telephoned to the two Groups of Armies, the message already mentioned ; "Armistice conditions of the Entente accepted. "All hostilities on land and in the air are to be stopped at "once ".

The Emperor Karl Changes His Mind and hands over Command of the Troops

Shortly after this, General Arz returned from his visit to the German-Austrian Parliament, without having been able to persuade the State Council to express approval of the Armistice terms; the Council would not, he was told "meet again until next morning " and its acquiescence was "quite improbable ". Thereupon the Emperor began to have doubts about accepting the terms without the concurrence of the State Council; he still had hopes that it would accede to his request; he particularly wished to avoid taking the blame for allowing the armies of the Entente to attack Germany from his territories. He therefore ordered General Arz to attend the next meeting of the Crown Council, and to recall all the orders with regard to the Armistice just given. The wireless message to General Weber via the Italian Comando Supremo had not gone off, and that could be stopped—as for the identical message via Trent, it seems to have been assumed that it would not get through. Field-Marshal Krobatin's Chief of the General Staff, on being told on the telephone of the counter-order, replied to Major-General Waldstätten that the original order, to cease hostilities, had already gone out in the *Eleventh Army* (on the Trentino front, and responsible for the sector containing the Val Sugana, Val d'Assa and the valley of the

Adige), and to cancel it would "lead to a catastrophe". After further discussion with the Emperor, although both the *Isonzo Army* and the *Sixth Army* were in a condition to continue fighting, standing in closed bodies on the Tagliamento, with, in the southern half, rear guards still on the western bank, the order to the Groups of Armies to cease hostilities was repeated to them at 3.45 a.m. (3rd November).

The wireless message to General Weber, which authorized him to sign the Armistice, was not sent off, as the Emperor still hoped to obtain the concurrence of the Austrian State Council. In the early morning, however, he resigned the chief command of the army of his many peoples, already in dissolution, and appointed General-Colonel Arz to take it over. The general informed him that he would sign the protocol of the Armistice, but begged that Field-Marshal Kövess von Kövesshaza, commanding on the Balkan front, as senior officer, should be given the Supreme Command, and stated that he would officiate until his arrival. To this the Emperor gave his sanction.

The Signing of the Armistice at Villa Giusti

It was unfortunate for the Austrian Armistice Commissioners that they were isolated from the High Command by slow communication, and that, coming from the Trentino front, some of them carried in their minds the picture of the scenes of disintegration and disaster which they had witnessed.

The next meeting of the two Armistice Commissions took place at 6 p.m. (2nd November), after the arrival from Paris of the officer with the full French text, 3 of the 7 Austrian members being absent at Trent. It was to the first point in the "Protocol attached containing the details and "executive clauses", which had not previously been communicated, that General Weber took exception. It contained the proviso that hostilities would not cease until twenty-four hours after the signature of the Armistice, whilst the first article of the Armistice read "immediate "cessation of hostilities". In vain he protested, begging that the period might be reduced to twelve hours for the Italian front. But, as was quite justifiably pointed out by his opponents, it would take, possibly, more than twenty-four hours to bring the signing of the Armistice to the notice of the front line troops, all being on the move.[1] He then asked who was to be the umpire in case of disagreement on any clause, and the Comando Supremo referred to the Supreme War Council, who decided that the Italian view must prevail. It was by now 2 a.m. (3rd November), and General Weber, in his belief that his report had been received announcing that the conditions must be accepted before midnight of the 3rd/4th November, begged by wireless via Pola for a decision as soon as possible whether he was to sign, and then sent off the " Protocol attached ". His first message arrived 5.10 a.m., after the decision at the Supreme Command had already been made. He received no answer, and was not informed of the decision until 4 p.m.

Meantime Colonel Schneller in Trent had at 1.20 a.m. (3rd November)[2] received by wire from Baden the original order for the acceptance of the terms, and had left for Padua with his fellow commissioners before the Emperor's cancellation arrived. Owing to the block of baggage and other wagons on the road, his progress was slow. At *XIV Corps* headquarters in Aquaviva (5½ miles south of Trent) he learnt that the order to cease fire had been issued to the troops, and that the Staff were puzzled what to do if the Italians who were in Calliano, only 4½ miles farther on, continued their march. Colonel Schneller advised that all further combat should be avoided; but, as he was leaving about 5 a.m., he received an order to return to Trent. There he was able to speak on the telephone to Major-General Waldstätten (Chief of the Operations Bureau), and obtained permission to proceed, but to pay no attention to and destroy the order authorizing the acceptance of the Italian terms contained in the summary. On arrival at the Villa Giusti at 1 p.m., he informed General Weber of the order accepting the terms and its counter-order, and of the issue to the troops of the order for the cessation of hostilities. General Weber decided to take on himself the responsibility for signing the Armistice, and formally declared his willingness to do so at a meeting of both Commissions at 3 p.m. He made the reservation that Article 4 of the Military Clauses (free movement in Austrian territory) and Articles 4 and 5

---

[1] On the Western Front hostilities on land and in the air ceased six hours after the signature of the Armistice with Germany, but there an extensive system of signal telephones and telegraphs was available.
[2] Thus A.O.A. vii, p. 730. The message had been sent at that hour.

of the naval clauses (free movement in the Adriatic and on the Danube, and the continuance of the blockade) would be brought up again at the Peace Conference. He informed General Badoglio that an order to cease hostilities at once had taken effect in the Austro-Hungarian army, and begged that the Italian Commission would endeavour to stop the fighting. To this, General Badoglio replied that it could not be done under 24 hours; but, looking at his wrist watch, which showed 3.20, he said, "Let us make "3 p.m. the exact hour of the breaking off of hostilities; "that is, the Armistice will come into force to-morrow, "4th November, at 3 p.m."

The protocol of the Armistice, with a map and the annexure containing the details and executive clauses, were formally signed at 6 p.m. Meantime, at 4.20 p.m., General Weber had, after acceptance of the terms at 3.20 p.m., received a telegram from General Arz authorizing him to sign.

On hearing at last, at 11 p.m. of the 24 hours' delay, General Arz addressed a protest to General Diaz. The latter, with justice, replied that the terms, including the 24 hours' delay, had been agreed to and signed by duly appointed plenipotentiaries, and that the interval was regarded as unavoidable in order to inform all troops on all fronts on land and on the sea of the cessation of hostilities; in accordance therewith, it was perfectly regular to take prisoners, and any captured before 3 p.m. on the 4th would be retained.

On 20th November a "Military Convention Regulating "the Application to Hungary of the Armistice Signed "between the Allies and Austria-Hungary" was signed at Salonika between the Allies and Hungary, by then a separate republic. Its clauses dealt with the demarcation line for the Hungarian troops' demobilization, the right of occupation by the Allies, the delivery of railway transport, river vessels, horses and arms, the reconstitution of telegraph and telephone systems, prisoners of war, the removal of mines, and the cessation of relations with Germany. On their part, the Allies covenanted not to interfere with the internal administration of Hungary.

NOTE

ECONOMIC CONDITION OF AUSTRIA-HUNGARY IN 1917–18

The terrible condition of Austria-Hungary in the later war years is described in "Hunger. Die Erschöpfungsjahre der Mittelmächte (The exhaustion years of the Central Powers) 1917–18", by General Landwehr, one time *Oberquartiermeister* (= Q.M.G.) on the Isonzo Front, and from February 1917 head of the Austrian "General Food Commission"; and in "The Cost of The World War to Germany and Austria-Hungary", issued by the Carnegie Endowment for International Peace.

Austria-Hungary suffered much more severely from food and other shortages than Germany—as the *Reich's* Allies always do. Everything failed, even manure in consequence of the poor feeding and rapid decline in numbers of the cattle. The total of cattle decreased in the war years from 17,324,800 to 3,518,197, and that of pigs from 7,678,000 to 214,000. There is a dreadful list of *Ersatz* substances. The situation was saved in 1917 by the occupation of Rumania, from which country immense supplies were drawn; but Austria got little out of the Ukraine in 1918, receiving only 4,622 trucks of corn and flour, although immense numbers passed through Vienna, as Germany refused to form "a common front" as regards food supplies—and simple want of food did more to bring about the downfall of the Dual Monarchy than anything else. Early in 1917 only four-fifths of the *minimum* amount of corn required was available, and nearly half of this came from Rumania, a source which was lacking in the next twelve months.

CHAPTER XXVI

THE END OF THE BRITISH FORCES IN ITALY
(Map IV; End-paper; Sketch 8)

PLANS TO INVADE BAVARIA

The days immediately following the Armistice of 4th November were spent by the British troops in refitting, collecting Austrian stragglers, and making attempts at salvage. The men fully expected they would be called on to continue operations and march into Germany or, at least into Austria.[1] Plans had indeed been made by the Comando Supremo for an advance into Bavaria, the suggestion being put forward that it should be carried out by Lord Cavan's Tenth Army. This would, for the purpose, consist of two Italian Corps (the XI and XVIII, which had already been under him), and the XIV Corps, with all 3 British divisions (7th, 23rd and 48th South Midland) in it, which would first be concentrated near Verona. It was subsequently proposed that a second Army should take part—no more than two Armies could be supplied—and in this case General Badoglio would be in command of the Group. After the Armistice with Germany on 11th November, however, General Diaz talked of sending four Armies into the *Reich*.

As early as 4th November Lord Cavan had informed the Chief of the Imperial General Staff that a project for the invasion of Bavaria was afoot, and suggested that the views of Maréchal Foch on its strategic value should be ascertained. He himself was not enthusiastic about the plan, as he did not believe that the Italian people and troops were keen about fighting Germans. Further, the distance from Trent to Innsbrück over the Alps by the Brenner Pass was more than eighty miles, and beyond Innsbrück lay the thirty-mile wide barrier of the Bavarian Alps. Thus, remembering the position of Trent, over a hundred miles of mountainous country would have to be traversed; it was pretty certain that the roads and tunnels would be damaged by enemy

---
[1] See End-paper.

agents; and, judging by the destruction done to the permanent bridges in Italy, there could hardly be a clear route by road or rail into Germany for a considerable time. Winter was approaching—the first snow in the British area in the Venetian plain fell on 17th November—which would make any advance into Bavaria hazardous. And a start could not be made at once; for Lord Cavan was informed that the roads and railways around Rovereto and Trent, and in the Val Sugana, were in a very bad state, and would take a month to put right; an advanced base would have to be established; and to get the Tenth Army back to Verona would take from sixteen to twenty days, as the roads were in a bad condition. The Piave too, the permanent bridges not having been restored, would have to be crossed by pontoon bridges, a slow, tedious process. The picture of German divisions falling on Italian columns as they debouched from the mountains after a winter march was hardly a cheerful one to contemplate.

At this time the German High Command, no less than the Austrian, was endeavouring to avoid defeat in the open field and to stop the War by means of an armistice, and was on the point of succeeding. On 5th November Maréchal Foch was placed by the Supreme War Council in supreme direction of all forces operating against Germany on all fronts,[1] and at the same time the German Government were informed by President Wilson that the proposals for an armistice had been accepted by the Allies and that they should apply to Maréchal Foch if they wished to know the terms on which an armistice would be granted. That no military reasons existed for further operations based on Italy was soon obvious, and, though the Comando Supremo continued to cherish the idea of Italian Armies marching into Germany or, failing that, into Austria, a decision was made by the Supreme War Council to do no more than occupy the Trentino. An appeal from the Emperor Karl, that the French and British should send troops to maintain order in Vienna and Budapest was not entertained by the Supreme War Council.

---

[1] For dynastic reasons, as the King was nominal Commander-in-Chief of the army, the forces of Italy had not theoretically been under the Generalissimo of the Western Front.

Withdrawal of the XIV Corps to the Trissino Area

On 6th November, through Br.-General Delmé-Radcliffe, the Comando Supremo informed Lord Cavan that it was getting out orders to move the British XIV Corps westwards, and that the G.O.C. Ninth Army (the reserve) would take over the Tenth Army front from him; the movement, it was added, was not easy to arrange, in consequence—as the British were to experience—of the number of Italian units in the back areas.

It was settled that the XIV Corps should concentrate, reorganize and refit " somewhere south of Vicenza ", where the 48th Division, the heavy artillery and all British personnel would rejoin it.

On 5th November the outposts of the XIV Corps over the Tagliamento were reduced to two British battalions and a cyclist company, with one battalion of the Italian 31st Division; the rest were withdrawn west of the river; but, as fighting was reported to be taking place at Cormons (6 miles west of the Isonzo, near Gorizia), the XI Corps was directed to send troops there, and trestle and pontoon bridges were constructed at Ponte della Delizia and Gradisca on the Tagliamento to take field artillery and 30-cwt. lorries; another such bridge was made at Sacile, and the pontoon bridge there replaced by an " Inglis " bridge. Next day, the Italian 31st Division was transferred from the XIV to the XI Corps, and all British troops east of the Tagliamento were withdrawn. On the 8th, in fine, cold weather, the 7th and 23rd Divisions, with corps units attached, started on the 40-mile march to Treviso where, on the 11th, the dismounted portions began entraining for the Trissino area, the artillery, corps mounted troops and transport continuing by road. The railway movement was completed on the 14th. There were a great many Italian troops in the area, and until they were transferred elsewhere, it was difficult to find sufficient quarters.

Withdrawal of the 48th Division

The supply route of the 48th Division before it was withdrawn from the Trentino front afforded some idea of the difficulties likely to be encountered in a campaign against

Germany via Trent. Supplies were brought from railhead at Villaverla (north of Vicenza) in two lorry stages to Granezza, the old divisional headquarters (4 miles south of Asiago)[1]; then light Italian lorries carried rations and stores to a depôt at Osteria del Termine, on the Austrian frontier; and then 27 British 30-cwt. Fiat lorries took them on to Caldonazzo, via the zigzag three-thousand feet descent. It was feared that should snow fall—and it was overdue—grave difficulties might arise, for wheeled traffic would become impossible, and sledges would be required; the country could furnish nothing, and the Austrian dumps contained little except forage and cigarettes too nauseous for British palates. The local situation was somewhat improved by the discovery of a new route from Vezzena to Caldonazzo by a road over the Lavarone plateau and down the valley in which Ceuta stands, thus avoiding the dangerous zigzag, but it was three miles longer.

On 6th November the 48th Division was warned that it would shortly be sent back to Granezza, and next day, in anticipation, the artillery, engineers and machine-gun battalion were concentrated at Caldonazzo.

The first order received by Major-General Sir H. B. Walker from the Italian XII Corps was that the 48th Division should march back via the Val Sugana and the valley of the Brenta; but as this would have entirely upset the supply arrangements, an appeal was made to the Sixth Army, and the division was allowed to return by the route, via Val d'Assa, by which it had come into Austria. The retirement was begun on the 8th, on the same day as the XIV Corps marched from the Tagliamento, in bad weather which lasted two days. The march was carried out by the divisional troops and the brigades in 3 stages, with halts at Vezzena and Val Portule, to Granezza. The last troops, except for a clearing-up detachment, left Austria on the 11th, the date of the Armistice with Germany. It was then continued in another 3 stages, the first of which was 18 miles to Thiene, at the foot of the mountains,[2] and thence west to the Trissino area, where it rejoined the XIV Corps.

---

[1] See Map IV and Sketch 8.
[2] See End-paper.

THE CONCENTRATION OF THE BRITISH FORCE AND DEMOBILIZATION

Then ensued an "era of spit and polish" with a view to a review by the King of Italy on 27th November, in which a composite infantry brigade and a field battery took part. Work was varied with such amusements and instruction as could be improvised, including football, cross-country running, boxing, hockey, wrestling on horseback, theatricals, a race meeting, educational courses and lectures on demobilization.[1] The first four "key men" left for the United Kingdom on 4th December, and other small parties followed; the first demobilization train left on 23rd December, followed by others on the 29th and 30th.

A proposal was made that the troops proceeding home, instead of travelling by rail, should march by the Col de Tenda and the Riviera route by which they had entered Italy, and thence to French ports; but investigation showed that, owing to the cost of preparing winter rest camps en route and of the road transport of supplies, this method would be more expensive than rail.

By 15th January almost exactly 10,000 men, about a fifth of the force, had gone, and from that date 650 left daily; battalions were amalgamated, some brigades ceased to exist as formations and were attached to others; divisions shrank to brigade groups. On 18th January Lord Cavan handed over command to the G.O.C. XIV Corps, and returned home, and Br.-General Pitt-Taylor became senior general staff officer in place of Major-General Gathorne-Hardy. On 3rd March, in his turn, Lieut.-General Sir James Babington passed the command to the senior divisional commander, Major-General Sir H. B. Walker, and Lieut.-Colonel D. H. Talbot succeeded Br.-General Pitt-Taylor.[2] At this date the force consisted of (1) a mixed brigade of occupation; (2) the cadres and remnants of the 3 divisions, each under a brigade commander; (3) the cadre and remnants of the heavy artillery; and (4) lines of communication units. Of these (2) and (3) soon passed out of

---

[1] The Y.M.C.A. opened eleven centres.
An account of the demobilization scheme and how it worked out will be found in the volume on the Occupation of the Rhineland, which is projected.

[2] The H.Q. Staff was reduced to G.S., 4; A. & Q., 3; Ordnance officer, 1; Army Pay, 3; Court Martial officer, 1; Intelligence, 3; D.A.P.M., 1.

existence.[1] There remained a total of 6,512 men in the mixed brigade and 4,296 on the lines of communication.

It had first been decided in London to maintain 10 battalions in Italy; this number was, on 3rd February, reduced to 4 (at a thousand strong), organized with detachments of other arms as a mixed brigade, the units being made up with men who had joined the colours in 1916 and after, volunteers,[2] and young soldiers sent out from home.

The 4 battalions selected were the 1/7th R. Warwickshire, the 8/York & Lancaster, the 22/Manchester and the 1/6th Gloucestershire. The other units were a new 102nd Brigade R.F.A.,[3] the 101st Field Company R.E., a Signal detachment of 3 officers and 82 other ranks, one company of the 48th Machine Gun Battalion, the 69th Light Stokes Mortar Battery, a company of the 23rd Divisional Train, the 1/3rd South Midland Field Ambulance, the 1/1st South Midland Veterinary Detachment, the 17th Mobile Laboratory, the 84th Sanitary Section, and a platoon of the 234th Employment Company, with Lines of Communication staff. The R.A.F. detachment was reduced to a flight, and this soon left for the United Kingdom.

The war material was for the most part sent to France for disposal, but lorries and cars were sold to the White Russians or the Swiss; the best mares were sent back to England, other horses were sold locally at good prices.

In the midst of demobilization and reduction, various duties fell to the British troops in Italy. On 23rd November, in consequence of trouble at Fiume between the Yugoslavs and Italians, Br.-General Herbert Gordon, with the 8/York & Lancaster (23rd Division) and an American battalion, was despatched there " to keep order "—by rail to Venice and thence by sea. They met with a great reception from the inhabitants, and although the Italian force in the town was 9 battalions, with cavalry and artillery, they had no difficulty in keeping the peace. Orders to send a battalion to Cattaro were received; but, owing to the difficulty of supplying it, the duty was transferred to the Navy.

On 28th November the H.A.C. battalion (7th Division)

---

[1] The 48th (South Midland, T.A.) Division was re-formed in England in 1920.

[2] By the middle of January only 732 men had volunteered to stay.

[3] Made up of one battery each from the 102nd, 103rd, 240th and 241st Brigades R.F.A.

was sent to the Trentino " to emphasise the Allied character " of the occupation ", and was stationed at Imst, on the west of Innsbrück. The difficulties of Alpine warfare in winter at once became apparent, Lieut.-Colonel O'Connor having to hire sledges to maintain communications and supply his men. When the mixed brigade was formed the H.A.C. battalion was relieved by the 22/Manchester.

The small number of British prisoners taken by the Austrians—20 officers and 144 (38 hospital cases) other ranks—rejoined at Trieste, and it then came to notice that some thousand Italian officers, ex-prisoners of war, with thousands of other ranks, were herded on the wharves, with hardly any shelter—and the winds from the Alps can be icy in November—the " men literally in the last stages of " exhaustion from hunger, some already dead ". As the Italian commander was completely apathetic, Lord Cavan felt it a duty to humanity to send food, and the British Red Cross also gave assistance.

It may be added that on 7th January a relief supply train with 200 tons of British army supplies was despatched to the inhabitants of Vienna, with a guard of 2 officers and a hundred men ; a second followed on the 25th with the guard reduced to half ; with the third, the guard was halved again.

Early in December trouble occurred in the 8 battalions of the British West Indies Regiment employed on dock duties in Taranto, the port terminus of the " overland " route " from Cherbourg to Salonika and Egypt-Palestine ; some men of one battalion refused to work, stones were thrown at two officers, and a bomb was thrown into the tent of a regimental quartermaster-sergeant. The main grievance of the men was that they had enlisted to fight, but had been employed continuously at bases and, the War being over, they wanted to go home. The disturbance was dealt with by the commandant, Br.-General J. H. V. Crowe, who, having five hundred British reinforcements and some R.A.F. machine guns at his disposal, disarmed two of the battalions ; but at first the situation appeared so serious that the 1/7th Worcestershire and a machine-gun company were despatched by rail, with Major-General H. F. Thuillier in charge. When they arrived on the 15th after a journey of three nights and three days, all was quiet, and another battalion and an artillery battery which had been warned,

CLOSING DOWN. 1919

were not sent. The West Indies battalions were sent home, their place in the docks being taken by Italians; but the Worcestershire remained at Taranto for three months, not rejoining in the Trissino area until 13th March.

The 1/6th Gloucestershire was sent to Scutari (Shkoder) on 19th February " to emphasise the Allied character of " control in Albania ", dropping one company at Taranto in relief of the Worcestershire.

The 8/York & Lancaster remained at Fiume until September 1919, where in May a Military Mission under Lieut.-Colonel S. C. Peck was assembled.

The other two of the battalions of the mixed brigade, the 1/7th R. Warwickshire, and 22/Manchester, with the other arms previously mentioned, went in April to Arquata, the base north of Genoa, whence, with the 1/6th Gloucestershire from Scutari, still as a mixed brigade, they departed towards the end of May under Br.-General Herbert Gordon, to Egypt, and the troops remaining in Italy were reduced to those necessary for clearing up, for the disposal of surplus stores, and for maintaining the Cherbourg–Taranto line of communication which was required for bringing troops and demobilized men home from the Middle East. In September, 40 officers and 700 men were passing through Taranto every three days.

On 26th June, Major-General Walker's G.H.Q. closed down, and command, including Fiume, passed to the I.G.C., Major-General Strick; but the Intelligence Section was transferred to the British Mission at the Comando Supremo.

Reductions were gradually carried out, so that by 1st November 1919, the strength of the British troops in Italy was 316 officers and 4,278 other ranks and at the end of December 180 officers and 2,100 other ranks, including 1,300 men employed on the disposal of stores. There still remained 3,700 tons of stores to go back to England. During September and October most of the " *haltes repas* " and police posts were closed down and withdrawn. The Taranto base was closed at 6 a.m. on 16th December, the staff of the C.R.E. and No. 7 General Hospital staying on, however, a few days to clear up. These reductions finally left parties only at Genoa, Arquata, the demobilization centre, Tortona, Milan and Pavia, at the last three for the disposal of stores. Finally the last remaining units, under

Lieut.-Colonel R. M. Campbell, the L. of C. headquarters, the L. of C. Signal Company, No. 2 R.A.S.C. Base Depot, No. 116 Auxiliary Petrol Company, No. 38 Stationary Hospital, No. 3 Company R.A.O.C. and No. 246 Base Park Company were disbanded on 15th April, 1920 and the personnel left for the United Kingdom by sea.

APPENDIX I
ORDER OF BATTLE OF THE BRITISH FORCES IN ITALY
NOVEMBER–DECEMBER 1917
GENERAL HEADQUARTERS

Commander-in-Chief ...	General Sir Herbert Plumer
M.G.G.S.	Major-General C. H. Harington
G.S.O. 1 (I)	Lieut.-Colonel C. H. Mitchell
D.A.G.	Major-General W. G. B. Western
D.Q.M.G.	Major-General A. A. Chichester
Director-General, Transportation	Major-General W. G. Grey
Commander Royal Artillery	Major-General C. R. Buckle
Chief Engineer	Major-General F. M. Glubb
Commander Royal Flying Corps	Br.-General T. I. Webb-Bowen
Liaison Officer with the C.I.G.S.	Br.-General J. H. V. Crowe
D.A.A.G., 3rd Echelon ...	Major M. B. Webb

ARMY TROOPS

Artillery :
    Field Artillery :
        XIV (Army) Brigade R.H.A., LXXII, LXXVI, 175th (Army) Brigades R.F.A.
        A/72, C/76, C/175, 400, Batteries R.F.A.
    Heavy Artillery :
        XV, XXIV, LXXX, XCIV, 104th Heavy Artillery Groups
        19, 90, 155, 1/1st Warwickshire Heavy Batteries R.G.A.
        105, 137, 171, 172, 176, 181, 197, 229, 240, 247, 289, 293, 302, 307, 315, 316, 317, 390, 391, 438 Siege Batteries R.G.A.
    Anti-Aircraft Artillery :
        No. 4 Group Lovat's Scouts (Yeomanry)
        S. Battery (72, 106, 117 Sections)
        23, 60, 63, 135, 136 A.A. Sections
        80, 81 Searchlight Sections
Machine Guns :
    12th Motor Battery
Royal Engineers :
    285, 290 Army Troops Coys.
    6 Field Survey Coy. (25, 29 Observation Groups ; E Sound Ranging Section)
    Detachment Meteorological Section
    No. 5 Pontoon Park (H.T.)
    No. 2 Boring Section

APPENDIX I

Royal Flying Corps:
  VII Brigade (Fifty-first and Fourteenth Wings):
    28, 34, 42, 45, 66 Squadrons
    7th Aircraft Park
    Aeroplane Supply Depot
    7, 22, 24, 33 Kite Balloon Sections
    4, 9 Balloon Wings
    20th Balloon Coy.

Signal Service:
  32, 34, 9 (Motor) Airline Sections
  N, WS, WT Cable Sections
  2nd Signal Construction Coy.
  5, 25 Motor Wireless Sections
  7th Army Wireless Observation Group
  15, 24, 80, 94, 104 H.A.G. Signal Sections
  70, 71, 72, 73, 74 Horse-drawn Pigeon Lofts

Army Service Corps:
  4th Pontoon Park (M.T.) (360th Coy.)
  Army Troops Supply Column
  443rd, 1047th Army Auxiliary H.T. Coys.
  1st Mobile Repair Unit (93rd Coy.)
  654th, 1037th Coys. (attached heavy artillery)
  369, 370, 374, 375, 377, 380, 383, 386 (M.T.) Sections
  No. 2 Section A.A. Workshop

Medical:
  26, 36, 41 Motor Ambulance Convoys
  9, 24, 37, 38, 39 Casualty Clearing Stations
  32, 33 Advanced Depots Medical Stores
  7, 14 Bacteriological Laboratories
  15th Hygiene Laboratory
  36, 57, 73, 75, 84 Sanitary Sections

Ordnance:
  3rd (Light), 11th (Medium) Mobile Workshops

XI CORPS

Arrived in Italy 1st December 1917
Returned to Western Front, 13th March 1918

Commander ...	Lieut.-General Sir Richard Haking
B.G.G.S. ...	Br.-General J. E. S. Brind
D.A. & Q.M.G. ...	Br.-General A. F. U. Green
C.R.A. ...	Br.-General E. W. Alexander, V.C.
C.H.A. ...	Br.-General R. H. F. McCulloch
Chief Engineer ...	Br.-General H. J. M. Marshall

APPENDIX I

Corps Troops :
  1/1st King Edward's Horse
  H.Q. Corps Heavy Artillery
  11th Cyclist Battalion
  Corps Topographical Section
  Signal Troops :
    L Corps Signal Coy., 27 (Motor) Airline Section, R, LC Cable Sections, Corps Heavy Artillery Signal Section
  Corps Siege Park
  Corps Ammunition Park (345th Coy. A.S.C., 25 Ammunition Sub-Park)
  Corps Troops Supply Column (321st Coy. A.S.C.)
  491st Coy. A.S.C. (attached Corps Heavy Artillery)
  5th (Light) Ordnance Mobile Workshop
  Area Employment Coy.
  Corps School

XIV CORPS

Arrived in Italy 5th November 1917
Became G.H.Q. Italy, 18th April 1918
Re-formed 9th–16th October 1918

Commander...	Lieut.-General Earl of Cavan
B.G.G.S.	Br.-General Hon. J. F. Gathorne-Hardy
D.A. & Q.M.G.	Br.-General H. L. Alexander
C.R.A.	Br.-General A. E. Wardrop
C.H.A.	[did not accompany the corps to Italy]
C.E. ...	Br.-General C. S. Wilson

Corps Troops :
  1/1st Northamptonshire Yeomanry
  14th Cyclist Battalion
  Corps Topographical Section
  Signal Troops :
    J Corps Signal Coy., 54 (Motor) Airline Section, AS, M, BU Cable Sections
  Corps Supply Column :
    No. 14 Corps Troops (391st Coy. A.S.C.) ,No. 17 Divl. (498th Coy. A.S.C.), No. 41 Divl. (494th Coy. A.S.C. No. 48 Divl., No. 50 Divl.
  Corps Ammunition Park :
    No. 17 (600th Coy. A.S.C.), 23 (607th Coy. A.S.C.) ; 50, 62 Ammunition Sub-Parks
  No. 7 (Light), No. 4 (Medium) Ordnance Mobile Workshops
  No. 273 Area Employment Coy.
  Corps School

APPENDIX I

5th Division

Arrived in Italy 27th November 1917
Left for Western Front 1st–9th April 1918

Commander	Major-General R. B. Stephens
G.S.O.1	Lieut.-Colonel G. C. W. Gordon-Hall
A.A. & Q.M.G.	Lieut.-Colonel R. F. A. Hobbs
C.R.A.	Br.-General A. H. Hussey
C.R.E.	Lieut.-Colonel J. R. White

Divisional Troops :
    XV, XXVII Brigades R.F.A.
    X5, Y5, Z5 Trench Mortar Btys. R.A.
    Divisional Ammunition Column
    59th, 491st (Home Counties), 527th (Durham) Field Coys. R.E.
    Divisional Signal Coy.
    Pioneers : 1/6th Argyll & Sutherland Highlanders
    205th Machine Gun Coy.
    Divisional Train (4th, 6th, 33rd, 37th Coys. A.S.C.)
    13th, 14th, 15th Field Ambulances
    Mobile Veterinary Section
    208th Divisional Employment Coy.

13th Brigade	15th Brigade
Lieut.-Colonel L. Murray acting until Br.-General L. O. W. Jones re-assumed command on 18th December 1917	Br.-General R. D. F. Oldman
14/R. Warwickshire	16/R. Warwickshire
15/R. Warwickshire	1/Norfolk
2/K.O.S.B.	1/Bedfordshire
1/R. West Kent	1/Cheshire
13th Machine Gun Coy.	15th Machine Gun Coy.
13th Trench Mortar Bty.	15th Trench Mortar Bty.

95th Brigade
Br.-General Lord E. C. Gordon-Lennox
    1/Devonshire
    12/Gloucestershire
    1/East Surrey
    1/D. of Cornwall's L.I.
    95th Machine Gun Coy.
    95th Trench Mortar Bty.

APPENDIX I

7th Division
Arrived in Italy, 17th November 1917
Demobilized in Italy 1919

Commander...	Major-General T. H. Shoubridge
G.S.O.1	Lieut.-Colonel G. W. Howard
A.A. & Q.M.G.	Lieut.-Colonel B. J. Lang
C.R.A.	Br.-General H. C. Stanley-Clarke
C.R.E.	Lieut.-Colonel A. W. Reid

Divisional Troops:
XXII, XXXV Brigades R.F.A.
X7, Y7, Z7 Trench Mortar Btys. R.A.
Divisional Ammunition Column
54th, 95th, 528th (Durham) Field Coys. R.E.
Divisional Signal Coy.
Pioneers: 24/Manchester
220th Machine Gun Coy.
Divisional Train (39th, 40th, 42nd, 86th Coys. A.S.C.)
21st, 22nd, 23rd Field Ambulances
12th Mobile Veterinary Section
210th Divisional Employment Coy.

20th Brigade	22nd Brigade
Br.-General H. C. R. Green	Br.-General J. McC. Steele
8/Devonshire	2/R. Warwickshire
9/Devonshire	1/R. Welch Fusiliers
2/Border Regiment	20/Manchester
2/Gordon Highlanders	2/1st H.A.C.
20th Machine Gun Coy.	22nd Machine Gun Coy.
20th Trench Mortar Bty.	22nd Trench Mortar Bty.

91st Brigade
Br.-General R. T. Pelly
2/Queen's
1/South Staffordshire
21/Manchester
22/Manchester
91st Machine Gun Coy.
91st Trench Mortar Bty.

23rd Division
Arrived in Italy 6th–16th November 1917
Demobilized in Italy March 1919

Commander...	Major-General Sir J. M. Babington
G.S.O.1	Lieut.-Colonel C. Evans
A.A. & Q.M.G.	Lieut.-Colonel E. F. Falkner
C.R.A.	Br.-General Sir Dalrymple Arbuthnot, Bt.
C.R.E.	Lieut.-Colonel E. H. Rooke

Divisional Troops:
    102nd, 103rd Brigades R.F.A.
    X23, Y23, Z23 Trench Mortar Btys. R.A.
    Divisional Ammunition Column
    101st, 102nd, 128th Field Coys. R.E.
    Divisional Signal Coy.
    Pioneers : 9/South Staffordshire
    194th Machine Gun Coy.
    Divisional Train (190th, 191st, 192nd, 193rd Coys. A.S.C.)
    69th, 70th, 71st Field Ambulances
    35th Mobile Veterinary Section
    223rd Divisional Employment Coy.

68th Brigade	69th Brigade
Br.-General C. D. V. Cary-Barnard	Br.-General T. S. Lambert
10/Northumberland Fusiliers	11/West Yorkshire
11/Northumberland Fusiliers	8/Green Howards
12/Durham L.I.	9/Green Howards
13/Durham L.I.	10/Duke of Wellington's
68th Machine Gun Coy.	69th Machine Gun Coy.
68th Trench Mortar Bty.	69th Trench Mortar Bty.

          70th Brigade
        Br.-General H. Gordon
        11/Sherwood Foresters
        8/K.O.Y.L.I.
        8/York & Lancaster
        9/York & Lancaster
        70th Machine Gun Coy.
        70th Trench Mortar Bty.

41st Division

Arrived in Italy, 16th November 1917
Returned to Western Front, 1st March 1918

Commander	Major-General Sir S. T. B. Lawford
G.S.O.1	Lieut.-Colonel R. G. Parker
A.A. & Q.M.G.	Lieut.-Colonel T. S. Riddell-Webster
C.R.A.	Br.-General A. S. Cotton
C.R.E.	Lieut.-Colonel E. N. Stockley

Divisional Troops:
    187th, 190th Brigades R.F.A.
    X41, Y41, Z41 Trench Mortar Btys. R.A.
    Divisional Ammunition Column
    228th, 233rd, 237th Field Coys. R.E.
    Divisional Signal Coy.

APPENDIX I

Pioneers : 19/Middlesex
199th Machine Gun Coy.
Divisional Train (296th, 297th, 298th, 299th Coys. A.S.C.)
138th, 139th, 140th Field Ambulances
52nd Mobile Veterinary Section
238th Divisional Employment Coy.

122nd Brigade	123rd Brigade
Br.-General F. W. Towsey	Br.-General E. Pearce Serocold
12/East Surrey	11/Queen's
15/Hampshire	10/R. West Kent
(Hampshire Carabineers)	23/Middlesex
11/R. West Kent	20/Durham L.I.
18/K.R.R.C.	123rd Machine Gun Coy.
122nd Machine Gun Coy.	123rd Trench Mortar Bty.
122nd Trench Mortar Bty.	

124th Brigade
Br.-General W. F. Clemson
10/Queen's
26/Royal Fusiliers
32/Royal Fusiliers
21/K.R.R.C.
124th Machine Gun Coy.
124th Trench Mortar Bty.

48th (1st South Midland) Division

Arrived in Italy 22nd November 1917
Demobilized in Italy 31st March 1919
Re-formed in the U.K. in 1920

Commander...	Major-General R. Fanshawe
G.S.O.1	Lieut.-Colonel H. C. L. Howard
A.A. & Q.M.G.	Lieut.-Colonel G. H. Barnett
C.R.A.	Br.-General W. Strong
C.R.E.	Lieut.-Colonel V. Giles

Divisional Troops :
240th (Gloucester), 241st (Worcester) Brigades R.F.A.
X48, Y48, Z48 Trench Mortar Btys. R.A.
Divisional Ammunition Column
474th, 475th, 477th Field Coys. R.E.
Divisional Signal Coy.
Pioneers : 1/5th R. Sussex
Divisional Train (459th, 460th, 461st, 462nd Coys. A.S.C.)
251st Machine Gun Coy.
1/1st 1/2nd, 1/3rd South Midland Field Ambulances
1/1st South Midland Mobile Veterinary Section
242nd Divisional Employment Coy.

APPENDIX I

143rd (Warwickshire) Brigade
    Br.-General G. C. Sladen
    1/5th R. Warwickshire
    1/6th R. Warwickshire
    1/7th R. Warwickshire
    1/8th R. Warwickshire
    143rd Machine Gun Coy.
    143rd Trench Mortar Bty.

144th (Gloucester & Worcester) Brigade
    Br.-General H. R. Done
    1/4th Gloucestershire
    1/6th Gloucestershire
    1/7th Worcestershire
    1/8th Worcestershire
    144th Machine Gun Coy.
    144th Trench Mortar Bty.

145th (South Midland) Brigade
    Br.-General D. M. Watt
    1/5th Gloucestershire
    1/4th Oxfordshire & Buckinghamshire L.I.
    1/1st Buckinghamshire Bn. Ox. & B. L.I.
    1/4th R. Berkshire
    145th Machine Gun Coy.
    145th Trench Mortar Bty.

LINES OF COMMUNICATION UNITS

Base
Large Rest Camp
XI Corps Reinforcement Camp
XIV Corps Reinforcement Camp
2 General Base Depôts
Royal Engineers :
    8th (Monmouth) Army Troops Coy.
    Half No. 32 Base Park Coy.
    Detachment Special Works Coy.
Signal Service :
    Detachment Signal Coy.
    Detachment L. of C. Signal Coy.
    No. 1 Telegraph Construction Coy.
Infantry :
    2 Base Depôts
    3 Coys. 1st Garrison Bn. R. Munster Fusiliers
Army Service Corps :
    2nd Base Depôt (1046th Coy.), H.T. & S.
    Branch Requisition Office
    6th Advanced H.T. Depôt (1045th Coy.)
    Advanced Supply Depôt
    Nos. 6, 32 L. of C. Supply Coys.
    Nos. 24, 25 Field Bakeries
    Nos. 11, 20 Field Butcheries
    Nos. 7, 39, 52, 62, 63, 64 Railhead Supply Detachments
    Base H.T. Depôt
    Base M.T. Coy. (1034th Coy.)

APPENDIX I

Nos. 82 (1035th Coy.), 83 (1036th Coy.) Auxiliary Petrol Coys.
Remounts :
    H.Q. Depot, Nos. 10, 19, 33 Remount Squadrons.
Medical :
    Nos. 1, 4, 14 Sanitary Sections
    Nos. 11, 60, 62 General Hospitals
    Base Depôt Medical Stores
    Nos. 7, 14 Mobile Bacteriological Laboratories
    Nos. 15, 23 Mobile Hygiene Laboratories
    Nos. 15, 18, 21 and 26 Ambulance Trains
Veterinerary :
    Nos. 1, 22 Veterinary Hospitals
    No. 6 Base Depôt Veterinary Stores
Ordnance :
    3, 68, 79, 83 Coys.
    Base Provision Office
    Medium Mobile Workshop
    Railhead Ammunition Detachments
    Railhead Ordnance Detachments
Army Pay Corps, Base Pay Unit
Base Post Office
Censor Section
Labour :
    4th, 6th, 7th, 8th, 10th, 11th Bns. British West Indies Regiment
    16, 172, 195 Coys.
Miscellaneous :
    Claims Commission Office
    Printing & Stationery Depôt
    Convalescent Depôt
    Graves Registration Office

APPENDIX II

ORDER OF BATTLE OF THE BRITISH FORCE IN ITALY

15TH JUNE 1918

Commander-in-Chief	General the Earl of Cavan
B.G.G.S.	Br.-General Hon. J. F. Gathorne-Hardy
D.A. & Q.M.G.	Br.-General H. L. Alexander
Commander R.A.	Br.-General A. E. Wardrop
Commander H.A.	Br.-General T. R. C. Hudson
Chief Engineer	Br.-General C. S. Wilson

APPENDIX II

D.M.S. ... ... Major-General F. R. Newland
Deputy-Director, Transportation ... ... Br.-General G. L. Colvin
Commander, 14th Wing R.A.F. Lieut.-Colonel P. B. Joubert de la Ferté

General Headquarters Troops

Mounted Troops:
    1/1st Northamptonshire Yeomanry
    14th Cyclist Battalion
    12th Motor Machine Gun Bty.

Heavy Artillery:
    XV, XXIV, LXXX, XCIV, 104th Brigades R.G.A.[1]
    19th, 90th, 155th, 1/1st Warwickshire Heavy Batteries R.G.A.
    105, 137, 171, 172, 176, 181, 197, 229, 240, 247, 289, 294, 302, 307, 315, 316, 317, 390, 391, 438 Siege Batteries R.G.A.

Anti-Aircraft Artillery:
    S, V, A.A. Btys.

Royal Engineers:
    285 (Army Troops) Coy. R.E.
    Half Monmouth A.T. Coy. R.E.
    5 Pontoon Park (H.T.)
    Advanced R.E. Park
    Detachment Meteorological Section, R.E.
    6 Field Survey Coy. (with 25, 29 Observation Groups and E Sound Ranging Section)
    34 Anti-Aircraft Searchlight Section R.E.
    Transportation Stores Coy. R.E.

Royal Air Force:
    Fourteenth Wing
    28, 34, 45, 66, 139 Squadrons
    7th Aircraft Park
    9th Balloon Coy.
    7, 33 Balloon Sections

Signal Service:
    G.H.Q. Signal Coy.
    34, 54, 102 Airline Sections
    M, BU Cable Sections
    No. 7 Wireless Observation Group
    15, 24, 80, 94, 104 H.A. Bde. Signal Sections

Pigeon Service:
    70, 71, 72, 73, 74 Horse-drawn Pigeon Lofts

---

[1] Heavy batteries of six 60-pdrs.; siege batteries of four 6-inch hows.

APPENDIX II

Army Service Corps:
  Corps M.T. Column ; Corps Troops M.T. Coy.
  7, 23, 48 Divisional M.T. Coys.
  Corps Siege Park (654th Coy.)
  No. 4 Pontoon Park M.T. (360th Coy.)
  No. 2 Auxiliary Pack Train (443rd Coy.)
  No. 6 Army Auxiliary H.T. Coy. (1047th)
  No. 1 Mobile Repair Unit (93rd Coy.), with 1 Type Press (L)
  Workshop Section for A.A. Btys. (part 423rd Coy.)
  1037th Reserve M.T. Coy.
  Directorate of Requisitions & Hirings, G.H.Q. Branch

Medical:
  36, 41 Motor Ambulance Convoys
  9, 24, 39 Casualty Clearing Stations
  32, 36 Advanced Depôts Medical Stores
  14, 36, 73, 75, 84 Sanitary Sections
  7, 14 Bacteriological Laboratories
  15th Hygiene Laboratory

Ordnance:
  3, 5, 7 Light Mobile Workshops
  4, 11 Medium Mobile Workshops
  No. 6 Heavy Mobile Workshop

Printing & Stationery Services:
  Press, Publications & Photographic Sections

Postal Censorship:
  1 Field Section

Miscellaneous:
  No. 4 Group Lovat's Scouts
  273rd Employment Coy.
  1 Coy. 1st Garrison Battalion, R. Munster Fusiliers
  Claims Commission
  Detachment 109th Light Railway Operating Coy.

7th Division

Commander...	Major-General T. H. Shoubridge
G.S.O.1	Lieut.-Colonel G. W. Howard
	(to 23rd October)
	Lieut.-Colonel W. B. G. Barne
A.A. & Q.M.G.	Lieut.-Colonel B. J. Lang
C.R.A.	Br.-General H. C. Stanley-Clarke
C.R.E.	Lieut.-Colonel E. Barnardiston
	(to 16th October)
	Lieut.-Colonel W. A. FitzG. Kerrich

APPENDIX II

Divisional Troops :
  XXII, XXXV Brigades R.F.A.
  X7, Y7 Trench Mortar Btys. R.A.
  Divisional Ammunition Column
  54th, 95th, 528th (Durham) Field Coys. R.E.
  Divisional Signal Coy.
  Pioneers : 24/Manchester
  Divisional Train (39th, 40th, 42nd, 86th Coys. A.S.C.)
  7th Machine Gun Battalion
  21st, 22nd, 23rd Field Ambulances
  12th Mobile Veterinary Section
  210th Divisional Employment Coy.

20th Brigade	22nd Brigade
Br.-General H. C. R. Green	Br.-General J. McC. Steele
8/Devonshire	2/R. Warwickshire
9/Devonshire*	1/R. Welsh Fusiliers
2/Border Regiment	20/Manchester*
2/Gordon Highlanders	2/1st H.A.C.
20th Trench Mortar Bty.	22nd Trench Mortar Bty.

91st Brigade
Br.-General R. T. Pelly
  2/Queen's
  1/South Staffordshire
  21/Manchester *
  22/Manchester
  91st Trench Mortar Bty.

23rd Division

Commander...	Major-General Sir J. M. Babington (to 15th October)
	Major-General H. F. Thuillier
G.S.O.1	Lieut.-Colonel H. R. Sandilands
A.A. & Q.M.G.	Lieut.-Colonel E. F. Falkner
C.R.A.	Br.-General Sir Dalrymple Arbuthnot, Bt. (to 28th July)
	Br.-General J. Byron
C.R.E.	Lieut.-Colonel E. H. Rooke (to 28th October)
	Major R. A. Turner, acting, to 13th November

---

* Transferred to Western Front in September 1918, on reduction of infantry brigades to 3 battalions.

APPENDIX II

Divisional Troops:
  102nd, 103rd Brigades R.F.A.
  X23, Y23 Trench Mortar Btys., R.A.
  Divisional Ammunition Column
  101st, 102nd, 128th Field Coys. R.E.
  Divisional Signal Coy.
  Pioneers: 9/South Staffordshire
  Divisional Train (190th, 191st, 192nd, 193rd Coys. A.S.C.)
  23rd Machine Gun Battalion
  69th, 70th, 71st Field Ambulances
  35th Mobile Veterinary Section
  223rd Divisional Employment Coy.

68th Brigade	69th Brigade
Br.-General C. D. V. Cary-Barnard	Br.-General A. B. Beauman
10/Northumberland Fusiliers	11/West Yorkshire
11/Northumberland Fusiliers	8/Green Howards
12/Durham L.I.	9/Green Howards*
13/Durham L.I.*	10/Duke of Wellington's
68th Trench Mortar Bty.	69th Trench Mortar Bty.

70th Brigade
  Br.-General H. Gordon
  11/Sherwood Foresters*
  8/K.O.Y.L.I.
  8/York & Lancaster
  9/York & Lancaster
  70th Trench Mortar Bty.

48th (1st South Midland) Division

Commander...	Major-General R. Fanshawe (to 20th June)
	Major-General Sir H. B. Walker
G.S.O.1	Lieut.-Colonel H. C. L. Howard
A.A. & Q.M.G.	Lieut.-Colonel G. H. Barnett
C.R.A.	Br.-General W. Strong
C.R.E.	Lieut.-Colonel E. Briggs

Divisional Troops:
  240th (Gloucester), 241st (Worcester) Brigades R.F.A.
  X48, Y48 Trench Mortar Btys. R.A.
  Divisional Ammunition Column
  474th, 475th, 477th (South Midland) Field Coys. R.E.

---

* Transferred to Western Front in September 1918, on reduction of infantry brigades to 3 battalions.

APPENDIX II

Divisional Signal Coy.
Pioneers : 1/5th R. Sussex
Divisional Train (459th, 460th, 461st, 462nd Coys. A.S.C.)
48th Machine Gun Battalion
1/1st, 1/2nd, 1/3rd South Midland Field Ambulances
1/1st South Midland Mobile Veterinary Section
242nd Divisional Employment Coy.

<table>
<tr><td>143rd Brigade
(Warwickshire)
Br.-General G. C. Sladen
1/5th R. Warwickshire
1/6th R. Warwickshire
1/7th R. Warwickshire
1/8th R. Warwickshire*
143rd Trench Mortar Bty.</td><td>144th Brigade
(Gloucester & Worcester)
Br.-General H. R. Done
1/4th Gloucestershire
1/6th Gloucestershire
1/7th Worcestershire
1/8th Worcestershire*
144th Trench Mortar Bty.</td></tr>
</table>

145th Brigade
(South Midland)
Br.-General D. M. Watt (to 27th August)
Br.-General W. W. Pitt-Taylor (to 14th October)
Lieut.-Colonel L. L. C. Reynolds, acting to 29th October
Br.-General G. W. Howard
    1/5th Gloucestershire*
    1/4th Oxfordshire & Buckinghamshire L.I.
    1/Buckinghamshire Battn., Ox. & B. L.I.
    1/4th R. Berkshire
    145th Trench Mortar Bty.

LINES OF COMMUNICATION UNITS

Administrative Areas :
    Taranto (including Base and Rest Camp) ; Faenza (including Rest Camp) ; Arquata (including Arquata and Genoa Bases) ; Cremona Area.
Royal Engineers :
    158th (Army Troops) Coy.
    8th (Monmouth) Army Troops Coy.
    No. 246 Base Park Coy.
    Detachment 13th Reinforcement Coy.
Signal Service :
    L. of C. Signal Coy. ; No. 6 Telegraph Construction Coy.
Infantry :
    2 Coys. 1st Garrison Battn. R. Munster Fusiliers
    No. 2 (Service) Coy. 1st Garrison Battn. Suffolk Regt.

---

* Transferred to Western Front in September 1918, on reduction of infantry brigades to 3 battalions.

APPENDIX II

Army Service Corps :
  No. 2 Base Depôt (H.T. & S.), 1046th Coy.
  Base Supply Depôt
  L. of C. Supply Coy. (32nd)
  24, 25 Field Bakeries
  7, 52, 62, 64 Railhead Supply Detachments
  11, 20 Field Butcheries
  Base M.T. Depôt (1034th Coy.)
  No. 116 L. of C. Auxiliary Petrol Coy. (1074th)
  Pavia Heavy Repair Shop (1081st Coy.)
  Advanced Supply Depôt
Remounts :
  Depôt, with 10, 19, 33 Remount Squadrons
Medical :
  4, 110, 112, Sanitary Sections (with 8 Sanitary Squads)
  11, 62, 79 General Hospitals
  29, 38, 51 Stationary Hospitals
  Faenza European Hospital
  Taranto Native Hospital (No. 6)
  No. 14 Base, No. 35 Advanced Medical Stores
  18, 22, 30, 31, No. 10 Italian Red Cross Ambulance Trains
  No. 23 Mobile Hygiene Laboratory
  No. 26 Motor Ambulance Convoy, Convalescent Depôt
Army Veterinary Corps :
  1, 22 Veterinary Hospitals ; No. 6 Base Veterinary Stores
Ordnance :
  Base Establishment
  3, 68, 79, 93, 137 Coys. ; No. 142 (Boot Repairing) Coy.
  Base Provision Office
  Cleaning and Repair Establishment
Army Pay Corps : Base Pay Unit
Postal : Base Post Office
Censor Staff : 1 Section
Labour :
  8th, 10th, 11th Battalions British West Indies Regiment
  196th Labour Coy.
  One Labour Coy. (authorized, but unnumbered)
Printing & Stationery Services :
  Army Printing & Stationery Depôts at Genoa and Taranto
Miscellaneous :
  Directorate of Requisitions & Hirings
  Claims Commission
  Expeditionary Force Canteen Staff
  Central Requisition Staff
  M.F.O. and R.T.O. Establishments
  Caesar's Camp (Reinforcements) ; Vaje Camp (Details)
  H.Q. Base Depôt

Subsequent Changes

In October the 7th and 23rd Divisions were formed into the XIV Corps under Lieut.-General Sir James Babington, the 48th being left with the Italian XII Corps.

APPENDIX III

ORDER OF BATTLE OF THE FRENCH FORCES IN ITALY

NOVEMBER 1917

TENTH ARMY

Commander... ... ... General Duchêne
Chief of the General Staff... Colonel Brion

Army Artillery :
    Attached XXXI Corps :
        Field : 219th F.A. Regt. (9 batteries of 75-mm.)
        Mountain : 6 groups of 3 batteries
        Heavy : 16 groups (6 of 155-mm. L.s. ; 8 of 155-mm. S.s. ; 2 of 155-mm. s.)
    Attached XII Corps :
        Heavy : 2 groups of 155-mm. L.s. ; 4 groups of 155-mm. S.s.

46th (Chasseur) Division (General Levi)

47th (Chasseur) Division (General Dilleman)

XXXI Corps (General Rozée d'Infreville) :
    64th Division (General Colin)
    65th Division (General Blondin)
    Corps Artillery :
        Field : 264th F.A. Regt. (6 batteries of 75-mm.)
        Heavy : 1 group of 105-mm. S. ; 1 group of 120-mm. L.

XII Corps (General Nourrisson) :
    23rd Division (General Bonfait)
    24th Division (General Odry)
    Corps Artillery :
        Field : 52nd F.A. Regt. (6 batteries of 75-mm.)
        Heavy : 1 group of 105-mm. S. ; 1 group of 120-mm. L.s.

TOTAL

    2 corps of 2 divisions each
    2 independent divisions
    32 groups of heavy artillery (**224 guns**)

APPENDIX IV

ORDER OF BATTLE OF THE ITALIAN ARMIES
24TH OCTOBER 1917

Third Army (Lieut.-General Duke of Aosta):
  XXIII Corps (45th, 28th, 61st Divisions)
  XIII Corps (54th, 14th Divisions)
  XI Corps reserve (58th, 31st Divisions)
  XXV Corps reserve (33rd, 4th Divisions)

Second Army (Lieut.-General Capello):
  VIII Corps, General Grazioli (7th, 59th, 48th Divisions)
  VI Corps, General Lombardi (24th, 66th Divisions)
  II Corps, General Albricci (8th, 44th, 67th Divisions)
  XXIV Corps, General Caviglia (10th, 68th, 49th Divisions)
  XXVII Corps, General Badoglio (64th, 22nd, 65th, 19th Divisions and 10th Alpine Group)
  IV Corps, General Cavaciocchi (43rd, 60th, 34th Divisions)
  Reserve:
    XXVIII Corps (23rd, 47th Divisions)
    XIV Corps (30th, 25th Divisions)
    VII Corps (3rd, 62nd Divisions)

Carnia Zone (Lieut.-General Tassioni):
  XII Corps (26th, 36th Divisions)

Fourth Army (Lieut.-General Nicolis di Robilant) (Cadore):
  XXVIII Corps (15th, 51st, 56th Divisions)
  IX Corps (17th, 18th Divisions)
  VI Alpine Group
  I Corps (1st Division)

First Army (Lieut.-General Count Pecori-Giraldi) (Trentino):
  XXIX Corps (27th, 37th Divisions)
  V Corps (55th, 69th Divisions)
  X Corps (9th, 32nd Divisions)
  XXVI Corps (11th, 12th Divisions)
  XXII Corps (2nd, 57th Divisions)
  XX Corps (29th, 52nd Divisions)
  Reserve: 1 brigade

III Corps (Lieut.-General Count Camerana) (West of Lake Garda):
  (5th, 6th Divisions)

Albania: (5 divisions)

Tripoli: (2 divisions, 16 battalions, 8 of which native)

Ægean: (3 battalions)

G.H.Q. Troops:
  In Third Army area : XXX Corps (16th, 20th, 21st, 63rd Divisions)
  In Second Army area : 13th, 53rd, 60th Divisions
  In Fourth Army area : 5 cyclist battalions
  1st, 2nd, 3rd, 4th Cavalry Divisions

APPENDIX V

ORDER OF BATTLE OF THE ITALIAN ARMIES
(Including French and British Contingents)

15TH JUNE 1918

(Additions in October in italics; Reductions indicated by Footnote References)

Third Army (Lieut.-General the Duke of Aosta) :
  (¹) XI Corps (23rd, 31st, 45th Divisions)
  (⁷) XXIII Corps (4th, 61st Divisions and 12th Cyclist Battalion)
  XXVIII Corps (25th, 53rd Divisions)
  2nd Cavalry Division
Eighth Army (Lieut.-General Caviglia) :
  VIII Corps (48th, 58th Divisions)
  XXVII Corps (51st, 66th Divisions)
  (⁷) XXX Corps (47th, 50th Divisions)
  XVIII Corps
  XXII Corps
Fourth Army (Lieut.-General Giardino)
  (²) I Corps (24th, 70th Divisions)
  VI Corps (15th, 59th Divisions)
  IX Corps (17th, 18th Divisions)
  (³) XVIII Corps (1st, 56th Divisions)
Sixth Army (Lieut.-General Montuori) :
  XIII Corps (14th, 28th Divisions)
  XX Corps (2nd, 10th Divisions)
  XII Corps
  (²) French XII Corps (23rd and 24th Divisions)
  (¹) British XIV Corps (7th, 23rd, 48th Divisions)
First Army (Lieut.-General Count Pecori-Giraldi) :
  V Corps (29th, 55th, 69th Divisions)
  X Corps (9th, 12th, 32nd Divisions)
  XXIX Corps (26th, 34th, 54th Divisions)
Seventh Army (Lieut.-General Tassoni) :
  III Corps (5th, 75th Divisions)
  (⁴) X IV Corps (6th, 20th, 21st, 22nd Divisions)
  X XV Corps

APPENDIX V

Ninth Army (Lieut.-General Morrone):
  (⁵) XII Corps (27th, 37th Divisions)
  (³) XXII Corps (57th, 60th Divisions)
  (⁶) XXV Corps (7th, 33rd Divisions)
  (⁷) XXVI Corps (11th, 13th Divisions)
  XIV Corps
  XXI Corps
  Storm Corps (Storm, Czechoslovak)
  4th Cavalry Division
G.H.Q. troops 1st and 4th Cavalry Divisions

Subsequent changes

On the 14th October were brought into existence :*

Tenth Army (General Lord Cavan):
  XIV Corps (7th and 23rd British divisions)
  XI Corps (23rd and 37th Italian divisions)
Twelfth Army (General Graziani):
  I Corps (24th and 70th divisions)
  XII (French) Corps (23rd French and 52nd)
Cavalry Corps (Count of Turin):
  1st, 2nd, 3rd, 4th Cavalry Divisions

(¹) In October to Tenth Army, British XIV Corps less 48th Division
(²) In October to Twelfth Army less French 24th Division
(³) In October to Eighth Army
(⁴) In October to Ninth Army
(⁵) To Sixth Army
(⁶) To Seventh Army
(⁷) Drop out

APPENDIX VI

ORDER OF BATTLE OF THE AUSTRO-GERMAN FORCES IN THE ITALIAN THEATRE AT THE BEGINNING OF THE CAPORETTO OFFENSIVE

Commander-in-Chief ... The Emperor and King, Karl
Chief of the General Staff... General Freiherr Arz von Straussenburg

A. GROUP OF ARMIES ARCHDUKE EUGEN ON THE SOUTH-WESTERN FRONT:
Commanding-in-Chief ... Field-Marshal Archduke Eugen
Chief of the General Staff ... Major-General Konopicky

---

* The reorganization is given at the beginning of Chapter XIV.

German Fourteenth Army (General Otto von Below):
    Krauss's (Alfred) Corps:
        3 Austro-Hungarian, 1 German (Jäger) divisions
    Stein's Corps:
        1 Austro-Hungarian division
        3 German divisions (12th, 117th, Alpine Corps)
    Berrer's Corps:
        2 German divisions (26th, 220th)
    Scotti's Corps:
        1 Austro-Hungarian division
        1 German division

Isonzo Command (General-Colonel von Boroevic):
    Reserve:
        3 Austro-Hungarian divisions

Second Isonzo Army (General Ritter von Henriquez):
    Kosak's Corps:
        3 Austro-Hungarian divisions
    XXIV Corps (Lukas):
        2 Austro-Hungarian divisions
    IV Corps (Schönburg-Hartenstein):
        2 Austro-Hungarian divisions
    II Corps (Kaiser) (in reserve):
        3 divisions

First Isonzo Army (General-Colonel Freiherr von Wurm):
    XVI Corps (Kralicek):
        3 Austro-Hungarian divisions
    VII Corps (Schariczer):
        3 Austro-Hungarian divisions
    XXIII Corps (Csicserics):
        3 Austro-Hungarian divisions
    21st Rifle Division (in reserve)

B. GROUP OF ARMIES CONRAD ON THE TRENTINO FRONT:

Commanding-in-Chief ... Field-Marshal Freiherr Conrad von Hötzendorf
Chief of the General Staff ... Major-General Richard Müller

Eleventh Army (General-Colonel Graf Scheuchenstuel):
    XIV (Edelweiss) Corps:
        1 Austro-Hungarian division
        1 Austro-Hungarian brigade
    III Corps:
        3 Austro-Hungarian divisions
        1 Mountain Group
    XX Corps:
        3 Austro-Hungarian divisions

Tenth Army:
  This Army (General-Colonel Freiherr von Krobatin), in the entirely mountain sector in the west, contained 1 division and 2 mountain brigades, totalling 29½ battalions and 10 companies and local levies. Until 31st October 1917, it belonged to Conrad's Command, but then passed from it to the Archduke Eugen's Group.

APPENDIX VII

ORDER OF BATTLE OF THE AUSTRO-HUNGARIAN ARMIES

15TH JUNE 1918

Commander-in-Chief ... The Emperor and King, Karl
Chief of the General Staff ... General-Colonel Freiherr Arz von Straussenburg

FIELD-MARSHAL FREIHERR CONRAD VON HOTZENDORF'S[1] GROUP OF ARMIES

Chief of the Staff ... ... Field-Marshal-Lieutenant Richard Müller

Tenth Army (Field-Marshal Freiherr von Krobatin):
  Group Archduke Peter Ferdinand:
    1st, 22nd Divisions; 163rd, 164th Brigades
  XX Corps (General Edler von Kaiser):
    49th Division; Riva Detachment
  XXI Corps (General Freiherr von Luegendorf):
    19th, 56th Divisions
  XIV Corps (General Edler von Verdross):
    Kaiser Jäger Division; 159th Brigade
  Reserve:
    9 battalions

Eleventh Army (General-Colonel Graf Scheuchenstuel):
  III Corps (General-Colonel von Martiny):
    6th Cavalry, 6th, 28th, 52nd Divisions
  XIII Corps (General von Csanady):
    5th, 16th Divisions; 38th, 42nd, 74th Honved Divisions
  VI Corps (General Edler von Kletter):
    Edelweiss, 18th, 26th Divisions
  XXVI Corps (General Edler von Horsetzky):
    4th, 27th, 32nd Divisions
  I Corps (General Kosak):
    55th, 66th Divisions

---

[1] In July he was superseded by the Archduke Joseph, who in October was succeeded, in turn, by Field-Marshal Krobatin.

XV Corps (General Scotti) :
  48th, 50th Divisions ; 20th Honved Division
Reserve :
  3rd, 10th Cavalry, 36th, 53rd Divisions

FIELD-MARSHAL RITTER VON BOROEVIC'S GROUP OF ARMIES :
Chief of the Staff ... ... Major-General Ritter von Pitreich

Sixth Army (Archduke Joseph) :
  II Corps (General Rudolf Krauss) :
    8th Cavalry Division
  XXIV Corps (Field-Marshal-Lieut. Goiginger) :
    31st, 13th, 17th Divisions
  Reserve :
    11th Cavalry Division ; Group of Cyclist Battalions
Isonzo Army (General-Colonel Freiherr von Wurm) :
  XVI Corps (General Kralicek) :
    33rd, 46th, 58th Divisions
  IV Corps (General Prince Schönburg-Hartenstein) :
    64th, 70th Honved, 29th Divisions
  VII Corps (General Freiherr von Schariczer) :
    9th Cavalry, 14th, 24th, 44th Divisions
  XXIII Corps (General von Csicserics) :
    1st Cavalry, 10th, 12th Divisions
  Reserve :
    57th Division, 201st *Landsturm* Brigade ; 2 Cyclist Battalions
G.H.Q. Reserve :
  9th, 35th, 41st, 51st Honved, 12th Mounted Rifle Divisions

Subsequent Changes

In September 1918, the left wing of the Eleventh Army, consisting of the I, XV and XXVI Corps, was formed into the Army Group Belluno (Field-Marshal Ritter von Goglia) and transferred to Boroevic's Group of Armies.

APPENDIX VIII

THE SECRET TREATY WITH ITALY

(THE PACT OF LONDON : 26TH APRIL 1915)

The following is the authorized English text of the Secret Treaty with Italy, published in 1920 as a Parliamentary paper :

Agreement between France, Russia, Great Britain and Italy, signed at London, April 26th 1915.

By order of his Government, the Marquis Imperiali, Ambassador of His Majesty the King of Italy, has the honour to communicate to the Rt. Hon. Sir Edward Grey, His Britannic Majesty's Principal Secretary of State for Foreign Affairs, and to their Excellencies M. Paul Cambon, Ambassador of the French Republic, and to Count de Benckendorff, Ambassador of His Majesty the Emperor of All the Russias, the following memorandum :

MEMORANDUM

Article 1

A military convention shall be immediately concluded between the General Staffs of France, Great Britain, Italy and Russia. This convention shall settle the minimum number of military forces to be employed by Russia against Austria-Hungary in order to prevent that Power from concentrating all its strength against Italy in the event of Russia deciding to direct her principal effort against Germany.

This military convention shall settle question of armistices, which necessarily comes within the scope of the commanders-in-chief of the Armies.

Article 2

On her part, Italy undertakes to use her entire resources for the purpose of waging war jointly with France, Great Britain and Russia against all their enemies.

Article 3

The French and British fleets shall render active and permanent assistance to Italy until such time as the Austro-Hungarian fleet shall have been destroyed or until peace shall have been concluded.

A naval convention shall be immediately concluded to this effect between France, Great Britain and Italy.

Article 4

Under the Treaty of Peace, Italy shall obtain the Trentino, Cisalpine Tyrol with its geographical and natural frontier (the Brenner frontier), as well as Trieste, the countries of Gorizia and Gradisca, all Istria as far as the Quarnero and including Volosca and the Istrian islands of Cherso and Lussin, as well as the small islands of Plavnik, Unie, Canidole, Palazzuoli, San Pietro di Nembi, Asinello, Gruica, and the neighbouring islets.

Note

The frontier required to ensure execution of Article 4 hereof shall be traced as follows :

From the Piz Umbrail as far as north of the Stelvio, it shall follow the crest of the Rhetiàn Alps up to the sources of the Adige and the Eisach, then following the Reschen and Brenner mountains and the Oetz and Ziller heights. The frontier shall then bend towards the south, cross Mt. Toblach and join the present frontier of the Carnic Alps. It shall follow this frontier line as far as Mt. Tarvis and from Mt. Tarvis the watershed of the Julian Alps by the Predil Pass, Mt. Margart, the Tricorno (Terglu) and the watersheds of the Podberdo, Podlaniscam and Idria passes. From this point the frontier shall follow a south-easterly direction towards the Schneeberg, leaving the entire basin of the Save and its tributaries outside Italian territory. From the Schneeberg the frontier shall come down to the coast in such a way as to include Castua, Mattuglia and Volosca within Italian territory.

Article 5

Italy shall also be given the province of Dalmatia within its present administrative boundaries, including to the north Lisarica and Tribani ; to the south as far as a line starting from Cape Planka on the coast and following eastwards the crest of the heights forming the watershed in such a way as to leave within Italian territory all the valleys and streams flowing towards Sebenico—such as the Cicola, Kerka, Butisnica and their tributaries. She shall also obtain all the islands situate to the north and west of Dalmatia, from Premuda, Selve, Ulbo, Scherda, Maon, Pago and Patadura to the north, up to Meleda to the south, including Sant'Andrea, Busi, Lissa, Lesina, Tercola, Curzola, Cazza and Lagosta, as well as the neighbouring rocks and islets and Pelagosa, with the exception of Greater and Lesser Zirona, Bua, Solta and Brazza.

To be neutralized :

(1) The entire coast from Cape Planka on the north to the southern base of the peninsula of Sabbioncello in the south, so as to include the whole of that peninsula ; (2) the portion of the coast which begins in the north at a point situated 10 kilometres south of the headland of Ragusa Vecchia extending southward as far as the River Voïussa, in such a way as to include the gulf and ports of Cattaro, Antivari, Dulcigno, St. Jean de Medua and Durazzo, without prejudice to the rights of Montenegro consequent on the declarations exchanged between the Powers in April and May 1909. As these rights only apply to the present Montenegrin territory, they cannot be extended to any territory or ports which may be assigned to Montenegro. Consequently neutralization shall not apply to any part of the coast now belonging to Montenegro. There shall be maintained all restrictions concerning the port of Antivari which were accepted by Montenegro in 1909 ; (3) finally, all the islands not given to Italy.

APPENDIX VIII 413

Note

The following Adriatic territory shall be assigned by the four Allied Powers to Croatia, Serbia and Montenegro :

In the Upper Adriatic, the whole coast from the bay of Volosca on the borders of Istria as far as the northern frontier of Dalmatia, including the coast which is at present Hungarian and all the coast of Croatia, with the port of Fiume and the small ports of Novi and Carlopago, as well as the islands of Veglia, Pervichio, Gregorio, Goli and Arbe. And, in the Lower Adriatic (in the region interesting Serbia and Montenegro) the whole coast from Cape Planka as far as the River Drin, with the important harbours of Spalato, Ragusa, Cattaro, Antivari, Dulcigno and St. Jean de Medua and the islands of Greater and Lesser Zirona, Bua, Solta, Brazza, Jaclian and Calamotta. The port of Durazzo to be assigned to the independent Moslem State of Albania.

Article 6

Italy shall receive full sovereignty over Valona, the island of Saseno and surrounding territory of sufficient extent to assure defence of these points (from the Voïussa to the north and east, approximately to the northern boundary of the district of Chimara on the south).

Article 7

Should Italy obtain the Trentino and Istria in accordance with the provisions of Article 4, together with Dalmatia and the Adriatic islands within the limits specified in Article 5, and the Bay of Valona (Article 6), and if the central portion of Albania is reserved for the establishment of a small autonomous neutralized State, Italy shall not oppose the division of Northern and Southern Albania between Montenegro, Serbia and Greece, should France, Great Britain and Russia so desire. The coast from the southern boundary of the Italian territory of Valona (see Article 6) up to Cape Stylos shall be neutralized.

Italy shall be charged with the representation of the State of Albania in its relations with foreign Powers.

Italy agrees, moreover, to leave sufficient territory in any event to the east of Albania to ensure the existence of a frontier line between Greece and Serbia to the west of Lake Ochrida.

Article 8

Italy shall receive entire sovereignty over the Dodecanese Islands which she is at present occupying.

Article 9

Generally speaking, France, Great Britain and Russia recognize that Italy is interested in the maintenance of the balance of power in the Mediterranean and that, in the event of the total partition of Turkey in Asia, she ought to obtain a just share of the Mediterranean region adjacent to the province of Adalia, where Italy has already acquired rights and interests which formed the subject of an Italo-British convention. The zone which shall eventually be allotted to Italy shall be delimited, at the proper time, due account being taken of the existing interests of France and Great Britain.

The interests of Italy shall also be taken into consideration in the event of the territorial integrity of the Turkish Empire being maintained and of alterations being made in the zones of interest of the Powers.

If France, Great Britain and Russia occupy any territories in Turkey in Asia during the course of the war, the Mediterranean region bordering on the Province of Adalia within the limits indicated above shall be reserved to Italy, who shall be entitled to occupy it.

Article 10

All rights and privileges in Libya at present belonging to the Sultan by virtue of the Treaty of Lausanne are transferred to Italy.

Article 11

Italy shall receive a share of any eventual war indemnity corresponding to her efforts and her sacrifices.

Article 12

Italy declares that she associates herself in the declaration made by France, Great Britain and Russia to the effect that Arabia and the Moslem Holy Places in Arabia shall be left under the authority of an independent Moslem Power.

Article 13

In the event of France and Great Britain increasing their colonial territories in Africa at the expense of Germany, those two Powers agree in principle that Italy may claim some equitable compensation, particularly as regards the settlement in her favour of the questions relative to the frontiers of the Italian colonies of Eritrea, Somaliland and Libya and the neighbouring colonies belonging to France and Great Britain.

Article 14

Great Britain undertakes to facilitate the immediate conclusion, under equitable conditions, of a loan of at least 50,000,000*l.* to be issued on the London market.

Article 15

France, Great Britain and Russia shall support such opposition as Italy may make to any proposal in the direction of introducing a representative of the Holy See in any peace negotiations or negotiations for the settlement of questions raised by the present war.

APPENDIX VIII

Article 16

The present arrangement shall be held secret. The adherence of Italy to the Declaration of the 5th September, 1914, shall alone be made public, immediately upon declaration of war by or against Italy.

After having taken note of the foregoing memorandum, the representatives of France, Great Britain and Russia, duly authorized to that effect, have concluded the following agreement with the representative of Italy, also duly authorized by his Government:

France, Great Britain and Russia give their full assent to the memorandum presented by the Italian Government.

With reference to Articles 1, 2 and 3 of the memorandum, which provide for military and naval co-operation between the four Powers, Italy declares that she will take the field at the earliest possible date and within a period not exceeding one month from the signature of these presents.

In faith whereof the undersigned have signed the present agreement and have affixed thereto their seals.

Done at London, in quadruplicate, the 26th day of April, 1915.

E. GREY.
IMPERIALI.
BENCKENDORFF.
PAUL CAMBON.

II

DECLARATION BY WHICH FRANCE, GREAT BRITAIN, ITALY AND RUSSIA UNDERTAKE NOT TO CONCLUDE A SEPARATE PEACE DURING THE COURSE OF THE PRESENT EUROPEAN WAR.

The Italian Government, having decided to participate in the present war with the French, British and Russian Governments and to accede to the Declaration made at London, the 5th September, 1914, by the three above-named Governments.

The undersigned, being duly authorized by their respective Governments, make the following declaration:

The French, British, Italian and Russian Governments mutually undertake not to conclude a separate peace during the course of the present war.

The four Governments agree that, whenever there may be occasion to discuss the terms of peace, none of the Allied Powers shall lay down any conditions of peace without previous agreement with each of the other Allies.

In faith whereof the undersigned have signed the present Declaration and have affixed thereto their seals.

Done at London, in quadruplicate, the 26th day of April, 1915.

> E. GREY.
> IMPERIALI
> BENCKENDORFF.
> PAUL CAMBON.

III

DECLARATION

The Declaration of the 26th April, 1915, whereby France, Great Britain, Italy and Russia undertake not to conclude a separate peace during the present European war, shall remain secret.

After the declaration of war by or against Italy, the four Powers shall sign a new declaration in identical terms, which shall thereupon be made public.

In faith whereof the undersigned have executed the present Declaration and have affixed thereto their seals.

Done at London, in quadruplicate, the 26th day of April, 1915.

> E. GREY.
> IMPERIALI.
> BENCKENDORFF.
> PAUL CAMBON.

APPENDIX IX

OFFICIAL REPORT OF THE CONVENTION IN THE EVENT OF CO-OPERATION OF BRITISH TROOPS IN ITALY

7TH MAY 1917

(A) PREMISES

(1) Should it become desirable to transfer a British force to the Italian theatre, the sending of such a force and its strength will depend upon the conditions existing at the time. The preliminary studies are based on the possible transfer of a force of six divisions with their own services (about 120,000 men and 26,000 animals).

(2) The Italian military authorities shall put at the disposal of the British Army :—

(a) The places necessary for the establishment of the Base and of the Advance Depôts. The Italian authorities will prepare all the necessary works, huts and sheds required for this in good time, and any works, huts and sheds that may be subsequently required.

(b) They will carry out the transport of the supplies from the frontier to the Bases and from the latter to the troops.

(3) Officers of the Italian General Staff will be attached to the British Command for purposes of liaison.

An officer from the transport service of the Italian General Staff will be attached to British Headquarters in order to insure the efficient working of the transport of British troops and material.

(4) During the period of concentration, maintenance, sanitation, etc., will be carried out by the Italian authorities through the intendance of the particular Army in whose district the British troops are assembling.

When the concentration is completed, these services will be carried out by the British authorities, at all events, for the first month ; subsequently, the Italian authorities will assist in the provision of supplies for men and horses of the British Force as far as the resources available permit.

(B) CONCENTRATION OF BRITISH TROOPS.[1]

(5) Intervention of British troops may take place towards the western frontier or towards the Trentino. The zone of concentration of British troops will be decided at the time according to the military situation. The zone in question, however, will be approximately as follows :—

(a) On the western side, the territory included in [Area 3].

(b) In the Trentino zone : [Area 1].

It is possible that the British intervention might precede the French. In that case, the zone of concentration would be that included in [Area 2].

(6) It is not possible to state what time will elapse between the moment when the order is given to begin the concentration until the moment when the first trainloads of troops cross the frontier, because that depends on the number of trains that France will put at the disposal of the British, and on the military situation at the moment.

Three full days would be required after the time that the movement was ordered before the trains on the Italian side would be in readiness to commence running.

---

[1] See Sketch 2.

(7) The transfer of troops from the frontier to these areas would be carried out by the Italian authorities on the plan already drawn up for the movement of a French force, viz :

12 through trains per 24 hours via Modane
16 ,, ,, ,, ,, Ventimiglia
8 trains per 24 hours ... from Aosta
6 ,, ,, ... ,, Susa
6 ,, ,, ... ,, Pinerolo
8 ,, ,, ... ,, Tenda
6 ,, ,, ... ,, Savona

in all 62 trains per 24 hours, which would be maintained until such time as the movement was completed.

(C) MAINTENANCE OF THE TROOPS DURING THE PERIOD OF CONCENTRATION

(8) *Medical Service.* The British troops will be sent with all the organization and material necessary for the working of their medical services. Such organizations will form part of each division.

The Italians will put at their immediate disposal in Hospital accommodation :

(a) About 5,000 beds in the zone into which the sick and wounded will be evacuated by motor transport, and definitely within Area 1 as follows :

Vicenza, 1,000 beds ; *Padua,* 1,000 ; *Montagnana,* 500 ; *Rovigo,* 2,000 ; *Este,* 500.

In Area 2 :

Vicenza, 1,000 beds ; *Verona,* 1,000 ; *Montagnana,* 500 ; *Legnago,* 500 ; *Este,* 500 ; *Rovigo,* 2,000.

In Area 3 :

Milan, 1,500 beds ; *Mortara,* 250 ; *Pavia,* 2,000 ; *Lodi,* 500 ; *Vigevano,* 500.

(b) About 4,000 beds in the hospitals situated near the Base into which the evacuation will be executed by ambulance trains :

Genoa, 2,000 beds ; *Celle Ligure,* 700 ; *S. Remo and environs,* 2,000.

The number of beds in the vicinity of the Base will be increased should the necessity arise.

(c) 100 beds (in huts) with the necessary administration buildings at the Base for the use of the troops actually employed there. The evacuation of the sick and wounded will be carried out as far as the frontier by means of Italian ambulance trains and beyond the frontier by English trains that are already in France.

(9) *Supplies.* The Italian authorities will provide the supplies for the troops which cross by road from the moment they enter Italian territory.

APPENDIX IX

The British troops coming through the whole way by train will bring with them two days' rations for consumption on arriving in the area of concentration in case the Italian authorities are unable to make provision in time.

In the concentration zone, the Italian authorities will provide the supplies from the third day of the arrival of the British troops. Therefore, the troops coming by road will be supplied, besides the rations for the journey, with two rations for consumption on arrival in the concentration area.

The ration which will be issued during this period to the English troops will be the same as that recently agreed upon by the Comando Supremo and the British Military Attaché (Gen. Delmé-Radcliffe) for the British batteries, viz.:

	Bread	700 g.
	Fresh meat	350 g. (or 330 g. if frozen)
	Cheese	70 g.
(1)	Potatoes	200 g. (or beans, g. 80)
	Beans	80 g.
	Roast coffee	15 g.
	Tea	10 g.
	Sugar	50 g.
	Wine	25 cl. (3 times a week)
	Sauce	one ration (or bacon or oil, g. 15)
	Salt	20 g.
	Pepper	0.5 g.
(2)	Lean bacon	60 g.
	Marsala wine	15 cl. (8 times a month)
(3)	or Aniseed Liqueur Quinine Liqueur 4 cl. (7 times a month)	
	Lemon	one

(Salted fish will not be accepted as a substitute for meat.)

Once the Base has started working everything will be furnished by the British authorities.

(10) *Service of the Lines of Communication.* The Italian authorities will establish the following posts on the lines of communication:

(a) at S. Dalmazzo di Tenda for the troops arriving by the Colle di Tenda;

(b) at Pragelato and Pinerolo for the troops coming down by the Monginevra [from Briançon];

(c) at Susa for the troops coming by Mont Cenis;

(d) at Aosta for the troops coming down by the Valley of Aosta.

During the period of concentration, they will establish suitable

---

(1) To be distributed whenever possible.
(2) In default, they will distribute an equal quantity of bacon.
(3) To be distributed only by the order of the commander of the troops.

depôts in the zone of concentration. One British officer and two non-commissioned officers will be attached to each depôt.

The Italian authorities will provide each of such stations with two soldiers who know English to act as interpreters.

At the detraining station in France there will be guides provided to show the British troops the way through the mountain passes.

(11) The Italian authorities will put at the disposal of the British Command 500 new motor lorries at Turin. The personnel for these lorries shall be previously sent by the British for their organization into companies. A portion of this number of lorries will be collected near the frontier for the use of the troops that are marching across it. Orders in connection with this service will be given by the British authorities at the right moment. Petrol and lubricating oil will be furnished by the Italian authorities.

The Italian authorities undertake to maintain these lorries in working order, furnishing the necessary spare parts, tyres, etc.

(12) *Postal Services.* Will be carried out in the same manner as the Italian and in the existing depôts, but by English personnel (two men per division will be allotted for this service).

(13) *Telegraph Service.* An Italian telegraph officer, who knows English, will be attached to the British Staff. He will be in possession of a plan showing all telegraph lines.

Existing telegraph and telephone lines can be utilized by the British forces.

The British will construct such telegraph extensions as may be required for their own use in the course of subsequent operations.

(14) *Billeting Arrangements and Camping.* In the zone of concentration the British troops will be billeted in the localities which have already been indicated. At the detraining station, however, on the frontier and during the halts at the end of each march which takes place on the Italian side, the troops which cannot be billeted will encamp. The Italian authorities will provide to send to the zone of concentration the number of tents required for the British troops. The British troops will retain the tents issued for use when they leave the zone of concentration and billeting is no longer possible. As to the march lines along which the billeting of troops should not be possible, the Italian authorities will prepare a convenient number of tents at the first halting place on the frontier.

(15) *Maps.* The Italian authorities undertake to provide the following maps :—

	1/100,000	1/200,000	1/500,000
For British Staff ...	50	50	10
For each division ...	900	1,750	100

APPENDIX IX

Maps will refer to the zone in which the operations may possibly develop. Such maps will be consigned in suitable cases to the G.H.Q. of the divisions as they arrive in the zone of concentration. On every case will be indicated the number of the maps contained by it, the scale of the maps and the zone to which they refer.

A key will be handed to the Chief of Staff of every division.

Maps on scale of 1/25,000 of zone of concentration will also be supplied in the following quantities:

> 12 for the H.Q. Staff.
> 6 for every division.
> 12 for the Base.

On these latter maps will be marked the various Sectors in which the Divisions will probably be billeted.

(16) *Interpreters.* The Italian authorities have consented to provide interpreters who will be detailed to the various units composing the British forces on the scale set forth below.

These interpreters will remain attached to those units during the period that the British force is operating in the Italian theatre.

In the case of the units detraining in French territory and marching across the frontier the interpreters will join such units at the frontier. Interpreters attached to units which make the whole journey by rail will join their units at the detraining station in Italy.

Interpreters will be provided upon the following scale:

> Per division 47
> H.Q. of a corps ... 4
> G.H.Q. 4

(D) THE WORKING OF THE SERVICES AFTER CONCENTRATION

(17) The Base which has been selected is at Arquata. Accommodation at the cold storages at Genoa, and if necessary at Milan, will be placed at the disposal of the British authorities for the storing of meat.

The internal working of the Base and advanced depôts is entirely in the hands of the British authorities.

The transfer to the British Command of the functions exercised by the Italian authorities during the period of concentration will be carried out by arrangement between the British and the Italian authorities as soon as the former are in a position to assume these functions.

For working parties at the Base at Arquata, the Italian Command will detail 500 men.

The maintenance of roads will be continued by the Italian authorities.

Dalla Sede dell'Intendenza Generale dell'Esercito
il 4 Maggio 1917.

LOMBARDI STEFANO,
Intendente Generale.
J. H. V. CROWE,
Br.-General, General Staff.

(1) *Discipline.*
The British authorities will deal with all offences committed by British troops, whether against British or Italian subjects.

(2) *Liaison Officers.*
The Italian authorities will provide Liaison Officers, as follows :
        To General Headquarters ... 2 Staff Officers.
        To each division ... ... 1 Staff Officer.
These officers will join on the arrival of the British Force in the area of concentration and will be provided with their own motor cars, etc.

GENERAL C. PORRO.
As regards No. 2; leaving No. 1 in abeyance.
J. H. V. CROWE,
Br.-General, General Staff.

Comando Supremo
7th May 1917.

SUPPLEMENT TO THE OFFICIAL REPORT OF THE CONVENTION IN THE EVENT OF CO-OPERATION OF BRITISH TROOPS IN ITALY

A. As it is not practicable to allot definite telegraph and telephone lines of the Italian systems to the British forces in the areas of concentration and between these areas and the base at Arquata, the lines and facilities will be so augmented as to ensure any service that may be required.

If so desired, British personnel may be attached to the telephone offices, in addition to the Italian personnel, for the communications in English. Any telegraph or telephone material which the British troops bring with them can be employed when, how and where desired by the British Military authorities, either to supplement existing communications or to construct new lines in the area of operations.

B. (1) No special arrangements have been made for halts for food (except the halte-repas* where coffee is to be supplied) as it is assumed that the rations carried by the troops will be eaten in the trains.

---

* The location of the halte-repas will be notified later.

APPENDIX IX

Should any further supply of fresh food (in addition to the rations supplied for the journey which include bread or biscuits) be desired at the halte-repas notice should be given to the Italian authorities, who will examine how this can be done.

(2) Good drinking water is abundant at all the stations. To facilitate the supply of water to the troops, metal buckets will be supplied at all the stations, where halts of some duration take place, on the scale of 100 buckets for each train.

(3) Field latrines, giving accommodation for 100 men at a time, will be constructed at Turin, Milan, Verona, Sampierdarena, Allessandria, Bologna, Monselice and Mestre ; also at the entraining stations. At all other places the troops would use the ordinary station latrines.

C. The Italian authorities will put up standing tent camps, as necessary in order to supplement billeting accommodation at halting places on the march over the Alps.

The Italian authorities will provide food at all halting places on the Italian side of the frontier for the troops that have to march across the frontier. This provision is covered by paragraph 9 of the Convention.

D. The Italian Port Authorities at Genoa have agreed with the Italian General Staff to reserve, for the exclusive use of the British forces, on three days' notice being given, lengthwise berths for 11 steamers simultaneously as a minimum. A daily rate of discharge from the steamers has also been guaranteed, with a minimum of 600 tons per steamer per day, rising to 2,000 tons per steamer per day according to the material to be unloaded. This rate of discharge is guaranteed on condition that the personnel of the " Consorzio Autonomo del Porto di Genoa " is employed for the work. A translation of the rules of the Consorzio and of the scale of charges for the unloading of ships will be furnished to the British authorities.

E. The Italian authorities agree to a representative of the British Directorate of Transportation being at the Headquarters of the Italian Commissione di Linea during the whole period of the movement by rail. Paragraph VI of the French Convention provides for a representative of the Directorate of Transportation to be at the Directorate of Transports of the Intendenza Generale of the Italian Army ; also for an officer to be at the Commissione di Linea at Turin and for another to be at the Commissione di Linea at Genoa ; further for a party of officers from the Directorate of Transportation to be detached to Milan to be employed when and where required.

F. The appointment of Liaison Officers, including a British General Staff Officer to the Headquarters of the Italian Army in the area of which the concentration is taking place, is agreed to by the Italian authorities. The name of the British officer selected will be communicated to the Italian authorities through the Head of the British Military Mission attached to the Comando Supremo ; the names of the Italian officer or officers to be attached to the British Headquarters will be telegraphed to the Chief of the Imperial General Staff at the War Office, London, on receipt of orders for the movement.

G. The Italian authorities agree that, at the proper time, orders shall be given to the Military Treasurers (Cassa Militare) under the Commissary-Generals of Army Corps (Commissariato di Corpo d'Armata), under the Intendance of the Armies (Intendenze di Armata), or under the Intendant-General of the Army (Intendenza Generale) for the exchange of English or French money and for the acceptance of English or French money in payment at current rates of exchange, whether in coin, bank-notes or cheques drawn by responsible officers.

H. The British authorities undertake that the personnel for the motor lorries (500) to be provided by the Italian Government (see paragraph 11 of the Convention) shall be dispatched to Turin as soon as the decision as to the movement of the British troops has been taken, in order that the necessary sections of lorries carrying the tents and supplies can be organized in time and dispatched to meet the British troops destined to march by road.

APPENDIX X

INSTRUCTIONS BY THE CHIEF OF THE IMPERIAL GENERAL STAFF TO GENERAL SIR HERBERT PLUMER WHEN LEAVING FOR ITALY

9TH NOVEMBER 1917

(1) You are appointed to command the British Forces now in course of dispatch to Italy and will take over this duty from Lieut.-General Lord Cavan, who is now in command, as soon as possible after your arrival in the country. Lord Cavan will revert to the command of an Army Corps.

(2) The immediate object of dispatching British troops to Italy is to assist the Italians in defending their country against invasion, and to give them time and opportunity to reorganize their Armies and generally to restore them to an efficient condition. The Prime Minister desires me to add that, in view of the low morale and poor fighting qualities of the Austrian troops, he trusts you will bear in mind the desirability of exploiting to the full any favourable opportunity for doing so which may arise.

(3) His Majesty's Government attach great importance to the early achievement of the above-mentioned object and, as information regarding the state of affairs is obscure and somewhat

unreliable, you will, as soon as possible after reaching Italy, forward to me a report on the situation, with special reference to the amount and nature of reinforcements, if any, which you consider to be required, in addition to those which have been already dispatched or are under orders, namely, 4 British and 4 French divisions, with a due proportion of heavy artillery.

(4) In pursuance of the object specified in paragraph 2 and in order effectively to co-operate with the French and Italian Armies, you will be good enough to conform to the wishes of the Italian Commander-in-Chief with respect to the dispositions and employment of your troops and to give him all the assistance in your power.

Subject to the above you will regard yourself as an independent commander and will be responsible to His Majesty's Government for ensuring that your troops are not placed in a compromising position. If, at any time, you are requested by the Italian Commander-in-Chief to carry out operations which in your opinion would unduly endanger the safety of your troops, you should make the requisite representations to Italian General Headquarters, and, if necessary, refer to me for the instructions of the War Cabinet.

No part of your force should be detached from your Command except as a temporary and urgent measure, and then only with your concurrence. The British troops are likely to render much more valuable assistance if kept together in a compact body than if disseminated amongst the Italian or French troops.[1]

(5) The supply and maintenance of your force will be controlled by the War Office. Major-General Grey, who is G.O.C. Mediterranean L. of C. (Cherbourg-Taranto) has been appointed to act as D.G.T. to the force, and in this capacity will be under your orders. The Base of the force in Italy is Arquata. The force is now concentrating at Mantua, but as the Italians are pressing for a more forward concentration, Lieut.-General Wilson has been ordered by the Supreme War Council to examine the matter and consult with Lord Cavan in regard to it. You will report direct to me regarding operations, and to the Secretary, War Office, on other necessary matters. You will send me a report of progress of events at least once daily and more frequently when engaged in important operations.

Paris,
9th November 1917

W. R. ROBERTSON,
C.I.G.S.

---

[1] The greater part of para 4 was communicated to the Italian Government with the addition after " in order effectively to co-operate " of the words " and then only with your concurrence ".

APPENDIX XI

PROTOCOL OF THE CONDITIONS OF ARMISTICE BETWEEN THE ALLIED AND ASSOCIATED POWERS AND AUSTRIA-HUNGARY

SIGNED AT VILLA GIUSTA, AT 3 P.M., ON THE 3RD NOVEMBER 1918

I. MILITARY CLAUSES

Attached : 1 protocol with sketch map [not found]

(1) Immediate cessation of hostilities by land, by sea and in the air.

(2) Total demobilization of the Austro-Hungarian Army and immediate withdrawal of all units operating on the front from the North Sea to Switzerland.

There will only be maintained on the Austro-Hungarian territory, within the boundaries mentioned below in paragraph 3, as Austro-Hungarian military forces, a maximum of 20 divisions, reduced to the establishment on the peace footing before the War.

Half the total material of the divisional artillery, corps artillery, as also the corresponding equipment, beginning with all that to be found on territory to be evacuated by the Austro-Hungarian Army, must be collected between points which will be fixed by the Allies and the United States of America, to be handed over to them.

(3) Evacuation of all territory invaded by Austria-Hungary from the commencement of the war and the withdrawal of the Austro-Hungarian forces, within a space of time, to be determined by the General Officers Commanding-in-Chief of the Allied Forces on the different fronts, beyond a line fixed as follows :

From the Piz Umbrail to the north of the Stelvio, it will follow the crest of the Rhetian Alps as far as the source of the Adige and of the Eisach, then passing over Mounts Reschen and Brenner and along the heights of the Oetz and the Ziller.

The line will then turn towards the south, will cross Mount Toblach and rejoin the present frontier of the Carnic Alps. It will follow this frontier as far as Mount Tarvis and, after Mount Tarvis, the watershed of the Julian Alps, by Col Predil, Mount Margart, the Tricorno (Terglou) and the watershed of the Podberdo, Podlaniscam and Idria heights. From this point onwards, the line will follow a south-easterly direction towards the Schneeberg, leaving outside of it the whole basin of the Save and its tributaries ; from the Schneeberg the line will descend towards the coast, so as to include Castua, Mattuglia and Volosca in the evacuated territory :

APPENDIX XI

It will also follow the present administrative boundaries of the Province of Dalmatia, comprising, to the north Lisarica and Tribani and, to the south, up to a line leaving the coast at Cape Planka and, in an easterly direction, along the summits of the heights, which form the watershed, so as to include in the evacuated territories, all the valleys and watercourses which descend towards Sebenico, such as the Cicola, the Kerka, the Butisnica and their affluents.

It will also enclose all the islands situated to the north and to the west of Dalmatia from Premuda, Selve, Ulbo, Scherda, Maon, Pago and Puntadura in the north to Meleda in the south, including Sant' Andrea, Busi, Lissa, Lesina, Tercola, Curzola, Cazza and Lagosta, as also the surrounding rocks and islets, and Pelagosa, excepting only the islands of the Big and Little Zirona, Bua, Solta and Brazza.

All the territories thus evacuated shall be occupied by the forces of the Allies and of the United States of America.

All military and railway material belonging to the enemy and situated on territory to be evacuated is to remain in its place.

All this material (including stores of coal and other supplies) is to be handed over to the Allies and to the United States, according to the detailed instructions, which shall be given by the General Officers Commanding-in-Chief of the Forces of the Associated Powers on the different fronts.

There shall be no further destruction, nor pillage, nor requisitioning by enemy troops in territories to be evacuated by the enemy and to be occupied by the forces of the Associated Powers.

(4) The Armies of the Associated Powers shall be free to move by all the necessary roads, railways and waterways on Austro-Hungarian territory.

Occupation by the Armies of the Associated Powers of all strategic points in Austria-Hungary, as these Powers may at any moment consider necessary, so as to render possible any military operations and the maintenance of order.

Right of requisition, on payment, by the Armies of the Associated Powers in whatever territory they may be.

(5) Complete evacuation, within 15 days, of all German troops, not only from the Italian and Balkan fronts, but from all Austro-Hungarian territories.

Internment of all German troops, who shall not have left Austro-Hungarian territory within this period.

(6) Evacuated Austro-Hungarian territories shall be provisionally administered by the local authorities under the supervision of the Allied or Associated troops of occupation.

(7) Immediate repatriation, without reciprocity, of all prisoners of war, interned Allied subjects and evacuated civil populations,

under conditions to be fixed by the General Officers Commanding-in-Chief of the Armies of the Allied Powers on the fronts.

(8) The sick and wounded, who cannot be evacuated, shall be attended to by Austro-Hungarian personnel, who will be left on the spot with the necessary material.

II. Naval Clauses

(1) Immediate cessation of all hostilities by sea and precise indication of the position and movements of all Austro-Hungarian vessels.

Neutral Powers shall be notified of the freedom conceded to the navigation of the Navies and Mercantile Marines of the Allied Powers and their associates within all territorial waters, without raising any questions of neutrality.

(2) Delivery to the Allies and the United States of America of 15 Austro-Hungarian submarines, completed between 1910 and 1918 and of all German submarines in or liable to enter Austro-Hungarian territorial waters. Complete disarmament and demobilization of all other Austro-Hungarian submarines, which must remain under the supervision of the Allies and of the United States of America.

(3) Delivery to the Allies and to the United States of America with their armament and equipment complete of 3 battleships, 3 light cruisers, 9 destroyers, 12 torpedo boats, 1 minelayer, 6 monitors from the Danube, to be selected by the Allies and by the United States of America.

All other surface war vessels (including river boats) shall be concentrated at the Austro-Hungarian Naval bases, to be selected by the Allies and by the United States of America, and must be completely demobilized and disarmed and placed under the supervision of the Allies and of the United States of America.

(4) Freedom of navigation for all ships belonging to the Navies and the Mercantile Marines of the Allied and Associated Powers, both in the Adriatic, including territorial waters, on the Danube and on its tributaries in Austro-Hungarian territory.

The Allies and the Associated Powers shall have the right to sweep all the minefields and to destroy all obstructions, the positions of which must be pointed out to them.

In order to ensure freedom of navigation on the Danube, the Allies and the United States of America may occupy or dismantle all fortified works and defences.

(5) Maintenance of the blockade by the Allied and Associated Powers under present conditions ; Austro-Hungarian ships, found at sea being subject to capture, except in cases which may be admitted by a Commission which will be nominated by the Allies and by the United States of America.

(6) Collection and immobilization of all Naval Air Forces at Austro-Hungarian bases, which shall be named by the Allies and by the United States of America.

(7) Evacuation of the whole Italian coast and of all the ports occupied by Austria-Hungary outside her national territory and surrender of all floating material, naval material, equipment and material for navigable routes of any description.

(8) Occupation by the Allies and the United States of America of the fortifications by land and sea and of the islands which form the defences of Pola, as also of the dockyards and the Arsenal.

(9) Restitutions of all commercial ships of the Allied and Associated Powers seized by Austria-Hungary.

(10) Prohibition of any destruction of ships or material before evacuation, delivery or restitution.

(11) Return, without reciprocity, of all prisoners of war belonging to the Navies or Mercantile Marine of the Allied and Associated Powers at present in the hands of the Austro-Hungarians.

The undersigned plenipotentiaries, being duly authorized, declare that they approve the conditions stated above.
3rd November 1918.

The Representatives of the Supreme Command of the Austro-Hungarian Army.	*The Representatives of the Supreme Command of the Italian Army.*
Victor Weber Edler von Webenau	Lt.-Gen. Pietro Badoglio
Karl Schneller	Maj.-Gen. Scipioni Scipione
Y. von Liechtenstein	Colonel Tullio Marchetti
J. V. Nyekhegyi	Colonel Pietro Gazzera
Zwierkowski	Colonel Pietro Maravigna
Victor Freiherr von Seiller	Colonel Alberto Pariani
Kamillo Ruggera	Captain Francesco Accini
	(Royal Italian Navy)

PROTOCOL ATTACHED CONTAINING THE DETAILS AND THE EXECUTIVE CLAUSES DEALING WITH CERTAIN POINTS IN THE ARMISTICE BETWEEN THE ALLIED AND ASSOCIATED POWERS AND AUSTRIA-HUNGARY

Military Clauses

(1) Hostilities by land, sea and air will cease, on all fronts of Austria-Hungary, 24 hours after the signature of the Armistice, that is to say at 1500 hours November 4th (Central European time).

As from that hour the Italian and Associated troops will refrain from advancing beyond the lines reached at that moment.

The Austro-Hungarian troops and the troops of the countries allied with Austria-Hungary will retire to a distance of at least 3 kilometres in a straight line from the line reached by the Italian troops of the Allied and Associated Countries. The inhabitants of the 3-kilometre zone included between the two lines indicated above, may apply to their own national army or to the Armies of the Associated Powers in order to obtain necessary food supplies.

All Austro-Hungarian troops, which, at the hour of cessation of hostilities are still behind the fighting line reached by the Italian troops, will be considered as being prisoners of war.

As regards the clause contained in Articles 2 and 3, dealing with artillery and its equipment and the war material, which is to be collected in the places indicated or left on the spot in the territory to be evacuated, the Italian plenipotentiaries, as representing all the Allied and Associated Powers, declare that they give to the said clauses an interpretation which shall have an executive character.

Every object which can be used for purposes of war, or of which the component parts can be so employed, will be ceded to the Allied and Associated Powers.

The Austro-Hungarian army and the German troops are authorized to take with them only such objects as form part of the personal equipment and arms of the officers and men evacuating the territory indicated in Article 3, as well as officers' chargers, the vehicles and horses forming part of the establishment of each unit for the transport of rations, kitchens, officers' baggage and medical materiel. This clause applies to all the different arms and services of the armies.

(*b*) As regards the artillery more especially, it is laid down that the Austro-Hungarian Army and German troops will leave all artillery materiel and all its equipment in the territory to be evacuated.

The calculation necessary to establish exactly and completely the total amount of the divisional and corps artillery in possession of Austria-Hungary at the moment of the cessation of hostilities, of which amount half will be ceded to the Associated Powers, will be carried out later in such a way as to determine, if necessary, the handing over of other artillery materiel of the Austro-Hungarian army, or possibly the return of materiel to the Austro-Hungarian army by the Allied and Associated armies.

All the artillery not forming part of the establishment of the divisional and corps artillery will be surrendered, without any exception, but it will not be necessary to calculate the exact quantity.

APPENDIX XI 431

(c) The handing over of all the divisional and corps artillery will be carried out, for the Italian front, at the following places: Trent, Bolzano, Pieve di Cadore, Stazione per la Carnia, Tolmino, Gorizia and Trieste.

The Commanders-in-Chief of the Allied and Associated Armies on the different fronts of Austria-Hungary will appoint special commissions, which will at once proceed, accompanied by the necessary escorts, to the places which they may consider best suited for carrying out the provisions indicated above.

(4) It is laid down that the names M. Toblach and M. Tarvis mean the groups of mountains dominating the Toblach saddle and the Tarvis basin, as shown on the attached explanatory sketch map, scale 1 : 500,000.

(5) The evacuation of Austro-Hungarian and Allied troops to beyond the line indicated in Article 3 of the Protocol of the conditions of the Armistice, must be carried out, as regards the Italian front, within 15 days from the day of the cessation of hostilities.

On the fifth day the Austro-Hungarian and Allied troops, as far as the Italian front is concerned, will be beyond the line Tonale – Noce – Lavis – Avisio – Pordoi – Livinallongo – Falzarego – Pieve di Cadore – Collemauria – Upper Tagliamento – Fella – Raccolana – Sella di Nevea – Isonzo ; they will, in addition, have retired from the territory of Dalmatia, as laid down in the Article mentioned above.

Such Austro-Hungarian or Allied land or sea forces as have not carried out their retreat from the territory laid down within the period of 15 days, must be considered prisoners of war.

(6) The payment for the requisitions, which the Armies of the Allied and Associated Powers may make in Austro-Hungarian territory, must be carried out according to the rules laid down in the first paragraph of page 227 of " Servizio Guerra—Part II—1915 edition ", at present in force in the Italian army.

(7) As regards the railways and the exercise of the rights assigned to the Associated Powers by Article 4 of the Protocol of the Armistice between the Allied Powers and Austria-Hungary, it is laid down that the transport of troops, war materiel, food and supplies for the Allied and Associated Powers on the Austro-Hungarian railway system outside the territory evacuated according to the clauses of the Armistice, as well as the management and working of the system, shall be entrusted to employees of the Austro-Hungarian railway administration, under the control, however, of special commissions nominated by the Allied Powers and of such military commands of railway stations as it may be deemed necessary to establish.

The Austro-Hungarian authorities will give precedence, over all others, to such transports and will guarantee their safety.

(8) In the territory to be evacuated at the moment when hostilities cease, steps will be taken to unload and make completely innocuous all mines on roads and railways, and all minefields and all other arrangements designed to interrupt road or railway communications.

(9) Within eight days from the cessation of hostilities all prisoners and civilians interned in Austria-Hungary will cease any work, with the exception of agricultural work in so far as concerns prisoners and interned civilians already employed in agricultural work before the day on which the armistice is signed. They must in any case be ready to leave as soon as the Commander-in-Chief of the Italian Army makes a request to that effect.

(10) Austria-Hungary will provide for the protection, safety and supply (of which the expense will be refunded) of the different commissions of the Allied Governments charged with taking over the war materiel and with exercising all kinds of controls that may be necessary, whether these commissions are in the territory to be evacuated or in any other part of the Austro-Hungarian territory.

Naval Clauses

(1) The hour for the cessation of hostilities by sea is the same as that for cessation of hostilities by land and by air.

By the same hour the Austro-Hungarian Government will have supplied the Italian and Associated Governments, through the Wireless Station at Pola, which will communicate with Venice, with the necessary information concerning the place where all Austro-Hungarian vessels will be and also concerning their movements.

(2) All the units, referred to in Article 2 or 3, which are to be surrendered to the Associated Powers, must reach Venice before 0800 on the 6th November. They will pick up a pilot when 14 miles from the coast.

An exception is made for the monitors on the Danube, which will present themselves at the port fixed by the Commander-in-Chief of the Associated Forces on the Balkan front, according to conditions which the said Commander-in-Chief may think fit to lay down.

(3) The ships which will proceed to Venice are the following:
Teghethoff,
Prinz Eugen,
Ferdinand Max,
Saida,
Novara,
Heligoland,

APPENDIX XI 433

> Nine torpedo-boat destroyers of the Tatra type, of at least 800 tons, of the most recent construction.
> 12 torpedo-boats of the 200-ton type.
> The mine-layer *Camaleon*.
> 15 submarines constructed between 1910 and 1918 and all the German submarines which are, or may be, in Austro-Hungarian territorial waters.

Any damage that may have been arranged beforehand or which takes place on board the ships to be surrendered will be considered by the Associated Governments as constituting most serious infractions of this armistice.

The Lake Garda Flotilla will be surrendered to the Associated Powers at the port of Riva.

All vessels not to be handed over to the Associated Powers will be assembled, within 48 hours of the cessation of hostilities, within the ports of Buccari and Spalato.

As concerns the right of sweeping all minefields and of destroying all booms, the Austro-Hungarian Government gives its word of honour that it will, within 48 hours from the time fixed for the cessation of hostilities, deliver to the Commander of the Fortress of Venice and the Commander of the Naval Forces at Brindisi, the plans of the minefields and booms of the ports of Pola, Cattaro and Fiume and, within 96 hours from the same time, the plans of the minefields and booms of the Mediterranean and of the Italian rivers and lakes, indicating, moreover, the plan of the minefields and barrages laid down by orders of the German Government of which it has knowledge.

Within the same period of 96 hours, a similar communication dealing with everything concerning the Danube and the Black Sea, will be delivered to the Commander of the Associated Forces on the Balkan front.

(5) The return of merchant ships belonging to the Associated Powers will be carried out within 96 hours from the moment of the cessation of hostilities, in accordance with the methods which will be laid down by the Associated Powers and which will be communicated to the Austro-Hungarian Government.

The Associated Powers reserve to themselves the constitution of the commission referred to in Article 5 and to communicate the details of its functions and the place of its assembly to the Austro-Hungarian Government.

(6) The Naval base referred to in Article 6 is Spalato.

(7) The evacuation referred to in Article 7 must be carried out within the time fixed for the withdrawal of the troops beyond the Armistice Lines.

No damage may be done to any fixed, mobile or floating material existing in the ports.

The evacuation may be carried out through the canals of the Lagoon by means of Austro-Hungarian boats, brought from without for the purpose.

(8) The occupation referred to in Article No. 7 will take place within 48 hours from the moment of the cessation of hostilities.

The Austro-Hungarian authorities must guarantee the safety of ships transporting the personnel destined to take possession of Pola, the islands and other places indicated in the Armistice for the Army.

The Austro-Hungarian Government will make the necessary arrangements to ensure that all vessels of the Associated Nations proceeding to Pola will find pilots, capable of indicating the safest course, at a distance of 14 miles from the said fortress.

(9) All damage done to persons or property belonging to the Associated Powers will be regarded as a very grave breach of this Armistice.

The undersigned plenipotentiaries, being duly authorized, declare that they approve the conditions indicated above.
3rd November 1918

The Representatives of the Supreme Command of the Austro-Hungarian Army	*The Representatives of the Supreme Command of the Italian Army*
Victor Weber Edler von Webenau	Lt.-General Pietro Badoglio
Karl Schneller	Maj.-Gen. Scipioni Scipione
Y. von Liechtenstein	Colonel Tullio Marchetti
J. von Nyekhegyi	Colonel Pietro Gazzera
Zwierkowski	Colonel Pietro Maravigna
Victor Freiherr von Seiller	Colonel Alberto Pariani
Kamillo Ruggera	Capt. Francesco Accini
	(Royal Italian Navy)

# GENERAL INDEX 435

A

Adige river, line, 71, 77, 94
Administration, 122
Air, Austrian, harass retreat, 67; master Italian, 109
Air, British, first aid to Italy, 59; increased, 96; total, 108; establish superiority, 109, 132, 133; 165, 178, 180, 183; at Asiago battle, 200; at Piave, 222–23, 224, 226, 236; 252, 254; at Vittorio Veneto, 269; photography, 271; 291, 298, 300, 305, 317, 350
Air, German, initiate night-bombing, 109, 132
Air, Italian, strength, 9; inactivity, 44, 50; at Caporetto, 56; inferior to Austrian, 109; A.A. defence useless, 109, 133; raids, 132; at Piave battle, 236; at Vittorio Veneto, 266
Albricci, Gen. (commanding Italian corps in France), 157, 405
Alexander, Br.-Gen. E. W., V.C. (C.R.A., XI Corps), 112, 141, 390
Alexander, Br.-Gen. H. L. (D.A. and Q.M.G., XIV Corps), 89, 268, 391, 397
Alfieri, Gen. (Italian Minister of War), 80
Alpine Corps, 12, 43, 44, 52, 66, 102, 142
American contingent, 244, 245; at the Monticano, 307, 318, 353, 354; battalion goes to Fiume, 385
Ammunition, reserve, 124
Anglo-Italian Army, proposed, 185
Aosta, Duke of (Italian Third Army), iii, 13, 75, 79, 81 (fn), 110, 264; congratulates Lord Cavan, 355; 405, 406
Arbuthnot, Br.-Gen. Sir Dalrymple, Bt. (C.R.A., 23rd Div.), 196, 393, 400
Armistice, German-Austrian appeal to President Wilson, 247, 250; Austrians send parlementaire, 304; 314, 315; Italians refuse to receive Commission, 325; receive it, 330; misunderstanding, 337, 339, 352, 354; announced, 343; time announced, 353; how the Villa Giusti armistice came about, 359; armistice or surrender, 366; Austrian army informed, 367; the terms, 369; no German representatives, 370; difficulty of promulgating, 372; the protocol, 372; mistake as to commencement, 374, 376; signature authorized, 376; Austrian protest, 378; application to Hungary, 378; text, 426–34
Artillery, Austrian, 17-inch, 174, 199
Artillery, British, loan to Italy, 31; reduced, 43; in retreat, 63, 67; reorganized on the Piave, 84; augmented, 89; in Montello sector, 108; in Asiago sector, 166; in Asiago battle, 196–97, 200; in Vittorio Veneto battle, 287
Artillery, Italian, 14, 16, 18, 20, 22, 26, 31, 34; weakest arm, 136; with British, 139; strength, 143; at Vittorio Veneto, 265, 267
Arz von Straussenburg, Gen. (Austrian C.G.S. from Feb. 1917), 36, 37, 39, 66; bad division of forces, 190; disappointed in June offensive, 220, 232; confesses Austrian weakness, 250, 373; 375; appointed to chief command, 376; protests re armistice, 378; 407, 409
Asiago plateau, 18, 19, 34, 76, 85, 98, 110, 117, 140; plan to attack, 158; British take over, 164; the ground, 167; the position, 168, 170, 197; plan, 178; offensive postponed, 181; forestalled, 185; Austrian offensive, 187; Battle of, 194 *et seq.*; reflections, 217; Austrian account, 219; offensive planned and abandoned, 238; urged by Foch, 243; offensive prepared, 244, 247; trench warfare, 251; Austrian withdrawal, 255, 258; Italians propose attack, 256; new offensive, 322; Austrians abandon, 327
Asquith, Rt. Hon. H. H. (British Prime Minister, 1914–17), 24; displaced by Mr. Lloyd George, 25
Austro-Hungarian Army, strength, 11; Fifth Army formed, 12; Eleventh Army formed, 17; shaky, 36; driven from last position, 37;

Caporetto plan, 48; short of rations and clothing, 100; re-organized into two groups, 142; Piave offensive, 187; strength, 193; not starved, 198, 258; plans in Italy, 249; shortage of men, 250; strength at Vittorio Veneto, 265; defences, 270, 273, 286; Hungarian and Slav troops give trouble, 314, 362–63; language difficulties, 364; breaks up, 366

B

Babington, Major-Gen. Sir J. M. (23rd Div.), 59, 195, 199, 252; commands XIV Corps at Vittorio Veneto, 268, 270, 291, 318; succeeds Lord Cavan and goes home, 384; 393, 400, 404
Babtie, Surgeon-Gen. Sir W. (Inspector Medical Services), 123
Back lines, 222
Badoglio, Gen. (Italian IV Corps), 47; becomes Deputy C.G.S., 81, 159, 183; wants offensive, 247, 249; on reliefs, 254; 255, 262; armistice plenipotentiary, 371, 378; to command against Bavaria, 380
Bainsizza plateau, 11; battle, 34, 35, 37, 53, 54, 55, 56
Banse, Professor E., quoted, 218
Barnardiston, Br.-Gen. E. (C.E., XIV Corps), 268, 399
Barne, Lieut.-Col. W. B. G. (G.S., 7th Div.), 399
Barnett, Lieut.-Col. G. H. (A.A. and Q.M.G., 48th Div.), 395, 401
Barratiere, Gen. Count (Italian 4th Cav. Div.), 353
Bartlett, Lieut.-Col. A. J. N. (1/4th Oxford L.I.), 205
Base, at Arquata, 29, 60, 128, 130
Basso, Gen. (Italian XVIII Corps), 287, 292
Bate, Major J. P. (1/7th Worcestershire), 210
Bavaria, plans to invade, 380
Beauman, Br.-Gen. A. B. (69th Bde.), 269, 290, 301, 401
Belluno Group, 410
Below, Gen. Otto v. (German Army commander), career, 49; in pursuit, 66, 69; orders at Tagliamento, 71; breaks line, 75, 76; differs with Krauss, 83; takes charge of attack, 101; leaves Italy, 142; 408
Berndt, Field-Marshal-Lieut. (Austrian corps commander), 296, 312

Berrer, Gen. (German corps commander), 52, 56; killed, 65; 408
Blindloss, Major E. A. M. (1/5th R. Warwickshire), 205; killed, 208
Bliss, Gen. T. H. (U.S. Military Representative), 156
Bombing, night, 109, 132, 180
Boroevic von Bojna Svetosar, Gen. (Austrian Isonzo Group commander), 12; counter-attack, 33; visited by Emperor, 36, 37; promoted field-marshal, 142; no plans, 188; 189; at Piave battle, 221, 226, 227, 230, 231, 233, 239, 240, 241; at Vittorio Veneto, 265, 314; considers situation hopeless, 315; evacuates heavy material, 361; reports increase of mutinies, 364; offers to evacuate Venetia, 365; troops hold on, 367; 408, 410
Bosnia, annexation, 1
Braganza, Duke of (Austrian cavalry general), 342
Briand, Monsieur Aristide (French Prime Minister), 24
Bridging, 141, 223, 224, 226, 227, 229, 230, 234, 236, 240; request for Inglis bridges, 249; at Vittorio Veneto, 266, 271, 272; Italian scows, 274, 276, 279; British equipment unsuited, 281, 282; 284, 285, 288, 294, 295, 298, 299, 303, 312, 313, 322, 349, 351, 382
Briggs, Lieut.-Col. E. (C.R.E., 48th Div.), 401
Brind, Br.-Gen. J. E. S. (B.G.G.S., XI Corps), 112, 390
British aid to Italy, project, 30; loan of heavy artillery, 31; more demanded, 35, 40; reduced, 43; divisions sent, 58; note on use, 72; arrival, 88; additional, 96, 99; enter line, 104; recall considered, 148; reduced, 150, 153–54; Italian protest, 151; three divisions remain, 162
British army, good discipline, 100; spearhead at Vittorio Veneto, 294; total strength, 355; demobilization, 384
Brusilov, Gen. (Russian general), offensive, 18, 34, 357
Buckle, Major-Gen. C. R. (G.O.C., R.A.), 94, 389
Buzzard, Lieut.-Col. C. N. (Heavy Artillery Group), 31; narrative of Eleventh Battle of Isonzo, 36
Byron, Br.-Gen. J. (C.R.A., 23rd Div.), 323, 400

GENERAL INDEX 437

C

Cadorna, Gen. Luigi (Italian C.G.S., 1914–17), 5, 13, 16, 19; fears attack in Jan. 1917, 27, 32; resumes operations in Aug., 34, 35; plans to resume, 37; contemplates defensive, 40, 41, 42; at Caporetto, 46; orders, 47, 53; his back lines, 53; retirement orders, 54; delays retirement, 55, 56; order for retirement, 57, 62; halt on Tagliamento, 70; considers retirement to Adige river, 71; misuse of Allies, 72; removal suggested, 80; succeeded by Diaz, 81; goes to Versailles, 120; leaves Versailles, 156
Campbell, Lieut.-Col. R. M. (L. of C. H.Q.), 388
Canteens, 127, 174
Capello, Gen., commands Italian VI Corps, 21; Gorizia Zone, 32; Second Army, 34, 35; sick, 46; at Caporetto, 53, 54, 55; 405
Caporetto campaign, planned, 38; battle, 40 *et seq.*; expected by Italians, 41, 44, 45; orders, 47; enemy plan, 48; bombardment, 51; first news, 58; end of campaign and casualties, 102
Carnia, 10, 12, 53, 56, 76
Carso plateau, 11, 13, 21, 22, 35
Cary-Barnard, Br.-Gen. C. D. V. (68th Bde.), 290, 309, 394, 401
Casualties, Austrian, 13, 15, 19, 21, 22, 33, 34, 38; at Asiago battle, 216, 220; at Piave battle, 237
Casualties, British, 115; at Asiago battle, 216; in raids, 258, 259, 260, 262, 310; in Trent operation, 345; in final phase, 355; total, 356
Casualties, German, incomplete, 103
Casualties, Italian, 13, 14, 15, 19, 21, 22, 33, 34, 38, 102, 140; at Piave battle, 237
Cavalry, failure of German, 66, 78; Italian cover retreat, 67, 78, 83; keep order, 79; Italian corps, 265; charge by British troop, 307; Italian ordered forward, 317, 321, 322; reach British front line, 324; cross Livenza, 349; push on when unopposed, 354
Cavan, Lieut.-Gen. Earl of, 59, 60, 89; report of 6th Nov., 90; 92; relieved by Gen. Plumer, 95; takes command of sector, 105; of British force, 150; on offensive plan, 161; on limited offensive, 176; reports on uncertainty of situation, 177; reports, 181, 182; doubts Italian information, 183; consults French, 184; opposes formation of Anglo-Italian Army, 185; conference before Asiago battle, 198; at battle, 210, 212, 215, 217; offensive cancelled by Italians, 238; stirs up Diaz, 247, 248; to command Italian Tenth Army, 249; commands temporarily Sixth Army, 253, 255; suggests exchange of divisions, 255; agrees to Asiago attack, 256; points out Italians ignore British effort, 258; in London, 261; presses C.I.G.S. to urge Italians, 262; secures cancellation of Italian orders, 263; at Vittorio Veneto, 264, 268; instructions, 270; orders, 287; Italian XVIII Corps under him, 292; orders for 28th Oct., 297; praise of Italians, 299; orders for 29th Oct., 304; on Italian slowness, 317; orders pursuit to Tagliamento, 348; congratulated by Duke of Aosta, 355; against invasion of Bavaria, 380; returns home, 384; 391, 397, 407
Caviglia, Gen. (Italian XXIV and VIII Corps), 53, 64, 69, 138; commands Eighth Army, 264; co-ordinates three Armies, 267, 285; 406
Chichester, Major-Gen. A. A. (D.Q.M.G.), 94, 389
Cholera, 124
Clarke, Lieut.-Col. H. T. (1/8th Worcestershire), 211
Clemenceau, Monsieur Georges (French Prime Minister from 16th Nov. 1917), 94, 154, 369
Clemson, Br.-Gen. W. F. (124th Bde.), 395
Clive, Br.-Gen. C. S. (British Mission at French G.Q.G.), 61
Coal, shortage of, 119, 125
Colvin, Br.-Gen. G. L. (Deputy Dir.-Gen. of Transportation), 398
Command, Foch wants united Anglo-French in Italy, 99
Commando Supremo (Italian G.H.Q.), *see under* Cadorna *and* Diaz
Concentration, area, 89, 91, 92, 98; not cleared, 101; 102; XI Corps, 112
Conferences, 1915, Chantilly, 14, 16; Paris, 16; 1916, Chantilly, 24;

Paris, 24 ; 1917, Rome, St. Jean de Maurienne, 27 ; London, 35 ; Udine, 40 ; Boulogne, 43 ; Rapallo (*q.v.*), 79
Conrad von Hötzendorf, Field-Marshal (Austrian C.G.S.), on Italian faith, 4 ; at Russian front, 11 ; attacks in Trentino, 16 ; begs for German help, 18 ; advocates Italy as main theatre, 26, 38, 39 ; superseded as C.G.S., 39 ; commands in the Trentino, 76 ; offensive, 85 ; commands group, 142 ; proposes offensive, 187 ; plans approved, 189 ; in June 1918 battle, 216 ; visited by Emperor, 232, 233 ; 235, 239 ; removed, 241 ; 357, 408, 409
Convention, Anglo-Italian on reinforcement, 29 ; text, 416–24
Cotton, Br.-Gen. A. S. (C.R.A., 41st Div.), 394
Cramon, Major-Gen. v. (German plenipotentiary at Austrian G.H.Q.), 232, 259
Crookshank, Br.-Gen. S. D'A. (Acting Dir.-Gen. Transportation), 147
Crowe, Br.-Gen. J. H. V., mission to Italy, 28, 30 ; C.I.G.S.' representative, 58 ; report adopted, 61 ; becomes liaison officer, 95 ; 125, 126 ; at Taranto, 386 ; 389
Csanady, Gen. (Austrian XIII Corps), 192
Cummins, Col. S. L. (medical officer with Crowe Mission), 30
Cyclists, Italian, 67, 313 ; British, 99, 318, 350, 351
Czechoslovaks, declare independence, 362 ; divisions organized, 365
Czech troops, give trouble, 314, 315

D

Dalton, Hugh, Lieut., R.A., 64 fn. 1
Dankl, Gen. (Austrian commander), 12, 17
De Angelis, Gen. (Italian 31st Div.), 307
Deception, 50, 51, 141, 251, 253, 259, 288
Defence, groups, 110 ; rear lines, 117, 118 ; in depth, 133 ; groups abolished, 137 ; doctrine, 196 ; Italian back lines, 222 ; 357
Delmé-Radcliffe, Br.-Gen. C. (head of British Military Mission), 13, 30 ; reports expected attack, 46 ; 58, 89, 102, 185, 264, 382

Demobilization, 384
Derby, Rt. Hon. Earl of (Sec. of State for War), 40, 149, 151
Deserters, Austrian, 44, 182, 183, 198, 241, 255
Diaz, Gen. Armando (second Italian C.G.S.), succeeds Cadorna, 81 ; his career, 81 ; holds the Piave line, 82 ; anxious, 86 ; on concentration area, 92 ; 95, 98, 101 ; visits British sector, 107 ; accepts group defence, 110 ; suggests retirement from Piave, 111; groups abolished, 137 ; objects to British reduction, 150, 151, 152 ; plans for 1918, 159–60 ; postpones offensive, 176 ; inaction, 183 ; change of plan, 184 ; favours Anglo-Italian Army, 183 ; no reserves, 215 ; at Piave battle, 227, 230, 234, 235 ; orders Sile attack, 238 ; minimum effort, 242 ; his excuses, 243, 244 ; goes to Paris, 245 ; still cautious, 246 ; agrees to offensive, 247 ; alarmed, 248; announces offensive, 249 ; conference before Vittorio Veneto, 264 ; plan, 266 ; anxious about Monte Grappa, 273 ; postpones crossing of Piave, 278, 284 ; removes a corps commander, 313 ; orders Third Army forward, 317 ; orders advance to Livenza, 321 ; decides on Asiago attack, 322 ; orders pursuit to Tagliamento, 348 ; armistice negotiations, 368, 370 ; plans to invade Bavaria, 380
Di Giorgio, Gen., commands reserve divisions, 63, 76
Di Robilant, Gen. (Italian Fourth Army), 78, 405
Done, Br.-Gen. H. R. (144th Bde.), 329, 396, 402
Dress, winter, 163 ; summer, 174 ; khaki in pine forest, 213 ; Italian uniforms worn, 269
Duchêne, Gen. (French Army commander), 59, 90, 95, 105 ; leaves Italy, 110 ; 404

E

Eberle, Lieut.-Col. G. S. J. F. (C.R.E., 48th Div.), 206
Engineer services, 123
Engineers, Italian, backward, 136
Entrenchments, Italian, out of date, 104, 106, 107
Establishments, reduction of brigades to three battalions, 260

GENERAL INDEX 439

Eugen, Archduke, commands against Italy, 12, 17, 19, 37, 49, 85; command abolished, 142; 407, 409
Evans, Lieut.-Col. C. (G.S., 23rd Div.), 393
Executive War Board, 148, 149, 151, 152, 153, 156

F

Falkenhayn, Gen. Erich v. (German C.G.S., 1914–16), 12; attacks Verdun, 16; removed, 21
Falkner, Lieut.-Col. E. F. (A.A. and Q.M.G., 23rd Div.), 393, 400
Fanshawe, Major-Gen. Sir Robert (48th Div.), 96, 195, 199, 205, 210, 211, 214, 215; leaves division, 252; 395, 401
Fayolle, Gen. (commander of French contingent), 99, 102, 110; on the Italian army, 137; submits plan, 158; returns to France, 158
Field-Marshal-Lieutenant, 221 fn.
Fiume, trouble at, 385
Flame-throwers, 101, 201
Foch, Gen. (later Maréchal) Ferdinand, sent to Italy, 28; 59; on aid to Italy, 59; goes to Italy, 62, 71; suggests halt on Piave, 71, 72; 75, 79; interviews Diaz and remains in Italy, 82, 92, 95, 98, 101; wants single command, 99; conference, 101; leaves Italy, 102; president of Executive War Board, 148; suggests return of Allied divisions, 152; stirs up Diaz, 183, 243, 244, 245; powers of coordination, 242; promoted Maréchal, 244; offers sound advice, 358; commands all armies against Germany, 381
Fog, 222, 225, 259, 276, 282
Food shortage, 120, 198
French help to Italy, guns, 37; reduced, 43; divisions sent, 58, 59; note on use of, 72; four divisions arrive, 84; two more, 96; movement, 97; line taken over, 106; reduced, 156, 162, 175
Frontier, Austrian, crossed, 334
Frugoni, Lieut.-Gen. (Italian Second Army), 13

G

Gas, 44; Italian mask, 48; at Caporetto, 51, 57.; at Asiago, 86, 199; British masks for the Italians, 134; 189, 198; at Piave, 222, 240, 357

Gathorne-Hardy, Br.-Gen. Hon. J. F. (B.G.G.S., XIV Corps), 89, 248, 262; M.G.G.S., Tenth Army, 268; goes home, 384; 391, 397
Gell, Lieut.-Col. W. C. G. (1/5th R. Warwickshire), 341
G.H.Q. Italy, places, 95, 132
German aid to Austria, 43, 44, 46
German army, Fourteenth Army formed, 49; use of reserves, 49; looting, 66; failure of cavalry, 66; bad staff work, 68, 69, 70; short of ammunition, 84; transport difficulties, 85; leaves Italy, 102
Giardino, Gen. (Italian Deputy C.G.S.), 81; becomes Military Representative, 156; commands Fourth Army, 264, 283, 406
Giles, Lieut.-Col. V. (C.R.E., 48th Div.), 395
Giolitti, Signor, Italian premier, 3
Girard, Col. (French liaison officer), 244
Glubb, Major-Gen. F. M. (C.E.), 94, 118, 123, 389
Goglia, Field-Marshal Ritter v. (Austrian Belluno Group), 365, 374, 410
Goiginger, Field-Marshal-Lieut. (Austrian XXIV Corps), 191, 221, 231, 233, 410
Gordon, Br.-Gen. H. (70th Bde.), 203, 319; goes to Fiume, 385; to Egypt, 387; 394, 401
Gordon-Hall, Lieut.-Col. G. C. W. (G.S., 5th Div.), 392
Gordon-Lennox, Br.-Gen. Lord E. C. (95th Bde.), 392
Gorizia, battle of (*see* Isonzo, Sixth Battle), 19
Gorlice-Tarnow, battle of, 11
Gravè, meaning of, 266
Graziani, Gen. (French corps commander), 156, 176, 184, 215; wants offensive, 247; conference with, 255; to command Twelfth Army, 263; at Vittorio Veneto, 264, 284; 407
Green, Br.-Gen. A. F. U. (D.A. and Q.M.G., XI Corps), 112, 390
Green, Br.-Gen. H. C. R. (20th Bde.), 291, 393, 400
Grey, Rt. Hon. Sir Edward (Minister for Foreign Affairs), 6
Grey, Major-Gen. W. H. (Dir.-Gen. Transportation), 60, 126, 128, 389
Guicciardi, Gen. Count (Italian 3rd Cav. Div.), 352, 353

440 GENERAL INDEX

H

Haig, Field-Marshal Sir Douglas, sends divisions to Italy, 58, 59 ; protests, 60 ; 94, 96 ; requests return of Plumer, 155

Haking, Lieut.-Gen. Sir Richard (XI Corps), 97, 112, 118 ; takes over front, 138, 141 ; 390

Hall, Major P. A. (1/1st Buckinghamshire Bn.), 205

Hamilton, Br.-Gen. P. D. (commander heavy artillery), 31

Hankey, Col. Sir Maurice (later, Lord) (Secretary, Cabinet), 26

Harington, Major-Gen. C. H. (Plumer's Chief General Staff Officer), 93, 149, 159, 389

Hartley, Major D. R. C. (R.F.A.), 206

Herzegovina, annexation, 1

Heywood, Captain W. B. (G.S.), 116

Hildebrand, Col. A. B. R. (Deputy Dir. of Signals), 129

Hindenburg, Gen.-Field-Marshal v., 21 ; wants Trentino attack, 85

Hoare-Nairne, Br.-Gen. E. S. (C.R.A., XIV Corps), 268

Hobbs, Lieut.-Col. R. F. A. (A.A. and Q.M.G., 5th Div.), 392

House, Col. (the American President's representative), 369, 370

Howard, Br.-Gen. G. W. (145th Bde.), 329, 393, 399

Howard, Lieut.-Col. H. C. L. (G.S., 48th Div.), 338, 339, 395, 401

Hudson, Lieut.-Col. C. E. (11/Sherwood Foresters), awarded V.C., 203

Hudson, Lieut.-Col. H. H. (11/West Yorkshire), 300

Hudson, Br.-Gen. T. R. C. (C.R.A., XIV Corps), 89, 268, 397

Hungarian troops, begin to give trouble, 314 ; talk of independence, 362 ; mutiny, 363 ; lay down arms, 366, 373 ; separate armistice, 378

Hussey, Br.-Gen. A. H. (C.R.A., 5th Div.), 141, 392

I

Imperiali, Marchese (Italian Ambassador), 6

Influenza, 181, 195, 217, 268

Intelligence Service, 130 ; summary, 146, 152 ; warnings of attack, 198 ; Italian, faulty, 80, 245

Interior lines, 10, 20, 265

Isonzo Armies, Austrian, 49 ; amalgamated into one, 142

Isonzo, river, 10, 11 ; front reinforced, 12 ; first four battles, 13 ; fifth battle, 15 ; sixth battle, 19 ; seventh, eighth and ninth battles, 22 ; tenth battle, 32 ; eleventh battle, 34 ; Ludendorff on this battle, 38 ; twelfth battle (see Caporetto)

Italian army (see also Armies, Italian, in Arms, Formations and Units index), state and numbers, 9 ; objective, 13 ; shortage of guns, 13, 14, 15 ; removal of officers, 14 ; material assistance to, 16 ; Third Army, 13 ; Second Army, 13 ; First Army, 17 ; causes of failure, 36 ; morale, 57 ; nervous, 86 ; no march discipline, 100 ; strength, 103 ; out-of-date defences, 104, 107 ; bad staff work, 108, 118 ; little confidence, 113–114 ; maps inaccurate, 116 ; telegraph and telephone system disorganized, 129 ; neglects training, 134 ; staff work theoretical, 135 ; Plumer on, 135–37 ; Fayolle on, 137, 143–44 ; strength and reorganization, 142 ; could spare ten divisions, 149 ; two divisions go to France, 156, 157, 241 ; lack of sanitation, 174 ; cease attending British schools, 175 ; exaggerated reports, 182 ; inaction, 183 ; strength, 193 ; short of drafts, 247 ; newspapers ignore the British, 258

Italy, plans to assist Germany against France, 2 ; plans against Austria-Hungary, 5 ; policy, 5 ; joins Entente, 6 ; campaign advocated by Mr. Lloyd George and also by Conrad, 26 ; reinforcement move prepared by Crowe's mission, 28, 30

J

Jäger, German division formed, 49, 66, 102, 142

Jardine, Major C. (R.F.A.), 207

Joffre, Gen. (French C.-in-C., 1914–16), his conferences, 14, 24 ; superseded by Nivelle, 25

Jones, Br.-Gen. L. O. W. (13th Bde.), 392

Joseph, Archduke (Austrian Sixth Army), 142, 189, 190 ; at Piave battle, 221, 226, 233 ; commands Trentino Group at Vittorio Veneto, 265 ; ordered to evacuate material, 361 ; vacates command, 365

GENERAL INDEX 441

Joubert de la Ferté, Lieut.-Col. P. B. (R.F.C.), 96, 398
Julian Alps, 10 ; front (see Isonzo), 11, 50

K

Karl, Kaiser of Austria, 85, 142, 190, 232, 233, 234, 235, 241 ; affected by German defeats, 260, 360 ; 314 ; orders evacuation of Venetia, 315 ; efforts to obtain armistice, 359 ; his manifesto, 361 ; appeals to the Pope, 363 ; decides to ask for armistice, 364 ; fatal effect of the manifesto, 365, 367 ; accepts armistice terms, 373, 374 ; tries to recall acceptance, 375 ; authorizes signature, 376 ; wants Allied troops to keep order, 381 ; 407, 409
Kay, Major-Gen. W. H. (C.R.A., Tenth Army), 268
Kerenski offensive, 34, 36, 49, 357
Kerrich, Lieut.-Col. W. A. FitzG. (C.R.E., 7th Div.), 282, 294, 295, 399
Knox, Lieut.-Col. J. M. (1/7th R. Warwickshire), 205, 211, 212
Konopicky, Major-Gen. (Austrian C.G.S., Italian front), 407
Kövess v. Kövesshaza, Field-Marshal, appointed to command the Austrian forces, 376
Krafft v. Delmensingen, Gen. (German C.G.S. in Caporetto campaign), 37 ; reconnaissance, 48, 49 ; at Caporetto, 55, 69
Krauss, Major-Gen. Alfred (Austrian commander), 17 ; commands corps, 50, 51 ; at Caporetto, 52, 56 ; at the Tagliamento, 76, 77 ; differs with Below, 83 ; sent to Ukraine, 239 ; 408
Krobatin, Field-Marshal (Austrian Group Commander, vice Archduke Joseph), 326, 365, 366, 367, 374, 409

L

Labour, 123
Lambert, Br.-Gen. T. S. (69th Bde.), 394
Lang, Lieut.-Col. B. J. (A.A. and Q.M.G., 7th Div.), 393, 399
Language difficulties, 91, 92, 106, 287
Lawford, Major-Gen. S. T. B. (41st Div.), 59, 394

Lawson, Lieut.-Gen. Sir Henry (Inspector-Gen. of Communications), 128
Leave, 175, 254
Libya, see Tripoli
Lido, meaning, 266
Linder, Col. Bela (Hungarian Minister of War), 366, 373
Linfoot, Captain H. A. (1/6th R. Warwickshire), 209
Livenza river, reached, 319 ; halt on, 321, 348 ; crossed, 349
Lloyd Baker, Lieut.-Col. A. B. (1/4th R. Berkshire), 210
Lloyd George, Rt. Hon. D. (Sec. of State for War), advocates Balkan campaign, 24 ; becomes Prime Minister and advocates Italian campaign, 25, 26 ; on Italy's inactivity, 27 ; orders divisions to Italy, 58 ; goes to Italy, 62 ; proposes Supreme War Council, 79 ; promises help, 80 ; sees King of Italy, 81 ; sees Gen. Plumer, 94 ; anxious to reduce B.E.F., 94 ; on railways, 245 ; on armistice terms, 369
Loans to Italy, 23
Looting, by Austrians, 341, 350, 367, 374
Lowther, Lieut.-Col. Sir C. B. (Yeomanry), 307, 351
Ludendorff, Gen. Erich (German First Q.M.G.), on eleventh battle of the Isonzo, 20, 28 ; insists on German participation in twelfth battle, 48 ; wants German divisions back, 66 ; nervous, 74 ; wants Trentino attack, 85 ; appeals for Austrian action, 191 ; for Austrian divisions, 232, 241 ; visited by Arz and refuses help, 250

M

McCulloch, Br.-Gen. R. H. F. (C.H.A., XI Corps), 112, 390
Macdonogh, Major-Gen. Sir George (D.M.I., War Office), 245
McNally, Sergt. W., awarded V.C., 310
Macready, Lieut.-Gen. Sir Neville (Adjt.-Gen. of the Forces), 40
Magniac, Col. C. L. (Deputy Dir.-Gen. of Transportation), 61
Maistre, Gen. (French Army commander), succeeds Gen. Duchêne, 110 ; returns to France, 156
Malaria, 250
Marshall, Br.-Gen. H. J. M. (C.E., XI Corps), 112, 390

Martigny, Gen.-Col. (Austrian III Corps), 340
Maurice, Major-Gen. F. B. (D.M.O., War Office), 40, 46
Medical services, 123, 181; stretcher difficulties on bridges, 298; sick and wounded cases, 356
Military Representatives (Supreme War Council), instructions, 115; names and report, 120; form Executive War Board, *q.v.*, 148; reduced duties, 242
Mills, Lieut.-Col. R. P. (R.F.C.), 59
Mining, Austrian, 140
Mitchell, Lieut.-Col. C. H. (Intelligence Branch), 130, 389
Moberly, Lieut.-Col. A. H. (Heavy Artillery Group), 31
Moltke, Field-Marshal v., on Italian help, 2
Moltke, Gen.-Col. v. (German C.G.S.), on Italian help, 3, 4
Monte Asolone, 116, 139, 160
Monte Grappa, 77, 83, 85, 86, 98, 101, 103, 111, 116, 117, 142, 192, 194, 238, 248, 263, 267; Diaz's anxiety, 270; fighting at, 282, 314, 321, 322; evacuated by Austrians, 320, 327
Montello, The, description, 72, 77, 104; British take over, 104, 116; in Piave battle, 190, 191, 215, 221, 222, 226, 227, 228, 230, 231, 233, 234, 235, 236, 240, 271
Monte Pasubio, 18; mining, 140
Monte Tomba, 101, 117, 133
Monticano river, reached, 301, 302, 303; description, 305; forcing of, 306; 312, 314, 315
Montuori, Gen. (Italian II Corps), 46; at Caporetto, 54; commands Second Army, 54, 63; Sixth Army, 159, 177, 184, 217, 253, 255, 262; at Vittorio Veneto, 264; 406
Morrone, Gen. (Italian Ninth Army), 265, 407
Motor lorries, purchase of, 126; pattern, 171
Mountain warfare, German instructions, 51, 52; equipment, 98, 111; transport, 164, 171; reliefs, 177; 217; employment of British, 254; supply in, 335; remarks on, 346, 386
Mules, pack, 171, 173
Müller, Major-Gen. Richard (Austrian C.G.S. Trentino Group), 408, 409

N

Nash, Major-Gen. P. A. M. (Dir.-Gen. Transportation), 96, 245
Newland, Major-Gen. F. R. (Dir. Medical Services), 123, 398
Nitti, Signor (Italian Finance Minister), 244, 245
Nivelle, Gen., becomes French C.-in-C., 25; plan, 26; visits Italy, 27; offensive fails, 32
Nourrisson, Gen. (French corps commander), 96, 98, 404

O

O'Connor, Lieut.-Col. R. N. (H.A.C.), 274, 276, 279, 280, 282, 352, 386
Odry, Gen. (French 24th Div.), 263, 328, 329, 404
Ogston, Br.-Gen. (D.A. and Q.M.G., XIV Corps), 268
Oldham, Lieut.-Col. H. (XXV Bde., R.F.A.) 207
Oldman, Br.-Gen. R. D. F. (15th Bde.), 392
Orders, operation, Cadorna's for Caporetto, 47
Ordnance services, 124
Orlando, Signor (Italian Prime Minister), 71, 75, 80, 151; cautious attitude, 246, 247, 369, 370
Ortigara, battle of, 33
Overland route, railway, *see* Taranto

P

Pact of London, 5; terms, 6; text, 410-15
Painlevé, Monsieur (French Prime Minister till 16th Nov. 1917), 62, 79, 80, 94
Panic, Italian, 57, 65, 68, 76; Austrian, 296; 358
Paolini, Gen. (Italian XI Corps), 287, 291, 311
Papadopoli Island, best place for attack, 188, 194; in Piave battle, 224, 227, 229, 231; in Vittorio Veneto battle, 266, 270, 271, 272; description, 273; seizure, 275; cleared, 280
Parker, Lieut.-Col. R. G. (G.S., 41st Div.), 394
Payot, Col. (head of French L. of C.), 26, 29, 60, 61, 96
Peace, propaganda, 33, 57; Austrian Emperor's proposals, 37, 43

GENERAL INDEX

Pearce-Serocold, Br.-Gen. E. (123rd Bde.), 395
Peck, Lieut.-Col. S. C. (Military Mission, Fiume), 387
Pecori-Giraldi, Gen. (Italian First Army), 264, 405, 406
Pelly, Br.-Gen. R. T. (91st Bde.), 291, 308, 393, 400
Penella, Gen. (Italian Eighth Army), 234, 235, 263; ceases to command, 264; commands corps, 331, 342, 405
Pétain, Gen., commands French Armies, 35, 37; pessimism, 79, 96
Piacentino, Gen. (Italian Second Army), 32
Piave river, Foch suggests halt on, 71; description, 77, 104; bridges destroyed, 83; Austrians win bridgehead, 86; evacuate it, 102; patrols across, 131; Arcade front, 138; offensive expected, 182; genesis of battle, 187; plan, 190; battle, 221 *et seq.*; quiet, 252; bridging, 281, 282, 286, 288, 294; passage by British, 294; bridgeheads expanded, 297
Piccione, Gen. (Italian Operations Branch), 89
Pitreich, Major-Gen. Ritter v. (Austrian C.G.S. Isonzo Group), 410
Pitt - Taylor, Br. - Gen. W. W. (B.G.G.S., XIV Corps), 116, 268; becomes chief G.S.O., 384
Plumer, Gen. Sir Herbert, arrives in Italy, 86, 93; his instructions, 94, 424; at Mantua and Padua, 95; first report, 95; 101; tact, 107; proposes defence groups, 110; refuses to retreat, 111; report of 14th Dec. 1917, 113; defence scheme, 117; report of 13th Jan. 1918, 132; of 20th Jan. 1918, 134; 141; returns to France, 150, 155; 389
Pollio, Gen. (Italian C.G.S., 1912-14), negotiations with German General Staff, 3, 4; death, 5
Pope, His Holiness, the, peace encyclical, 33, 360
Porro, Gen. (Italian sub-C.G.S.), 13, 15, 16, 29, 40, 80
Prisoners, Austrian, 299, 308, 310, 334, 335, 342, 343, 344; British captures, 293, 345; in final phase, 354
Prisoners, British, small numbers, 386
Prisoners, Italian, 33, 38, 54, 69, 70, 77, 84, 102, 227, 231, 237, 386

Propaganda, 33, 57, 117
Pryor, Lieut.-Col. W. M. (1/6th R. Warwickshire), 205, 215, 342
Purefoy Robinson, Lieut.-Col. J. A. (Heavy Artillery Group), 31

R

Raids, 179, 253, 256, 258, 262, 263, 327
Railways, Taranto route, France to Italy, 29; project for movement to Italy, 30; final programme, 61; movement, 88; Italian breakdown, 91; additional divisions, 96; feeding arrangements, 127; return journey, 146-47
Rain, 50, 51, 63, 69, 131, 141, 226, 228, 259, 269, 276, 278, 279, 289
Rapallo Conference, 79; first session, 80; becomes Supreme War Council, *q.v.*, 80
Rawlinson, Gen. Sir Henry (Fourth Army), 93; becomes Military Representative, 156
Recreation, 118, 174
Red Cross, British, assists Italian prisoners, 386
Reid, Lieut.-Col. A. W. (C.R.E., 7th Div.), 393
Reliefs, 177, 255, 261, 262
Reserve, General, 148, 151-52
Rest areas, 174
Reynolds, Lieut.-Col. L. L. C. (1/1st Buckinghamshire Bn.), 204, 211
Riddell-Webster, Lieut.-Col. T. S. (A.A. and Q.M.G., 41st Div.), 394
Riga, German offensive at, 49
Roads, responsibility, 123, 333
Robertson, Gen. (later Field-Marshal) Sir William (C.I.G.S.), visits Italy and sends Crowe's Mission, 28, 29; on aid to Italy, 59; goes to Italy, 62, 71; note to Cadorna, 72; 75; at Rapallo Conference, 79, 82; conference at G.H.Q., 94; objects to united command, 99; on recall of troops, 148; superseded, 148
Rodd, Sir Rennell (British Ambassador in Rome), 75
Rohr, Gen. (Austrian commander), 11, 12
Romer, Ritter v. (Austrian parlementaire), 338
Rooke, Lieut.-Col. E. H. (C.R.E., 23rd Div. and C.E. XIV Corps), 349, 393, 400

Ross, Lieut.-Col. H. A. (2/Gordon Highlanders), killed, 292
Rozée d'Infreville, Gen. (commanding French corps), 59, 98
Rumbold, Lieut.-Col. S. D. (9/York & Lancaster), 323

S

Sacile, strongly held, 320; capture, 323; traffic jam, 350
Salonika, 24, 25
Sandilands, Lieut.-Col. H. R. (G.S., 23rd Div.), 400
Sanna, Gen. (Italian 33rd Div.), 292
Schäffer v. Bernstein, Col. (German G.S.), 370
Schariczer, Gen. (Austrian VII Corps), 236, 410
Scheuchenstuel, Gen.-Col. Graf (Austrian Eleventh Army), 187, 340, 409
Schilhawsky, Lieut.-Col. Ritter v. (Austrian Operations Staff), 188
Schlieffen, Gen. Graf v., on Italian help, 2
Schneller, Col. (Austrian Armistice Commission), 371, 374, 377
Schomberg, Lieut.-Col. H. (1/6th Gloucestershire), 211
Schönburg-Hartenstein, Gen. Fürst (Austrian Sixth Army), at Vittorio Veneto, 265
Schools, 128, 134, 175
Searchlights, 257, 279, 288
Sette Communi (see Asiago), 19, 159
Shellard, Major E. (1/4th Gloucestershire), 210
Shoubridge, Major-Gen. T. H. (7th Div.), 96, 195, 252, 261, 272, 279, 291, 319, 352, 354, 393, 398
Siesta, 106
Signal Service, 129; visual, 163; at Asiago, 170, 199, 277
Sile river, 139, 140, 187; attack, 238; practice bridging, 274
Sladen, Br.-Gen. G. C. (143rd Bde.), 204, 205, 331, 337, 342, 396, 402
Smoke, 239
Smuts, Rt. Hon. Gen. J. C., at Rapallo Conference, 79
Sonnino, Baron (Italian Foreign Minister), 27, 35, 75, 80, 152
Stanley-Clarke, Br.-Gen. H. C. (C.R.A., 7th Div.), 196, 393, 399
Steele, Br.-Gen. J. McC. (22nd Bde.), 269, 274, 279, 352, 393, 400
Stephens, Major-Gen. R. B. (5th Div.), 141, 392

St. Hill, Lieut.-Col. A. A. (11/Northumberland Fus.), killed, 290
Stockley, Lieut.-Col. E. N. (C.R.E., 41st Div.), 394
Strick, Br.-Gen. J. A. (Base Commandant), 60, 387
Strong, Br.-Gen. W. (C.R.A., 48th Div.), 196, 395, 401
Strongpoints, how dealt with, 293
Supplies, 125, 172; in the mountains, 335, 345, 382; 354
Supreme War Council, proposed, 79; formed, 81; instructions to military representatives, 115; 156; supports Foch, 242; on Armistice terms, 369, 371, 377; places Foch in command of all armies against Germany, 381; decides to occupy the Trentino, 381
Surrender, Austrian, 337, 338; British terms, 339
Swabey, Col. W. S. (Director of Transport), 171
Switzerland, rumoured attack through, 27; plans to meet it, 28, 115

T

Tagliamento river, defence line, 53; retirements to, 56, 58 et seq.; bridges, 63, 67, 69; Italians reach, 70, 71; halt on, 74; retirement from, 78, 83; advance to, 351; nature, 351
Talbot, Lieut.-Col. D. H., becomes chief G.S.O., 384
Tanks, not required, 40; Diaz's request for, 244; 245
Tappen, Col. (chief of German Operations Section), 4
Taranto route (Cherbourg to Taranto, by rail), 29, 41, 386
Tassioni, Gen. (Italian XII Corps), 406
Tassoni, Gen. (Italian XIV Corps), 160; Seventh Army, 264
Telferage lines, 116, 172, 310, 313
Theatre of war, 10; Caporetto, 50; 356
Thuillier, Major-Gen. H. F. (23rd Div.), at Vittorio Veneto, 268, 290, 319; at Taranto, 386; 400
Tolmino, bridgehead, 35, 44, 51
Tomkinson, Lieut.-Col. F. M. (1/7th Worcestershire), 210, 211, 212
Tonale Pass, action, 194, 240, 252, 331
Torre river, 65, 66

GENERAL INDEX 445

Townley, Sergt.-Major R. (1/5th R. Warwickshire), 208-209
Towsey, Br.-Gen. F. W. (122nd Bde.), 395
Traffic control, absence of, 64, 65, 67, 68, 99, 298, 311, 350
Transport, of troops to Italy, see Crowe, Payot *and* Railways
Transportation (*see also* Transport, Railways and Motor lorries), 126
Treaties, see Triple Alliance *and* Pact of London
Trench warfare (*see* Raids), on Asiago front, 251
Trent, British reach, 338 ; Italians appear, 340 ; 342, 344
Trentino, 10 ; Austrian offensive, 16 ; Italian offensive, 33 ; offensive in autumn unlikely, 41 ; offensive feared, 72, 73 ; Conrad in command, 76 ; Conrad's offensive, 187
Trieste, 11 ; Italian objective, 13 ; in danger, 33, 35
Triple Alliance, treaty, 1 ; no military value, 2 ; Italo-German plan, 3, 4 ; denounced, 6 ; terms, 7
Tripoli, 1, 3, 5, 9
Trissimo (rest area), 165, 174, 195, 382
Turin, Gen. Count of (Italian Cav. Corps), 265, 352, 407
Turkish Empire, Italy wants share, 7, 27
Turner, Major R. A. (acting C.R.E., 23rd Div.), 400

V

Val d'Assa, 331 ; nature, 332
Val Sugana, 333, 334, 336
Veneto island, 272, 281, 298
Versailles Council, *see* Supreme War Council
Veterinary Service, 127
Victor Emanuel II, King, removes Cadorna, 81 ; receives Lord Cavan, 89 ; receives Gen. Plumer, 95 ; Foch can only advise, 242
Vigliani, Gen. (Italian 56th Div.), 292
Vittorio Veneto, battle of, 264 *et seq.* ; rations carried, 287 ; Austrian account, 295, 314, 325

W

Waldstätten, Major-Gen. (Deputy Austrian C.G.S.), 232, 240, 249, 375, 377
Wales, H.R.H. Prince of (A.D.C.), 89
Walker, Major-Gen. Sir H. B. (48th Div.), 252, 262, 263, 328, 331, 332, 336 ; offers terms to Austrians, 338 ; on mountain warfare, 346 ; succeeds to chief command, 384 ; goes home, 387 ; 401
Waller, Major N. H. (1/5th Gloucestershire), 205
War Cabinet, 149, 151, 152, 153, 154, 156, 244
Wardrop, Br.-Gen. A. E. (C.R.A., XIV Corps), 89, 200, 391, 397
Water supply, 123-124, 172, 173
Watt, Br.-Gen. D. M. (145th Bde.), 396, 402
Weather (*see also* Rain *and* Fog), frost, 99, 105 ; snow, 110, 116, 132, 137, 152, 158 ; Italians frozen to death, 116 ; cold the enemy, 119, 163 ; mud, 139 ; cold, 345, 382, 383
Webb, Major M. B. (D.A.G.), 389
Webb-Bowen, Br.-Gen. T. I. (R.F.C.), 96, 389
Weber, Edler v. Webenau, Gen. (Austrian Armistice Commissioner), 360, 367-68, 370, 371, 372, 374, 376, 377
West Indies Regiment, British, 386, 387
Western, Major-Gen. W. G. B. (D.A.G.), 94, 389
Wetzell, Gen. (head of German Operations Section, 1916-18), 26, 38
Weygand, Gen. (Foch's chief assistant), visits Italy and Switzerland, 28 ; 82, 95 ; military representative, 120
White, Lieut.-Col. J. R. (C.R.E., 5th Div.), 392
Whitehouse, Major P. H. (1/8th R. Warwickshire), 205
Wilson, President, armistice appeal to, 247, 250, 360 ; his 14 points, 361 ; accepts Austro-German armistice proposal, 381
Wilson, Br.-Gen. C. S. (C.E., XIV Corps), 89 ; C.E. of Tenth Army, 268 ; 391, 397
Wilson, Gen. (later Field-Marshal) Sir Henry, sent to Russia by Mr. Lloyd George, 25 ; at Rapallo Conference, 79 ; interviews Diaz, 82 ; on concentration, 92 ; gloomy reports, 94 ; goes to Versailles, 98, 120 ; becomes C.I.G.S., 148, 151, 152 ; opposes offensive, 175 ; proposes Anglo-Italian Army, 185 ; 244

Winter operations, 139 ; equipment, 163
Wood fighting, 213, 214, 218, 240
Wood, Private W., awarded V.C., 301
Woodroffe, Br.-Gen. C. R. (British Mission at French G.Q.G.), 61, 96
Wurm, Gen. Freiherr v. (Austrian Army commander), 142, 189 ; at Piave battle, 221, 227, 234, 239 ; 408, 410

Y

Youll, 2/Lieut. J. S., awarded V.C., 204

Z

Zuccari, Gen., to command Italian help to Germany, 4

INDEX TO ARMS, FORMATIONS, AND UNITS 447

American unit—
  332nd Regiment—307, 318, 353, 354
Armies, Italian—
  First—10, 17, 44, 113, 134, 144, 160, 264, 330, 405, 406
  Second—9, 13, 15, 20, 22, 32, 34, 35; success, 36, 41; reorganized, 42; at Caporetto, 44, 53, 56, 63, 64, 65, 67; loses equipment, 70; on the Tagliamento, 74; panics, 76, 77; retirement to the Piave, 83; abolished, 132, 135; 405
  Third—9, 13, 15, 20, 22, 32, 34, 35, 41; reorganized, 42, 53; retirement ordered, 54, 56, 62, 63; loses equipment, 70; on the Tagliamento, 74, 75, 77; on the Piave, 78, 83, 84, 134, 144, 160; 254, 267, 271, 303, 311, 317, 320, 324, 348, 349, 353, 405, 406
  Fourth—10, 22; after Caporetto, 74, 77; on the Piave, 78, 83, 84, 113, 117, 134, 144, 160, 264, 267, 269, 283, 285, 313, 321, 325, 331, 405, 406
  Fifth—18, 132, 135, 145, 160
  Sixth—159, 160, 175, 177, 183, 185, 217, 238, 264, 265, 266, 267, 330, 338
  Seventh—160, 264, 330, 406
  Eighth—234, 248, 264, 266, 271, 284, 285, 303, 312-21, 325, 350, 406
  Ninth—265; relieves the Tenth, 382; 407
  Tenth—Lord Cavan to command, 249; formed, 263; 264, 267, 271, 284; Piave assault, 286; 297, 303, 304; at the Livenza, 320, 348; at the Tagliamento, 351; is relieved and the British concentrate at Trissino, 382; 407
  Twelfth—formed, 263; 264, 266, 267, 283, 284, 285, 304, 313, 321, 325, 348, 407
Army Ordnance Corps—
  Units with Force—390, 391, 397, 399, 403
Army Service Corps—
  Units with Force—388, 390, 391, 392, 393, 394, 395, 396, 398, 400, 401, 402
Army Veterinary Corps—
  Units with Force—385, 392, 393, 394, 395, 397, 400, 401, 402, 403

Artillery—
  Batteries, Field—
    12th—207, 211, 212; 35th—206; 104th—206; 105th—206, 308; 400th—389; A/LXXII—389; C/LXXVI—389; A/102nd—206; C/175th—389; D/240th—207, 212
  Batteries, Heavy—
    19th—389, 398; 90th—108, 389, 398; 155th—389, 398; 1/1st Warwickshire—108, 389, 398
  Batteries, Siege—
    105th—108, 398; 137th—108, 398; 171st—389, 398; 172nd—108, 389, 398; 176th—108, 389, 398; 181st—108, 389, 398; 197th—389, 398; 229th—108, 389, 398; 240th—389, 398; 247th—108, 389, 398; 289th—108, 389, 398; 293rd—389; 302nd—31, 389, 398; 304th—31; 307th—31, 389, 398; 314th—31; 315th—31, 389, 398; 316th—31, 389, 398; 317th—31, 389, 398; 320th—31; 322nd—31; 334th—31; 390th—31, 389, 398; 391st—31, 389, 398; 392nd — 31; 394th — 31; 395th — 31; 396th — 31; 438th—398
  Brigades, Field—
    XV—392; XXII—202, 206, 287, 294, 301, 305, 393, 400; XXXV—204, 287, 393, 400; LXXII — 108, 155, 389; LXXVI — 154, 155, 389; 102nd—202, 206, 287, 305, 319, 323, 385, 393, 401; 103rd—202, 203, 287, 293, 385, 393, 401; 175th—154, 155, 389; 187th—395; 190th—395; 240th—204, 207, 385, 395, 401; 241st—204, 385, 395, 401
  Brigade, R.H.A.—
    XIV—108, 155, 389
  Brigades, Heavy (H.A.G.)—
    XV—133, 154, 166, 197, 389, 398; XXIV—108, 166, 197, 389, 398; LXXX—108, 166, 187, 389, 398; XCIV—31, 89, 108, 133, 154, 166, 197, 389, 398; XCV—31; 101st—31; 104th—154, 166, 197, 389, 398
Cavalry—
  Special Reserve — 1/1st King Edward's Horse, 391

448 INDEX TO ARMS, FORMATIONS, AND UNITS

Cavalry (continued)—
  Yeomanry — 1/1st Northamptonshire, 307, 318, 319, 350, 351, 391, 398

Corps—
  XI—move to Italy, 96, 97, 102, 110, 112; 126, 127, 128, 129, 131, 133; in Arcade sector, 137, 138-9, 140-41; returns to Western Front, 150, 153-55; order of battle, 391
  XIV—move to Italy, 59, 60, 88, 91-92; in the Montello sector, 99-100, 101-102, 104-105, 123; artillery with corps, 108; group plan of defence, 110-111, 133; 115, 126, 127, 128, 129, 138, 154; on the Asiago plateau, 160-166; merged into G.H.Q. Italy, 18th April 1918, 162; re-formed 9th Oct., 263, 404; in Battle of Vittorio Veneto, 24th Oct-4th Nov., 264, 266, 268-69, 270, 271, 272-83, 287-95, 297-98, 299-301, 304-311, 317-19, 322-23, 348-52, 353-54; casualties, 355; 380, 382, 384; order of battle, Nov. 1917, 391-96

Cyclists—
  XI Corps—391
  XIV Corps—99, 318, 350, 351, 391, 398

Divisions—
  5th—97, 110, 111, 118, 138-39, 140-41, 154-55, 157, 162, 393
  7th—move to Italy, 96, 97, 102; in reserve, 105, 106, 110, 111, 117; move to France cancelled, 150, 154; in the Montello sector, 153; strength 12th Mar. 1918, 162; on the Asiago plateau, 164, 165, 178, 181; in reserve, Battle of Asiago, 15th/16th June 1918, 195, 201, 210, 216; 249; minor operations July-Oct. 1918, 252, 253, 254, 256, 259, 260, 261, 262, 263; moves to Piave sector, 268; in Battle of Vittorio Veneto, 24th Oct.-4th Nov. 1918, 269-70, 272, 274-82, 287, 288, 289-94, 295, 301-302, 305-309, 310, 317-19, 348-54; casualties, 24th Oct.-4th Nov., 355; 380; withdrawn to reserve, 382; order of battle, Nov. 1917, 393; June 1918, 399-400
  21st—97

Divisions (continued)—
  23rd—move to Italy, 88, 89, 91; to Vicenza position, 95, 99, 101; in the Montello sector, 105, 106, 108, 110, 116, 162; on the Asiago plateau, 163, 164-65, 178, 181; in battle of Asiago, 15th June 1918, 195, 201, 202-204, 217, 219; casualties, 15th June, 216; 249; minor operations July-Oct., 252, 253, 254, 259, 260, 262, 263; moves to Piave sector, 268, 269; in Battle of Vittorio Veneto, 24th Oct.-4th Nov., 277, 278, 279, 281, 287, 288, 289-92, 294, 295, 299, 300-301, 305, 307, 309-10, 318-20, 322-24, 349, 350, 354; casualties 24th Oct.-4th Nov., 355; 380, 382; orders of battle, Nov. 1917, 393; June 1918, 400
  41st—88, 89, 91, 95, 99, 100, 101, 102, 105, 106, 108, 110, 116, 150, 153, 395
  47th (2nd London)—261
  48th (1st South Midland)—arrival in Italy, 88, 96, 97; moves to front line, 110, 111, 112, 188; relieved, 138, 139; in the Montello sector, 154, 162; in reserve, 163, 165, 178; on the Asiago plateau, 181; battle of Asiago, 15th/16th June 1918, 195, 199, 201, 204-206, 217-18; casualties, 15th June, 219; minor operations, July-Oct., 249, 252, 256, 259, 260, 262, 263; operations on the mountain front, 1st-5th Nov., 327-35, 336-37; casualties, 1st-5th Nov., 345; 382-83, 385; orders of battle, Nov. 1917, 395; June 1918, 401

Engineers (R.E.)—
  Bridging Train—4th/5th, 266
  Field Companies—
    54th—282, 393, 400; 101st—276, 288, 294, 385, 394; 128th—282, 394; 285th—349, 389, 398; 290th—154, 389; 474th—210, 333, 395, 401; 475th—333, 395, 401; 477th—206, 209, 211, 214, 266, 333, 395, 401
  Field Survey Company—
    6th—288, 389, 398
  Engineer units with Force, 389, 392, 393, 395, 396, 400, 401, 402

INDEX TO ARMS, FORMATIONS, AND UNITS 449

Flying Corps (R.F.C. and R.A.F.)—
 Balloon Companies—
  20th—154, 155, 390
 Balloon Sections, Kite—
  3rd—269 ; 7th—269, 390, 398
 Balloon Wing—
  No. 4—108, 155, 390
 Brigade—
  VII—96, 130, 155, 390
 Squadrons—
  5th—96 ; 28th—59, 108, 155, 165, 180, 269, 390, 398 ; 34th—59, 108, 155, 165, 269, 390, 398 ; 42nd—96, 108, 154, 155, 390 ; 45th—96, 108, 154, 165, 180, 223, 390, 398 ; 66th—96, 108, 154, 165, 180, 223, 390, 398 ; 139th—269
 Wings—
  Fourteenth—96, 155, 162, 165, 269, 298, 390, 398 ; Fifty-first—59, 155, 389

Infantry Brigades—
 13th—139, 392
 15th—139, 392
 20th—256, 282, 289, 291, 292, 302, 306, 307, 308, 317, 319, 350, 352, 354, 393, 400
 22nd—256, 269, 274–82, 306, 311, 318, 349, 350, 352, 354, 393, 400
 68th—165, 202, 203, 278, 288, 290, 292, 293, 299, 300, 306, 307, 309, 310, 319. 394, 401
 69th—165, 204, 216, 269, 278, 279, 288, 290, 292, 293, 300–301, 306, 307, 309–10, 319, 350, 394, 401
 70th—165, 202, 216, 290, 306, 310, 311, 319, 322–24, 394, 401
 91st—165, 210, 216, 256, 282, 289, 291, 292, 301–302, 306, 307–309, 319, 393, 400
 95th—139, 392
 123rd—102
 143rd—204–215, 256, 331, 332–34, 336–37, 339, 343, 344, 396, 402
 144th—195, 210, 211, 213, 214, 256, 328–30, 331, 332–34, 336, 342, 343, 344, 396, 402
 145th—195, 204–215, 218, 328–30, 331, 332–34, 336–39, 342, 343, 396, 402

Infantry Regiments—
 Argyll & Sutherland Highlanders, 1/6th Bn., 392
 Bedfordshire, 1st Bn., 392
 Berkshire, Royal, 1/4th Bn., 205, 207, 210, 214, 259, 329, 330, 396, 402

Infantry Regiments (*continued*)—
 Border Regiment, 2nd Bn., 180, 253, 257, 291, 302, 308, 354, 393, 400
 Buckinghamshire Battalion, Oxford L.I., 1/1st, 180, 205, 206, 209, 214, 259, 327, 396, 402
 Cheshire, 1st Bn., 392
 Cornwall L.I., 1st Bn., 392
 Devonshire, 1st Bn., 392
 —8th Bn., 179, 291, 292, 293, 294, 393, 400
 —9th Bn., 260, 393, 400
 Duke of Wellington's, 10th Bn., 216, 259, 290, 293, 300, 308, 394, 401
 Durham L.I., 12th Bn., 202, 290, 300, 301, 309, 394, 401
 —13th Bn., 202, 260, 394, 401
 —20th Bn., 395
 East Surrey, 1st Bn., 392
 —2nd Bn., 393
 —12th Bn., 395
 Gloucestershire, 1/4th Bn., 195, 210, 211, 212, 263, 329, 337, 342, 344, 396, 402
 —1/5th Bn., 195, 201, 205, 207, 208, 214, 260, 396, 402
 —1/6th Bn., 195, 211, 213, 214, 257, 329, 358, 387, 396, 402
 —12th Bn., 392
 Gordon Highlanders, 2nd Bn., 291, 292, 293, 351, 393, 400
 Green Howards, 8th Bn., 180, 278, 279, 290, 300, 301, 307, 309, 310, 394, 401
 —9th Bn., 253, 260, 394, 401
 Hampshire, 15th Bn., 395
 H.A.C., 2/1st Bn., 179, 253, 274, 275, 276, 277, 278, 280, 351, 352, 385, 386, 393, 400
 King's Own Scottish Borderers, 2nd Bn., 392
 King's Royal Rifle Corps, 18th Bn., 395
 —21st Bn., 395
 King's Own Yorkshire L.I., 8th Bn., 202, 203, 290, 319, 401
 Manchester, 20th Bn., 179, 257, 260, 393, 400
 —21st Bn., 253, 260, 291, 393, 400
 —22nd Bn., 253, 293, 302, 308, 385, 386, 387, 393, 400
 —24th Bn., 393, 400
 Middlesex, 19th Bn., 395
 —23rd Bn., 395
 Munster Fusiliers, Royal, 1st Garr. Bn., 396, 402
 Norfolk, 1st Bn., 392

INDEX TO ARMS, FORMATIONS, AND UNITS

Infantry Regiments (*continued*)—
Norfolk, 1st Garr. Bn., 402
Northumberland Fusiliers, 10th Bn., 204, 253, 288, 293, 300, 309, 394, 401
—11th Bn., 180, 202, 203, 204, 206, 290, 291, 293, 301, 309, 394, 401
Oxfordshire & Buckinghamshire L.I., 1/4th Bn., 204, 206, 207, 209, 210, 213, 214, 219, 260, 330, 332, 343, 344, 396, 401
Queen's (R. West Surrey), 2nd Bn., 291, 302, 307–8, 400
—10th Bn., 395
—11th Bn., 395
Royal Fusiliers, 26th Bn., 395
—32nd Bn., 395
Sherwood Foresters, 11th Bn., 179, 202, 203, 260, 401
South Staffordshire, 1st Bn., 179, 257, 291, 292, 302, 308, 393, 400
—9th Bn., 306, 319, 323, 394, 401
Sussex, Royal, 1/5th Bn., 196, 210, 333, 342, 395, 402
Warwickshire, Royal, 2nd Bn., 179, 279, 280, 318, 349, 354, 393, 400
—1/5th Bn., 205, 207, 208, 209, 213, 214, 215, 257, 331, 340, 342, 395, 402
—1/6th Bn., 179, 196, 205, 209, 212, 213, 215, 262, 331, 332, 333, 342, 396, 402
—1/7th Bn., 196, 205, 210, 211, 212, 213, 214, 257, 262, 331, 332, 333, 334, 336, 337, 385, 387, 396, 402
—1/8th Bn., 205, 213, 214, 260, 396, 402
—14th Bn., 392
—15th Bn., 392
—16th Bn., 392

Infantry Regiments (*continued*)—
Welch Fusiliers, Royal, 1st Bn., 179, 257, 274, 276, 277, 278, 280, 318, 319, 349, 354, 393, 400
West Kent, Royal, 1st Bn., 392
—10th Bn., 395
—11th Bn., 395
West Yorkshire, 11th Bn., 216, 253, 277, 278, 293, 300, 301, 307, 310, 394, 401
Worcestershire, 7th Bn., 195, 210, 211, 212, 213, 214, 331, 332, 386, 396, 402
—8th Bn., 195, 211, 214, 257, 260, 396, 402
York & Lancaster, 8th Bn., 179, 202, 204, 319, 385, 387, 394, 401
—9th Bn., 202, 310, 319, 320, 322, 323, 394, 401
Labour—
Units with Force—397, 402
Lines of Communication units—396–97, 402–403
Machine Gun Corps—
7th Bn.—257, 400; 23rd Bn.—319, 395, 404; 48th Bn.—385, 395, 402
Motor Battery, 12th—99, 100, 318, 389, 398
Units with Force—392, 393, 394, 395, 396, 402
Medical—
Units with Force—123, 154, 385, 387, 388, 390, 392, 393, 394, 395, 397, 399, 400, 401, 402, 403
Signal—
Units with Force—129, 390, 391, 392, 393, 394, 395, 396, 398, 400, 401, 402
Trench Mortar—
Units with Force—385, 392, 393, 394, 395, 396, 400, 401, 402

Printed in Great Britain under the authority of
HIS MAJESTY'S STATIONERY OFFICE
by COLE & CO. (WESTMINSTER), LTD.

S.O. Code No. 70—540*

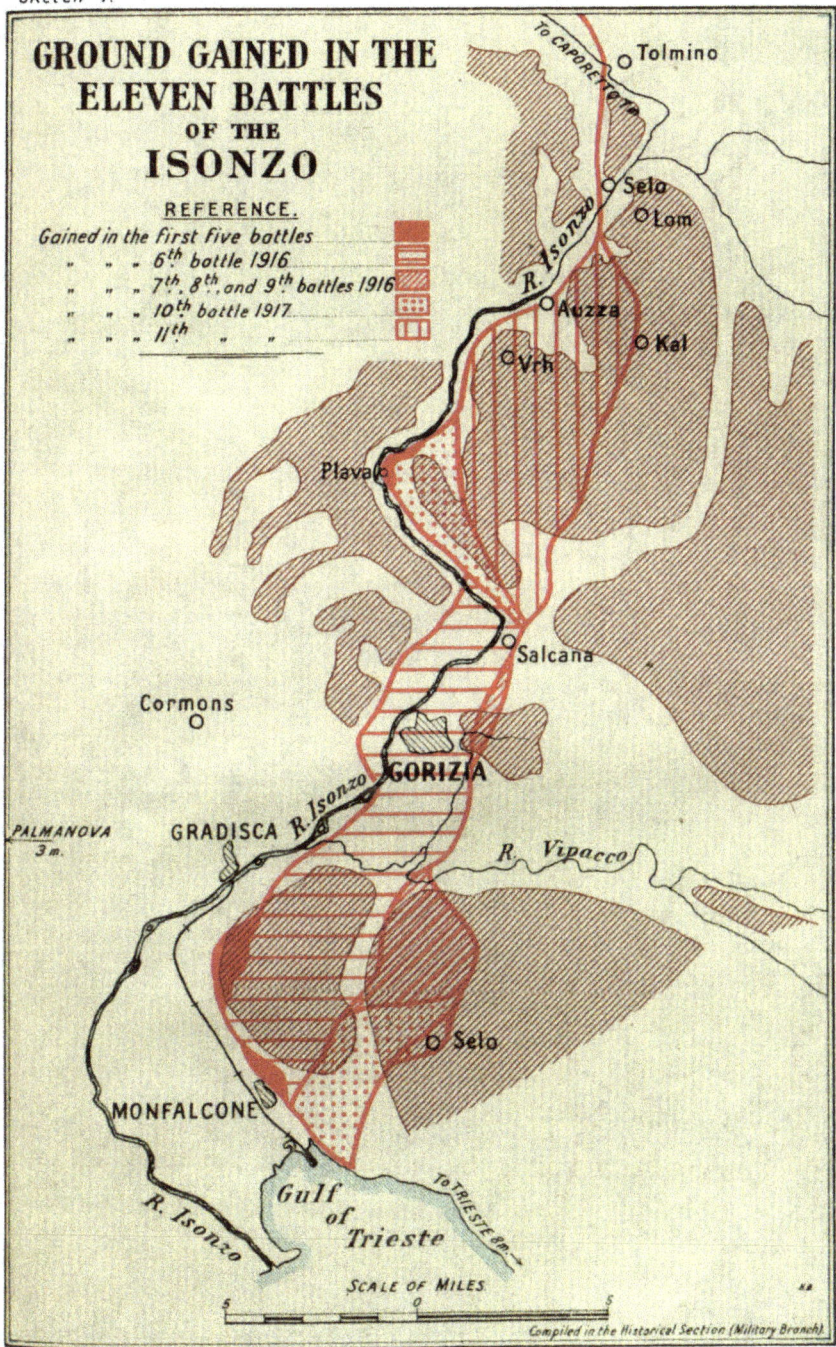

Sketch 2.

Sketch 3.

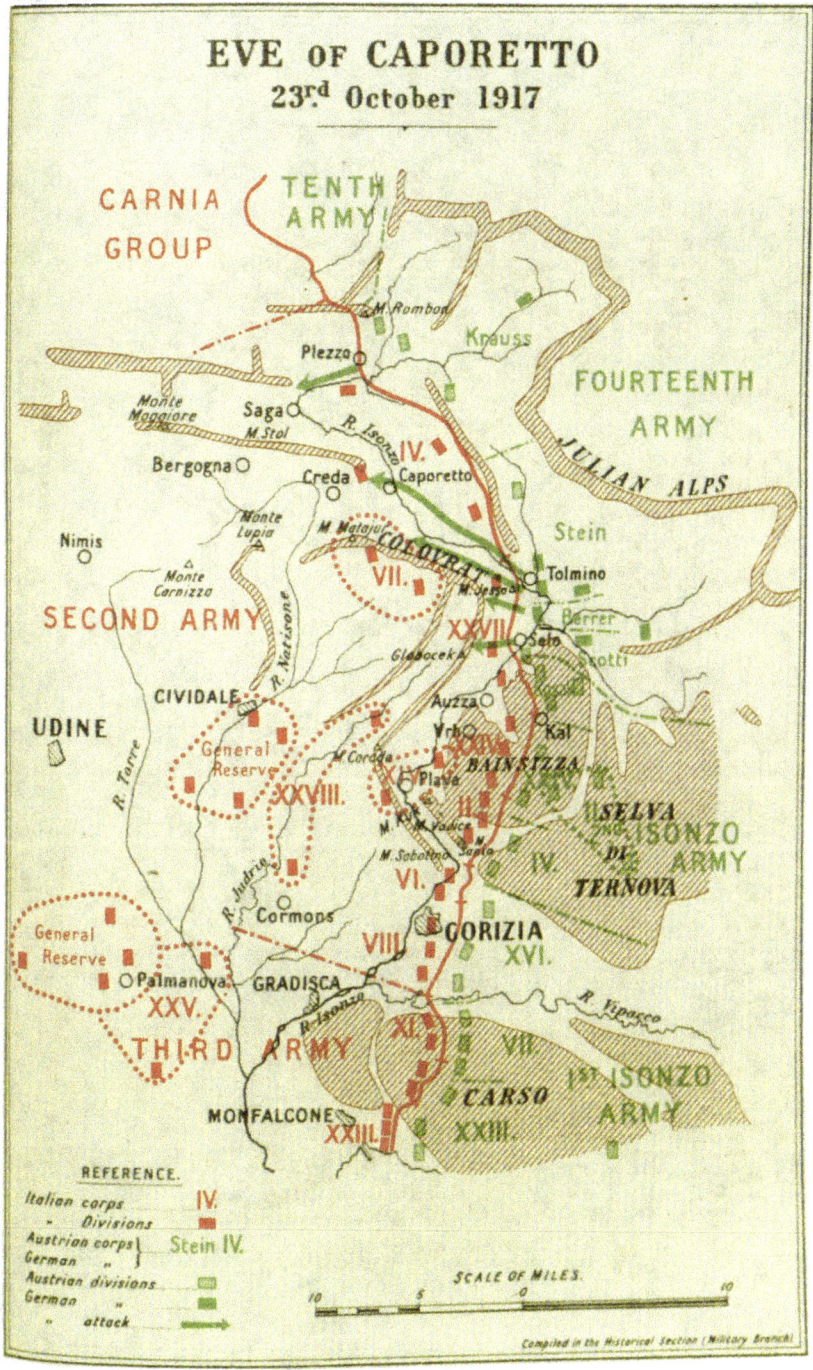

Sketch 4.

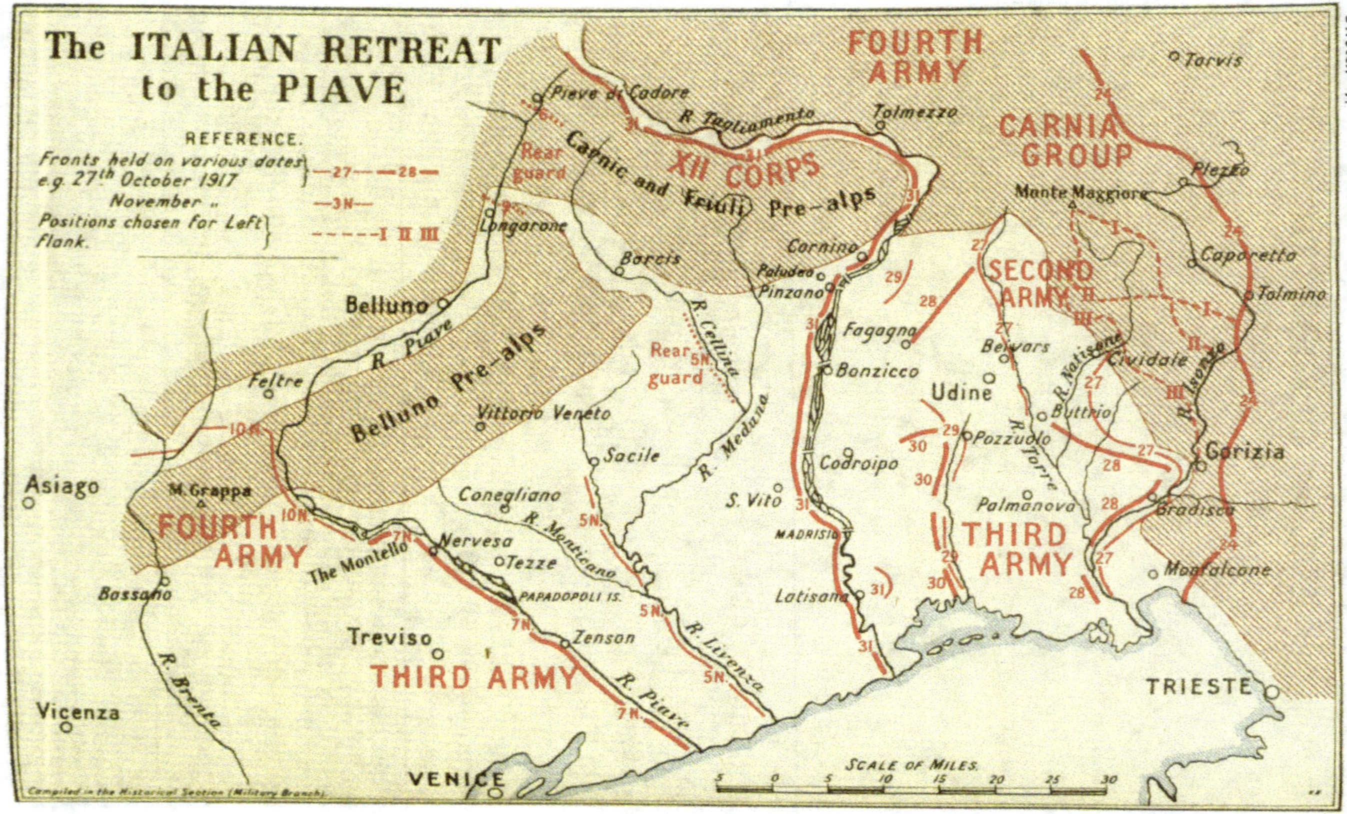

The ITALIAN RETREAT to the PIAVE
REFERENCE.
Fronts held on various dates e.g. 27th October 1917 —27— —28—
November " —3N—
Positions chosen for Left flank. -----I II III
FOURTH ARMY
CARNIA GROUP
XII CORPS
SECOND ARMY
THIRD ARMY
FOURTH ARMY
THIRD ARMY
Carnic and Friuli Pre-alps
Belluno Pre-alps
Rear guard
Rear guard
Tarvis
Plezzo
Monte Maggiore
Caporetto
Tolmino
Cividale
R. Isonzo
R. Natisone
Gorizia
Bradisca
Monfalcone
TRIESTE
Pieve di Cadore
R. Tagliamento
Tolmezzo
Longarone
Barcis
Cornino
Paludea
Pinzano
R. Cellina
Fagagna
Bonzicco
Beivars
Udine
Buttrio
Pozzuolo
R. Torre
Palmanova
Codroipo
S. Vito
Madrisio
Latisana
R. Medana
Belluno
R. Piave
Feltre
Vittorio Veneto
Sacile
Asiago
M. Grappa
Conegliano
R. Monticano
Nervesa
Tezze
The Montello
Papadopoli Is.
Bassano
Treviso
Zenson
R. Livenza
R. Piave
R. Brenta
Vicenza
VENICE
SCALE OF MILES.
5 0 5 10 15 20 25 30
Compiled in the Historical Section (Military Branch).

Sketch 5.

Sketch 7.

AUSTRIAN PLAN FOR OFFENSIVE 1918

Sketch 8.

The BATTLE OF ASIAGO
15-16 June 1918

Sketch 9.

BRITISH MULTIPLE RAID
OF THE 8TH/9TH AUGUST 1918
AND THE
AUSTRIAN RETIREMENT

Sketch 10.

ITALIAN PLAN
AND
Situation on 24th October 1918

Sketch 11.

CAPTURE OF
PAPADOPOLI ISLAND
23rd — 26th October 1918

Sketch 12.

CAMPAIGN OF VITTORIO VENETO
DAILY ADVANCES

www.ingramcontent.com/pod-product-compliance
Lightning Source LLC
Chambersburg PA
CBHW070756300426
44111CB00014B/2410